GW01149696

CROATIA THROUGH HISTORY

Branka Magaš

CROATIA THROUGH HISTORY

The Making of a European State

SAQI

London San Francisco Beirut

ISBN: 978-0-86356-775-9

This first edition published by Saqi Books
© Branka Magaš, 2007

The right of Branka Magaš to be identified as the author of this work has been asserted by her in accordance with the Copyright, Designs and Patents Act of 1988.

All rights reserved. No part of this book may be reproduced or transmitted in any form or by any means, electronic or mechanical, including photocopying, recording or by any information storage and retrieval system, without permission in writing from the publisher.

This book is sold subject to the condition that it shall not, by way of trade or otherwise, be lent, re-sold, hired out, or otherwise circulated without the publisher's prior consent in any form of binding or cover other than that in which it is published and without a similar condition including this condition being imposed on the subsequent purchaser.

A full CIP record for this book is available from the British Library.
A full CIP record for this book is available from the Library of Congress.

Manufactured in Lebanon

SAQI

26 Westbourne Grove, London W2 5RH
825 Page Street, Suite 203, Berkeley, California 94710
Tabet Building, Mneimneh Street, Hamra, Beirut
www.saqibooks.com

Contents

Maps and Illustrations	7
Introduction	11

Part One: From Roman Dalmatia to Habsburg Croatia

1.	Dalmatian Beginnings	19
2.	The Triune Kingdom	54
3.	The Ottoman Wars	85
4.	Borderland	115
5.	Language and Literacy	151
6.	The Politics of State Right	185

Part Two: From Kingdom to Nation State

7.	Illyrian Croatia	217
8.	Interregnum	255
9	The Croatian-Hungarian Compromise	287
10.	Croatia and its Serbs	323
11.	Redeeming Dalmatia	363
12.	Educating Istria	404

Part Three: Yugoslavia and Beyond

13.	The Road to Yugoslavia	435
14.	Between Italy and Serbia	479
15.	Reform, Reaction and Revolution	530
16.	The Promised Land	594

Acronyms	665
Notes	669
Select Bibliography	702

Sources 728
Index 729

Maps and Illustrations

In-text Illustrations

Image of Salona, by Vicentius Paternus, 1751	20
Roman Illyricum, circa 400	21
The Ostrogothic kingdom, circa 500	23
Europe under Charlemagne, ninth century	32
Croatia, ninth to eleventh century	35
Seal of King Krešimir IV, 1070	46
Iadra ad cedem. Zadar surrenders to the Crusaders in 1202	57
King Louis I arrives in Zadar, 1358	62
Relief of Ban Paul I Bribirski, 1380	67
Seal of the royal free city of Gradec/Zagreb, fourteenth century	74
Ruins of Cetingrad	80
Ottoman *akıncı* burn villages and take slaves	89
Vuk Frankapan's address to Emperor Charles V, 1530	91
The battle of Sisak, 1593	95
The fortress of Novi Zrin, 1664	102
The fortified defence line between Karlovac and Sisak	105
Zrinski lands in the second half of the sixteenth century	124
Vuk Krsto Frankapan	128
The burning of the Süleyman Bridge at Osijek, 1664	129
Execution of Petar Zrinski, 1671	131
The battle of Virovitica, 1684	133
The Military Border, eighteenth century	141
Napoleon's Illyrian Provinces, early nineteenth century	148
Euclid and Herman the Dalmatian, by Matthew of Paris, circa 1259	155
Marginal notes by Henry VIII in Marko Marulić's *Evangelistarium*	157
The first edition of *Judith*, Venice 1521	158
Faust Vrančić's parachute in his *Machinae Novae,* Venice 1595	161
Matija Vlačić Ilirik – Mathias Flacius Illyricus	163

Markantun de Dominis	166
The Augsburg Confession, 1564	169
Ritual Rimski by Bartol Kašić, 1640	172
St Jerome with the 'Illyrian' arms, by Natale Bonifazio	176
Pavao Ritter Vitezović's historical, Illyrian and Slav Croatias	181
Joseph II as a ploughman	191
Ban's Croatia, 1785	193
Janko Drašković	202
Rijeka welcomes Emperor Charles VI, 1728	207
Ivan Kukuljević	224
Zagreb in 1844, by J. Lechner	226
Ivan Mažuranić	228
National Demands, 1848	231
Patriarch Josif Rajačić	235
Habsburg generals, 1848–9	242
Ante Starčević	260
Vuk Karadžić with Mrs Karadžić	261
Croatian Parliament, 1861, by I. Zasche	277
Austria-Hungary, 1867	290
Josip Juraj Strossmayer	312
Ban Khuen-Héderváry welcomes King Francis Joseph, Zagreb, 1895	321
Ban's Croatia, end of nineteenth century	322
Tsar Dušan crushes the Turks, 1741	327
The battle of Klis, 1648	329
Pavle Jovanović	349
The Serb Orthodox community building	360
Miho Klaić	370
Mihovil Pavlinović	373
Arrival of Francis Joseph in Zadar, 1875	388
The National Reading Room building in Split	398
Map of Istria	405
Distribution of Glagolitic inscriptions in Istria	408
Juraj Dobrila	412
Cover page of *Pro Patria*	421
Frano Supilo	450
Ante Trumbić	467
The Treaty of London line, 1915	469
Nikola Pašić	481

Maps and Illustrations

Territorial formation of Yugoslavia, 1913–9	499
Ban on the use of Croat by Fascists of Vodnjan, Istria, 1920	507
Svetozar Pribićević, Ante Trumbić and Josip Smodlaka, circa 1920	511
Stjepan Radić	520
Vladko Maček	523
General Petar Živković, prime minister of Yugoslavia, 1929	525
Vladko Maček and Dragiša Cvetković, Zagreb 1939	539
Banovina Croatia, 1939–41	541
Partition of Yugoslavia, 1941	547
Slavko Kvaternik and Ante Pavelić, Zagreb 1941	550
The Zagreb synagogue, built 1867, destroyed 1941	558
Projected Great Serbia, 1941	564
Joakim Rakovac, circa 1943	582
'Long Live Croatian Istria!', 1945	585
Julian Region boundary proposals, 1946	589
Croatia's international frontiers	593
Andrija Hebrang on liberated territory, Croatia 1944	600
The first Communist government of Croatia, Split 1945	606
Nasser, Nehru and Tito, Brijuni 1956	613
Wall plaque at Split	616
Latinka Perović, Savka Dabčević-Kučar and Aleksandar Ranković at Karađorđevo, 1964, photographed by Tito	624
Savka Dabčević-Kučar, Miko Tripalo, Pero Pirker and Tito, 1968	628
Tito on bier, May 1980	650
Projected Great Serbia, 1991	654
Birth of the Second Republic, Zagreb 1990	656
Croatian banknotes in 1994	659
Dubrovnik burns, December 1991	660
Head of a young woman, Šibenik cathedral, fifteenth century	663

Colour Illustrations

Between pages 128–129
Relief of King Krešimir IV, 11th century
Map of Croatia by Al Idrisi, 12th century
Zadar as shown in *Pilgerreise von Konstanz nach Jerusalem*, 1486
The castle of Klis
The walled city of Dubrovnik
Diocletian's palace, the core of Split, 4th century

St James's cathedral in Šibenik, 15th century
The oldest known map of Zagreb, 16th century

Between pages 224–225
St Jerome, by Gentile Bellini, 15th century
The Rheims Gospel, 1395
A Croat-language prayer book, c. 1450
Canaletto, Riva degli Schiavoni or Riva of the Croats, c. 1736
Marko Marulić, by Ivan Meštrović, Split
Bribir (Roman Varvaria)
The church of St Mary in Vrboska
Ozalj on the Kupa, a 13th century Frankapan citadel

Between pages 320–321
The Zrinski palace in Čakovec, 16th century
Croatia after the Peace of Zadar, 1358
Ottoman incursions into Croatia, 1391–1490
Croatia, 1606
Croatia, 1741
Trakošćan
The country house of Gornja Bistra
The castle of Sisak

Between pages 416–417
Arms of the Croatian *regnum*, 1830
Arms of the Dalmatian *regnum*, 1701
Arms of the Slavonian *regnum*, 1701
Arms of imaginary Illyria, 1701
Ban Jelačić's banner, 1848
Banner of the Zagreb National Guard, 1848
Flag of the Triune Kingdom, second half of the 19th century
Flag of the Independent State of Croatia, 1941
Arms of the Socialist Republic of Croatia, 1947
Flag of the Republic of Croatia, 1990
The first Zagreb Christmas Fair, Ljubo Babić, 1926
Adriatic Day, Pavao Gavranić, 1933
Opatija, Edo Murtić, 1955
Krvatska!, Boris Ljubičić, 1991
The 29th Split Summer Festival, Boris Bućan, 1983

Introduction

This book is concerned with Croatia's evolution from a medieval kingdom into a nation state. It concentrates, therefore, on the development of its political institutions, the forging of a common identity among its people and the unification of its state territory under a single authority.

The modern nation state is based essentially on three principles: civic equality, popular sovereignty and participatory democracy. Their functioning assumes a bounded territory and political independence, since it is otherwise not possible to establish the domain of law, define citizenship or exercise sovereignty. Creation of the nation state thus involves the establishment of clear political borders, which separate its sovereign domain from all others, and simultaneously create conditions for its internal consolidation as a particular community. Nation states are in consequence territorially based constructs, irrespective of the existence of a historically evolved emotional tie between state and nation – a quality for which French political theory has invented the term 'nationality'. This work concerns itself with the establishment over time of Croatia's borders, the evolution of governance within them, and the changing nature of the sovereign will that identified it as a state.

The formation of nation states is an intensely political process, involving institutions of authority within a given polity as well as that polity's relations with others. It is also highly individual, in that each nation traverses the path towards modernity in its own way, in its own time and under conditions that are specific to it. The main purpose of this work is thus to chart the uniquely Croatian itinerary towards modern nationhood. Yet the starting point, the stages passed through and the aim of the journey undertaken are typically European in their impulses, constraints and ambitions. They cannot be understood outside the historical framework of the transformation of Western Christendom into a community of sovereign nations. At the same time, however, the Croatian medieval state arose from the decaying Roman order at the confluence of the Mediterranean world with that of central Europe; it was the interplay between these, a process involving both assimilation and opposition, that helped to define the specifically Croatian national identity.

The conversion of a feudal land into a nation state is a long, arduous and by no means unilinear process. Setbacks along the way can sometimes be so great that they appear to imperil the very possibility of success. This is certainly true for Croatia. Any study of its history confronts the problem of its prolonged territorial fragmentation and the incorporation of the individual parts into other state structures. The Ottoman invasions of the fifteenth and sixteenth centuries, in particular, stunted its organic development and turned it for several centuries into a buffer zone and a site of intermittent warfare. Each of its parts consequently underwent a separate evolution, and in the Ottoman case a drastic restructuring. Each accordingly demanded a different strategy of integration into the common Croatian state. At the same time, Croatia's union with Hungary in the early twelfth century, the inclusion of both kingdoms into the Habsburg Monarchy at the start of the sixteenth century, and Croatia's entry into Yugoslavia at the start of the twentieth century, intertwined the histories of these states and supra-states to such an extent that Croatia's own – viewed from outside – became at times practically invisible. One of the intentions of this work is to disentangle Croatian history from the history of those state associations, albeit without seeking to deny or minimise their influence, which is both complex and profound.

Perhaps the most remarkable aspect of Croatian history has been the sheer ability of the state to survive in highly adverse conditions, and to fuse its diverse parts together into a single nation. This work consequently traces in some detail the formation and programmes of political parties in the context of transformation of the Habsburg Monarchy into a quasi-parliamentary democracy. Croatia's national consolidation in the modern period derives, in fact, not so much from the political leverage of its elites, powerful friends or military triumphs, as from the arrival – over the second half of the nineteenth century and the first half of the twentieth – of universal (in the first instance male) suffrage, which welded together its cities and countryside. This democratic device could function, however, only on the basis of an already entrenched sense of national unity among the elites. Modern Croatia in this sense provides a good example of a state as a democratic undertaking – insofar as this can be dissociated from warfare: for the ability to raise armies served equally to establish the early kingdom and to maintain it in the centuries that followed, and this work pays due

Introduction

attention to that side of Croatian history. It is even more concerned, however, with the constitutional struggles waged in both the Habsburg Monarchy and Yugoslavia, the forms and aims of which emerged from a political dialogue taking place within Croatia's own society. With the advent of political parties in the nineteenth century, this internal dialogue took the form of party disputes; it is from the conflicts between the dominant parties and their dissidents, in particular, that the full import of the momentous changes that gave birth to modern Croatia may be gleaned. Beginning in the second half of the nineteenth century, Croatian politics came also to address the problem of Croat-Serb unity and division; due attention is accordingly paid here to the relationship between the Croat and Serb components of the Croatian nation.

This book concerns itself primarily with the evolution of the Croatian state and the interplay between its centre and its historic regions. The somewhat crab-like movement of the account presented here reflects in part the diachronic quality of the development of Croatia's component parts – a state of affairs that lasted until the end of the Napoleonic Wars. It is a history viewed from above rather than from below: a history of institutions, and of political projects and movements concerned with state power and territorial integration, rather than of the social, economic and cultural transformations that gave them life in the first place. Important topics not directly covered in this book include the internal history of the Dubrovnik Republic; the history of the Croats of Bosnia-Herzegovina, which falls outside the scope of this volume; and that of the large Croat diaspora, despite its significant involvement in political life in the twentieth century. Also left aside here is a detailed account of Yugoslavia's slide into war in the late 1980s, or of the war itself, since these are covered at length in my *The Destruction of Yugoslavia – Tracking the Break-up 1980-1992* (1993), and in a work I co-edited with Ivo Žanić, *The War in Croatia and Bosnia-Herzegovina, 1991-1995* (2001).

At the same time, however, the circumstances of Yugoslavia's break-up and the emergence of new sources, books and information (albeit sometimes only anecdotal) rendered it both necessary and desirable to review long-standing beliefs. Many of the insights concerning the recent period came from extensive conversations conducted over the years with Albanian, Bosnian, Macedonian, Montenegrin, Serbian and Slovene friends. My late friend Miklós Krassó helped greatly, in retrospect, by his recollections of the old Croatian-Hungarian ties (and impressed me too with his ability to recite the names of the Croatian counties at the start of the twentieth century). Particular thanks go to Stanko Andrić for sharing with me his extensive knowledge of the history of medieval Slavonia; to Ivo Banac for many discussions on the progress of contemporary Croatia; to Neven Budak for helping me understand the difference between the monarch of the land and the monarch of the people; to Noel Malcolm and Ivo Žanić, who both at different times read parts of the manuscript and provided most welcome moral support; to Aleksandar Stipčević for stimulating conversations and for introducing me to the ever-helpful staff of the National and University Library in Zagreb; to Stanka and Martin Špegelj for their generous hospitality; and to Jagoda, Ivo and Iva Rusan for being such good friends. I remain indebted also to Sonja Biserko, Norman Cigar, Marshall Freeman Harris, Luka Markešić, Nermin Mulalić, Ines Sabalić and Steve Walker for sharing with me their insights into the policies associated with the wars of the Yugoslav succession.

The Croatian community here in Great Britain has been a great source of learning and inspiration: Chris Cviic, Vesna Domany-Hardy, Vivian Grisogono, Jasna Nardini, Marija and Vlado Pavlinić, and Flora Turner are thanked here for their interest and support. I wish to record my special appreciation of the contribution made by the late Adrian Hastings, who read drafts of the first two chapters of this work and provided much encouragement. The late Jill Craigie and her husband Michael Foot won my affection and admiration with their efforts on behalf of Bosnia-Herzegovina and Croatia, while it was Norman Stone who urged me to write the book in the first place. Warm thanks are due also to Grant McIntyre and Mike Shaw for their consideration and patience during an earlier stage of this work.

I have been working on the present volume for most of the past decade. During this time my family became the recipient of long and involved historical monologues, which they bore with great fortitude. Leo Kublai proved throughout a tower of strength, while his wizardly computer skills saved many sticky situations. It was a great kindness on the part of Marko Attila to undertake a critical reading of the manuscript and to offer invaluable scholarly advice regarding its form and content. Quintin's careful perusal of the various drafts and proposals for improvement made all the difference to the final outcome. My parents Nevenka and Šime provided a vital generational perspective with their comments and observations on Yugoslavia's dissolution. André Gaspard and the sadly missed Mai Ghoussoub gave me both their friendship and their guidance in the closing stages of this work; I am delighted that it is being published by their Saqi Books, founded by friends from another Mediterranean country, which has recently extended to an impressive coverage of southeastern Europe. It has been a great pleasure

Introduction

to work with Lara Frankena, Lynn Gaspard and Rukhsana Yasmin during the preparation of this book for publication. To all those mentioned here, as well as to many who while not directly acknowledged will recognise their input, I can only express my deepest gratitude – while in no way wishing to associate them with any of my misconceptions or failures.

PART ONE

From Roman Dalmatia to Habsburg Croatia

ONE

Dalmatian Beginnings

The Roman foundations

The Croatian state emerged during the eighth century on the territory of the Roman province of Dalmatia, one of the two administrative units (the other being Pannonia) into which the subdued Illyricum had been divided at the start of the new era. Roman Dalmatia comprised a triangular area extending from the river Raša in Istria to the mouth of the river Drin and from the Julian Alps to a point on the river Sava southwest of Belgrade.[1] Salona on the Adriatic coast, a port built by the Delmatae, an Illyrian people who gave the province its name, became the seat of Roman governors. As the administrative, juridical, military, economic and later also ecclesiastical centre of Dalmatia, Salona experienced a spectacular growth – accommodating at the height of its development, at the end of the third century, some 60,000 inhabitants.[2] Its authority embraced the coastal and island cities and spread up to the Pannonian plain and into the interior of what is now Bosnia, along the roads the Romans built beyond the nearby mountain pass of Klis. Together with the main roads leading across the southern edge of Pannonia and along the Dalmatian coast, these transversals created a cultural space that belonged to the Latin world but remained also open to cultural influences from the East, whence Christianity started to spread in the third century.[3] Early in the fourth century Emperor Diocletian, who was born close to Salona, built himself a magnificent palace in its proximity to which he withdrew after his abdication in 305 AD.[4] Julius Nepos, the last legal emperor of the West, also spent his final days in the palace. In the fourth century, when Christianity became the empire's official religion, the Church came to provide an additional element of Dalmatia's territorial organisation, its influence resting on state subsidy and land ownership. Salona became the seat of an archbishop: as bishop of the capital city the archbishop was

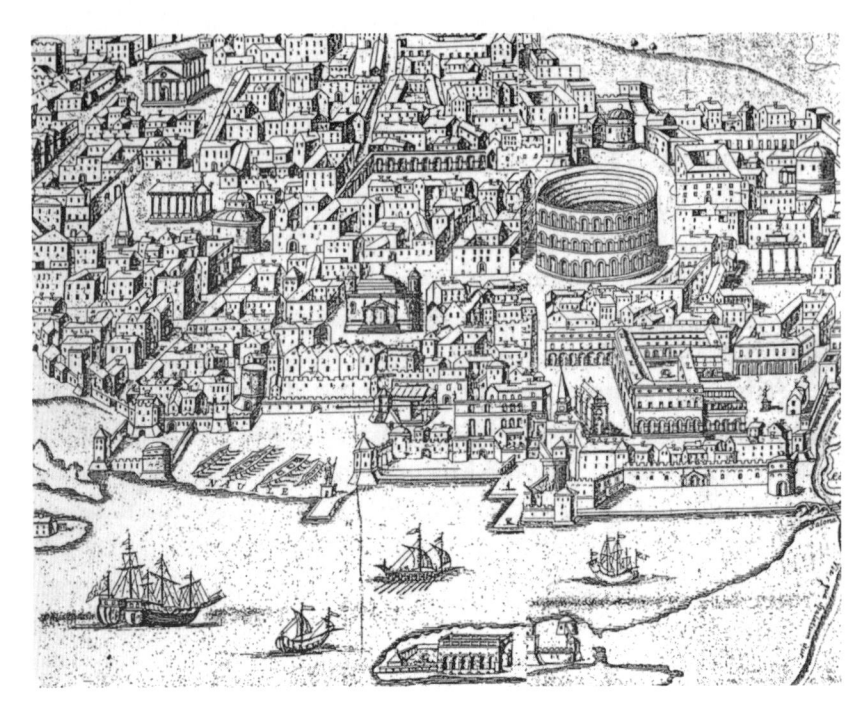

Image of Salona, by Vicentius Paternus, 1751

also head of the Dalmatian church.[5] The city, albeit much weakened by that time, would disappear in the early seventh century under the impact of the Avaro-Slav invasion, which inadvertently gave rise also to the city of Split, its successor and heir. Split arose out of the old imperial palace, which – having become a sanctuary for the Salonitans and others fleeing the invaders – transformed itself into the present-day capital of what remains of the ancient province. Its patron saint became St Domnius, the third-century bishop of Salona martyred by Diocletian.

In administrative reforms conducted by emperors Diocletian and Constantine, whereby the empire was divided into four prefectures, Western Illyricum, which comprised Pannonia and Dalmatia, was included in the Italian prefecture, with Rome as its capital. Dalmatia's southern extension, the area south of Kotor, was simultaneously detached and under the name of Praevalis added to the Eastern Illyrian prefecture that included also Dacia and Macedonia.[6] These reforms effectively divided the empire into two halves, West and East, along a line that followed Dalmatia's eastern border and extended across the Mediterranean Sea to the Gulf of Sirte. Dalmatia's fate remained closely linked with that of Pannonia. In the second century this large province had been subdivided into Upper (western) and

Dalmatian Beginnings

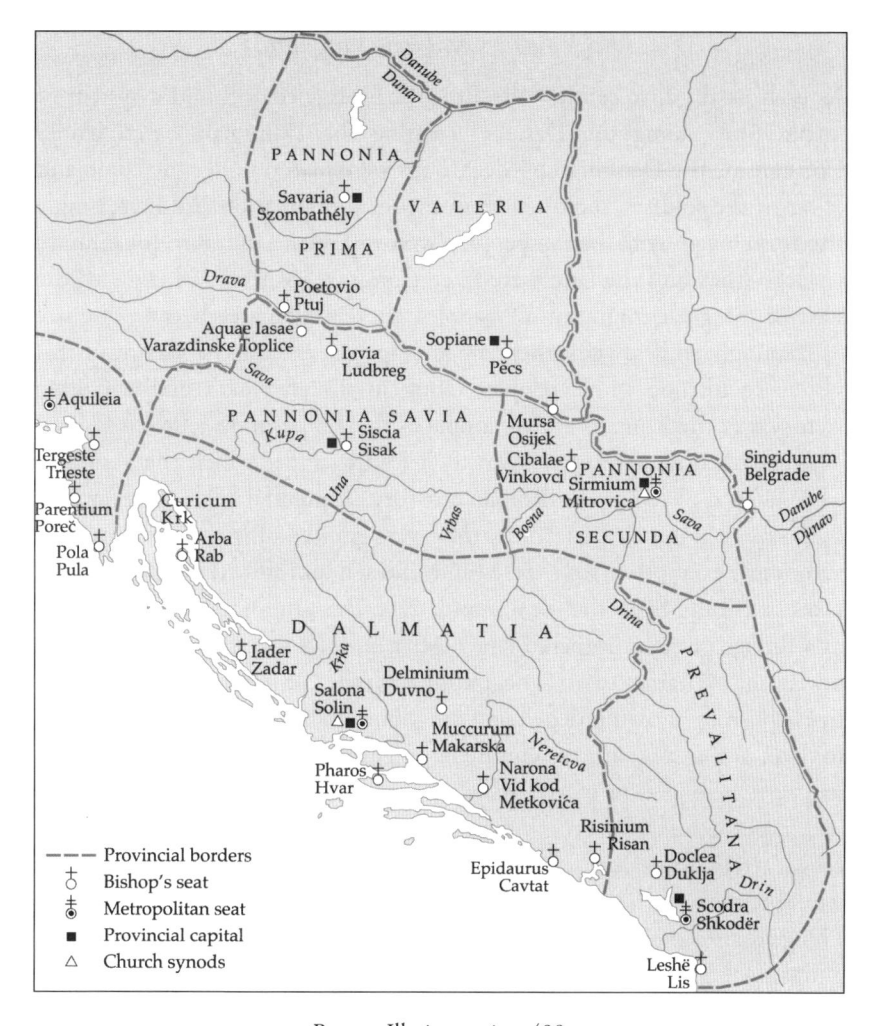

Roman Illyricum, circa 400

Lower (eastern) Pannonia, with the border between them drawn from the confluence of the rivers Vrbas and Sava to Lake Balaton. Under Diocletian, each of the two halves was further subdivided. Of the four Pannonias that emerged as a result, two lay south of the river Drava: Pannonia Savia, named after the river Sava, with Siscia (now Sisak) as its capital; and Pannonia Secunda, which was governed from Sirmium – another great city that has since disappeared, but whose name still identifies the lowlands between the Sava and the Danube (Srijem/Srem). Several centuries later these two southernmost Pannonias would acquire a new – Slav – population and a new name to match, becoming Slavonia.

Old frontiers and new kingdoms

As early as the first century the Romans proceeded to build a system of fortifications along the Danube, creating the Danubian *limes*. Under Constantine the Danubian border troops were placed under the command of *duces*; the soldiers, recruited from the local population and increasingly also from invading barbarian peoples, were given land in return for military service – they and the land were freed from taxes as well. When, with the start of the great migration of peoples, the Danube area became the site of seemingly endless wars, the Roman emperors extended a variant of this system to include whole peoples. Thus, in the aftermath of the Gothic victory over the Romans at Adrianople in 378, Emperor Theodosius I (379–95) concluded an agreement with their leaders under which the Visigoths were allowed to remain on Roman territory as imperial allies; in return for their service in the imperial army they were granted official titles, complete autonomy, exemption from taxes and, most important, the right to draw taxes or tribute from the local population. This amounted to recognition of a foreign state on imperial land.[7] After an initial submission to Roman power, the barbarian rulers – beginning with the Germanic kings – went on to establish their own independent kingdoms on the territories surrendered to them in this way; but the empire never gave up its claim to the lands that had once belonged to it, and which to its representatives were inalienably and in perpetuity its own. This commitment to the reincorporation of the crown territory was carried over into the Europe of the Middle Ages, and would acquire special significance in the case of the kingdoms of Croatia and Hungary after their great territorial losses to the Ottomans in the fifteenth and sixteenth centuries: their kings habitually swore at their coronation that they would regain the lost lands and reincorporate them under the crown and into the respective kingdoms.[8]

At the close of the fourth century it was the turn of the Ostrogoths to come to an understanding with Constantinople, after which they were settled in Lower Pannonia. A century later their king, Theodoric (474–526), became the master of Italy, or more precisely of the Italian prefecture bereft of Africa. He had inherited Dalmatia and probably also Pannonia Savia from his predecessor Odoacer: both provinces formed the Italian king's own patrimony for tax purposes. Theodoric proceeded to unite Dalmatia with Pannonia Savia into a single administrative unit headed by a *comes* who sat in Salona, and it seems that at this time the Savian bishopric of Sisak was placed under the jurisdiction of the archbishop of Salona.[9] Dalmatia spent over fifty years under Gothic rule, during which its Church greatly prospered; and it is

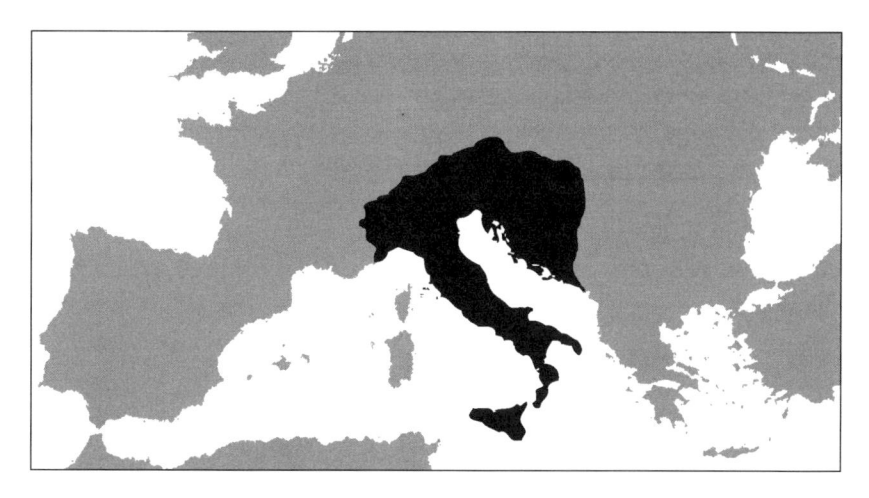

The Ostrogothic kingdom, circa 500

probable that the transformation of Diocletian's mausoleum into a Christian cathedral took place during this period. By creating a single administrative and ecclesiastical structure for Savia and Dalmatia, the Gothic king fashioned the mould in which the Croatian nation was cast.[10]

Dalmatia's strategic importance for the defence of Italy became visible during the long war against the Ostrogothic kingdom initiated by Emperor Justinian (527–65), with both sides fighting hard to win and keep it.[11] After the Goths were finally defeated, Justinian restored the earlier administrative system in Dalmatia and extended to it his legal system, within which the administrative and ecclesiastical borders were made to conform. The diocese of Sisak, however, remained part of the Dalmatian Church organisation. This ecclesiastical protrusion of Dalmatia into Pannonia would play an important role in the formation of the Croatian state.

In the second half of the sixth century Pannonia came under Avar rule, which was consolidated with the capture and destruction of Sirmium in 582. Under the protection of the Avar qagan Slavs now spread throughout the area between the Adriatic and the Aegean Sea, creating in the process a number of *Sclavinias,* areas in which the already decaying Roman order and civilisation came to be replaced by Slav rule organised in accordance with Slav law and custom. Salona's fall to the Avaro-Slav armies in 614 marks a decisive turning point in Dalmatia's history in that it would henceforth become closely bound to that of Croatia. Little is known of the circumstances of this change, since the Avaro-Slav invasion ushered in two 'dark centuries' characterised by the absence of eyewitness reports. Contemporary records, while noting the appearance of Slavs as an increasing menace to Roman Dalmatia, say nothing about the actual conquest of Salona and what happened subsequently in Dalmatia. At the end of the eighth century, however, after Charlemagne had destroyed the Avar empire and the Franks conquered Pannonia and much of Dalmatia, the sources began to register the presence of an organised Croat people ruled by a *dux*, but without offering any clues as to where they came from and how they got to Dalmatia. Only much later, in the middle of the tenth century, did the Byzantine emperor Constantine VII Porphyrogenitus (913–59) and his officials provide – in a work later named *De administrando imperio* (*DAI*) – a first account of the arrival of the Croats in Dalmatia, which was based on the Croats' own recall as transmitted to imperial officials by their Dalmatian neighbours, in particular those living in Zadar and Split.[12]

According to *DAI,* the Croats came to Dalmatia not in the first Slav wave but soon after the fall of Salona; once there, they overthrew Avar rule and established their own. The story, in fact, appears in two versions. In the first version the Croats, led by their military leader or *dux,* arrived from an area situated north of Hungary and close to the Frankish kingdom, and settled in Dalmatia with the permission of Emperor Heraclius (610–41). They recognised Roman sovereignty and entered into a written contract with the emperor – that is, they became *foederati*, a foreign kingdom on Roman soil. Initially a pagan people, after their arrival they were converted to Christianity by clergy sent from Rome at Heraclius' request. The other version does not mention Heraclius, but concentrates instead on the Croats' relations with the Franks, to whom they were allegedly subjected in both their old and their new habitats, but from whose overlordship the Dalmatian Croats managed to free themselves after a difficult and bloody struggle. According to this version, their country of origin was White Croatia, situated north of Bavaria; they were baptised after their successful rebellion against the Franks in Dalmatia. In this version the Croats came to Dalmatia led by seven brothers, or five brothers and two sisters, one of whom was called Croat (*Chrobatos*). This memory of the Croats' Dalmatian beginning was still alive in the thirteenth century when the Split cleric Thomas the Archdeacon used it in conjunction with his study of the archives of the Split (former Salona) Church to produce his own version of the coming of the Croats, their capture of Salona and the birth of the city of Split. According to Thomas's narrative, seven or eight noble clans arrived from Poland, or perhaps Bohemia, and 'when they saw that Croatia was suitable for settlement, since it was largely uninhabited, they demanded it and gained it from their *dux*. So they remained there and started to oppress the natives and forced them into becoming their servants.' Here both the land and the natives in question are firmly identified as Croat: 'Since ancient times this region was called Curetia and the people now called Croats were once called Curetes or Coribantes.' However, 'many called them Goths and also Slavs after the particular name of those who arrived from Poland or maybe Bohemia'.[13] According to Thomas's account, it was under the new ruling class that the native population acquired the Croat name and became identified as Slavs and Goths.

The Croatian state arose indeed in an area that before the arrival of the Romans had been dominated by two Illyrian peoples, the Liburni and the Delmatae, and came to include the central territory of another Illyrian people, the Iapodes. In Istria, meanwhile, the Croats came into contact with the local Histri. These native peoples and their cultures took part in a new ethnic symbiosis carried out under the Croat name, and joined the elite that in the wake of the empire's retreat began to fashion a new order between the river Drava and the Adriatic Sea.[14] That the Croat immigrants did not displace the local population but rather merged with them finds support in recent studies of the genetic origin of Europe's population, according to which most Croatians descend from the population that had lived for thousands of years in the area where the medieval Croatian state first arose.[15]

Stories of origin

As for the origin of Croat rule, both versions presented in *DAI* share the Byzantine point of view, according to which barbarian settlement appears as a consequence of imperial will rather than of conquest: by legalising the invaders' presence and by converting them to Christianity, the empire asserted its sovereignty over both the people and the land. As in the earlier case of the Goths, the terms of the arrangement are not recorded; but subsequent developments suggest that the Croats did indeed enter into a formal relationship with the empire, which did not actually rule over them.[16] Its authority in Dalmatia, insofar as it existed, had by now been reduced to discontinuous segments of the Adriatic coast made up of three arrays: the islands of Cres, Krk and Rab in Dalmatia's north; the cities of Zadar, Trogir and Split in the centre; and the cities of Dubrovnik and Kotor in the south.

The account of the Croat origins and arrival presented in *DAI* belongs to the medieval literary genre known as *origo gentis,* the story of origin, through which the histories of the peoples who had not been part of the ancient world yet came to rule over portions of the Roman empire were integrated with that of the empire itself.[17] As a rule, the story of origin recapitulates in a concise and schematic form the long and complicated history of the formation of a particular *ethnos*, by taking from it events deemed worthy of record and arranging them into a chronological order. Such stories are typically made up of three elements. First there is a people, which for some reason leaves its homeland under divine guidance. There follows a primordial deed, such as the crossing of a sea or river (the Rhine for the Franks, the Danube for the Slavs) or victory over a superior enemy or both, the successful completion of which creates conditions for the legitimation of a central core made up of leaders, or representatives of well-known families with proven leadership qualities, who are the bearers of the dominant tradition. Around this core a new gentile formation appears, through the separation of the existing community or its transformation. The new *gens* henceforth forms a privileged layer or nobility in relation to the local population. The final primordial act is religious conversion.[18] The Croat story of origin as recorded in *DAI* exhibits a similar pattern: an original separation from a larger tribal association (White Croats living beyond the Carpathians), the crossing of the Danube, the victory over the Avar or Frankish enemy, and conversion to Christianity. The newcomers brought with them a shared tradition, including their gentile name, and a core represented by the seven leaders and their followers, or by the *dux* and his retinue. They gave the name to the privileged or noble layer which came to rule over the Slavs already settled in Dalmatia as well as over the indigenous Illyrian and Roman population.

Apart from the name and the story of origin, however, there is little to link the White Croats with the *gens Chroatorum* that emerged in early medieval Dalmatia. Given the persistence over centuries of the legend of origin, some relationship between them did doubtless exist; but it has proved difficult to derive one directly from the other. In fact, rather than having a unique territorial focus, the Croat 'ethnic' name is found widely scattered over the area between the Baltic, the Adriatic and the Black Sea: as well as in Croatia, it has been registered in Ukraine, Poland, Germany, the Czech Republic, Slovakia, Slovenia, Montenegro, Macedonia, Albania and Greece. Although highly visible on the ground, however, it offers few clues to an earlier formation of the people. As noted by a Ukrainian scholar, it is as if one were looking at 'a strange shining object lying at the bottom of the sea, the contours of which fade as soon as we try to grasp what it is'.[19] Rather than constituting a nation in embryo, the migrating Croats – like other barbarian peoples who eventually settled on Roman soil – must have formed an ethnically diverse army kept together by the political skill and military achievements of their leaders. Such a formation would have fragmented at times, with parts joining other tribal formations, or become reinvigorated through new ethnic infusions. What can be said of those who made their way to Dalmatia, on the other hand, is that they were forged in close contact with the increasingly permeable Danubian *limes,* where during the sixth and seventh centuries a new constellation of peoples appeared whom the Roman sources called Slavs.[20]

The Slav progress at this stage is not unlike that of the Franks. The Franks appeared in the third century on the right bank of the lower Rhine as plunderers of Roman territory lying across the river. Their name, which probably meant 'free', emerged as the common designation of the Germanic peoples living north of the Rhine who united against the Roman Empire. It was only in the second half of the fourth century that the leading tribe of Salians came to be known as Franks.[21] The primordial act of crossing the Rhine had been accomplished at about this time, after which they were settled on Roman territory as imperial allies with the task of guarding the river frontier. There followed conversion to Christianity under Clovis at the end of the fifth century. The Slavs appeared somewhat later, on the northern bank of the lower Danube, from where they too raided Roman territory. If the Franks shared the west German language of the lower Rhine, the Slavs developed their own lingua franca, which survived for a long time across a large area covering a host of different idioms. The origin of their name is also uncertain, though it most likely involves self-definition, that is, the people who can speak, unlike their Germanic neighbours whom they called 'mute'.[22] Unable to defeat them, the Romans sought to contain them with bribes in money and land; but, as the Greek historian Procopius wrote, 'once they had tasted the Byzantine wealth it was impossible to keep them from it, or to make them forget the road to it'. In the case of the people called Croats, their movement ended with the establishment of their rule on territory conquered from, or ceded under contract by, the Romans. State formation now became the vital element of their development, and the main agency of their integration into the Roman world. The emergence of the Croat kingdom in Dalmatia accordingly marks the real as opposed to the mythological starting point of Croat history, the true beginning of the Croat beginnings, since it was within the medieval state or *regnum* that Europe's tribal formations evolved into legally constituted nations. Croat history thus properly begins as history of the Croato-Roman, or more precisely Croato-Dalmatian, synthesis.

Name as mark of identity

In their efforts to unravel the constellation of factors which set off the process of transformation of this heterogeneous community into a national people, historians are faced with the problem of the two 'dark centuries', the seventh and the eighth, during which the Croatian medieval kingdom emerged on the territory of Roman Dalmatia. In the search for clues as to the nature of the earliest forms of its legal and political organisation, the Croat name has come under particular scrutiny, since the name of a people lies at the core of its tradition. However, while the immigrants, to judge by their language, were undoubtedly a Slav people originating in the area adjacent to the Baltic Sea, the names of the leaders who according to legend brought them to Dalmatia are not of Slav origin. Neither are the constitution and terminology of the rule they established on their arrival, as reflected in the titles of their dignitaries: ban for military leader, *župan* for head of the primary unit of territorial division (*župa /županija*). These terms point instead to a Eurasian nomadic inheritance, associated with the area that was previously under Avar rule. This, and the fact that the Croat name (as Horoathos/Horuathos) appears on Iranian tombs from the second or third century found in the ruins of the old Greek settlement Tanais that once flourished at the mouth of the river Don, suggest a distant Iranian, indeed Sarmatian, origin of the people called Croats.[23]

Some scholars have argued that the Croat name echoes the cult of the sun-god Hors brought to the Slav world by Iranian-speaking people – that is, that it identifies a people (Hor-vat) in whose cosmology the sun played a central role.[24] It was accordingly the cult of the dominant social group rather than any single *ethnos* that, in its successive adaptations, travelled from the Asian grasslands to Europe. The wide diffusion of the Croat name suggests that it was transmitted by military elites who supplied the core of the migratory movements. Others too have argued that Croat was originally not an ethnic name but denoted a social rank, this time within the Avar empire – that it named the warrior caste which on behalf of the Avars governed the subjugated Slav peoples inhabiting the borderlands of their empire.[25] As Avar power weakened in the seventh and eighth centuries, this military elite was in a position to organise local revolts and replace the Avar government with its own. Thus the Bulgar leader who led an anti-Avar rebellion in the early seventh century and established a Bulgarian kingdom was called Kuvrat, rendered also *Crovatos/Crobatus*.[26] The Bulgarians and the Croats, indeed, have a similar myth of origin. In the second half of the seventh century a new wave of Asian horsemen appeared and took over Kuvrat's state, but along its edges the descendants of Kuvrat's armies survived, imprinting the area with their Croat name. The account given in *DAI* could thus refer to two distinct phases of settlement: one taking place during the Bulgarian phase of Avar rule, and another that occurred at the end of the eighth century, when the Franks fought their victorious wars against the Avars.[27] All these explanations, and others besides, associate the Croat name with a martial tradition. There is much evidence, indeed, that the government the Croats established in Dalmatia had a military foundation, whose sinews were provided by the chain of military outposts that emerged during the seventh century along the Roman roads connecting Pannonia with Istria and Dalmatia.

Territorialisation

The nature of the territorialisation of Croat rule is indicated by the fact that the Croatian counties named in *DAI* do not bear the names of individual tribal settlers, but evoke territory instead: they are named after rivers (for example, the county of Cetina), or refer to geographical locations (for example, the county of Sidraga/Convallis) or existing Roman settlements (for example, the county of Varvaria/Bribir).[28] Three of these counties – Gacka, Lika and Krbava, all situated in Liburnia's interior and providing the shortest and most favourable route between western Pannonia and central Dalmatia – formed together a distinct administrative domain governed by a ban, a post which in the Frankish area was associated with the office of *dux*. Liburnia was in late antiquity constituted as a separate province of Dalmatia, because of its great importance for the defence of Italy; its strategic aspect would explain its quasi-military constitution. With Liburnia in their hands, it was possible for Dalmatian Croats to move to southern Pannonia and establish another realm there, which, according to *DAI*, while autonomous from the Dalmatian Croatia, remained closely linked to it. The ban's territory thus acted as a buckle holding together the main areas of the Croatian state: Istria, Slavonia and Dalmatia.

If one accepts the Byzantine interpretation according to which Emperor Heraclius ceded territory to the Croat-dominated political association in exchange for recognition of his sovereignty and service in defence of the empire, then the Croat presence in Dalmatia, in contrast to that of the Avars, was recognised and made legitimate in Roman eyes. It was indeed this pact, some have argued, that stimulated an early transformation of a fragmented society into a unified political body.[29] As imperial allies the Croats would be exempted from taxes and the religious discipline of the empire, might acquire official titles and be vested with the right to draw tribute from the local population. The Croatian state, however, had its own independent legitimation and enjoyed sufficient internal cohesion to successfully resist all attempts to restore an active imperial presence in that part of Dalmatia. The revival during the two 'dark centuries' of the Dalmatian church, and on the other hand the rise of the new cities of Split and Dubrovnik, attest to largely amicable if not always harmonious relations between the old and the new Dalmatians.

Early adoptions into the Croat language of a large number of place-names in the east Adriatic area – from Koper and Poreč in western Istria to Dubrovnik and Kotor in southern Dalmatia – as well as of the names of the major rivers and mountains suggest that ethnic and cultural amalgamation began soon after the Croats' arrival, since they could have come about only through direct contact with the local population. In view of the closely intertwined nature of their habitation, moreover, the new Dalmatians must have been exposed quite early on to the Christian influence of the cathedral cities, but the tempo of their conversion depended on the ability of the local church to undertake sustained missionary work. The fact that a large number of places bearing names of Christian saints traditional to the area have survived in archaic Croat forms – such as Supetar for St Peter, Sućidar for St Isidorus, Stobreč for St Laurentius, Stombrata for St Martha, Sutvara for St Barbara – shows not only that Christian life survived in areas under Croatian rule, especially in the vicinity of the Roman cities, but argues also in favour of an early date of Croat conversion to Christianity.[30] Croatia's early history was thus one of steady assimilation into the bi-polar Roman–Christian world and the civilisation of the Adriatic and southern Pannonian regions. It was the lands of the interior, however, where the establishment of Croat dominance was swift and complete, that provided the core of the new state. Along the coast, meanwhile, where the Roman legacy was initially dominant, its spread involved a slower process of social and political integration. The continuity of Roman civilisation in this area endowed Croatia with a specific personality, which came to be reflected also in the kingdom's medieval name: it became *Croatia atque Dalmatia* or Croatia with Dalmatia. The church played a key role in this process of mutual adaptation. At the time of the Croat arrival the unity of the Dalmatian church remained to be restored, although the Bishop of Split – who now occupied Emperor Diocletian's old quarters in the Split palace – was treated as *primus inter pares*. The Dalmatian church was under Rome's jurisdiction, but the papacy, squeezed between Roman emperors residing in Byzantium and the barbarian rulers of Italy, was having a hard time: following the death of Pope Gregory I (590–604) Rome saw twenty popes in less than a century. In 732 Emperor Leo III sought to remove the Roman pontiff's jurisdiction over the Dalmatian bishoprics, on the grounds that imperial bishops could not be directed by a church leader who was himself the subject of a foreign ruler, in this case the Lombard King of Italy. This was the beginning of a major ecclesiastical dispute, associated with the iconoclast crisis, which poisoned relations between Constantinople and Rome for over a century. One result of this was that in the middle of the eighth century Pope Stephen II placed the Roman Church under the protection of the Frankish kings.

The Carolingian inheritance

At the close of the eighth century the whole order in Dalmatia became caught up in the whirlwind of wars waged by Charlemagne, against first the Lombards and then the Avars. By 774 Lombard Italy was in his hands, soon after that Byzantine Istria too. The acquisition of Istria opened the door to Dalmatia and to *Hunia*, or Avar Pannonia. In 791 Charlemagne moved his troops against the Avars from Bavaria along the Danube, while his son Pippin took the old Roman road through Liburnia from Tarsatica (now Rijeka) to Senj, crossed the Kapela Mountains and proceeded into Pannonia. The war lasted eight years (791–9) and ended with the conquest of the Avar empire, which soon disintegrated under the combined pressure of internal dissension and foreign occupation. Various Slav armies drawn from the edges of the Avar realm fought on the Frankish side and gained land and titles in return.[31] A string of Slav states appeared along the eastern border of Charlemagne's empire, which the Franks made part of their imperial system by turning their military leaders into vassals and enlisting them in their wars against the Avars and other imperial enemies. These states, however, were named in the Frankish chronicles not after the peoples who established them, but after the old Roman provinces, which now re-emerged as constitutive elements of the new political order, providing an organisational framework for the emergent Slav polities: they became their homelands or *patriae*. The Slav collectivity consequently became differentiated by these *patriae*: they became known as the Slavs of Carniola and Carantania, of Pannonia and Dalmatia.[32]

The Croatia that emerged at the end of the Frankish-Avar war was a politically unified territory governed by Christian rulers allied to the emperor of the West. Whether it was Charlemagne's power that actually created this princely Croatia, or whether that power only accelerated the consolidation of an already existing state order by furnishing additional military muscle in

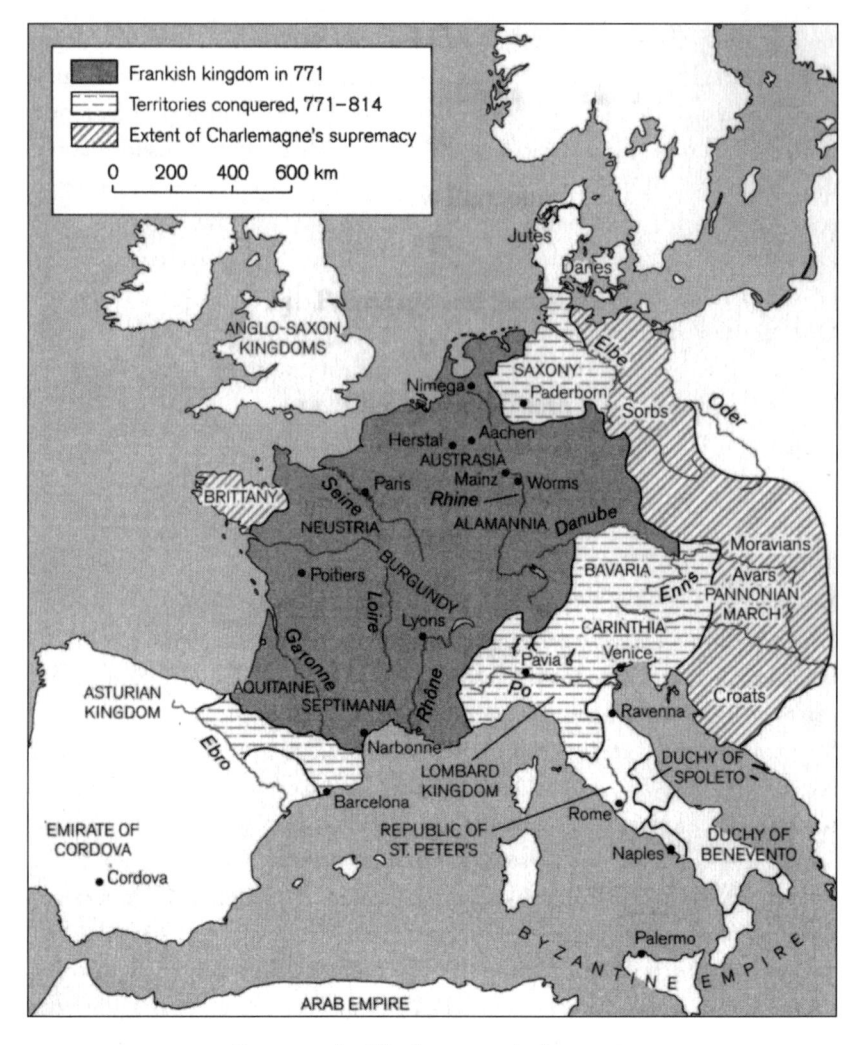

Europe under Charlemagne, ninth century

the form of auxiliary armies or access to more advanced weapons, is disputed among historians. What is certain is that the war provided an opportunity for ambitious local rulers to advance their own interests by siding with the Franks, and that the Croatia which came out of it was to all appearances a Carolingian formation. Charlemagne's reach into Western Illyricum clearly had supplied the compelling stimulus enabling the nascent state finally to overcome local resistance to its consolidation under the authority of a single prince.

Croats played a crucial role in the Frankish conquest of Dalmatia and Pannonia. The central residence of the Avar kings, indeed, was destroyed in

796 by a Slav leader called Vojnomir, who probably came from the Croatian area, given that his expedition was organised by the Frankish margrave Eric of Friuli.[33] The strategic importance of the Croat lands was highlighted at the start of the ninth century, when Ljudevit, leader of the Pannonian – or Slavonian – Croats, rose with the support of the Slavs of Carniola and Carantania against the enforced assimilation of his society into the hierarchical order of Charlemagne's feudal system. It took the Franks three years (819–22) to suppress this rebellion, seen by contemporaries as the greatest challenge confronting the empire after Charlemagne's death in 814, given the ongoing conflict with Byzantium over Istria and parts of the former Lombard kingdom, and more generally over imperial rights and religious orthodoxy. The earlier alliance between the Pannonian and Dalmatian Croats now came unstuck, for in their efforts to crush the uprising the Franks were aided by Ljudevit's southern neighbour, Borna. Frankish sources name him in 819 as *dux Dalmatiae*, and in 821, the year in which he died, *dux Dalmatiae atque Liburniae,* that is, of both Dalmatia and Liburnia. When the vanquished Ljudevit sought refuge with one of Borna's relatives, he was killed in confirmation of the Dalmatian principality's unswerving loyalty to the Western emperor; it is possible that at this time Dalmatian Croatia came to incorporate the western, Savian, part of Ljudevit's Slavonia.

Croatia's outline at the start of the ninth century can be established with some accuracy. In the east the border ran along the river Cetina to the point where the river bends sharply to the north, and from there to the source of the Vrbas, after which it largely followed the river's right bank up to the river Sava and thence continued northwards in a nearly straight line to the Drava, and then upstream to Croatia's present-day border with Slovenia. The area to the east, namely Pannonia Secunda, came briefly under Bulgarian rule and would remain a contested area. The lands to the west were under direct imperial control, which made the border stable: with a minor modification on the river Kupa, this border has remained unchanged to the present day. South from it Croatia held the eastern coast of Istria up to the river Raša, though it would lose this in the twelfth century, despite the fact that much of Istria was at this time settled by Croats under Frankish patronage. The territory south of the river Cetina as far as the Neretva, including the central Dalmatian islands, became the home of the *Narentani* (Neretva) Slavs, who in the ninth century entered the Croatian political orbit for good. East of the river Vrbas another political formation would appear in due course: Bosnia with Usora.[34]

Croatia's border with Byzantium was settled by negotiations between the two empires. In 805 Charlemagne's Croat allies, backed by a naval expedition led by the Friulian margrave, were poised to take the Byzantine part of Dalmatia too, prompting the Zadar *dux* and bishop to travel to the imperial court at Diedenhofen, where they met Venetians invested with a similar mission: to offer their city's formal submission. In the following year, however, a much stronger Byzantine navy sailed into the Adriatic, and the conflict was in the end resolved by compromise. The Peace of Aachen of 812 confirmed the existing territorial disposition between the Frankish and Byzantine empires, leaving Venice as well as the Dalmatian cities to Byzantium – thus out of Croatia's reach. In the second half of the ninth century the Eastern empire, faced with Arab incursions into the Adriatic, organised its part of Dalmatia as a separate military-administrative unit or *thema* with Zadar as its capital. The *thema* would henceforth be supported with a varying degree of determination by Byzantine naval power and diplomacy; but the new arrangement remained largely a formality, since this remnant of the Roman past soon reverted to its by now well-established existence as a set of loosely connected self-governing urban municipalities separated from each other by stretches of Croat-controlled coast.

In contrast to the situation further north, where the Alpine Slav principalities became submerged into Charlemagne's state system and saw their leaders replaced by Frankish counts, Croatia retained its autonomy. In Frankish eyes the Croatian king was *dux,* a vassal of the Western emperor who acted as the military and civilian governor of this frontier part of the empire, bound to perform military duties and appear at imperial councils. Hierarchically he was subordinated, initially at least, to the margrave of Friuli, who had overall responsibility for the newly acquired territories of Istria, Dalmatia and Slavonia. But the Croatian *dux* was no mere imperial official – he was also the elected ruler of the Croats. This dual underpinning of his legitimacy was evident at times of dynastic succession: when Borna died, his nephew Ladislav was proclaimed the ruling prince 'at the request of the people and with imperial consent'.[35]

The integration of the Croat state into the Frankish empire not only aided the development of administrative and judicial machinery, but also altered perceptions of the nature of political power. Trpimir (845–64), who ruled in Croatia as a vassal of King Lothar of Italy, appears in the documents produced at his court as *dux Chroatorum* 'by divine benevolence'. A Saxon cleric called Gottschalk, a dissenting theologian and friend of the margrave of Friuli, who spent two years at Trpimir's court at Klis, wrote that in the eyes of his people Trpimir was *rex*.[36] Trpimir was thus a *kralj*, the Croat Charlemagne

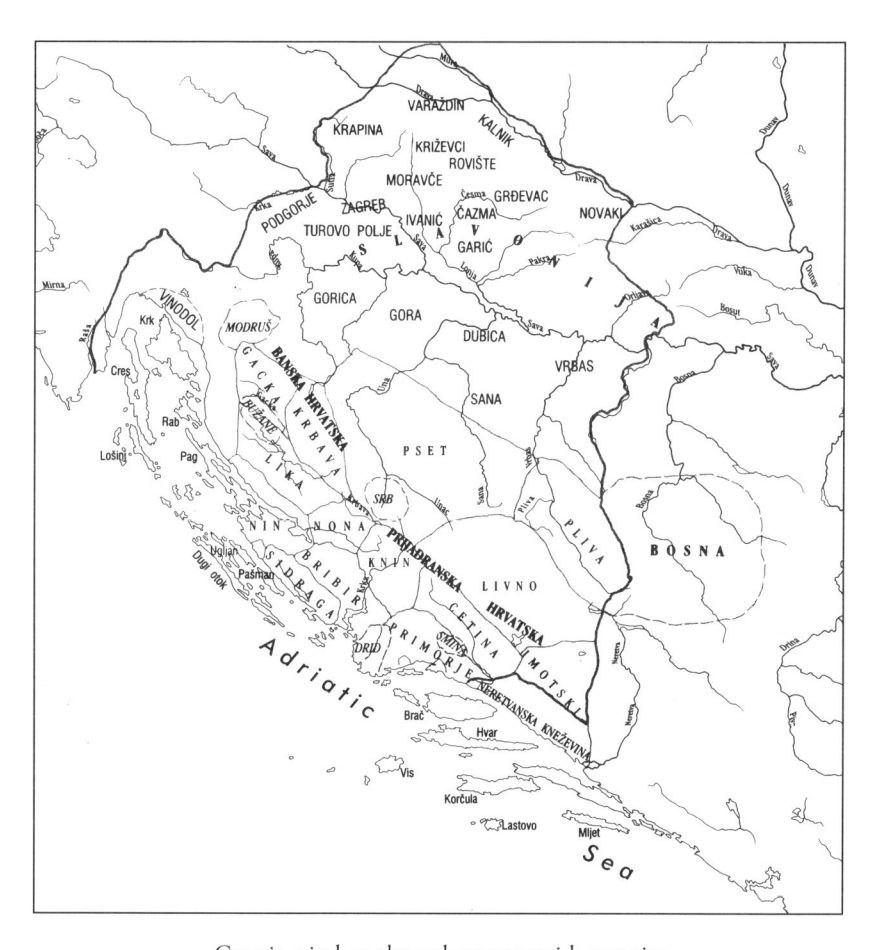

Croatia, ninth to eleventh century, with counties

(*kralj* being a derivation from Carolus), whose power was both personal and territorial. He was the supreme ruler, military commander and judge within his realm, with the right to tax the population and demand hospitality. His administration was modelled on the system that prevailed in other parts of Frankish Europe, its basic division being the county (*županija*), which acted as the unit of tax collection and of military and ecclesiastical organisation, governed by officials residing in fortified centres. Their heads (*župani*) formed part of Trpimir's court.[37] The army under the king's command was recruited within the counties, which fielded hundreds of soldiers, based on local clans. The Croatian administration also incorporated elements of the older imperial order, in which the city and its surrounding territory (*civitas*) and the bishoprics associated with it dominated the countryside. Documents issued by his court name this territorial power *regnum Chroatorum* –

kingdom of the Croats. In fact, according to Gottschalk, Trpimir's officials habitually referred to their king not as *rex* but *regnum,* in the same way that officials of the Byzantine cities of Split and Trogir evoked the emperor in Constantinople as *imperium*. The Dalmatian cities supplied a good number of Trpimir's officials, recruited from the clergy, who brought with them an understanding of government based on bureaucracy, and the concept of unitary state that Byzantium had inherited from Rome.

Although after Charlemagne's death Europe's regional kingdoms, including Croatia, began to consolidate on lines of their own, they nevertheless remained self-consciously part of a unified Christian society that had emerged out of the collapse of the Roman Empire in the West. Croatian rulers and their family members made pilgrimages to the same holy places in Friuli as did the Frankish rulers and other Slav princes under their influence,[38] and they organised their court in the Frankish manner. The Croatian court thus typically included a palatine or court judge, a chamberlain who headed the royal household, a court chaplain, a chancellor who ran the writing office and took care of the royal treasury, and state officials (*župani*). By the end of the ninth century the court became even more elaborate. The king was advised by the court council attended by the *župani,* and all state documents were issued in Latin. When in the 870s Carolingian chanceries introduced Christian-era dating, the Croatian court scribes soon followed suit. Crown revenue derived from several sources: the royal lands, land tax, custom levies, fines, gifts, hospitality (which could take a monetary form), and later also tribute paid by the Dalmatian cities.

Since in Frankish eyes the Croat *patria* was Dalmatia, however, Trpimir was *dux Dalmatinorum,* even though the imperial court knew that he did not rule throughout all the old Roman province. But with much of the western part of Roman Dalmatia having become Croatia, the Dalmatian name in time became restricted to the cities remaining in the Byzantine sphere of influence, and will hereafter be used in this sense. Trade and other contacts which the Dalmatian cities continued to maintain with the opposite coast of the Adriatic Sea kept alive their Roman and Latin civilisation, whence it radiated into the Croatian interior, as well as to the new ports of Šibenik and Biograd founded by the Croatian kings in the tenth century. Though the cities were oriented towards Constantinople and the sea, their peace, security and economic prosperity vitally depended on friendly relations with the Croat state dominating their hinterland. Major decisions regarding Dalmatia continued to be made in Constantinople, but in reality the cities were left to their own devices in fashioning their relationship with the Croat ruler.

Their inhabitants spoke the local Dalmatian dialect and, if literate, wrote in Latin, while their Croat neighbours spoke a Slav language and initially at least were illiterate. Nevertheless, the cities' chronic lack of land and people stimulated an early Croat inflow, and with it an ethno-cultural symbiosis starting with the elites. The Croatisation of Dalmatia proceeded faster in Trogir and Split, somewhat more slowly in Zadar, and still more slowly in Dubrovnik; but by the tenth century Croats formed the majority of their populations. Studies of personal names current in the tenth century within the upper social layer of Zadar, capital of the Dalmatian *thema*, show that 75 per cent of them were either Croat or of Croat derivation.[39] As in the Dalmatian cities, their church and their notables bought or gained land and rights on Croatian territory – through royal donations or by marriage, through the granting of citizenship to individual Croats or in other ways – Croat customary law invaded their legal practice, at the same time as Latin clergy recruited from the cities became employed by the royal court to record such land transactions in the area of its authority.[40] The realities of everyday life thus inexorably drew together the Adriatic cities and the kingdom encamped outside their walls, in the process changing the nature of both. Croatian rulers sought from the start to win control over this Dalmatia, by application of military pressure or diplomatic tact or both, and were at times encouraged in this direction by the pope or the Byzantine emperor seeking regional allies. However, it was the determination on the part of the Roman Church after 800 to regain control over its West Illyrian dioceses that proved decisive in overcoming the political division between Frankish Croatia and Byzantine Dalmatia.

Church organisation

The spread of Frankish power during the late eighth and the early ninth centuries was as a rule accompanied by an extension of Christianity to the previously pagan areas, or where an older church organisation survived by its transformation in accordance with Frankish norms and understanding. Istria thus used to be the domain of the patriarchs of Grado, but they proved too loyal to the Byzantine emperor, so after some hesitation the Istrian church was transferred to the authority of the patriarch of Aquileia, who became responsible also for conversion of the rest of the area governed by the margrave of Friuli, including Croatia. In the areas north of the river Drava, this task was entrusted to the archbishop of Salzburg.

Up to this time there had been no organised church in the Croatian lands, but after the Peace of Aachen both empires were able to concentrate on re-establishing the ecclesiastical structure in their respective orbits. In the middle of the ninth century a new bishopric was accordingly established at Nin, one of the principal seats of the Croatian kings where Christian life had survived the migrations. The bishop of Nin, whose jurisdiction included the whole Croatian area between the Drava and the sea, was made a suffragan of the patriarch of Aquileia, and his church became the main conduit for missionary activities undertaken at this time by Frankish priests. They encouraged the growth of monastic orders, necessary for training the local clergy, beginning with the order of St Benedict. Benedictine monasteries established by kings Trpimir and Branimir in the last quarter of the ninth century and run by Frankish clergy became the nurseries of Croat Latinity. Crown land and income were used to endow the Croatian church and the monasteries, support the renovation of old churches and aid the construction of new ones, whose patron saints became the saints venerated in the Frankish empire, particularly in the patriarchate of Aquileia.

The Croatian kings, however, endowed also the Dalmatian church in tacit recognition of its traditional primacy. The intimacy between Croatian kings and Dalmatian prelates was aided by the fact that the state's centre had become firmly established within the triangle formed by Nin/Zadar, Knin (ancient Tenin, known also as 'the gate to Zadar') which the Romans had built on the river Krka, and Klis guarding the approach to Split. Klis became one of Trpimir's principal seats and he built a Benedictine monastery just below the castle. The nature of his relationship with the Split archbishop can be gleaned from a document issued by his court in 850, when the king, unable to find enough silver for the monastery, turned for help to Archbishop Peter of Split, who was also godfather to one of his sons. The bishop gave eleven pounds of silver in return for a portion of land with tied labour near Solin (Salona), that is, in the area of the Croatian church's jurisdiction, on which Trpimir's father had built a church dedicated to St George, as well as the tithe from the royal estate of Klis. The Croatian bishops resented royal donations to the Dalmatian church, which they saw as an infringement of their own wealth and authority, and after Trpimir's death this bequest was challenged by Bishop Aldefred; but Trpimir's son, Muncimir, confirmed it as a possession of the Split church. At about this time Croatian kings started to acquire Christian saints' names in addition to traditional Croat ones, a custom which it seems began with Trpimir's son Peter, the godson of the archbishop of Split.

The re-christianisation of the Croatian area was by now well advanced. The ecclesiastical leaders in the areas ruled by Frankish kings had understood very early on that religious conversion, education and spiritual care demanded use of the vernacular. Whereas before this time only Hebrew, Greek and Latin were recognised as church languages, by the end of the eighth century religious education in other languages was authorised, since only in that way could the illiterate population be brought to understand the difference between virtue and sin. Once Charlemagne's empire came to include Slavs, religious literature appeared also in the Slav language, written with Latin letters. Depending on the political circumstances, Rome approved the use of Slav as the language of the church. The Western church insisted, however, on the primacy of Latin in liturgy, the education of the clergy and Church administration. The Eastern church, by contrast, was accustomed to use of the vernacular. The Byzantine Empire indeed produced an outstanding scholar in Constantine (St Cyril, 827–69), who is credited with creating a new Slav script – the Glagolitic, or Glagolica, alphabet – into which liturgical and scriptural texts necessary for evangelical missions and the training of Slav clergy were translated.

In 862-3 Constantine and his brother Methodius arrived in Moravia at the invitation of its prince, spending three years there before being forced out by the Frankish clergy, even though – and because – their mission enjoyed strong support from Rome. Their mission fell victim, in fact, to the bitter conflict between Rome and Salzburg over religious jurisdiction in post-Avar Pannonia. Popes Hadrian II and John VIII insisted that Western Illyricum had always been under papal authority, while the Bavarian clergy rested their case on Charlemagne's decision that Pannonia north of the river Drava was their concern. One outcome of this was that Rome endorsed the use of the Slavic language and alphabet in the Catholic Church, justifying this departure on the grounds that 'He who created the three principal languages, to wit Hebrew, Greek and Latin, created also all other [languages] for His praise and glory.'[41] Constantine, who became a monk and assumed the name of Cyril, died in Rome in 869 and was buried there. His brother Methodius was eventually appointed archbishop of Sirmium, with authority over all Pannonia north of the Drava, but upon his death in 885 his leading disciples were expelled from Moravia. It was after the debacle of the Moravian mission that the Slav liturgy started to spread into Croatian lands. Contrary to a widely accepted view that it took root first in the area under Croatian rule, it was in fact the Dalmatian Byzantine cities which, having by now acquired a sizable Christian Slav constituency, were the first to welcome the appearance of Slav-speaking Glagolica clergy.[42] Successive popes would subsequently ban the use of Slav in celebrating the mass and 'the most sacred offices' on pain of excommunication, and limit the use of Slav to the religious education of 'simple and unlearned people'; but the use of Slav in the liturgy nevertheless survived in Croatia, and through Croatia became integrated into the life of the Catholic Church.

The establishment of a large Croatian bishopric at Nin under the jurisdiction of Frankish Aquileia complicated the renewed attempts by the Roman pontiffs to re-establish ecclesiastical unity in the former Roman Dalmatia under their authority. The accession of Basil I (867–86) to the imperial throne proved helpful in this regard, since the new Byzantine emperor, unsure of his position, wished to heal the long-standing feud with Rome over theological issues and church jurisdiction. At the last united Christian synod held in Constantinople in 869, it was decided that Bulgaria would remain under its patriarch, while Roman Dalmatia was tacitly left under papal authority. Further negotiations in regard to Croatia and Dalmatia between the Eastern emperor and Pope John VIII (872–82) took place in 878–9. But an agreement between these two powers was not enough – the pope had to win also the consent of the Croatian king in his role as protector of the church. Keen to promote closer integration of Croatia and Dalmatia, Trpimir supported the restoration of the old Salona church organisation; yet this could not advance so long as Croatia remained part of the Frankish imperial system. During much of the ninth century Croatian rulers continued to recognise the overlordship of the kings of Italy and fought wars on their behalf. In 871, for example, the Croatian navy joined an imperial expedition to free Bari in Apulia (Puglia) from the Arabs. However, as the Western empire became torn by dynastic rivalries, its influence over Croatia declined, until, following the abdication of Emperor Charles III in 887 and his death a year later, the ties were effectively broken. The authority of the Aquileia patriarch also faded as a result. Three events occurred at the end of the 870s which confirmed Croatia's new political orientation: Basil I instructed the Dalmatian cities to pay the tribute normally paid to his representative in Zadar to the Croatian king and other Slav princes, in return for their nominal submission; Pope John VIII re-asserted Rome's rights in Dalmatia in fresh negotiations with the Byzantine emperor; and Croatia acquired a new ruler in Branimir who promptly announced his desire to renew his kingdom's ties with Rome. Armed with little more than diplomacy, the pope wrote four letters addressed to, respectively, 'our dearest son Branimir'; the Croatian people and clergy; and the newly elected, though as yet unconsecrated, Croatian bishop Theodosius; the fourth, more threatening in tone, was directed to the Dalmatian clergy and people, demanding their return to the fold of the Roman Church on pain of excommunication.

The correspondence between the pope and Branimir suggests that they were negotiating terms under which the pope's ecclesiastical and possibly also secular authority would be extended to Croatia. Branimir's chief concern, however, was to strengthen his own influence in Dalmatia, so Theodosius gained his pallium not in Rome but in Aquileia, during the king's visit in 880 to a nearby place of pilgrimage.[43] This left the pope with no other option but to recognise the new bishop, whom he appointed as his envoy to the Bulgarian king (there was still hope that Bulgaria would return to Rome). In 882, however, the pope died, to be followed in 886 by Basil I. King Branimir quickly moved to strengthen his position in Dalmatia. Taking the opportunity presented by the death of the incumbent bishop of Split, he got the local clergy to elect Theodosius in his place. Pope Stephen V (885–91), accepted, under protest, the fait accompli and even offered to recognise Theodosius as the Dalmatian archbishop, provided he submitted to papal authority; but this attempt by the Croatian king on the one hand and the pope on the other to unite Croatia and Dalmatia through the medium of the Church failed, since Byzantium under Basil's successor Leo VI (886–912) re-asserted its influence in Dalmatia, while the papacy entered a state of prolonged crisis. The course for Dalmatia's integration into Croatia was nevertheless set, maintained by Croatia's own growing power.

Constantinople, which had shown little interest in Moravia, could not overlook Croatia. Church unity in the Croatian lands might have been achieved under the authority of the patriarch of Constantinople, as happened in Bulgaria and Serbia; but this would have required Croatia's absorption into the Byzantine commonwealth.[44] There was a distinct possibility of this happening during the time of Basil I, but Croatian resistance proved too strong. Basil I did manage to install a pro-Byzantine ruler, Zdeslav (878–9), but he was soon killed by an anti-Byzantine court faction in the forging of which Theodosius, then merely an archdeacon, played an important role. Unwilling to exchange a weak Frankish overlordship for a more intimate Byzantine one, Branimir sought support in Rome; but, as we have seen, negotiations between the interested parties proved inconclusive. In the circumstances prevailing at the time, any lasting progress in achieving a political union of Croatia and Dalmatia needed the goodwill of Byzantium. A new situation arose in the early tenth century when, in response to a very real threat from Simeon's Bulgaria, Byzantine emperors sought help from regional Slav rulers and found an effective ally in the Croatian king Tomislav (910–28). Tomislav's successful campaign against the Bulgarians, as well as against Magyar tribes which appeared at this time north of the Drava, led to his appointment as imperial proconsul in Dalmatia with the right to a proportion of the taxes normally paid by the Dalmatian cities to the imperial treasury. This rapprochement between Croatia and Byzantium helped to create the political conditions for the unification of the Croatian and Dalmatian churches, and provided also the background against which Emperor Constantine VII and his clerks composed the Byzantine version of Croatian history in which Tomislav's Croatia appears as a major regional power.

It was in 925, during the reign of King Tomislav, that Pope John X (914–28) finally managed to persuade the Dalmatian bishops to return to Roman jurisdiction, by promising them the restoration of their earlier dioceses on Croatian state territory. The Dalmatian prelates, and in particular the bishop of Zadar, found the continued existence of the Nin bishopric unacceptable, however, on the grounds that ancient Aenona, the precursor of Nin, had not been a bishop's seat but part of the diocese of Zadar. The pope appealed to Tomislav in his capacity as king of Croatia-Dalmatia, and Tomislav – albeit reluctantly – acquiesced. Despite the protests of Gregory, the Nin bishop, whom the king initially backed, it was decided that the huge Croatian bishopric would be abolished and its parishes distributed among the Dalmatian dioceses.

The other important issue which this synod and the following one, held in 928, had to resolve was that of hierarchy. The bishop of Split claimed primacy on the grounds that Split was Salona's successor; the bishop of Nin believed that he should be the archbishop, not only because his church was by far the largest in the kingdom, but also because his predecessor had been confirmed bishop of Split; while the bishop of Zadar felt that this honour belonged to him, since Zadar was Dalmatia's capital. The bishops of Zadar and Nin travelled to Rome to argue their respective rights, but in the end the metropolitan power was acquired by the bishop of Split on the basis of the alleged apostolic tradition of the Salonitan church: 'Since blessed Domnius was in ancient times sent to preach in Salona by Peter the Apostle, it is decided that the church and the city where his relics rest should have the primacy over all other churches in this province and acquire the legitimate title of metropoly over all other bishoprics.'[45] The pope also confirmed that the authority of the Split church included also 'all of Croatia'. Its suffragans became the bishops of Zadar, Rab, Krk and Osor in the north, and those of Ston, Dubrovnik and Kotor in the south; their bishoprics too were to 'realise the same fullness of their seats and borders and at all times the dogma of the Catholic faith'. The dissatisfied parties – the bishops of Nin and Zadar, and possibly also the Croatian king and nobility – were warned to respect this decision. The church organisation thus reverted once again, nominally at least, to the form that had prevailed before the Slav invasion, with Split now playing the role of Salona. The deposed bishop of Nin was offered a choice of four dioceses, including the Savian one of Sisak, but chose instead the restored bishopric of Skradin.

With the metropolitan centre established in Split, Dalmatia gained an even greater importance for Croatia. Church unification, on the other hand, furthered the area's cultural amalgamation. Slav liturgy and the Glagolitic script spread throughout Croatian parishes at the same time as unity with Rome demanded the removal of all influence of the Eastern rite from the Dalmatian church. Despite recurring papal attempts to impose full linguistic and spiritual congruence on the united church, Slav liturgy survived. Latin remained the privileged language of the Croato-Dalmatian church, in that all priests had to know Latin; but the overwhelmingly Slav nature of their congregation forced the local clergy to rely also on texts written in Slav letters. At the end of the twelfth century the Cyrillic script, a closer adaptation to the Greek alphabet, made its appearance in the Croatian lands, soon to be followed by texts written in the Latin alphabet. The result was that Croatian literature emerged from the Middle Ages displaying its characteristic – and in the Slav world unique – scriptural trialism.[46]

A united kingdom

Croatian-Byzantine relations became close under Emperor Basil II and King Stephen I Držislav (969–97). The Croatian king recognised nominal Byzantine sovereignty and was in return invested with the government of Dalmatia. Such acts were, however, more a matter of international diplomacy than of the regional balance of power. Beginning with Držislav, the Croatian kings regularly called themselves kings of Croatia-Dalmatia. Držislav's mother Helen, born into the powerful Zadar family of Majo, built the church of St Mary and St Stephen on the rivulet of Jadro in Solin (the former Salona), which became the royal family's burial place. Situated on the old Roman road leading from Salona/Solin to Split, it epitomised Croatia's presence in Dalmatia. Its hold over Dalmatia, however, was now increasingly being challenged by Venice. In 1000, following a successful campaign along the east Adriatic coast directed mainly against the unruly Neretva Slavs, the Venetian doge Pietro II Orseolo, who was also Držislav's father-in-law, proclaimed himself *dux Dalmatiae* – a purely fictional title, in fact, since Venice did not gain actual possession of Dalmatia.[47] Venice did, however, stop paying to the Croatian rulers the customary annual 'peace tax' for undisturbed sailing along the Croatian coast. Having won at this time important trade concessions in Constantinople, the republic's need to control the east Adriatic coast in order to protect its ships sailing to and from the Levant turned it into Croatia's most determined rival in Dalmatia.

The kingdom's ties with Byzantium weakened in the middle of the eleventh century, with the arrival of Normans in southern Italy and Turks sweeping into Asia Minor. In the situation of the empire's near collapse, King Peter Krešimir IV (1058–74) won indisputable control of Dalmatia from Emperor Romanus IV Diogenes (1068–71). The united kingdom was by now perceived as a single political and administrative entity, although the Dalmatian name remained attached to Croatia's in recognition of the autonomy of the Dalmatian municipalities, and at times also of Byzantium's ultimate sovereignty over it. Under Peter Krešimir IV the medieval state reached the zenith of its development, permitting the king to proclaim that during his reign 'our kingdom has been extended on land and sea' and that the Adriatic had become 'our Dalmatian sea'.[48] Krešimir emphasised his state's Adriatic orientation by moving his capital to Biograd, which now became a cathedral city, and by granting a charter to the city of Šibenik. Peter Krešimir IV ruled 'by divine grace', but also by right of inheritance. Named after his grandfathers Krešimir III and the Venetian doge Peter Orseolo II, he was brought up in Venice and gained the crown in the course of a dynastic struggle in which his elder brother perished. That the king was responsible for his brother's death was denied, however, in testimony sworn by the king and twelve of his counts before the papal legate Abbot Mainard, who met the king at Biograd. His innocence having been established in this way, he was confirmed king of Croatia-Dalmatia by Pope Nicholas II. The church became the main pillar of Krešimir's rule in Dalmatia, and the king the main protector and benefactor of the church. His image is preserved on the marble relief adorning the font of the baptistry in Split cathedral, which in its overall composition and relevant details testifies to Croatia's immersion in the cultural mores of eleventh-century Carolingian Europe. The relief shows the crowned king sitting on his throne, holding a cross in his right hand and an orb in his left: the customary symbols of the dignity and power of a Christian monarch, who is the bearer of divine law and justice on earth. On his right stands a court official partially turned towards the king, carrying what must have been a roll in his arms symbolising the king's law, which now governed the realm. A figure lies prostrate at his feet in complete submission to royal power and its divine inspiration. The erased inscription above referred, in all probability, to the king as justice.[49]

This was the time of the great schism between the Eastern and Western churches, and the pope, wishing to prevent any disorder in Croatia that could leave his church exposed to Byzantine pressure, sent Mainard to Biograd. The Roman Church was in the full throes of the reform movement that had started at the turn of the tenth century in Cluny in France, and which aimed to reorganise the Church administration, codify the Roman rite, and remove all secular influence over the church's internal affairs. The reign of Peter Krešimir IV coincided with those of three reforming popes: Nicholas II (1058–61), Alexander II (1061–73) and Gregory VII (1073–85). Mainard thus came to Croatia not only in order to sit in judgement on the new king, but also to appoint new bishops capable of vigorously promoting the reform that would establish 'the primacy of St Peter' in Croatia. This undertaking relied in the first instance on the Benedictine order, which had emerged as one of the most ardent proponents of the reform and whose centre in Monte Cassino played a decisive role in the election of the three reforming popes (Mainard himself came from there). In 1060 Lawrence, the bishop of Osor whose Benedictine monastery had supplied a number of key reformers, was, in the royal presence, unanimously elected archbishop of Split. The new metropolitan introduced the custom of bishops having to swear loyalty to their archbishop, and generally encouraged them to act also as secular leaders. The reform movement reached its high point under Pope Gregory VII, whose belief in the ultimate supremacy of the pope (*dictatus papae*) over the secular rulers of Christendom would lead to an open breach not only with the emperor, but also with the Croatian king. Krešimir, while endorsing many of the reforms, refused to become an obedient vassal of a pope who believed that his right to rule Christendom derived from St Peter, that the emperor and the regional kings could rule only by a delegation from him, and that he could absolve a defiant ruler's subjects from allegiance to their king.[50]

The king and the archbishop worked at first in harmony, with Krešimir joining Lawrence in sanctifying new churches and establishing new monasteries. A large number of smaller churches were built or renovated at this time. The extent of Peter Krešimir's generosity towards the church is illustrated by the establishment of eighteen new Benedictine monasteries,

Seal of King Krešimir IV, 1070

two of which were for women. They were built mainly along the coast, and include St Mary in Zadar and St John the Evangelist in Biograd (subsequently destroyed by Venetians). This great industry stimulated in turn a major revival of architectural skills and the visual arts in Croatia. Consonant with the revival of interest in the early church, the king and the archbishop paid particular attention to the holy sites of ancient Salona, in whose proximity three Benedictine monasteries were built. One of these, a convent dedicated to St Euphemia, was erected at a place associated with St Domnius situated just outside Split's northern wall at the point where the road from Salona/Solin enters the city. The inscription placed above its door was to remind passers-by of the close rapport established between Church and State, which animated and drove forward the religious reform movement in Croatia: 'This work was completed in AD 1069, when Krešimir reigned in Dalmatia and you, Lawrence, were bishop.'[51] In that same year the Croatian king built a dazzling basilica in Solin dedicated to St Peter and St Moses as a symbolic counterpoint to Lawrence's cathedral in Split. Grafted upon the foundations of Salona's largest church, built in the sixth century but now in ruins, and incorporating the worked stone that had survived, its design was conceived as homage to the land's early Christian past. The relief described above was carved from one of the residual marble tablets, and placed in front of the altar in salute to the king as God's vicar on earth. The frequency of Church synods held at this time indicates the great pace of the reform, but also the strength of the resistance that it was generating. The reform party, made up of the upper secular and Church dignitaries, including the bishops and the royal court dominated by Benedictine monks, regularly denounced as heretics the defenders of existing social and religious customs, such as the right of priests to marry or wear beards and long hair. Krešimir managed to check this reaction, which may explain his depiction in such a prominent place as a dispenser of justice. On the other hand, Lawrence's attempt to suppress the Slav liturgy, by closing churches that offered Slav services, remained a great source of friction, especially in the Adriatic north where that liturgy had taken deep root. The popularity of the Glagolica clergy, and the support it gained from Counter-Pope Honorius II (1061–4) backed by the emperor, led to a compromise by which the Slav liturgy would not be banished, but its spread would be restricted.

In this tense alliance between the Church and the crown, the Church proved to be the more determined and better-organised side. The second half of the eleventh century witnessed great political turbulence in Western Europe, associated with the investiture contest between pope and emperor. The king, as was usual in Croatia, watched with great interest what was happening in Italy. During the 1070s Byzantium finally lost Bari to the Normans, who were papal allies, and the assertive Cardinal Hildebrand became Pope Gregory VII. Krešimir joined the fray by aiding the Bulgarians in their revolt against Constantinople. It seems, however, that there now occurred an irreparable breach between the pope and the king, who must have proved too independent for Gregory's liking. There was a fear that Krešimir might seek in Constantinople a balance against Rome, thus endangering the pope's hold over Dalmatia, which he considered his own. In 1074 the king was captured by a dispossessed Norman noble somewhere in the Adriatic, possibly on Gregory's orders, after which he disappeared. In the following year the Croatian ban of Slavonia, Demetrius Zvonimir, who had married the sister of the Hungarian king Géza I Árpád (1074–7), twice visited the pope in Rome offering himself and the kingdom to papal protection. The Byzantines also showed their interest: in 1075–6 the Venetian doge, acting in the name of the Byzantine emperor, made the representatives of Split, Trogir, Biograd and Zadar promise that they would not invite 'Normans or other foreigners to Dalmatia'. Finally, in 1076, the year in which Pope Gregory VII excommunicated Emperor Henry IV, Zvonimir was invested by papal envoys as King of Croatia-Dalmatia. Krešimir's legitimate successor, Stephen, was forced to retire to the monastery attached to the church of St Mary and St Stephen on the river Jadro. There is no doubt that Archbishop Lawrence played a crucial role in this denouement.

Zvonimir's crowning was a highly conspicuous event. It took place in Krešimir's basilica in the presence of the higher clergy, the Croatian nobility and the representatives of the Dalmatian cities. On the eve of the coronation Krešimir's marble image underwent careful alteration: the roll was removed from the arms of the official and the inscription, in which the word 'law' remains barely visible today, deleted. King Zvonimir (1075–89) swore fidelity to the pope and received from his envoy sword, sceptre, crown and the papal flag. The coronation oath was drafted by the Roman curia: 'In the name of the holy and indivisible Trinity, in the year of our Lord 1076 I Demetrius called also Zvonimir, by divine grace king of Croatia and Dalmatia, was empowered by our lord Pope Gregory and vested with the government of the Croats and Dalmatians, and constituted king [...] in the Salonitan basilica of St Peter and St Moses through joint and united choice of the clergy and the people.'[52] The new king promised to promote justice, respect human dignity (that is, banish the slave trade), prevent illegal marriages and protect the poor, widows and orphans. He also vowed to aid the church in its struggle against simony and clerical marriage, and to pay an annual tribute of 200 gold coins to the Holy See. Zvonimir ceded to the pope the wealthy abbey of St Gregory on Lake Vrana near Biograd with all its contents for the use of papal envoys. To the Split church he donated the county of Cetina with all its revenue, the church on the Jadro where Croatian kings were buried – and Krešimir's basilica.[53] True power in Dalmatia was to remain in Archbishop Lawrence's hands. A partial compensation was the re-establishment of the bishopric of Nin, albeit over a smaller area, and the creation of a 'Croat bishop' (later the bishop of Knin), who acted as royal chancellor and whose authority extended to the river Drava. Zvonimir, in all probability, was aided in his rise to the Croatian throne by his Hungarian relatives. His alliance with the church ensured peace in his lands during the difficult period that opened with the enforced exile and death of Pope Gregory VII, which was closely followed by Zvonimir's own. Legend has it that Zvonimir was killed by his people, but there is no evidence that he died a violent death. His successor Stephen II (1089–91) inherited an orderly kingdom, but he died without leaving a legitimate heir and so precipitated a wider struggle for the crown of Croatia-Dalmatia.

Stephen's death coincided with the ejection from Rome by imperial troops of Pope Urban II (1088–99). The Hungarian king Ladislav I (1077–95), having defected to the emperor's camp, immediately moved against the Croatian kingdom by seizing Slavonia and installing his nephew Álmos as its *dux*, after which he informed the abbot of Monte Cassino – and through him the pope – that he had 'gained almost all of Slavonia' (meaning Croatia). Ladislav's hope was that the pope would recognise Álmos as King of Croatia, but nothing came of it, because he was unable to move further south due to strong Croatian resistance. In 1092, moreover, the Byzantine emperor Alexius I Comnenus (1081–1118) sent his navy into the Adriatic, took control of Dalmatia and formally claimed the Croato-Dalmatian kingdom. According to the medieval Split historian Thomas the Archdeacon, Ladislav's Croatia now remained limited to Slavonia, that is, the area north of the Kapela Mountains.

The end of an era

The dynastic tie with Hungary established under Zvonimir may explain why the Hungarian king met little organised resistance from the Slavonian *župani* after crossing the Drava. Those who promptly swore loyalty to the new king were rewarded with confirmation of their property and privileges. It was a different matter with the church. The Slavonian capital, Sisak, had survived the migrations as a cathedral city and served as the principal seat of the local rulers before becoming firmly attached to the Croatian kingdom. The bishopric of Sisak, which formed the core of the county of Zagora or Gora (Gora being the name of the bishop's seat at this time), was now once again a possession of the archbishop of Split. With Dalmatia remaining outside his reach, the Hungarian king was faced with the problem of a potentially hostile ecclesiastical authority in Slavonia.

During the preceding centuries Slavonia had welcomed Slav missionaries, who were spearheaded most probably by Moravian clerics who, supported by local Croatian nobles, had set up a number of Benedictine monasteries using the Slav liturgy. Ladislav's first step towards bringing the Slavonian church under his control was to proclaim this liturgy a form of heresy, *error idolatriae*.[54] His next step was to break the bishopric's tie with the Croatian church by bringing in a new bishop, a Slav cleric named Duh, who was made suffragan first of the Hungarian archbishop of Esztergom and then of the archbishop of Kalocsa. The bishop's seat was soon after moved from Gora to an old Benedictine monastery close to the citadel (*castrum*) of Gradec, the precursor of Croatia's present-day capital of Zagreb, and new – Hungarian – clergy imported to run the bishopric. In contrast to the rest of Croatia the centre of the bishopric of Zagreb thus emerged in a place where there was no city to begin with; nor, indeed, would one exist there for a long time to come, since Gradec would acquire a royal charter only in 1242. The Glagolica monasteries, denied all support, underwent a rapid decline; some of them must have been destroyed, which would account for the almost complete absence of Glagolica documents or inscriptions in Slavonia, in contrast to their proliferation in the surrounding areas. The presence of the older church organisation is recalled, however, in the facts that the oldest possessions of the Zagreb bishop lie in the Sisak area; that the oldest rite of the Zagreb church, with its roots in Glagolica liturgical books, was named after Gora; that the archdeacon of Gora ranked first on the list of Zagreb archdeacons; and that the church of Sisak was treated as the first church within the diocese.[55]

Ladislav's failure to take the rest of Croatia thus led him to create a new church administration in Slavonia. The pope was presented with the need to accept not the establishment of a new bishopric – an act beyond the powers of the Hungarian king – but a transfer of jurisdiction: that is, with a 'correction' of borders between the archbishoprics of Split and Kalocsa. Rome at first refused to acknowledge the Hungarian fait accompli; long after the Hungarian kings had indeed acquired all Croatia, the pope continued to address them solely as kings of Hungary. Once their rule appeared secure there, however, Rome finally accepted the border revision. This was not the only change in the Croatian-Dalmatian church. The bishopric of Dubrovnik had become now a separate archbishopric, its area of jurisdiction formally defined in 1022.[56] In 1154 Zadar too became a separate archbishopric, so that by the middle of the twelfth century the original unity of the Croato-Dalmatian church established under native Croatian kings had disappeared for good.

As for Croatia south of the river Kupa, it is not clear what actually happened there after the death of King Stephen II. It seems that two pretenders to the crown emerged: Petar Snačić (or Svačić) from Knin, and Slavac from Split; but the Croatian nobility proved unable to unite around a king from its own ranks, and the question of the succession in Croatia became a subject of international dispute. The Hungarian king Ladislav claimed the kingdom on the grounds of dynastic ties, but this was contested by the Byzantine emperor, in whose eyes the kingdom had always been part of his empire. Pope Urban II felt that the decision as to who should rule in Croatia-Dalmatia belonged to him, since both Croatia and Hungary were vassal states of Rome. Venice insisted that Croatia-Dalmatia had been transferred to its administration by the previous Byzantine emperors. Finally Emperor Henry V argued that the kingdom was rightfully part of his domain, since Western Illyricum belonged to the Western empire; to emphasise this claim, he even sent his army against Hungarian-held Bratislava. A certain count of Havichsburg took part in this campaign – the first registered evidence of the Habsburg family's presence in this part of Europe.[57]

In 1097, however, the Hungarian king Coloman (1095–1116) crossed the Drava, defeated Petar's army at the mountain of Gvozd in the Kapela range and arrived in Biograd. Military victory alone, however, could not secure international recognition of his rule in Croatia – he had also to be formally crowned. After prolonged negotiations an agreement was reached between the Croatian nobility and the Hungarian king, known in Croatian historiography as *Pacta Conventa* after the document in which it appears. According to this document, the news of Coloman's army on the Drava moved the Croatian nobility to prepare a defence. Seeking to avoid war Coloman sent his deputies to negotiate, after which a formal meeting took place between the Hungarian king and the heads of leading aristocratic families. They recognised Coloman as their king in return for his confirmation of their status, property and rights, including freedom from taxation for themselves and their subjects. The agreement also contained a military clause: in the event of a foreign attack on the two kingdoms joined in this way, the Croatians would supply armed knights up to the Drava at their own expense, and beyond the Croatian borders only if paid for by the king. The military side of the agreement clearly assumed that both parties treated the Drava as the political border between the two kingdoms. The agreement allowed Coloman to be crowned king of Croatia-Dalmatia in 1102 in Biograd. The new king confirmed also the existing rights and privileges of the Dalmatian cities.[58] Coloman secured Byzantium's acquiescence by aiding Emperor Alexius' efforts against the Normans, and by marrying his sister to the emperor's son, John. The Croato-Hungarian kingdom's close involvement with the Byzantine empire lasted throughout the twelfth century, despite occasional wars fought for control of eastern Slavonia and of Dalmatia which, during the lifetime of Emperor Manuel I Comnenus (1143–80), reverted for the last time to Byzantine rule.

This account of how Coloman became king of Croatia appeared in the middle of the fourteenth century, when Croatia and Hungary were ruled by another – Anjou – dynasty, and at a time when royal counties were once again being established in central Croatia, raising anew the issue of the nature of royal power in the kingdom. Headed 'How the Hungarians gained the realm of Dalmatia and Croatia', the *Pacta Conventa* aimed to correct the interpretation given by Thomas the Archdeacon in the previous century, who, relying on Hungarian sources, had presented the union as resulting from conquest. In this (the fourteenth) century, however, this explanation had been replaced by another: King Louis I of Anjou had gained Croatia by dynastic right, but it was Coloman who actually subdued the kingdom and joined it to Hungary. The Croatian document rejected both assumptions – that of conquest and that of a lawful succession – stressing instead that Coloman became Croatian ruler by mutual agreement of the king and the nobility. Deposited in the archives of Split cathedral where the Croatian kingdom's land books were kept, *Pacta Conventa* was subsequently reproduced in each and every subsequent copy of Thomas's own chronicle. In this presentation of the origin and legal nature of the union of Croatia and Hungary, the term 'Croats' refers to the community made up of 'all Croat noblemen, aristocrats and landowners' of the kingdom, who are portrayed, moreover, as direct descendants of the seven clans which, according to the old legend, had come to Roman Dalmatia and established the Croatian state there. The document's main message was that the Hungarian king ruled in Croatia only by consent of the nobility, meaning that no final and absolute political authority existed outside the Croatian political body; and, by extension, that Croatia was a political subject distinct and separate from Hungary.[59]

The end of the Trpimirović dynasty and the arrival of the Árpáds re-oriented Croatia towards Pannonia. By this time, as attested by Archdeacon Thomas's *Historia salonitana,* the kingdom had become firmly identified with Roman Dalmatia. The work's very first sentence states that Dalmatia and Croatia had since ancient times been one and the same country. Salona – to which, Thomas alleges, St Peter had sent St Domnius to preach – had been the 'capital of Dalmatia and Croatia'. John of Ravenna, who is said to have revived the Dalmatian church soon after the Avaro-Slav invasion, was active throughout 'Dalmatia and Croatia'. The *dominium* of the Croatian kings was 'Dalmatia and Croatia', which included also Slavonia. Thomas's narrative, though punctuated by frequent references to fights between the people of Split (called also *nostri)* and the highlanders ('Croats'), has only praise for the Croatian kings and their generosity towards the Dalmatian church. He was fully aware of the fact that the Pannonian Árpád dynasty showed little interest in Dalmatia and its church. Thomas was a leading cleric in a city whose bishops used to bear the title of metropolitan of 'Dalmatia and all of Croatia'. This title subsumed the long formative period of both the church and the state in the early Middle Ages, which ended with Pope Gregory VII playing the role of honorary godfather of the Croato-Dalmatian nation: the oath that Zvonimir swore on the occasion of his coronation refers to him as ruler of the 'kingdom of the Croats and Dalmatians'. The unification of the Dalmatian church had as its corollary the political unification of Dalmatia and Croatia, which ensured the harmonisation of the state and ecclesiastical borders. This unity inferred in retrospect the identity of the two, as illustrated by the map of the Mediterranean drawn by the great Arab cartographer Al-Idrisi (1100–65) in which Croatia extends from Istria to Dubrovnik – although Dubrovnik had in fact never been ruled by native Croatian kings.[60] The understanding that Croatia, Dalmatia and Slavonia formed a single kingdom informed, of course, all the external claims to the Croatian crown raised after the death of King Stephen I: those of the eastern and western emperors, Rome, Venice and the kings of Hungary.

Although the unity of the Split church had disappeared by the time Thomas wrote its history, the perception that the kingdom should have its own autonomous church organisation did not. In 1240 Herzeg Coloman, the brother of the Croato-Hungarian king Bela IV (1235–70), who ruled as a near-sovereign prince in Croatia, made one last attempt to create a unified church hierarchy for the kingdom. Keen to rid the bishopric of Zagreb (by far the wealthiest part of his realm) of the influence of the Hungarian court, he appealed to Pope Gregory IX to allow a merger of the Split and Zagreb churches, in view of the great impoverishment of the Dalmatian church. He even offered to surrender his title to the future archbishop of Zagreb. The annual income of the bishop of Zagreb at this time was nearly four times that of the bishop of Split and three times as large as that of the bishop of Zadar. The parlous state of the Split church made it difficult, indeed, to fill the bishop's seat: all six bishops elected to the post between 1217 and 1220 declined the honour on the grounds of likely penury. Stephen, the bishop of Zagreb at this time (1225–47), was a scion of the powerful Slavonian family of Babonić. A graduate of the University of Paris, he completely transformed the life of his large diocese by inviting in the Franciscans and Dominicans, and by turning the canonical chapters in Zagreb and Čazma into public notaries. Bishop Stephen supported Herzeg Coloman's project, as did the Split bishop and municipal leaders, but the enterprise failed in the end. Rome did not wish to surrender its traditional rights in Dalmatia to the Hungarian king, but strong resistance came also from the Hungarian church.[61]

TWO

The Triune Kingdom

When the Árpáds became also kings of Croatia they established a separate administrative apparatus for its government, headed by either the crown prince or the next son who bore the title of *rex* or *dux* of Dalmatia-Croatia, or alternatively of 'all Slavonia' – meaning all the Croatian lands between the Drava and the Adriatic Sea. To ensure succession, the crown prince would usually be crowned during his father's reign, whereupon he became 'the younger king' and was entrusted with the government of Croatia. When he became king himself, this position would pass to his younger brother. The establishment of the king's son in Croatia was more a recognition of the power of the territorial lords than a forceful intervention in the kingdom's internal affairs. The resident nobility retained the Croatian legal system, which underpinned the autonomy of the land and their own and their people's collective identity.

In the fourteenth century, the role of royal representative in Croatia was assumed by the ban, who – alone or in the assembly of nobles and officials – executed the king's justice. At such assemblies the ban discussed the affairs of the kingdom, heard complaints, issued documents affirming individual or collective rights and privileges, and implemented any particular decision made by the king. These assemblies became in time permanent institutions. The ban also led the army of the kingdom, alone or alongside the king; supervised the collection of taxes; and at times acted as arbiter between the Dalmatian cities. After an initial period of reliance on their own imported officials, the Árpád kings regularly appointed Croatian magnates as Dalmatian city governors, but the cities retained the right and power to challenge any individual choice.

The differing historical evolution and organisation of government in Dalmatia, central Croatia and the Slavonian lands north of the river Kupa – together with the contrasting ways in which the new dynasty established itself in each of these parts and the nature of the obstacles that the kings faced in their efforts to rule over them – produced, however, by the middle of the fourteenth century three differently articulated systems of regional government or *regna*, leading to Croatia's constitution as the Triune Kingdom of Dalmatia, Croatia and Slavonia. A terminological clarification is necessary here. The fact that the Latin term *regnum* is normally translated as 'kingdom' may give the impression that at this point in history the Kingdom of Croatia dissolved into three separate kingdoms. Dalmatia and Slavonia, however, never became separate kingdoms: they continued to belong to the Croatian crown. They differed, however, in the way in which they were governed: the term 'triune' refers solely to this aspect. 'Croatia' consequently refers to two different albeit related things: the realm of the Croatian crown, and the narrower area of the Croatian *regnum*. It should be clear from the context to what the term actually refers in each case.

The *Dalmatian* regnum

The Dalmatian cities acquired very early on the capacity for self-rule and evolved self-governing institutions, similar in many ways to those of Italian city-states. They deferred to Byzantium in the sense that they helped the imperial navy to maintain control of the Adriatic, in return for its protection. While never actually repudiating imperial authority, they obeyed it, however, only to the extent that it did not infringe their autonomy, which remained grounded in individual city governments dominated by secular and clerical notables. The cities' location on the empire's edge inevitably strengthened their self-reliance; but their traditional autonomy and territorial scatter prevented the creation of a unified regional government, even when Dalmatia became organised as a *thema*.

The cities kept their freedom also under Croatian rule. It is a moot point whether their institutionalised autonomy or the kingdom's failure fully to absorb them was the primary cause of their continued separateness. The unity realised under the Croatian rulers was certainly strong enough, on the other hand, to permit the emergence of a realm-wide church organisation – a feat that would elude all their successors. Union under the same crown brought considerable advantages to both sides and created a bond that survived long periods of political separation.

With equal stubbornness the cities resisted falling under Venetian control, despite the fact that their Mediterranean trade inclined them to cooperation with whomsoever controlled the Adriatic Sea. This Janus-like nature of the Dalmatian ports did not disappear when the Croatian crown was acquired by the Árpáds; it became if anything more visible, since the new rulers, preoccupied mainly with their Pannonian possessions, abandoned the native kings' Adriatic orientation. A pattern was soon established, with the cities accepting Venetian overlordship at times when the king threatened their autonomy by imposing his own bishops or placing his troops within their walls; when his prolonged absence left them exposed to Venetian threats or to the local lords' pressure; or when dynastic conflicts threatened anarchy in their hinterland. But they would return to royal rule as soon as the king was able to defend them from Venice, or in other ways guarantee their freedoms. At the same time, since the cities also clashed with each other, usually over territory and church jurisdiction, they sought support among all the interested parties, including the local Croatian counts and the pope. This offered much scope for outside interference in their internal affairs. The Croatian kings' main enemy in Dalmatia remained Venice, against whom they fought intermittently and with varying success for centuries. Lacking a strong navy, however, and with the cities refusing to be garrisoned, their enterprise proved to be one of ever-diminishing returns.

In the interregnum that opened with the death of King Stephen II in 1091, the cities recognised first Byzantine and then Venetian rule. Dubrovnik switched directly from Byzantine to Venetian authority. As king of Croatia Coloman regained most of Dalmatia, but by the time of his death the coast was again in Venetian hands. His son Stephen II (1116–31) won back Biograd, Šibenik, Trogir and Split, but Venice kept Zadar and the northern or Kvarner islands of Osor, Krk and Rab. In 1125–6 Venice, supported by the Eastern and Western emperors, was back in Šibenik, Trogir and Split; on this occasion it razed Krešimir's former capital of Biograd to its foundations, forcing its bishop to remove himself to Skradin. Ten years later Šibenik, Trogir and Split returned to royal rule, but not Zadar. A decade later still Venice took the central Dalmatian islands of Brač, Hvar and Vis; by winning control also of the Istrian cities it became the true mistress of the Adriatic Sea. In 1154 the bishopric of the now Venetian Zadar was raised to the status of an archbishopric, and the bishops of Osor, Krk and Rab (for a while also of Hvar) were made its suffragans. Disregarding the city's wishes, however, the pope placed the new archbishop under the authority of the patriarch of Grado, who headed the Venetian church. Venice's ability to influence the choice of the Zadar archbishop supplied an important instrument of rule in northern Dalmatia. Zadar rose three times against Venice during the twelfth century, to which Venice responded by, among other things, exiling leading members of its nobility.

Iadra ad cedem. Zadar surrenders to the Crusaders in 1202

After the brief Byzantine interlude, Biograd, Šibenik, Trogir and Split again recognised the Croato-Hungarian king Bela III (1173–96). So too did Zadar, which was this time successfully defended by the ban's army. Unable to crush the city, in 1202 Venice made a deal with a passing Fourth Crusade army led by French knights, according to which, in return for favourable terms of hire of Venetian ships to take them to the Holy Land, they were to seize 'Zadar in Slavonia' and hand it over to Venice. The quest to liberate Jerusalem from the Muslim 'infidel' was thus to begin with the destruction of the Christian city of Zadar. Two Old French chronicles, one written in 1208 by Geoffrey de Villehardouin from Champagne, the other penned in 1216 by Robert de Clari from Picardy, describe in some detail the knights' negotiations with Doge Henrik Dandolo, the divisions which his proposition caused among them, how they arrived at their decision, the ensuing siege of the city, and its surrender.[1] After spending the winter in Zadar the Crusaders went on to seize Byzantium too, where they established the short-lived Latin Empire (1204–61), a large portion of which was assigned to Venice together with the privilege of appointing the patriarch of Constantinople. Although the Venetians would later be expelled from Constantinople, they managed notably to retain Crete.

Zadar's fate was in fact sealed by the dynastic struggle that erupted after Bela's death between the new king, Emerik (1196–1204), and his brother, Andrew. To prevent future claims to his Adriatic possessions by Byzantium or Venice, Bela had Emerik crowned separately as king of Croatia. This ended the custom according to which the king's brother ruled in Croatia as a semi-sovereign prince.[2] The conflict began with Andrew claiming his rights in Croatia, which he soon won: in 1198 he became duke of 'all of Croatia, Dalmatia and Hum [Herzegovina]'. This, however, did not end his defiance, which led to his temporary arrest and imprisonment. In this situation King Emerik applied to Pope Innocent III for the return of Zadar, but the pope, who had done nothing to prevent its fall, was unable to rectify the deed. The archbishop of Split tried to help Zadar, but it was the Croatian count Domald of Sidraga who managed to liberate the city, after which he was elected its *comes*. Domald could not hold Zadar, however: a year later the Venetian navy appeared once again in its waters and the city, realising its impotence, returned to Venetian rule. The story of its earlier fall repeated itself, albeit in not so drastic form, in 1216 when Andrew, now King of Hungary and Croatia (1205–35) and intent on joining the Fifth Crusade, gave up his rights to Zadar in return for passage on Venetian ships. Zadar rose again in 1242, during the visit to Dalmatia of Andrew's heir, Bela IV (1235–70); but Bela's army was defeated and he too surrendered his rights to Zadar. This time the city was forced to sign a punitive peace with Venice, which gained the right to appoint its *comes* as well as to control its economy and its navy.

A new star now appeared on the Dalmatian horizon: the Neapolitan Anjou dynasty. In 1264, at the instigation of Pope Urban IV and with the material support of the French Church, Charles of Anjou, brother of the French king Louis IX, won the crown of Sicily from Emperor Frederick II's son Manfred. Together with the crown he acquired the desire to conquer Constantinople. In 1271 he crossed the Adriatic, took Durrës (Durazzo), and proclaimed himself King of Albania. His progress was checked, however, by uprisings in Sicily itself, which led to his losing the island to the rival Aragon kingdom. This outcome gave rise to two Sicilian kingdoms: Sicily and Naples. Charles became King of Naples.

Bela IV's successor, Stephen V (1270–72), established close ties with the Neapolitan royal house by marrying his heir, Ladislav, to Charles's daughter Isabella and his daughter Mary to the crown prince also called Charles (later

King Charles II). Stephen's early death, however, meant that both Ladislav IV (1272–90) and his brother Andrew, duke of Croatia, were under age, so the governance of the kingdoms devolved to their mother, Elisabeth. Her rule, however, was not acceptable to a number of important Croatian and Hungarian lords. When in 1278 the Croatian duke died, another Andrew – the youngest son of Bela IV, born after his father's death and brought up in Venice – stepped forward to claim the right to rule in Croatia. The rebellious magnates then invited Andrew to take the Croato-Hungarian crown. After Ladislav's death in 1290 the Hungarian lords, after some hesitation, invited Andrew to assume the throne. But there were other claimants to this crown, who raised objections to Andrew's accession.

The German king Rudolph I Habsburg (the first Habsburg to hold this title) argued that during the Tartar invasion of 1241–2 Bela IV had left Hungary and Croatia under the protection of Emperor Frederick II, so the crown properly belonged to his own son Albrecht of Austria. Ladislav's sister, Queen Mary of Naples, supported by Pope Nicholas IV, declared that she – or rather her son, Charles Martel – was the rightful heir: in 1292 Charles Martel was indeed crowned King of Hungary and Croatia by a papal envoy in Naples. The Habsburg claim was settled by Albrecht's military defeat, but the Anjou problem proved more difficult, given that much of Croatia sided initially with the Anjou pretender. In the end its nobility too accepted Andrew III (1290–1301) as their king, whereupon his Venetian mother was installed as ruler in Croatia. When Charles Martel died in 1296, his claimed right to the Croato-Hungarian throne passed to his son, Charles Robert.

King Andrew, who had no son, appointed in 1299 his Venetian maternal uncle Albert Morosini as his successor, thereby provoking a fresh rebellion among the magnates. In 1300 the Croatian ban, Paul Count of Bribir, sailed to Naples and returned with Charles Robert. In 1301 Andrew, last of the Árpád line, died. After Croatia, Hungary too was left without a native dynasty. Ban Paul's brother George now took the Neapolitan prince to Zagreb, where he was met by a Hungarian party which took him to Esztergom to be crowned. Croatia and Hungary acquired not only a new king, Charles I (1301–42), but also a new dynasty with a vested interest in the Adriatic. Economic and cultural ties between Dalmatia and the Adriatic lands of the Kingdom of Naples were both ancient and strong – Dalmatia imported wheat from Apulia and exported salt, timber, cattle and agricultural product to Romagna and Marche – but Dalmatia now acquired a strategic importance for the House of Naples. If the Anjou kings were to rule in Dalmatia, however, they had to beat Venice, which – taking the opportunity created by the dynastic change – had managed to acquire Split, Trogir and Skradin. The republic's advance explains the Croatian lords' early endorsement of the Anjou succession.

Charles Robert was only twelve years old at the time of his crowning, a situation which encouraged other claims and a factional struggle within the Hungarian nobility, leading to the crowning of yet another king (Otto of Bavaria). Charles II's chief concern was to consolidate his grandson's position in Hungary, which involved prolonged negotiations with the Croatian and Hungarian nobility. By the time he died in 1309, his project of gaining for his family the Croato-Hungarian crown had proved successful. His own kingdom was inherited by his youngest son, Robert. The link between the two branches of the family was now further strengthened by the betrothal of Charles I's brother Andrew to Robert's granddaughter Joanna. In 1336–7 a cadet Anjou branch received Durrës and its hinterland as a fief from Robert of Naples; the Albanian nobility remained loyal to the House of Anjou, which defended them against the Serbs.

Charles I was succeeded by his son Louis I (1342–82), who decided it was time to reclaim Dalmatia. In 1345 the young king took a large army to Croatia and set up his camp outside the walls of Zadar. His presence encouraged the city to rise yet again, but the royal army was routed by the Venetians. After a two-year siege Zadar was finally forced to surrender, its leaders appalled to learn that Louis had accepted an eight-year peace with Venice. The king's determination to reclaim Dalmatia, nonetheless, is indicated by the fact that contemporary court documents for the first time registered Dalmatia as a separate *regnum*. Louis's attention was in fact distracted by events in the Kingdom of Naples. His brother Andrew, who had married Joanna, now Queen of Naples, was murdered in 1345 by, it seems, supporters of another Anjou line.[3] Louis made two attempts to seize the Neapolitan kingdom, but in the end a close victory was won by Joanna's side.

In 1356, after the expiry of the eight-year peace, Louis prepared for a new war against Venice by consolidating his military presence in Croatia. As a result, Split, Trogir and Šibenik expelled their Venetian governors, with Zadar planning to do the same. Dubrovnik too decided to change sides. Determined to escape the pressure of the Bosnian and Serbian rulers and increasingly constricted in its development by its Venetian overlord, the city started to negotiate – for the first time in its history – terms of surrender to a continental king, in whom it perceived a new Adriatic power. In 1358, backed by the ban's army operating in Croatia, Louis managed to inflict a heavy defeat on the Venetian republic at Treviso, and forced it to sign the

Peace of Zadar. Venice gave up its claims to Dalmatia 'from the middle of Kvarner to the borders of Durrës, with all its cities, lands, castles, islands [and], in particular, the cities of Nin, Zadar, Skradin, Šibenik, Trogir, Split and Dubrovnik on the land, as well as the cities and land on the islands of Osor, Cres, Krk, Rab, Pag, Brač, Hvar and Korčula'. The Venetian doge simultaneously surrendered his title *dux Dalmatiae et Croatiae*.[4] Louis hurried back to Dalmatia where Zadar prepared him a triumphal welcome, celebrating the end of 'Venetian tyranny'. Dubrovnik now recognised Louis as its sovereign. In the charter of privileges issued to Dubrovnik, the king confirmed its borders and promised to respect its autonomy and to defend it from Bosnian and Serbian rulers. Dubrovnik engaged in return to pay an annual tax to the royal treasury, contribute ships to the royal navy in times of war, and elect mayors only from among his majesty's subjects.[5] It was this dramatic change along the east Adriatic coast that produced the Dalmatian *regnum* as an area of special interest of the Anjou kings. As specified in the treaty, this Dalmatia formed a continuous territory that included not only the old Byzantine *thema*, but also the cities and islands that belonged initially to Trpimir's Croatia and the associated principality of Neretva.

Venice viewed Dalmatia as a set of self-governing communes united by a common culture and its own authority, and haggled over each of them individually with the king – offering Louis material and other inducements in return for keeping Zadar, and hoping to retain at least Dubrovnik. Louis, by contrast, saw Dalmatia as an entity acquired by the kings of Hungary with Coloman's coronation as King of Croatia. The Venetians argued that Dubrovnik in particular had never recognised the Hungarian king's rule; but in Louis's eyes Dubrovnik had always been an integral part of Dalmatia. The royal charter issued to Dubrovnik, the text of which incorporates both parties' understanding of the city's past position, states that although Dubrovnik 'had not since time immemorial been in real possession and government' of the king's predecessors, and had in fact been ruled by the Venetians for over a century, albeit 'under certain conditions and agreements', this did not mean that 'it should not have been theirs'. The king, indeed, knew for certain that Dubrovnik 'was built and founded in our *regnum* of Dalmatia, and for that reason belonged to us by right'. At all events, 'by the grace of God and through a splendid victory, our *regnum* of Dalmatia is now in our hands, and the Doge and the Venetian commune have surrendered all their rights together with the title, insofar as they had any'.[6] Venice responded by imposing an economic embargo against the Dalmatian cities.

This Dalmatian *regnum*, however, was no more organised as a unified

King Louis I arrives in Zadar, 1358

political body under the new regime than it had been in the past. Royal government rested instead on discrete agreements reached between the king and the individual cities. It is not that this Dalmatia lacked coherence though, given the congeneric development of its parts, which during the previous two centuries had produced a distinct order based on the self-governing commune. The Dalmatian commune, headed by a *comes*, was made up of the urban centre or *civitas* and the outlying rural district. The unity of the Split commune and its members, for example, was expressed in the formula 'the commune and people of the city of Split'. During the thirteenth century, power in the commune devolved to a governing council, made up of a limited number of local notables, which in the following century separated off to form a closed and self-perpetuating body representing the city nobility (*nobiles cives*). The system of laws governing the life of these Dalmatian communes was drafted in accordance with the practice adopted by the other, Italic, side of the Adriatic. Based on revived Roman law as taught at the University of Bologna, they were, with some exceptions, written in Latin.[7] Thomas the Archdeacon, one of the Dalmatians who studied jurisprudence at this university, was responsible for bringing a *podestà* from Ancona, who in 1240 drafted the first statute of the commune of Split. Judging by the date of the oldest preserved versions, Korčula had a statute in 1265, Dubrovnik in 1272, Zadar and Brač in 1305, Šibenik in 1315, Trogir in 1322, Hvar in 1331 – and so forth. By 1350 all the communal societies of the eastern Adriatic – from Istria in the north to Kotor in the south – had codified their legal practice, creating in the process a set of discrete worlds, of highly localised *patriae,* with the ambition to regulate their lives and the will to resist the encroachments of all outside powers – including the king, the territorial lords and Venice – into their internal affairs. Cities and islands that were initially 'Croatian' also became 'Dalmatian', in consequence of this tide of legalistic congruence which came to form the basis of a distinctive regional identity.

In 1370 Louis I was also crowned King of Poland. He now ruled a huge realm stretching from the lower Vistula to Kotor on the Adriatic Sea. And there was also the 'unredeemed' part, the Kingdom of Naples, for which an opportunity presented itself in 1381, when Queen Joanna was excommunicated by Pope Urban VI. Louis promptly dispatched to Italy his cousin Charles of Durazzo, who in the following year was crowned King of Sicily by the pope. Louis died a year later, leaving behind as his heir a twelve-year-old daughter, Mary, promised to Sigismund of Luxemburg, son of Emperor Charles IV. A wing of the Croato-Hungarian nobility, dissatisfied with the new queen and even more with her Bosnian-born mother Elizabeth, offered the crown to Charles of Durazzo. Mary was forced to retire, and in 1385 Charles was crowned King of Croatia and Hungary. His reign was brief, however, for in early 1386 he was murdered in his palace in Buda by the queen's party, which restored Mary to the throne.[8] Soon after her marriage to Sigismund, however, she and her mother were captured by their mainly Croatian opponents and imprisoned at an abbey near Zadar, where Elizabeth was murdered. In this situation the anti-Anjou faction crowned Sigismund King of Hungary and Croatia (1387–1437). His queen, whom he liberated from prison, died in 1395.

Unlike Louis, Sigismund took great interest in the Ottoman advance into Europe. Three decades earlier the Ottomans had seized Adrianople (now Edirne) and made it their new imperial capital. The Byzantine emperor John V Palaeologus (1341–91) had visited Louis at Buda to seek his help against the Ottomans, but neither Louis nor indeed any of the Western rulers had paid much heed to his request for common action. Sigismund, however, gathered a large army, which confronted Sultan Bayezid I at Nicopolis in 1396. The Christian side suffered a heavy defeat, and it was not known for several months whether Sigismund had survived. The supporters of the Anjou line took this opportunity to declare Ladislav of Naples, son of the murdered Charles, king of Croatia and Hungary. Sigismund returned in time to stop this design, but was himself deposed in 1401 and imprisoned. Though released soon after, his enemies nevertheless invited Ladislav to assume the throne.

The dynastic conflict left Dalmatia exposed to the Venetian threat. Zadar, which had initially affirmed its loyalty to Queen Mary, sided with Ladislav in 1402. In 1403 Ladislav landed at the city, where he was crowned by the archbishop of Esztergom. Mindful of his father's fate, however, he refused to travel north and, after a few months spent in Dalmatia dispensing titles and privileges to Croatian and Bosnian magnates, he returned to Naples. Venice had in the meanwhile gained control of the entrance to the Adriatic, having taken the former Anjou inheritance of Durrës and Shkoder. During the first decade of the fifteenth century the republic's territory expanded further on both land and sea, seizing on the one hand Vicenza, Verona and Padua and on the other Ulcinj, Bar and Budva (all now in Montenegro). In this situation, and given Sigismund's strong comeback, Ladislav decided to cut his losses, so in 1409, after some haggling, he sold his rights in Dalmatia to Venice for 100,000 ducats. Zadar, followed closely by Rab, Osor and Nin, now surrendered to Venice also.

Sigismund lost his first war against Venice (1411–13) and with it Šibenik, which submitted to Venetian rule after a prolonged siege. He lost also the second war (1418–20), after which Trogir, Split, Korčula, Brač and Hvar also capitulated to Venice. With the exception of Dubrovnik, the Dalmatian cities would hereafter remain under Venetian rule until the republic's demise in 1797. Venice took full possession of them without formally suspending their statutes.[9] Formally speaking they became vassals of the doge and had to swear loyalty to the republic; but their condition was that they would not be asked to fight against the Croato-Hungarian king. The republic placed soldiers within their walls; appointed their governors and influenced the choice of their bishops; directed their trade and acted as the supreme legal instance; but otherwise it did not interfere much in their everyday affairs. Although Sigismund was unable to regain Dalmatia, he never surrendered his rights there. In 1411, however, he was elected King and Emperor of Germany, which brought him new responsibilities and diminished his interest in the affairs of Croatia-Hungary.

The *Croatian* regnum

Whereas in Slavonia the Hungarian kings were able to create new administrative and ecclesiastical structures, in Croatia proper they found these already in place. Their authority was supreme in matters of war and justice, but in practice they were able to rule only by forming alliances with Croatian lords and the Dalmatian cities. During the twelfth and early thirteenth centuries a number of powerful families had emerged in the Croatian heartland, which acquired control of the individual counties and became hereditary counts. Castles that under the native kings had acted as administrative centres became under their Árpád successors the seats of these semi-independent magnates. Their success depended to a large extent on their skill in dealing with individual kings, but also on their relationship with the cities, which in the absence of the monarch or his deputies relied on the Croatian lords to ensure the rule of law and to protect them from their enemies, especially Venice. Given that their own lands were devoid of major urban centres, the Croatian lords' ambitions remained focused on the cities, which led them to compete for their allegiance with both Venice and the king.

Of these baronial families, by far the most eminent were the Šubić, counts of Bribir. The Bribir castle, set on a hill not far from Zadar and Šibenik, commanded a panoramic view over the nearby land and sea. If Knin was the key to Croatia (*Tinini sit clavis Sclavoniae*), Bribir was the key to Zadar. Together with the castle of Ostrovica, another possession of the family, Bribir guarded the main road along the Dalmatian coast, the old Roman *via magna*, linking Split, Knin, Zadar, Nin and beyond. With Skradin in their possession, the Šubić were able to control Šibenik too. The earliest mention of the Šubić name dates to the eleventh century, when members of the family acting as county heads or judges received land and privileges from successive Croatian kings. By the end of this period the Šubić had become hereditary counts of Bribir – whence the family's name Bribirski – with the family as a whole (*nobiles de Berberio*) participating in the exercise of power. As one of the noble families that had signed the *Pacta Conventa*, they retained their prominent status under the new Hungarian kings; but also during the brief Byzantine rule in the late twelfth century the Šubić held on fast to their lands. At the time of the Árpáds' return to Croatia the family head was one Miroslav, whose younger brother was bishop of Knin. Miroslav appears in contemporary documents as *župan* of Bribir, but his son Gregory I (1184–1234) is identified as *comes*. In the early thirteenth century Gregory Bribirski and his brother Stephen fought Domald, count of Sidraga, for regional supremacy, a contest so intense at times that one Zadar scribe likened it to a religious schism. Domald (c.1160–1243), son of the *župan* of Klis, whose lands lay between the river Krka, Zadar and the sea, was in 1203 elected *comes* of Zadar, having freed the city from Venetian occupation. During the first two decades of the thirteenth century this (according to Thomas the Archdeacon) 'circumspect and thoughtful man' acted at time also as *comes* of Šibenik and of Split. At some point, however, he came into conflict with King Andrew II, after which his lands passed to the Bribirski family. Gregory and Stephen now became governors of Split and Trogir.

The sudden arrival of King Bela IV in Dalmatia in the middle of the century for a while checked Bribirski power. The king, escaping from the Tartars, was helped in his flight from Slavonia by the counts of the island of Krk, whom he now appointed governors of Split and Trogir. Bela wished to avoid any concentration of power in this part of his realm in the hands of a single family, and also to remove magnate influence over the Dalmatian cities; but he could not afford to alienate the Bribirski family, so he confirmed their possession of the county of Bribir. After Bela's return to Hungary, the Bribirski returned to their pre-eminence. The period 1270–1320, during which the Árpád line died out, saw the zenith of the Bribirski ascendancy.

Stephen had three grandsons, Paul, George and Mladin, who, captained by Paul (1272–1312), gradually extended the family's rule over much of central Croatia. Paul's elevation started in 1272 when he was elected *comes* of Trogir. A year later he became also governor of Split and the ban's deputy; shortly afterwards he himself became ban and soon after that hereditary ban, which gave him a position of near equality with the king. An early supporter of the Anjou succession, he played a decisive role in bringing Charles Robert to the throne of Croatia and Hungary. The nature of the family's power is illustrated by the fact that they were able to secure for Šibenik – which they treated as their own port – the status of a cathedral city, thus dividing the old diocese of Trogir into two. Ban Paul, who minted his own coins, governed his realm from Knin; his brothers administered Split, Trogir, Nin and Klis on his behalf. At the end of the thirteenth century the Bribirski extended their presence deep into Bosnia: Paul became also 'the ruler of all Bosnia'. He now invested George with the government of the maritime cities, and handed to Mladin the government of Bosnia. Mladin, however, soon met his death there, probably as the result of a religious feud.[10] Before his death in 1312 Paul divided the honours and rule of his various lands between his sons. The eldest, Mladin II, became the new ban. The family's dominance reached a symbolic climax when Zadar sent the Venetian governor packing,

Relief of Ban Paul I Bribirski, 1380

after which Mladin triumphantly entered the city and took the title *comes Dalmatiae*. Paul appears in contemporary documents as 'ban of the Croats', his son Mladin as 'ban of the Croats and of Bosnia'. Mladin was also 'the supreme lord of all Hum'.

The inclusion of Zadar into the Bribirski realm concluded a trajectory that in many ways mirrored that of the rise of the early medieval Croatian kingdom: the concentration of power in a single family, territorial integration, rule over the Dalmatian cities and the drive towards sovereignty. Bribir, indeed, lies within the core of the old Croatian state territory, the flat and fertile part of which – now called Ravni Kotari – encircles Zadar. The land here belonged to some of the oldest Croat families, the most important of which had negotiated the original settlement with the Hungarian king Coloman. Their heads traditionally met at a field situated halfway between Zadar and Bribir, at a place where King Branimir built a church in the ninth century.[11] It is possible that the Croatian state emblem, the red-and-white chequerboard, derives from this same area.[12] Its nobility laid great stress on Croatia's old traditions, which accounts for the fact that Ban Paul and his son Ban Mladin II preferred to call themselves bans of 'the Croats' rather than of 'Croatia' – a denotation that involved a kingly understanding of the nature of the ban's authority. In his private correspondence with Charles II of Naples, Paul referred to himself as 'ban of all Slavonia [i.e. Croatia]'.[13] Like other dynasts of their time the Šubić counts held their own court, influenced the organisation of the Church on their territory, built and endowed churches and monasteries, donated land and privileges, aided the development of the cities and market places, and mediated conflicts between the different constituencies. With Paul's death, however, the family's fortunes began to decline. The following year Mladin was forced to return Zadar to Venice.

Most damaging for the family perhaps was the fact that the formal division of the Bribirski realm worked against its unity. Mladin's brothers found it necessary to side with the cities they governed against the ban. Division among the brothers was also fuelled by disputes between the cities, such as the war between Split and Trogir over the communal boundary, or the quarrel between Trogir and Šibenik over church jurisdiction. There was also a permanent state of tension between the cities and their rural environs, against which they sought to expand – meeting fierce resistance on the part of the villagers. The Croat highlanders, on the other hand, periodically pillaged the city districts, and robbed their merchants as they travelled inland. Another ingredient in this brew of problems was the resentment felt by the other magnates towards the family. At the end of the first decade of his rule Mladin II was confronted with a broad coalition of forces composed of the king, the cities, and members of the Croatian and Bosnian nobility. Charles Robert, having consolidated his position in Hungary, sought to reduce the power of the Bribirski in order to be able to reign effectively also in Croatia. In 1322 Mladin II was defeated on the battlefield and taken to

Hungary, where he died in captivity. The Bribirski lords, humbled in this way, retired to their castles of Bribir, Skradin, Ostrovica and Klis. It was the chaotic situation created by this finale that encouraged Šibenik and Trogir, and somewhat later Split and Nin, to turn to Venice.

Mladin III of Klis, eldest son of the unlucky *comes Dalmatiae* and now the king's mortal enemy, concentrated on forging links with his regional opponents. He married the sister of the Serbian ruler, Stephen Dušan; one of his brothers married the daughter of the Venetian doge, while his sister married into the Bosnian ban's family. In 1343 the Bribirski brothers took Venetian citizenship. Two years later, however, Louis I arrived with his army in Croatia, and in 1347 succeeded in persuading Mladin's uncle, Gregory, to cede to him the important castle of Ostrovica, in return for the castle of Zrin and a nearby manor in Slavonia. Ostrovica belonged in fact to Gregory's brother, Paul, who on his death in 1346 made his son, George III, a ward of the Venetian doge. In his will, Paul specifically asked that Ostrovica never be surrendered to the king but, if necessary to Venice. Gregory broke the terms of the will in delivering the castle – and young George too – to the king. Beginning with George, this branch of the Šubić clan called itself Zrinski. Mladin III died soon after and was buried in Trogir. The inscription on his crypt describes him as a 'paragon of virtue' and 'the mighty shield of the Croats'.

Having gained Knin also, Louis was in a position not only to wrench Dalmatia from Venice, but also to establish a military presence in Croatia. This permitted him to institutionalise his own authority in the land. Croatian bans became once again royal appointees and counties became self-governing communities of the small and middle nobility. The Croatian Estates' parliament first met c. 1350 in the presence of a new ban. This part of Croatia thereby acquired an administrative structure similar to that of Slavonia: it became, in fact, a distinct *regnum*. One response to this assertion of royal authority was the *Pacta Conventa*, the document describing the circumstances under which Coloman had acquired the Croatian crown, the implication of which was that the king could rule in Croatia only with the consent of the nobility. This document was deposited in the cathedral of Split, a city which the Šubić had treated as an integral part of their realm. Half a century of Bribirski rule had clearly laid the basis of a new national sensibility.

The defeat of the Bribirski family altered for good the strategic situation in Zadar's hinterland. Those of the Šubić clan who remained in the Bribir area were reduced to the rank of lower nobility or became royal knights;

some moved permanently to Zadar. From the end of the fourteenth century, indeed, there followed a general alienation of the land owned by the wider Šubić clan, mainly by sale to Zadar nobles or to the Venetian state. Louis's victory proved in the end to be a Pyrrhic one, since without a strong resident aristocracy the Croato-Hungarian kings were unable to keep Dalmatia. Venice alone in the end profited from the fragmentation of this power, though it too would lose much of Dalmatia – in due course and for the same reason – to the invading Ottomans.[14] Its acquisition of Dalmatia coincided, in fact, with the start of Ottoman raids into Croatia.

Throughout the preceding period the Dalmatian cities and the Croatian nobility fought each other, but also relied on each other in their struggle against third parties. Depending on the circumstances, they aligned themselves, together or apart, with the king against Venice, or with Venice against the king. Notwithstanding their conflicts and differences, they felt part of the same land. Croatia would thus enter the age of Ottoman wars with a crystallised sense of national identity. When, several decades after the arrival of the Venetians, a Croat nobleman was killed by Ottoman raiders near Split, Marko Marulić, the foremost poet of Croatian humanism, wrote the epitaph on his tomb in Split cathedral, in which he calls him 'the flower and glory of all Dalmatian knights' and commits his body to 'the ancient motherland' for which he had fought and died with honour.[15] The understanding that Dalmatia belonged with Croatia and not with Venice was to remain alive in subsequent centuries, and informs such major works as the first modern history of Croatia, the six-volume *Regnum Dalmatiae et Croatiae* written by the Trogir patrician Ivan Lucić-Lucius and published in 1666 in Amsterdam.

It was during the period of Ban Paul's rule that events in Croatia became closely intertwined with those in Bosnia. Bosnia had emerged as a separate *regnum* after the retreat of Byzantium, and by the end of the thirteenth century it had grown strong enough to absorb the three Croatian counties situated along the river Vrbas. These formed the core of a distinct territorial entity called Donji Kraji – *partes inferiors*, or Lowlands. That the Bribirski were able to acquire Bosnia was due largely to the support of the lords of Donji Kraji, who it seems had retained a sense of belonging to the Croat noble community. Their head at this time was called Hrvatin, meaning someone from Croatia.[16] Not all the family members supported the Croatian ban – yet even such a person as Vukac Hrvatinić, who remained stubbornly loyal to the Bosnian ruler throughout this historical episode, named one of his sons Hrvoje. After Mladin II's defeat in 1322 the pendulum swung back, and Bosnia started to expand again into Croatian territory. The Bosnian ban took three additional Croatian counties in what is now western Bosnia, the coast between the estuaries of the Cetina and the Neretva, and briefly also the cities and islands of central Dalmatia. In 1377 the Bosnian ban Tvrtko, who proclaimed himself king in that year, was forced to return these gains to King Louis; but after Louis's death the three counties reverted again to Bosnian rule. Hrvoje Vukčić Hrvatinić, on the other hand, aligned himself with Ladislav of Durazzo, who before returning to Naples appointed him his deputy in Croatia-Dalmatia and lord of Split. Hrvoje for twenty years ruled parts of Croatia and Bosnia as if they were a single unit. He recognised Sigismund as his king, but in the end rebelled against him. In 1415 he defeated a punitive expedition sent against him by inviting the help of the Ottomans, after which there followed the first recorded Ottoman incursion into Croatia.

The waning of Bribirski power was attended by the rise of another magnate family, the Frankapan, which succeeded in establishing its presence throughout Dalmatian Croatia. Its progenitor Dujam governed Krk in the middle of the twelfth century as an appointed Venetian official, but his sons became hereditary counts of Krk. In contrast to the Bribirski, Dujam's family began their climb by entering the service of the Croato-Hungarian kings, commencing with Andrew II. Bartul (Bartholomew), the founder of the family's fortunes, who fought on the side of Bela IV against the Austrian Babenberg family, is said to have killed Friedrich of Babenberg, archduke of Austria and Styria and lord of Carniola, at Wiener Neustadt in 1246. Babenberg's lands, initially divided between the German and Croato-Hungarian kings, eventually ended up as Habsburg possessions. In the middle of the thirteenth century the counts of Krk gained from the grateful Bela IV confirmation of their rights to the counties of Modruš and Vinodol opposite Krk, thus establishing themselves on the mainland. Soon afterwards they acquired also the port of Senj, which mainly served Venetian trade with Croatia, Austria and Hungary. Marriage brought them estates in Slavonia. They supported the Anjou dynasty, aided Zadar's rebellion against Venice in 1345–6, and sided with King Louis against the Bribirski. On the other hand, the Frankapan also played a crucial role in making peace between the branch of the Bribirski who became Zrinski and the king, since the first Zrinski's mother was a Frankapan.[17] After Louis's death they aligned themselves with Sigismund. The family played an active part in the politics of the Croatian kingdom, and supplied numerous city governors and bans in the fourteenth and fifteenth centuries.

Ban Nicholas (1426–32), the only heir to the Frankapan family estates, held Krk, Vinodol, Modruš, Senj and Lika in Croatia, and Cetin, Slunj and Ozalj in Slavonia. When King Sigismund, in return for 28,000 ducats, mortgaged to him a number of places between the Una and the Cetina, including Bihać, Knin, Ostrovica, Skradin, and Poljica near Omiš, Nicholas acquired practically all of the old Croatia. In keeping with the humanist fascination with ancient Rome, Nicholas now took the name 'de Frangepanibus', or Frankapan, claiming descent from an old Roman patrician family. Sigismund later sought to break up the greatly expanded Frankapan territorial base, encouraging the family to enter the service of the Habsburgs, who had in the meantime become their neighbours.

The Frankapan derived their wealth and prestige from their control of a significant part of the Croatian Littoral, which after the loss of Dalmatia provided the Croato-Hungarian kingdom with its only outlet to the sea. In the fourteenth century, with Rijeka in the hands of local Habsburg allies, this part of the Croatian coast became the site of stubborn competition, including small wars, between Venice, Austria and Croatia-Hungary over the flow and terms of trade, which only enhanced the importance of the Frankapan family. In order to prevent family feuds, Nicholas's nine sons divided his realm among themselves, with the exception of Krk and Senj which they continued to govern together. The family's strength was henceforth sapped by persistent family feuds, Ottoman assaults, and the desire on the part of the crown to gain control of Senj. The Frankapan nevertheless retained their regional preeminence by forming in the fifteenth century a marital alliance with the Zrinski family.

The Slavonian regnum

In contrast to Croatia's old Dalmatian heartland, where royal power was consolidated only in the middle of the fourteenth century, Slavonia offered a far freer hand, under the Árpáds, in organising counties, establishing bishoprics and collecting taxes. At the end of the twelfth century Slavonia comprised eight counties: Varaždin, Zagreb, Križevci, Virovitica and Požega in the west, and Vukovar, Baranja (between the Drava and the Danube) and Srijem (between the Sava and the Danube) in the east. Baranja was later incorporated into one of the counties of southern Hungary, but ended up, together with Vukovar and Srijem, under the authority of the bans of Mačva, or of Belgrade military commanders or captains.[18] Whereas western Slavonia was encompassed by the see of Zagreb as early as the eleventh century, in eastern Slavonia the church organisation took shape only with the re-establishment in 1229 of the bishopric of Srijem. In 1247, moreover, Đakovo in the county of Vukovar became the seat of the bishop of Bosnia.

The thirteenth century was a time of a rapid colonisation of the land, encouraged by the king, the royal princes and the bans, leading to the emergence of chartered towns. Varaždin acquired a royal charter in 1209, followed by Petrinja, Vukovar, Virovitica, Samobor, Zagreb (in 1242), Križevci, Jastrebarsko and Bihać (now in Bosnia). The greater part of the land in Slavonia was owned until 1200 by the king and the Church; but during the thirteenth century practically all the royal land was given away to religious orders, the new cities, or the king's allies. The position of the Slavonian nobility was strengthened by the acquisition of civil jurisdiction over their estates, and following the Tartar invasion in 1242 the right to fortify and garrison their seats. Slavonia as a result became a patchwork of practically autonomous territorial units, constantly at war with one another as the magnates tried to unify or extend their estates. The county system virtually fell apart, but royal interest, combined with the concerns of the small and middle nobility, led to its revival, with the difference that counties now became self-governing communities run by noble assemblies. This supplied the basis for the emergence of a parliament of the Estates. The Slavonian parliament met for the first time in 1273, when noble rights and the legal life of the land as a whole were codified. It became a regular institution under the Anjou kings, convened by the ban, who acted as the king's representative. Official documents register this Slavonia as a *regnum*, that is, a community with its own legal system based on the Slavonian customary law codified that year. The Slavonian *regnum* was thus composed of Slavonian counties governed in accordance with the Slavonian statute; but it was also a *banatus*, since it was governed by a ban.[19]

King Sigismund, whose imperial duties demanded frequent absence from the kingdom, relied on a small number of local barons of whom the most prominent in Slavonia were the Celjski, a German family from Styria whose main seat was Celje (now in Slovenia), which they gained from the Habsburgs in 1322. Sigismund, who married the daughter of Herman Celjski, helped the family to acquire extensive properties also in western Slavonia, which made Herman eligible for the post of Slavonian ban. Herman's son married a Frankapan and gained a number of fortified places in Croatia – the two families would fight over them after her death. The bulk of the Celjski family estates was ultimately inherited by the Habsburgs.

Sigismund died in 1437 after nominating as his heir his son-in-law, Albert Habsburg (1437–9), King of Bohemia and later also German emperor.

Seal of the royal free city of Gradec/Zagreb, fourteenth century

During Albert's brief reign the Ottomans reached the Danube, where they took Smederevo, capital of what remained of the Serbian state. Albert tried to drive them back, but his army was decimated by the plague – of which he too died after his return to Vienna. He left two daughters and a pregnant wife. Queen Elisabeth's right to rule was contested by the majority of the Croato-Hungarian nobility, who, fearful of the Ottomans, chose the Polish king Vladislav Jagiełło. A party of Hungarian and Croatian magnates set off for Cracow to bring the newly elected king to the royal capital of Buda; but by the time they got back Elisabeth had given birth to a son, Ladislav, known also as Posthumous, whom she had promptly crowned king (1440–57) and entrusted to the care of Emperor Frederick III Habsburg. On his arrival in Hungary Vladislav too was crowned (1440–44), so Croatia and Hungary now had two kings – a state of affairs which led to civil war. Sultan Murat II took the opportunity to lay another siege to Belgrade, 'the gate to Hungary', but the city was saved by the Croatian magnate Ivan Talovac (the captain of Belgrade) whose brothers were at this time bans of Croatia and Slavonia.

This strengthened Vladislav's negotiating hand, and with the help of the pope a deal was reached in 1442 according to which Ladislav Posthumous would rule after Vladislav's death.

Vladislav was chosen in the hope that he would be able to stop the Ottomans. In 1443, supported by the duke of Transylvania, John Hunyady, he led a large army south to Bulgaria, winning a number of battles on the way. Sultan Murat II offered a ten-year peace, which was accepted; but in the following year Vladislav took another army to Varna on the Black Sea – where, however, he suffered a decisive defeat and was killed in the battle. The nobility then elected Sigismund's five-year-old grandson, Ladislav, and appointed John Hunyady as regent of the realm. Emperor Frederick, however, refused to give up the boy-king, who after some negotiations was committed to the care of his cousin, Ulrich, son of Herman Celjski.

In 1456 Murat's successor Mehmed II laid yet another siege to Belgrade; but the city held out this time too, defended by Hunyady's military skill and – even more importantly according to legend – by the miraculous powers of St John Capistran, a Franciscan monk who had joined Hunyady.[20] But both men died from plague in the following months. More deaths were to come. That same year the unpopular Ulrich was executed in Belgrade by Hunyady's elder son, John whereupon the enraged king had him put to death and his younger brother Mathias imprisoned in Prague. Ladislav himself died without an heir soon afterwards, leaving Croatia-Hungary – and Bohemia too – with the problem of finding a new king.

In 1458 the Estates of Croatia and of Hungary chose Matthias (1458–90) – called Corvinus after the raven that formed part of the family's emblem – as their king. He was then fifteen years old. Matthias was in fact the choice of the lower, county-based nobility, who appreciated his father's anti-Ottoman achievements. The Bohemian Estates too chose a native noble, George Podiebrad, in preference to a Habsburg.[21] George promptly engaged his daughter to Matthias and supplied an armed escort for his return to Hungary. In the eyes of the Croatian and Hungarian grandees, however, Matthias's humble origins made him unfit to rule over them, so they offered the crown to Frederick Habsburg. Matthias solved this problem by making a deal with Frederick, according to which if he died without a male heir the crown would go to Frederick or one of his sons. The agreement was sponsored by Pope Pius II, who wished to see a new engagement against the Ottomans.

In 1463 Bosnia fell to Mehmed II and its king was captured and killed. Matthias managed to salvage the strategic city of Jajce (Hrvoje's old seat) from the kingdom's ruins, and to create a defence system in Bosnia against Ottoman expansion into Croatia and Hungary. After 1465, however, having won only tepid support from the West, he abandoned anti-Ottoman offensives to concentrate instead on his realm and his own position in Central Europe. Matthias's radical overhaul of the tax system – which came to include also the nobility – and creation of a standing army gave his lands a much wanted stability. But his centralising tendencies, his reliance on 'new men' drawn from the lower nobility and his incessant involvement in dynastic conflicts in Austria and Bohemia – directed mainly against Frederick – in preference to confronting the Ottomans, led eventually to a revolt among the magnates. Two of his initially most loyal Slavonian allies (John Vitez of Sredna and Janus Pannonius) would also turn against him.

Vitez, a petty noble from the county of Križevci, canon of Zagreb cathedral, bishop of Oradea/Nagyvarad (now in Romania) and diplomat of the realm, was an old friend of Matthias's father, who appointed him tutor to his two sons. After Matthias's coronation, Vitez became chancellor of the realm and the king's main political adviser. In 1465 he became archbishop of Esztergom. Like Vitez, his nephew Janus – a foremost poet of the humanist period in Croatia-Hungary – was educated in Italy and destined for a church career. He eventually became bishop of Pécs, a thriving city in lower Hungary, and at one point also ban of Slavonia. In 1467 Vitez and Janus were able to defuse a rebellion among the Transylvanian nobility, directed against heavy taxation and the king's neglect of the Ottoman front. In 1471, however, they sided with Matthias's opponents. After the rebellion was crushed, Janus died in the castle of Medvedgrad near Zagreb, followed within a few months by his imprisoned uncle Vitez.

For Matthias, the Frankapans were the most important family in central Croatia, given their control of what remained of the Croatian coast. Two of its members, John and Stephen, were to play key roles in this period. John gained the island of Krk, after surrendering his claim to the rest of the inheritance. Feeling insecure nonetheless, he placed himself under Venetian protection, and in 1453 he drafted a will leaving the island to Venice in the event of his dying without a male heir. Stephen, on the other hand, gained the burg of Modruš, a staging post for the Adriatic trade starting at Senj, which in 1460 became a bishop's seat. He played a particularly active role in the events leading to Matthias's accession. With the Frankapan lands exposed to Ottoman attacks, Stephen became Matthias's envoy in various negotiations aimed at the formation of an anti-Ottoman European alliance. After the fall of Bosnia he was appointed ban of Croatia and Dalmatia, and found himself seeking aid not only for his kingdom but also for his manors. In 1465 he too placed himself under Venetian protection, and in 1469 he asked Emperor Frederick for help. These acts were interpreted by Matthias as a threat to his rule in this part of Croatia, so in 1469 the king sent his army to take over Senj; but when the army tried also to take the island of Krk, skilful Venetian diplomacy managed to secure it for the republic.

The Frankapan were eventually persuaded by the Venetians and the pope to make peace with the king, but they never regained Senj. This prompted them to develop Bakar, a small port north of Senj, as their main Adriatic trading post. Bakar was part of their fiefdom of Vinodol, a narrow strip of land between Rijeka and Senj, which the Frankapan had gained in the first quarter of the thirteenth century, and which juridically was subject only to their own and the royal authority. In the middle of the fifteenth century Bakar became one of the three most important ports in the northeastern Adriatic – the other two being Senj, now held by the crown, and Rijeka, now in direct possession of the Austrian Habsburgs.

In 1481 Matthias asserted his authority in Croatia-Slavonia by staging a political trial at which all the main magnates, including the Frankapan, the Zrinski and the bishop of Zagreb, were accused of treason: of having taken part in the 1471–2 conspiracy and collaborated with the Germans and the Ottomans. The trial was in fact designed to win their acceptance of a new tax on land and additional military obligations – after accomplishing which Matthias immediately amnestied them. The Frankapan once again made their peace with the king: both sides needed each other in this time of troubles. Stephen's son Bernardin took part in negotiating Matthias's second marriage to Beatrice Aragon of Naples, and joined the royal family by marrying the new queen's niece. Matthias's Neapolitan connection once again revived the issue of Dalmatia. In 1486 the king gave a speech before the Croato-Hungarian parliament in which he accused Venice of usurping Dalmatia; and on the eve of his death he complained also to the pope that all Venetian possessions in Croatia and Dalmatia belonged in fact to the Hungarian crown.

With Bosnia in Ottoman hands, the attention of the Frankapan became focused on the increasingly difficult task of defending their estates. King Matthias, on the other hand, worked hard to secure the succession for his only, albeit illegitimate, son, John. He died in Vienna in 1490, in the middle of yet another war against Frederick of Habsburg, without achieving this aim. There were several candidates for the Croato-Hungarian throne: John Corvinus; the King of Bohemia, Vladislav II Jagiełło; his younger brother, John Albert; and Frederick's son and heir, Maximilian Habsburg. The Jagiełło brothers claimed the crown on account of family ties, and Maximilian on the basis of the agreement that Matthias had reached with his father. The Croato-Hungarian nobility, who favoured Vladislav, came to an arrangement with John Corvinus, whereby he gave up his claim to the throne in exchange for the title of hereditary duke of Slavonia and life-long ban of Dalmatia and Croatia. John Albrecht's claim was settled by military defeat. Maximilian Habsburg also took to arms, ejecting Croato-Hungarian troops from Austria and marching into Hungary. A number of Croatian magnates, including two of the Frankapan, rallied to his cause. However, Croatia was secured for Vladislav II Jagiełło by John Corvinus, and the unlucky Habsburg pretender was forced to accept a compromise according to which he or his successors would rule in Bohemia, Hungary and Croatia in the event of the Vladislav branch of the Jagiełło dynasty dying out. In 1492 this agreement was formally accepted by the Estates of Hungary and Transylvania, and separately by those of Croatia and Slavonia. Slavonia had in the meantime become the 'shield of Hungary' against the Ottomans, and the new king, Vladislav II Jagiełło (1490–1516), granted it its own coat of arms.

Vladislav II surrendered many of the powers wielded by Matthias, especially in regard to the financial and military obligations of the nobility. His freedom of action, in fact, became heavily conditioned by the will of the Croatian and Hungarian Estates. He was not allowed to wage offensive wars without the permission of their parliaments, and was expected to pay also for defensive wars. Nor was the king any longer permitted to appoint the palatine, that is, the king's deputy in Hungary, without the Hungarian Estates' approval. Stephen Zapolya, a member of a Slavonian family that rose to prominence in Matthias's service – and who was chiefly responsible for Vladislav's accession – now became the Hungarian palatine.[22] This was the beginning of the formation of a 'national' party in Hungary, a political alliance resting on the lesser nobility, whose individual members had won the right to attend the parliament in person. In 1502, under their influence, the Hungarian parliament passed a law making any attempt to support a foreigner's claim to the throne high treason. This measure was aimed in the first instance at Maximilian, but also against those Croatians who, in their desperate efforts to save their lands from the rising Ottoman tide, were turning towards the Habsburgs. Hungary became torn between the 'national' party led by the Zapolya family, which had support in eastern Hungary and Transylvania, and the loyalist 'court' party made up of the higher nobility and clergy who were strong in western Hungary. In this situation Vladislav and Maximilian met again in 1515 and reaffirmed their earlier agreement on the succession, which they sealed this time by the engagement of the crown prince Louis to Maximilian's granddaughter.

The reigns of Vladislav II and his son Louis II (1516–26) were marked by further Ottoman advance and widespread peasant revolts. Louis, who was only ten years old when his father died, inherited a bankrupt state steeped in anarchy. He came of age at the same time as Süleyman II became sultan; the latter promptly took from him the crucial castles of Belgrade (1521) and Knin (1522). At a meeting of the Croatian Estates in early 1526, a number of leading magnates led by Bernardin Frankapan's son Christopher demanded that they designate Ferdinand Habsburg of Austria as their king, since he would be able to defend Croatia. Later that year Süleyman crushed the Croato-Hungarian army on the field of Mohács in southern Hungary. The young king, fleeing from the battlefield, drowned in a nearby brook. Ferdinand now claimed the crowns of Bohemia, Hungary and Croatia. Playing safe after so many setbacks, he asked each of the Estates' parliaments – the Bohemian, the Hungarian, the Croatian and the Slavonian – to confirm him as their king. In Hungary itself the nobility split between the minority pro-Habsburg 'court' party and the majority 'national' party led by John Zapolya. In late 1526 the 'national' party crowned Zapolya King of Hungary, while the pro-Habsburg party accorded the same title to Ferdinand. France, Poland, Venice and the pope promptly recognised Zapolya. A long and bitter civil war followed, leading Zapolya to place himself under Süleyman's protection.

Croatia too divided: the Croatian Estates opted for Ferdinand, while the Slavonian Estates chose Zapolya. On 1 January 1527 the Croatian Estates formally elected Ferdinand I Habsburg (1527–64) King of Croatia. The momentous meeting took place at the Franciscan monastery in Cetin, a Frankapan seat. Those who attended included the Zrinski, the Frankapan, the titular bishop of Knin (which was now in Ottoman hands), and other important magnates from this part of Croatia. Ferdinand lobbied hard to gain the Croatian crown, bribing the magnates with money and promises.[23] His election a few weeks earlier as king of Hungary was noted by those who favoured him in Cetin, but this made no real difference, since the Hungarian parliament alone could not secure him the Croatian crown. He had to win over the Croatians, and in order to do so he had to promise them what they needed most: an effective military protection against the Ottoman threat. Through the medium of his envoys, present at the meeting, Ferdinand

Ruins of Cetingrad, where Ferdinand I Habsburg was elected King of Croatia

promised them 1,000 paid horse soldiers and 200 foot. He also promised to maintain a sizable army on the border between Croatia and his duchy of Carniola, and to pay for the repair and supply of Croatian castles and fortifications. In sum, he assured them that 'they and their glorious kingdom would always remain under [his] mighty protection'. In addition, Ferdinand bound himself unconditionally to respect 'all privileges, rights, freedoms and decisions of the Kingdom of Croatia'.

Croatian needs were great and urgent, but the new king clearly failed to heed them, since three months later the Estates met again and wrote to the king protesting that he had not kept his promises. They stressed that it was they who had made him king of Croatia: 'His Majesty should know that there is no evidence to show that any ruler took Croatia by force; but that after the death of our [cherished] King Zvonimir [we] freely joined the holy Hungarian crown, and now Your Majesty.' The Croatians told Ferdinand also of various advantageous offers they had received from the sultan, the Venetians and John Zapolya, which they had however refused. They added for good measure that many of their countrymen were starving because the king had failed to honour his financial commitments. It would appear from the letter that they had interpreted Ferdinand's promises rather generously, and had moreover assumed that he would join Croatia to the Habsburg Austrian hereditary lands. Ferdinand, however, was too busy with his war against Zapolya to be able to do much about the situation in Croatia. In 1535 the Croatian Estates even threatened to depose him, telling him that 'since

Your Majesty has wholly abandoned us, those who live in extreme danger', they wanted him to return the election diploma, for in this situation 'we ourselves must take full responsibility for our situation'. Knowing full well that this was an empty threat, Ferdinand replied asking them to be patient, for he would 'never abandon them'. He did not: the Habsburgs would remain kings of Croatia until the end of World War I.

The *regnum* of Slavonia pursued a different course. Meeting in early January 1527, its Estates noted that foreigners could not become kings of Hungary. The assembly was convened by Christopher Frankapan, who in the meantime had defected to Zapolya, and the bishop of Zagreb, Simeon Erdödy. Christopher was now ban of Dalmatia-Croatia-Slavonia, appointed to this post by 'the illustrious prince and lord John, by divine grace king of Hungary, etc.' These two dignitaries delivered Slavonia to Zapolya. The Estates, fearing civil war, also instructed Ban Christopher to seek reconciliation between Ferdinand and Zapolya. Although Christopher had sided with the 'national' party, he remained suspicious of its intentions; as he wrote to the bishop of Senj, however, he hoped that the Hungarians had learnt their lesson at Mohács. He died that year trying to seize Varaždin from Ferdinand. When the Slavonian Estates eventually did recognise Ferdinand, he added Slavonia to his royal title.

Contested sovereignty

The three systems of government or *regna* established in Croatia during the thirteenth and the fourteenth centuries differed in their origin, meaning and design. The borders and division of authority between the three parts remained fluid throughout, as reflected in the titles of the bans who were variously called bans of 'Croatia-Dalmatia', of 'all of Slavonia', of 'Croatia-Slavonia', of 'Croatia-Dalmatia-Slavonia'. Croatia remained a single kingdom, despite the triple name under which it appeared in the royal title – a title which took no account of the fact that the bulk of the old Anjou Dalmatian *regnum* had been lost to Venice, or that the separate nature of the Croatian and Slavonian *regna* would disappear with the fusion of their Estates in 1558. The merged Estates of Croatia-Slavonia inherited the perception of Croatia (inclusive of Dalmatia) as a realm that was distinct and separate from both the kingdom of Hungary and the other lands ruled by the house of Austria. In 1578, for example, the Estates' parliament passed a motion directed against Hungarian interference in Croatia's internal affairs, which contained some of the key elements informing the *Pacta Conventa* and Ferdinand's election diploma: the Croatian nobility accept the authority of the Hungarian king, but not of the Hungarian kingdom; kings of Hungary rule in Croatia only with the consent of its nobility; King Ferdinand rules in Croatia irrespectively of whether he reigns also in Hungary. By the end of the sixteenth century, the term 'Croatia' was habitually used for the territory represented directly or indirectly in the Zagreb parliament, despite the fact that official documents commonly referred to it as 'Croatia and Slavonia'.

The conviction that Croatia and Hungary were united solely through the person of a king enjoying Croatia's confidence was not shared by influential Hungarian officials and jurists, for whom the crown, not the king, guaranteed the lasting unity of the two kingdoms. This view was set out in the Tripartite Code, a new interpretation of the laws pertaining to the lands of the Hungarian crown published by the Hungarian jurist István Werbőczy in 1516, which reformulated and re-affirmed 'ancient' individual and collective rights of the nobility, such as full seigneurial rights over the serfs, exemption from all direct taxation, and maintenance of their hold on the land through the right of entail. The Code affirmed also the noble Estates' rights and privileges in contradistinction to those of the king. In this interpretation of the nature of political authority, *sacra corona*, or the holy crown, stood for the supreme power which the king could wield only if legally crowned. For this to happen, however, the consent of the nobility was indispensable, since the nobility represented the body of the kingdom. The holy crown, in other words, symbolised the essential sovereignty of the noble nation and the integrity of its lands: the territory of the crown was inalienable and indivisible – even the parts lost to other powers – since it was the legal property of the nobility.

This interpretation of the relationship between king and Estates involved also a novel understanding of the nature of association of the lands adjoined to the holy crown. At the time of the Habsburg accession, the only institutional link between the kingdoms of Croatia and Hungary was the person of the king: they behaved otherwise as separate political and legal entities. The establishment of the Estates parliaments in Croatia and Hungary served, indeed, to demarcate 'Hungary of the crown' – that is, the historic association of kingdoms and lands each with its own customary law and parliament – from Hungary of the Estates, which was only one, albeit the most important, component of the association. The affirmation of the power of the Estates in regard to the king could not be limited, however, only to those of Hungary, since they represented only one of the lands of the Hungarian crown. The consent that a king might gain in the kingdom of Hungary did not automatically oblige the kingdom of Croatia:

the Hungarian king could rule lawfully in Croatia only by agreement of the Croatian Estates. This is why the agreement reached in 1492 between Maximilian Habsburg and Vladislav II Jagiełło on the succession issue had to be approved by the Estates of Croatia and Slavonia meeting separately from those of Hungary and Transylvania.

According to the Tripartite Code, however, the rights enjoyed by the king as well as the virtual rights of Hungarian and Croatian kingdoms derived from the power of the 'holy crown'. Since the associated kingdoms and lands were subject to the crown, and since the 'holy crown' was the crown of Hungary, the kingdom of Croatia was subject to the kingdom of Hungary and to its laws.[24] The rights and privileges of the Croatian Estates were consequently deemed to be not original in nature, but conceded to them by the (legally crowned) king of Hungary, who could therefore withdraw them in the future, if that was the will of the Hungarian diet. From the Croatian Estates' point of view, however, the power of the crown was consonant with its obligation to defend Croatia's legal individuality; failure in this regard left the kingdom free to abrogate the union with Hungary and elect a different king – which is what happened in 1527 when the Croatian nobility elected Ferdinand I Habsburg quite independently.

Up to 1527 the Croatian nobility had never questioned the act of union with Hungary, despite the fact that its members did not always support the same king or dynasty as did the Hungarian nobles, or that some of the Croatian magnates rebelled against a particular ruler. The lines of political division within 'Hungary of the crown', in fact, hardly ever followed state-territorial borders. This was true also in 1527, when Croatia and western Hungary opted for Ferdinand, while Slavonia with the rest of Hungary and Transylvania chose Zapolya. What happened at Cetin in 1527 was of a wholly different nature, in that the Croatians felt no longer bound to the Hungarian crown. The election diploma approved in Cetin indeed makes no reference to Hungary as such: it begins by addressing Ferdinand as 'King of Bohemia and archduke of Austria', and ends by naming him 'King of Bohemia and Croatia'.

By electing Ferdinand I Habsburg in 1526–7, however, Hungary and Croatia came once again to share the king, the act of coronation, and audiences with the king at which matters demanding direct royal participation were decided. The concept of the holy crown, on the other hand, proved a useful device in the Estates' battles against royal power. The Habsburg kings, for their part, never accepted the existence of an essential distinction between the king and the crown, since in their view the crown was an emblem of royal dignity, not the bearer of royal power. The Croatian and Hungarian Estates inserted references to the crown and its powers in the texts of the decisions formulated at their joint meetings, and the king as a rule sanctioned these, for pragmatic reasons. But in reality constitutional matters were decided by relations of power: *de jure* and *de facto* royal power differed greatly in the subsequent period, and the same was true too of the quality of the relationship between the kingdoms of Croatia and Hungary.

THREE

The Ottoman Wars

Croatia's history between the middle of the fifteenth century and the middle of the eighteenth was largely shaped by its position on the border of the Ottoman Empire. During the fifteenth and sixteenth centuries the country suffered great territorial losses to the latter, culminating with the transformation of a large part of what remained of its territory into a Military Border, settled in due course by a sizable population of the Orthodox faith, thus altering for good the earlier purely Catholic character of its society. Despite the fact that by the end of the seventeenth century most of the lost area had been regained, the Military Border was to endure for another 200 years. Once crucial to the country's survival, after 1700 it became the main impediment to its development.

The Ottoman wars played a decisive role in the country's metamorphosis from a primarily Mediterranean to a predominantly Central European state. This geopolitical realignment was consolidated with the Habsburgs becoming kings of Croatia, the emigration of the nobility and wider population from the lands incorporated into the Ottoman Empire, and the fusion of the Estates of Croatia and Slavonia. At the same time, the prolonged defensive positions of Croatia and Hungary, both severely reduced in size, created an objective need for their closer cooperation, leading to a regular participation of Croatian representatives in the working of the Hungarian parliament.

Ottoman expansion

The Ottoman state established its first foothold on the European Continent at about the same time as Louis I of Anjou gained Dalmatia from Venice. It proceeded to expand to the north and west through major battles fought by standing (*janissary*) and locally raised (*timar*) armies led by the sultan, but also by advance raids carried out by *akıncı* – light cavalry organised by the commanders (*begs*) of the military districts or *sandžaks* that the Ottomans established along their new borders. These frontier *begs* played a crucial role in pushing the Ottoman borders outwards, and in absorbing the conquered territory into the Ottoman system.[1] The task of the *akıncı*, who were paid from disposable war booty, was repeatedly to plunder enemy territory and, by destroying its material and human resources, make it an easy target for the final occupation.

A Croat captive who fought in the janissary army described the Ottoman thrust in the following manner: 'The power of the Ottoman forces is like that of the sea, which neither grows nor diminishes yet is of such a nature that it is always busy, pulling back and moving forward, so that, calm in one part, it rushes and batters the coast elsewhere.'[2] The image of Ottoman expansion as an elemental force is preserved also in this description of the *akıncı* style of warfare: 'They are like a stormy rain that pours from the clouds and creates a flood, like streams that rise up and overflow their banks. Whatever the water reaches is carried away, while the damage done cannot always be easily made good.'[3]

By the time of Louis's death in 1382, *akıncı* units were raiding deep into Greece, Macedonia, Albania and Serbia. Bosnia soon came within their range. Ottoman expansion into Bosnia was facilitated by the inability of the Christian states to muster an effective military response to the large and centrally organised Ottoman armies – but also by a struggle for power among the territorial lords. Since Louis had married the daughter of the Bosnian king Stephen Kotromanić, the dynastic struggle that followed his death between his son-in-law Sigismund and the Anjou rival fanned civil war also in Bosnia. Sigismund's forces were ejected from Bosnia with the aid of *akıncı,* after which the latter proceeded to torch royal estates in Slavonia and Croatian manors and abbeys beyond the river Una. After Sigismund's defeat in 1396 at Nicopolis, the *akıncı* appeared in Slavonia and central Croatia.

Sigismund fought several battles against Ottoman armies in Wallachia and Serbia with mixed results, but he did manage to gain Belgrade from the Serbian despot George Branković. When a few years later he once again had to leave, he entrusted Croatia to Ban Nicholas Frankapan and Slavonia to his father-in-law Ban Herman of Celje, but the kingdom immediately reverted to fighting among the magnates. In Bosnia the enemies of King Tvrtko II were actively aided by the Ottomans. In 1434 Sigismund's forces invaded Bosnia and occupied several strategic towns, including Jajce and Hodidjed (present-day Sarajevo); but the subsequent conflict between the king and the Frankapan for the control of key castles in southern Croatia permitted the armies of Sultan Murat II to capture Hodidjed. Responding to the Estates' concerns, Sigismund proposed a defence system based on the creation of a sequence of militarised areas in Croatia, Bosnia and Hungary, but nothing came of this plan. By the time he died, he had managed to gain control of western Bosnia, but the Ottomans had crossed the Drina and occupied Bosnia's heartlands, whence, descending into the valley of the Neretva, the *akıncı* plundered the entire area down to the Adriatic coast.

Sigismund was succeeded by his son-in-law Albert, but the latter's early death caused another round of dynastic struggle. This permitted Sultan Murat II to seize Smederevo and establish a new *sandžak* there, which became the main outpost for the war against Hungary. Albrecht's successor, Vladislav I Jagiełło, ruled for only four years. He met his death at Varna, where the Christian army under his command was crushed by the Ottomans. After John Hunyady's defeat in 1448 in Kosovo, the Ottoman power south of the Danube was assured. In May 1453 Sultan Mehmed II took Constantinople and made it into the empire's new capital. The war against the Ottomans henceforth took on a largely defensive character.

The fractious Estates of Croatia and Hungary, however, proved unequal to the task of organising an effective resistance. It was not until Hunyady's son Matthias Corvinus became king that something resembling a defence system emerged. The Ottomans took the opportunity presented by the dynastic change, however, to swallow up what remained of Serbia and seize the fortress of Avala next to Belgrade. In 1463, in a lightning attack, Mehmed moved into Bosnia, captured the Bosnian king Stephen Tomašević and had him executed at Jajce. Although Matthias managed to regain Jajce and the whole of northern Bosnia, the defence henceforth had to reckon with the appearance of a new *sandžak* of Bosnia. Almost immediately Ottoman raiders appeared in the hinterland of the Dalmatian cities. In 1466 the Bosnian *sandžak-beg* Isa-beg Ishaković took Mostar, which became the seat of a new *sandžak* of Herzegovina. The two *sandžak-begs* proceeded to coordinate their attacks on central Croatia and Venetian Dalmatia. In 1468–9 *akıncı* pillaged the area between Zadar and Šibenik, and attacked the Frankapan cities of Senj and Modruš. Croatia also became increasingly the conduit for Ottoman raids into Austrian Carniola. Ottoman attacks continued for the rest of the fifteenth century, targeting central Croatia, western Slavonia, Styria and Carniola.

Matthias's preoccupation with his interests in Bohemia and Austria left the Croatian nobility to fend for themselves. Unable to resist the growing Ottoman pressure on their own, they sought outside help. A vicious circle was soon established. Since the king could not help with the defence of their lands, and with their material and human resources rapidly diminishing, Croatia's leading families were forced to look for help to Venice and Habsburg Austria – and even to contemplate surrender to the Ottomans. This made them suspect in the eyes of their king, who responded by seizing strategic castles or appointing outsiders to positions of responsibility in Croatia. The resulting conflict further undermined Croatia's defence. Matthias's successor, Vladislav II Jagiełło, proved even less able to organise an effective defence.

The Croatian armed forces were at this time organised according to a pattern established under the Anjou kings, in which the magnates and middle nobility fielded their own armies, whose size depended on the size of their estates. The ban had his own standing army and the lower nobility contributed their units to county armies. Croatia's military weakness was fully revealed in 1493 when the ban's army, flanked by cavalry and soldiers commanded by local nobles, was destroyed by the Ottomans on the field of Krbava. Leading members of the Frankapan, Zrinski and Karlović (counts of Krbava) families, the ban of Jajce, and hundreds of knights, perished on the battlefield. The Croatian ban himself and other notables were captured. The defeat accelerated the exodus, partly spontaneous and partly organised, of the local population from this part of Croatia. The Ottomans soon after this occupied the Adriatic coast between Omiš and the Neretva, and *akinci* returned to raid Croatia, targeting in particular the counties of Lika and Krbava.

The hard-pressed Croatian nobility were now forced to contemplate an understanding with the Ottoman foe. Some of those with estates surrounded or about to be seized accepted Ottoman suzerainty and service in the sultan's army. The majority appealed for help to Pope Alexander VI and Emperor Maximilian. At a meeting held in Bihać a few months after the battle of Krbava, the Croatian Estates made their situation very plain:

> We shall not be able to continue to resist the Turks unaided, since their wars have destroyed us. Our cities and homes are becoming increasingly deserted as our subjects and serfs are taken away and our estates seized or devastated. Up to now we have resolutely refused all offers from the Turks, in the belief that the Emperor and [the German] princes would be able to destroy the Turkish might, thus permitting us to remain part of Christendom. Now, however, we know that we cannot sustain ourselves much longer. The Turks have left us until the spring or summer to respond by offering our subjugation to them.[4]

Ottoman *akıncı* burn villages and take slaves

Matthias's able son, John Corvinus, ban of the Triune Kingdom, did what he could to shore up Croatian defences and even scored some victories; but not even the better positioned Venice was able to prevent Ottoman raids into Dalmatia, Istria and Friuli. Ceasefires agreed between King Vladislav and Sultan Bayezid did not apply to cross-border raids. The new sultan Selim I (1512–20), did not in any case feel himself bound by these agreements. The defence system established in northern Bosnia by Matthias was soon destroyed, leaving Jajce an exposed outpost. The Ottomans also drew closer to Split by capturing Sinj in its immediate hinterland.

Vladislav's son Louis inherited a land wrecked by peasant insurrections and feudal tyranny. In 1514, two years before his accession, a mass rebellion of Hungarian peasantry had been suppressed with great violence. A Hungary divided in this way could not defend itself. The papal nuncio predicted its early demise, stating that only a divine miracle could save the kingdom. Archduke Ferdinand, the new head of the Habsburg Austrian patrimony and Louis's brother-in-law, shared this judgement: 'If the Turk – God forbid! – comes, I feel Hungary will be finished, after which it will be my land's turn.'[5] Croatia stood as 'a rampart and a living shield before our Inner Austrian lands, [which] if not helped will become the Turks' booty.' No miracle occurred. In 1520 Sultan Selim was replaced by his son Süleyman. In the early summer of 1521 his army crossed the Sava and seized Belgrade. The following year the Bosnian Husrev-beg took Knin and Skradin. The Croatian magnate Bernardin Frankapan, who had fought at Krbava, reminded the German Estates meeting at Nürnberg in 1522 of the strategic danger presented by an eventual installation of Ottoman power in Croatia: 'If the Turk by misfortune were to seize Croatia, it would be very difficult for the Christian armies to dislodge him from there, such is the [geographical] nature of Croatia and such are its castles.'[6] Ferdinand of Austria too stressed the need to help Croatia defend itself. He wrote to the Nürnberg assembly that unless 'the gallant Christian Croatian nation, which as a bulwark and a strong shield stands before our Inner Austrian lands, is helped, they too will become the Turks' booty. If this were to come to pass, the whole burden of defence would then fall to our Inner Austrian lands. However, trusting the Christian and gallant bravery of the Croats, we believe that if helped they will be able to withstand the Turks.'[7]

These considerations encouraged Ferdinand to become directly involved in Croatia's defence. He sent soldiers into Croatia, contributed financially to the maintenance of its key castles and garrisons, and in general actively cooperated with the local lords and the Croatian ban. This aid tied the Croatian lords to the Habsburg dynasty. But the latter's help, however welcome, proved insufficient. In 1523 the Ottomans ended count Karlović's resistance by seizing a key fortress south of Bihać. Two years later Ottoman forces attacked the Adriatic port of Bag, endangered Senj, and burned down the Frankapan city of Modruš, causing a flight of population along the whole of this part of the Croatian coast and inducing fear in the neighbouring islands of Pag, Rab and Krk. The Venetian governor of Dalmatia wrote at this time that Croatia was effectively in Ottoman hands. To place the whole country under Habsburg protection seemed now the only option.

Hungary too was in mortal danger. In 1526 Süleyman again marched his army north, and was joined at Belgrade by forces under the command of the Smederevo and Bosnian *sandžak-begs*. During the summer they took Petrovaradin and Ilok on the Danube, crossed the Drava at Osijek and invaded Hungary. The Hungarian and Croatian armies led by the king were wiped out in less than two hours on the field of Mohács. Two archbishops, five bishops, a large number of nobles and some 10,000 soldiers were killed on this occasion. In 1529 Süleyman took the Hungarian capital of Buda, and there installed Ferdinand's rival for the crown of Croatia-Hungary, John Zapolya. The Bosnian Ottoman forces took advantage of the confusion caused by the conflict between Ferdinand Habsburg and John Zapolya to capture Udbina and Obrovac in Lika-Krbava, leaving the key fortresses of Klis, Bihać and Jajce isolated islands in an Ottoman sea. Ferdinand was supposed to do something about Croatia's defences, but this was not possible

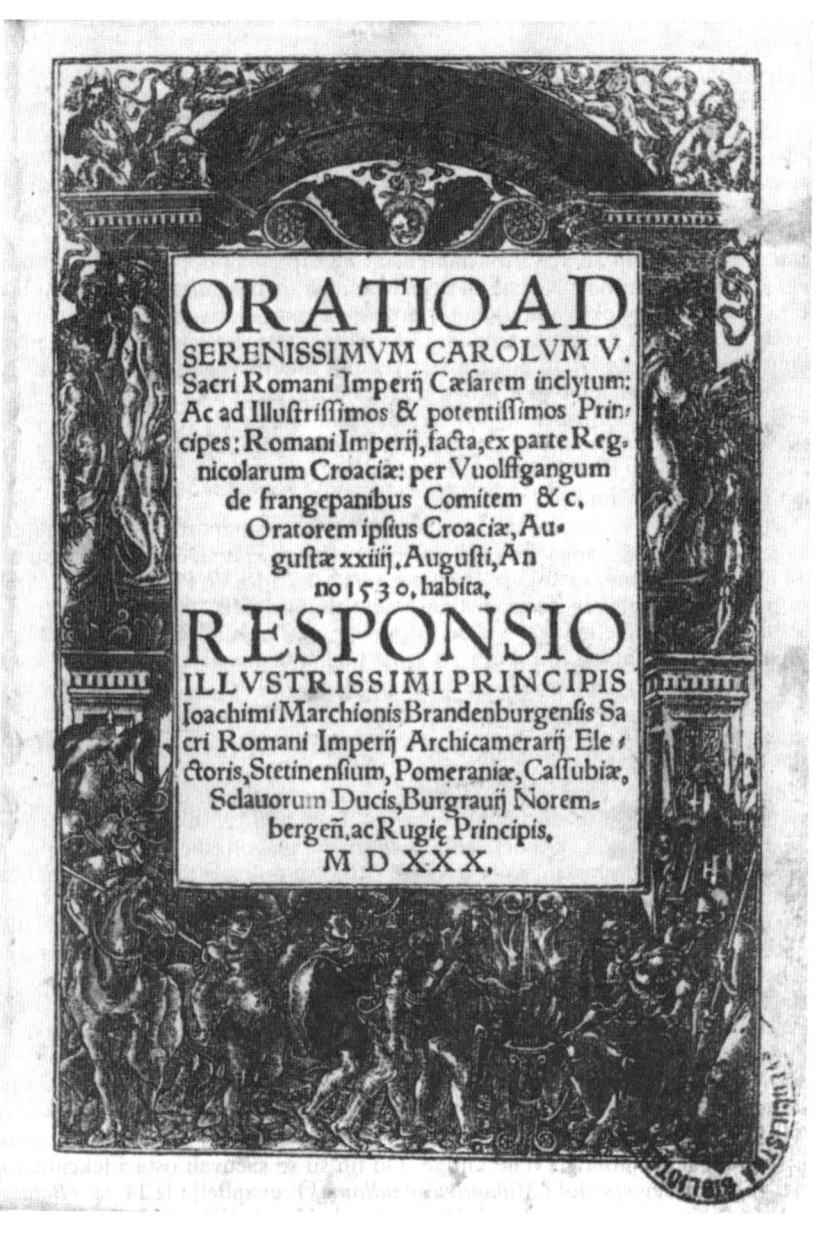

ORATIO AD
SERENISSIMVM CAROLVM V.
Sacri Romani Imperij Cæsarem inclytum:
Ac ad Illustrissimos & potentissimos Principes: Romani Imperij, facta, ex parte Regnicolarum Croaciæ: per Vuolffgangum de frangepanibus Comitem &c, Oratorem ipsius Croaciæ, Augustæ xxiiij, Augusti, Anno 1530, habita,

RESPONSIO
ILLVSTRISSIMI PRINCIPIS
Ioachimi Marchionis Brandenburgensis Sacri Romani Imperij Archicamerarij Electoris, Stetinensium, Pomeraniæ, Cassubiæ, Sclauorum Ducis, Burgrauij Norembergeñ, ac Rugię Principis,
M D XXX.

Vuk Frankapan's address to Emperor Charles V seeking aid for Croatia, with Margrave of Brandenburg's reply, 1530 in the conditions of civil war. Jajce, held by Zapolya supporters, surrendered to Bosnia's Husrev-beg, followed by Banja Luka. The Slavonian counties of Požega and Križevci were now directly exposed to Ottoman attacks.

At the end of 1528, as Süleyman began to muster his forces for an attack on Vienna itself, Ferdinand called upon the Slavonian counties of Požega and Vukovar to prepare for war; but the defence of Slavonia proved difficult in view of the continuing support for Zapolya among its nobles. In the summer of 1529 Süleyman crossed the Drava, met with Zapolya at Mohács and continued to Vienna. His failure to seize the city did not end the war of succession. The Austro-Turkish ceasefire of 1530 indeed made little difference to Croatia: between 1530 and 1532 Ottoman forces fanned out across Lika and Krbava, attacked Klis, pillaged western Slavonia, and torched Požega. In 1533 the Estates of Croatia and Slavonia met together in order to coordinate their defences, but the Slavonian nobility remained too divided.

The border now underwent a major shift to the west. In 1536 the Ottomans gained a foothold on the Sava's left bank by capturing Brod and Đakovo in southeastern Slavonia. Požega fell next and was made the seat of a new *sandžak*. The population and nobility in this part of Slavonia were promised leniency if they would accept Zapolya as their king, which most did, with relief. In March 1537 Klis also fell and was made the seat of a new *sandžak* of Klis.[8] That year King Ferdinand I mounted a campaign to drive the Ottomans out of Slavonia with an army gathered from the Austrian provinces and Bohemia; this proved no match, however, for the far more experienced Ottoman forces commanded by the local *sandžak-begs*. A deputation of the Croatian Estates visited the king in Graz, the capital of Styria, pressed him to come to an agreement with Zapolya, and supplied him with a list of places to be fortified and garrisoned. However, the religious conflict in Germany and the war with France kept Ferdinand busy – and also out of pocket. He turned to the Estates of Inner Austria for help, but there was never enough money to maintain the defences in Croatia-Slavonia. Neither could the latter's own parliament provide the ban with the necessary means. The defence as a result suffered from a chronic lack of guns, ammunition, food and manpower, all of which the Ottoman interior had in abundance. In this situation some of the Croatian nobility, including the Zrinski and the Frankapan, agreed to pay tribute to the sultan in order to protect their estates from the raids. This further weakened Croatia's capacity to resist.

Following Zapolya's death in 1540, Ferdinand repeatedly tried to retake Buda, but without success. The continuous Habsburg pressure, on the other hand, led Süleyman to re-organise Ottoman Hungary as a separate province or *eyalet*, to which he joined the *sandžak* of Srijem. Zapolya's son renounced the Hungarian throne and was given instead the running of the principality of Transylvania, now an Ottoman dependency. Elsewhere the war continued. By the middle of the 1540s the Ottoman army had established a bridgehead on the right (that is, the Slavonian) bank of the Drava near Virovitica. After lengthy negotiations, Ferdinand I and Emperor Charles V managed to win a year's peace from the pasha of Buda. At a joint meeting in Bratislava the Croatian and Hungarian Estates urged the king to greater efforts, and in that context pressed him to pay the new Croatian ban Nicholas Zrinski so that he could maintain his army. In lieu of payment the king invested Zrinski with permanent possession of the city of Čakovec, and in effect much of Međimurje (the area between the rivers Drava and Mura). The Zrinski were now the leading family in Croatia.

The five-year peace which the Habsburgs signed with Süleyman in 1547 in return for an annual tribute was spent in preparation for a new war. Ferdinand's involvement in an internal struggle in Transylvania triggered off fresh attacks on Slavonia. In 1552, the Požega *sandžak-beg* took the Slavonian towns of Virovitica and Čazma and made the latter into the seat of a new *sandžak*. Čazma, Zrinski wrote to the king, had to be retaken if the rest of Croatia-Slavonia were to be saved. With Ottoman raids now seriously threatening Varaždin, the Styrian Estates faced the prospect of the Ottoman Empire arriving on their own doorstep. Ban Zrinski resigned his post, telling the king that Croatia was falling apart. Ferdinand refused to accept his resignation and concentrated instead on persuading the Estates of Inner Austria that it was in their own interest to pay for a standing army in Croatia-Slavonia. In 1553 the Croatian parliament accepted the king's plan for defence of the border, which was to be paid for by the Estates of Styria, Carniola and Carinthia. In 1556 a permanent War Council was established at Graz – to which Carniola, Carinthia and Styria but not Croatia sent their representatives – with the task of establishing a secure defence line against the Ottomans.

Nicholas Zrinski was sent that year to inspect the defences of the strategic fortress at Sziget, north of Mohács, which was being besieged by Grand Vizier Mehmed-pasha Sokolović. In his absence the Ottomans took his manor of Kostajnica, breaking the Croatian defence line on the Una. All of Croatia now became a war zone. Confronted with the possibility that the rest of Croatia might fall too, Zrinski resigned once again from the post of ban and was replaced by his son-in-law, Peter Erdödy.[9] The war intensified for the rest of the decade, but there were also the first signs that a new military balance was being established, symbolised by the Ottoman decision to destroy Čazma and remove the *sandžak*'s seat eastwards to Pakrac.

In 1564 Ferdinand died and was succeeded by Maximilian (1564–76). Süleyman took this opportunity to start a new war aimed at securing the communications between Buda and Istanbul by seizing Sziget, defended by Zrinski. He built for this purpose a permanent, all-weather bridge across the Drava at Osijek. In 1566 he crossed the Drava over the magnificent new bridge and joined the siege of the city. He died three days before Sziget's fall. All its defenders, including Nicholas Zrinski, perished in the battle. The eight-year peace signed in 1568 was not observed by the Bosnian commanders, however, whose forces continued to harass the Dalmatian cities. In 1571 they established themselves in the immediate vicinity of Zadar. The peace of 1573 between the Porte and Venice permitted the Bosnians to concentrate on the area between the Una and the Kupa. Heavy fighting took place there throughout the decade, causing further population exodus. The systematic battering of Croatian defences led in 1576 to the loss of most places in what is now northwestern Bosnia. A new eight-year peace signed in Istanbul did not end the cross-border war. When in the spring of 1577 the Ottomans began to settle Vlachs in Lika-Krbava, the new king, Rudolf II (1576–1608), ordered their expulsion, but this proved impossible. The Ottomans responded by taking Zrinski's silver mine at Gvozdensko and the old family seat of Zrin, thereby shifting the Croatian border towards the rivers Korana and Kupa.

Severely pressed, in 1578 the Croatian parliament finally surrendered control of the border area to King Rudolf's brother, Charles, the archduke of Styria. Charles took an immediate decision to build a new fortress at the confluence of the Korana and the Kupa, on land bought from the Zrinski. Completed in 1579 it was named Karlstadt, the forerunner of the present-day city of Karlovac. It was also decided to rebuild the port of Bag, once property of the Karlović family, after which Bag was renamed Karlobag. The creation of the Military Border under the command of the War Council stimulated a reorganisation of border defences on the Ottoman side too, leading to the emergence in 1580 of a Bosnian *eyalet* that included four *sandžaks* established on Croatian territory: Pakrac, Požega, Lika and Klis. War remained the chief concern of the Croatian parliament throughout the second half of the sixteenth century. With military matters in the hands of the War Council, its contribution was reduced to supplying the army of the Military Border with food and manpower, maintaining the communications

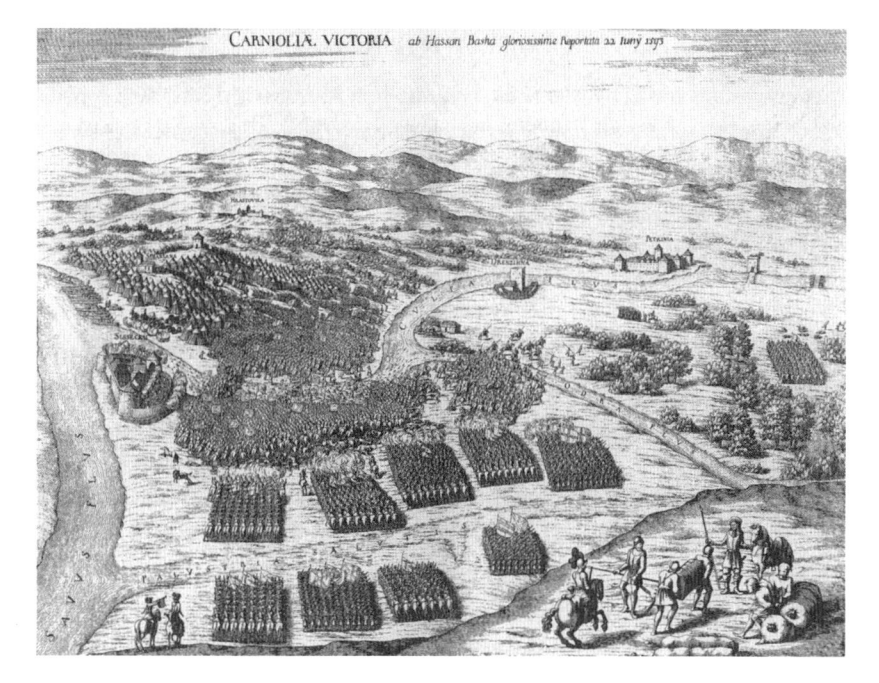

The battle of Sisak, 1593

and defences of the cities in the interior, and paying for the the upkeep of the ban's own army. As the new military balance stabilised, cross-border raids turned into a series of local wars, during which the Croatian side targeted in particular the newly settled population on the Ottoman side of the border.

The sixteenth century closed with what turned out to be the decisive battle of Sisak. In the spring of 1593 the Ottomans assembled an army drawn from Bosnia and Ottoman Slavonia, which greatly outnumbered the ban's and king's forces waiting for them on the other side of the river at Sisak. The battle, which took place on 22 June 1593, decided Croatia's fate. The enemy was driven into a sharp corner made by the Kupa and one of its tributaries, and its retreat cut off. The Bosnian pasha, the *sandžak-begs* and thousands of lower commanders and ordinary soldiers perished in the Kupa. Exactly one century after the battle of Krbava, Ottoman expansion into Croatian territory had finally been halted. The 1606 Peace of Zsitva formalised the situation on the ground. The frontier thus established between Croatia and the Ottoman Empire was to remain largely unchanged until the end of the seventeenth century.

A hundred-year retreat

A century and a half of Ottoman conquest had severe effects on Croatia. According to one estimate, during the fifteenth and sixteenth centuries the country lost three-quarters of its territory and over 60 per cent of its population. Around three-quarters of its towns, villages, hamlets, castles and forts were destroyed, together with over 500 churches and monasteries. Lika and Krbava, in particular, were so devastated that the Ottomans could not establish any kind of administration there for several years.

The Catholic Church lost the bishoprics and parishes of Makarska, Knin, Krbava, Bosnia (whose centre was in Đakovo) and Srijem, as well as the clerical chapters of Požega and Čazma, which had belonged to the bishopric of Zagreb. Parish records, manuscripts, artefacts and books – the cultural wealth collected over centuries – and much of the educated class were gone for good. The trade between Venice and Pannonia that used to start at Senj and continue by way of Modruš, Topusko, Zagreb and Križevci towards Hungary in the north, or by way of Sisak and Požega towards the Danube in the east, was now diverted to Carniola. Towns and market places that had served as important centres of trade and craft along these routes declined into insignificance or were lost to the Ottomans, including Bihać and Kostajnica on the Una, which had once served the movement of goods and people from Bosnia to Slavonia or to Senj.

The population fled to Venetian Dalmatia and Istria, to the Italian Marche, Abruzzi and Puglia, to the Austrian provinces, to western Hungary, and in particular to what remained of Croatia. A large number of those who stayed behind were either killed or taken into slavery. The mass flight to more secure areas left large tracts of land permanently uninhabited and ungoverned. Pastures, plough-lands and vineyards reverted to wilderness as the secular nobility, the episcopate, the clerical chapters and the monasteries lost their manors and servile labour. Some of the nobles who moved away from the border area took their serfs with them. Nicholas Zrinski took his serfs from Slavonia and the Una area to Međimurje, Francis Batthyány to his Hungarian estates across the Drava. Peter Erdödy took his serfs from central Slavonia to western Hungary, the Zagreb bishop moved his to Carniola. The descendants of the once all-powerful Slavonian Babonić family settled in Carniola for good. The large landowners suffered great losses, but their economic strongholds were as a rule located in the interior, where estates could be repopulated as the population returned, or settled with refugees from other areas. It was the lesser nobility, including the cadet branches of the great families, whose lands lay wholly contained within the border area, that suffered most. A large number were killed or made destitute. Many ended up serving in the army of the Military Border. The greatest victims of the Ottoman wars, of course, were the peasants themselves. Ferdinand's military advisers sent to help set up Croatia's defences described it as a 'devastated and hungry country'. The disappearance of manors as centres of economic and administrative life obliterated the very foundation of the feudal order within a broad band of territory that materialised along the whole length of Croatia's frontier with the Ottoman Empire: to the east, cutting right across Slavonia, it ran for 100 kilometres between the rivers Sava and Drava. It was three times as long to the west, stretching as it did from the Sava to the Adriatic Sea. This territory became in due course the site of the unique institution of the Military Border (*Vojna Krajina* in Croat, *Miltärgrenze* in German).

Ottoman Croatia

The Ottoman part of Croatia came to be organised according to the usual imperial pattern, in which the larger administrative unit was the *sandžak* headed by the military commander or *sandžak-beg*. A group of *sandžaks* formed a *beglerbegluk* or *eyalet*, run by a *beglerbeg*. *Sandžaks* were divided into smaller units or *kadiluks*, headed by a *kadi* or judge, and these into *nahiye* or subdistricts. The *kadiluks* as a rule carried the name of the larger urban centres. Some of the *nahiye* were based on pre-Ottoman parishes and kept their old names, derived from rivers, previous manors or other established features.[10]

The Ottoman system of government involved a complete break from the previous feudal administration. It differed above all in its far higher degree of centralisation, rooted in the fact that the land belonged to the sultan, who was also the highest religious authority. Its formation and maintenance were consequently the responsibility not of the landed class, but of the state itself. It differed also in that its organising principle was military need not territory. The *eyalet-sandžak-kadiluk* division was in fact the territorial aspect of the pattern of allocation of the army's revenue, and mirrored the distribution of taxes deriving from a given territory among the different state officials.[11] The installation of the Ottoman order, nevertheless, did not amount to a complete rupture with the past. Continuity was embedded in the territory's geographical features, its largely agrarian character, and the cultural, ethnic and family affinity of the population, which often transcended the religious and political divide.[12]

Until such time as a regular administration could be established, the newly acquired border areas were administered from the neighbouring *sandžaks*. The area seized from the Croatian *regnum* was initially governed from Bosnia, but was later included into the *sandžak* of Klis. In the last quarter of the sixteenth century a new *sandžak* of Krka-Lika emerged, which embraced northern Dalmatia, Lika, Krbava, and the area between Senj and the Una. The vilayets of Srijem and Požega were at first governed from the *sandžak* of Smederevo, but in the middle of the sixteenth century Požega and Osijek became the seats of two new *sandžaks*: Požega and Srijem. The Požega *sandžak*, which comprised a large part of Slavonia between the Drava and the Sava, reached its greatest extent with the conquest of Virovitica and Čazma, when it also gained the *kadiluk* of Osijek. The seat of the *sandžak* of Srijem was then moved to Ilok. The two *sandžaks* of Požega and Srijem were later added to the *eyalet* of Buda, but in 1580 the Požega *sandžak* was transferred to the Bosnian administration and then, in 1600, to the newly established *eyalet* of Kanizsa in the Ottoman part of Hungary. The large area between the rivers Una and Sava, and part of Slavonia on the right bank of the Sava, were originally incorporated into the Bosnian *eyalet*, but in 1547 came to form a separate *sandžak* of Čazma. A few years later the seat of the *sandžak* of Čazma was moved to Pakrac, and later still to Cernik. In 1580 this *sandžak* was again incorporated into the Bosnian *eyalet*.[13]

The Ottoman administration took over or rebuilt the towns and villages once the worst of the war was over. This was true especially after the peace of 1606, when Slavonia underwent an accelerated development.[14] Due to the presence of the Süleyman bridge, Osijek in particular developed rapidly to become the largest 'Croatian' city. The main initial problem facing the new administrators was the scarcity of population. Areas that had fallen in a lightning conquest retained most of their inhabitants, but those exposed to prolonged attack became severely depopulated. A good part of the land remained unworked until the new order stabilised, after which there followed an influx of Muslim settlers from other parts of the empire, but mainly from Bosnia. There was also a significant settlement of Orthodox population coming mainly from Bosnia, especially in the *sandžak* of Pakrac and, in the case of eastern Srijem, from Serbia. Catholic immigrants came too, some voluntarily, some not. Thus a sequence of risings among the Catholic Vlach population of the Klis and Krka *sandžaks* led in 1627 to a forced resettlement of some 2,000 families into Slavonia. There was also considerable internal migration. A main characteristic of Ottoman Croatia was indeed a high mobility of population and a great fluidity of the state's approach to the settlers.

By the end of the sixteenth century a pattern was established according to which the Muslim population, made up mostly of soldiers and administrators, predominated in the towns, while the Christian population lived in their outskirts or in the countryside. The town of Ilok, for example, had 237 Muslim and 27 Christian households, but its *nahiya* had 320 Muslim and 836 Christian settlements. There were 412 Muslim and 52 Christian households in Požega, but in the *nahiya* only 21 Muslim compared with 385 Christian settlements. In the Požega *sandžak* as a whole, on the other hand, there were 9,950 homesteads, of which 2,463 were owned by Muslims: this was the only part of Slavonia with a significant presence of Muslim villages. In the case of the Cernik (formerly Čazma) *sandžak*, its southern part along the Sava retained a significant Catholic population, but a row of Orthodox Vlach villages emerged around Okučani to form Little Wallachia.

The Ottoman conquest led to the effective disappearance of the previous Catholic Church organisation. Some of the churches in the main towns were turned into mosques, while those that survived generally suffered from lack of priests. As the size of the Muslim population grew, new mosques were built, so that by the end of the seventeenth century there were probably 100 mosques in Ottoman Croatia, of which two-thirds were in the towns and larger settlements.[15] With the establishment of the Orthodox bishopric of Buda in 1541, and the restoration of the Patriarchy of Peć in Kosovo in 1557, conditions were created for the establishment of an Orthodox Church administration. An Orthodox bishopric was established in Požega, but the spiritual centre of the Orthodox population became the monastery near Orahovica, where a new church was built in 1594.

That the Catholic Church survived at all was due mainly to the Franciscan order. A charter granted by Sultan Mehmed II in 1463 to the Bosnian Franciscans permitted the establishment of the Franciscan Bosnian Province in 1517, which subsequently came to include also Ottoman Croatia and Hungary. In the late sixteenth century the order built a new monastery near Požega, which became the religious centre of the *sandžak*'s Catholics. According to one estimate, in the late seventeenth century Ottoman Slavonia had around 220,000 inhabitants, of whom 48 per cent were Muslim, 33 per cent Catholic, 14 per cent Orthodox and 5 per cent Protestant.[16] According to another, the Muslims formed no more than a quarter of the total population of Slavonia and Srijem in the sixteenth century, and no more than a third in the seventeenth.[17]

The Ottoman state lightened the earlier feudal burden of the Christian peasantry, particularly in regard to the *robot* or obligatory free labour, which was either reduced or abolished altogether; it also permitted some movement on the land. The social and material conditions of the peasantry improved considerably as a result, in comparison with their counterparts on the other side of the border. Bartol Kašić, a Croatian Jesuit who in the early seventeenth century travelled through Ottoman Croatia, wrote favourably about the Ottoman system of administration. Such immediate benefits were offset, however, by a cultural regression of the predominantly Christian rural society attendant upon the disappearance of the indigenous educated elite. Neither the surviving Franciscan order nor the growing Orthodox clergy could remedy this loss. The abandonment of the social and territorial stratification associated with the feudal system encouraged, moreover, a reversion among the Christian peasantry to pre-feudal, patriarchal and highly localised forms of social organisation.

The peace that came in the early seventeenth century permitted a reconstruction of the economy and society on both sides of the Ottoman border. In the longer run, however, continued peace had a detrimental effect on the viability of the Ottoman system in Croatia. As territorial expansion came to an end and with it the acquisition of land and treasure, which had been the main source of enrichment for the military class, fiscal and other forms of exploitation of the peasantry by the Ottoman state increased, while surplus rural population and irregular forces turned to brigandage. The worsening situation by the end of the seventeenth century produced growing social unrest among the Christian population, leading at times to open rebellion. As a result, groups, predominantly of Vlachs, started to cross into Habsburg territory, settling in the largely deserted area within the Military Border.

The Military Border

When in 1527 Ferdinand Habsburg became King of Croatia, he inherited together with his title responsibility for the kingdom's defence. In the conditions of a dynastic war, however, the king's overriding problem became not fighting the Ottomans but defeating his dynastic rival, now aided by the Porte. With Slavonia divided into two warring camps, money and armies raised for fighting the Ottoman armies in Slavonia were in 1529 used to defend Varaždin and to wrench Zagreb and central Slavonia from John Zapolya's supporters. It was only after Ferdinand and Zapolya had made peace that defence could be given the necessary attention. Ferdinand's repeated failure to regain Buda after Zapolya's death, or to prevent the steady Ottoman advance into Slavonia, showed that the enemy could not be defeated in a set battle, and that the answer lay in erecting a strong system of defences.

An effective defence of Croatia and Slavonia required a solution to three sets of problems.[18] The first involved finding a workable concept of defence. This comprised repairing the existing castles and fortifications, and building new fortresses that would be made part of a unified system by the erection of a network of watchtowers between them to be kept in mutual touch by light cavalry. A border army had to be recruited and organised, and supplied with the necessary arms and provisions on a regular basis. Labour, mainly of serfs but also of skilled craftsmen and architects, had to be found to maintain or build the fortifications, and to establish a secure system of communications between them and the land in the interior.

The second set of problems involved finding a source of stable and regular financing of the border. This could not be supplied by Croatia. In 1544, for example, the war tax in Slavonia brought only one-hundredth of the sum needed for its defence. Indeed, throughout the sixteenth century the cost of defence of Hungary and Croatia greatly exceeded the income collected in taxes from the two kingdoms: the Habsburgs were consequently forced to seek financial assistance from the Estates of Inner Austria. Ferdinand's argument that defence of Croatia provided for their own security did not initially evoke a sympathetic response; but in the end the directly exposed duchies of Carniola and Styria accepted the main responsibility for financing the emerging system of border defence in Croatia.

The third set of problems involved the relationship between the king and the Croatian Estates – that is, the delineation of authority on the one hand between king and parliament over the border army, and on the other hand between the royal captains and the magnates whose estates and castles were to be included in the defence system.

In the case of Slavonia, the construction of a defence network proceeded relatively fast, due to the flat nature of the terrain and the absence of conflicting feudal rights. A new system of walls and towers was built in Varaždin (the 'gate of Styria'), and Zagreb's defences too were strengthened. New fortresses according to the latest designs were built at Koprivnica, Križevci and Ivanić, which became the seats of royal captains in charge of an array of forts and watchtowers erected in their vicinity. Much of this work was paid for by Styria, or by the king himself, usually by forfeiting state taxes. The land involved was in any case part of the royal fisc, added after the previous owners had died without leaving a legal heir. Ban Nicholas Zrinski built at his own expense a modern castle – which he called Novi Zrin (New

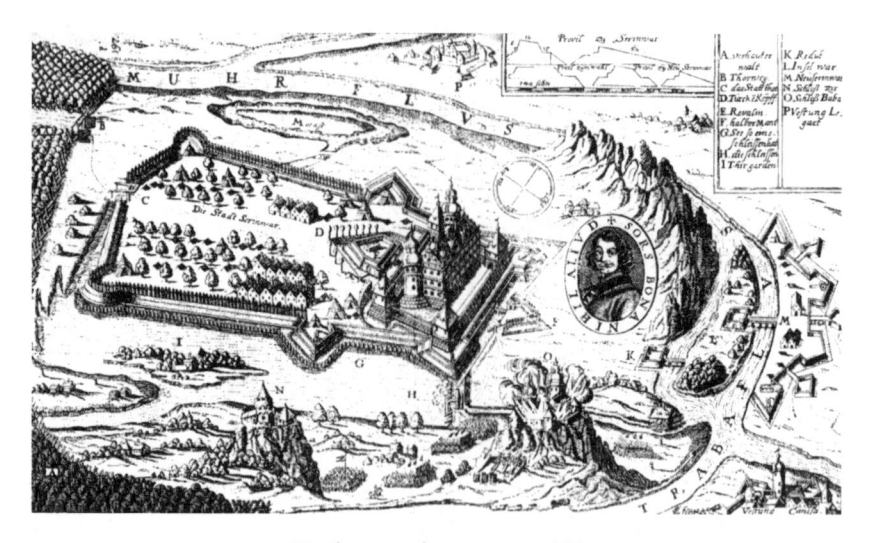

The fortress of Novi Zrin, 1664

Zrin) – to protect the newly acquired manor of Čakovec. The bishop and canons of Zagreb built a new fortress at Sisak to defend the approach to Zagreb. The last in the chain of the new castles in Slavonia was that of Karlovac, paid for by the Estates of Inner Austria.

In central Croatia, the creation of a unified defence system proved more complicated, since much of the land on which it was to emerge was in the possession of influential local lords and the church. The agreement forged between Ferdinand and the Croatian Estates was that the king would help Croatia's defence both by fielding his own army and by contributing directly to that of the nobility. This assumed that the king would be able to honour his commitments and that the nobility would preserve its economic and military strength. However, with their manors repeatedly torched and the population constantly haemorrhaging, the Croatian lords were forced to rely increasingly on royal help to maintain their castles, forts and garrisons. Located in a mountainous territory subdivided by rivers, these formed a dense patchwork which proved, initially at least, an effective barrier to any permanent occupation. Many, however, were small and/or poorly maintained. Given the population loss they could not be easily held or supplied, so frequently ended up as islands surrounded by an effective wilderness, easily bypassed by the Ottoman light cavalry on their raids further north and west. The king and his captains, concerned with the rationalisation of the defence system as a whole, pressed the nobles either to defend their castles and citadels better or, if unable to do so, to destroy them or surrender them to the king. But this demand was regularly rejected on the grounds that it would facilitate Ottoman advance, encourage a further exodus of the population and ultimately lead to Croatia's obliteration. Abandonment of estates, moreover, frequently amounted to the loss of ancient family seats. In the view of the Croatian lords, the solution lay not in abandoning the territory, but in a more effective royal assistance.

Ferdinand's initial base in Croatia was the castles and towns that Matthias Corvinus had managed to acquire half a century earlier. Of these the most important for Croatia's defence were Senj and Bihać, each commanded by a royal captain. As the Ottomans pushed forward from the south and east, however, the area under royal control widened, since the nobility, unable to resist, surrendered their land and castles to the king or the ban for protection. The Zrinski thus surrendered Kostajnica, the key fortress on the Una; the Frankapan gave up Otočac and Brinje in the hinterland of Senj. The king increased the territory under his control too, by buying land from local landowners in order either to consolidate the two captaincies or to create new ones: the great new fortress of Karlovac was built on land bought from the Zrinski.

Transfer of territorial control to the king, however, did not guarantee success. The loss of Kostajnica showed that the royal army did not necessarily perform better then the local lords. Once the area between Jasenovac (at the confluence of the Sava and the Una) and Novi (at the confluence of the Sana and the Una) came under Ottoman control, the centre of gravity of Croatia's defence moved to the Kupa. In 1558 the parliament rejected once again the king's demand to destroy indefensible forts and surrender the key ones to his captains; it made instead the crucial decision to establish by its own efforts a defence line along the Kupa – subsequently known as the Ban's Border – between Karlovac and Sisak. But this could be only a small part of the total: by 1563 thirteen out of eighty-five fortified places facing the Ottoman forces were owned by the king, forty-five were garrisoned by the king's army, while twenty-seven were deserted. Only fourteen were maintained by their owners, six of them by the church.

That year Ferdinand, concerned with the rising cost of defence of Croatia, sent a commission to survey the existing situation and make proposals that would be presented to the Estates of Inner Austria, by now the greatest financial contributor. The commission's conclusion was that a new type of military institution should be established, preferably under a single command, which would deal with all aspects of the border defence. In its estimate, the maintenance of the two borders – the Slavonian and the Croatian – required an annual sum of over 324,000 forints, a sum far greater than Styria and Carniola were providing at the time. It was necessary, therefore, in the view of the commission, that Carinthia be brought in to share the burden. At a meeting of representatives from the German empire and the Austrian lands held in 1577 in Vienna, the estimate of the necessary monies was if anything revised upwards. It was agreed that the empire would supply an additional annual sum of 140,000 forints and the emperor-king another 60,000. At the request of the Estates of Inner Austria, the new emperor and king, Rudolf (1576–1608), entrusted the responsibility for the whole border to his uncle, Archduke Charles.

Charles was thus made the supreme commander and governor of a complex of border garrisons and forts – fifty-three in central Croatia and thirty-seven in Slavonia – and all auxiliary units and military services. He was allowed to dispose freely of the financial aid supplied by the German empire, which was to be spent on public works, armaments and provisions. The two generals appointed to command the Slavonian and Croatian border armies were to be subject to him. The archduke indeed was to have full autonomy of decision in all matters of defence, except in regard to the appointment of the top commanders, which the king retained for himself. The right to offensive action against the Ottoman Empire was also retained by the king. In military matters the Croatian ban – effectively the kingdom's own army – was also subordinated to the archduke. The king agreed also to the formation of a War Council in Graz, which was to advise the archduke on such problems as the building and maintenance of fortifications, military discipline and supplies. In the following year the Estates of Inner Austria, meeting at Bruck on the Mura, approved these decisions. Geographic location dictated the division of labour: Styria took responsibility for maintenance of the border in Slavonia, while that in central Croatia fell to Carniola and Carinthia. It was at this meeting that the decision was taken to build the new fortress of Karlovac.

This string of decrees created a new source of authority in Croatia. The decrees were immediately challenged by the Croatian parliament, which, aided by the Hungarian Estates, denounced as illegal the subjugation of the ban to the archduke. The king confirmed his decision, but he also added a clarification: 'the ban of Croatia-Slavonia, together with all the forces subject to him, is in our name directed to the archduke in military matters, and in other matters to us as king of Hungary.' Formally speaking, the ban remained an equal to the archduke in military matters, but in reality defence policy was henceforth decided in Graz. As a result, by the end of the sixteenth century two separate levels of authority had appeared in Croatia:

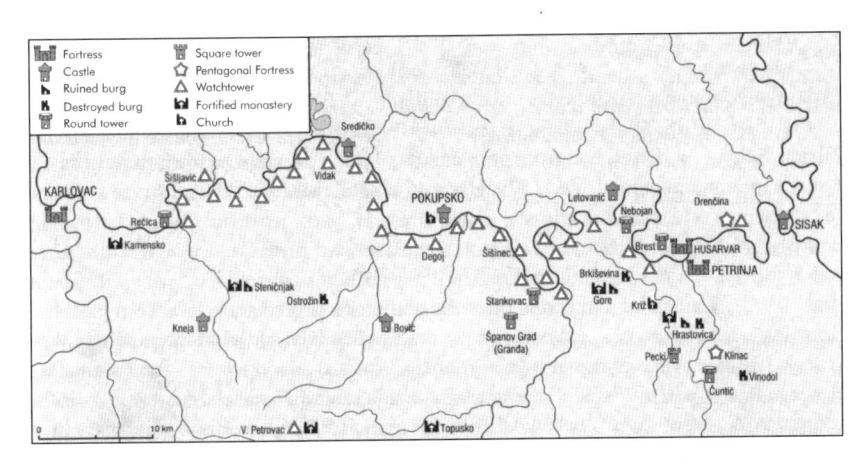

The fortified defence line between Karlovac and Sisak, sixteenth century

the traditional one involving the ban, the parliament and the manorial lords; and a military one vested in the commanders of the royal garrisons that was independent from all these levels. Out of this divided authority there emerged a special territorial and military institution in the area facing the Ottoman Empire: the Military Border. The Slavonian Border became eventually organised as three captaincies, with their headquarters in Ivanić, Koprivnica and Križevci. Since its commanding officer – with the rank of a general – resided in Varaždin, it was known also as the Varaždin *Generalität*. The Croatian Border for similar reasons became the Karlovac *Generalität*. Between them lay the Ban's Border, controlled by the Croatian Estates.

The Estates of Inner Austria treated as their right the privilege of filling top command posts and supplying the garrisons with food and uniforms at prices which they themselves determined. The financial resources which they could, or were willing to, provide proved insufficient to meet all the border's needs, however, despite the fact that the Croatian parliament regularly provided unpaid serf labour for the repair of battlements and the transport of supplies. Soldiers' pay was the most costly item, and various ways were sought to minimise this, usually at the soldiers' expense. The border regularly suffered, in fact, from delayed payment and corrupt officials, so that the border army often resorted to pillaging nearby villages, to the dismay of the peasants and their lords alike. A strong ban like Nicholas Zrinski regularly fined offending commanders, after bringing them before his court; but the military exhibited an increasing tendency to disregard the laws of the kingdom, and to apply their own in matters outside their authority. The parliament made regular complaints to the War Council, usually to little effect. An answer to the permanent problem of manpower and expenditure was in the end supplied by the Vlachs, who from the 1530s on started to cross over from Ottoman territory. Contemporary documents give them a host of names reflecting their status, ethnicity and place of origin – such as Vlachs, Turkish Vlachs, Rascian (that is, Serbian) Vlachs, *uskoks* or runaways – but eventually the term Vlach prevailed as their common designation.

The presence of Vlachs in Croatia predates the Ottoman arrival. Documents from the fourteenth century show the existence of a substantial Vlach population in the area between the Zrmanja and the Cetina. Their influx into Lika and Krbava and the Dalmatian interior was encouraged in particular by population loss as a result of the Great Plague of 1348. They were settled on the estates belonging to the Croatian lords or the king and were called, respectively, Private Vlachs and King's Vlachs.[19] Being of the Catholic faith they quickly assimilated, judging by their names and their speech inscribed in the Glagolitic documents issued by their leaders. They nevertheless preserved their individuality, due partly to the inaccessibility of their villages and partly to the king's and the local nobility's need for soldiers.[20]

The Porte, too, used Vlachs as military auxiliaries. They formed the bulk of the *akıncı* units, served as frontier guards, and were the source for the repopulation of the conquered areas. The policy of settling Vlachs in the *sandžak* of Požega in Slavonia is described by an Ottoman official in these terms:

> The stated [Vlachs] are settled in the given empty land of the border *vilayet*, which they then cultivate. Some till the land and others graze cattle and sheep. A tax of 83 *akçe* [silver coins] on each household has been decided as a counter-value for the use of the land and as a levy on the cattle, in accordance with the Vlach custom in other *vilayets*. [They] are obliged to keep watch over and guard these borders and to perform military service at imperial demand. This being a border *vilayet*, it could not be settled without the Vlachs. Quite apart from this, the roads are infested by infidel thieves. It is both useful and necessary that they [the Vlachs] should inhabit this area.[21]

Most of the Vlachs who settled in the Ottoman part of Croatia came from Bosnia. The colonists were granted by the authorities tax reductions, and traditional local self-government based on elected village judges or *knezi*, and military leaders or *vojvode*. As the border moved westwards, however, the Vlachs in the interior lost their distinct social status and become part of the non-privileged Christian population. In an extended process that subsumed waves of immigration and integration, by the end of the sixteenth century Vlach society came to exhibit a wide range of degrees of social and legal assimilation into the Ottoman order. The Vlachs also became ethnically more heterogeneous. They could perhaps best be described as a community with its own customs and privileges, attachment to which proved stronger than the eventual ethnic or religious identification of its members. Their migration to the Habsburg side of the border was encouraged by the erosion of their privileged status, caused on the one hand by the consolidation of the Ottoman state and on the other by the weakening of the empire's offensive power. For, as the Croatian-Ottoman border stabilised, the military service performed by the Vlachs became less important than their taxes, while the cross-border raids that had once brought easy booty came to elicit an increasingly punitive response from the Military Border army.

Vlach immigration posed the problem of where, and under what conditions, they would be allowed to settle. The few groups that, led by their *vojvode* and sometimes accompanied by their cattle, arrived in the early sixteenth century were willing at first to submit themselves to manorial jurisdiction, provided they be freed from taxes for a certain period – as indeed was customary in such situations. The lords, though keen to repopulate their estates, proved unwilling to accept them, however, fearing the reaction of their own peasants whose cattle and produce the immigrants, devoid of other means of life, frequently stole. For want of a better solution they ended up on the manor of Žumberak, a Habsburg property in Carniola bordering Croatia. The area of their habitation was organised as a distinct administrative unit – the District of Žumberak – and placed in charge of a captain. Since their basic task was to act as frontier guards, the district was eventually joined to the Slavonian Border. Of the 3,000 soldiers who normally guarded the Slavonian frontier in the sixteenth century, around one-third were of Vlach origin.

Since the Žumberak Vlachs became, in effect, King's Vlachs, this arrangement did not disturb the existing legal order. The inherent problems posed by the existence of dual authority in Croatia came to a head, however, during the Long Turkish War of 1593–1606, when at least 10,000 armed Vlachs crossed into Habsburg Slavonia. They came mainly from the border *sandžaks*, but some also from further in the Ottoman interior. The initial response of the Croatian and Styrian Estates was to decline all responsibility for the immigrants. But something had to be done, and in the end the Border commanders pressed the Estates of Styria to come up with a solution. This was found in directing the Vlachs to the empty land surrounding the main garrisons, with or without the permission of its owners, as a result of which the previously deserted border area started to fill up. Everyone agreed that as peasants and soldiers the colonists would contribute to the economic and military needs of defence. If they were to stay, however, it was necessary to grant them the kind of privileges they had enjoyed on the other side. In 1597 Archduke Ferdinand, who had replaced Charles as the border's supreme commander, issued a guarantee promising the immigrants land and exemption from taxes, as well as respect for their customs.

His proclamation did not refer, however, to the vital issue of jurisdiction. This problem did not arise in the case of the Vlachs who had settled on land where manorial jurisdiction was still in existence, and who consequently acquired the status of Private Vlachs. It was not a problem either in regard to the majority that had ended up on land belonging to the royal fisc. Many, however, established themselves on empty property belonging to the ecclesiastical and secular lords who, once it became clear that this arrangement would be permanent, demanded payment of the usual feudal dues. The first to protest against an effective usurpation of his property was the bishop of Zagreb, since most of the privately owned land settled by these Vlachs belonged to the church. He insisted that the Vlachs should recognise him as their lord (*dominus terrestris*) and negotiate with him the issue of rent. The rest of the nobility followed suit. The Croatian Estates, supported by those of Hungary, backed this demand out of concern – justified as it turned out – that the surrender of jurisdiction over the Vlach colonists would inevitably lead to the border territory being alienated from the kingdom. The Zagreb parliament demanded of Styria to stop the frontier commanders settling Vlachs without the prior agreement of the legal owners. They also asked King Ferdinand II (1618–37) that the border land belonging to the royal fisc be administered by royal and not Styrian officials.

The Croatian and Hungarian diets, in fact, spent much of the seventeenth century struggling with the king and the Inner Austrian Estates over the terms of Vlach settlement. Consecutive sessions of the joint Croatian-Hungarian parliament during the seventeenth century passed laws aimed at subjugation of the Vlachs to the jurisdiction of the lords, the ban and the Croatian parliament. Three of these – in 1635, 1659 and 1681 – emphatically declared that Vlach privileges issued by the king were null and void. The Croatian Estates knew that the Vlachs could not be made into serfs and were willing to recognise the privileges they already enjoyed; but only on condition that they submit themselves to the laws of the kingdom. Both parties to the conflict – the Croatian Estates backed by those of Hungary, and the Vlachs supported by the Styrian Estates and the border commanders – appealed to the king. Ferdinand could not lawfully give away the nobles' land, since this amounted to expropriation – an illegal act which he could not contemplate in any case, given that the affair coincided with the Thirty Years War (1618–48), and he needed the support of the Croatian and Hungarian nobility. But he also needed the Vlachs, both as border soldiers and as recruits for his own armies – several thousand of them were drafted to fight in Germany. The king offered to buy the land from the nobles or to exchange it for land of his own in Hungary; but this was rejected since it amounted to a loss of Croatian state territory. He also tried to persuade the Vlachs to pay some rent to the lords, but they refused. The king was consequently forced to play a double game: he sanctioned the decisions of the Croatian-Hungarian diet and sent mixed commissions to Slavonia to adjudicate the matter; but he also allowed the commissions' work to drag on inconclusively, during which time he kept reaffirming the Vlachs' existing privileges.

With the commissions unable to agree, the matter was in 1628 brought before the crown court in Bratislava. Its ruling involved a compromise: where a claim to deserted land could be proven, the land was to be returned to the rightful owner. The Vlachs who lived on it, however, were to pay only the usual public taxes, and in regard to their military duties were to obey not the lord but the ban, that is, the king. On the basis of this decision the Croatian parliament in the following year drafted its own Vlach Law. According to this, the Vlachs were not to be treated as serfs; they would be exempt from the *robot*, and they would give to their lords what they were already giving to the border generals and captains, or as privately agreed. The Vlachs, however, were to 'voluntarily surrender to the kingdom' and perform military service under the ban's command. This possibility of a lasting settlement between the Croatian Estates and the Vlach immigrants, which would ultimately have led to their integration into Croatian society, was thwarted by Styria, which played on the Vlachs' fear of losing their formal privileges based on the use of land conditioned only by military service.

The return of a considerable part of the territory of the Slavonian Border to Croatian administration was something that King Ferdinand II would not allow either. In 1630, in his capacity as King of Croatia, that is, as the supreme executive and lord of the land, he signed the portentous *Statuta Valachorum*, the Vlach Code, which set out the terms of settlement for the Vlach community (*communitas Valachorum*) living between the Drava and the Sava. The Vlachs were granted full use of their land holdings, which carried no rent other than public *robot*; but land tenure was conditional upon military service to the king. The land was not actually given to the settlers, since it remained the property of its legal owners; but control over it was assumed by the king. Other Vlach privileges, including the right to elect their *vojvode* and *knezi* and, in the case of the Orthodox, to practise their religion freely, were endorsed; but – in recognition of the Croatian state right to the territory of the border – in civic disputes not covered by the code the Vlachs were to be tried according to the laws of the kingdom. The response of the Croatian and Hungarian Estates came in 1635, in the form of their joint diet's full revocation of the code and all other earlier Vlach privileges; but they did not have the actual power to realise this or any other subsequent similar decision.

The Vlach Code, however, did not specify the scope of the authority of the elected Vlach officials, as opposed to that of the border commanders. This allowed the latter, particularly after the removal of the Croatian parliament's influence from the border, to negate Vlach rights in practice and generally to interfere in the internal affairs of their community, as a result of which a Vlach rebellion broke out as early as 1631. By 1650 the Slavonian Vlachs were ready to come to an agreement with the Croatian Estates, whereupon the parliament produced a new draft of its earlier Vlach Law, which now included some of the provisions of Ferdinand's code. The Vlachs were this time to be subject to the ban's authority in civilian matters too, and would be allowed also to elect their own local leaders. They would be treated like the soldiers of the Ban's Border, and eventually enjoy the usual rights of the kingdom's inhabitants, such as the right to take their manorial lords to court. The colonists were to pay only the usual public taxes, while the small rent for the land they enjoyed would be paid not directly to the lord but indirectly through their elected leaders, thus preventing seigneurial abuse. The draft, in other words, satisfied the Vlachs' main concern not to be subjugated to individual lords, but only to the king. Although the Croatian parliament's offer in some respects fell below what the *Statuta* promised, the Vlach leaders found the offer attractive. Actual agreement was in the event prevented by Styria, but in a deeper sense by the fact that the Vlachs never quite gave up their preference for being free peasants and soldiers. Periodic Vlach rebellions against abuse, generally perpetrated by military commanders, continued until 1666, when one such mutiny was suppressed with great force, after which the Vlachs' autonomy was significantly reduced.

The Vlach Code triggered a process of enclosure of the area of the Military Border and its separation from the rest of Croatia. The Croatian and Hungarian Estates tried to limit the application of the code solely to Orthodox Vlachs, so it became necessary to establish the precise domain of the code's validity. The area between the Drava and the Sava, to which it vaguely referred, embraced in reality not just Vlach colonies entitled to the given privileges, but also villages inhabited by Private Vlachs, villages in which Vlachs lived alongside non-Vlachs, villages inhabited by native Slavonian serfs whose feudal burden had been reduced because of their service on the border, and land holdings of manorial serfs who had joined the Border society having fled their lord's jurisdiction. The immigrant population, moreover, contained Catholics, who were not treated as 'true Vlachs', and whose continued allegiance to the Catholic faith was of great concern to the bishop of Zagreb.

The commission that was set up to separate the two kinds of border population had only a limited success. Even where the commission managed to establish the actual legal situation, it often proved in practice impossible to divide 'true Vlachs' from others claiming the same status, partly because of the solidarity displayed by a peasantry keen to avoid servile status, but also – and more importantly – because of the staunch resistance put up by the border commanders. It was decided in the end that Ferdinand's privileges applied to all Vlach hamlets and villages in Slavonia except those inhabited by Private Vlachs, that is, those who came under seigneurial jurisdiction. This ruling demarcated off the territory under purely military administration, in effect the territory of the Slavonian Border. Križevci and Koprivnica as royal free cities were not included in it, but since some of their battlements were, they remained permanently restricted in their spatial development, while their privileged status came under constant threat from the Border commanders. Being the seats of local captains, moreover, they acquired a strongly military character.

With the application of the Vlach Code the previous separation of the civilian from the military government associated with the garrisoning of the king's army in the Slavonian Border area acquired a territorial form. The population and territory of this part of the Croatian kingdom were henceforth divided into two distinct parts, subject to two different legal systems and two different authorities. The Slavonian Border became, in other words, not simply a militarised area, but the site of a differently constituted society, whose formative force throughout remained the link between land tenure and military service. The peasant had the right to land if and only if he was also a soldier, and the land remained his basic form of pay. He could sell the land or pass it to someone else, but would then have to leave the Border, since the land was the only source of life. Enlarging his existing landholding made no sense, since military service allowed him little time for farming or stock-breeding. Insofar as there was any division of labour, it occurred within the extended family, which remained the basic economic unit of Border society. The Military Border as initially constituted was a land devoid of towns, since there was no need for them. As a result, border society remained throughout its existence a socially undifferentiated community based on self-subsistence agriculture, in which the only form of hierarchy was that supplied by the army. Since the border arose on land from which the feudal order (and so the manor as the basic unit of economic and administrative life) had been removed, the War Council in Graz and the local commanders became responsible also for regulating the social and economic life of the peasant population living within it.

Once the War Council took charge of the defence effort, the Croatian Border also acquired a definite military organisation, the centre of which became the new fortress of Karlovac. Carniola contributed to the maintenance of the captaincies of Senj and Ogulin, while Carinthia took care of the Karlovac garrison and the area to its east. The situation here, however, was different from that prevailing in Slavonia. To begin with, by the end of the sixteenth century most of the devastated area had ended up in the Ottoman Empire. In the part which remained in Habsburg Croatia, the local lords – the Zrinski and Frankapan families and the Church in particular – did not lose control of their estates, and were able after the conclusion of the Long Turkish War in 1606 to organise resettlement. As a result, no clear-cut separation of the territories under manorial and military authority – of the kind that emerged in Slavonia – was to materialise in the Croatian Border.

The great influx of Vlachs, which began in 1600, moreover was here not sudden but gradual, while the settlers themselves were more mixed in origin than was the case in Slavonia. The main groups were supplied by Orthodox Vlachs, Catholic Vlachs and immigrants from the Venetian area. Local inhabitants also took part in repopulation of the border. The outcome was a complex amalgam of different juridical areas and types of colonist, which made it impossible for the settlers' status to be regulated with a single document analogous to the Vlach Code. Each group of settlers was forced instead to negotiate its status with the individual lord or military commander, so that some villages inhabited by local populations escaped manorial jurisdiction, while other purely Vlach villages did not. Vlachs in the Croatian Border, moreover, could rarely appeal to military commanders or the king to protect them from the resident lords, since the local magnates often also held posts of command in the border. This situation would change dramatically with the destruction of the Zrinski and Frankapan families in 1671 and the confiscation of their estates, some of which lay at the border's very centre. This permitted a territorial consolidation of the Croatian Border and its organisation on the Slavonian model.

Consolidation of the Military Border entailed sub-division of the much reduced Croatian kingdom between Civilian Croatia-Slavonia, headed by the ban, and Military Croatia-Slavonia, run by the War Council in Graz. Although the Military Border remained formally a part of the Croatian kingdom, the ties between the two parts became quite tenuous, since the military authorities in the Border, backed by the king in Vienna, worked hard to minimise the influence of all outside authorities – of the Croatian parliament as much as of the Catholic Church.

A fragmented kingdom

Of all the South Slav kingdoms and principalities that had emerged during the Middle Ages, Croatia alone survived, albeit in a truncated form. The irresistible push of the Ottoman armies during the fifteenth and sixteenth centuries had reduced it to a narrow strip of land adjacent to the German empire, whose money, soldiers and organisational skills helped it to hold out as part of the empire's own defence effort. The fragmentation of its territory reached a peak, however, at the start of the seventeenth century. Venice still held the bulk of the Dalmatian seaboard and the associated islands – though by now the republic had become more of an ally than an enemy. The Dalmatian interior and the coast between Split and Dubrovnik had been absorbed into Ottoman Bosnia. The Dubrovnik republic managed to survive – and thrive too – as a trading partner of the Ottoman Empire. There was Ottoman Slavonia, attached alternately to the *eyalets* of Bosnia and Buda. The rest of Croatia was divided into two separate areas: a civilian one governed by the Croatian parliament, and a purely military one answering solely to the king. Different communities and cultures evolved within the individual boundaries of these fragments, but never radically enough – at least in the minds of the indigenous elites – to fully escape the gravitational pull of the Croatian state tradition. A main, though not the only, factor activating this historical imagination was the view shared by the Croatian kings, bans and parliament that the Croatian remnant stood for the whole of the Triune Kingdom. However insubstantial this may have appeared in the realities of the sixteenth and seventeenth centuries, it nevertheless kept alive irredentist dreams. As long as the Ottoman foe appeared invincible, the country concentrated on defence; but as soon as the border stabilised, the urge to regain the lost lands returned. This could not be accomplished, however, without the support of the German empire.

FOUR

Borderland

The defeat at Mohács in 1526 was an expression of the deep crisis of the whole social and political order in a realm marked by weak central authority, noble infighting, peasant rebellions and territorial haemorrhage. The reign of Matthias Corvinus, which ended at the close of the fifteenth century, represented in many ways a historical watershed, after which the country increasingly fell out of step with developments in western Europe.

Between the thirteenth and the sixteenth centuries, northern Croatia (with Hungary) had undergone a structural transformation similar to that taking place in Western Europe, with the separation of secular and religious authority, and the emergence of chartered cities and Estates which, gathered in their parliaments, represented noble lands in their relationship to the king. The codification of rights, privileges and duties underpinning this social complex included also the relationship between the landowners and their dependent peasantry, since both became bound by the laws of the land. This was a period also of growing economic prosperity, shared by all social classes. During the fifteenth century, indeed, natural rent – the rent in kind owed by the peasant to the lord – became increasingly replaced by monetary payment, reflecting the peasantry's increased production for the market. The peasants became free to leave the noble estates and, with minimal restrictions, to dispose of their property. One result of this broad-based commercialisation of agriculture was the growth of urban centres, including the rise of numerous market towns, especially on the manorial estates: 70 per cent of known Slavonian urban settlements appeared in the course of the fifteenth and early sixteenth centuries.[1]

At the start of the sixteenth century, however, Croatia and Hungary entered a process known as the coming of the second serfdom, for at the end of this period the peasantry became once again tied to the land and subjected to the full juridical authority of their lords. The change was fuelled in part by the price inflation that engulfed Europe in the early sixteenth century, which in Croatia and Hungary was exacerbated by defence needs, since the army and auxiliary services were supplied from local sources. Inflation devalued money rents while simultaneously increasing the value of agricultural products. The lords consequently became interested in production from their own demesne lands and in blocking the peasants' access to the market. This led to a return of natural rent and to the restriction of the peasants' mobility and other rights. By the middle of the sixteenth century, natural rent in Slavonia formed up to three-quarters of all feudal rent. Although it proved impossible fully to bind the peasants to the land, because of the great movement of population caused by the Ottoman invasion, peasants were no longer allowed to change their social status by, for example, moving to the towns. These measures led to an urban crisis in Slavonia, with previously thriving market places becoming reduced to the status of villages and their population to that of serfs. The worsening economic and legal position of the peasantry resulted in waves of peasant rebellion, which significantly reduced the kingdom's ability to resist Ottoman invasion. The struggle continued throughout the seventeenth century, with the peasantry frequently joined by the towns and the lower nobility.[2]

Re-feudalisation and an emphasis on the *robot* rather than the size of landholding had by the end of the sixteenth century led to a fragmentation of the large estates into smaller units, and to a consequent growth in the size of the gentry class, some of which was recruited from wealthy peasants and burghers. This trend continued into the seventeenth century, when a new class of self-made landowners appeared. During the seventeenth century, which was a period of relative stability, the process of re-feudalisation entered a second stage, with the *robot* increasing at the expense of natural rent, until it came to form between one-half and three-quarters of the total obligations of the serfs.[3] However, the spread of second serfdom was not everywhere uniform. Western Croatia, with its Adriatic orientation, retained an emphasis on monetary rent. Settlers who had been brought in to repopulate areas left deserted by Ottoman warfare were exempt from many of second serfdom's worst forms of exploitation. Peasants who served in the lord's army or on the border were also freed from some of the regular obligations, though as a rule once the immediate Ottoman danger had subsided the privileges of this layer of peasantry too came under threat, producing further waves of rebellion.

The noble nation

Among the nobility the greatest power was wielded by the magnates, who in the second half of the sixteenth century formed 3 per cent of the total landowning class but held 75 per cent of all enserfed land. Below them extended a layer of well-to-do and middling nobility, owning around 17 per cent of the land, and below these again a still more numerous, petty nobility – 75 per cent of the total noble class – who between them held only 7 per cent of the land. The petty nobility, who lived either as vassals on magnate land or formed their own noble communes, generally differed from the free peasantry only in their political rights.

The king ruled together with the Estates gathered in parliament, or *sabor*, which remained a single chamber throughout its existence. The Estates were composed of prelates (bishops, abbots, heads of clerical chapters or monasteries in possession of royal fiefs); the magnates (the ban and high state officials, county heads, counts and barons); the nobility (hereditary, service and otherwise defined); and royal free cities and privileged noble districts. Only the prelates and the magnates had the right to attend the sabor in person. Each city sent two representatives, but otherwise formed a legally closed territory subject only to the king's justice. The counties also sent two deputies each. When, in the early seventeenth century, members of the privileged districts lost the right to sit in parliament, they were represented by two elected deputies for each district. The sabor had legislative and executive powers: its decisions were recorded and became laws, except in cases involving a precedent, when royal consent was required. When the sabor was not in session, political life continued at the level of county assemblies.[4] During the sixteenth and seventeenth centuries the volume of work conducted by the sabor contracted as a result of territorial losses to the Ottoman Empire, the transfer of sovereign rights to the king in the area of the Military Border, and more generally in consequence of a growing concentration of power in the crown.

The governing class was thus made up of the first two Estates and of regularly elected members of the middle and lower nobility, including the cities (which were treated as noble districts). Together they formed the political nation. The ban acted as the parliament's chief executive, and was in fact the intermediary between the king and the kingdom. He was nominated by the king and, being his representative, swore loyalty to him not to the sabor; but he had to be confirmed by the latter in order to be able to discharge his duties. When he assumed his post, the parliament delivered to him the state banner as the symbol of his military powers – he was *supremus capitaneus croaticus* – and the sceptre as symbol of his juridical authority. Although, at the height of the Ottoman threat, the sabor was forced to surrender to the king most of the ban's military prerogatives, it continued stubbornly to defend his juridical autonomy.

The functioning of the sabor was influenced also by an alteration of the relationship between Croatia and Hungary, as the two kingdoms drew closer together in reaction to the growing centralism of royal rule. In 1625 the Croatian ban was formally invited to join the upper house of the Hungarian parliament (which after the fall of Buda met in Bratislava), and a few decades later this invitation was extended also to other high Croatian lords. In 1700 the Croatian sabor, too, became formally represented at the Hungarian diet, by way of an elected delegation: of the three deputies it elected for the purpose one sat in the upper and two in the lower house. This parliamentary connection, however, did not of itself limit the Croatian sabor's independent law-making powers. The king's decisions were discussed and decided together, but demands to the king were raised and voted on separately. All matters pertaining to the two kingdoms were jointly decided by consensus. If the Hungarian side raised matters that affected also Croatia, the Croatian deputies could agree or disagree, but as a body they remained bound by the instructions of the sabor. It is a matter of dispute whether the joint sittings of the Croatian and Hungarian representatives in Bratislava amounted to the Hungarian diet being transformed on these occasions into a joint parliament (which is the view upheld by most Croatian historians), or whether (as some Hungarian historians assert) it was simply a Hungarian parliament in which Croatia – being a land of the Hungarian crown – was bound to participate, and which thus had the right to dispense laws also for Croatia. During this period, the actual constitutional relationship between the two kingdoms could best be described, in fact, as confederation: an association of two states each with its own parliament but having a common king. Problems arose when the interests of the two kingdoms clashed directly. In the skirmishes between Croatia and Hungary over the relative competences of the two parliaments, the king regularly supported Croatia: if the powers of the holy crown protected Croatia from royal absolutism, royal power protected Croatia from Hungarian domination. This may explain the fact that in Hungarian documents of the seventeenth century the term 'conjoined lands' (*partes adnexae*) used commonly to described Croatia's relationship to Hungary began to be replaced by 'subjected lands' (*pars subjecta*), prompting the sabor to insist on Croatia's equality with Hungary.

Zrinski's Croatia

In Croatia itself by far the most prominent magnate family were the Zrinski. So far as the Ottomans were concerned, indeed, Croatia in the sixteenth and seventeenth centuries was a Zrinski *vilayet*.[5] Croatia at this time was in effect divided into three spheres of authority, exercised respectively by the Zrinski, the sabor, and the border commanders. As territorial lords, as bans of Croatia and as high officials on the Military Border, the Zrinski bridged all three. Their pre-eminence derived from the fact that a substantial part of the reduced Croatia was made up of lands united through intermarriage between the Zrinski and the Frankapan families. The various branches of the latter still held extensive estates between the Kupa and the Adriatic Sea, while the Zrinski had acquired considerable land in Slavonia, including the large manor of Čakovec. Stretching thus between the Mura, the Kupa and the Adriatic Sea, the Frankapan and Zrinski families' possessions covered much of the Croatian core.

The foundation stone of the two families' strategic alliance was laid in 1544, when Ban Nicholas Zrinski (c.1508–66) married Bernardin Frankapan's granddaughter Catherine. Bernardin had left Catherine and her brother Stephen to King Ferdinand's care, but the appointed managers of their estates proceeded to abuse their positions, and Zrinski came to the aid of the siblings in their struggle to win back control over them. As part of the marriage settlement Nicholas and his brother-in-law agreed to divide the estate of Vinodol between them, leaving Zrinski in possession of some twenty-five fortified places, including Modruš and the port of Bakar: after more than two centuries, the old Šubić clan was back on the Croatian shore. Following Catherine's death, her brother surrendered to the Zrinski family the remaining part of the Frankapan possessions in this area, including the important castle of Ozalj. The Zrinski thus gained much of what remained of the Croatian seaboard, hence control of trade between the Adriatic Sea, Inner Austria and Hungary. This brought them into conflict with the king, seeking to build up his own port of Rijeka. Ferdinand's persistent efforts to divert sea trade from Zrinski's port of Bakar to Rijeka failed, however, in the face of the resistance coming from the Croatian and Hungarian parliaments. Trade war between the two ports continued under Ferdinand's successor, Maximilian, which is why Nicholas Zrinski did not submit the two families' agreement to King Maximilian for his confirmation.

The Zrinski lands were grouped around three centres: Čakovec in Međimurje, Ozalj in central Croatia and Bakar on the Adriatic Sea. Since Međimurje was included in the Hungarian county of Zala, the Zrinski became also a leading magnate family in Hungary. Hungary's possession of Međimurje was in fact disputed by Croatia, since in terms of church jurisdiction it belonged to the bishopric of Zagreb. But the frontier between the two kingdoms was at this time more notional than real, given that the magnates owned land on either side. It was less important for them, in fact, than the borders between their own lands. As large landowners in both Croatia and Hungary, the Zrinski took part in forming the policy of both kingdoms, although they preferred to attend – together with the Croatian ban (when the latter was not a Zrinski) – the upper house of the Hungarian parliament rather than the unicameral Croatian sabor.

Hungary was at this time run by an oligarchy composed of some fifteen magnate families, which collected taxes and organised the defence of the kingdom. The Zrinski, who held the honorary title of royal chamberlains, belonged to this exclusive club. Officers from Inner Austria came to command the border garrisons in Hungary as well as in Croatia, but it was magnates who filled the highest positions within the border army. The pursuit of war remained the main vocation of this frontier aristocracy, with the attendant cult of knightly virtues based on military skill and personal courage in battle.[6] As ban of Croatia, Nicholas Zrinski was paid to maintain the Croatian army; when he resigned this post, he continued to receive pay as a high-ranking official elsewhere on the border. For many petty nobles too, some locally born and others arriving from elsewhere in Europe, service in the border army supplied the initial step for ascent within the social hierarchy.

Possession of a sea port not only brought wealth and prestige to the Zrinski family, but also provided the possibility for conducting an autonomous foreign policy. It allowed them to maintain contact with Dalmatian cities, and in particular with the Dubrovnik republic, which notwithstanding its annual tribute to the Porte remained nominally part of the Croato-Hungarian realm. Bakar, indeed, had become a main port for Dubrovnik, which had been deprived of its traditional inland routes by the Ottoman conquest of Bosnia and parts of Croatia. Zrinski's Adriatic ports thus maintained a sense of national unity through trade, travel and personal contacts. The ships plying the Adriatic trade carried not only salt, timber, oil, honey, wax and skins, but also newly published books, regional news, and intelligence on the movement of Ottoman troops, supplied in particular by Dubrovnik merchants. A score of works by Dalmatian authors published in Venice and elsewhere came to be dedicated to the Zrinski family, extolling their cultural and martial achievements. Their active presence in the Adriatic led a Dubrovnik poet of the seventeenth century to declaim triumphantly:

> Italy would long ago have
> sunk into a sea of slavery
> but for the Croatian shore
> taming the Ottoman sea.[7]

The Croatian and Hungarian magnates treated the Ottoman conquests as a passing phenomenon, however, and considered the lost lands as waiting to be redeemed. The frontier's frequent shifting resulted, moreover, in a fluid understanding of sovereignty in the frontier area, as a result of which its unlucky inhabitants frequently ended up paying taxes to both states. Nicholas Zrinski, for example, was able to force the peasants of Baranja, which was under Ottoman control, to pay taxes to the royal treasury. The border, in fact, never became an impermeable physical or cultural barrier: although the Zrinski had dedicated their lives to the destruction of Ottoman power, they also adopted some of the dress and lifestyle of their foe. The correspondence between them and the neighbouring Ottoman officials, many of whom were locally born and brought up, displays at times a considerable degree of personal warmth and mutual esteem.

Though the Zrinski rarely attended the sabor, as local landowners, bans and border commanders they retained a keen interest in Croatian affairs. Habitually wary of the power of the family, which was able to evade any decision that did not suit them, the sabor nevertheless found the Zrinski useful allies, not least because of their contribution to the kingdom's defence. In reality, however, neither the Croatian nor the Hungarian parliaments could impose their will on the Zrinski or the other magnates – only the king could do so. The Ottoman proximity, and the continued existence of the semi-independent principality of Transylvania, imposed constraints even on the king's own ability to exercise his prerogatives in regard to the magnates; but the fact that they were subject to his justice, and that their kingdoms could not defend themselves without his help, made his power real enough. The border thus acted as a political factor in its own right, contributing vitally to an essentially unstable equilibrium established between the two poles of political authority: the king in Vienna backed by the War Council, on the one hand, and on the other the aristocracy in control of the parliaments in Zagreb and Bratislava, which under magnate influence frequently made and implemented laws without submitting them to royal sanction.

The axiom of the Ottoman policy adopted by the War Council was that peace should be maintained at all costs. Its report in 1576 to King and Emperor Rudolf had made this very plain: 'One should not begin or undertake an offensive war against such a superior enemy; rather, all available means should be employed to keep a lasting peace.' This strategy of permanent defence was rejected by the Croatian and Hungarian Estates, committed to regaining the lost lands. Hungarian magnates such as the Batthyány and the Nádasdy, close neighbours, friends and relations of the Zrinski, as well as the Zrinski themselves, tried at times to sabotage the building of the defensive barrier against the Ottomans, which they saw as consolidating the division and permanent loss of their lands. They resisted too the garrisoning of German soldiers on their lands, although they did eventually accept it. This defiance was practised especially by those Hungarian magnates whose estates were located at some distance from the actual frontier, and who were consequently able to retain a degree of independence by fielding their own armies. Given, however, that their own lands were more exposed to Ottoman raids, the Zrinski cooperated more readily with the king and the War Council.

Excepting the Zrinski and the Frankapan, the Croatian nobility could not afford armies of their own, since they had either lost the land that could support soldiers or held estates directly exposed to attack. This situation ultimately led to the border area being withdrawn from the jurisdiction of the Croatian parliament. What was true for both Croatia and Hungary, on the other hand, was that the cost of war was always greater than the funds collected or granted for defence. The magnates consequently engaged in various forms of war profiteering, including smuggling and the pillaging of enemy territory, thus contributing to the depopulation of the frontier area. The Zrinski themselves engaged in piracy in the Adriatic and in the smuggling of salt and other war materiel through their ports. The Habsburgs, while condemning cross-border raids when these threatened signed peace agreements, condoned them at other times because they lowered the cost of army maintenance. Much money, on the other hand, could be made from supplying the frontier garrisons. The lion's share of the profit, however, went to Austrian merchants and trading companies, which bought goods in Italy and Germany and sold them at a much higher price in the Military Border.

Nicholas Zrinski was ban of Croatia for fourteen years (1542–56) before becoming commander of the Hungarian citadel of Szigetvár, which guarded the approaches to Buda and his own Međimurje. He had three sons, but one died young leaving George and Nicholas to inherit the family estates and honours. In the will he drafted on the eve of his death, Nicholas of Sziget begged the king to recognise his sons' possession of the Frankapan estates; after his death, Maximilian in fact tried unsuccessfully to claim it for the royal fisc. George, as the elder son, took over the management of Međimurje and Čakovec, while from his seat at Ozalj, Nicholas concerned himself with Vinodol and central Croatia. After the fall of Szigetvár the whole border had suddenly shifted westwards towards Kanizsa (now Nagykanizsa), so that Zrinski's Međimurje, located on the opposite side of the Drava, became a border area.

The family's overriding commitment to the preservation of their patrimony ensured that George would choose a military career – he was the only member of the family who never became Croatian ban. Concerned primarily with the defence of Međimurje, the family's most important possession, George Zrinski preferred instead the post of supreme commander of the highly active Transdanubian border established between the Drava and Lake Balaton. He would spend seventeen years defending this part of the Hungarian border. By marrying the daughter of his father's close friend, Peter Erdödy, he gained estates also in the nearby Hungarian county of Vas, so that Zrinski lands came to be included in all the three Borders: the Croatian, the Slavonian and the Hungarian. Since the Austrian duchies and the German empire paid for the maintenance of these, conserving full control over the family's possessions within them demanded a great deal of skill and effort on the part of the two Zrinski brothers. The fortress of Karlovac, built on Zrinski's land, protected the Ozalj manor so that George was able to concentrate on defending Međimurje; but he nevertheless kept at Karlovac his own unit of hussars as a sign of the family's presence. Marital ties served as another form of war insurance. Most of the Zrinski girls married into the Hungarian aristocracy, but one of George's daughters was wedded to Baron George Lenković, captain of Senj and one of the most trusted royal officials, while a sister married Johann Thurns, another Croatian Border commander. As part of the same policy of strategic alliances, George Zrinski chose his wife from an old Styrian family.

The wealth of the Zrinski derived in large part from the location of their lands along the Croatian border with Austria and the Adriatic Sea. Croatian-Hungarian trade at this time went in two main directions: along the Danube to Germany, and along the 'Ljubljana road' to Italy. That part of the trade which passed through Croatia – to Zagreb on the one hand, and to Bakar and Rijeka, or to Modruš and Senj, on the other – had to traverse their lands. When Senj became endangered and the route through Ljubljana gained in

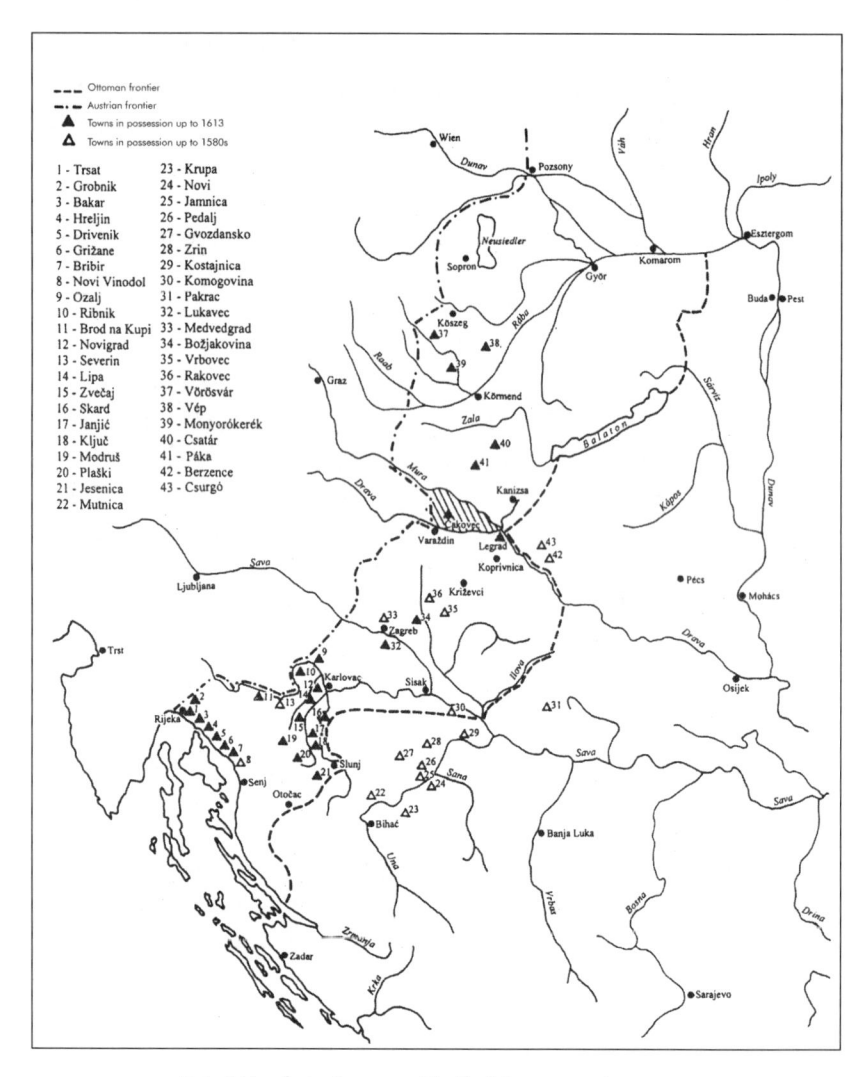

Zrinski lands in the second half of the sixteenth century

importance, the main transit post along it became Zrinski's Nedelišće in Međimurje: 50 per cent of all customs dues paid on the border between Inner Austria and Croatia-Hungary in 1565 was collected at Nedelišće.[8] Apart from their percentage of customs dues, the Zrinski derived income also from the sales tax and various tolls paid on Međimurje's roads and river crossings, which brought a handsome revenue in the second half of the sixteenth century in particular. The income from Vinodol and the estates grouped around Ozalj came largely from taxes paid by the Adriatic ports and towns, through which timber, wine, wheat and cattle were exported to

Italy and Italian luxury goods arrived in exchange. After 1600, when a good part of the Hungarian trade (especially of cattle) with Venice was diverted through Croatian territory, passing through Bakar and other smaller ports, the 'Zrinski route' became so profitable that in the early seventeenth century the family started to build a new port at Kraljevica, south of Bakar.

Nicholas and George Zrinski studied at the University of Padua, as had their father before them. They corresponded with each other in Croat, occasionally in Hungarian, but communicated with ease also in Latin, Italian and German. They could also speak Turkish. Their offices issued letters and documents in the Latin, Glagolitic, Cyrillic and Arabic scripts. Their sister Dora was married to the Hungarian magnate Balthazar Batthyány, and their home became a meeting place for leading humanists of the day.[9] The Zrinski brothers, like their father, inclined to Protestantism, as did most of their peers: 90 per cent of the Styrian and Hungarian nobility were at this time Protestant.

Despite the terms of the Augsburg Peace of 1555, which allowed him to remove all Protestants from his lands, the Austrian archduke in charge of the Military Border was forced to make significant concessions to the Styrian nobility in return for their financial support. The Habsburgs were similarly unable or unwilling at this time to impose Catholicism upon the Hungarian and Croatian nobility. The Croatian sabor sided on the religious issue with the king, but was too weak to confront the magnates. The only exception was George Drašković, ban of Croatia and bishop of Zagreb, who on his return in 1563 from the Council of Trent ensured the passage of a law through the sabor prohibiting non-Catholics from owning property or performing public service in Croatia. This law was never fully implemented: the Zrinski and other Croatian noble families who inclined to Protestantism simply ignored it, while Drašković never insisted upon its enforcement: he himself belonged to the liberal Catholic current. Bearing in mind the long-standing tradition of Glagolitic liturgy in Croatia, he favoured use of the vernacular by the church. He supported also suspension of the rule of celibacy for priests. Since, moreover, the Border area accommodated not only Catholics but also Orthodox and Protestants – practically all German soldiers and officers of the border were Protestant – religion failed to create a strong line of division in Croatia.

Working together with the Croatian parliament, however, Drašković was able to limit the spread of Protestantism in northern Croatia, a task facilitated by the ongoing conflict between the (mainly Protestant German) border commanders and the (purely Catholic) Croatian parliament. By the end of the sixteenth century Protestants had been driven out of the Military Border and in 1604, during the regime of Drašković's nephew, Ban Ivan (John) II Drašković, the Croatian parliament formally banned Protestants from Croatia. The Hungarian parliament's decision of 1606 that, where the nobility and free cities were concerned, the edict on religious toleration that it had negotiated with King Rudolf (1576–1606) should also apply in Croatia was successfully rebuffed, with the sabor warning the king that failure to respect its will would lead Croatia to reconsider whether it should continue to be 'tied to the holy crown [of Hungary] or separate from it'.[10] In the seventeenth century the Zrinski family would revert to Catholicism, together with many other Croatian and Hungarian nobles.

The court of the Zrinski at Čakovec attracted a host of Croatian writers, some Protestant, some not, whose books and translations into the Croat language were printed on the family's presses. The reputation of the Zrinski as anti-Ottoman warriors and their active presence on the Adriatic made them a source of inspiration also for the Dalmatians. This was true especially for writers from Dubrovnik, whose works were in great demand among the Croatian nobility. Thus the sixteenth-century Dubrovnik poet Dominko Zlatarić dedicated his *Electra*, published in Venice in 1597, to George Zrinski, noting that 'on the very news of your arrival the enemy forces scatter, and the frightened guards of their castles and forts prefer to surrender rather than to confront you'.[11] The book, the author wrote, must please him since it was written in his Croat language. Zrinski wrote back apologising for not replying sooner, but the book had reached him in 1600, the year in which Kanizsa finally fell into Ottoman hands; he could not immediately read it, for 'when arms speak, the muses fall silent'. He died soon afterwards, in 1603. His son, also called George, fought on the Habsburg side as ban of Croatia and commander of its army during the Thirty Years War.

The role played by the Zrinski family in Hungary's defence and politics, and their Hungarian possessions and marriage ties with leading Hungarian families, make them an important part of Hungarian history. One must add to this also their penchant for poetry. George's son Nicholas thus wrote an epic poem in Hungarian – on the siege of Sziget and his grandfather's heroic death – that remains greatly appreciated in Hungary.[12] The family played a far more important role in Croatian history, however, not only because of their Croat origins (which was important in the eyes of their Croatian contemporaries), their long service as bans of Croatia, and their role as regional patrons of arts and science, but also because by holding onto their lands they kept Croatia together.

Rebellion and defeat

George Zrinski died in 1626, leaving two under-age sons born within a year of each other: Nicholas and Peter. The importance of the Zrinski–Frankapan inheritance was such that the two boys became wards of King Ferdinand II (1618–37). They were entrusted to a carefully selected group of tutors, made up of magnates and high crown officials, consisting of three Croatians, two Hungarians and one German. The Croatian and Hungarian Estates likewise retained a keen interest in the boys' progress. When the king tried to resolve the trade dispute between the ports of Bakar and Rijeka by offering the two brothers considerable estates in Hungary in exchange for Vinodol, this was vetoed by the Estates. For what was at stake was Croatia-Hungary's access to the coast. In 1630 the Styrian treasury advised the king to remove the Zrinski from the coast 'for the sake of the common good', by if necessary replacing the Zrinski tutors 'who are not of the German nationality' with a single person enjoying his confidence.[13] Ferdinand was in fact warned by several crown commissions sent to investigate the trade conflict that the coast should not be left in the hands of a traditionally rebellious nobility. That their warnings were not wholly groundless was to be proved several decades later, when Peter Zrinski invited King Louis XIV to land his army at Bakar and assume the role of Croatia's protector.

Like generations of Zrinski before them, Nicholas and Peter spent lives dominated by war. Both fought in the Thirty Years War. Nicholas was an admirer of Tasso and Machiavelli, while Peter was interested in military innovations, especially in artillery. As was the custom in the family, Nicholas, as the elder son, took over Međimurje; he became head of the county of Zala and joined the royal court. Peter managed Vinodol and Ozalj. Nicholas married a Drašković and, after her death, a German baroness. Peter married a Frankapan, the sister of his friend Vuk Krsto, captain of Karlovac. In 1647 Nicholas was appointed ban of Croatia, a post which he held until his death in 1664. Peter became captain of Senj, and, after Nicholas's death, ban (1665–70). As captain of Senj, Peter joined the Venetian side during the Candian War against the Ottomans. Nicholas wrote poetry in Latin and in Hungarian, his brother Peter in Croat. Peter also translated some of his brother's Hungarian poetry into Croat, which he dedicated to Croatian knights.

Ban Nicholas encouraged the Croatian parliament's demand in 1655 that, in a document issued that year by the Hungarian state chancellery, Croatia be cited by its proper name and not as 'subjected lands'. The document in question involved recognition by the Estates of the right

Vuk Krsto Frankapan, commander of the Croatian
Military Border, seventeenth century

of Leopold, son of Ferdinand III, to succeed his father as king of Croatia and Hungary. The Croatian parliament instructed its representatives to accept Leopold as king, and also to support Nicholas's candidature for the post of Hungarian palatine – or, failing that, the candidature of a Catholic recommended by the ban.[14] Leopold I (1657–1705) was duly crowned King of Hungary and Croatia, after promising to respect the established rights of the two kingdoms. The Hungarian magnate Ferenc Wesselényi was elected palatine instead of Nicholas Zrinski, the candidate of 'the national party'. It was during Leopold's reign that the long-simmering dissatisfaction of the Croato-Hungarian nobility with the Habsburg defensive stance came to the boil. Ever since the end of the Thirty Years War in 1648, the magnates had felt that peace in the West should be used to make war in the East. In his pamphlet *Remedy against the Turkish Opium,* published in 1663, Nicholas Zrinski made the case for a professional army that would expel the Ottomans from Croatia and Hungary.[15] The answer came that same year, when a large Ottoman force gathered at Osijek under the leadership of Grand Vizier

Relief of King Krešimir IV, 11th century, baptistry of Split cathedral.

Map of Croatia by Al Idrisi, 12th century.

Zadar as shown in *Pilgerreise von Konstanz nach Jerusalem* by Konrad von Grünemberg, 1486.

The castle of Klis. Established by the Delmatae and fortified by the Romans, it became a seat of Croatian kings.

The walled city of Dubrovnik.

Diocletian core of Split, 4th century.

St James's cathedral in Šibenik, 15th century.

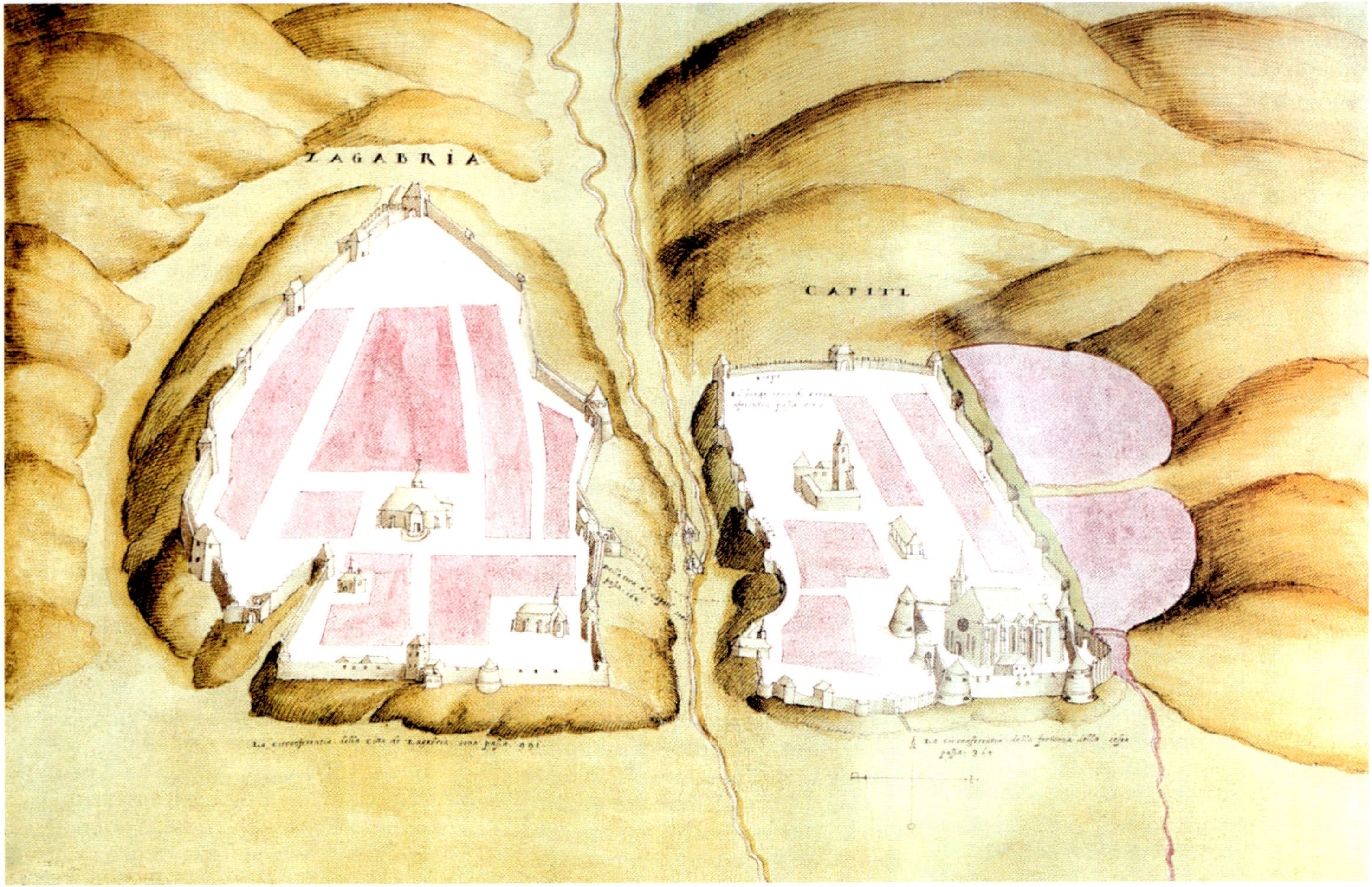

The oldest known map of Zagreb, 16th century.

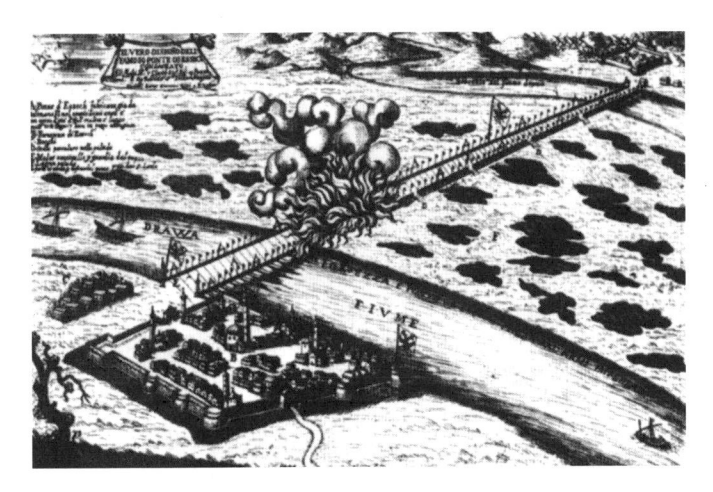

The burning of the Süleyman Bridge at Osijek, 1664

Ahmed-pasha Köprülü. Its immediate target was the recently built fortress of Novi Zrin, the main defence post against Ottoman Kanizsa. The Kanizsa *beglerbeg* demanded of Zrinski to pull the fortress down, and when this was refused its destruction was added to the list of Istanbul's demands for the continuation of peace. As negotiations broke down, Ahmed-Pasha with his army crossed the Drava by way of the Süleyman bridge and proceeded to Buda. After another round of negotiations had failed, the Ottomans laid siege to Nove Zamky, which soon fell. On his journey back to Osijek, the grand vizier ordered the pillage of the estates belonging to Zrinski and other magnates. Nicholas then proposed a lightning winter raid across southern Hungary, with the aim of destroying the Süleyman bridge, that crucial supply and communication line to Ottoman Hungary. The daring raid proved successful, making Zrinski the toast of Europe.

The bridge was quickly rebuilt, however, and the war continued. In the following spring Zrinski besieged but failed to take Kanizsa. Ahmed-Pasha, however, managed to occupy and destroy Novi Zrin, which the Austrian army commander Raimondo Monteccucoli refused to defend.[16] Zrinski's complaints to the king and the War Council fell on deaf ears. After removing this obstacle to 'the rest of the West', the Ottoman army marched on to the line formed by the Zala and Raba rivers, where they were routed by the imperial army led by Monteccucoli. The Bosnian *beglerbeg* was among those who perished. Instead of pursuing its advantage, however, Vienna (then in conflict with France) sued for peace on the basis of the status quo, and in August 1664 a new twenty-year peace was signed at Vasvár to the consternation of the Estates of both kingdoms. One of its conditions was that Novi Zrin would not be rebuilt. Pamphlets appeared attacking the court in Vienna. Zrinski's relative and Hungarian chief justice Francis Nádasdy claimed in a strongly worded anti-German pamphlet that Croatia was being attacked on all sides: with German generals entrenched in Varaždin and Karlovac and German officers in command of the Slavonian and the Croatian Borders, one part of the country was being snatched by Styria and the other by Carniola, while those parts of Dalmatia not taken by the Turks were left to the Italians as if they belonged to them.[17]

The dissatisfied nobility was led by the Croatian ban Nicholas Zrinski, the Hungarian palatine Francis Wesselényi and the Hungarian primate George Lippay. Francis Rákóczi, a wealthy descendant of the Transylvanian princely family and Peter Zrinski's son-in-law, would also join the plotters. In December 1664, however, Nicholas suddenly died, gored by a wild boar during a hunt. There were rumours that he had been murdered, and even that he had chosen to die. Solemn masses were held for him in Vienna, Munich, Paris, Madrid and Rome. The leadership of what in reality was a highly chaotic and amateurish intrigue passed in the end to Peter Zrinski, Francis Nádasdy and the Styrian count Hans Tattenbach. Francis Christopher Frankapan, Peter's brother-in-law, was also brought in, mainly as a translator of correspondence. The plotters relied most of all on the Habsburg's determined enemy, Louis XIV of France, even envisaging a French prince as King of Croatia-Hungary.[18] They hoped to make a separate peace with the Ottoman Empire, permitting them to use the border army in an eventual showdown with the king. At one point they counted also on Polish support. But nothing worked out for them. The Porte had no desire to start a new war; Louis XIV made peace with Leopold I in 1667 over the issue of the Spanish succession; and the Candian War between Venice and the Ottoman Empire, fought over Crete but mainly on Dalmatian soil, ended in 1669. The court in Vienna was now ready to move against the conspirators.

In April 1670 the Croatian population was informed that Peter Zrinski was a traitor; he was accused, among other things, of wishing to become king of Croatia. He and his brother-in-law were arrested, stripped of their titles and had their lands confiscated. In the Zrinski case the seizure applied to only half of Međimurje, since the other half belonged to the late Nicholas's son, Adam, whose inheritance was spared because his father had died before the conspiracy was revealed. The imperial army seized Čakovec and the border army Ozalj and Bakar. Although they met no resistance, all the Zrinski and Frankapan estates, including the property of their tenants, were submitted to systematic pillage.[19] Against Leopold's own personal preference, Zrinski

Execution of Petar Zrinski, 1671

and Frankapan were condemned to death.[20] Peter left behind his only son, John. Francis Christopher, who had married into the Roman Barberini family, left no heir. The two Croats were executed in Wiener Neustadt on 30 April 1671. Nádasdy was executed on the same day, Tattenbach some months later. Around 200 others were also condemned for taking part in the conspiracy. Rákóczi escaped by paying a huge ransom and by informing against his friends. The Croats were buried in a small local church and their grave marked with the following inscription: 'Here lie Peter Zrinski, Ban of Croatia, and Marquis Frankapan, the last of his family, who like blind men leading each other both fell into this pit. Learn, you mortals, from our example to keep faith with God and King. Anno Domini 1671, 30 April, 9 o'clock. The price of vanity is death.' A stone tablet with a similar inscription was placed at the site of their execution. In 1802, when the church was turned into a granary, their bones were removed to the local parish church. In 1919 the bones of the Croat 'martyrs' were brought to Croatia and buried in Zagreb cathedral.

The rest of the Zrinski family was intentionally scattered. Peter's wife, Catherine, a noted poetess, died in a convent in Graz in 1703, her youngest daughter in a convent in Klagenfurt, and her middle daughter in a convent in Zagreb. The eldest daughter, Helen, after the death of her first husband, Francis Rákóczi, married the Hungarian magnate Thököly and joined him in organising a major rebellion against the Habsburgs whose initial success would prompt the Porte in 1683 to undertake yet another siege of Vienna.

She died in exile in Nicomedia and was buried in Istanbul. Peter's son John fought against the Hungarian rebels, but, charged with seditious intentions, died in a Graz prison in the same year as his mother. Frankapan's wife, Julia, died in Rome. Nicholas's son, Adam, the last of the line, was killed in 1691 at the battle of Slankamen, where the Ottoman army suffered a historic defeat. His death from a bullet in the back has led to the belief that he fell victim to Habsburg revenge. Whatever the truth, his demise permitted the crown to appropriate the rest of the Zrinski possessions. Some of the Zrinski and Frankapan lands were included into the Croatian Border, but most of them went to the state treasury, after which parts were sold off to private individuals.

The destruction of the Zrinski and Frankapan families marks the end of the chivalric period of Croatian history. The kingdom never quite recovered from the sudden and violent disappearance of two families which for half a millennium had dominated its politics. The loss was acutely felt in Dalmatia in particular, where Peter's engagement in the Candian War had stimulated great hope for a final liberation from Ottoman rule. In 1651 Ivan Lučić (Ioannes Lucius), a Trogir patrician, started to write a history of his homeland, with the aim of establishing the political individuality of Dalmatia, which he saw as part of the same kingdom with Croatia. He met Peter Zrinski in Venice a few years later and continued to correspond with him. The six-volume *History of the Kingdom of Dalmatia and Croatia* was published in Amsterdam in 1666, to be replaced two years later by a new and corrected edition dedicated to Peter Zrinski as ban of Croatia, Dalmatia and Slavonia.[21] The edition included also the first accurate map of 'Contemporary Illyricum', consisting in this case of Croatia and Bosnia-Herzegovina. The map was subsequently included in the publisher Blaeu's *Atlas Maior* under the title *Illyricum sive Slavonia*. Whereas previous maps of the area had been decorated with the emblems of Austria, Turkey and Venice, this one carried only the state symbols of Croatia and Bosnia: in the Dalmatian eyes the Croatian ban was regent of the Illyrian realms a symbol of their unity and autonomy. Lučić finalised his historical work in Rome. Discouraged by Zrinski's execution, he never returned home: he died in Rome a few years later and was buried in the church of St Jerome the Illyrian.

The Reconquista

In May 1682 Leopold sent his envoy to Istanbul with the aim of extending the Peace of Vasvár, but the Austrian overtures were rejected. The following spring Grand Vizier Kara Mustafa arrived in Osijek, accompanied by the

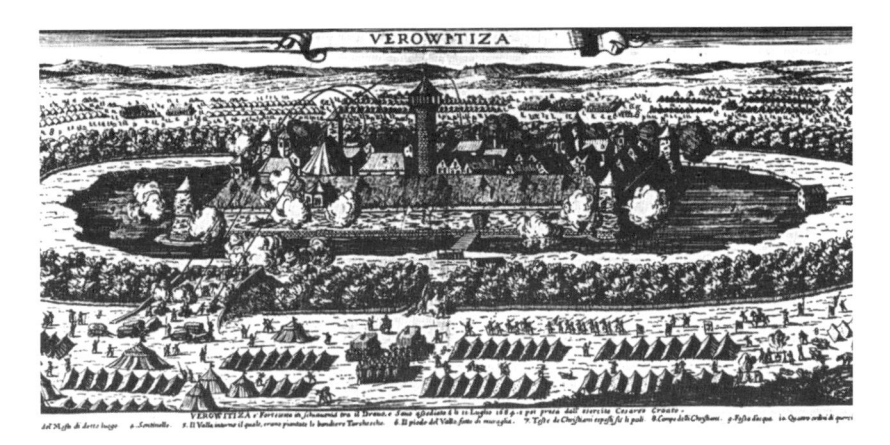

The battle of Virovitica, 1684

heads of all of the Ottoman provinces, whence he proceeded to Vienna. The siege of Vienna, in which thousands of rebel Hungarian soldiers took part on the Ottoman side, began in June 1683, to be broken in the following September by a combined army from Saxony, Bavaria and Poland led by the Polish king Jan Sobieski. Although Vienna sued for peace, the opinion of the War Council prevailed: that war should be continued until the Ottoman Empire was expelled from Hungary and Croatia. The campaign was to be fought on two fronts, in Hungary and in Slavonia. In Slavonia the aim was to take Osijek, in order to cut off Ottoman supplies from Bosnia and Serbia. The bulk of the army was to attack the Ottoman strongholds in Hungary itself.[22]

In July 1684 Virovitica fell to the imperial and royal army after a stubborn defence. Slavonia soon descended into anarchy as the local Christian population joined the war on the Habsburg side. Muslim houses were burned down and thousands of civilians killed. The advance continued in 1685, when the Croatian ban entered the *sandžak* of Cernik and, aided by local insurgents, seized and destroyed a number of its settlements. An Ottoman counter-attack from across the Una was repulsed. Osijek could not be taken, however, while the Ottomans held key positions across the Drava, so the Slavonian army withdrew to Virovitica to await developments further north. In the Croatian south the *sandžaks* of Klis and Krka-Lika also started to dissolve. The Ottoman forces retreated to Obrovac and Knin; but armed local irregulars, aided by the border army, soon forced them out of Obrovac. At the end of 1683 the commander of the Croatian Border attacked Bihać, and after burning its environs took Drniš in northern Dalmatia, thus freeing the hinterland of Zadar and Šibenik from the Ottoman presence. Venetian forces failed to take Sinj, but an Ottoman counter-attack in the Split area was repulsed by local militias. In 1685 a combined operation of Venetian and Habsburg troops devastated Krbava and Lika, but the Ottoman garrisons there did not yield.

Both sides prepared for renewal of the war in the spring of 1686. The Austrian strategists decided to go for Buda, the siege of which began in June of that year. The Ottoman side counter-attacked in Slavonia, in order to relieve the pressure on the garrison in Buda; but their units were vanquished as they moved towards Virovitica, after which the surrounding area was subjected to plunder and general terror. Buda fell on 2 September 1686: after a break of a century and a half, the Hungarian capital was once again in the hands of Hungarian kings – and was heavily looted by the liberators. The Slavonian army, commanded by Ludwig of Baden, took Pécs and Siklós in southern Hungary before moving on to destroy the great Süleyman bridge at Osijek. In the south, Venice, aided by local volunteers, finally managed to seize Sinj.

The fall of Buda shocked the Porte, which decided to raise a fresh army to recover the lost territories. War resumed in the spring of 1687, when some 40,000 soldiers under German command gathered at Pécs, while an army of approximately equal strength assembled at Belgrade and Osijek under the leadership of Grand Vizier Süleyman-pasha. Victory went to the Christian side. King Leopold now issued a proclamation inviting the Christian population to rebel against the sultan, promising his protection and respect of their rights. The Muslim population of Slavonia began to leave en masse, burning their houses as they withdrew across the Sava into Bosnia. The bulk of the imperial army next moved in the direction of Transylvania, while a force of 10,000 soldiers continued the operations in Slavonia. The approach of the Austrian troops brought panic to Osijek, which surrendered and thus survived largely intact. After the fall of Osijek, the last of the Muslim population left Đakovo, Vukovar, Ilok and other places in eastern Slavonia. The collapse of the Ottoman government in Slavonia allowed the occupation of the land to proceed with relative ease.

At Osijek the imperial army divided into two, one part remaining to pursue the war in eastern Slavonia and Srijem, while the other circled back towards Orahovica and Požega, both of which were quickly taken. Their Muslim population fled towards the Sava, many falling victim to Christian violence on the way. At the Sava they were met and helped across by Bosnian forces. Ilok, the seat of the *sandžak* of Srijem, fell to the imperial army in the summer of 1688. Here the army again divided into two parts. The smaller, under Ludwig of Baden, was left to continue the war in Slavonia, while the rest proceeded towards Belgrade, which fell on 6 September. Brod and Gradiška on the Sava were taken next. Baden moved to Sisak, met there with the Croatian ban Erdödy and proceeded to Kostajnica, which soon surrendered. The imperial army also took Jasenovac. On the other side of the Una, the Bosnian *beglerbeg* Hussein Topal-pasha assembled an army with the aim of preventing the Habsburg forces from crossing the river. Baden moved into Bosnia, however, seizing Brčko and all the towns on the other side of the Sava as well as Zvornik on the Drina.

In the Adriatic zone the Venetian units, aided by local insurgents, continued with their attacks. Knin fell a few days after Belgrade, raising the possibility of Venice also taking Lika and Krbava, which would have posed a grave threat to the Habsburg port of Senj. Vienna could not allow this to happen, so in the spring of 1689 the Croatian Border army moved into Lika, proceeded into Krbava and forced the surrender of the Ottoman garrison at Udbina. Most of the local Muslim population fled to Bosnia.

In the meantime Baden took his army into Serbia, where he defeated the Ottoman forces at Niš and went on to take Vidin. Another wing of the imperial army moved further south to Macedonia, Kosovo and Albania. The Ottoman state had by now, however, acquired a more vigorous grand vizier, whose Tatar units forced the imperial army to retreat. Baden advised King Leopold to withdraw the army to the other side of the Danube and the Sava, fortify Belgrade, take the Banat of Temesvár, and leave the defence of the Sava to the Croatians. But the king was persuaded that the local Christian population would rebel, and that with their aid he would be able to expel the Turks from Europe. The Ottoman army's advance, however, proved irresistible and Baden had to withdraw across the Danube. As the tide of war turned, Ottoman raids across the Sava multiplied. The fall of Belgrade to the Ottomans in September 1690 was the signal for an all-out Bosnian attack across the Sava. Within a month practically all central Slavonia found itself once again within the Ottoman Empire.

War returned with the spring. The Ottoman army gathered again at Belgrade and the Habsburg at Osijek. The decisive battle took place at Slankamen in Srijem, in August 1691, and it is here that the imperial army won decisively. The grand vizier perished in the battle together with a large number of his top commanders. But the Austrian side suffered numerous casualties too: Baden wrote to Emperor Leopold that it was the bloodiest battle of the century. The defeat at Slankamen induced the Ottoman army in Slavonia to retreat to Brod, Gradiška and Pakrac. Požega and Pakrac, however, soon fell to the army of the Military Border, while the imperial army regained Brod and Gradiška. The war for Slavonia was over.

The land was by now completely devastated and had lost over half its population. Hardly anything was left that recalled the previous Ottoman order. The same was true for Lika and Krbava. Recovery was slow, as the badly supplied imperial army proceeded to live off the land. However, beginning with the spring of 1692, people began slowly to return to renew their villages and homesteads. Both Catholic and Orthodox groups left Bosnia and moved across the Sava into Slavonia and Srijem, where they settled in existing villages or built themselves new ones. Settlers came also from southern Hungary, Serbia and the Croatian Border area. As part of the same wave of immigration, people from the areas of Senj and Vinodol moved into Lika and Krbava, as did a large number of Vlachs from Bosnia. Bosnian settlers appeared also in the valleys of the Una and the Kupa.

In the summer of 1693 the imperial army tried and failed to take Belgrade, with the result that the year 1694 passed in peace. In 1695 Sultan Ahmed II died and was succeeded by Mustafa II. Two years later the new sultan's army was literally annihilated at Zenta by imperial forces commanded by Eugene of Savoy. The twenty-five-year Peace of Karlovci was signed on 26 January 1699 on the basis of the new status quo. Peace with Venice was agreed separately on 7 February 1699. The Ottoman Empire had lost Hungary (though not yet the Banat of Temesvár) and Transylvania, together with almost all it had taken of Croatia (though not the important area between the Una and the Vrbas). Croatia's border with Bosnia-Herzegovina, fixed by these treaties, has with only minor alterations remained in place until the present day.

The Ottoman wars were not quite over, however. When in 1714 the Porte attacked Venetian territory in the Peloponnese, Vienna decided to join the war on the side of Venice. The imperial army took the Banat of Temesvár, while Venice gained the part of Herzegovina in the hinterland of Dubrovnik. In 1717 German imperial troops seized Belgrade, while Venice took Imotski in the Dalmatian interior. The war ended with the signing of the Peace of Požarevac in June 1718. The Habsburg Monarchy gained thereby a 6–10 kilometre-wide band of land south of the Sava, between the Una and Bijeljina. Venice, however, lost its new gains in Herzegovina. The Ottoman Empire (hence its heir Bosnia-Herzegovina) acquired an outlet to the Adriatic Sea at Sutorina in the Boka Kotorska, and another between Neum and Klek south of the Neretva. These two strips of land were intended to protect the Dubrovnik republic from Venice.

In 1737 Austria joined Russia in another war against the Ottomans. Advancing along the Morava its army took Niš, while the border army tried and failed to take Banja Luka.[23] The imperial army was soon forced to retreat, though, and by the end of the year the Ottoman Empire had regained all the recently lost territories. With the Peace of Belgrade of 1739 the Habsburg Monarchy lost everything it had gained at Požarevac. The last Austro-Turkish war was initiated in 1788 by Joseph II, who hoped to seize Serbia and Bosnia and, with Russian help, push the Ottomans out of Europe. The war ended in 1791 with the Peace of Svištovo, which confirmed the borders established by the Peace of Belgrade. Austria (that is, Croatia) returned to the Ottoman Empire (that is, Bosnia) the towns of Gradiška, Dubica and Novi, gaining in their place Dvor on the Una, Cetin and a few more places in the vicinity. This territory was included in the Military Border. The wars against the Ottoman Empire were now finally over. But Croatia was left to fight another protracted war, albeit a purely diplomatic one, against the king in Vienna over the status and future of the Military Border, which rather than being abolished after the disappearance of the Ottoman threat was not only retained but also enlarged and consolidated in consequence of Austria's continued interest in the Balkans.

A limited reintegration

The court in Vienna had no clear idea at first regarding the future disposition and government in the newly liberated lands. But its initial approach was based on the assumption that Leopold was their sovereign master, not bound by the rights of their pre-Ottoman owners. Leopold, however, had given a written promise to the parliament at Bratislava in 1687 that these lands would be returned to Croatia and Hungary, in exchange for two concessions: the Estates' surrender of the right of insurrection, and their acceptance of the automatic law of succession for male members of the Habsburg family. Although the Habsburgs ruled in Croatia and Hungary as hereditary monarchs, up to 1687 the order of dynastic succession was not defined. The dynasty had the right of inheritance, but the Estates and Orders of Croatia and Hungary had the right to choose their king from among the members of the ruling house. This is why until 1687 the act of crowning was important. On his coronation the king had not only to swear to respect the rights of the kingdoms of Hungary and Croatia, but also to affirm the nobility's right to resist by force of arms illegal royal measures – the *ius resistendi*, granted by Andrew II Árpád in the Golden Bull of 1222. Since *ius resistendi* applied not only to the totality of the Estates but also to their individual members, it provided a legal pretext for the Croatian and Hungarian magnates' revolt in the wake of the Peace of Vasvár. In 1687, however, with the victorious imperial army in charge of large parts of Croatia and Hungary, this right was surrendered by the Estates together with the acceptance of automatic Habsburg succession in the male line.

With the argument that the land had first to be pacified, however, the government of the newly acquired territory was entrusted to the state treasury, which established a Slavonian branch of its commission in Osijek. At this time the possibility of a renewal of war led Vienna to conclude that the probable frontier with the Ottoman Empire would be on the Sava, and to accept the War Council's proposal that villages and settlements along this river should be included in a new Military Border to be established along its length. Headed by General Antonio Caraffa, the commission's task was to organise Slavonia's administration and to demarcate areas of civilian and military authority. The Croatian parliament followed the commission's work closely, even despatching its representatives to Osijek to discuss re-establishment of the previous county system, and to instal county heads of its own choice in Požega and Virovitica. Caraffa, however, firmly rejected this initiative, on the grounds that the time was not ripe to establish a county system, since this would additionally burden the impoverished population

In the spring of 1702 the area of the new Slavonian Military Border was measured up, and its future soldiers drafted into the army. The border absorbed the land along the Sava to the width of one German mile, amounting in total to some 2,500 square kilometres. The rest of Slavonia, an area of around 10,000 square kilometres, remained under the control of the treasury, which now established offices also in the border area. In matters pertaining to the use of land, the peasant remained subject to its judicial authority; but as a soldier he came under the army's control. It was expected at first that some of the settlers would serve on the new frontier with the Ottoman Empire in return for being exempt from taxation; but the fact that the soldier and his immediate family were not taxed, while the rest of their extended family was taxed, created practical problems for the treasury's tax collectors. This was especially true for mixed villages, where the soldiers came under the authority of the War Council and the civilians under that of the state treasury. Once again a solution was sought in separating the areas of civilian and military jurisdiction, in other words, dividing the population in line with their rights and duties. This resulted in the division of Slavonia too into two parts, one under military and the other under civilian control.

The commission in the meantime proceeded to determine the situation on the ground, drawing up a list of former landowners, and deciding the size of the annual tax on land. Property whose previous owners could not be found was to be sold to the highest bidder. Some estates were returned to the church, some rented to creditors of the crown, and some sold outright. There was no legal basis, however, for relating the level of tax to the size and type of land, nor was the status of the peasantry clear. In relation to the latter the treasury behaved in fact like a feudal lord, to whom the serfs paid a tax on the land, a tax for maintenance of the border, and a tax for commutation of the *robot*. The peasants also paid a tithe in kind to the church. The Slavonian peasantry, on the other hand, were not bound to the land. This temporary arrangement made no provision, however, for those peasants who ended up on privately owned land. In the absence of a legal code governing their status, the peasantry as a whole suffered considerable deprivation at the hands of the treasury officials, the new landlords and the military commanders, leading to a series of rebellions and, in 1737, to the first Slavonian land law. The law was never implemented, though, and it was left to Maria Theresa (1740–80) to impose a new land law and to complete the administrative organisation of Slavonia.

Since Maria Theresa's accession to the throne practically coincided with Prussia's invasion of Austrian Silesia, it was possible to make a deal according to which the Estates voted a military levy of 40,000 soldiers in return for her recognition of the kingdoms' privileges and autonomy, including restitution of the regained territories. Maria Theresa's promise to return to Croato-Hungarian jurisdiction the areas that would not be included in the new Military Border accelerated the efforts to separate the military from the civilian territory. Once this was completed, the civilian area was organised as three counties: Srijem, with Vukovar as its capital; Požega, with its centre at Požega; and Virovitica, governed from Osijek. The three Slavonian counties were placed under the jurisdiction of the Croatian ban, and sent their representatives to the parliament in Zagreb; but in tax matters they received orders from the Hungarian crown council. This dualism produced a constitutional crisis in 1751, when the Hungarian parliament – despite the protests of the Croatian representatives – invited the Slavonian counties to elect deputies to the Hungarian parliament

South of the Sava the situation developed differently. The treasury placed Lika and Krbava under its control, and in 1692 sold them together with the port of Karlobag to a Styrian count. This sale was rescinded, however, after the War Council informed Leopold that it was dangerous to surrender this strategically important territory bordering Venice and the Ottoman Empire to a private person; that turning the population into serfs would leave the area without soldiers; and that the population was in any case bound to resist, which could result in the return of the Ottomans. Their arguments prevailed. Various attempts to divide the territory between military and civilian government failed, so Lika and Krbava were incorporated into the Croatian or Karlovac Border as a separate district of Lika. The district was repopulated relatively rapidly by Vlachs, coming mainly from western Bosnia; according to the military census of 1712, 74 per cent of the new population was made up of Vlachs.[24] The immigration was largely spontaneous, giving rise to a pattern of scattered villages of irregular construction. The immigrants paid no tax on the land, which they insisted they had won by the sword. The absence of local lords, however, resulted in greater freedom for the border captains, some of whom became *de facto* feudal lords: at one point as much as one-third of the Karlovac Border population was reduced effectively to servile status.

The area between the Kupa and the Una, meanwhile, had been liberated by the ban's army and, after some dispute with the Habsburg generals, was for the most part added to the Ban's Border. The battle over jurisdiction in this area focused in particular on Kostajnica on the Una, an important centre for trade with Bosnia. Vienna's position was that because the territory between the Kupa and the Una was inhabited by Vlachs, it belonged *ipso facto* to the Karlovac Border. In the end a compromise was reached, whereby the whole area was incorporated into the Ban's Border, and its Vlachs subordinated in military matters to the ban and in civilian matters to the kingdom. The Croatian parliament's jurisdiction in this part of the Military Border initially prevented the emergence of a separate Vlach society, which here too was made up mostly of Orthodox Christians: according to the military census conducted in the middle of the eighteenth century, of the 55–57,000 males registered in the Ban's Border four-fifths were of the Orthodox faith. The parliament, however, was obliged to support the Ban's Border from its own resources, which came to consume two-thirds of its total military expenditure. One consequence of this was that the fortress of Petrinja ended up in the Varaždin Border, since the Estates could not pay for its upkeep. Some of the land was sold to individuals such as deputy-ban Stephen Jelačić, and to the Erdödy and Drašković families, while some was restored to the original owners, for example the Keglević family and the Catholic Church. The Ban's Border did not escape, however, from the overall regulation imposed by the War Council.

After the Peace of Karlovci the Varaždin Border ceased to be a frontier

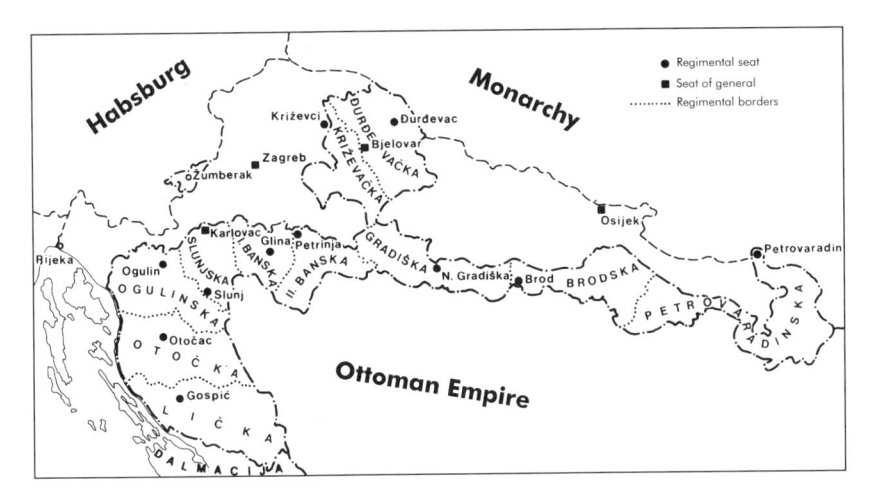

The Military Border, eighteenth century

area. Despite Leopold's promise that it would be dissolved, it survived intact, due to a new outbreak of rebellion in Hungary for whose suppression it supplied some 3,000 soldiers. Led by Francis II Rákóczi, the grandson of Peter Zrinski, and aiming to achieve independence for Hungary, it ended in 1711 with the compromise peace of Szatmár. The Varaždin Border's main purpose henceforth would be to safeguard Habsburg interests in Hungary and Croatia. Unpaid duty on this 'border' was reduced to a minimum, but the Grenzer (soldier of the border) became obliged for the first time to fight in Habsburg wars abroad.

The reorganisation of the Military Border

The problem facing Vienna was that the extension of the Military Border to the east – along the rivers Sava, Danube and Tisza – greatly increased the number of Grenzer (Krajišnici in Croat) at a time when the Ottoman threat had radically declined. This fact, and the need to justify the retention of the Varaždin Border, led the War Council in Vienna to review the whole purpose of the border army. The decision was soon reached to integrate it into the regular army, with the difference that in its case land would remain the basic form of the soldier's pay. Since this amalgamation demanded that the Grenzer units be recast to fit the regular formation, the whole of the border system had to be refashioned. The first step in the reform was to exclude the Estates of Inner Austria from having any say in the organisation and management of the Military Border. In 1743 the War Council office in Graz was abolished, after which the central state assumed full financial responsibility for the Military Border as a whole.

The other important step was to rationalise the border's internal structure. In 1732 the boundaries of the captaincies in the Varaždin Border were redrawn so as to equalise the number of basic units in each, and the units themselves were organised as companies. The War of the Polish Succession (1733–5) and the renewed campaign against the Ottoman Empire (1737–9) increased the need for soldiers, however, and it was decided that the Varaždin Border should supply more men, enough to make up two regiments of 4,000 soldiers each. Its area was consequently divided into two approximately equal parts: the area of the Križevci regiment and the area of the Đurđevac regiment. Five mounted or hussar companies were raised as well. As a result of this reorganisation the Varaždin Border was able to supply 8,500 unpaid soldiers. For this number to be reached, however, each family rather than each landholding became obliged to place one unpaid soldier at the disposal of the War Council. A new Border Code *(Statuta Confinorum Varasdiensium)* was consequently passed that year, replacing the old *Statuta Valachorum*. While formally confirming the Grenzers' earlier privileges, it in fact restricted their right to dispose of the land.

The reorganisation of the Karlovac Border followed the same pattern. Its existing captaincies and basic units were dissolved and the previously enserfed villages within it set free. Three new regiments, or regimental areas, appeared, with headquarters at Slunj, Ogulin and Otočac. The Karlovac Border as a whole, including its hussar companies, supplied 18,000 unpaid soldiers. A few years later the Ban's Border too was subjected to the same reorganisation. The existing forms of Vlach self-government within it were abolished, and two regiments (regimental areas) – the Ban's 1st and the Ban's 2nd – were created. In the case of the Slavonian Border, following the establishment of the county structure in the civilian part of Slavonia, it was similarly divided into three regimental areas: Petrovaradin (Mitrovica); Gradiška (Gradiška); and Brod (Vinkovci).

These reforms fundamentally changed the nature of the Military Border. It continued to guard the frontier with the Ottoman Empire, but its main function now was to provide ever-ready regiments at the disposal of the king and emperor. In 1763, for example, this part of Croatia provided one-fifth of the total number of soldiers drafted for the war against Prussia. Between 1769 and 1862 the Military Border supplied between one-fifth and one-quarter of the total Habsburg infantry. The changes, on the other hand, made the border a much more expensive institution. The actual cost was made greater by the fact that the border's original territory proved insufficient to raise the requisite number of regiments, so the War Council was obliged to buy additional tracts of populated land to add to it. The danger arose that the cost of a Grenzer might rise above that of a soldier of the line; yet it was difficult to offset the difference by taxing the Border population, in view of the fact that the soldier's insertion into the imperial army had greatly increased his own economic burden. Participation in frequent military campaigns abroad, and the additional training that was now required of the Grenzer, led to prolonged withdrawal of able-bodied males from the self-subsistence economy that formed the basis of Border society. The burden on the Grenzer and his family was compounded by the need to buy the new uniforms that he now had to wear: the cost of these, deducted from the serving soldier's pay, was, apart from public *robot*, the only form of direct taxation.

The problem of rising expenditure both for the state treasury and for the individual soldier encouraged the War Council to search for a new source of revenue within the border itself. The solution was found in the inclusion of towns into the border system. Whereas up to this point towns had been treated as a subversive influence upon its wholly agrarian society, it was now intended that they should play a key role in transforming the border into an economic system capable of financing the reformed structure. The urban population was to be treated as soldiers, but would be able to buy their freedom from military service by paying taxes. This would permit the real Grenzer to escape taxation and thus remain able to give full attention to military duties. It was intended that the towns would also play a part in making the Military Border a self-sufficient economic zone. They were to supply the Grenzers with the goods they needed, such as uniforms and boots, while the Grenzer villages would supply the towns with the necessary raw materials. The upshot of this was that the regimental headquarters were given a special status as military municipalities. Petrovaradin and Zemun in Srijem, Brod, Karlovci and Gradiška in Slavonia, were the first to acquire these rights. They were followed by Gospić, Otočac, Brinje and Ogulin in the Karlovac Border, and Bjelovar, Kostajnica and Ivanić in the Varaždin and Ban's Borders. (Karlovac itself became part of Civil Croatia by acquiring the status of a royal free city in 1778.) By 1785 there were about twenty of these privileged military townships, including the ports of Senj and Karlobag.[25] The hope that they would greatly increase tax revenue, however, remained unfulfilled: in 1819 they contributed only about 17 per cent of direct taxes.[26] The townships in the Karlovac Border lost their special status as a result.

The reorganisation and centralisation of the border system and the striving to make it a self-sufficient *corpus separatum* – a territory with its own laws, judiciary, administration, army and economy – were conducive to the full bureaucratisation of Grenzer society. A new border law was enacted in 1754, which replaced all the different previous legal codes and provided a uniform legal basis for the functioning of the new system. Land tenure became more sharply qualified, in that the state – in the person of the emperor-king – became the legal owner of the land: if a Grenzer left the Border, his holding reverted to the emperor-king, who could freely dispose of it. Sale or donation of land within the Border also became limited: now that the family and not the individual male was 'enlisted' into the army, land transactions had to be controlled so as to leave each family with a certain land minimum, large enough to ensure its physical survival.

The transformation of the Military Border into an autarchic quasi-state led inevitably to the emergence of a new level of administration, responsible for civilian matters such as justice, economy, religion, education, crafts and trade. A new breed of economic managers appeared, trained in special colleges established in Graz and Vienna. This brought to life, however, the old conflict between the 'civilian' and 'military' sides of border administration over the allocation of revenue and competencies, from which the latter emerged victorious. Saving rather than spending, and spending on military rather than on civilian needs, remained throughout the War Council's main concern, as a result of which the Military Border became subject to constant experimentation driven by the need to reconcile the socio-economic and military demands of this bizarre institution. The desire to simplify administration led eventually to the fusion of the different border commands. Between 1823 and 1851 two main commands were established: one in Zagreb for the Varaždin, Karlovac and Ban's Borders, and one in Petrovaradin for the Slavonian and Srijem Borders. When in 1849 Croatia and Hungary formally separated, the Slavonian regiments were added to the command in Zagreb.

The reorganisation of the border undertaken in the second half of the eighteenth century led in the end to the land itself being taxed. The process was initiated by the desire of the War Council to equalise the burden of military service among border inhabitants. Families which had more or better land, or which did not have actively serving males, became liable to a land tax, the revenue from which was used to compensate the families that were either too small to supply a soldier (no family could be left without an able-bodied male in an economy based on self-subsistence) or which did not have enough land – that is, those that could or did suffer disproportionately from the loss to active service of the labour of the males. What began as an improvisation was subsequently both simplified and generalised, leading to the emergence of a system in which each Grenzer family had to pay a certain amount of tax, depending on the size and quality of its landholding, and every family with a serving male was eligible for monetary compensation. All males not in active service became obliged to perform free public labour. This socialisation of Grenzer welfare involved the whole of the Military Border: the better-off regiments were taxed more so that they could subsidise the poorer ones. Such a system of taxation and distribution required close control and supervision of each and every aspect of Grenzer society, and simultaneously helped to maintain a social balance by weakening tendencies towards social differentiation. Most important was the fact that, when all the revenues and expenditures were added up, the Military Border paid for itself. Different calculations involving comparison between the cost of maintenance of a soldier of the border and that of a soldier of the line agree that a Grenzer was four to five times cheaper.

On the positive side, the drive to make the Military Border a self-sufficient economic institution led in the last quarter of the eighteenth century to a concentrated effort to improve its material infrastructure. A number of roads were built to facilitate trade and communications between the regimental centres, from Zemun in the east to Senj and Karlobag in the west. Regulation of the rivers Kupa and Sava was also undertaken, re-establishing the old trade route between the Danube and the Adriatic by way of Sisak and Karlovac. These improvements encouraged trade between the border as a whole and Civilian Croatia, Venetian Dalmatia and Ottoman Bosnia, where the crucial role was played by Kostajnica. The problem the military authorities never managed to solve, however, was that the border hardly produced any surplus with which to trade. With the partial exception of Srijem in the east, the peasant-soldier had neither the time nor the incentive to produce for the market or to engage in trade and crafts. Since the main purpose of the Border system was to produce cheap soldiers, transition to a fully monetary economy was in fact neither sought nor achieved. As a result, and despite the military administration's efforts to stimulate internal trade and production, the barter economy continued to dominate its internal life.

One consequence of this was that the growth of the border economy failed to match that of the population, so that bad harvests led to famine in the poorer regiments of the Karlovac Border in particular. Here the state of near-permanent agricultural crisis became chronic by the end of the eighteenth century, causing emigration to more fertile parts of the border. The poor quality of the land increased reliance on sheep farming, but since the animals' seasonal movement involved crossing state borders it was discouraged by the military authorities. The Grenzer population of the Karlovac Border became as a result permanently dependent on the complex system of food relief set up by the military authorities, a dependency which strengthened its loyalty to the border system.

Population growth, on the other hand, increased pressure on land. Land was initially given to a single family – each landholding was to supply an able-bodied soldier – but a generation or two later it might no longer be able to sustain the families of the descendants. The extent of the problem varied from one part of the border to another, depending on the size and quality of the original land grant, but was present throughout. Demand for land grew also as a result of the subdivision of the extended family traditional among the Vlachs, among whom land was collectively owned by the adult males. A sedentary existence encouraged a large family's separation into its nuclear components, leading to a subdivision of the landholding. But subdivision of land in a society in which all males had equal rights of inheritance carried the danger that individual plots might end up being too small to sustain a family. In those parts of the Military Border, such as the Varaždin Border, that had reserve land for distribution or where initial land plots were large, this did not cause immediate problems. The problem became acute in the Karlovac Border, where the land, particularly in the coastal region and in Lika, was of poor quality. Unchecked subdivision of land could not be allowed to proceed without endangering the very foundation of the Border; hence, preservation of the extended family or *zadruga* – in effect demographic control – became one of the border commanders' main concerns. The first attempt to prevent *zadruga* division was made with the Border Law of 1754, when it was made conditional on the permission of the regimental commander and on each branch of the divided family being left with a certain land minimum. In 1807 an even more restrictive law was brought in, according to which each branch of a divided family had also to contain at least three able-bodied males. Subdivision henceforth had also to be fully consensual: all adult males had to agree not only to the act of division but to its modalities, too.

But it was the transition from a natural to a money economy – which began in the last quarter of the eighteenth century – that posed the gravest threat to the *zadruga* family. The possibility of additional earnings emerged, but the *zadruga* framework greatly inhibited individual mobility and initiative. If, for example, an individual acquired land by marriage or by purchase, it became the collective property of his *zadruga*. *Zadruga* members who worked outside the family – who sold cattle they themselves raised, distilled alcohol for sale, engaged in crafts, for instance – had to share their income with other family members, since the land on which the cattle grazed or the fruit and wood used in distilling were collectively owned. The tendency towards the break-up of extended families proved irresistible with time. Restrictions imposed in 1754 and again in 1807, when a married couple was even banned from having their own bedroom, did slow down family divisions, but the effect of such measures could be only of short duration. Divisions soon resumed, but were now conducted in secret.

The perpetuation of the Military Border well after its original purpose had disappeared led to its transformation into a quasi-state designed to preserve two of its basic pillars: land tenure conditioned by military service, and a form of family that maximised the number of available males. The desire to make the Border self-financing brought about a degree of economic modernisation; but this remained limited at all times by the desire to minimise its effects upon border society. As land became taxed and the burden of military service greatly increased with the Grenzer integration into the imperial army, the relative advantages once enjoyed by the Grenzers over the enserfed peasantry in the rest of Croatia disappeared. Frequent absences of able-bodied males and demographic oscillations caused by repeated war losses further undermined an economy based on self-subsistence. Freedom from serfdom as the only advantage offered by the border vanished in 1848, when serfdom was abolished in the rest of Croatia-Slavonia. By that time, however, the Eastern Question had made its appearance, infusing new life into an increasingly moribund institution.

Old militarism and new Europe

The link between the Military Border and the future of Turkey-in-Europe was placed in a new light at the start of the nineteenth century, with the arrival of French troops in Croatia. In 1806 Napoleonic France acquired Istria, Dalmatia, and the Republic of Dubrovnik, following which the Republic was dissolved and joined to the rest of Dalmatia. A year later Vienna was also forced to cede to France the Croatian Border area south of the river Sava, that is, the six Karlovac and Ban's regiments. This *Croatie militaire*, together with Carniola, Carinthia, Istria and Dalmatia, were then constituted as the Illyrian Provinces. Napoleon told his government in 1809:

Napoleon's Illyrian Provinces, early nineteenth century

> The Illyrian Provinces bring the borders of my great empire to the Sava. Contiguous with the empire of Constantinople, I shall find myself naturally in a situation to oversee the highest interests of my trade in the Mediterranean, the Adriatic and the Levant. I shall protect the Porte provided it wrenches itself from the fateful influence of England, but remain ready to punish it, if it allows itself to be ruled by perfidious and dishonest [British] advice.[27]

The French policy was to secure for France dominance in the Mediterranean, to prevent Russian access to the latter, and to keep Britain away from the Adriatic. The Illyrian Provinces were consequently placed under tight control from Paris, especially in regard to military matters, which were entrusted to General Auguste Marmont.

The French administration in Croatia, however, soon displayed the same conflict of interest between its civilian and military wings that had informed

Vienna's own contradictory reforms in the Military Border. The debate was set off by the desire of the French government to establish as soon as possible a civilian administration, beginning with civilian courts, in the Croatian Border, as part of its efforts to create a uniform system of taxation for all the Illyrian Provinces. The proponents of its abolition saw the Illyrian Provinces as an important link in the trade between French Europe and the Middle East. The continental blockade, which made the Danube-Sava-Kupa-Adriatic route important to trade between Pannonia and the Mediterranean and between Central Europe and the Balkan peninsula, only served to underline the importance of this design. If Sisak, Karlovac and Kostajnica were once again to become important trade centres for the wider region, *Croatie militaire* had to be abolished. However, General Marmont was firmly against this. He saw the border as a springboard for military conquest of the Ottoman Balkans, and was keen to extend it into the Dalmatian interior. The Croatian Border's great virtue, in his view, was that 'it supplies and maintains sixteen thousand soldiers organised as well as the best trained units in Europe, always ready to move as units of the line, while at the same time providing indispensable service on the border'. In purely monetary terms, 'this impoverished land' was by virtue of its military status 'as valuable to His Majesty in time of war as the alliance with one of the most important members of the Confederation of the Rhine'.

General Antoine-François Andreossy summed up the civilian case against the Military Border in terms that echoed the new spirit in Europe. According to Andreossy, the institution of the Military Border served the Austrian government well, in that it provided a cheap frontier guard in the form of 'a well-armed and semi-barbarian militia warring constantly with neighbouring peoples of an equally barbarian disposition'. Its maintenance, however, was 'wholly inimical to the economic development and therefore to the welfare of the people who inhabited it'. It was possible, the general went on, to argue an economic case for the Border, provided its regiments were used only as frontier guards. This whole 'primitive institution' was bound to fall apart, however, as soon as the Ottoman Empire, as the result of a war or treaty, evacuated the neighbouring lands, since Croatia would then cease to be a border land. It was impossible, in any case, to imagine that Military Croatia could be sustained as part of the Illyrian Provinces 'governed by laws common to all civilised nations', since 'the disparity and injustice of it would be greatly felt' by its inhabitants. The decision to retain *Croatie militaire* was in the end made by Napoleon himself. In 1812 two of the border regiments joined Napoleon's campaign in Russia. As long as the Habsburg Monarchy remained allied to France, the border remained docile. In August 1813, however, Vienna declared war on Paris and within days Military Croatia reverted to Habsburg rule. Supported by British naval action along the coast, a combination of border and regular armies moved into Dalmatia, and by the end of January 1814 the Illyrian Provinces were in Austrian hands. At the Congress of Vienna of 1815 they were formally awarded to the Habsburg Monarchy. The whole of Croatia now found itself under the same crown – but not as yet under the rule of the parliament in Zagreb.

FIVE

Language and Literacy

Literacy in its Latin form came to the Croats with their conversion to Christianity. The task of turning pagans into Christians, initially undertaken by Dalmatian bishops, was with the inclusion of Croatia into Charlemagne's empire assumed and skilfully executed by the Frankish Church of Aquileia, backed by the Croatian kings. In the ninth century, however, the arrival of Church Slavonic broke the established monopoly of Latin in the Croatian area, mainly as a result of the papacy's own policy. Keen to reduce the influence of the Frankish clergy, Rome supported the mission undertaken by Constantine (later Cyril) and Methodius at the invitation of like-minded Slav princes in the Danubian area, and even appointed Methodius bishop of the diocese of Sirmium, with authority over the whole of former Roman Pannonia (other than Savia). When, following Methodius' death in 885, the Slavonic clergy was summarily expelled, some of them ended up in Dalmatia, so that the Dalmatian church became a source not only of Latin but also of Glagolitic literature and priests.

When the Dalmatian church was finally restored to full papal jurisdiction and the Croatian church incorporated into it, the area between the Adriatic and the Drava, including much of the Istrian peninsula, became the site of a bilingual ecclesiastical order. Successive popes insisted on the primacy of Latin in the Church and sought to curtail the influence of the Glagolitic clergy by confining them to the lower ranks and to monasteries; but the autonomy of the Croatian kingdom secured a permanent presence for the Slavic liturgy in its parishes. Although linguistic duality produced periodic conflicts within the Church, no permanent split occurred: Glagolitic churches and monasteries were not closed down, but continued to flourish in much of Croatia. Latin, however, remained the official language of the Church and the state, thus depriving Church Slavonic of the kind of institutional protection that it came to enjoy in the Orthodox Slav world.

It was this absence of an ultimate authority that could insist on its purity, or secure for it exclusive use in public life, that led to an early rise of literacy in the vernacular. Among the first recorded examples of the vernacular is the eleventh-century report of King Zvonimir's donation of land to the church of St Lucy on the island of Krk, written in Glagolitic letters and engraved on a stone tablet kept in the church.[1] In the following centuries all manner of legal texts – bequests of land and rights, parish church registers, accounts and ledgers, monastic and municipal records, statutes of local communities, rules of religious fraternities and of professional associations, inscriptions on public buildings and graves and personal correspondence – came to be written in the Glagolitic script.

The script's official protector became St Jerome, translator of the Bible into Latin, the Vulgate, whose use Charlemagne had made obligatory in his realm. Indeed, to better resist the pressure of Latin the Croatian Glagolitic clergy embraced the proposition that the Slav script had been invented by St Jerome, himself a native of Roman Dalmatia.[2] This convenient interpretation was accepted by the Catholic Church. In the late thirteenth century Pope Innocent IV confirmed in a letter to the bishop of Senj his permission for continued use of Glagolica in the areas where it had become customary, adding that the clergy in 'Sclavonia' insisted 'that they have received it from St Jerome'.[3] To medieval Croatian scholars Glagolica was the Croat script. Thus George of Slavonia, a Croatian cleric who taught at the University of Paris at the start of the fifteenth century, called it *alphabetum chrawaticum*, the Croat alphabet, and the Church Slavonic used in Croatian churches the Croat language. For the benefit of his French colleagues he wrote down the Glagolitic alphabet and supplied also the list of the bishoprics in which it was permitted to conduct liturgy in the Croat language. These were Krbava, Knin, Nin, Krk, Rab, Osor, Senj, Split, Trogir, Šibenik and Zadar. In Istria also, he suggested, the clergy said Mass in Croat, since 'Istria too is a Croat land'.[4] As the supposed inventor of Glagolica, St Jerome became the founding father of Croat literacy and by extension the patron saint of the Croatian linguistic nation. Jerome indeed became a highly popular name in the Croatian Adriatic area.

The adoption of St Jerome did not mean that Cyril and Methodius were forgotten. They too were naturalised and became Dalmatians. According to the fifteenth-century author of a Glagolitic breviary, the two brothers were born 'in the city of Salona in Dalmatia from the lineage of Emperor Diocletian'.[5] The constitutive elements of this myth – Slavic liturgy, Salona and Diocletian – were part of a wider Dalmatian recollection of an alleged golden age when close collaboration between the secular and ecclesiastical authorities kept Dalmatia and its people united. One of its sources was the chronicle *Sclavorum regnum* (Kingdom of the Slavs), an extensive account of a true and imagined past of this part of Europe based on oral tradition and written documents. It was composed (or possibly translated from an earlier Croat version) by Gregory, a Benedictine priest from Zadar, who in the second half of the twelfth century became briefly archbishop of Bar. The chronicle includes information that has shown surprising tenacity, such as that Slavs (or Croats in the Croat version) were the same people as Goths, that St Cyril had worked as a missionary in Croatia, that the 'great and marvellous city of Salona was [once] the capital of the king of the Dalmatians', and that King Zvonimir was killed by 'cursed and unfaithful Croats' resisting his call to join the first crusade.[6] According to the chronicle:

> during the reign of good king Zvonimir the whole country lived a joyous life, since it was abundant and adorned with all kind of riches, and its cities full of silver and gold. The poor did not fear the greed of the rich or the weak the strong, or the servant his lord's injustice, since the king protected all and, himself taking only what was rightly his, insisted that others did the same. Great was the wealth enjoyed in both the highlands and along the Littoral at the time of the good King Zvonimir.[7]

This marvellous time ended with regicide. The dying king, the story continues, pronounced a curse on the Croats, saying that 'that they will never have a king of their own tongue, but will forever be ruled by foreigners'. Copies of this work were kept in a number of Dalmatian monasteries and became an influential, if unreliable, source of the Croatian historical imagination. For, if Cyril was a missionary in Croatia, then his alphabet was meant for the Croats – it was the Croat alphabet.[8] These early centuries produced a number of historical works written in Latin or Croat by patricians and clerics from all over Dalmatia, including the history of the Salona/Split church by Archdeacon Thomas of Split. The scholarly prestige of the Dalmatian Glagolitic clergy led Charles IV of Luxembourg in 1347, the year in which he established the University of Prague, to invite the Glagolitic Benedictine clergy to set up a centre for study of the script and language in Prague. Their monastery, which survived for around seventy years, helped among other things to stimulate a movement for use of the Czech language in the church, which reached a high point under the leadership of Jan Hus in the early fifteenth century.

If vernacular literacy was owed in the first instance to the work of monastic schools and scriptoria, it was use of the 'Croat' script by the courts of magnate families such as the Bribirski, the Zrinski, the Frankapan or the nobility of Lika and Krbava that made it a familiar medium of social interaction. Since the Cyrillic alphabet, which came to be used also in central Dalmatia, was likewise perceived as a Croat alphabet, the terms 'Glagolitia' and 'Cyrillic' were often treated as synonyms. The continued dominance of Latin in the affairs of church and state ensured, on the other hand, that the literary language would evolve in close interaction with Latin and with the Latin culture of western Europe.[9] In contrast to the Venetian state, however, which was fully oriented towards the Mediterranean, Adriatic Croatia remained tied to Central Europe by way of its Slavonian twin. Cultural exchange between the two regions was crucially aided by the Church, whose organisational network ensured that clergymen born in one part would often end up serving in the other. Those who reached high positions within the church or at the royal court were as a rule educated at the universities of Paris, Bologna or Padua, which attracted scholars from all over Croatia and became an enduring source of Latin influence in the land.[10] Among the first was Herman Dalmatin from Istria, who studied and taught at the cathedral schools of Chartres and Paris in the 1230s. A noted Arabist, he translated (together with Robert of Ketton) parts of the Qur'an, as well as Arabic and Greek texts on mathematics and astronomy. Ugrin from Čazma in Slavonia, who was archbishop of Split in the first half of the thirteenth century, his uncle Stephen Babonić, bishop of Zagreb, who hoped to merge the Zagreb and Split dioceses, and the Trogir-born Augustin Kažotić, who in the early fourteenth century became bishop of Zagreb and established there its first cathedral school, were all, for instance, graduates of the Sorbonne.

This Croat-Latin culture took wing in the fourteenth century, when the Latin script began to replace Glagolica and when the Dalmatian urban elite, which had previously written only in Latin, began to produce works also in the vernacular. Once embraced by the cities, the practice of writing in the native language spread along the Adriatic coast and laid the foundations of a unified national culture. The arrival of humanism in the early fifteenth century produced an outburst of works in Latin and Croat, ranging from poetry and theology to history and natural science. Practically every Dalmatian city, including Kotor, acquired its own humanist circle, whose members – animated by the idea of the need to improve man and society – engaged in writing and translating and kept in close touch with their peers abroad.

Euclid (left) and Herman the Dalmatian, by Matthew of Paris, circa 1259

The crucial breakthrough in the spread of literature in Croat came with the invention of printing and the establishment of the first printing press in Venice in 1470. The city had in the meantime acquired a substantial colony of Croats, many of whom worked in its arsenal or in its navy. They settled around Riva degli Schiavoni, also known as Riva of the Croats,[11] the hub of Venetian trade with the Levant, where Dalmatian ships had their own berths. Croat emigration to Venice escalated between 1450 and 1525 under the impact of the Ottoman offensive, and in 1451 the Fraternity of St George and St Triphonis – registered by the Venetian authorities as the Fraternity of Illyrians or Dalmatians – was established in the parish of San Pietro di Castello behind the Riva to care for their collective needs. St Jerome was another of the fraternity's patron saints. A printing press was soon set up for publication of religious literature in the Latin and Glagolitic scripts, where the first book – a Glagolitic Missal According to the Roman Rite – was produced in 1483. This was the first printed book in a Slavic language.[12]

Although printing centres were soon afterwards established also in Croatia, Venice remained a major publishing centre for Croatian authors and a place where they could also purchase the latest works produced elsewhere in Europe. A cursory glance at some of the titles published in Venice by Croatian authors between the end of the fifteenth and the start of the seventeenth century in Latin, Croat and Italian reveals a wide spectrum of interests: *Elegies and Poems* (Juraj Šižgorić, 1477); *The Origin and History of the Slavs* (Vinko Pribojević, 1532); a translation into Italian of Pedro de Medina's *L'arte del navegar,* together with a map of Spain (Vicko Palatin, 1554); a collection of poems and plays (Hanibal Lucić, 1556); a collection of poems and stories based on the everyday life of Dalmatian fishermen (Petar Hektorović, 1568); a pastoral novel *The Highlands* (Petar Zoranić, 1569); *Considerations on the Nature of Currents and Eddies in the Oceanic Sea* (Nikola Sagrojević, 1574); *Family Rule* and *On the State of the Republics* (Nikola Gučetić, 1589 and 1591); *Dictionary of the Five Most Noble European Languages* and *Principles of Logic* (Faust Vrančić, 1595 and 1608); and *An Introduction to Aristotle's Metaphysics* (Antun Medo, 1596).

Our mother tongue

An insight into the functioning and scope of this multilingual Croatian culture at the start of the modern era is provided by the opus of Marko Marulić (1450–1524), a Split patrician whose Latin works, inspired by the contemporary movement for spiritual and institutional renewal of the Catholic Church, were read widely and continuously in western Europe between the late fifteenth and late seventeenth centuries. Marulić's *Evangelistarium,* in which the teaching of Christ is declared to be the source of all ecclesiastical doctrine, first came out in Venice in 1487 and went to seventeen editions by 1601. Even more acclaimed was his *De Institutione bene vivendi*, a treatise on Christian morality illustrated with examples taken from the Bible and the lives of the saints. First published in Venice in 1498, it had undergone thirty more editions by 1691. Marulić's circle of readers widened beyond the Latin-language circle, with a thirty further editions of this book appearing in Italian, German, French, Spanish, Portuguese and Czech translation. The book reached also into the New World, since the Portuguese translation was read not only in Portugal, but also in the Portuguese possessions in Africa, Asia and Latin America.

Marulić's writings were also read attentively in England. Henry VIII used them to compose his *Defence of the Seven Sacraments* in 1521, which earned him the title Defender of the Faith from the grateful pope.[13] Thomas More too relied on them when writing his *Supplication of Souls*. Marulić's influence on More is visible also in the latter's *Dialogue of Comfort against Tribulation,* written in captivity in 1534, which closely follows the text of *Evangelistarium*. Extensive quotations and borrowing from these books by sixteenth-century biblical scholars enlarged further the area of their influence. The two books were particularly popular with Italian Franciscans,

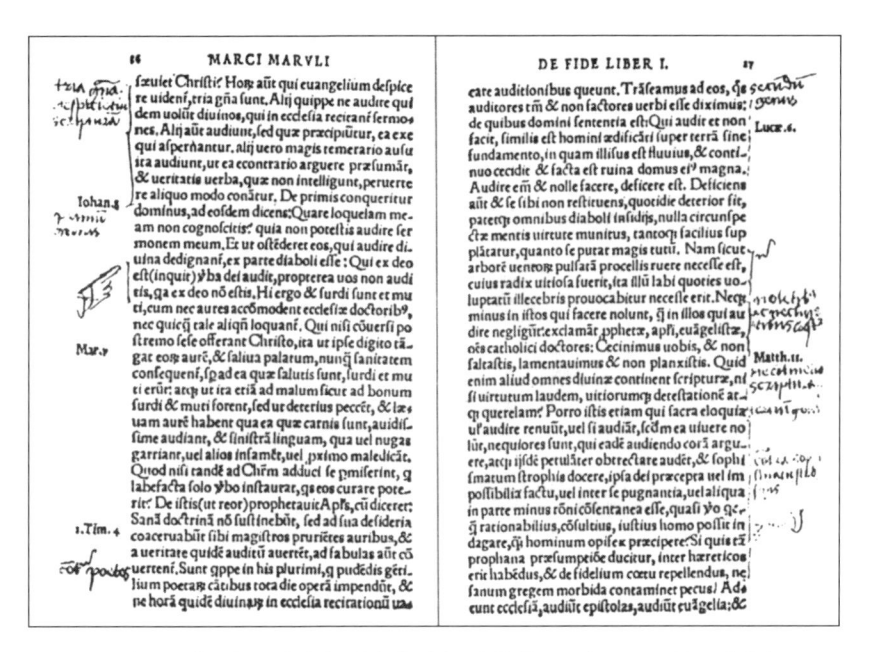

Marginal notes by Henry VIII in Marko Marulić's *Evangelistarium,* British Library

which is perhaps not surprising given Marulić's great admiration for Francis of Assisi – like Archdeacon Thomas, Marulić was buried in the courtyard of the Franciscan monastery in Split. But they were an inspiration also to the Jesuits, who quickly adopted *De Institutione* as required reading for the brethren, including those trained at the Illyrian College established in 1580 at Loreto near Ancona for missionary activity in the Ottoman lands, as well as those active in missionary centres in the New World. When in 1542 Francis Xavier went to the Far East, he took only two books with him: his breviary and Marulić's *De Institutione*.[14]

The latter's widespread appeal is indicated also by the fact that the first Italian translation was organised by Florentine enemies of the Medici and sympathisers with the teachings of Savanarola, whereupon they came to the attention of the Church censors. Marulić's claim that in certain circumstances it is morally acceptable to lie was particularly open to attack. The Spanish Inquisition, in particular, took great exception to the argument that there are times when 'it is justified and even necessary to dissemble and lie', and insisted on purging such heretical passages from all copies of *De Institutione,* including the one which St Francis Xavier took with him to Goa. In 1546, indeed, the Inquisition burned a copy of the Italian edition in Sienna, together with Machiavelli's *Prince*; but this did not prevent eleven more editions from appearing between 1563 and 1610.[15]

**C Libar Marca Marula Splichianina Vchomſe
uſdarſi Iſtoria Sfeçe udouice udit u uerſih
haruacchi ſloſena/chacho ona ub: uoi
uodu Olopherna Poſridu uoiſ
che gnegouc/i oſlodobi pu-
ch iſraelſchi od ueli
che pogibili.
✠

Prodaiuſe ubnecih umarcarii uſtacũ
chidarſi libar ſa ſignao.**

The first edition of *Judith*, Venice 1521

Marulić's writings were admired not only by Catholics but also by Protestants. His profound knowledge of the scriptures, his rejection of ancient heroes and philosophers as sources of spiritual inspiration, his avoidance of theological controversy and his sober presentation of the

Christian norms of devotion appealed to such admirers of Luther as the Basel publisher Adam Petri de Langendorf, who in the early sixteenth century printed elegant editions of both books, thus assuring them wide dissemination outside of Italy. After Marulić's death his works were used as a weapon against Lutheran ideas, however; reprinted in Cologne, then a citadel of Catholic orthodoxy, they were sold in all the major cities of Europe. Distribution of *De Institutione* soon succumbed to censorship in the Catholic lands, but interest in it revived after John Fowler, a fugitive from Elizabethan England, published a new edition of the work in Antwerp, after which it was republished several more times in Holland, France and Germany. Philip Howard, Earl of Arundel, another Catholic imprisoned in the Tower, translated Marulić's *Carmen de doctrina* into English (as *Dialogue betwixt a Christian and Jesus Christ Hanging on the Crosse*), and had it printed, together with the Latin text, secretly at his castle in 1595, the year of his death.

Marulić's works in Croat, on the other hand, earned him the attribute of 'the father of Croatian literature'. He won this accolade with his epic poem *The Story of the Holy Widow Judith Composed in Croat Verse* – or, as he wrote to his friend Cipicco, archdeacon of the Split cathedral, in *lengua nostra materna*, our mother tongue. The poem, in which the biblical story is rendered with the aid of classical Greek and Latin into the Croat vernacular, is not only a testimony to Marulić's own artistic talent, but also a reminder of the maturation of literary engagement during the preceding period. Writing in the vernacular meant writing for one's own national constituency: composed in one great surge in 1501, in an atmosphere of imminent danger posed by Ottoman attacks, *Judith* was meant for those of his countrymen who could not read Latin or Italian.[16] Throughout Western Europe at this time national languages were challenging the primacy of Latin, and Croat was no exception. By writing *Judith* Marulić wished to demonstrate in the poetic form of the period that the Croat *volgare* too was, or could be, as versatile as Latin. His intention to invest Croat with the full dignity of a literary language was revealed in a letter to a friend inviting him to acknowledge, after reading the manuscript, that 'the Slav [Croat] language too has its Dante'.[17] Though published with a delay of twenty years, for reasons that are not clear (although church censorship comes to mind, because of the work's celebration of female sexuality), the epic was an instantaneous success, encouraging its Venetian publisher quickly to produce two more editions.

Among Marulić's various compositions written in Latin, Croat and Italian – some (erotic verses) only in Latin, some (sonnets) only in Italian, some (patriotic poems) only in Croat[18] – one finds also translations between the three languages: for example, of part of Dante's *Divine Comedy* into Latin, and of Petrarch's *Canzioniere* into Croat. This was a common practice in Dalmatia. Marulić thus translated the Croat version of *Sclavorum regnum* into Latin, while Mavro Orbini, a Bendictine monk from Dubrovnik, rendered a Latin version of the chronicle into Italian and had it published under the title *Il Regno degli Slavi*.[19] The development of the Croat language proceeded thus to be shaped through a creative dialogue with its two regional companions: with Latin, as the universal language of the educated class; and with Italian, which had arrived with the Venetian administration, but whose lasting presence was secured by its role as the lingua franca of Mediterranean trade. Croats wrote in all three languages, depending on the prospective audience. When Benedict Kotruljević (Cotrugli), a native of Dubrovnik who spent much of his adult life at the Aragonese court of Naples, decided in the middle of the fifteenth century to write a guide to trade and double-entry bookkeeping, he opted after some hesitation for Italian rather than Latin on the grounds that it would be more useful to uneducated merchants.[20] A sense of the literary effervescence present in Dalmatia in the sixteenth century is conveyed in a letter sent in 1549 to the Venetian government by its local representative: 'The citizens of Split live in accordance with Slav [i.e. Croat] customs and tradition, and their mother tongue is so melodic and elegant that it holds the first place in Dalmatia, just as Tuscan is acclaimed in Italy as the flower of Italian dialects, the most beautiful and the best.'[21] The same feeling of cultural accomplishment inspired Faust Vrančić at the end of the century to include Croat (which he called Dalmatian) among the 'five most noble languages of Europe'. By reading and borrowing from each other's works, Dalmatian authors transformed what began as individual local efforts into a single literary culture, in which the norm cultivated in the Republic of Dubrovnik – already hailed as 'the pride and glory of the Croat language'[22] – would in the eighteenth century acquire pre-eminence.

The foundations of this achievement had been laid down by the native clergy officiating in the Glagolitic parishes dotting the coast and its hinterland. An incident recorded in Cres in 1668, after more than two centuries of continuous Venetian government, brings out the role played by the vernacular church in bolstering a sense of national individuality. That year one Gaspar de Lio, a trainee priest (of Venetian origin, incidentally) interrupted a sermon delivered by the parish priest at the time of Lent by calling him – in Venetian Italian – a pig. The young man was provoked by the fact that the parson had addressed the congregation in Italian. Hauled

Faust Vrančić's parachute in his *Machinae Novae,* Venice 1595

before the bishop's court, Gaspar declared (again in Venetian) that what he had done could not be construed as a public insult, given that hardly anyone had attended the church that week – a state of affairs which he blamed on the introduction of Italian, because 'we Croats [literally: *Schiavoni*] are not attracted by sermons in a foreign tongue'.[23] This incident is one of many illustrating the long-lasting duel between the local clergy used to preaching in Croat and the higher church officials, appointed in effect by Venice, who sought to replace Croat by Latin or Italian. For Venice itself, the linguistic issue was a political, not a doctrinal, problem: in 1480, when it acquired the Frankapan island of Krk in the teeth of King Matthias Corvinus's opposition, the new governor was promptly instructed to drive out the clergy sermonising in Church Slavonic. If Venice discouraged the use of Croat in Dalmatian and Istrian churches, it was because to do so served its political interests in the Adriatic area. In the sixteenth century, however, when liturgy in the vernacular became associated with Protestantism, the latent conflict over the language of the Mass and the sacraments acquired a wider theological significance. In 1562 the Council of Trent, convened originally to debate religious differences in the hope of safeguarding the unity of the church and the faith but now ending up as a purely Catholic gathering, decided after prolonged deliberation that the Mass and the sacraments had to be delivered in Latin, and that 'those who say that the Mass should be celebrated only in the vulgar tongue be anathemised'.[24] This decision did not of itself excommunicate those who used the Croat liturgy, but it was nevertheless used to further restrict use of the Croat vernacular in Catholic churches.

Rebellion against Rome

It was inevitable, perhaps, that clerics from Istria and the cities and islands of the north Adriatic, these strongholds of Slavic liturgy, would supply the most active Croatian Protestants. Protestantism came to Adriatic Croatia largely from Venice, where the large German colony imported and circulated Protestant literature without hindrance from the state, keen to maintain its valuable trade with German cities and principalities. Under pressure from the pope and Emperor Charles V, however, Venice did permit the establishment on its territory of the Holy Office, a special commission created by the papacy for the persecution of Protestants. Balthazar (Baldo) Lupetina, an Istrian from Labin, a small town facing the island of Cres, and a popular preacher who became guardian of a Franciscan monastery in Venice, would in the middle of the sixteenth century become one of its victims. Lupetina is remembered largely because it was he who persuaded his young cousin Matija Vlačić (1520–75) to study at the University of Basel. The life of Matthias Flacius Illyricus, called by some the 'Achilles of pure Protestantism', became henceforth inextricably linked with the progress of the German Reformation.[25] Vlačić soon left Basel for the newly established Lutheran university in Tübingen, where he joined the household of another Istrian Croat, Matthias Grbac-Garbitius, also called Illyricus, professor of Greek and friend of Philip Melachthon. Armed with Grbac's commendations Vlačić arrived at Wittenberg in 1541, where he spent eight years teaching Greek and Hebrew and working closely with Melachthon and Luther. The vernacular Bible was one of Luther's most lasting gifts to the German nation, yet one language Vlačić never fully mastered was German: he wrote in Latin and, if he could help it, also taught in Latin. He was to spend all his adult life in Germany, yet he never quite made it his home, and it is possible that this intimate sense of alienation, this inability to adapt to the world around him, contributed in part at least to his theological intransigence, which made him a prominent leader of the so-called Gnesio-Lutherans who, following Luther's death in 1546, believed themselves to be his sole legitimate heirs.[26]

Matija Vlačić Ilirik –
Matthias Flacius Illyricus

The split between Vlačić and Melachthon occurred soon after Luther's death, when the defeat of the Protestant princes and the capture of Wittenberg by imperial troops opened the door to a religious settlement based on compromise. Melachthon accepted, but Vlačić rejected the need for an accord. Disappointed with what he saw as a betrayal of the Lutheran credo by his old friend and mentor, Vlačić moved to Magdeburg, which had become the centre of resistance to any understanding between the pope and the Emperor. He spent eight highly productive years there writing (in addition to a stream of fiery pamphlets, some of which appeared under pseudonyms) his major work, *Catalogus Testium Veritatis,* and organising and contributing to the publication of the first three volumes of *Ecclesiastica Historia*, the authoritative Protestant Church history known also as the *Magdeburg Centuries*.[27] Jan Blahoslav, a member of the Czech Brothers, a Protestant current not recognised by either of the two Lutheran camps, visited both Flacius and Melachthon in 1556 in order to understand the nature of their conflict. He left a telling description of Vlačić at Magdeburg: 'Illyricus is a passionate and learned man and it seems that what he does he does from his heart, yet in a manner that is too proud, rigid and implacable. It is my impression too that in his pride, argumentativeness and refusal to accept criticism he can be likened to Osiander, for while we were speaking his hands were shaking with anger.'[28] Vlačić's position in Magdeburg became untenable, however, in the aftermath of the Augsburg Peace of 1555, which left the secular lords and the free cities to decide on the religious orientation of their territories. Two years later, at the invitation of the Weimar princes, he moved to Jena, where he assumed the chair of theology at the newly established university. Vested by his patrons with more authority than he wished for or could realistically wield, Vlačić became increasingly isolated and was eventually asked to leave. He moved next to Regensburg, where he planned the establishment of a school and publishing house for books in Slav languages – a project that was never realised, although some books in Slovene and Croat were published there in 1566–8. He began to write there his most important work, *Clavis Scripturae Sacrae*; but his inflexible theological stance led to another effective expulsion five years later, after which he found no permanent position. He died in 1575 in a convent in Frankfurt, aged fifty-five, practically an outcast in a Protestant Germany which he had helped to create.

The call for a fundamental Church reform, if not necessarily in the form advocated by Luther, had in the meantime acquired supporters in every major Croatian city. The generation that came after Marulić and Vlačić faced a different situation, however, in that the Catholic Church had succeeded in stabilising itself by conducting its own reform at the same time as keeping up a vigorous anti-Protestant campaign, to which the Jesuits were making a significant intellectual and organisational contribution. One of these was Markantun (Marcus Anthonius) de Dominis (1560–1624), a noble from Rab whose life and fate came to be shaped by the contradictory and unpredictable progress of the Catholic renewal in this part of Europe.[29] In contrast to the complete uprooting experienced by Vlačić, Dominis began his career in a leisurely manner typical of his class. He studied at the Jesuit colleges in Loreto and in Padua, where he taught mathematics and natural sciences. By all accounts he was a highly gifted student and a popular teacher.[30] Dominis left the Jesuit order, however, in order to become bishop of Senj, that bastion of Glagolitic clergy, replacing his uncle who had died fighting the Ottomans at Klis in 1596. But he was soon forced to flee before the *uskoks*, the anti-Ottoman guerrillas ensconced in the city, who were enraged by his role in an attempt coordinated between the Venetians and the Habsburgs to demobilise and resettle them.

Dominis now sought a new position for himself and, at the invitation of the local clergy and with the support of the two powers, he became archbishop of Split in 1602. Here Dominis composed his most important work, *De republica ecclesiastica*, in which he argued that the Catholic Church had become too secular and too alienated from its spiritual nature. The main cause of this deviation, in his view, was papal primacy, which not only represented an illegal usurpation of power but was also alien to the true spirit of Christianity. Such a spirit, he was convinced, could properly be nurtured only in a community organised on the model of the early church. Dominis did not stop at describing the state of affairs, however; he also acted. When in 1606 Pope Paul V, as part of a power struggle with the Venetian senate, placed the republic under an interdict prohibiting the clergy from administering the sacraments on its territory, he publicly sided with Venice, arguing that papal interference in secular affairs was contrary to canon law and religious principles.

Rome and Venice soon made peace, but Dominis had to reckon henceforth with a hostile Roman curia, whose ranks and importance had been swelled by the demands of the Counter-Reformation. Motivated by a growing sense of impotence in managing the affairs of his diocese as well as by resentment at his treatment by the Roman curia, he finally decided after some negotiations with the highly active English envoy to Venice to make his way to England. He resigned his post in Split in favour of his nephew and in 1616 began a secret and hazardous journey to London, for in the meantime the Holy Office had banned not only his existing but also all his future works, and had instructed papal representatives abroad to have him arrested. On his arrival in London he was welcomed as an 'exotic trophy' won in the battle for authority being waged by the new Anglican Church against Rome.[31] Warmly received by the archbishop of Canterbury and King James I, Dominis was appointed dean of Windsor and elected an honorary doctor at the University of Cambridge. A year later the first four volumes of his *De republica ecclesiastica* were published in London. They received much attention in Europe and strong condemnation in Rome, which he managed to provoke further by organising the publication of his Venetian friend Paolo Sarpi's critical *History of the Council of Trent*.

Although comfortably settled, Dominis soon came into conflict with the local establishment. When in 1621 his teacher and friend became Pope Gregory XV, he felt encouraged to profess more openly his ideal of church unity. This greatly displeased the English Anglicans and prompted the king to expel him from Britain. He travelled to Rome, confessed he had been wrong, and was forgiven. In that same year, however, Gregory died and his more militant successor, Urban VIII, decided to re-open the case against Dominis, who was consequently imprisoned in Castel Sant'Angelo, where he soon died; but the trial against him continued nevertheless, and he was found guilty. The verdict stated:

> We condemn the memory of the deceased Mark Anthony, former archbishop of Split, to eternal disgrace and deprive him of all honours, functions and entitlements, and confiscate all his possessions and goods in favour of the Holy Office. We banish his memory, his body form present here, his portrait and his works from the church of whose mercy he proved unworthy during his

Markantun de Dominis

life, [and] demand that his writings be publicly burnt.[32]

His body, portrait, papers and books were taken to Campo de' Fiori, where they were solemnly burnt and the ashes thrown into the Tiber. Dominis' progress from Catholic orthodoxy to rebellion against Rome, followed by return to the Catholic Church, was not untypical for the cities and nobles of Adriatic Croatia – where authentic, articulate and at times stringent criticisms of the corruption of the Church and the papacy as an institution had emerged early on, yet had never led to a lasting breach with Rome.

The Protestant Croat Bible

Protestantism was an intensely national phenomenon, not least because of its insistence on the use of the vernacular in church. The first officially approved English Bible of 1540 was published in 20,000 copies, 'more than enough to provide one for every parish church in England'.[33] Luther's translation of the New Testament into German appeared in 200,000 copies between 1522 and 1534; eighty-three editions of the German Bible came out in Wittenberg alone up to the time of Luther's death. In the Croatian case, however, despite widespread use of the vernacular in churches, and translations into Croat of parts and even the whole of the Bible made at different times by committed individuals, the first Croat Bible was printed not in Croatia itself but in Protestant Germany, in 1563, and enjoyed only a brief life.

Vlačić's *Dialogue between a Papist and a Lutheran* published in 1555 was the first Protestant work to appear in Croat.[34] Shortly afterwards, in 1561, a Croat Biblical Office with a printing press was established at Urach, near Tübingen, by the Styrian nobleman John Ungnad, a close friend of the Zrinski and Frankapan families, under the protection of Christopher of Württemberg. Ungnad had served the German empire for several decades as a high official and military commander in Styria and Croatia; but he came into conflict with Ferdinand I (who in 1556 replaced his brother Charles V as German emperor) when Ferdinand refused to legalise Protestantism in the Habsburg hereditary lands. So Ungnad left his estates to his sons and defected to the Württenberg princes. It was his desire to aid the cause of Reformation in Slovenia and Croatia that prompted him to establish a centre on his Urach estate for printing religious works in their languages.[35] During its three years of operation – which had to be discontinued after Ungnad's sudden death in 1564 – the Croat Biblical Office managed to produce fourteen titles in the Glagolitic, eight in the Cyrillic and seven in the Latin script, including the Catechism, the New Testament and parts of the Old Testament, amounting to a total of 25,000 books. The books were transported by way of the Danube to Vienna and Ljubljana, before ending up in Croatia where the translations were checked for accuracy by local scholars. In 1563 Nicholas Frankapan was able to confirm reception of three translations produced in Urach – The New Testament together with the Epistles, Johann Brenz's *Postilla* and Melachthon's *The Augsburg Confession* – and also that they were published 'in our true Croat language, so that every Croat should find it easy to read and understand them'. He added that 'the people of our language desire and pray to God that he give them the Bible in our Croat language, so that they may understand the Old and New Testaments'.[36]

Since the Bible was meant to be read and heard in common worship, what mattered in the first instance was the ability of the congregation to understand its word. The task of the Croat translators working at Urach was complicated, however, by the fact that in Croatia, as in Italy, more than one fully-fledged literary language based on local speech had emerged during the Middle Ages. These languages are commonly grouped into three intersecting sets called *čakavian*, *štokavian* and *kajkavian* after the respective words for 'what' (*ča, što, kaj*). *Čakavian* speech predominated in Istria, on the Dalmatian coast, and in the area between the Kupa, Una and Cetina rivers. Western Slavonia spoke *kajkavian,* while the *štokavian* idiom was common in eastern Slavonia and – with Bosnia acting as a bridge – along the southern Dalmatian Littoral from the river Cetina to the Bay of Kotor. The large-scale migrations caused by Ottoman expansion during the fifteenth and sixteenth centuries changed this pattern, however, leading to a considerable expansion of the area of *štokavian* speech, mainly at the expense of *čakavian*. This idiomatic diversity did not hinder the formation of a common literary culture. Marulić wrote in the *čakavian* idiom of his area, but he borrowed also from the Croat version of Church Slavonic, from Dubrovnik authors who wrote in their local *štokavian* idiom, and from other *štokavian* dialects: in his eyes all were forms of the same language. The *štokavian* language of the Dubrovnik writers, on the other hand, came to be influenced by *čakavian* works produced in central Dalmatia, while writers in the Adriatic north and in Lika and Krbava – that is, in the area of confluence of *čakavian* and *kajkavian* speech – introduced *kajkavian* into their *čakavian* language. In the *kajkavian* area around Zagreb, literature in the vernacular that appeared in the early fifteenth century was written in Glagolica and contained *čakavian* elements; and the Ottoman-induced migrations further strengthened *čakavian* intrusions into *kajkavian*. Given the initial dominance of central Dalmatia, it seemed at first that *čakavian,* fertilised by additions from the other two idiomatic sets, would supply a nationwide standard language; but this contingency was ultimately checked by Venice's administration of Dalmatia, and by the spatial and economic decline of the Dalmatian cities (other than Dubrovnik) caused by the Ottoman invasion.

The Protestant translators of the sixteenth century came from the *čakavian* area, but they wished to produce a Bible comprehensible to all, so they continued the existing tradition of using a language that included all three idioms. The Croat Protestant Bible, had it survived, could have played the same role in forging linguistic unity in Croatia as its counterpart had done in Germany or England; but despite the fact that leading Croatian magnates had endorsed the reformed religion, Habsburg Croatia remained an overwhelmingly Catholic land. The Zrinski cancelled the church tithe, expelled the Catholic clergy from their Čakovec estates, and replaced them with Protestant pastors and preachers. Ungnad's brother-in-law Peter Erdödy, ban of Croatia (1557–67), helped with the distribution of the works published in Urach, disregarding the protests of the Croatian parliament and the bishop of Zagreb. Yet the appeals sent out by Ungnad's sons after his death elicited no adequate response, and the Biblical Office had to close down because of lack of funds.[37] Much of the typographical wealth of the Urach office ended up in Rome, where it became the property of the Congregation for the Propagation of Faith, the famous Propaganda Fide established in 1622 by Markantun Dominis's friend, Pope Gregory XV, to coordinate the international evangelical efforts of the Catholic Church, and of the Jesuits in particular. Of the 25,000 books published in Urach, only 1 per cent survived the Counter-Reformation. Nevertheless, the approach adopted by the Croat translators at Urach of forging a standard language based on all three Croat idioms continued to be pursued by scholars meeting

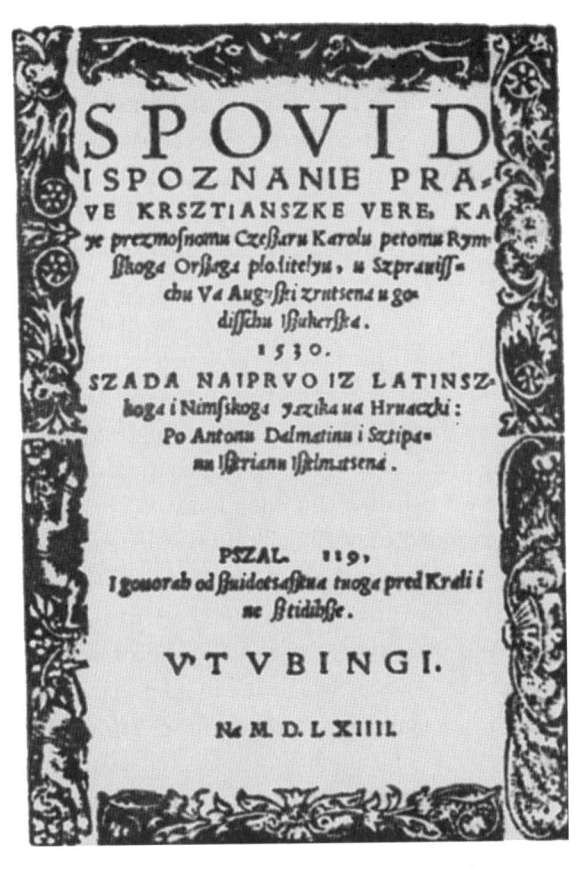

The Augsburg Confession, translated into Croat by Anton
Dalmatin and Stipan Istranin, 1564

at the Zrinski-Frankapan court in Ozalj, an area which itself embraced all three. This was perceived as a national necessity, given that 'our language [i.e. nation] is scattered among many states'.[38]

The person most credited with keeping Protestantism out of the key area of the Zagreb county was George Drašković (1525–87), who as bishop of Zagreb created his own humanist circle as well as a seminary for training a new generation of priests. He was born in the vicinity of Knin into a family that belonged among the oldest in Croatia: his father took part in the 1527 assembly which elected Ferdinand king of Croatia. The family had to flee their estates, however, in the face of the Ottoman advance. Having become utterly destitute, they settled on the Zrinski manor where the fortress of Karlovac would later be built. They were helped by their relative Bishop (later Cardinal) George Utišenić from Skradin, who began his career at the court of Matthias Corvinus and, after filling some of the highest posts at the court of John Zapolya, joined the new Croatian king, Ferdinand Habsburg. Utišenić provided an excellent education for all his nephews, thus laying the foundations for the family's ascendency. The Drašković, known for their loyalty to the Habsburg dynasty and their Catholic orthodoxy, became one of the leading families in Croatia, supplying a number of royal and imperial court officials, Croatian bans and Hungarian palatines, generals and prelates.

George himself was sent to study in Cracow and Vienna and finally Padua, where he composed his first work, which contested Calvin's views on the Eucharist. He became secretary to Emperor-King Ferdinand, and accompanied him to the imperial assembly at Augsburg in 1555, where he played a moderating role. Drašković also attended the last year of the Council of Trent, this time on behalf of the kingdoms of Hungary and Croatia; characteristically he signed the Council's decrees by adding *Croatus* to his name. In that same year, 1563, the year of publication of the Croat Protestant Bible, he relinquished his title of bishop of Pécs to his schoolfriend and fellow humanist Andrew Dudić,[39] in order to become bishop of Zagreb and soon after also ban – a post which at times he shared with others.[40] A committed Catholic yet a great supporter of church reform, what concerned him most was the issue of church unity, for the sake of which he had sought compromise with the Protestants. He argued for tolerance towards those who disagreed, but was also diligent in implementing the Tridentine decisions in his diocese and countering Protestant beliefs. One consequence of his success was the consolidation of Latin at the expense of his native language in the churches of the Zagreb diocese.

The Catholic Croat Bible

Following the collapse of the doomed Protestant effort, the task of producing the Bible in Croat was assumed by the Jesuits. Croatian parishes, and especially the Glagolitic ones, were at this time faced with the problem of the lack of liturgical and other religious books in the vernacular, made worse by the fact that after the Council of Trent, with its strict attitude towards religious texts, new and corrected books were slow in arriving while the old books were falling apart because of incessant use.[41] Following the repeated request of the Croatian clergy to be given new and corrected religious books, in 1599 Claudio Acquaviva, the superior general of the Jesuit Order, instructed Bartol Kašić from the island of Pag to write a Croat grammar for use in the Illyrian College at Loreto. Kašić, like Dominis, had been educated at the college, and after additional study in Rome joined the Jesuit order. His Croat grammar, based on the organising principles of the Latin language, was published in Rome in 1604 under the title *Foundations of the Illyrian Language*. Kašić was a *čakavian* speaker, however, and the grammar he produced was based on the *čakavian* idiom, albeit with a significant presence of *štokavian* elements. But he spent the next several years living in Dubrovnik, as well as travelling through Ottoman Bosnia, Slavonia and Serbia, which made him aware of the great spread of the *štokavian* idiom. In 1622, the year of the establishment of Propaganda Fide, he began to translate the New Testament into the *štokavian* or 'Illyrian' idiom, after which he was asked to translate the whole Bible. The translation was completed by 1637 and submitted to the Propaganda, which decided against its publication, however, on the grounds that it was 'not expedient that a version of the Holy Scriptures in the vernacular Illyrian language [and] in Latin script be published'.[42] What the Propaganda needed, or thought it should have, was a Bible and other religious literature in 'the Slav literary language' – meaning Church Slavonic – that could be used throughout the Orthodox Slav world. Given the nature of this project, the 'Illyrian' vernacular – and indeed any Slav vernacular – was ruled out in favour of Church Slavonic as used in the churches of Ukraine and Russia, which was perceived to be the oldest version, or the least corrupted by common speech, of the language used by 'the apostle to the Slavs' St Cyril. In the Propaganda's view, furthermore, the vernacular suffered from genetic instability (that is, constant change) as well as from dialectal differences. And there was also the lack of a unified orthography for the 'Illyrian' language written in the Latin script. Kašić's Bible was thus set aside.[43] This unfortunate decision was made at a time when a host of books written in the Croat vernacular and in Latin script were being published in Venice.

With the Latin script ruled out, it was a matter of choosing between the Glagolitic and the Cyrillic scripts. After some struggle between the pro-Glagolica camp, made up largely of Dalmatians, and the pro-Cyrillic camp, dominated by Ukrainian Uniate clerics, the commission set up to consider the alternatives eventually decided to publish liturgical books in both scripts. As it turned out, the hope that the 'schismatics' would prefer the Roman rite on the grounds that it was simpler, more beautiful and more dynamic than the Greek rite proved largely unfounded. The decision also left the Croatian Glagolitic clergy with Russified liturgical books that were quite useless to them. Although Kašić lost the argument over the Bible, he was nevertheless asked by the Propaganda to produce a Croat translation of the Roman rite.

RITVAL RIMSKI

ISTOMACCEN SLOVINSKI
po Bartolomeu Kaſsichiu Popu Bogoslovçu od Druxbæ Yeſuſovæ Penitençiru Apoſtolskomu.

V R I I M V, Iz Vtieſteniçæ Sfet : Skuppa od Razplodyenya S. Vierræ. 1640.

Ritual rimski by Bartol Kašić, 1640

He again used *štokavian* and the Latin script, this time strongly resisting the Propaganda's desire to have it published in Glagolica. His *Ritual rimski*, published in 1640, was used in churches throughout Croatia until 1929, when a new translation came out in Zagreb based on its predecessor.[44] By bringing *štokavian* into all Croatian parishes, *Ritual rimski* tilted the balance in favour of this idiom as the basis of the Croat standard.

The seventeenth century was a turning point in the formation of the national standard language, precisely because – under pressure of the Reformation and Catholic Renewal – literacy started to spread beyond the educated elite to embrace wider social strata. The need to give the popular language a uniform structure now became paramount. Those concerned with the standardisation of the Croat language had to grapple, however, with its historical and cultural singularity – its three-pronged dialectal form. There were only two ways in which a uniform norm could be achieved – by using elements of all three dialects, or by choosing one of them as the basis. The translators of the Croat Protestant Bible sought an integration all three idioms, and the same approach was pursued later by scholars gathered at Peter Zrinski's Ozalj. The area of Ozalj, which included part of the Military Border, was ideally suited for this, because of its location at the confluence of all three idioms. The activity of the Ozalj circle ended, however, with Peter's execution. The suppression of Protestantism on the one hand, and the destruction of the pivotal Zrinski-Frankapan family on the other, precluded the possibility of an inter-dialect becoming the national standard. The virtual disappearance of literature in *čakavian* by this time, moreover, had encouraged the emergence of two poles of literary production: self-governing *štokavian* Dubrovnik in the south and the *kajkavian*-speaking Zagreb area in the north. Nevertheless, the *čakavian* Glagolitic religious and vernacular literature of the earlier period had bequeathed a permanent heritage to both these idioms, in the form of common lexical and stylistic foundations that remained characteristic of the Croat language.

In order to understand the role of the early religious literature in maintaining this linguistic unity, it is necessary to return briefly to the Biblical Office at Urach. Working closely with the Croat translators at Urach was Primož Trubar, a Slovene Protestant pastor from Carniola who was responsible for translating the New Testament into Slovene, and who consequently became known as 'the father of the Slovene language'. In 1559 Trubar was accused of having produced a heretical translation of the Bible. On the advice of Ungnad, he wrote to Maximilian – Ferdinand's heir and the Bohemian king – whose sympathies lay with the Protestants, asking him to have his work examined by competent authorities. Within a month a judgment arrived, written in Latin by an unnamed author, affirming Trubar's religious orthodoxy. The reviewer took the opportunity, however, to comment also on the quality of the translation. He complained that Trubar's language, while being Slav, was nevertheless 'confined solely to the lay language used in the provinces of Styria, Carniola and Carinthia', so that his Bible would not be of use to other Slavs, including 'the Illyrians and those in the Zagreb area'. Trubar, in other words, was criticised for having translated the Bible into the Slovene language. The reviewer, moreover, disapproved of Trubar's use of German words that had become assimilated into the Slovene language, and proposed Slav alternatives. Trubar was also taxed with relying on the German spelling of certain Slav sounds, rather than on the solutions prevalent in the Zagreb area. For the sorely tried Slovene translator, it was not necessary for the reviewer to state – which he did – that the Croat translation of the Bible would do the trick, in order to guess that his detractor was a Croat from Zagreb.

The reviewer, it later turned out, was Paul Skalić, a native speaker of *kajkavian* – which, in fact, has much in common with the Slovene language.[45] Responding to these charges, Trubar described Skalić as one of those Slavs who 'in religious matters behave like Croats, although their priests conduct Mass in Latin'. This, in Trubar's view, ruled him out as a qualified judge of his translation. Trubar defended his Slovene language with its German words on the grounds that this was how the local people spoke; he had intentionally chosen for his Bible the 'peasant Slovene language' rather than resorting to 'unusual Croat words or inventing new ones'. His own spelling, he argued, would be comprehensible also to German speakers, whereas the Croats, the Czechs and the Poles had adopted, in his view, an unnecessarily complicated spelling. This dispute, focused on the language of a Bible intended for the popular masses, highlights the fact that when it came to the written word, and to that of religious texts in particular, Slovenes and Croats were two different nations. Stable state borders and the cultures that developed within them had separated the Slovenes from the Croats just as firmly as they had united the Pannonian with the Mediterranean Croats.

The ultimate victory of *štokavian* over *kajkavian* as the basis for the national standard language was ensured in the eighteenth century with the incorporation of the overwhelmingly *štokavian* areas previously under Ottoman rule. The extensive literature of devotional texts which the Bosnian Franciscans translated into – or wrote in – *štokavian* for the education of their parishioners helped the literary tradition of the Dubrovnik republic to expand northwards, reaching by way of Bosnia deep into Slavonia. The Franciscans also ensured the dominance of the Latin over the Cyrillic script in Bosnia, so that use of the latter after the eighteenth century remained confined to Orthodox Serb communities, becoming known accordingly as the 'Serb script'. By 1728, when the Jesuit Ardellio della Bella published his *Dizionario italiano-latino-illirico*, *štokavian* had been confirmed as the

Croat language standard outside the *kajkavian* area.[46] Following Kašić's *Ritual rimski,* a most important role in its promotion was played by *The Pleasing Story of the Slav People* published by the Franciscan priest Andrija Kačić Miošić in Venice in 1756. This history in verse of past Slav kings and states, based in part on Venetian and Croatian documents and influenced by Mavro Orbini and Pavao Ritter Vitezović (of whom more below), was intended to make the overwhelmingly rural population of Dalmatia proud of their Croatian and Slav heritage.[47] Dedicated to 'farmers and shepherds', it proved hugely popular.

Croats as Slavs and Illyrians

In the eyes of the Roman world, the early Croatia was first of all a Slav land (Sclavinia, Sclavonia or Slavonia), the term Slav designating a people living in accordance with Slav laws and customs. Croat and Slav became synonyms as a result. When Pope John X writing in the tenth century addressed 'all the people inhabiting Slavonia and Dalmatia', the Slavonian-Dalmatian distinction referred not to ethnicity but to the different legal systems, one Slav and the other Roman, under which the people lived. As Slav Croatia and Byzantine Dalmatia grew together and legal differences between them diminished, the Slav name came to embrace also Dalmatia. In the early thirteenth century, for example, the French chronicler of the Fourth Crusade noted that Zadar was in 'Slavonia'. In 1351 the anti-Venetian bishop Nicholas Matafar called himself 'bishop of Zadar in Slavonia'. Marulić's French publisher, on the other hand, placed his native Split in 'Croatia'. The fifteenth-century Dubrovnik historian Louis Crijević Tuberon wrote that 'most of Dalmatia is in Croatia'. Croatia in his writings appears as Dalmatia's interior, extending to the river Drava beyond which lay the Hungarian Pannonia. In 1453 the pope established a hostel in Rome bearing St Jerome's name, for the use of pilgrims from the 'nation of Dalmatia and Slavonia', jointly defined as the 'Slav nation'.

The rediscovery of the ancient world by the humanists, however, encouraged the identification of Croatia with ancient Illyricum, so that Croats became known also as Illyrians. It was, in fact, the humanist scholar and bishop of Senj and Modruš, Nicholas (1427–80), himself born in Kotor, who introduced the concept of *natio Illyrica* into the European political vocabulary.[48] A translator working in Trogir in 1441 on a Croat text written in Glagolica stated that it was written in 'the Illyrian or Slav language and alphabet'. In 1490 the renowned humanist Enea Silvio Piccolomini, who became Pope Pius II, presented the Slavs as direct descendants of the ancient

St Jerome with the 'Illyrian' – Croatian and Bosnian – arms,
by Natale Bonifazio, sixteenth century

Illyrians. The college established at Loreto for training missionaries for work among the South Slavs became inevitably the 'Illyrian College'. When in 1589 Pope Sixtus V established a chapter for the church attached to the hostel of St Jerome in Rome, he named it 'Illyrian': according to the terms of foundation of the chapter, the canons had to be 'of Illyrian origin' or know 'the Illyrian language'.

Croatian scholars of the sixteenth and seventeenth centuries made their own contribution to the theory that Croats and other South Slavs were the original population of the area they now inhabited, that is, that they derived from ancient Illyrians. Vinko Pribojević argued in his history of the Slavs, published in 1532, that all Slavs – not only the Croats, but also the Czechs, the Poles and the Russians – derived from Dalmatia, which they had left under the leadership of three brothers called respectively Czech, Lech and Rus. Faust Vrančić's ancient Dalmatia stretched from the Adriatic to the Danube; but he limited 'contemporary' Dalmatia to the lands of the South Slavs – from which he excluded, however, the Slovene territories. Mavro Orbini, whose *Il Regno degli Slavi* came out in 1601, likewise upheld the view that the Slavs were the original population of Roman Illyricum. In 1652 Juraj Rattkay, a canon of the Zagreb cathedral chapter, incorporated this view into his history of Croatia, with the difference that he located the original birthplace of the three Slav brothers in Krapina, close to Zagreb. Ivan Zakmardi, deputy chief justice of Croatia in the middle of the seventeenth century, placed on the cabinet containing the Croatian state documents an inscription acclaiming Croatia as the cradle of the Czech and Polish kingdoms. There were those who argued otherwise, however. Juraj Križanić, an outstanding proponent of Slav cooperation active at this time, relied on contemporary scholarship to argue that the Slavs derived not from Roman Dalmatia, but from the territory of the ancient Slav Kingdom of Rus.

The educational and publishing activity of the Catholic Church in the era of Catholic Renewal needed, however, a more precise understanding of the term 'Illyrian'. When in the middle of the seventeenth century a clergyman of Slovene descent (whose father came from Trubar's Carniola) applied to join the chapter of the Illyrian or St Jerome church in Rome, his suitability for the post was contested by prominent Dalmatian scholars and clerics – such as Jeronim and Ivan Paštrić from Split[49] – on the grounds that Carniola was not an Illyrian land. Others, including even Križanić, argued that Slovenes were Illyrians because they were Slavs. The Sacra Romana Rota, the supreme papal court, had to decide, therefore, whether Carniola was part of Illyricum and the Slovenes part of the Illyrian nation. It was a judgment the importance of which went beyond the immediate case, since it involved a matter of principle: whether nationality pertained to territory rather than to language. The opposing sides based their arguments on a mass of geographical, historical and linguistic evidence.[50] The final verdict, reached in 1655, was that the contemporary Illyrian province properly speaking was 'Dalmatia, which is composed of Croatia, Bosnia and Slavonia and completely excludes Carinthia, Styria and Carniola'. The Zagreb canon Rattkay praised the decision of the papal court and criticised his friend Križanić for trying surreptitiously to introduce 'foreigners' into the Illyrian, meaning Croatian, nation. Ivan Lučić, whose *Kingdom of Dalmatia and Croatia* appeared ten years later, identified nationality even more closely with political territory. Like Križanić he also rejected the view that the Slavs were the original population of Dalmatia. While downplaying the ethnic unity of Croatia and Dalmatia in the past, he emphasised their political unity in history: it was not any common descent of their population, but rather their common political past that made Dalmatia and Croatia a single kingdom.

Contemporary attempts to fathom the origin of the Slavs, to deduce their movement in space and time, and to publish books understandable to as many Slavs as possible, led to the term 'Illyrian language' embracing all Slav languages. The *natio Illyrica* entrusted to the care of Propaganda Fide thus came to include all Slavs. In his bull of 1627 Pope Urban VIII stated that the people of the Illyrian tongue inhabited large parts of Europe and Asia, where they had once had flourishing states and kingdoms. Many of these had since been conquered by the Turks, while those that had not were in part infected by the 'poison' of the Eastern schismatics (that is, the Greek Orthodox Church) and the northern heretics (the Protestants). The duty of the Church was to remedy this situation. Impressed by the growing power of the Muscovy principality, whose rulers – convinced that they were direct descendants of the Roman emperor Augustus – now called themselves tsars, the Catholic Church sought ways of influencing this self-proclaimed Third Rome. Juraj Križanić was one of those entrusted by the Propaganda with the task of bringing Russia closer to Rome.[51]

Born into a minor noble family living on the Zrinski estate of Ozalj a decade after the Austro-Turkish peace of 1606 had concluded an exhausting thirteen-year war, Križanić grew up at a time when the Military Border had begun its transformation into a separate juridical area. This generational experience left him with strong anti-Ottoman as well as anti-German sentiments. Križanić attended the Jesuit college in Ljubljana and the universities of Graz and Bologna, after which he joined the Greek-Ruthenian (Ukrainian) College in Rome in order to prepare for missionary activity in Russia. As he understood his assignment, he was to work on the education and enlightenment of the Russian court as a necessary first step on the road to church unity; but he was also to encourage the tsar to undertake, with the help of other Christian kings, the liberation in particular of the Slavs living under Ottoman rule. Križanić believed that the Slavs formed a single ethnic family derived from the Russian area, which had once spoken the same language. This language had in the meantime become corrupted under the influence of foreign rule (though least so in his Ozalj homeland), but could be reformed through interaction of all its various idioms. Russia, fortunate because it alone was governed by native princes and spoke only the native language, embodied in his eyes 'the necessary external force' which, when applied, would enable the subject Slav nations, including his own Croat one, to regain their rightful place in Europe: 'He who prepared the Roman Empire to preach the gospels of our Eternal King can be considered to have chosen this new Muscovy principality as a light for the illumination of our wretched [Slav] peoples.'[52] As he wrote to the bishop of Zagreb, his work was dedicated to 'the glory of God and the good of our [Croatian] homeland'.

Križanić's Slavic ideology was thus born in reaction to foreign, in particular German, domination of the western Slavs. In one of his addresses to the Russian tsar he begged him to 'lift the German yoke from their necks'. Russia's historic mission was to help the Slav nations regain government by their own princes – in other words, to help them rid themselves of German and Turkish overlordship. The Slav nations would then find themselves united within the Catholic Church, although not unnecessarily subjected to the Roman rite and discipline. By reuniting the Christian world, the Slavs would help create a new society in which Church and State would work in close cooperation while remaining autonomous from one another. On his second visit to Russia in 1659, Križanić joined the court circle and sided with the Church reform being conducted by the tsar and the patriarch. For some reason, however, he was exiled in 1661 to Siberia, where he spent fifteen years. His long captivity did not prevent him from writing his magisterial *On Government,* an extensive treatise involving economy, geo-strategy and state policy, intended for Russia's rulers and designed to make Russia a great power, strong enough to free the subjected Slav nations. This work later became favourite reading for Peter the Great.[53] After his release from Siberia in 1677 Križanić ended up in Vilnius, where – wishing to return to Rome – he joined the army of the Polish king, Jan Sobieski, rushing to relieve the Ottoman siege of Vienna. He died within Vienna's walls in 1683, and was thus unable to witness the long awaited *reconquista* – undertaken not by Russia, however, but by western Christian powers united under the name of the Holy League – during the initial stages of which the armies of the hated German empire gained such impetus that at one point they appeared actually capable of expelling the Ottoman power from Europe.

Resurrected Croatia

This achievement encouraged the hope in the Croatian parliament that Croatia would regain not just eastern Slavonia, but also its old territory between the rivers Una and Vrbas; and that Leopold I might even be persuaded to push Venice out of Dalmatia. The expectation in the event remained unfulfilled; but the moment produced a vision of a reborn Croatia that would never again be lost. One of its early manifestations was the publication in 1700 of *Croatia Rediviva* by Pavao Ritter Vitezović, a Croat nobleman born into an assimilated Alsatian family Ritter (*Vitez* in Croat, hence Vitezović) that had settled in Senj, which at that time was governed by Peter Zrinski. Vitezović began his education at the Jesuit Academy in Zagreb, which he left at the high point of the Zrinski-Frankapan conspiracy. He was back in Zagreb in 1695, when he became head of the state printing press.[54] As a volunteer in the ban's army he took part the defence of Vienna, and after demobilisation was seconded by the Croatian parliament to represent its interests in the border commission set up after the Peace of Karlovci in 1699 and headed by the court official Luigi Ferdinando Marsigli, to which he delivered written submissions specifying the borders of 'all of Croatia'. *Croatia Rediviva*, or 'Resurrected Croatia', dedicated to Leopold I, was based on these documents.

According to the author, he 'undertook this great work in order to *resurrect* from the existing bloodied ashes the great *name* of Illyricum, of our Croatia [Slavonia], which in the course of never-ending changes during a long wartime had become suppressed and almost buried'.[55] Central to Vitezović's preoccupation was the status of the newly liberated parts of Dalmatia, which became the subject of prolonged negotiations between Vienna and Venice. Venice claimed all land that had ever been covered by the name Dalmatia, while Vienna sought to reduce the Venetian presence to a few Dalmatian cities, that is, Zadar, Šibenik, Trogir and Split. Vitezović relied a great deal on Lucić's history of Dalmatia and Croatia, but unlike Lucić he insisted that Dalmatia's separate identity was nothing but a Venetian ruse. This province, he argued, was and always had been an integral part of historic Croatia – hence, part of the Habsburg lands – having never had either defined borders or a ruler of its own. Dalmatia, in Vitezović's view, had died with Roman rule. This argument, of course, was welcomed by Marsigli – whose brief included 'the affirmation of our [Habsburg] claims' at Venetian expense – as well as by the Croatian Estates, who paid for the printing of his book. One of its telling features is that it does not even mention the detested Military Border.

Croatia Rediviva articulates a state-national ideology that rests on a close integration of legal history (the establishment, continuity and evolution of political institutions and law), culture (language, origin and customs) and territory. In this work, however, Vitezović followed the tradition that identified the Croats, and indeed all Slavs, with the Illyrians. Echoing the

Language and Literacy

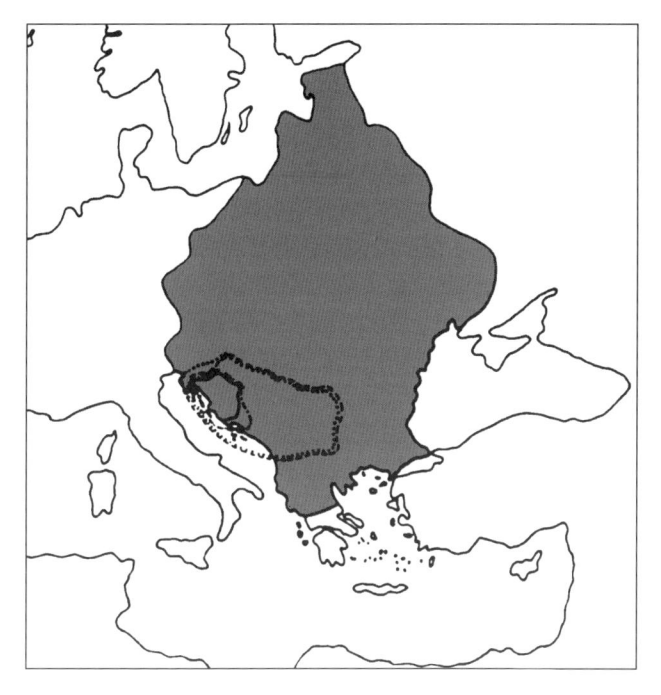

Pavao Ritter Vitezović's historical, Illyrian and Slav Croatias as they appear in his works

views of Pribojević and Rattkay, on the other hand, he assumed that all Slavs were descendants of Croats. He consequently imagined a Great Croatia that embraced all the lands which, according to different and often conflicting theories, the Slavs actually inhabited or had done in the past. The picture that emerges from his considerations is one of concentric circles, with an Inner Croatia – Croatia in its widest historical borders – at the centre, surrounded by the South Slav territories, and finally by Slav lands from the Baltic to the Black Sea. The second, South Slav, circle reflected in its extent the Habsburgs' original negotiating position vis-à-vis the Porte, the idea being that if and when they were gained they would be united with Croatia. This 'South Slav' Croatia to emerge in consequence of the Ottoman retreat from the Balkans, however, was not conceived as an exclusively Croat national territory, but rather as an overall name for the union of South Slav lands: it was, in other words, an Illyria called Croatia. After the Russian victory over Sweden in 1709, Vitezović, treading the same path as Križanić, invited Peter the Great to destroy the Ottoman Empire and seize Istanbul. In 1711 the Russian tsar did indeed for the first time in Russian history announce to 'Illyrian' Christians the start of a joint battle against the Ottomans.

Vitezović died in 1713 as an exile in Vienna, but his influence survived him, since his *Croatia Rediviva* was accepted not as a historical construction, but as a political programme.[56] Balthazar Krčelić, a canon of Zagreb cathedral, did much to propagate Vitezović's ideas in the eighteenth century, when the book was reprinted several times. In the early decades of the nineteenth century it would become the Bible of the Croatian national politics pursued under the name of the Illyrian movement. Ljudevit Gaj, one of the movement's main ideologues, exclaimed in 1848: 'Vitezović's task has been completed; Gaj's remains to be done.' What is characteristic of this shared Croat belief that the Slavs – and the South Slavs in particular – were a single people is that it did not involve denial of the differences that existed among them, nor did it entail the creation of a single Slav state. Its adherents counted on Slav solidarity to bring about the emancipation of the subject Slav nations; but how that solidarity was to be achieved – through Church union, adoption of a common literary language, mutual diplomatic support, or in relation to the Ottoman Empire's joint military action – was a matter of individual imagination.

Binding the nation with a common standard

By the end of the eighteenth century, standardisation of the language became an urgent task in view of the decision of the government in Vienna to reform the education system in Croatia-Slavonia. Language and grammar commissions were consequently set up, textbooks, dictionaries and grammars published. The primacy of *štokavian* was not challenged, but two problems remained to be solved. One was the problem of orthography. The other was the fact that *štokavian* itself was not a unified dialect, but contained three subdivisions – *ikavski, ijekavski* and *ekavski* – based on the reflexes of the Church Slavonic 'yat'. Most of the *štokavian* population of the kingdom spoke *ikavski*, but *ijekavski* was dominant in parts of the Military Border. The Serbs living in Croatia's eastern county of Srijem, on the other hand, spoke *ekavski*. The writers of the Dubrovnik circle, however, used *ijekavski*, which in the end proved decisive for the Croat literary standard.

Writers who addressed the *ikavski* population of Dalmatia and Slavonia wrote in *ikavski*. Since the previous Ottoman period had produced no secular literature in the native language, however, they had to rely on *štokavian* literature published elsewhere, mostly in Dubrovnik, and this brought in the *ijekavski* idiom. As Slavonia became integrated with western Croatia, its writers also introduced elements of *kajkavian*, but by this time fascination with the *štokavian* Dubrovnik literature had gripped central Croatia, and this worked to the detriment not only of *ikavski* but also of *kajkavian*. At the start of the nineteenth century Joakim Stulli, a Franciscan priest, published a three-volume Latin-Italian-Illyrian dictionary based on *ijekavski štokavian*, with the support of the French governor of Dalmatia, Marshall Marmont, and the Croato-Hungarian king and German emperor, Joseph II. A native of Dubrovnik, Stulli took words not only from the spoken language and from written works, but also from Church Slavonic; Russian, Polish and Czech. Russian imports were used with the Orthodox population in mind. Up to the eighteenth century Serb literature, overwhelmingly religious in nature, was written in the Serb variant of Old Church Slavonic; at the start of the eighteenth century, however, the Serbs who settled in southern Hungary invited in Russian teachers to make up for the absence of their own, and these brought with them books written in the new Russian literary language, based on a reformed Russian Church Slavonic. As a result, Serb literature in the eighteenth century was written in a mixture of Serb Church Slavonic, Russian Church Slavonic, and Serb and Russian vernacular forms. The hybrid was called *slovenosrpski* or Slavo-Serb.

There was also a growing convergence in the field of orthography. The Franciscans trained at the Illyrian College brought to Slavonia and southern Hungary the Italian orthographic tradition, while the Jesuits from the *kajkavian* Zagreb area used the Hungarian-style spelling. The two wings of the Catholic Renewal used in fact a mixed approach, and by constant experimentation produced a Slavonian spelling system that was simple and consistent, and which became used also in the Military Border. It was Zagreb in the end – or rather the nationally minded politicians and intellectuals who in the first half of the nineteenth century formed the Illyrian movement – which not only affirmed the primacy of the *štokavian-ijekavian* dialect as the Croatian literary language, but also produced a new system of spelling by recourse to the diacritics used by western Slavs and favoured by a number of their predecessors, including Vitezović.

Their approach did not pass unchallenged, however. The *kajkavian* area was far smaller than the *štokavian*, but it had been the centre of the Croatian state and politics since the sixteenth century. To Canon Ignac Kristijanović, a talented writer and one of the staunchest defenders of *kajkavian*, language belonged to the people and could not be changed at will and from above. With Zagreb determined to uphold *štokavian*, the *kajkavian* reaction was soon swept aside. But the resistance offered by supporters of the *ikavski* subdialect proved more serious, and involved two arguments. One was that most *štokavian* Croats spoke *ikavski*. The other was that the Dubrovnik idiom was too 'artificial', too distant from the speech of the popular masses: if the nation was to be unified, the popular *ikavski* not the literary Dubrovnik language should be adopted as the standard. This was the view of Šime Starčević, a clergyman from Lika whose *Illyrian-French Dictionary* appeared on the eve of Austria's seizure of the French Illyrian Provinces. Lika, however, could not mount an effective challenge to Zagreb. Far more dangerous proved to be the Dalmatians' response, articulated by Ante Kuzmanić from Split, editor of *Zora dalmatinska* (Dalmatian Dawn) published in Zadar. The application for permission to publish this journal submitted in 1842 to the Dalmatian government stated that it would be published in the Croat language, since the people called themselves Croat – as opposed to 'Illyrian' or 'Slav', which were names invented by intellectuals.[57] To mould Dalmatia in a pattern decided in Zagreb was, in Kuzmanić's view, sheer arrogance: compared to the 'brilliant Latin civilisation of Dalmatia', northern Croatia epitomised an essentially rural culture. But when the Dalmatian clergy accepted the Zagreb language reform, the already weakened resistance of Kuzmanić and his supporters was ended. For it was not that these Dalmatians sought to keep Dalmatia apart from Croatia. On the contrary. The northern Croats were to them 'our brothers', people who 'remember the crown of Krešimir and Zvonimir'. The unification of 'the three sisters Croatia, Slavonia and Dalmatia will restore vitality to the Croatian crown', Kuzamnić argued, and thereby permit the Croats to be the agents of their own freedom.[58]

The Croat language had by this time lost its former tri-scriptural appearance in favour of the Latin script. It now seemed on the verge of losing also its dialectal complexity, but this did not happen. The adoption of the *štokavian* dialect thus did not amount to a complete break with past literary production, so that the Croat language, despite the dominance of *štokavian*, remained in essence an inter-dialectal formation.

SIX

The Politics of State Right

The close cooperation with Hungary pursued by Croatia during the seventeenth century came to an abrupt end with the collapse of the magnate conspiracy in 1671. The religious conflict had already taken its toll: in 1606, when the Hungarian parliament had voted that the edict on Protestant toleration negotiated with King Rudolf (1576–1608) should apply also to Croatia, the Croatian Estates had warned the king that failure to respect their will would lead them to reconsider the union with Hungary. Croatia's Catholic probity and absence of significant rebellion now meant that it was not punished like Hungary: during the 'dark decade' of 1671–81 when Hungary came to be governed by diktat, the Croatian parliament continued to meet regularly. Croatia's alienation from Hungary increased further with the Rákóczi rebellion in Hungary, which lasted from 1703 to 1711: the Zrinski-Frankapan anti-Habsburg revolt notwithstanding, the Croatian Estates had always found it hard to contemplate Croatia's separation from Austria.

The adoption of a new political orientation based on loyalty to the Habsburg dynasty was made easier by the fact that the disappearance of the two most powerful magnate families allowed the middle nobility to gain greater influence in parliament. The Croatian gentry had grown in size during the seventeenth century by recruitment from the wealthy peasantry and burger class. This social layer, stiffened by the arrival of industrious self-made men, saw Croatia as a self-governing kingdom headed by the king, and insisted that in legal matters it should be treated separately from Hungary. Vitezović's works, with their integration of the Croatian state tradition and cultural formation, were a condensed expression of this vision. Guided by a strong quest for territorial and political unification, the Croatian parliament asked in 1700 for the return of the newly liberated areas, as well as for the right to be consulted about appointments in the Border army. Croatia's autonomy from Hungary, on the other hand, demanded also the acquisition of its own church hierarchy. In 1701 the bishop of Zagreb asked that 'Lower Slavonia', that is, the regained portion of historic Slavonia, be included into his diocese, which provoked a conflict with the Hungarian bishop of Pécs; and in 1709 his successor requested that the Zagreb bishopric be made into an archdiocese. Hungarian opposition proved too strong, however, and both requests were declined.

The conflict over church jurisdiction in Slavonia, with its implications for Slavonia's eventual incorporation to Croatia rather than Hungary, took place immediately after the Croatian parliament had decided to send its representatives to the Hungarian parliament as a form of insurance that the liberated lands would be reincorporated into Croatia as one of the lands of the Hungarian crown: Croatia and Hungary both relied on the argument of historic right to territories earlier lost to the Ottomans, in order to assert their exclusive jurisdiction over them. Vienna, on the other hand, appealed to *ius belli* in defence of the king's unquestioned right to their government and disposal – although it too used the argument of historic right in its negotiations with Venice and the Ottoman Empire. The new institutional link between the Croatian and Hungarian parliaments, on the other hand, only encouraged the latter in the belief that it had the right to legislate also for Croatia. Whenever the interests of the two kingdoms clashed and Hungary tried to impose its will on its weaker partner, the Croatian Estates' only recourse was to rely on the king to protect their state interest.

The disappearance of the Ottoman threat had in fact removed the main motive for the old cooperation between Croatia and Hungary, which would henceforth be replaced by increased confrontation. The disparity in their size and in the wealth of their landowning class became if anything more pronounced in the post-Ottoman period. Hungary's struggle with Vienna over the reincorporation of the newly liberated territories was combined with the desire of its parliament to unify all the lands of the Hungarian crown under its authority. This, and the fact that it denied Croatia's right to eastern Slavonia, strengthened Zagreb in its determination to negotiate directly with the court in Vienna. The thrust towards disengagement from the framework of the Hungarian crown reached a high point in 1712, when the Croatian Estates once again asserted their right to choose their king independently of Hungary. The opportunity was provided by the Habsburgs' own need to clarify the order of succession within the family. In 1687 the Estates of Hungary and Croatia had been persuaded by Leopold I to accept automatic Habsburg hereditary succession in the male line, following which Leopold's elder son Joseph was crowned King of Hungary and Croatia. When Joseph died in 1711 leaving no male heir he was succeeded by his brother Charles, who wished to make his line on both the male and the female sides have legal precedence over Joseph's. The succession law of 1687, however, did not recognise inheritance in the female line, and consequently left open to Croatia and Hungary the right to choose their king from another dynasty in the eventual absence of a male heir.

Croatia now seized its chance. In 1712, acting on the advice of the bishop of Zagreb, Emeric Esterházy, upheld by a strong lobby led by the influential magnate Ivan Drašković, the Croatian Estates – guided, as they insisted, by the care and desire to safeguard their homeland from the threats that sometimes accompany 'the dangerous times of interregna', but also in order to win greater sympathy and a more benevolent attitude on the part of the dynasty – decided that the original terms of 1527 (when Ferdinand Habsburg was elected King of Croatia) would apply also to the female line: that is, that they would accept as their king the person of either gender who legally succeeded to the rule of Inner Austria.[1] This decision was conveyed to Charles on the eve of his coronation as King of Croatia and Hungary, in the form of an address stressing that Croatia was and always had been at liberty to choose its kings independently of Hungary. The sabor informed the future king that, although Croatia was associated with Hungary, 'we are not its subjects'; and that Croatia had once had its own kings. The address stressed: 'No power, no enslavement subjected us to the Hungarians – we have of our own free will subjected ourselves to their kings, not to their kingdom. We shall continue to recognise their king [i.e. remain linked to Hungary] only while he rules in Austria.' So, as far as the parliament was concerned, Croatia was united with Hungary only in the person of the monarch, and even then only on condition that he or she ruled also in Austria: for Croatia, its relationship to Austria was more important than its relationship to Hungary. Croatia's decision was welcomed in Vienna as a way of putting additional pressure on Hungary, which made clear that it itself favoured no change. Not wishing to alienate Hungary, the aspirant king did not sign the Croatian parliament's decision as a law, promising instead to protect the kingdom's traditional liberties and privileges. Charles III (1711–40) was consequently crowned King of Croatia and Hungary on the basis of the 1687 provision. Nevertheless, the fact that Croatia accepted the new arrangement freely and separately from Hungary boosted the Croatian Estates' sense of independence.

What happened next was of the greatest importance for the future relationship between Croatia, Austria and Hungary. In 1713 Emperor Charles VI (King Charles III in Croatia and Hungary), acting as head of the dynasty and Holy Roman Emperor, issued a declaration known as the Pragmatic Sanction, which specified a common order of succession for all the lands ruled by the dynasty in its capacity as the sovereign house in Austria. According to this, the family possessions would pass, in primogeniture, first to Charles's male issue; in default of that to his female issue; and in default of that again to Joseph's line, in the same order of precedence. In the lands of the Hungarian crown, the Pragmatic Sanction was adopted first by Croatia (1712), followed by the Free City of Rijeka (1720), Transylvania (1722) and finally also Hungary (1722–3). This settlement, in which the House of Austria appears as a constitutive factor in its own right, created the Habsburg Monarchy – a new power embracing the largest European territory outside Russia.[2]

By contrast with the Monarchy's western lands, where the Pragmatic Sanction was a unilateral imperial declaration (though subsequently ratified by the regional parliaments), its adoption by Hungary rested on a compromise between the king and the Estates. The Hungarian parliament, with Croatia's participation, accepted the Pragmatic Sanction and with it the lasting unity of Hungary with Austria – but in a form that asserted also the lasting unity of the lands of the Hungarian crown. The reason for Croatia's acquiescence to this affirmation of the permanence of its union with Hungary becomes clear when one considers the terms of the Hungarian version of the Pragmatic Sanction. These obliged the monarch to respect the constitutional set-up and territorial integrity of the lands of the Hungarian crown, and in particular to reintegrate the liberated lands into the respective kingdoms. The Pragmatic Sanction was passed into law in a manner that confirmed the Monarchy's constitution as a complex of distinct historical-territorial units. At the same time, however, the different way in which the sanction was adopted across the Monarchy established also a clear line of division between the eastern, or Hungarian, crown lands – made up of the kingdoms of Hungary and Croatia (including Rijeka) and the principality of Transylvania – and the western or 'Austrian' lands, consisting of the kingdom of Bohemia (with its associates Moravia and Silesia) and the Habsburg hereditary and other lands.

Once Hungary had accepted a lasting union with Austria, Croatia's link with the former would be used to compensate for the weakness of its nobility, who were faced with a growing royal absolutism whose power now took also a military form, given that the two kingdoms had accepted in 1715 the stationing of the regular army on their territory. This had been justified at the time by defence needs; but once the Pragmatic Sanction became law, the king's army acted also as its guarantor. The fact that this army was able to conduct exercises without prior permission from the Croatian ban or the Hungarian palatine made it a permanent threat to any resurgence of disloyalty to the king in Vienna. At the same time, the Hungarian parliament's repeated attempts to assert its authority in Croatia were resisted by the sabor's appeals to the king, who – wishing to keep Hungary out of the Military Border – as a rule refused to sanction those decisions of the Hungarian parliament perceived to be injurious to Croatia's constitutional autonomy. Croatia's balancing act between the two powers could not be sustained during the eighteenth century, however, when – reacting against the centralising, unifying and modernising drive that earmarked the rule of Maria Theresa (1740–80) and Joseph II (1780–90) – it turned once again towards Hungary. It was thus not Hungarian but Habsburg power that bound Croatia more firmly to Hungary.

The change occurred in the first instance at the level of the central state organs, whose growing importance weakened the prerogatives of the ban and sabor in matter of internal administration, including the dispensation of justice and collection of taxes, in favour of central bodies concerned with the lands of the Hungarian crown. One of these was a Vienna-based Croatian court council, created in 1767 by Maria Theresa and entrusted with the collection of taxes as well as the administration of the district of Rijeka. Three decades later, however, this body was dissolved as a cost-cutting exercise, and its responsibilities transferred to the similarly Vienna-based Hungarian court council. The Rijeka district was at the same time attached to the Hungarian crown as a *corpus separatum,* in order to keep Rijeka – formerly a Habsburg family possession – out of reach of both Croatia and Hungary. When Joseph II succeeded Maria Theresa, he created a new territorial unit made up of the district of Rijeka and the old Zrinski possessions of Bakar and Vinodol, which he likewise placed under the control of the Hungarian court council. The centralisation of the government of Croatia in the hands of state bodies located in Vienna consequently now included its military and civilian parts alike.

These administrative reforms did not at first change the relationship between Hungary and Croatia. During the eighteenth century Croatia's parliamentary connection with Hungary, and the existence of common court bodies, were not incompatible with Croatia's standing as an autonomous state, since the Hungarian parliament did not legislate for it: as a rule, agreement on issues of common concern were reached by consensus in the upper house of the joint parliament. It was possible for the Croatian sabor to refuse to communicate with the Hungarian court bodies, on the grounds that Croatia was not part of the Hungarian kingdom. The sabor, indeed, repeatedly rejected the right of the Hungarian court council to interfere in Croatian internal affairs. What finally tipped the established balance were the Josephine reforms enacted at the end of the eighteenth century, which abolished the last vestiges of the Estates' self-government.

The belief that the Habsburg Monarchy was in need of urgent and comprehensive economic and governmental reforms grew in the wake of the serious military and political setbacks it suffered in the first half of the eighteenth century, including the loss to Prussia during the War of the Austrian Succession (1740–48) of Silesia, a land of strategic importance for Austria's position within the German empire; and the temporary loss in 1742 of the imperial title to Bavaria, whereupon much of the Bohemian nobility had defected to the new emperor. During the Seven Years War (1756–63) Vienna failed to regain Silesia, despite support provided by Russia and France. Convinced of the need for a radical, indeed revolutionary, change, Joseph II emancipated the serfs, dissolved the monasteries, proclaimed religious tolerance, introduced an advanced penal code and reformed the working of the law courts. A new professional civil service came to the fore, secular primary education was made compulsory, and church affairs made the concern of the state. Not only did the central state assume the right to collect taxes, but also – as a final and necessary act – the traditional exemption from taxation enjoyed by the Croatian and Hungarian nobility was abolished. Emancipation of the serfs and the threat of taxation compounded the fears of the nobilities on both sides of the Drava, and led to their open revolt.

Joseph II saw no difference between provinces understood as administrative units and territorially organised political entities such as Croatia and Hungary. He refused to be crowned separately in Croatia-Hungary, or to convene their parliaments. In a final push to create an effective modern government for all of his realm, he suspended the traditional county system run by the local nobility, replacing it with districts or 'circles' run by royal officials responsible to the Hungarian court council in Vienna, which he now invested with full authority in financial matters regarding the eastern half of the monarchy. This new, vertically organised chain of government created by Joseph II for Hungary and Croatia unified for the first time the lands of the Hungarian crown, and made them simultaneously autonomous from the rest of the Monarchy. Reacting against these measures, the Croatian

Joseph II as a ploughman

parliament moved paradoxically in the same direction. Mindful of the army in the Military Border and conscious of Hungary's far greater capacity of resistance, it enacted in 1790 a series of measures strengthening Croatia's link with Hungary. Having rejected this in the past, the Estates now voted to accept the competence of the Hungarian court council in Croatian internal affairs, including taxation, albeit for a limited period – that is, until the reincorporation of the Military Border, Venetian Dalmatia and the Croatian lands still under Ottoman rule (this was the time of a renewed war with the Ottoman Empire). The Hungarian Estates accepted this proposal, but, despite the sabor's protests, removed all reference to the temporary nature of the arrangement.

The sabor repeated its old positions that the union of Croatia and Hungary was a voluntary one, and that neither kingdom could make laws binding the other without its consent. At the same time, however, it took the momentous decision to allow the joint diet (i.e. the Hungarian parliament sitting together with Croatia's representatives) to decide on matters of common interest, including taxation, which up to then had been the sabor's exclusive prerogative. It qualified this move subsequently by specifying that the taxation of Croatia was a matter to be decided solely between the king and the Croatian delegation to the joint parliament, and that it preserved the right to decide autonomously on all issues relating to internal government. But the Hungarian majority took no notice of this evasion. The sabor, in fact, placed these decisions within the context of an effective federalisation of the two kingdoms, proposing that affairs of common interest should be run by a senate elected by the two parliaments, and that a joint body should also be set up to administer the Military Border. The language of the army of the border was to be Croat, though, while the army would be obliged to swear not only the customary loyalty to the king, but also loyalty to the Croatian nation.[3] The earlier authority of the ban was to be restored through the Croatian parliament regaining its old right to nominate candidates for the post, and through returning to the ban the right to convene the sabor without prior royal permission. These proposals, however, were rejected by the Hungarian parliament, this time with royal support. Since the concept of 'common affairs' was not specified in the Croatian proposals, they were in the end reduced to the affairs handled by the Hungarian court council. At this stage the council was little more than a royal executive organ; so long as the executive power was in royal hands, Croatian self-government was unaffected by the existence of joint offices with Hungary. This would change, however, in the first half of the nineteenth century, when the Hungarian court council transformed itself into a Hungarian national government, which sought to appropriate for itself most of the rights previously held by the king in person, or exercised through other bodies set up in Vienna.

Joseph's difficulties mounted in the meantime. In 1789, the year of the French Revolution, the Austrian Netherlands (modern Belgium) rebelled against the government in Vienna at the same time as Joseph was losing the war against the Ottoman Empire that he had joined the previous year as a Russian ally. Before he died in 1790 he was forced to rescind most of his measures except for the emancipation of the peasantry, church reform and religious tolerance. His successor, Leopold II (1790–92), began his reign by returning to constitutional rule, whereupon the Hungarian and Croatian parliaments revoked the laws dealing with peasant emancipation and taxation of noble land. The collapse of the Josephine system re-established also the old status quo in the legal relationship between Croatia and Hungary, since none of the decisions detailed above had been confirmed by the king. Resistance to a common foe had brought the two closer than ever before, but they moved apart as soon as the immediate danger was removed.

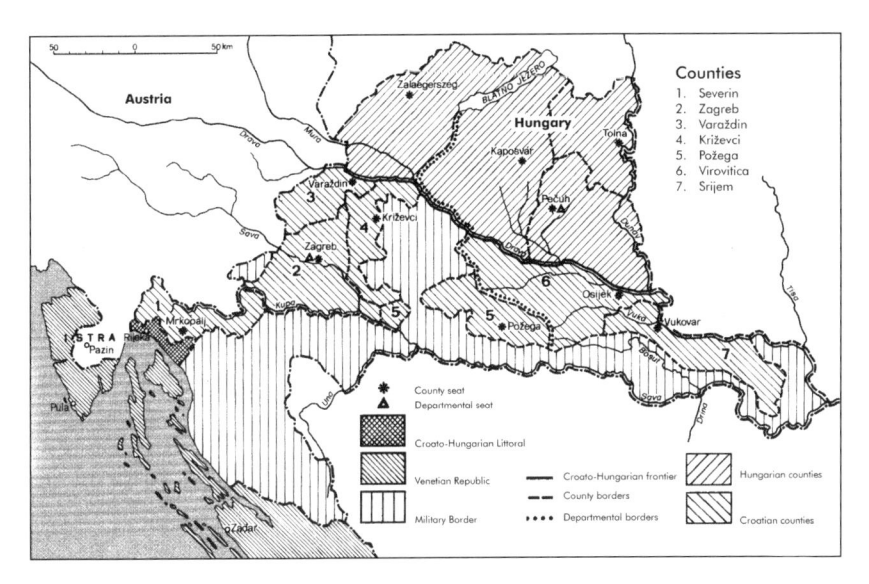

Ban's Croatia, 1785

Differences between Hungary and Croatia would henceforth only grow in scope and intensity, and with the return of parliamentary life they could be openly aired.

The essential conflict involved the alleged legal rights of the two kingdoms, or more precisely the nature and extent of the authority of their respective parliaments. It was an old issue which was now brought to bear on the political status of Slavonia, which both kingdoms claimed for themselves, as well as the governance of Rijeka. It involved also, however, the novel problem of language. Joseph II had opened the language issue with his decree of 1784, which made German the language of state administration throughout the Habsburg Monarchy on the grounds that this was the language of his most advanced lands. The decree was rescinded by Leopold II, but the 'Pandora's box of multinational discontent'[4] could no longer be closed. The non-German nationalities refused to accept the pre-eminence of the German language, and into the struggle was added the question as to which language should replace Latin in the public life of the Monarchy's disparate lands. The struggle would be embittered by the fact that in much of the Monarchy the nation of Estates and the nation of language did not as a rule coincide. It did so in Croatia, though, where the congruence of the legal and the linguistic nation would decide the form of political struggle during much of the nineteenth century.

The conflict between Hungary and Croatia over state, territory and language was waged in the first instance in legal and constitutional terms, but also and increasingly at the symbolic level. In the early nineteenth century the Hungarian Estates dropped the customary term 'holy crown' in favour of 'St Stephen's crown', in order to emphasise its Hungarian origin; to distinguish it as much as possible from the Habsburg imperial crown; and to remove all implicit reference to Croatia's distinct statehood. The Croatians similarly sought to defend their positions by reference to 'Zvonimir's crown'. Hungary would henceforth concentrate on merging the 'lands of St Stephen's crown' under the auspices of the Hungarian parliament, Croatia on escaping this embrace and (re)uniting the 'lands of Zvonimir's crown'. The Hungarian project insisted on unity of the Hungarian crown lands, the Croatian on their differences. Each side appealed to the historic legitimacy of their claims, encapsulated in the concept of state right.

Nationhood as a medieval inheritance

In the political vocabulary of the eighteenth century, the Croats were a nation because Croatia was a kingdom: they were a nation bounded by the laws of the kingdom. Being in possession of a national nobility, the Croats were thus one of the Habsburg Monarchy's six 'historical nations' (along with the Germans, the Czechs, the Poles, the Hungarians and the Italians), that is, a national group defined primarily as a political-territorial category, by contrast with those of the Monarchy's peoples (Slovaks, Slovenes, Serbs, Romanians and others) who did not possess an upper social layer that had traditionally enjoyed state-political privileges. This distinction between 'historical' and 'non-historical' nations reflected the constitution of the Habsburg Monarchy, which had developed as a union of state-like entities, such as kingdoms, principalities, duchies and so on.

This concept of the nation was hence a political not an ethnic category, expressing the unity of state, territory and political representation. Croatian state right insisted on the political and territorial unity of the Croatian lands in the same way that Bohemian state right insisted on the unity of the lands of the Bohemian crown, or Hungarian state right on the indivisibility of the lands of the Hungarian crown. Each of these state rights involved historical and legal arguments, and each was contested by a variety of other claims, including those raised within the component lands. The Croatian policy of state right rested on two axioms: the kingdom's political individuality, rooted in the sovereignty of the Estates which, together with the king, formed the 'political nation'; and its territorial integrity. As in the kingdoms of Bohemia and Hungary at this time, the Croatian politics of state right emanated from the conviction that the rights of the kingdom and of its constituent parts were not granted by the king but derived from the original or historical rights of the nobility.

The Estates of Croatia-Slavonia consequently inherited Croatia's historical claim to Dalmatia, calling itself the sabor of the kingdoms of Croatia, Dalmatia and Slavonia (*congregatio regnorum Croatiae, Dalmatiae et Slavoniae*). The state right, however, was Croatian in that the sabor traced the Triune Kingdom's political lineage to that of the early medieval Croatian state and saw its own sovereignty grounded in the latter's original independence. Although the political unity of 'the lands of Zvonimir's crown' had been shattered during the preceding centuries, it remained preserved in the virtual domain of state right as an essential aspect of Croatia's enduring statehood. Dynastic change and the Ottoman invasion had shifted the state's centre away from its Dalmatian cradle towards Pannonia; but from the point of view of state right the kingdom never changed its location or extent – its historic lands remained forever a single political unit. The Croatian parliament consequently represented Dalmatia also, even though it could not make laws for it. In the eighteenth century, however, a more urgent question was posed in regard to the governance of the former Ottoman Slavonian area, which in the middle of the eighteenth century became organised into three counties: Virovitica, Požega and Srijem.

The Croatian parliament had laid its claim to this Slavonia even before the conclusion of the Peace of Karlovci in 1699, but it was only in 1745 that the newly established Slavonian counties were formally returned to its own and the ban's authority. The question of actual sovereignty in Slavonia was not fully settled, however, since the three counties remained subject to the Hungarian state council in matters of taxation, as did Hungary (but not the rest of Croatia) – a state of affairs that derived from Slavonia's initial post-war status as royal land. The three counties consequently sent their representatives to both the Croatian and the Hungarian parliaments, and thus became subject to two different legal systems. At the joint sessions of the Hungarian parliament, the Croatian parliamentary delegation insisted that it represented also Slavonia – as did the Slavonian delegates sitting on the Hungarian benches. This duality had important consequences in the domain of civic law, for example in regard to the issue of religious freedoms. In 1790–1 Orthodox Christianity became formally recognised in both Hungary and Croatia; but Protestantism, whose adherents had been tolerated in the Ottoman period, remained proscribed in Croatia, hence also in Slavonia. Since a significant proportion of the Hungarian nobility was Protestant, the Hungarian parliament argued against the extension of

Croatian laws to Slavonia, on the grounds that the rule of the Croatian ban had never applied outside Slavonia of the Estates, from which it followed that the sabor's authority did not extend beyond the three westernmost 'Croatian' counties of Varaždin, Zagreb and Križevci. Slavonia, in other words, was part of the kingdom of Hungary. Royal edicts repeatedly confirmed the whole of Slavonia to be part of the Croatian kingdom, but they also failed to separate fully the areas of the Croatian and Hungarian jurisdictions.

Slavonia's difference derived also from the more recent implantation of the feudal order, in an area colonised, moreover, by a new and nationally more diverse population. Servile dues were lighter there, particularly in regard to obligatory labour; and the separation of rustical (peasant) from dominical (the lord's own) land was more straightforward than in 'Croatia'.[5] The different conditions prevailing in Slavonia and 'Croatia' in the eighteenth century led in the end to two separate land laws codifying the respective rights and privileges of the peasant and the lord. More troubling for the Croatian Estates was the fact that the new Slavonian nobility, composed mainly of magnates, was largely of foreign extraction, originating for the most part from Austria or Hungary – such as the Prandau, Eltz, Odeschalchi and Héderváry families. The Slavonian landowning class numbered no more than twenty families, eighteen of which owned over 99 per cent of all enserfed land. Only two of these twenty families could be classified as middle nobility (that is, possessing fewer than 100 serfs), as opposed to 450 such families in 'Croatia'. The Slavonian nobility was hence not only far wealthier than its 'Croatian' counterpart, but also shared little of the state tradition embedded in the Croatian parliament. Rather then journeying to Zagreb, the Slavonian magnates preferred to join their peers in the upper house of the Hungarian parliament. The retention of the Varaždin Border, which physically separated Slavonia from 'Croatia' but not from Hungary, further encouraged Slavonia's orientation towards Hungary. And whereas in 'Croatia' public functions at the level of the counties and the parliament were traditionally performed by the indigenous nobility, in Slavonia this was largely the task of a bureaucracy ennobled for the purpose but which as a rule did not own land. Slavonia, finally, was marked by the absence of towns with an uninterrupted urban tradition, making it far more rural in outlook.

The prolonged conflict between Croatia and Hungary over Slavonia well illustrates the functioning of the concept of state right and its adaptation to new realities. At the end of the eighteenth century the Hungarian parliament started to appropriate for itself the authority previously vested in the Hungarian crown, and consequently to conflate the rights of the crown with that of the Hungarian kingdom. Once the conflict over Slavonia came to be posed in terms of the superior rights of the Hungarian state, the differing interpretations of Slavonia's status became submerged into a wider legal and constitutional dispute over the history and nature of the Croatian-Hungarian association. The legal contest over Slavonia – conducted at joint sittings of the parliament or in communications with the king – became in fact part of a wider struggle over whether Croatia would survive as a separate state, or disappear within a Great Hungary; one conceived, moreover, as the state of the Magyar nation.

The Croatian claim to Slavonia rested on the inalienable right of the kingdom to all its territory, that is, not only to the part actually governed by the parliament but also to its 'alienated' or 'virtual' lands. At a joint session of the Hungarian parliament in 1790-1, the Croatian delegation insisted that the territory of 'Lower Slavonia' had always been a natural and legal part of the 'kingdom and duchy of Slavonia', and hence belonged to Croatia. The argument was articulated at three levels. The first referred to geography: Slavonia, defined as the area bounded by the rivers Drava, Sava and Danube, formed a natural geographical unit, which is why the Romans themselves had organised it as a single province. The second addressed ethnicity: this province had been inhabited by Slavs long before the arrival of the Magyars (i.e. ethnic Hungarian), and constituted as Slavonia by 'our forefathers' arriving from Dalmatian Croatia. The third element was purely legal in nature, and involved citations from documents – some going back to the thirteenth century when the Slavonian *regnum* was first established – dealing with such matters as taxation and other forms of the exercise of lawful authority on the part of Croatian state bodies which did not cease to operate even during the period of Ottoman occupation.[6]

The Croatian state right was evoked also in regard to Dalmatia. When in 1797 Austria gained Venice and its possessions in Istria and Dalmatia from France in return for Lombardy, the Croatian and Hungarian parliaments united in demanding Dalmatia's incorporation into Croatia, which the king refused on the grounds that he had won it in war. The same happened in 1814, after the Habsburg Monarchy had regained Dalmatia (which now included the Dubrovnik republic). The possibility of protest on the part of the Croatian Estates against the illegality of this act was precluded by the fact that in the period 1812–25 the emperor-king ruled without recourse to the local parliaments. As soon as parliamentary rule returned, however, the sabor instructed its representatives to place on the joint parliament's agenda the question of the unification of ban's Croatia – that is, the part of Croatia governed directly by the sabor – with Dalmatia and the Military Border. The dispute over Slavonia also revived, prompted in part by the language issue, of which more will be said below. The sabor consequently set up a special committee in 1827 to collect and sort out Croatian state documents, a collection of which was published three years later and copies distributed to the parliamentary deputies and local government officials.

In 1835, when the Slavonian issue was once again formally raised at a joint session of the Hungarian parliament, the Croatian position, based on the historic rights of the kingdom, was advanced in a new form. Whereas before the case had been approached mainly from the Slavonian angle, this time Croatia itself took centre stage. The argument was divided neatly into four parts, each covering a specific period: from Coloman to Matthias Corvinus (1102–1490); from Corvinus to the battle of Mohács (1490–1526); from the arrival of the Habsburgs in 1527 up to 1715 (when the first royal decision on Slavonia was made in Croatia's favour); and from 1715 on. The *Pacta Conventa*, described as an agreement reached between the Croats and King Coloman acting as equal partners, was now introduced as the cardinal proof that the river Drava had always formed the political border between Croatia and Hungary. A number of legal references were also added to the times when royal princes as dukes, or royal officials as bans, ruled in 'all of Slavonia', that is, in Croatia inclusive of 'Lower Slavonia'. But the Hungarian side was not impressed. The Hungarian parliament's response was to add the three Slavonian counties to the list of the Hungarian ones, and to advise their representatives to cease attending the parliament in Zagreb.

In 1845, when the issue came up again, the sabor felt forced to elaborate further its right to the government of Slavonia. Its legal experts had been hard at work, and came up with additional documents to back up the claim. More importantly, the whole tone of the presentation altered. In the part entitled *epocha prima* it was forcefully stated that Croatia's relationship to Hungary was one of a free association, based on the accord reached between the 'leaders of the Croat nation' and King Coloman. The Hungarian king's entitlement to the Croatian crown was this time limited to family ties with King Zvonimir. This document, like the two previous ones, was written in Latin and was largely legalistic in form; but its implications were nevertheless quite radical, since the nobility appeared explicitly this time as representative of the nation as a whole. The suggestion that Croatia had joined Hungary as a result of the free will of its people signalled the beginning of a new era in

Croatian politics. The Croatian state right would henceforth serve as code for the right of the nation to full sovereignty.

The contest between Croatia and Hungary, increasingly tinged with nationalist rhetoric, gave rise also to new national historiographies as the two sides got down to assembling and analysing old archival records in order to fight new battles. The main Croatian aim was to prove that Croatia had always been an independent state: far from being a subjugated kingdom as some Hungarian deputies were claiming, Croatian state right had remained unbroken and operative from the earliest times to the present day. The Hungarian parliament for its part instructed the appropriately named István Horvath (Stephen Croat), custodian of the newly established Hungarian National Museum, to examine 'objectively' the legal state relationship of Croatia with its Hungarian 'motherland'. As was to be expected, this work, published in 1844, proclaimed the *Pacta Conventa* document to be a forgery, and 'proved' that the sabor's claim that Croatia had never been conquered by Hungary was both false and spurious. The sabor then instructed its legal adviser, Ivan Kukuljević, to elucidate the history of the kingdoms of Croatia, Dalmatia and Slavonia before and after their incorporation to the Hungarian crown, and to collect all the relevant documents, which would be published at state expense. Kukuljević thus became Croatia's first official historian.[7]

Like all state traditions, the Croatian one too involved a mythical dimension: while resting on real events, it carefully selected these and organised them into a coherent whole. The new national ideology inherited from the feudal state's tradition its assimilation of the whole 'historic' territory under the Croatian name. But it also adjusted this tradition to the demands of the new age, by replacing the feudal concept of *natio* with one that embraced all the population. Modern Croat nationalism was thus born as a corollary of Croatia's statehood. Irrespective of whether its ideologues sought over time outright independence for their country or a place for it within a wider state association – the Habsburg lands, a federated Europe, or a union of the South Slavs – they would rely as much on the Croatian state right as on the people's 'natural right' to self-government.

Nationalisation of the state

The battle over Croatia's status and political jurisdiction pursued at the turn of the eighteenth century and in the early decades of the nineteenth was inextricably tied to the issue of the language of public affairs. It was obvious to the Hungarian nobles that Hungarian should replace Latin throughout the lands of the Hungarian crown. At the end of the eighteenth century,

Croatia had fewer than 10,000 nobles while Hungary had over 155,000, and this disparity was reflected also in the make-up of the joint parliament. The decision in favour of the Hungarian language becoming the working language of the joint parliament thus might have appeared justified.[8] Yet choosing the language of this and other public bodies was not simply a matter of practical expediency, since both sides perceived language as an essential element of state power – and now also of nation-building. Until 1790 the joint parliament had worked on the basis of consensus, involving a lengthy and complicated process of consultation and harmonisation of the different interests represented by the magnates, the counties, the royal free cities and the king. But in 1790 there was a new emphasis on majority voting, and the Croatians found themselves in a permanent minority. They were thus unable to prevent the parliament from adopting the proposal that Hungarian should replace Latin as the official language in the lands of the Hungarian crown, beginning with the parliament itself. In Croatian eyes the ruling was not only illegal, but also anti-Croat. It was illegal because, as Ban Petar Erdödy (1790–1806) – the fifth ban from this family of Hungarian origin – insisted, one kingdom could not impose laws on another. It was anti-Croat because, in the words of the Croatian deputy Adam Škrlec, 'to be made to speak someone else's language is a sure sign of slavery'.[9] By insisting on the linguistic status quo, that is, on the continued use of Latin, the Croatian representatives felt they were defending not only their country's freedom, but also their national honour.

It was one thing, however, for some to learn the Hungarian language, quite another for the country as a whole to be obliged to speak it. In 1805 this possibility was raised with the demand on the part of some Hungarian deputies that Hungarian be taught in Croatian schools. The Croatian deputies' response was that they had nothing against the promotion of the Hungarian language in Hungary, but not in Croatia, where the law stipulated the use of Latin. The Croatian kingdom was a nation just as the kingdom of Hungary was a nation. If Hungary upheld the right to promote Hungarian, Croatia had an equal right to promote its own language. The fact was that hardly anyone in Croatia knew Hungarian. The administration had for centuries used Latin, and in the Military Border German also. The upper class talked to each other in Croat, or when necessary in Latin or German. The Hungarian parliamentary majority nevertheless decided that knowledge of the Hungarian language should be made compulsory for those working in the central bodies; when the Croatians protested that this automatically excluded them, they were told that not all Croats but only those employed in the central administration should be able to speak Hungarian.[10]

A power struggle cloaked in legalistic terms was a natural outcome of the manner in which politics was organised in the Habsburg Monarchy. Unable to reach agreement in the joint parliament, Croatians and Hungarians each had traditionally appealed to the king. But there were issues such as the language of common institutions that had no immediate precedent. The question of whether they represented a single 'Hungarian nation' which preferred to speak in Hungarian was essentially one of who had the right to decide the issue. The language question divided the Croato-Hungarian nobility as well as the Catholic Church. The bishop of Zagreb, for example, used his jurisdiction in majority-Croat Medimurje, which belonged to the Hungarian county of Zala, to sabotage the introduction of Hungarian into its schools. Both he and the Croatian parliament believed that Medimurje should be in Croatia. In the following years the Croatian sabor would repeatedly seek royal help in redressing the balance, and the king tended to oblige since Vienna did not favour concentration of power in the hands of the Hungarian parliament. But constitutional disputes were power disputes; the king, when forced to choose, found it easier to risk alienating Croatia than Hungary. Although it was agreed in the end to leave Latin as the official language in Croatia, Hungary felt free to replace it with Hungarian in Slavonia, thus fostering the latter's alienation from Croatia. Fearing exclusion from the joint parliament and the common crown bodies, which increasingly relied on Hungarian, the sabor finally agreed in 1827 that Hungarian should be taught as an obligatory subject in Croatian secondary schools and the Zagreb Academy. The turning point came with the 1832–6 session of the joint parliament, when the Hungarian benches voted to make Hungarian the official language in Croatia. At Croatian insistence, King Francis I (1792–1835) refused to sanction the Hungarian parliament's decision; but the issue was too important to be set aside.

During the ensuing decades the Croatian parliament's defence of its sole right to make laws in Croatia produced a conceptual shift in national politics, whereby the nation came to include all the kingdom's inhabitants: irrespective of their social or ethnic affiliation, they now became 'politically' Croatians. State right now stood for the 'natural' right of this nation to free development. The process that led to this change was in retrospect called national rebirth, but in the first instance it involved a 'rebirth' of the political elite, in that the nobility was joined by a middle class that brought its own understanding of national politics. The 'democratisation' of the nobility was

Janko Drašković

thus accompanied by an '*étatisation*' of the middle class: excluded in the past from affairs of state, the latter now entered the political arena as a force in its own right. State right would henceforth no longer be limited to defence of the traditional rights of the kingdom, but would also be an instrument for forging the nation. This nationalisation of state politics involved the construction of clear territorial borders and a new emphasis on internal social cohesion.

The transition from the feudal to the modern national idea was the work of a movement that called itself Illyrian. Its patron was Count Janko Drašković, who not only lent it his illustrious name, but also made his house in Zagreb the meeting-place for its leaders. In 1832, on the eve of the opening of what promised to be a momentous session of the joint parliament which he was to attend as a member of the Croatian delegation, Drašković published a pamphlet in the *štokavian* or 'Illyrian' idiom called *Disertatia*, or Considerations, intended as a guide for the Croatian deputies. In this programmatic work he insisted on the historical autonomy of the Croatian kingdom. He also asked that it be given its own state council; recommended that Latin be replaced by 'Illyrian' as the official language; stressed the importance of economic development and of an improved judiciary and administration; demanded better education for the people (and in that respect assistance for the Orthodox clergy); called for the return to Croatia of Dalmatia and the Military Border; and proposed the federalisation of the Habsburg Monarchy.

Croatia, in Drašković's view, should take 'evolutionary' England rather than 'revolutionary' France as the right model to follow, because '[England] is the leader and its laws most advanced among the nations'. Croatia lay 'in the middle of Europe, squeezed between the east and the west, the former threatening us with its darkness and the latter with its blinding light'.[11] This is why it was necessary for it to follow a middle road, which, however, required great wisdom and educated officials. It also needed a united national effort. In his brochure *To the Most Noble Daughters of Illyria*, published in German in 1838, Drašković appealed to upper-class Croatian women to involve themselves in national politics. This was radical enough. But he went a step further by inserting Croatia into the framework of a Great Illyria that would include, in addition to Croatia, first Slovenia and later also Bosnia. This ambitious project captured the imagination of the country's young elite. At this juncture, most of the movement's ideologues and activists were in their teens or early twenties. Ljudevit Gaj, responsible for introducing the new Croat orthography, was twenty-three, as was Vjekoslav Babukić, who became the first professor of the Croat language. Bogoslav Šulek, a central figure of the movement, was sixteen, as was Ivan Kukuljević, the future official historian. Antun Mažuranić, author of the first Croat primers, was twenty-seven, while his brother Ivan, future ban and poet, was eighteen. Josip Juraj Strossmayer, the bishop of Đakovo and founder of the Yugoslav Academy, was seventeen. Others were a little older: the future ban, Josip Jelačić, was thirty-one; the writer of the Croatian anthem, Ivan Mihanović, thirty-eight. Drašković at sixty-two was by far the oldest.[12] It was this young generation, drawn from all social layers, that gave voice to the new national mood. Some of the activists came from the nobility, but most were of plebeian origin: law and philosophy students from the Zagreb Academy, theological students drawn largely from the countryside, young cadets from the Military Border studying at the military academy in Graz. Destined for employment in the main branches of the state – the church, the administration and the army – they formed a generation that would dominate Croatian political and cultural life for much of the nineteenth century.

The fervour with which the Illyrians adopted the new credo of 'political Croatism' was that of a generation entering political life at a time of great social and political change in the Habsburg Monarchy. Some of the Illyrians attended the 1832–6 diet in Pest as legal advisers to the Croatian delegation. There they met Ljudevit Gaj, an energetic organiser and inspired orator, and on their return to Zagreb they decided actively to promote the Croat language and Croatian political interests. Gaj's application for permission to publish the first political journal in the Croat language was supported by all the 'Croatian' counties and royal free cities. This led to the founding in 1835 of *Hrvatske novine* (Croatian Journal), written in the local *kajkavian* idiom and spelling, with its literary supplement called *Danica* (Morning Star). The journal was soon renamed *Ilirske Narodne Novine* (Illyrian National Journal), however, and henceforth published (*Danica* included) in the *štokavian* idiom with Gaj's reformed spelling. The task of these journals was to advance national development by raising 'our dear mother tongue to the place of honour it deserves'. The editors declared that they were merely following the example of other European nations, which by publishing works of culture and science in the national language ensured that they would be read and studied 'not only in palaces, but also in modest homes'. Some of them expressed their national sentiment by Croatising their names: Ignatius Fuchs, who wrote the music for the Croatian national anthem, became Vatroslav Lisinski; Lajos Farkas became Ljudevit Vukotinović.

They were heirs to a tradition that saw Croats as part of the Slav and in particular South Slav world; but, as they insisted, their Illyria was 'politically' Croatian. As Dragutin Rakovac, one of the leading Illyrians, explained, 'given that the Croatian name had become restricted to the three western counties', a more general name was required and 'Illyrian' appeared the most suitable. They could not use 'South Slav', since there were many South Slavs living outside the Habsburg Monarchy. One could use the names 'Croat', 'Slovene' and 'Serb', but they wanted to unite them all under a general name.[13] According to Ljudevit Vukotinović, they were not seeking to create an Illyrian state: 'We Illyrians have nothing to do with *political Illyrianism*.' Their Illyrianism should be understood in the national sense only in that they were seeking to awake among their people the knowledge of its own self. 'Our political programme, however, is *Croatism*: in the constitutional sense we are all Croats.'[14] They used the term Illyrian 'in the political sense', Dragutin Rakovac added, 'only in regard to our Triune body of Croatia-Dalmatia-Slavonia, for which the Illyrian name was often used in the past'. This Illyrian nation was divided by religion, but education would weaken the mistrust, particularly as they were committed to the equality of the Latin and Cyrillic scripts in public use.[15] Despite its name, the Illyrian movement was a Croat and Croatian national movement. The national idea which guided them was state-territorial, not ethnic, just as the feudal state which they now claimed for the nation was not based on ethnicity. The main purpose of the Illyrian movement was to achieve Croatia's consolidation and raise its regional prestige by uniting around it all the south Slav lands of the Monarchy – and Bosnia too at some point in the future.

Great Illyria

Drašković's Great Illyria was in many ways a by-product of the Napoleonic Wars. Two decades before the appearance of *Disertatia*, Croatia bordered in the southwest with France – or, more precisely, with the Illyrian Provinces that Napoleon created in 1809 out of Venetian Albania (the Bay of Kotor), the Dubrovnik republic, Venetian Dalmatia, the Croatian territory south of the river Sava, Istria, Carniola, Gorizia-Gradisca and a large slice of Carinthia. The Croatian Illyrian province, whose capital became Karlovac, included the key seaports of Rijeka and Senj (as well as one of Drašković's manors). In 1812, however, Napoleon's Russian campaign ended in disaster, the Habsburg Monarchy joined the camp of his enemies and in the autumn of 1813 its troops occupied the Illyrian Provinces and added them to the newly created Austrian empire proclaimed in 1804 after Emperor Francis was forced by Napoleon to surrender his German imperial title. Since this empire formally excluded the lands of the Hungarian crown, the inclusion of Croatian territory amounted to annexation. Ignoring Croatian demands for an immediate return of at least the civilian part of former French Croatia, Vienna proceeded to establish a new entity called the Kingdom of Illyria, based on the French Illyrian Provinces. The local nobility, fearing that they would be annexed to Carniola – which, they argued, would deprive them of their 'nationhood, homeland, language and custom' – appealed in the spring of 1814 to the Croatian and Hungarian state bodies to save them from 'German laws' and reunite them with Croatia. Nevertheless, the emperor-king decided to unite this Kingdom of Illyria with his Austrian hereditary lands 'for all time'; on the grounds that he had won it in battle. There followed a heated dispute involving the king, the army, the parliament and the local nobility, as well as the Croatian ban and the Hungarian palatine – who protested, among other things, that a customs border on the Sava would cripple Croato-Hungarian trade, which needed access to the sea. In 1822 the civilian parts of the Croatian Littoral, including the port of Rijeka, were returned to the jurisdiction of the Hungarian crown. The Illyrian kingdom survived in a reduced form until 1849, when it was effectively dissolved, although the Habsburgs kept the title 'king of Illyria' until their abdication in 1918. Gorizia-Gradisca, Istria and Trieste, on the other hand, were now administered together under the name of the Austrian Littoral.

The dispute between Vienna on the one hand and Croatia-Hungary on the other was thus about control of the ports of the Croatian Littoral, which formed a key building block also of Drašković's Great Illyria. Drašković's key argument for Great Illyria rested on the fact that both the French and the Austrian Illyrian provinces were inhabited mainly by South Slavs or 'Illyrians'. Since Croatia (and Bosnia too) was also inhabited by 'Illyrians', the projected Great Illyria was in fact a South Slav kingdom centred on Croatia – in effect a Great Croatia, since Croatia alone was a kingdom.

Drašković's vision of a kingdom that would embrace the Habsburg South Slav population was a construction articulated at the time of increasing conflict with Hungary, which came to involve also the status of the port of Rijeka. Since Croatia and Hungary fought over Rijeka until the very end of the Habsburg Monarchy, it is necessary to review briefly here its history.

Rijeka (Flumen St Vitus in Latin, successor to the Roman city of Tarsatica) was originally part of the Croatian kingdom, but in the twelfth century Emperor Henry V included it into the German empire, so that the Croatian Border shifted from the river Raša in Istria to the river Rječina (*Flumen*) which today runs through the middle of Rijeka. In the thirteenth century the Frankapans joined it to their Vinodol estates. In the fifteenth century, however, Rijeka became the property of the Habsburg family. At this time the local parish church used the Slav liturgy and kept records in Glagolica, the local nobility spoke Croat and Latin and the soldiers German, while the sea trade relied on Venetian Italian. Rijeka acquired a royal charter in the sixteenth century. During the seventeenth century its potential was limited by the tremendous growth of the Zrinski port of Bakar, but the family's disappearance removed this obstacle. Rijeka's development really took off in the early eighteenth century, when Austria proclaimed the Adriatic an open sea and Trieste and Rijeka free ports. In 1728 Rijeka and the former Zrinski port of Bakar became linked to Karlovac by road – the only road to the sea outside the Military Border – after which Rijeka became the main port for Croatian and Hungarian wheat exports to Lombardy. Duty-free imports, on the other hand, led to the development of industry, beginning with a sugar refinery. The relative economic strength of this part of the Croatian coastal area can be deduced from the fact that in 1787 Bakar had around 7,600 inhabitants, Rijeka 6,000, Varaždin 5,000, Karlovac and Zagreb 3,000 and Požega 2,000.

In 1775, at the suggestion of Joseph II, the free trade area was divided into three autonomous zones. Trieste was to become the main port of Austria, Rijeka of Croatia-Hungary, while the coast between (and including) Senj and Karlobag was joined to the Military Border. The port of Rijeka and its district were added to Croatia and placed under the administration of the Croatian state council. The city, which had enjoyed a separate existence for over three centuries, now joined its hinterland as an integral part of the new county of Severin. Maria Theresa also established separate governments or *gubernia* for Trieste and Rijeka. A few years later, however, Joseph II dissolved the county of Severin and created a *corpus separatum* linked to the Hungarian crown that was made up of three districts: Rijeka, Bakar and

The Politics of State Right

Rijeka welcomes Emperor Charles VI, 1728

Vinodol. This territory was run by the governor of Rijeka, appointed by the king. Rijeka's municipal council was replaced by a magistrate subject to the Hungarian state council in Vienna.

In 1809, this time under French rule, the city was linked to Karlovac by a new road. In 1813, however, Laval Nugent, an Austrian general of Irish extraction, took the Illyrian Provinces from France. He was married to a descendant of the Italian Sforza family, and since the Frankapan too had been related to the Sforza Nugent felt himself to be their relative, which turned him into a Croatian patriot. He bought a number of former Frankapan and Zrinski castles and lands, including the castle of Trsat above Rijeka, which became the family's main seat. The choice of Trsat was influenced by the fact that it had been established allegedly by Celts: although the Nugents were of Norman descent, they strongly identified with Ireland's Celtic nature. Laval's love of Croatia made him a patron of the Illyrian movement. In 1849 he became, along with Windischgrätz and Radetzki, one of the Habsburg Monarchy's three field marshals. As a close friend of Archduke John, he was in a position to sponsor in 1848 the appointment of the Croatian Border officer Josip Jelačić as ban of Croatia, which led his Hungarian opponents to accuse him of wishing to make his son Albert king of Illyria.

In the early 1820s when the Greek uprising closed the Straits to Russian wheat, and again in the late 1820s when the Russian-Turkish war once again stopped Russian wheat exports, the Croatian area experienced a trade boom. Vukovar on the Danube, Osijek and Varaždin on the Drava, Brod and Zagreb on the Sava, Sisak and Karlovac on the Kupa, and Rijeka and Senj on the Adriatic coast were its main beneficiaries, since they acted as intermediaries for Austria's exports of industrial goods and for Hungary's booming wheat exports from its southern counties, as well as for products originating from northern Serbia and Bosnia. These ports also saw a growing export trade in local produce, such as timber. One consequence of this resurgence in the economic importance of the Croatian trade routes was the rise of a new class of merchants, among whom the most prominent were the Vranyczány brothers, whose headquarters was in Karlovac. This family, headed by Ambroz, traded in wheat and timber, owned a steamer on the Sava and dreamed about a railway linking Vukovar on the Danube with Rijeka on the Adriatic Sea. Ljudevit Gaj, Ivan Kukuljević and Ambroz Vranyczány (who was thirty-one in 1832) formed the central core of Croatian political activity in 1848. If the true sinews of the movement were supplied by non-nobles such as the Vranyczány brothers, at a time when the nobility alone had political representation the support of aristocrats like Janko Drašković and Nugent Laval proved decisive.

Since for both Croatia and Hungary the Danube-Sava-Kupa-Adriatic trade route had become vital for export activity, and since the status of the Croatian Littoral as a *corpus separatum* of the Hungarian crown was not clearly defined, the question was now posed as to which of the two kingdoms of the crown did Rijeka actually belong.[16] In Drašković's view Rijeka was obviously Croatian: its population was overwhelmingly Croat, while Hungary was miles away. In 1848, when the Illyrians became responsible for guiding Croatia's affairs, the city had 8,000 inhabitants and its district 12,000, of whom (according to the census of 1851) all were Croat except for a small number of Italians (691) and Magyars (76). Great Illyria was a device designed to win for Croatia control over this vital trade route, and therewith the economic basis for its recovery, resurgence and emancipation from both Vienna and Pest.

Great Illyria versus Great Hungary

During the 1830s and 1840s the Hungarian lower nobility and the intelligentsia drawn from it, frustrated by the reduction of county powers in favour of central government, came to see themselves as the true representatives of the Hungarian nation and embraced the ideas of popular sovereignty and representative government. Many rallied to the newly formed Liberal Party, which believed that Hungary's economic backwardness could be remedied only by state interventionism. The introduction of Hungarian was seen as a necessary condition for the modernisation of state and society, but the problem was that the majority of inhabitants of 'historic Hungary' did not speak that language. Magyars (ethnic Hungarians) in fact formed less than half the population of the kingdom of Hungary (3 million out of 6.4 million), and just over one-third in the lands of the Hungarian crown (3.4 million out of 9.2 million).[17] This posed a grave problem for the transformation of the noble *natio Hungarica* into a Magyar national state. Hungarian nationalists also had to reckon with the fact that in their own kingdom of Hungary half the aristocracy, one-fifth of the lower nobility and the entire bourgeoisie – which was supposed to play a key role in Hungary's industrialisation – were not ethnically Hungarian. In view of these circumstances, the advocates of the Magyar national idea embraced the view that a centralised state would of itself produce a unified nation.

They were convinced that 'historic Hungary', that is, Hungary of the crown, could become a Magyar national state only if it were ruled by Magyars and spoke their language. Count István Széchenyi, founding father of the Hungarian Liberal Party, stated in 1848: 'Now that we have created [a fully autonomous] Hungary, we need to create Magyars.'[18] According to Lajos Kossuth, who emerged as spokesman for the radical county of Pest, 'the Magyar language is not only unknown abroad, it is not even spoken in many places [in Hungary itself]. It has failed to gain its rightful place in public life despite half a century of struggle, while in private life it faces thousands upon thousands of opponents.' If the Magyar nation was to overcome this dismal situation, it had to 'develop, spread and consolidate'. This demanded the creation of a strong middle class, but 'our cities are largely German – so German, indeed, that they show only a minimal degree of Magyar presence'. The Hungarian German cities favoured the Monarchy's adhesion to the German customs union; but if this were to happen, 'our nation would be endangered, not because Magyars would become Germans, but because it would prevent the Magyarisation of our cities and thereby the creation of a Magyar middle class.'[19]

For Hungarian Liberals, therefore, national integration meant in the first instance unification of the lands of the Hungarian crown under a Magyar-speaking administration. Inspired, on the other hand, by contemporary German economic theories – such as Friedrich List's *The National Approach to Political Economy*, which appeared in 1841 – they accepted as a basic postulate that progress lay in 'the development of a national industry by all social and political means available'.[20] Hungary's economic backwardness would be overcome by means of state-sponsored industrialisation coupled to a policy of economic protectionism. Protection of the Hungarian market as the condition for a self-sustaining industry and trade, however, required free access to the sea. Hungary did not have any sea, but Croatia did. The problem was solved by claiming that since Croatia was part of 'historic Hungary' (meaning the lands of the Hungarian crown), and since the Hungarian court council administrated the civilian part of the Croatian Littoral, Rijeka was automatically part of the Hungarian kingdom. According to Lajos Kossuth, 'our raw materials demand a market, the great world market, the door to which we shall find in Rijeka and Bakar'.[21] Kossuth's slogan of 'responsible government and administrative centralism', which the Liberals endorsed as their own, threatened to reduce Croatia to a mere geographical concept. The 'Illyrian' movement was a response to this threat. Their Great Illyria was to be a barrier to Hungary's drive towards the Adriatic Sea.

Like the Illyrians, the Hungarian Liberals also endorsed a territorial definition of the nation: in their view all citizens of 'historic Hungary' were 'politically' Hungarians. Croatia, however, was linguistically far more homogeneous than Hungary: in 1840 Magyars and Germans formed no more than 1 per cent of the total population of Croatia-Slavonia. Its Orthodox population, which increasingly identified itself as Serb, did indeed form about a quarter of the total;[22] but the fact that it too spoke the *štokavian* idiom meant that the Croatian nation could be defined also as a linguistic – and in that sense ethnic – community.

The Illyrian movement arose at a time of growing acceptance of the view that language identified a nation. The adoption of an all-Croatian language standard was thus seen as a precondition for achievement of the supreme national task of state unification. Drašković had recommended *štokavian* or Illyrian because it was the most commonly spoken language in Croatia and in the projected Great Illyria. 'We have no future', wrote Kukuljević in 1842, 'unless we behave as Croats in Croatia, as Slavs in the world, and as Illyrians towards our dear Yugoslav brothers, and until we begin to speak our mother tongue.'[23]

Among those responsible for ensuring that Latin would be replaced by *štokavian,* only a small minority were in fact native *štokavian* speakers. Most of them spoke *kajkavian* or *čakavian* at home, some German or Hungarian. Some (including Ljudevit Gaj) belonged to recently Croatised families of varied foreign descent. Their efforts to persuade the most important part of Croatia to give up its own *kajkavian* idiom derived from their understanding of its geographically limited scope. The choice of *štokavian* as the national language was thus both pragmatic and programmatic. It had, moreover, to be made binding without delay, given the Magyarisation of the institutions that Croatia shared with Hungary and the expansion of education initiated in the preceding period of reforms. It was necessary to persuade the sabor to give up Latin, to prevent it from choosing *kajkavian* as a replacement, and above all to exclude the Hungarian language from Croatia's schools and institutions. 'We are a free kingdom. Let those ashamed of being Croat bow before the wild Huns [the Magyars] and be their servants!' – that is how a patriotic poet writing at the start of the nineteenth century saw the issue.[24]

In 1843 Ivan Kukuljević established a historical precedent by addressing the Croatian parliament in Croat rather than the customary Latin. He urged the Estates to abandon Latin without delay, on the grounds that anything else threatened the survival of the Croatian nation. The decision of the sabor in 1847 to replace Latin by Croat as the official language in the kingdom was welcomed in the following terms: 'Our Estates and Orders have finally discovered that the time has come to make our national language the state language. It is the first duty of every legislator and politician to acquaint themselves with the position and needs of the people. This is what our sabor did when it decided to do what was of the greatest importance: to strengthen our nationhood.'[25]

In the eyes of the sabor, the Croatian kingdom's territory included not only those actually governed by it, but also the alienated lands. In 1780, at the start of the reign of Joseph II, present-day Croatia was divided into six distinct parts.[26] The Republic of Dubrovnik was an independent state. Dalmatia, including the Kvarner islands of the upper Adriatic, was a Venetian province. Istria was divided between Venice and the Habsburg duchy of Pazin. Baranja in the northeast and Međimurje in the northwest were part of Hungary. The Military Border was run from Vienna. Only the so-called Civilian Croatia was governed by the sabor – but the latter's right to Slavonia, as we have seen, was disputed. The contemporary Croatian republic covers 56,538 square kilometres. In 1780 Zagreb administered just under one-third of it. Of around 1,500,000 inhabitants who lived in the whole territory at that time, the sabor governed less than half that number.

When, following the Napoleonic Wars, the Habsburg Monarchy gained Dalmatia and the Venetian part of Istria, the Croatian territories were united under the same crown. But Vienna refused to return them to Croatia. Some territorial consolidation was nevertheless achieved. The unification of Istria and the reabsorption of the Dubrovnik republic into Dalmatia had reduced the number of components from six to four. By the 1830s, when the sabor was drafting its elaborate documents, the population under its jurisdiction had risen to one million, but a similar number continued to live outside that jurisdiction: around 660,000 in the Military Border, 125,000 in Istria, 360,000 in Dalmatia, and an estimated 62,000 in Baranja and Međimurje. National unity demanded erasing the borders that criss-crossed Croatia in order to create the single territorial and institutional framework necessary for national development. This is what the Illyrians set out to achieve. Reclaiming the other half of Croatia, however, involved confronting other interested parties with far superior political clout – as well as resistance in Dalmatia to the sabor's rule.

Croatia in 1850[27]

Territory	Area in sq. km.	Population
Civilian Croatia	20,740	955,950
Military Croatia	20,910	621,733
Dalmatia	11,758	356,460
Istria	3,130	141,700
Total	56,538	2,075,843

The argument with Hungary over Slavonia was a dispute between two parliaments, open in the last instance to royal arbitration; but in the estranged lands of the Military Border the sabor faced directly the power of the emperor-king. In 1825, indeed, the king refused for the first time to recognise unconditionally that the border was an inalienable part of Croatia, on the grounds that its army might be used against the interests of the Monarchy as a whole. Croatia's demand for restitution of the border was traditionally supported by Hungary, but the sabor's reliance on Vienna in its disputes with Hungary weakened the chances of any speedy recovery of this vital territory.

Dalmatia too remained out of reach. At the Congress of Vienna in 1815, Austria sought Venetian Dalmatia and the Dubrovnik republic on the grounds that they belonged to the Habsburgs as elected kings of Croatia; but having gained them it refused to return them to Croatian rule. The sabor's repeated demands that this 'allied kingdom' be joined to Croatia were as persistently rebuffed, with the argument that Dalmatia belonged to the empire as a whole. This dubious proposition on the part of a dynasty allegedly cherishing legitimism was soon abandoned as unnecessary, however, given the strong resistance of the Dalmatian patrician class to union with Croatia. In his *Genius patriae*, published in 1832, the Illyrian poet Ivan Derkos argued that 'we are part of the same state', people who 'ever since the times of Petar Krešimir, king of Croatia-Dalmatia, have enjoyed the closest relationship', so that 'a brotherly and mysterious tie of love exists between us, making our hearts open to each other'.[28] As the Illyrians soon discovered, however, the Italian-speaking city oligarchies of Dalmatia represented a community to which they could appeal neither in the name of state right nor in that of the Croat national idea, since the cities might admit to being Slav, but certainly not Croat and Croatian. In their protests to the emperor in Vienna against Dalmatia's addition to Croatia, Dalmatian representatives used arguments evoking real and imagined political privileges, historic rights and national differences. They asserted that with the collapse of Venetian rule the Dalmatian crown had reverted to the 'Dalmatian nation', which had then voluntarily surrendered it to the Austrian emperor. This 'Dalmatian nation' was represented by the Italian-speaking ruling stratum, not the Croat-speaking majority. 'We are not persuaded', wrote the Split municipality to Zagreb in April 1848, 'that the uneducated layer of the population identifies the nation rather than its educated part. Unification with Croatia-Slavonia and adoption of a Slav language in our administration would lead to our surrender to Croatian-Slavonian officials [and] to a veritable Croat invasion.'[29] They consequently asked for their own administration and for Italian as the language of that administration.

The Illyrians could counterpose to these centrifugal tendencies only the Croatian state right, which they now interpreted in accordance with liberal political thought and the philosophy of natural right. They replaced the idea that the Estates alone together with the king formed 'the political nation' with one in which sovereignty resided in the nation as a whole: the state to which they aspired was to be based on popular representation and administered by 'sons of the nation'. Gustaf Dollhopf, a member of the Illyrian circle that in 1848 gathered around the journal *Slavenski Jug* (The Slav South), elaborated this liberal-democratic reinterpretation of the Croatian state. He wrote that for nations who think themselves free and independent, state and nation could be separated only conceptually.[30] The most complete realisation of the national idea, indeed, was the state which the nation creates by itself, without outside intervention, since a nation could realise itself fully only as a sovereign subject. In order to be sovereign, however, it must be democratically constituted – the form of state in which 'the nation governs itself' could be only democracy. A true national government could not be the prerogative of a minority, because a state ruled by a single class could not express the popular will. For 'national statehood' to be fully realised, therefore, the popular masses must be given freedom and political rights in every sense: 'national liberty' was rooted in 'popular liberties'. The nation state was hence the kind of state which integrated all social classes by actively involving them in political life. The capacity of a 'state structure' to express the nation as a 'living body' depended entirely, however, on how it achieved this social unity. It followed from this that the main task of 'any minimally mature nation' was to transform the state into a state of citizens. Once freed from 'the chains of feudal privilege and medieval charters', 'the national spirit' would create by way of popular institutions a 'nation state' capable of resisting outside interference. Dollhopf also touched upon the issue of South Slav unity. According to him, the South Slav nations would be free from the threat of Germanisation and Magyarisation only after having acquired 'popular governments', because only a sovereign and democratic state could create and reproduce the collective will necessary for national survival. The path towards the unity of the South Slavs consequently lay in the development of their individual nation states, and only after this evolution had been completed could they proceed to unify 'politically'. It followed from this that the future state of the South Slavs, if and when it appeared, could be only a confederation of nation states.

Croat nationalism of the nineteenth century was 'traditional' in that it inherited the nobility's preoccupation with upholding, or regaining, Croatia's political autonomy and territorial unity. But it was also revolutionary in that it sought to create the foundations necessary for Croatia's transformation into a nation state. At times it embraced elements of ethnic nationalism – visibly so in regard to the language – but it never fully succumbed to this. The ethnic principle entered national politics chiefly in regard to the wider 'Illyrian' strategy aimed at uniting the Monarchy's South Slavs around Zagreb. Since this involved alteration of the existing political borders, Illyrian politics displayed a permanent tension between, on the one hand, stubborn defence of Croatia's own territorial unity and, on the other, advocacy of frontiers based on ethnicity.

PART TWO

From Kingdom to Nation State

SEVEN

Illyrian Croatia

The Illyrian initiative came at the right moment, given the decision that study of the Magyar rather than the Croat language should be made obligatory in Croatian secondary schools and the Zagreb Academy. The sabor had accepted this, while reaffirming Latin as Croatia's official language; but it also permitted that Croat be taught as an optional subject at the academy – where it became a vehicle for expounding patriotism to a highly receptive student body. The Illyrians now busied themselves with opening reading rooms, first in Varaždin, then in Karlovac, and finally in 1838 in Zagreb itself, whence they spread to the rest of the country. These reading rooms – a Croatian version of the Jacobin clubs – became crucibles of a new national elite. The Illyrian generation understood that Croatia had by now become so integrated with Hungary that the sabor had retained few institutional tools with which to resist. Their movement was designed to encircle the nation from above, by 'nationalising' the state structure, and from below, by educating it in the national spirit. Unlike their 'ancestors', who in the sabor's recollection had first won Dalmatia and then Slavonia, the Illyrians would first win the north then use it as a base from which to woo and win Dalmatia and Istria.

However, their adoption of the Illyrian rather than the Croatian name, and of the *štokavian* idiom, compounded the abundant difficulties they faced in winning adherents in the central *kajkavian* part of Croatia. Extracts from a diary kept by Dragojla Jarnević, herself destined to become a notable writer, trace the path of their progress in 1836–9. Jarnević lived in the former border town of Karlovac, where German remained the language of education and public life. The entries quoted below exhibit the characteristic interplay between the terms Croat and Illyrian.

1836: Our friends from the [Zagreb] seminary write to us [in

Croat] and my sister and I answer them in German: Croat does not please us! The Croats are invoking their language, but I cannot sympathise with them. I am a Croat and do not wish to call myself Illyrian. Let them call themselves what they wish. I greatly prefer Schiller, Goethe, Koerner and others to their Illyrianism, and in any case I do not see why I should have to study [Illyrian] in order to be Croat.

1837: My brother came this afternoon with his friends Vranić and Neralić. They talked mainly of Illyrianism. I cannot like the Illyrian as opposed to the Croat name, but since this is what the maestros – that Gaj in Zagreb and his supporters – have decided, that is how things will be. I find the Illyrian or Croat language difficult, and there was much laughter when the young men tried to make me speak in Croat.

May 1838: I have written a short story in German. I tried to write it in Croat, but did not get far. I cannot think in Croat, let alone write in it. My brother Josip occasionally writes to me from Zagreb in Croat, but I am quite unable to do so myself. Let Croatism be – it is of no use to me!

September 1838: Our guests have gone, [leaving] me with the benefit of being able to listen to, and learn a little of, my mother tongue. I feel greatly ashamed that I do not speak my own language well. But how can I learn it, when there are no books which I can study? I cannot afford the annual subscription to *Danica*. I am nevertheless determined to speak Croat, and that is what I do during my frequent meetings with Vranić and Neralić. Yet the Croat language remains alien to me, since I am unable to use it in everyday life. With whom can I practise it? Our visitors speak German, the schools are in German, so how can I improve my Croat?

1839. Trnski has brought a big Dalmatian-German-Italian dictionary which I will use to study Illyrian. They tried to persuade me to write a poem in Croat. I write a poem? In Croat? These young men are crazy! It is strange, you could almost call it fate, that I should have met them, for I indeed feel a new spirit awakening within me. My homeland is becoming increasingly dear to me. I gladly speak Illyrian, though I find it very hard. I should be able to find in books what my young acquaintances speak about, but where can I find such books in a place like Karlovac?[1]

The reading rooms and debating societies which the Illyrians established in the 1830s catered for such a need. The small size of 'Croatia' allowed the new ideologues to maintain personal contact with each other, and to concentrate their efforts on winning over for the national cause the key centres of noble power: county assemblies and the sabor. When, under their pressure, the Croatian sabor finally decided in 1847 to introduce Croat into schools and public administration, the first stage of national 'awakening' had been completed. Until then, however, they had been running a tight race, given the earlier decision that the Hungarian language be taught in Croatian secondary schools. Working in their favour was the fact that few Croatians knew Hungarian, which created a problem of finding qualified Hungarian-language instructors. The Hungarian government believed that some of these would come from Hungary itself, while others would be recruited from the native population. The education of Ivan Mažuranić, Croatia's great nineteenth-century poet and statesman, demonstrates the importance of the Illyrian effort to halt what amounted to a state-sponsored denationalisation of the Croatian elite.

The Mažuranić family originated from Split, which it must have left by the end of the Middle Ages, since local records show that in the sixteenth century one of Ivan's ancestors entered the service of the Frankapan counts as a free soldier on the Ottoman border. Ivan was born in Novi Vinodolski, a small town facing the island of Krk. His primary school, which taught in German, registered his name as Johann. His first preserved letter addressed to his brother Antun in Zagreb was written in German. Mažuranić next attended the *gymnasium* in Rijeka, where his name was changed to Giovanni. The language of instruction was typically Latin, but the students were also taught the Italian and Hungarian languages and literatures. Mažuranić's first printed poem, penned in honour of the Hungarian deputy governor of Rijeka, was composed in Hungarian. Under the influence of his Hungarian teacher – a noted poet who saw himself as an 'apostle' of his own national language – Mažuranić began writing poetry in Hungarian.[2] His formidable scholarly talents and proficiency in the Hungarian language won him a Hungarian state scholarship. He was supposed to go to Győr in western Hungary to improve his spoken Hungarian, but since he could not afford to live there he attended instead the secondary school in the nearby city of Szombathely, where his name was changed for a third time: he became János. He began to hate his situation, which he tried to remedy by improving his

French and English. When he learned of the appearance of *Danica,* one of whose editors was his brother Antun, he immediately submitted a poem – his first published poem in his mother tongue. He was then twenty-one. He wrote to the editors on this occasion: 'I have almost forgotten my own language.' Aware of his straitened circumstances, they offered to pay him for the poem, but he loftily declined: 'It is one's duty to love one's homeland. All I wish with my poems is to express my love for my country.' After completing his studies in Szombathely, he returned to Zagreb, enrolled in the academy and joined the Illyrian circle. In April 1848 he wrote an open letter, 'From the Croats to the Hungarians', in which he challenged the Hungarian liberals to choose between democracy and war. Drawing upon his personal experience, he insisted:

> There is no true freedom of the individual that is not rooted in national freedom, that does not derive from national sovereignty. Those who think that by liberating the individual they have liberated the nation are wrong, since both are necessary: it is erroneous and unnatural to separate the two. The idea that nations are nothing but an amorphous mass of individuals is a deception.[3]

National politics as pursued by the Croatian Estates at this stage was essentially defensive, designed to protect their autonomy as the only shield of their established way of life. But this now required state-building measures implying surrender of their monopoly of political representation – measures which they approved hesitantly and grudgingly. The Illyrian movement arose in the first instance against the old mentality of Croatia of the Estates, embedded in the 'Hungarian' constitution; and the real target of their anti-Hungarian polemics was the Croat noble nation fearful of change. The latter, lacking decisive leadership until the arrival of the Illyrians, was retreating step by step in the face of a persistent and ever-growing pressure from a Hungary motivated by its own urgent national needs and interests. It was the Croat nobility that had to be shaken up in the first instance and forced to act. The Illyrians avoided posing radical social demands, in order to win the nobility's cooperation and maintain national unity against Hungary; but they also sought to divide it, by fanning anti-Hungarian Croat nationalism. As for the policy of the imperial bureaucracy towards Croatia, it wavered between determination not to challenge the integrity of the lands of the Hungarian crown, fear of growing Magyar nationalism, and suspicion that the Illyrian movement – given its Slav orientation – might end up as an instrument of Russian foreign policy.

Capturing Zagreb

If Croatia was to survive, let alone reclaim its 'virtual' lands, it had first to regain control of its own state institutions. Ivan Kukuljević stated this need in very blunt terms at a meeting of the Zagreb county assembly in 1842: 'Now or never: our language and our government.' Addressing the sabor in Croat, he argued that the sabor should 'embrace our own language and make it sovereign in our lands'. Throughout the early 1840s he persistently demanded a government independent of the Hungarian court council, since the latter was 'dominated by the Magyar idea and the ideal of Magyarisation'. Croat as the state language and a separate government were the only protection against the mortal danger in which the nation found itself.[4] Only the national language, that primary bond between social classes, could ensure national cohesion. One of the leading Illyrians, Bogoslav Šulek (who was in fact an ethnic Slovak), wrote that the Hungarians had learnt from the Western nations – where nearly every peasant, burger, artisan or merchant could read books on agriculture, economy, manufacture, etc. – that education in the national language was the key to prosperity. Unfortunately, however, he went on, they wished to increase their bulk by trying to assimilate their neighbours linguistically. They had created for this purpose a Hungarian theatre, a Hungarian academy and a Hungarian museum, and had replaced Latin with Hungarian as the official language in Hungary. They had tried to make it the official language also in Croatia, he added, but the Croatians woke up to the fact and became concerned with the need to improve the parlous state of their own country. This could come about, however, only through cooperation of all social classes, and that can be achieved only through the medium of the national language. The main reason why the Croatian lower classes were illiterate was that the Croatian elite had been using Latin and German as the language of state and education. The Croats could not, however, become an educated nation by adopting a foreign, Magyar tongue.[5]

The emergence in the early 1830s of the Conservative and Liberal parties in Hungary stimulated a similar political division in Croatia itself, where two parties made their appearance in the early 1840s: a conservative Croato-Hungarian Party (quickly dubbed the Magyarones or Pseudo-Magyars by its opponents), which saw itself as the guardian of the established order; and the liberal Illyrian (later National) Party representing the forces of change.[6]

The Croato-Hungarian party, composed mainly of the anti-Austrian nobility, allied itself with the Hungarian Liberals and defended the teaching of Magyar in Croatian schools and even Hungary's rights in Slavonia. The National Party, prompted by Vienna, allied itself with the Hungarian Conservatives, who did not wish to see Hungary break away from Austria.

In the key county of Zagreb, the Croato-Hungarian Party enjoyed the support of the numerous petty nobles of Turopolje (the area south of Zagreb), whose only privileges were freedom from taxation and the right to bear arms. These had been temporarily taken away when Turopolje was included in the French Illyrian Provinces. This, and their experience of Austrian rule when they came under the Kingdom of Illyria, strengthened their dislike of the Illyrians. In 1819, in a tactical move designed to put pressure on the *sabor*, Vienna had granted this petty nobility the right to vote in the Zagreb county assembly in order to influence the composition of the *sabor*, as a result of which the Turopolje faction became an important force in political life. The Magyarones charged the Illyrians with wishing to separate Croatia from Hungary and join it to Austria, as well as with seeking to unite with Muslim Turks (that is, Bosnians) and Orthodox Vlachs (that is, Serbs). They supported the Hungarian proposal that the three western counties should follow the Slavonian example by sending their representatives directly to the Hungarian parliament; and, in an application of the principle of 'one nobleman, one vote', they demanded direct representation in the *sabor* itself. In order to minimise the number of recruits to the Magyarone party's cause, the Illyrians adopted the slogan: 'Long live the Hungarian constitution, the Croatian kingdom and the Illyrian nation.'

These pseudo-Magyars, Rakovac complained in 1842, had established a club to further the Magyar language. They write their names in Hungarian orthography, bring up their children in the Hungarian spirit, wear Hungarian dress, refuse to read anything in the Croat language, vote against 'our constitutional rights' and collaborate with Croatia's bitter enemies largely for opportunistic reasons. As for the Magyars themselves, he went on, they were seeking to erect a Magyar nation on the ruins of other Hungarian nationalities, resorting to just and unjust, legal and illegal means to realise their aims. They were working hard to raise 'the phoenix of their language from the ashes of other languages' by forcing the German, Slav and Romanian inhabitants of Hungary to learn their language, and had turned the churches too into Magyar-language schools. They were even trying to make it the language of command in the Military Border. Once Hungarian became the state language in Croatia, however, it would be used to assimilate the Croats.

They would soon introduce it also in the churches and schools, leading to the disappearance of the Croats' own national language. Once Hungarian became the official language in Croatia, indeed, Hungarians would gain administrative posts far more easily than Croatians and so, step by step, the Croatians would find themselves excluded from public life in their own country. To sum up: if Hungarian became the official language in Croatia, the Croatian kingdom would disappear and so would the Croat language and the Croat nation. Education in the mother tongue was, however, a basic right. Just as individuals had the right to improve their spirit and mind, so did nations – and this could be done only in their mother tongue. It was, indeed, 'a sacred duty of Croatian men and women to preserve and develop their language'.

The Croatian nation was insisting on its constitutional rights because: 'if the Magyars succeeded in abrogating just one of them, they would persevere until all were removed'. Since the Croatian constitution denied to the Hungarians the right to impose their language on Croatia, it had to be defended at all costs. This is why it was most important for Croatia to regain its own government, since this would be not only more efficient from the administrative point of view, but would also prevent the Hungarians from intervening in Croatian affairs. Some Hungarian deputies were trying to persuade the Croatians that their special status as a separate kingdom was a luxury they could not afford, that it would be better for the counties to be directly represented in the joint parliament, etc. If, however, the Croatian counties were to send their deputies to the joint parliament, there would be no need for the Croatian sabor; and without the sabor the six counties of Croatia-Slavonia would be overwhelmed by the far larger number of Magyar deputies in the joint parliament. The Illyrians, Rakovac insisted, did not seek in fact a complete break between Croatia and Hungary.

> What is it that we [Illyrians] want? Our language, without which we will disappear; our literature, in order to sustain our language; our nation's education, which can be realised only in our language; the preservation of our state right; to remain with our Hungarian brothers under the same constitution. What is it that we reject? We do not wish to be treated as raw material for the enlargement of another nation; we do not wish to be degraded. Our motto is: Long live the Hungarian constitution and the Illyrian nation![7]

The trouble was that in this *kajkavian*-speaking region there was strong resistance to making *štokavian* the language of public life. Šulek defended the

Ivan Kukuljević

Illyrians' language policy: 'It is fortunate that Croatian patriots understand the need to adopt the Illyrian language, which with small variations is spoken by twelve million South Slavs. This is meant to be only the language of literature, however, which as such will not replace *kajkavian* as the spoken language in Croatia. One can be both Croatian and Illyrian.'[8] He admitted that: 'many Zagreb citizens find the language difficult to follow at present, [but] with time and good will this will cease to be a problem.' It was not easy, however, to win the county of Zagreb. In May 1842 its assembly ended in a brawl costing lives, after which the pro-Illyrian county head Nikola Zdenčaj excluded the Turopolje 'masses' from the meeting and allowed the Illyrian Party to appoint county officials and sabor deputies.

It was in response to this event that the young nobleman Ivan Kukuljević resigned from the newly established Hungarian military academy in Pest and returned to Croatia to become, together with Ljudevit Gaj, the party's most prominent orator.[9] In a fiery speech to the Zagreb assembly he denounced Magyar nationalism for its 'contempt for other nations', its destructive

St Jerome, by Gentile Bellini, 15th century, Trogir cathedral.

The Rheims Gospel written in the Glagolitic script, 1395.

A Croat-language prayer book written in the Latin script, Dubrovnik, c. 1450.

Canaletto, Riva degli Schiavoni or Riva of the Croats, c. 1736. Courtesy of Sir John Soane Museum, London.

Marko Marulić, by Ivan Meštrović, Split.

Bribir (Roman Varvaria), seat of the Šubić family in the 13th century.

The church of St Mary in Vrboska on Hvar was fortified in the 16th century against the Ottomans.

Ozalj on the Kupa, a 13th century Frankapan citadel.

nature, and its 'lust for rule and domination'. He recommended that Croatian deputies to the joint parliament be recalled, and argued that the Croats should 'respond to Magyar fanaticism with greater fanaticism and to their terror with greater terror, if we do not wish to perish before the eyes of the rising Slav nations, if we do not wish the world to say that we do not deserve to be called a nation'.[10] Croatia's salvation, he insisted, demanded unity and cooperation of all social classes, and he pressed the nobility to place itself at the head of the movement for national revival by building schools and other national institutions. More immediately, it was necessary for Croatia to have its own government: 'Now or never: our language and our government.' Kukuljević was the first deputy to address the Croatian parliament in Croat rather than the customary Latin in May 1843 with a memorable speech in which he said:

> We [Croats] are a little Latin, a little German, a little Italian, a little Hungarian and a little Slav – and altogether, bluntly speaking, nothing at all! The dead Roman language and the living Hungarian, German and Italian ones are our tutors. The living ones threaten us while the dead one is holding us by the throat: it suffocates us and, having rendered us impotent, is surrendering us to the living ones. As of now we have enough strength to confront the dead one, but we will not be able for long to overcome the living ones unless we stand firmly on our feet, that is, unless we establish our own language in our homeland and make it sovereign.[11]

Under Hungarian pressure, however, Vienna banned use of the Illyrian name, after which officials suspected of pro-Illyrian sympathies were removed from their posts and replaced by supporters of the Croato-Hungarian party. It was now that the Illyrian party and journals renamed themselves 'National'. The Hungarian lower house, controlled by the Liberals, now voted that the Croatian deputies should not be recognised or be permitted to speak in Latin; but the upper house, controlled by the Conservatives and backed by Vienna, defeated these proposals. The upper house itself, nevertheless, adopted a general law on the Hungarian language and nationality, according to which Magyar became the official language also in Croatia. Although the king vetoed this decision, he did accept that within six years Croatians should be obliged to address the joint parliament in Magyar. In 1845, however, faced with a growing anti-Austrian opposition in Hungary, Vienna once again altered its policy towards Croatia. The Illyrian name was again permitted, albeit only for cultural purposes. Furthermore, the Turopolje

Zagreb in 1844, by J. Lechner

nobles were henceforth denied the right to vote individually in the Zagreb county assembly; this secured for the Nationals control of the Croatian parliament, which in 1847 introduced Croat alongside Latin as the language of debate and record. The sabor voted in addition that half the parliamentary seats should be given to the counties, which were instructed to send to it – in addition to their allocated two deputies apiece – also five intellectuals (*honorarii extremisii*). It also voted in favour of a separate government for Croatia, unification of Croatian territory, the introduction of Croat into schools, and turning the Zagreb bishopric into an archbishopric and the Zagreb Academy into a university. Finally, it decided that, in addition to a Croat-language chair, another chair be established at the academy for teaching Croatian history.

Given their plebeian birth, most of the Illyrians were barred from county assemblies and the sabor, so that the course of national politics was in the end decided by the struggle within the noble class itself. The outcome was ensured by the Illyrians, who between 1832 and 1847 had succeeded in forging a liberal-conservative alliance against Hungarian hegemony, the voice of which became their National Party. Fearing a 'premature' split in the National Party, the Illyrians did not demand the abolition of serfdom. They knew that the bonded peasantry formed the bulk of the nation, and they wished to see the end of serfdom – but they could not risk conflict with the nobility. In early 1848, when the joint parliament was set to debate the question of liberation of the serfs, the sabor divided on the issue; but the nobility eventually resigned themselves to its inevitability and instructed the Croatian deputies to vote in favour, albeit with full compensation for landowners.

1848: equality and liberty for all!

January 1848 brought revolutionary and constitutional changes in southern and central Italy. In February there was a revolution in Paris, leading to the abdication of the king and the establishment of the Second Republic. March saw unrest in Vienna, resulting in the fall of the Metternich regime, after which the central government practically ceased to exist. A meeting in Pest formulated Hungarian national demands, key to which was the formation of an independent Hungarian government. A national assembly convened in Prague to demand equality for the Czech people. Italians rebelled against Austrian rule in northern Italy, whereupon Piedmont declared war against the Habsburg Monarchy and occupied Milan. Revolution erupted in Berlin too, demanding Germany's unification. In April the Slovenes formulated their own national programme: equal rights for the Slovene language and formation of a separate Slovenian kingdom embracing the Slovene lands of Inner Austria and the Slovene Littoral. Having declined the prospect of becoming 'Illyrians', they were charting their own national path.

Also in April the Hungarian parliament, under Liberal leadership, voted to abolish serfdom and to institute a mildly representative but highly centralised and independent government for the lands of the Hungarian crown. The king could henceforth act as a monarch only when in Hungary, otherwise the palatine was the chief executive. Royal decisions had to be countersigned by the relevant minister. Hungary thus made itself an independent state with only a minimal link to the rest of Austria. The April laws offered nothing, however, to the non-Magyar nationalities: they would have no cultural or religious autonomy, and every demand on their part for territorial autonomy was treated as treason. The emergent Great Hungary was identified simply as the national state of the Magyars, which contained also a few national minorities. Transylvania, Rijeka, Slavonia and Medimurje were declared integral parts of the kingdom of Hungary. Slavonia and 'Croatia' were allocated thirty-six directly elected seats (six per county) in the house of representatives, and the Military Border six seats (one per regiment), which meant that Croatia would have forty-two out of a total of 377 seats in the Hungarian parliament. There was a vague promise of some autonomy for 'Croatia'. The new Hungarian government was headed by Lajos Batthyány, but real power lay with Lajos Kossuth. Addressing the parliament, Kossuth asked rhetorically: 'Where is Croatia? I cannot find

Ivan Mažuranić

it on any map.' The Croatians were nevertheless invited to join the struggle against 'the tyrannical Austrian bureaucracy', allegedly responsible for Croatian-Hungarian conflicts. In view of the revolutionary situation in Vienna and the need for Hungarian troops in Italy, the king confirmed all these decisions, except for that envisaging the establishment of a Hungarian ministry of defence with authority over all troops based on the territory of the Hungarian crown, including those of the Military Border.

In his letter 'From the Croats to the Magyars', drafted before the new laws were passed, Mažuranić welcomed the new democratic mood in Pest. Now that the Hungarians had 'embraced the modern European idea of brotherhood and equality and liberty for all', it was possible for Croatians to address them as friends. The purpose of his letter was to acquaint them with how the Croatians understood 'the sacred words equality, liberty and fraternity as applied to our common homeland'. Mažuranić then offered a three-point platform for a Croatian-Hungarian accord:[12]

1. 'Equality, liberty and fraternity for all peoples and languages embraced by the Hungarian crown.'

Those who believed that the unity of crown, government and state would disappear if the unity of nation and language were abandoned should bear in mind the Austrian example. Austria had granted personal liberties but not national rights, which is why its component nations had arisen 'under the banner of national liberation'. The future belonged to free nations, and wars would henceforth be won only by armies inspired by the national idea. True, the Magyars had abolished the rule of the aristocracy, but 'the spirit of the day is mightily hungry and demands more: it demands also surrender of the principle of national supremacy, since its time too has run out'. Citing the examples of Poland and Ireland, he argued that 'every present and future distress of undeveloped or subjugated nations will bring pain to those pursuing anti-national policies'.

2. 'Equality, liberty and fraternity for all religions existing under the Hungarian crown.'

'Religious freedom and equality [he wrote] is the best measure of national enlightenment. Let us put aside the grim monopoly of the heavens. Every church must be allowed its language, all clergy must enjoy equal status.'

3. 'Equality, liberty and fraternity for all states and lands under the Hungarian crown. Here too must be established in law that there is no dominant state, no alleged "mother-country". [Full] territorial integrity must be restored to our Kingdom of Croatia-Dalmatia-Slavonia.'

'The true cause of the unfortunate conflict between us', wrote Mažuranić, was that, 'you do not distinguish between "Hungarian" and "Magyar"'. Croatia was part of the Hungarian, not the Magyar, crown or state:

> Hungary as a Magyar state exists only in your mind, not in reality. [By] what right, indeed, is the Hungarian land and crown Magyar? By the right of numerical majority? This cannot be maintained, since in numerical terms the others are two or three times larger than you. By privilege that is natural or earned? This cannot be argued either, since in nature you are not better then they. [By] the right of original conquest? This is equally untenable, since those who appeal to the right of conquest [appeal] to the sword, and those who appeal to the sword will, I assure you, be answered by the sword.

Hungary could win Croatia as a friend if it gave up its unreasonable claims; if not, it would have a permanent enemy: 'I promise you that Ireland can never pose such a threat to the survival of the English as Croatia-Slavonia can to the future and survival of the Hungarian.' He concluded: 'We as a nation cannot trust the Hungarian government as long as we witness the injustice with which it treats non-Magyar nations in Hungary itself.'[13]

Breaking with Hungary

When news of the revolution in Vienna arrived, the sabor was not in session. In its absence a packed meeting, convened by the Zagreb magistracy on 17 March 1848, acquired the character of a national assembly. Kukuljević demanded immediate action: Croatia could not stand aside while its future was being decided in Vienna and Pest. He welcomed the arrival of political and civic freedoms and the end of feudalism, and insisted on the sabor's immediate convocation. The assembly then drafted an address to the king asking for recall of the Croatian parliament in order to be able to deal with the new situation. It stressed that Croatia, though part of the Hungarian crown, was a free and independent country, and asked for closer Croatian ties with Austria as well as restoration of Croatia's territorial integrity. On the same day, however, the king confirmed the new independent Hungarian government, thus negating Croatia's traditional right to appeal directly to the king.

A series of meetings held in late March formulated a national programme, in the form of national demands which included Croatia's territorial integrity, independent government, Croat as the sole official language, the independence of courts and trial by jury, legal and religious equality, civic rights including freedom of press and assembly, a parliament representing all social classes, taxation of the nobility, a national bank and army, a university for Zagreb, abolition of the customs border between Croatia and Austria and abolition of celibacy for the Catholic clergy. These demands endorsed the abolition of serfdom, and upheld union with Hungary provided that the latter was organised as a community of equal nations within the Habsburg Monarchy. The institution of the Military Border would be retained for a while, but its population would enjoy all civic rights (a way out of this contradiction continued to be debated).[14] Copies of this proclamation were sent out to all local authorities. A summary of the demands was next taken to the king for confirmation, but he refused to grant them, given the court's policy of appeasing Hungary. On 2 April the king nevertheless asked the acting ban, Bishop Haulik, to convene the sabor.

National Demands, 1848

One of the national demands was that Colonel Josip Jelačić, commander of the Ogulin regiment of the border army, be appointed ban. (The first to be offered the honour was in fact Count Drašković, who declined it on the grounds of old age.) Jelačić's landowning background and family tradition of dynastic service recommended him to the court and the army, while his anti-Magyar sentiments and Slav orientation made him an Illyrian. The choice was confirmed in late March by the king, who also made Jelačić

Feldmarschalleutnant and commander of the Croatian Border. The Slavonian Border, however, remained under the command of Jelačić's fellow border officer, General Johann Hrabowski. The loyalty that Jelačić commanded among the Serb Grenzer[15] was an important asset at a time when, with the countryside in a state of unrest following the abolition of serfdom, Croatia was sliding towards war with Hungary. The national make-up of the border army would underscore the sabor's authority, without the need to call on forces from outside. Jelačić's appointment as ban was formally approved by Hungary, but he refused to attend the Hungarian parliament.

In the middle of April the leaders of the Croato-Hungarian Party, which opposed the national demands and denounced Croatia's 'separatism', were arrested and the party banned. The magnates either tacitly supported Hungary (especially those in the counties of Virovitica and Srijem) or remained passive. The county of Srijem wished to keep the link with Zagreb, but also for Croatia to remain united with Hungary. The city of Osijek, with its sizeable German population, decided to keep Latin and fly only the Slavonian flag; it approved most of the national demands, but not the one about an independent Croatian government. The county of Virovitica voted in favour of the national language and the link with Croatia, and asked for two Croatian ministers to be included in the Hungarian government. The county of Požega adopted Croat immediately as its language of business, and became a bastion of the national movement. Slavonia as a whole favoured Croatia remaining in union with Hungary, provided that its right to self-government and its national language be respected.[16] In May 1848, when the royal-imperial family fled Vienna and moved to Innsbruck, most of the Magyarones emigrated to either Austria or Hungary.[17]

Jelačić toured the country announcing the end of serfdom and informing 'the Croat and Serb nation of the Triune Kingdom'[18] that the old constitutional link with Hungary had been severed and would be replaced by a new arrangement 'on the basis of freedom, independence and equality as befits our free and heroic nation'. 'We are faced with a great task of national transformation,' he declared, which could be undertaken only with the support of 'the nation and our educated patriots'. The sabor would soon convene to 'provide the great labour of our nation's political rebirth with natural and legal foundations'. These foundations would be based on 'the principle of national representation, so that the will of the whole nation regardless of social status may be articulated'. He greeted the clergy of both faiths and called for unity across religious lines. He ended his message with: 'God be with our king and our nation! Let harmony, freedom and brotherhood prevail.'[19] The 'educated patriots' were then invited to join the ban's council, which became a de facto government and got down to the task of producing a new electoral law.

Drafted mainly by Ivan Mažuranić, this electoral law was inspired by the principle that the representation of non-noble layers should be considerably greater than that of the nobility. Each county, royal free city and privileged township was allocated seats in proportion to their population. An at least passive vote was to be held by all male citizens, provided they were literate and aged twenty-four or over. There was a property qualification for both the urban and the rural vote, though it did not apply to university graduates. But whereas the towns were to elect their deputies directly, a two-step procedure was adopted in the countryside: voters first elected electoral colleges, which in turn elected deputies to the sabor. Despite initial resistance, Jelačić was persuaded to allow the Military Border to elect its own deputies, four for each regiment.

Dalmatia was invited to send deputies, elected by rules of its own choice. The ban wrote to the Dalmatians inviting them to send their representatives, as did others. The city of Zagreb wrote to Zadar, the county of Križevci to Dubrovnik. The Otočac border regiment invited the towns of Dalmatia's interior to 'join your Croatian-Slavonian brothers'.[20] The county of Varaždin too wrote to its 'dear Dalmatian brothers': 'Let our deputies meet in our common parliament in Zagreb.' Karlovac sent its own message to Dubrovnik: 'All for one and one for all!' None of these letters mentioned Hungary. The Dalmatians, however, went their own way. In the same month of April the emperor-king issued a provisional constitution for the Austrian lands, and Dalmatia decided to send its representatives to Vienna. Its municipalities either did not respond to the brotherly calls from the north or, if they did, excused themselves on the grounds that they were committed elsewhere.

Croatia's severance of formal links was causing problems for Hungary, cutting off access to Rijeka and the potential import of arms. The Hungarian palatine and government protested against the 'illegal' sabor, and warned that unless it were banned and 'traitors and separatists' stopped there would be a civil war. In May 1848 the Hungarian palatine managed to get the king to place Ban Jelačić and the border under the authority of the Hungarian government. When the ban refused to obey, the king proclaimed all his decisions null and void and appointed General Johann Hrabowski royal commissar in Croatia, with the task of investigating Croatian 'misdeeds'. This led to public burning of portraits of Hrabowski, the palatine and the Hungarian ministers on Zagreb's central square. Throughout May, the

Croatian and Slavonian counties wrote letters to the king protesting against the Hungarian treatment of Jelačić. Hrabowski, like all German officers of the border, was hostile to the Hungarian government, which he saw as a threat to the unity of the Habsburg Monarchy; but he felt he had to obey orders. His main task was to prevent the election of Slavonian deputies to the Croatian sabor, and to harass the newly proclaimed Serb Vojvodina (of which more below). Some counties refused to permit him access to their territories; others, prompted by the Slavonian Border units, accepted all Jelačić's decisions. The Slavonian counties refused in the end to elect deputies to the Hungarian parliament due to meet in July 1848.

At the end of May the two border commanders met and agreed to avoid conflict. The king, however, now ordered Jelačić not to convene the sabor, but instead to report to him at Innsbruck. But it was too late. The Croatians could not be cowed, because their back was covered by the army of the border. The ban's council for its part charged the Hungarian government with secessionism and causing trouble in Croatia. It argued that the king had permitted the sabor to meet; that it had to meet in order to legalise the 1847–8 decisions of the joint parliament; and that the ban in any case always had the right to convene the Estates. It assured the king that the kingdom was peaceful, while its members remained his most loyal subjects. The ban was prevented from travelling to Innsbruck before the opening of the parliament, because his presence was needed to make it legal.

The new sabor met in early June 1848. It was composed of 192 deputies most of whom had never before been active in public life. The property qualification limited the franchise to about 40,000 males, but the sabor was nevertheless the first representative parliament of ban's Croatia – and indeed the most representative that it would have in the whole century. In the absence of the Zagreb bishop Haulik, the Croatian ban was installed by the Orthodox patriarch Josif Rajačić, as the most senior churchman present. This met with the full approval of the bishops of Senj and Đakovo. Jelačić was the first Croatian ban to swear the oath to the king and the nation in Croat. On his inauguration he referred to the need to remain loyal to the king with the same zeal as he, Jelačić, was loyal to 'the new message of our age: freedom, equality and brotherhood'.[21] The Croatians had been resisting Magyar 'hegemonic behaviour' since before March 1848, he added, and had now destroyed it in their homeland. They were ready to defend their rights 'with sword in hand', since the age of national supremacy was over. He expressed his faith in the revival of 'our Dalmatian brothers' patriotism', and promised to work hard to make 'our ancient unity' a reality. His speech

Patriarch Josif Rajačić

was greeted rapturously by the deputies, after which Patriarch Rajačić made a suitable riposte on their behalf.

During 1848 a strong Serb national movement developed in eastern Croatia and southern Hungary, relying on the organisation of the Serb Orthodox Church, sympathetic border units and the proximity of the semi-independent principality of Serbia. Since the Hungarians refused to recognise the Serbs as a political subject in their own right, in the middle of May the latter proclaimed in Karlovci a Serb Vojvodina – composed of two

Hungarian counties and (to the consternation of the Croatian parliament) the county of Srijem – as an autonomous unit within the Monarchy. A border officer was elected as its head or *vojvoda* (hence the name Vojvodina), and Josip Rajačić as the Serb Orthodox patriarch. Fearing Hungary and seeking links with other Croatian Serbs, they expressed a wish to enter into union with Croatia based on equality. In early June a Serb delegation on its way to Innsbruck to petition the king stopped in Zagreb to participate in the work of the sabor and win Croatian support, which is why Rajačić (who was born in the Ogulin regimental area) was in a position to present Jelačić formally to the sabor. The sabor welcomed the appearance of Vojvodina, but denied it the right to Srijem until after Vojvodina's unification with Croatia.

During the sabor's debate on Hungary, arguments were put forward in favour of continued union with Hungary on the grounds of Croatia's financial weakness, as well as the fact that all Croatian state property and funds were in Hungary's hands; the majority, however, still voted to join the Austrian lands. The decision to break with Hungary was not easily taken, given that there was no certainty that the new Reichstag, the Austrian central parliament, would accept Croatia's annexation. The sabor adopted a definite position on Croatia's status within the monarchy as Article 11/1848, which included the following points:

1. The Triune Kingdom, which has always been independent from Hungary, cannot and will not recognise the existing Hungarian government until the latter forswears all those of its decisions that the kingdom finds unacceptable. Croatia, however, will have its own independent government.
2. A responsible government should be constituted for the whole Monarchy, dealing with defence, foreign policy and trade, in which Croatia would be represented by a minister responsible to the sabor and appointed by the king. The common government should be responsible to the central parliament and concerned solely with common affairs.
3. The Croatian government's authority should extend to the Military Border in regard to civilian affairs, while the ban as before should be in charge of all troops stationed on the territory of the Triune Kingdom.
4. Croat is to be the only official internal and external language of Croatia.[22]
5. Croatia's internal affairs are subject solely to the sabor.
6. Dalmatia is to be united with Croatia. The Triune Kingdom will also enter into a closer union with the newly established

Serb Vojvodina and with the Slav lands of Lower Styria, Carinthia, Carniola, Istria and Gorizia.
7. Croatian-Hungarian relations as defined by the Pragmatic Sanction are to be reestablished on the basis of freedom, equality and brotherhood and Croatia's sovereign will. This decision, however, remains subject to the king's fulfilment of the nation's just demands and Hungary's endorsement of the Monarchy's unity.[23]

The National Party's stance was based on the political doctrine of Austro-Slavism, supported at this time by all Habsburg Slavs other than the Poles. Its essential idea was that the Austrian Slav nations should remain within the Habsburg Monarchy, reorganised on the federal principle and governed constitutionally, as a protection against the rising Germany and autocratic Russia.[24] The party's acceptance of Austro-Slavism derived from its view that in the given circumstances Croatia could not survive as a fully independent state, while in a reformed Monarchy it could count on the support of other Slav nations. According to Mažuranić's concept, Croatia would be represented in the central parliament by deputies elected by and responsible to the sabor. It would have its own independent finances and a government responsible only to the sabor, while the ban would remain the supreme military commander. A Croatian minister appointed to Vienna would counter-sign all central decisions affecting the country. A similar schema for separation of powers between regional and central governmental bodies was adopted by the Czech National Committee in May 1848.

During the debate on the future of the Military Border, its deputies demanded the latter's outright dissolution; but the sabor could not do that and opted instead for reform. Croatian laws were applied to the area in regard to civic affairs, and Croat replaced German as the official language. Military laws applying to the border would in future be decided by the sabor. Military service was divided between regular service on the Ottoman Border and in the national guard, which could be send abroad only with the sabor's permission. The border army was to be under the ban's command. The moment of unification, however, was postponed.

But while the sabor was still in session, the king signed two decrees, one for the civilian and the other for the military part of Croatia, divesting Jelačić of all his positions and accusing him of treasonable activity. He also issued an imperial manifesto to the Croatians informing them of the reasons for Jelačić's dismissal. These included sedition; forcing the population to demonstrate against Hungary; persecution of individuals and officials supporting Croatia's union with Hungary; seizure of funds belonging to the Hungarian state treasury – using, moreover, royal troops; and imposition of new taxes. The king also complained of Croatian ingratitude in regard to the good efforts he had expended on their behalf.[25] The Hungarians published the royal manifesto in 100,000 copies and distributed them throughout the land. The Croatian government declared it a forgery, but the county of Virovitica now switched sides. On 12 June General Hrabowski attacked Karlovci, the unofficial capital of the Serb Vojvodina, triggering a war between Croatia and Hungary.

War with Hungary

The court in Vienna found itself in a difficult position. It needed Hungarian troops and money to pursue its military campaign in Italy, but it did not wish either to alienate Croatia, which if pressed could recall the border army from Italy. The king received the Croatian delegation bringing the sabor's decisions for his confirmation privately on 19 June, told them that the sabor was illegal, but also informed them that he had charged Archduke John to act as an intermediary between them and the Hungarians. News of revolutionary events at home and Hungary's assault against Vojvodina was in the meantime causing unrest and even desertions among the border units deployed in Italy, but Jelačić succeeded in halting this by appealing to them to remain loyal to the Austrian commander General Joseph Radetzky and promising them protection for their families at home. This strengthened his negotiating position with regard to Hungary. The archduke's attempt to reconcile Croatia and Hungary failed, however. The Croatian representatives insisted that the sabor and ban be recognised as legal, that Hungarian troops should leave Slavonia, that the Hungarian Serbs should be included in the negotiations, and that Hungary should recognise common bodies for the Monarchy. The Hungarian government found unacceptable all the Croatian demands, especially in regard to Vojvodina, support for which Kossuth proclaimed high treason. The Croatians could not give up Vojvodina, however, not only because they had endorsed its case as their own, but also because its military subjugation threatened the loss of Slavonia. During their negotiations, moreover, the Hungarian prime minister, Batthyány, could not promise Jelačić that Croatia would regain Slavonia, Rijeka and Međimurje. The Hungarian parliament, for its part, wrote to the king saying that Croatia's incorporation to Austria would undermine the latter's German nature, and asked that the sabor be dissolved. Kossuth argued that the Croatians were engaged in a dangerous rebellion aimed at the creation of a South Slav empire. His proposal that the Hungarian parliament begin recruiting 200,000 soldiers was accepted. Kukuljević insisted that the Croatian parliament was a lawful body, since it had been elected by the nation, and that the king should confirm its legitimacy as a condition for its negotiating with Hungary. Unable to agree, the two sides prepared for war.

The Hungarians formed their own national guard, while Jelačić instructed the counties to raise volunteer units in preparation for a mass mobilisation. These units marched under a new national red, white and blue tricolour combining the Croatian red and white and the Slavonian white and blue stripes. The press appeared with messages such as 'To arms! We must choose between war and slavery, independence and bondage, sovereignty and tyranny, glory and subjugation, pride and shame. Who can hesitate?' Fran Kurelac, a philologist of some note who was in charge of propaganda, called on the border to rise against the Magyars and their domestic supporters. The imperial war council, which never lost its grip on the situation, made a significant contribution to the Croatian defence effort and secretly pressed Jelačić to act against Hungary. It became clear by the end of the summer of 1848 that the differences between Croatia and Hungary would have to be resolved by war, all the more so since throughout the summer Slavonia had come under increased Hungarian pressure, and Vojvodina had been exposed to a strong military attack that it found itself increasingly unable to resist. A war psychosis now gripped Croatia, resulting in vitriolic attacks on Hungary's 'perfidious' policy towards Croatia and its repression of non-Magyar nationalities, which at times acquired an openly chauvinistic form.

Throughout the anarchic conditions of 1848–9 the sabor behaved like an independent body. It sent a delegation to negotiate with the Austrian parliament; the Reichstag, however, was too busy with its own problems to be able to focus on Croatia, quite apart from the fact that there were no established procedural rules for accepting the participation of a land belonging to the Hungarian crown. The German and Polish deputies were openly against receiving the Croatians, while the other Slav deputies felt there was little they could do. In the end the Croatians did not press their case, limiting themselves instead to issuing a manifesto to the Austrian and other European nations explaining that their cause was both just and lawful. According to this manifesto, drafted by Mažuranić, there were two positions from which one could view the movement of all nations: that of natural and that of historic right. The Croatian cause was based on both of them. Natural right, however, was the strongest right, since the foundation of every right rests on nature. Convinced that all nations were born free and equal, the Croatians' main wish was to be 'a free nation within a free Austrian empire'.

The Croatian cause found little support in the European press, which as a rule portrayed the Hungarians as freedom fighters and the Croats and other Slavs as supporters of Austrian absolutism and reaction. This was true especially of German public opinion, which viewed the Hungarian as natural allies against the alleged danger of Panslavism acting as a cover for Russia's westward expansion.[26] The Hungarian government and press readily fanned such fears, portraying Croatian policy as the work of a few fanatics and of Austrian reactionaries, but simultaneously also as an expression of Panslavism in the service of the Russian tsar. In late summer, however, Vienna adopted a more hostile stance towards Hungary. After the Austrian victory against Piedmont at Custozza in July 1848, which secured Lombardy for Austria, the court felt able to take on Hungary. The imperial family returned to Vienna in August, and at the end of the month the court chaplain, Josip Juraj Strossmayer, informed Ban Jelačić that the king wished him to take his army into Hungary. In early September Patriarch Rajačić too urged Jelačić to 'cross the Drava and clear Slavonia of the Magyars', threatening that unless the ban moved immediately he would be left with no other option but to annul the alliance with the Croatians and 'call on all Serb forces wherever they are to gather around us'. Zagreb too pressed Jelačić to act. On 4 September the king rescinded 'with singular satisfaction' all his decrees removing 'my dear Baron Jelačić' from his posts, and expressed the hope that Jelačić would strive to secure Austria's happiness, the integrity of the Hungarian crown, and beneficial development of the 'associated lands'.[27] Before proceeding to Hungary Jelačić took control of Rijeka in a bloodless coup, secured the full support of the Slavonian regiments, and regained the county of Virovitica. On 7 September the ban issued a proclamation to the nation in which he blamed the 'egoistical party' in Hungary for repressing the non-Magyar nationalities; attempting to enslave Croatia and annex its Slavonian territory; and destroying the unity of the Monarchy. Hungary's rejection of Croatia's rightful demands meant they would have to be realised through war. Backed by other Austrian generals, he crossed the river Drava on 11 September at Varaždin at the head of 50,000 badly trained and supplied recruits from the border, who immediately proceeded to plunder Međimurje, which Jelačić promptly annexed to Croatia.

The Austrian government, determined to rescind all the concessions it had been forced to grant to Hungary, now accused its government of acting contrary to the spirit and letter of the Pragmatic Sanction, and of wishing to destroy the Croatian parliament and take control of the Military Border. Hungary's attempted secession, by weakening the Monarchy, was also threatening Europe's stability. The Hungarian parliament sent a delegation to Vienna asking that Jelačić be stopped, and approached the Reichstag directly with the same message; but the latter refused to receive the Hungarians on the same grounds as it had refused to receive the Croatians. In late September 1848 Hungary was placed under imperial control. In early October, following the lynching of the imperial commander in Pest, the Hungarian parliament was formally dismissed, its decisions declared unlawful, and the whole country placed under a state of emergency. Jelačić was appointed royal commissar and commander of the royal and imperial troops in Hungary and Transylvania. The Hungarian and Croatian parliaments were ordered to obey him in full. Both prime minister Batthyány and the palatine Archduke Stephen now resigned, after which control of the Hungarian parliament passed to Kossuth and his circle.

Ivan Kukljević wrote on the eve of the war that it would be fought *against* unification of the 'Slavo-Austrian states' with the German *Bund*, and *for* the monarchy's territorial integrity, conditioned by 'equality and freedom for all Austrian nations and nationalities'.[28] War aims included also 'destruction of Magyar hegemony'; liberation of the oppressed Hungarian non-Magyar nationalities; and realisation of the Croatian sabor's and the Serb assembly's demands. But he also worried that the Croatian army might be used to realise not this vision but another, one inimical to Croatian national interests. Šulek wrote that once Pest was taken, the non-Magyar Hungarian nationalities should set up their own states, which would then federate; the problem of drawing their borders should be easily solved, since the union would be based on friendship. In Dollhopf's view the revolution's task was to create a new world in the European southeast, and to conduct a thoroughgoing social and democratic reform. His colleague, Nikola Krestić, writing for *Slavenski jug* wrote that Hungary – 'that conglomerate of nations' – could not exist as an independent kingdom, but should 'for civilisation's sake' be dissolved into its national components, which would then combine with their co-nationals in Austria, leading to a rejuvenated Austrian federation. But the arrival of the imperial army rallied the Magyar population behind the newly formed Committee of National Defence headed by Kossuth. There was a new uprising in Vienna and the court once again fled the city, together with the majority of the Reichstag's deputies. The imperial army, commanded by Prince Windischgrätz, proceeded to put down the rebellion. The Croatian press had roundly denounced the uprising,

Habsburg generals Alfred Windischgrätz, Joseph Radetzky and Josip Jelačić, 1848–9

which they saw as the work of anti-Slav German and Hungarian nationalists. It reprinted Jelačić's endorsement of František Palacký's view that the 'Slavs are Austria's greatest supporters, since Austria is for the Slavs of existential importance', and that 'if Austria did not exist, it would have to be invented'. Later that month the king endorsed for the first time the equality of the Hungarian nationalities, after which Jelačić issued a proclamation to his co-nationals stressing that he had gone to Vienna not in order to crush national rights, but in order to create conditions for national equality to prevail in the Monarchy – his struggle was consequently the struggle of all Croatians.

In December 1848 the emperor-king Ferdinand abdicated in favour of his nephew Francis Joseph (1848–1916), but Hungary refused to acknowledge the new king. In early March 1849 the new monarch dissolved the Reichstag and proclaimed a new centralist constitution for the entire Monarchy. The Hungarian response was to dethrone the dynasty, proclaim Hungary an independent state, and instal a regency headed by Kossuth. Hungary was now fighting for its very existence, and so successfully in fact that Vienna was eventually forced to seek Russian help. Mažuranić expressed a general feeling in Zagreb when he wrote in April 1849: 'If the Magyars win, they will again subjugate our country, hang some patriots and seduce our people with their lies. They will, I know, end badly, but there will be much suffering until that happens. This is why, given our difficult state, we cannot but hope that they be brought down as soon as possible.'[29] On the eve of the Russian intervention, he added: 'God willing, we shall come out of this war with much of our skin intact, but one can only imagine the distress and misery that await Hungary and Transylvania.'[30] The Hungarian national army surrendered to the Russians at Világos on 13 August 1849, after which the country was placed under military rule – justified on the grounds that Hungary had forfeited its separate institutions guaranteed by the Pragmatic Sanction.

The shifting sands of constitutionalism

The brutality with which the imperial army had subjugated Vienna, Jelačić's subordination to Windischgrätz and the emergence of a counter-revolutionary imperial government headed by Prince Felix Schwarzenberg created grave doubts in Zagreb. Šulek wrote that the Croatians had fought against the Hungarian government for national reasons, not against the idea of representative government. Kukuljević asserted that although Austrian German and Hungarian Magyar revolutionaries had refused to honour the principle of 'liberty, equality and fraternity', one should not rejoice in their defeat, since 'the old Austrian [centralist] spirit' was reviving, and the liberation which the Austrian Slavs had so eagerly awaited had not come. He attacked the new practice of appointing German officials to run Slav lands and condemned those Slavs who were ready to obey them. At the same time, some of the measures proclaimed by the new government in Vienna were welcome, such as Jelačić's appointment as governor of Rijeka and Dalmatia (which made little difference in reality) and the promise of local self-government. The imposed March Constitution aimed at creating a unified system of administration for the whole Habsburg Monarchy. The latter was now perceived as an association of crownlands, whose parliaments were retained, but with limited powers. Feudal land laws and legal systems based on them were abolished. The police was removed from the jurisdiction of crownlands, while their churches, schools and municipal affairs were to be run in accordance with common imperial laws. Equality of nations and languages was promised, single citizenship and common private and public laws introduced. The customs barrier between the Austrian imperial and Hungarian crownlands was removed, and the Austrian tax system extended to the latter. The constitution envisaged the creation of a central parliament which in time, it was hoped, would create a single Austrian 'state people'. It was to be composed of two chambers: an upper house, made up of deputies elected by crown land on the basis of stiff property qualifications, and a lower house composed of deputies elected on a proportional basis (one deputy per 100,000 inhabitants). The powers of the central parliament, however, were strictly limited in favour of the monarch. The monarch was to be crowned only once, as Emperor of Austria, and retained an absolute right of veto:

a vetoed decision could not be reconsidered by the same parliament. The emperor had the right to appoint a governor (*Staathalter*) for each crownland to ensure respect for imperial and regional laws. The emperor had the sole right to convene and dissolve central and local parliaments, appoint and dismiss the prime minister, confirm ministers and approve decisions of the legislative bodies. He also nominated all senior crownland officials, including the palatine in Hungary and the ban in Croatia. This centralisation was to be offset, however, by a considerable degree of autonomy vested in local municipal governments. According to Šulek, this should remove supporters of the Magyars in Hungary, of the Italians in Dalmatia, and of the Germans in Slovenia.

The Croatian-Hungarian constitution was confirmed, except where in conflict with the new constitution, but not the unity of the Hungarian crownlands as established by the Hungarian laws of 1848. Transylvania was detached from Hungary and given self-government. The Serbs of Vojvodina, however, were guaranteed only protection of their 'Church and nationality'. Croatia, inclusive of Rijeka and the Littoral, was proclaimed 'wholly independent from the Kingdom of Hungary', and Dalmatia was invited to discuss with the sabor terms of unification under the auspices of the central government, with the proviso that the results of the negotiations would be submitted to the king for confirmation. The institution of the Military Border, however, was retained under the control of the imperial war ministry 'for the defence of the state as a whole'. Its regiments were incorporated into the imperial army, but the border population was promised the same civic rights as those enjoyed by the rest of the emperor's subjects. Croatia acquired also its own supreme court, subject only to the supreme court in Vienna.

The March Constitution thus legitimised Croatia's independence from Hungary and endorsed the principle of national equality. While some saw the new constitution as the beginning of a new absolutism, others, including Mažuranić and Kukuljević, preferred to look at it as a possible path to a desired Austrian federation. The old idea that Croatia should participate in the Austrian parliament now revived, this time supported by the Czechs, who hoped that the arrival of Croats and Serbs would strengthen its Slav component. But the omens were not good. In a Hungary under the control of the imperial army, local government was entrusted to the magnates of the former Conservative Party, who were as intolerant towards non-Magyar nationalities as their more rebellious countrymen. The Croatian press wrote that the Slavs had supported the war against Hungary in the hope of ending Magyar hegemony and making Hungary a more humane and democratic land, but that their hopes had been disappointed given the behaviour of Hungarian officials who were not only enforcing Magyarism, but also openly working against state unity. The new Austrian government was accused of wishing to subjugate the Slavs in Austria to German domination and those in Hungary to Magyar domination.

In so far as it was implemented the March Constitution replaced the old chaotic Croatian administrative system based on diffused authority and seigneurial rights with a centralised structure resting on strict discipline and close supervision. Former officials (drawn as before from the nobility and the urban class) had to reapply for their posts, while county heads were appointed directly, largely from the magnate class. The upper ranks of the civil service in Croatia continued to be filled by Illyrians, however, and included at Jelačić's behest many nationally minded Serbs. But the Croatian tricolour adopted in 1848 as the symbol of national and state unity was now banned. The change in the style of government was both fundamental and sudden and it shook the entire country. Its unfamiliarity was compounded by the fact that its introduction coincided with implementation of new laws regulating social and economic relations in the towns and villages following the dissolution of serfdom.

The 'sons of the nation' remained to be educated in the new governing ways, and in the meantime officials were sent from the Austrian part of the monarchy to implement the reforms. Since most of the imported bureaucrats did not speak Croat, the German language came to dominate the internal administration. Orders issued by the central government were translated into Croat by native officials who had no time to polish their translations, as a result of which the official Croat acquired many German-language elements, which in turn provoked a linguistic reaction in the form of exaggerated purism and inflexibility. An unintended by-product of this period was that German became the second language of the generation entering public life in the 1850s and early 1860s, eradicating – as it turned out, for good – the earlier gains made by the Hungarian language in Croatia. However, this German-speaking administration had great trouble in communicating with the local population, which caused grave problems at the crucial level of the lower courts, confronted with the competing claims of lords and peasants in regard to the land and monetary compensation arising from the transfer of ownership.

Following the proclamation of the March Constitution, Croatia's demands were limited to protecting its political autonomy from Vienna and regaining its territories. In Croatian eyes the new government in Vienna, with its stress on centralised rule and use of the German language, threatened to negate the great sacrifice the country had made in its efforts to rid itself of Hungarian rule. Writing to Jelačić in Hungary, Mažuranić summed up the situation as follows:

> Our territorial borders have not been secured in accordance with our demands, nor is there hope that they will be. The country is made unstable, moreover, by unfulfilled expectations and inclines to the old – and at times even pro-Hungarian – sentiments. The peasantry is being provoked by attempts to re-introduce the *robot*, while the Border is upset by the supreme command's open intention to uphold the inimical status quo. The policy of the ban's council, which does not conform to the new national spirit, is becoming unsustainable and could also be described as inept. The country is pressed from outside by an administration whose character is foreign to us and which – impelled by the desire to restore the Monarchy's integrity and to win for itself the glory of having solved an insoluble [national-constitutional] puzzle – restricts itself to encouraging words, but does nothing for us. [The] country is still too weak and reacts against the firm, decisive, liberal but anti-national [Austrian] leadership.[31]

Mažuranić wrote this from Vienna, where he arrived with the Croatian deputation in order to protest against the imposed constitution and gain from the king legalisation of the sabor's decisions. The Croatians' greatest concern was that the country's emancipation from Hungary was not accompanied by any formal recognition of its frontiers; without fixed borders it was impossible to organise a national administration. They argued that, while the country had made considerable sacrifices for the king and the empire, its parliament's decisions had not been confirmed, thus leaving the country's status within the Monarchy undefined. The March Constitution did address this issue, but not in a manner that met Croatian aspirations, especially in regard to the Military Border. Neither could negotiations with Dalmatia proceed in the absence of the sabor, which the king refused to convene. Indeed, Ban Jelačić was now replaced by General Lazar Mamula of the Military Border as Dalmatia's new governor.

The ban's council consequently refused to proclaim the imposed constitution, largely on the grounds that it had to be first approved by the national parliament. Kukuljević wrote to Jelačić:

> If our nation were to accept today a patent or rescript – however

good it may be – in an unlawful manner, who can guarantee us that tomorrow it might not have to accept an unbefitting and even a dangerous one? If we accepted the imposed constitution, we should be surrendering our sabor's political authority, our old sovereignty, and the vital union with our Border, [which] alone can realise, sooner or later, our ideas. We should have to give up having any direct influence in Bosnia and Serbia, and our aspirations to unite with our Slav neighbours in Dalmatia, Istria, Carniola, etc.[32]

The country divided between a minority that believed that Croatia's modernisation needed Vienna's intervention and a majority that asserted that political autonomy was the only guarantee of national development. The latter argued that the old system of government could have been modernised rather than abolished outright – that the ban's council could institute the required changes, if only given the necessary powers. Despite their misgivings the Croatian administrators adopted a pragmatic stance, in the belief that the imposed constitution was not all that negative for their country, and that cooperation with Vienna could secure realisation of at least part of the national programme.

Awaiting the end of the war and recall of the sabor, the ban's council concentrated on drafting Croatia's own constitution – which fundamentally disagreed with the March Constitution. The 'draft law on the relationship between the Triune Kingdom and Austria' defined Croatia as 'a single whole governed by a single law and constitution that can never be divided or broken up', and specified its territory: the six counties of Civilian Croatia, the Military Border, Dalmatia, Rijeka, Srijem and Međimurje (Istria was not included, despite agitation by some Istrians). The draft envisaged Croatia's eventual unification with the Hungarian Serb and Austrian Slovene areas, but resisted the Monarchy's inclusion into the German Federation favoured by many Austrian Germans. It offered a vision of a fully sovereign Croatia within an Austrian confederation. Croatia was to sign inter-state agreements with the king and with individual crownlands in regard to common affairs, which could not be unilaterally altered. Each of the central government ministries was to have a Croatian department linked to equivalent bodies in Zagreb. Croatia would have the right to veto all measures infringing its internal autonomy. Communication between Vienna and Zagreb would take place only in Croat. The central government would have the right to establish in Croatia neither bodies of higher authority than its government, nor ones of equal or lower authority but independent from it. In regard to internal administration the county system was retained, but it was democratised and made more professional. The government, headed by the ban, would be responsible to the sabor and concern itself with all affairs except those left to the central government. Royal decisions would henceforth be countersigned by the ban and the relevant minister. The sabor would convene annually, and the right of participating in it by virtue of social status would be abolished. The parliament was divided into two houses with equal powers, on the basis of taxable wealth. Laws would be proclaimed by the king-in-parliament and published in the national language. In the sphere of education, the Croatians simply adopted the new Austrian law on education. Teachers would be trained and subjected to the authority of the government, which would also run the schools in the Military Border. Primary education was to be available to all. Primary schools would be supported by the municipalities and secondary schools by the state. Zagreb would acquire its own university. The churches were to be removed from the educational system.

The discussion on the national army involved a geopolitical assessment, whose basic idea was that the Habsburg South Slavs should work together to remove the Ottoman state from the Balkans, in order to strengthen their position vis-à-vis their German, Italian and Hungarian neighbours. It was necessary on this score to unite the interests of the Habsburg dynasty and those of the South Slavs. Because of Croatia's strategic importance in regard to the Eastern Question, its military organisation had to be different from that of other Austrian lands. The national army, modelled on the national defence forces of Prussia and Baden, would come under the authority of the Croatian ministry of defence headed by the ban, and its main role was to guarantee Croatia's constitutional and political liberties. Croatia's army would form a separate component of the imperial forces.[33]

These drafts, in sum, provided a blueprint for the transformation of Croatia into a modern state coexisting with other similar liberal-democratic formations within a federated Monarchy. They remained, however, words on paper, since the king refused to convene the sabor. Croatia's relative freedom of action had been made possible by Austria's own war against Hungary; but as that war wound down the interregnum too came to an end. In July 1849 the king proclaimed a land law for Croatia, which sanctioned the decisions already made by the sabor in 1848 but without any reference to that session, held to have been illegal. This intervention in Croatia's internal affairs was badly received. At the end of the month Ban Jelačić issued a proclamation stating that the March Constitution – which 'guaranteed self-government to each and every crownland and the free development of every nationality',[34] and secured also the Monarchy's unity – was in the spirit of the national will expressed by the previous sabor. The nation's most important task now was to forge new political and governing institutions based on that constitution. The ban's council, however, refused to proclaim the new constitution, on the grounds that it was 'contrary to our own and still binding constitution, according to which the only laws valid in our country are those drafted by the sabor and confirmed by the king'.[35] The council could not usurp authority which belonged only to the parliament. The ban should accordingly present the March Constitution to the sabor. The decreed constitution, however, not only negated Croatia's 'fundamental political and historic rights', but also infringed its territorial integrity by maintaining the separation of the Military Border. The country had risen against Hungary to protect its constitution and would continue to defend it.

According to Jelačić, it was necessary to adopt the decreed constitution in order to regulate Croatia's status within the Monarchy, thus ending the crippling *provisorium*. His supporters argued that Croatia should not erect a Chinese Wall between itself and the Austrian Slavs, since this would lead to its cultural and economic regression as well as to loss of political influence. The stance of the ban's council mainly aided the Hungarian conservatives. The pro-Austrian Croatian press insisted that Croatia could no longer behave like a state within a state, that the March Constitution was an established fact, and that Croatia could renew its political institutions only on that basis. The South Slavs united with Austria could play an important role in recovering their lands now in the Ottoman Empire. The Monarchy's independence from Germany, moreover, could not be secured without it first achieving internal stability.

Josip Juraj Strossmayer joined the fray. According to him, the Slavs would be in a majority in the central parliament, where in any case the constitution's worst aspects could be removed. The council should proclaim the constitution while expressing suitable reservations about its possible negative effects on Croatian autonomy. He himself did not like the March Constitution, but it was time for Croatia to compromise, since it could not win. He and others of similar view, including the Zagreb bishop Haulik, believed that the adoption of a common constitution would usher in constitutional rule throughout the Monarchy, thus allowing Croatia to realise at least some of its basic aims, such as regaining Dalmatia. Unless the Croatians accepted the constitution, the central government would leave them to the tender mercies of Hungary. Šulek, however, argued that in 1848 Vienna had asked only for the centralisation of some affairs, whereas now it was imposing a constitution, replacing regional governments by imperial officials, and insisting on German as the language of central administration. German centralism was even more dangerous than Hungarian. Croatia should join Austria only if the latter could guarantee it more self-government than it had enjoyed under Hungary. To deny Croatia the Military Border was to endorse an usurpation that the Croatian parliament had never accepted. The Croatian constitution might not be perfect, but it was up to the sabor to change it. Though feudal in the past, it was being modernised quite painlessly and could undergo further improvement. The March Constitution favoured only German bureaucracy.[36]

Croatian public opinion was thus divided between those who believed that nothing more could be gained by resisting while something could be gained by cooperation, and those who believed that only tenacity could secure the fulfilment of important demands, especially those relating to self-government and territorial integrity. The differences were tactical, not strategic. One side stressed the importance of institutional modernisation, which could be achieved only in cooperation with Vienna, the other that of national emancipation, which Vienna was obstructing. This debate became somewhat abstract after the capitulation of the Hungarian rebel army to Russian forces in mid-August 1849. At the end of that month, under pressure from both Vienna and Austrian Slav public opinion, the ban's council finally proclaimed the new constitution, after which it was dissolved and replaced by a state council headed by the ban acting as the executive of the central government. County self-government was abolished and a new vertical bureaucratic structure erected in its place, subject to control by the central interior ministry. The Croatian press became subject to strict censorship. In April 1850 the sabor of 1848 was formally dissolved, though a limited number of its decisions were confirmed, including endorsement of the Monarchy's unity, Croatia's separation from Hungary, national equality, and Croat as the official language. By the end of 1850 all oppositional activity had been either banned or drastically curtailed, and the whole country had been brought under central control. On 31 December 1851 the monarch suspended the contested constitution by the so-called Sylvester Patent, which affirmed legal equality of citizens, the end of serfdom and religious tolerance, but said nothing about national equality.

The Aftermath

In October 1849 Croatian representatives led by Ban Jelačić and Serb representatives headed by Patriarch Rajačić met to negotiate relations between Croatia and Vojvodina. The Croatian side and a minority of the Vojvodina Serbs wished for a common legislature, while the majority of the Serb politicians wished Vojvodina to become a separate crownland, which might eventually unite with Croatia. A month later Vojvodina, including the Banat of Temesvár and eastern Srijem, was proclaimed a separate crownland, governed by an Austrian general.

The Military Border representatives, under Jelačić's supervision, had drafted a basis for reform of the border system, which envisaged an immediate dissolution of the Varaždin Border and the introduction of civic reforms in the rest. The border was to be represented in the sabor. These proposals were rejected by Vienna in favour of the Basic Law on the Border of May 1850: this promised limited social and economic reform, but reaffirmed the border's separation from Croatia, obligatory military service and German as the official language.

In 1850 the Zagreb bishopric was given the status of an archbishopric, thus completing Croatia's separation from Hungary. This 'secession' of the Croatian Church offended the Hungarian clergy's national pride, which experienced it as yet another blow against the unity of the Hungarian crown lands. The formal independence of the Croatian Church was confirmed by the pope in 1856, when the Zagreb archbishop Juraj Haulik was named cardinal. The Vatican placed under his authority the bishoprics of Senj and Đakovo, the Uniate bishopric of Križevci, and the bishopric of Belgrade and Smederevo *in partibus*.[37] Upon Jelačić's recommendation, Josip Juraj Strossmayer was appointed bishop of Đakovo – hence, also of Srijem and Bosnia – and Catholic vicar for Serbia. This was an important post, in view of the fact that Austria had acquired responsibility for the Catholic population living in the Ottoman Empire. On his inauguration Strossmayer declared that he would be guided by the principle 'For faith and homeland!' He inherited the wealthy manor of Đakovo, the proceeds of which he would thereafter use to finance Croatian cultural and national institutions and initiatives.

In 1848 the pro-Hungarian nobility had either withdrawn into private life or emigrated. Those of more conservative outlook had gone to Austria, others to Hungary where they became officials or deputies in the parliament. Their departure was universally condemned in Croatia, and when the 1848 war started they were treated as public enemies. Those who had fled were banned from returning, and their property was sequestrated in order to prevent them using the income from their estates to pursue 'anti-state activities'. An identical course was followed by the Hungarian government, which confiscated the property of its opponents in Slavonia, including Patriarch Rajačić's manor of Dalj. After the invasion of Hungary by the imperial troops, it became clear to the 'Magyarones' that they had joined the losing side. As the Hungarian revolution radicalised, moreover, the Croatian immigrants became increasingly ostracised. As a result, requests to be permitted to return to Croatia multiplied. The right to return was made conditional, however, upon signature of an oath of loyalty. Some of those who returned were put on trial, and in such places as the county of Virovitica there was a systematic purge of officials. By the middle of 1849, however, the desire for revenge waned in reaction to Austrian centralism and the terror in Hungary. During the 1850s the 'Magyarones', who in 1848 were persecuted for agitating against king and country, became the pillars of the new absolutist regime. Prominent nationals, by contrast, were now viewed by the court in Vienna as dangerous radicals.

It is often said that, in the aftermath of the defeat of the 1848 revolutions in the Habsburg lands, Croatia received as reward what Hungary gained as punishment. This is only partially true. Relying largely on its own resources, the country was able to secure its autonomy and ensure that Slavonia would remain in Croatia. On the other hand, one of the great gains of 1848 – the liberation of the serfs – was not accomplished as part of the national movement. It is true that the abolition of serfdom in the lands of the Hungarian crown had the consent of Croatian representatives, that the ban proclaimed it valid in Croatia, and that the sabor gave it the necessary legal base. But the measure was decided on by Hungarian Liberals, fearful that it might otherwise be imposed by Vienna. The new agrarian law gave the peasants, in return for full compensation for the lords, only the secessional land upon which they had in any case enjoyed security ever since Maria Theresa's land laws. Meanwhile, the cancellation of feudal dues was not extended to land rented or otherwise gained from the allodium, nor to vineyards and pastures; nor did it include *iura regalia minora*, which was the source of considerable noble income. Only in Slovenia and Slovakia, where no national nobility existed, did the national movements of 1848 throw up agrarian demands more radical than those proposed in Vienna, Zagreb or Pest.

That serfdom should be abolished was something that the Illyrians supported wholeheartedly. 'It is not possible to imagine our country's happiness so long as inequality exists between the nobility and the peasantry', wrote Vukotinović in early 1848.[38] The National Demands drafted by Kukuljević and Gaj incorporated the abolition of serfdom, and called for representation of the peasantry in the national parliament. The legislative initiative, however, came from outside and, once made public, its effects could not easily be controlled by the Croatian government. The peasants interpreted the new laws in accordance with their own understanding, taking over the land they considered their own, refusing to pay customary dues, and occasionally putting noble mansions to the torch. The alliance with the conservative nobility in the name of national unity made it practically inevitable that the peasantry, seeking its own social and economic emancipation, would remain largely oblivious to the calls for national independence and democratic reform emanating from the cities and county assemblies. One of the first measures undertaken by Jelačić on assuming office as ban was indeed to institute summary courts directed as much against peasant brigands as against local sympathisers with Hungary. The fear of peasant anarchy in Croatia was compounded by the fact that the grip of the ban's council on the county administration was weaker than in Hungary. Whatever the differences among the Illyrians in regard to the justice of the new land laws, they situated themselves firmly on the terrain of legality; but the state which they were creating was not yet securely established. Fear of the peasantry, however, proved unjustified. As in Hungary, the initial wave of peasant unrest died down with the convocation of the national parliament. The newly liberated peasant population nevertheless remained to be educated in the national spirit, whose first principle was respect for law. The liberal journal *Slavenski Jug*, whose foundation coincided with a second wave of peasant unrest related to the wine tithe, addressed this need by publishing a supplement entitled *Friend of the People*, with the aim of inculcating national and democratic ideas in the countryside. In the first issue its editor, Dragutin Kušlan, a prominent noble member of the National Party, described feudalism as a foreign import and stressed the need for unity between nobility and peasantry. The nobility had to understand that peasant subjugation weakened the national will, while the peasantry had to acknowledge that 'one cannot be without masters, since they guarantee the rule of law'.[39]

The National Party, keen to keep the nobility's support, had endorsed the principle of compensation to the lords for land surrendered and for all cancelled feudal dues – while leaving the level and manner of payment to be decided in the future. However, given that the new agrarian laws were introduced against a background of preparations for war with Hungary, the sabor voted to extend their scope to cover also *iura regalia minora*. The peasants' unhindered access to pastures and forests was also left standing until such time as a proper decision could be made in the legislature. Similar laws were enacted in Hungary as soon as Jelačić crossed the Drava. But the traditional gulf between town and countryside was not significantly narrowed by the revolutionary year of 1848. Important for the future was the impact of the new land laws on the national economy. In the course of the discussion in the sabor in this regard, doubts were expressed as to whether the country would be able to sustain the level of taxation implied by the principle of total compensation for landowners, and there was concern that the burden might lead to peasant impoverishment 'on the Irish scale'. This fear was subsequently vindicated. Given the poverty in the countryside, the land reimbursement fund was constantly in deficit, creating an acute sense of dissatisfaction among the nobility. Since the configuration of land tenure and feudal dues was far more complex in 'Croatia' than in Slavonia, there was also a resurgence of Slavonian separatism. Isolated from the countryside and working in adverse international conditions, the National Party would be unable to sustain its struggle for Croatian autonomy against both Vienna and Budapest.

EIGHT

Interregnum

The various attempts ushered by the 1848 revolutions to reform the Habsburg Monarchy by finding a compromise between its component nationalities on the one hand and to establish a constitutional government based on elected bodies on the other ended with the dissolution of the Austrian parliament in March 1849 and the imposition of a new March Constitution, which itself was suspended with the February Patent of 1851. The Habsburg Monarchy now entered a period of the so-called neo-Absolutism in that all power became vested in the person of the monarch, and in the government in Vienna formally appointed by him, which ruled without resort to the local parliaments. This state of affairs continued until 1860, when another attempt at political reforms was made and, having failed again, led to a settlement in 1867 creating the dual state of Austria-Hungary.

During the period of direct rule exercised by Vienna, which lasted from 1850 effectively up to 1865, the Croatian feudal state was dismantled in all respects, economic, administrative and judicial. But the new order was slow to establish itself, and met, moreover, with strong resistance. Vienna's great gift was introduction of the liberal Austrian civil law; but the new legal system could not operate without the appropriate institutional framework, which was in its infancy and which continued to change in accordance with the nature of central rule itself. This was most visible in the application of the new land laws abolishing feudal dues, noble justice and church tithes. The legal separation of demesne and serf land proved relatively easy, but the same was not true for other categories such as forests and pastures, newly cleared land, vineyards, un-allotted land, or serf plots established on demesne land. Since the dissolution of serfdom was carried through in a legally, politically and administratively confusing situation, the struggle between former lords and newly emancipated peasants could not always be conducted through the courts. Special land commissions were established to investigate individual cases and decide the level of compensation, but the lords and the peasants had different views on the nature of individual land or rights. Judgments by the land commissions were frequently contested, leading to endless litigation that soon overwhelmed the land courts set up to adjudicate such complaints Disputes between the peasants and the lords consequently often ended in violent confrontation. The lack of qualified legal experts, land surveyors, and accurate maps and records – combined with the absence or poor condition of roads – further aggravated an already difficult situation. The state tried to protect the peasant, but the commissions were as a rule controlled by landowners or staffed with their sympathisers. The resulting peasant unrest was further stimulated by hunger, which became endemic in the 1850s. By 1857 the land commissions were nevertheless able to conclude their work and assess the extent of reparations due to the landowners.

Since the state had inherited the responsibility for indemnifying the nobility, a special fund was established for the purpose, financed from direct taxation. Some of the money was paid out immediately, albeit in a staggered form; but most payments took the form of state bonds which were transferable and carried interest. Some of these bonds were bought outright, others sold on the Vienna stock exchange. The central government subsidised the payments in the economically more passive eastern lands, but the bulk of the cost was borne by the crownlands. In the case of Civilian Croatia-Slavonia, the vast majority of the population belonged to the lowest tax category and was unable to pay its share. The local government's obligation to divert part of its revenue into the funds for reimbursement of landowners limited other budgetary allocations, while creating a soaring public debt. Croatian-Slavonian differences now re-emerged: impatient with the delay caused by the complexity of the situation in central Croatia, Slavonian landowners demanded (albeit unsuccessfully) that a separate land fund be set up for Slavonia.

Central government did nothing to remedy the economic stagnation that resulted from the change. It dictated the tempo of modernisation, but was neither able to invest nor indeed interested in furthering Croatia's economic development. The compensation which the nobility received was significant enough to impoverish the peasantry but not large enough to allow investment, given that it was paid over time and in bonds of rapidly decreasing value. Croatian landowners soon discovered that they could not sell land at its nominal value, but could not work it either in the absence of serf labour. The majority of landowners knew that technical advance was not possible using serf labour; but at a time when their lands lacked both labour and capital investment they sought to put off implementation of the new land laws. The odium for this state of affairs was directed at Vienna. The liberal-minded national administration had the potential to make modernisation more acceptable to the masses, but it was prevented from doing so by the institution of direct rule as well as by its own mistrust of Vienna's intentions.

In order to codify the new land laws and establish a uniform tax base, it was necessary to produce an accurate register of the land, and also of other forms of individual and public revenue. This demanded a national census. The first attempt at this, conducted in 1851, was largely the work of the military authorities aided by local parish priests, and was consequently unreliable. It was the census carried out in 1857 for the Habsburg Monarchy as a whole that gave a first insight into the social, ethnic and religious composition of the Croatian lands. According to this census, the Triune Kingdom had around 2,000,000 inhabitants, of whom 44 per cent lived in Civilian Croatia-Slavonia (henceforth Ban's Croatia), 35 per cent in the Military Border and 21 per cent in Dalmatia.[1] Ban's Croatia was an overwhelmingly agrarian land in which only three cities – Zagreb, Osijek and Rijeka – had more than 10,000 inhabitants.[2] Civilian 'Croatia', which formed the larger and more populous part, contained 70 per cent of its overall population, mostly (over 97 per cent) Catholic. The Orthodox population was more evident in Civilian Slavonia, where it was concentrated in the counties of Požega and Osijek.[3] The royal free cities and smaller towns in Ban's Croatia were almost exclusively Catholic, with only Osijek showing a significant Orthodox presence.

Population of Croatia by religion in 1857[4]

Region	Number	% Catholic	% Orthodox
Ban's Croatia	845,503	89.6	9.8
Dalmatia	415,305	81.3	18.6
Military Border	674,864	58.8	40.3
Total	1,935,672	77.1	22.3

Population of Ban's Croatia by county in 1857[5]

County	Number	% Catholic	% Orthodox
Zagreb	241,098	98.9	0.9
Varaždin	252,884	98.7	0.6

County	Number	% Catholic	% Orthodox
Rijeka	86,669	97.7	2.3
Požega	63,341	60.0	39.0
Osijek	101,559	70.5	24.8

The proportions of Catholic and Orthodox in the Military Border varied from regiment to regiment, with those of the Orthodox faith forming majorities in five out of eleven regiments, while the inhabitants of the military townships were, with the exception of Karlovci and Zemun, overwhelmingly Catholic. In the case of Dalmatia, 60 per cent of its Orthodox population lived in the interior of northern Dalmatia and 30 per cent in the area of the Bay of Kotor. The urban population of Dalmatia was also overwhelmingly Catholic (93 per cent).[6]

Military Border population in 1857[7]

Regiment	Number	% Catholic	% Orthodox
Lika	76,856	33.6	66.4
Otočac	67,809	55.2	44.8
Ogulin	73,318	53.7	42.3
Slunj	61,424	44.5	46.8
Križevci	61,532	73.0	26.9
Đurđevci	78,534	78.7	21.2
Brod	72,064	92.3	7.6
Gradiška	66,398	75.9	24.1
Ban's 1st	61,141	33.2	66.8
Ban's 2nd	53,279	36.4	63.6
Petrovaradin	75,730	14.0	76.0

An attempt to identify this population by nationality in the first census of 1851 was frustrated by the fact that central government had only a very hazy idea of how to classify Croatia's Slav population. Guided by a theory propagated by the Slovak philologist Pavel Šafařik and the Slovene philologist Jernej Kopitar which identified nation with language, the census treated *štokavian* speakers as Serbs, *kajkavian* as Slovenes and *čakavian* as Croats, which led to the absurd conclusion that most of Croatia was totally devoid of Croats. In subsequent censuses, the category of nationality was replaced by those of confession and language. Nationality defined by language would anyway have produced a confusing picture, since in the early 1850s there was no unanimity in Ban's Croatia on what to call 'the national language' that the sabor had proclaimed as Croatia's official language.

Naming the language

When the Serbian linguist Vuk Karadžić (1787–1864) chose the *ijekavski štokavian* speech of eastern Herzegovina as the basis for his reform of the Serb language, it seemed that the stage was set for the creation of a linguistically unified 'Illyrian nation'. This, however, soon proved illusory. One reason was that the Croat and Serb standards could not be made to coincide without doing violence to both, since the Croat variant of *štokavian* included within its corpus the *kajkavian* and *čakavian* tongues, while the 'pure' *štokavian* standard advocated by Karadžić did not. Since both the Croats and the Serbs were pursuing the same goal of creating a single *štokavian* standard, a degree of cooperation between them was inevitable; but the paths they followed were necessarily different and so too was the ultimate product.[8] At the same time, given that the Croat and Serb elites were primarily interested in the cultural and political unification of their own individual nations, the question of the language, instead of uniting them, emerged as a decisive battleground between the Croat and the Serb national ideas.

Whereas the Croat propagandists of the Illyrian idea saw the 'Illyrians' as a diverse group of historically defined Slav or South Slav polities, among the Serbs the term 'Illyrian' had become synonymous with 'Serb'. This view was expounded publicly for the first time in an article headed 'All and Everywhere Serbs' published by Karadžić in 1850, which acquired immediate notoriety since in it he proclaimed *štokavian* to be an exclusively Serb language, and *štokavian* speakers of Muslim and Catholic faith to be Serbs. *Kajkavian* speakers, on the other hand, were in his view Slovenes. The idea that most Croats were not Croat at all but Serb was naturally unacceptable to the Croats. The disagreement on how to standardise the *štokavian* language henceforth went hand in hand with the more emotive dispute over its national character. The debate set off by Karadžić was taken up in particular by writers from Novi Sad in Southern Hungary, which had emerged as the most important economic and cultural centre of the Hungarian Serbs.

A prompt response to the appropriation of the majority of Croats to the Serb and Slovene nations was supplied by Ante Starčević from Lika, a former Illyrian. Reacting against the view expressed in a Novi Sad journal that 'the Croats wish to write in our Serb language', Starčević not only claimed that *štokavian* was a Croat language but also made fun of the

Ante Starčević

belated birth of Serb vernacular literature. Belgrade voices soon joined the fray. After insisting that Dubrovnik (hence, also the much admired poet Ivan Gundulić) wrote 'the same language that Serb kingdoms and empires used to write', a respondent went on to say: 'Ljudevit Gaj wished to destroy the Serb name, and having failed to achieve that with Illyrianism he is now trying to turn us into Croats, by insisting that those who think of themselves as Serbs should use the educated Croat language,' i.e. the *štokavian* standard favoured by Zagreb philologists. Starčević in the end responded by negating the negation. The argument that all *kajkavian* speakers were Slovenes and all *štokavian* speakers Serbs could equally well lead to identifying both Slovenes and Serbs as Croats. If everyone was Croat, then the Illyrian language could be only the Croat language. There was indeed no Illyria, only Croatia. If there were to be unification of the South Slav lands, it would take place within Croatia.

The debate now became more politically charged. The Serb side upped the stakes by claiming that all Dalmatians were Serbs, and that all past literature written in the *štokavian* idiom was in fact Serb literature. As a sign of their increasing concern, the Croats changed the name 'Illyrian' in their publications to 'Croat'. In an attempt to calm the public quarrel, Bogoslav Šulek in 1852 published an article in which he argued that the Croats' readiness to unite with other South Slavs under a common Illyrian or Yugoslav name had given the false impression that the Croats did not value their own name, as a result of which 'in recent years Serb writers have started to extend their name to Croats and other Slavs'. This was not just a matter of individual views, but had become widespread. In contrast to the Croat side, which had condemned Ante Starčević for claiming that all Serbs were Croats, the Serb side had failed to respond in similar fashion. Since, however, neither the Croats nor the Serbs wished to give up their names, they should stop trying to impose them on others. He reminded over-zealous

Vuk Karadžić with Mrs Karadžić

Serbs in Dalmatia, Bosnia and eastern Herzegovina, only immigrant Serbs called their language Serb. At the same time, the fact that some Croats called themselves Slavonians, Dalmatians, and so forth reflected only current political borders, not separate national names. He ended by recommending cooperation on the basis of equality and the abandonment of any desire for domination between Serbs and Croats, precisely because they had a shared language.[9]

Šulek's argument neatly summed up the Zagreb point of view, but had a limited effect. The debate continued. Karadžić, who had been responsible for the debate in the first place, finally responded to his critics in 1861 by reiterating his earlier views. In the 'present-day Kingdom of Croatia', he wrote, from which one should exclude Slavonia and the Military Border, since they did not in fact belong to it, apart from a few *čakavian* speakers who lived on the coast there were in reality no Croats, but only Slovenes and the occasional Serb. The Croatian kingdom consequently did not represent a nation – it was 'only a political and geographical concept like, for example, Switzerland'. If, however, 'the Croat patriots do not agree to this reasonable basic [ethno-linguistic] division, then the only thing one can do for the time being is to separate ourselves according to religion: those of the Orthodox faith, wherever they live, will never give up their Serb name, while those of the Catholic faith can call themselves Croats, if they so desire'.[10]

What began as a dispute over standardisation of the *štokavian* idiom thus quickly became transformed into a dispute over its national name – a slide that was inevitable given the prevailing scholastic view of the relationship between language and nation, but which had important implications in forming a modern sense of nationhood. More ominous for the future was the fact that the name of the language had emerged as a territorial marker, an instrument of demarcation not just of national, but also of political borders.

Educational dilemmas

It was generally accepted that the emancipated peasant majority had to be educated in their new role as citizens, but for this to happen it was necessary first to overcome their illiteracy. In 1848 the sabor had set up a committee to deal with the education of the population 'in humanities and national values'; but its 'fundamental guide' could be implemented only in 1850–1 when the Croatian educational system was organised on the Austrian model. In 1855, following a concordat with the Holy See, the churches became responsible for the primary schools' 'internal' needs – such as teaching, choice of the curriculum, and textbooks – while central government and local authorities looked after finances, including school building and maintenance. The Croatian government's request that a unified education system be created for both the 'civilian' and the 'military' parts of Croatia – on the grounds that dioceses cut across their borders – was rejected. Separation of children along confessional lines found strong support among Croatian ecclesiastical and secular leaders, for various and often contradictory reasons. In the Military Border, too, education involved the churches, particularly after 1829 when the border administration finally accepted the idea of separate education for the Orthodox population. The churches' involvement in education thus made an important contribution to separating the Croatian population along confessional liens.

The ban's council invested great effort in producing textbooks in the national language, and invited competition for primers dealing with national literature, history and geography. Some of these readers, however, proved unacceptable to the Catholic Church. One textbook, for example, was rejected on the grounds that it celebrated Jan Hus, the founding father of the Czech Reformation. A textbook by Bogoslav Šulek was criticised for a 'materialist' slant and for being 'too political'. Teacher training also suffered from hostility displayed by the Catholic Church towards the natural sciences (including mathematics) and history. Orthodox schools were in an even worse state than the Catholic ones, since the teachers, drawn largely from the clergy, were paid even less by their community and were often barely literate. Another problem was that the language of instruction in the Orthodox schools was Slavo-Serb, which the children did not understand. Jewish schools taught exclusively in German, but most Jewish children attended Catholic schools. Quite apart from such problems, the educational reform soon became mired in the chaos generated by the dissolution of the feudal system and by the frequent administrative changes dictated from Vienna. Many peasants refused to send their children to school, because their childrens' labour had become additionally important on the newly acquired farms. Progress was visible in the second half of the 1850s in the quality and number of schools; in 1869, nevertheless, 88 per cent of the village population and 52 per cent of the urban population in Civilian Croatia-Slavonia remained illiterate.

Crucial for the production of a national elite were the high schools or gymnasia in Zagreb, Varaždin, Karlovac, Požega, Osijek and Rijeka. During the 1850s they became eight-year schools, in which students were taught philosophy, Greek, Latin, history, geography, mathematics, natural sciences, Croat and German. Since Vienna saw these schools as the source of future officials, after 1851 some subjects were taught exclusively in German. German became the language of instruction also in the Zagreb Academy, although knowledge of the 'Illyrian' language remained a condition of entry. In the Karlovac gymnasium, which served the Military Border, the German language continued to reign supreme. In 1854 German became the only language of instruction in secondary schools, with Croat used only to teach the Croat language and religion. In some of the primary schools, separate German and 'Croato-Illyrian' departments were introduced. Ignorance of German grammar was consequently added to ignorance of Croat grammar. Since, moreover, the majority of students could not follow classes in German, teachers had to spend a good deal of their lessons explaining German terms before proceeding to teach their subjects. In 1857 German became also the language of religious instruction. Croatian national leaders were confronted with the realisation that they had succeeded in excluding Hungarian from public life only to see it replaced by German.

Central government also assumed control over the content, printing and distribution of textbooks, which were written in German and translated into the other national languages of the Monarchy. Local governments were permitted to alter their content by introducing elements of local national culture; but central government placed a particular emphasis on the teaching of 'the national history of Great Austria'. It sought to adapt individual national histories to that model, since the absence of such a common history from the schools was perceived by it as one of the main causes of 'narrow-minded national separatism'. The Croatians, however, approached the subject of history with the opposite aim in mind: they wished to provide a scientific and ideological legitimation of the Croatian national and state individuality.

There was, in addition, the problem of what to call the printed language. The language reader produced by Antun Mažuranić in 1856 was called *The Illyrian Reader*, but its contents derived mainly from Croatian literature (though a few works by Serb authors were also included). The introduction described *štokavian* as 'the proper Croat language', while noting that Serbs called it the Serb language. The first volume of the language primer by the same author was meanwhile called *Croat Grammar*. The introduction to this volume pointed out that, although Croat and Serb were one and the same language and Croats and Serbs one and the same people, the term 'Croat' had been chosen partly for the sake of brevity but also because it was most widespread. The second volume, written by another author, was called *Illyrian Language Syntax* – but 'Illyrian' here stood for Croat. By the end of the decade, at all events, the term Croat/Croatian prevailed as the name of both the language and the nation.[11] But other terms were also used in particular contexts – for example, 'the Croato-Slavonian nation', when it was necessary to stress the political unity of Croatia-Slavonia.

Ban Jelačić referred to the nation variously as 'Serb and Croat', 'Croatian-Slavonian', 'Dalmatian-Croatian-Slavonian', 'Croatian', and at times also 'Yugoslav' (meaning South Slav). Most Croat politicians were not quite sure what the term 'Serb' referred to. When, for example, in 1850 the Uniate Bishop Evgenije Jovanović called the Orthodox population of the Military Border 'Serb by nationality', he was told by the Border Colonel Josip Maroičić that he was confusing religion with nationality: in Maroičić's view the border had been inhabited 'since time immemorial' only by Croatians of the Catholic and Orthodox faiths, who had fought together for centuries under that name. He agreed that there were 'eastern Serbs' who at a late date had settled in Vojvodina; but they, in his view, were the product of a different evolution from that of the 'Croato-Dalmatians'.

The resurgence of Croat national sentiment was encouraged by centralist rule and by the Germanisation of public life, under the impact of which the former Illyrians finally gave up the Illyrian ideology. They recognised that, though a laudable project in itself, their attempt to unite the Monarchy's South Slavs under that name had failed, and that Croat, Slovene and Serb political projects were moving in different directions. Franjo Rački noted at this time that 'the younger generation is rallying around the ancient and glorious Croat name', in the knowledge that the territories of Croatia, Dalmatia, Slavonia, Dubrovnik, Istria and so on formed one country, because they were all inhabited by the same Croat people. Such displays of national self-esteem were treated by Vienna as separatism, which is why during the 1850s those who addressed national themes tended not to sign their articles. Kukuljević, however, speaking at Jelačić's funeral in 1859, recalled the late ban's pride in being Croat.

Rejection of the Illyrian name did not necessarily amount to rejection of the idea that the Croats belonged to a wider South Slav space. But the number was growing of those who, like Ante Starčević, believed that the Illyrian or South Slav orientation had been a grave strategic blunder, especially after Karadžić and his supporters proclaimed all *štokavian* speakers to be Serbs and the area of their settlement to be Serb land.

Problems of modernisation: the case of the county of Rijeka

The case of Rijeka provides a good example of the problems that the Vienna-led institutional reform of the Habsburg Monarchy faced in the Croatian area. The March 1849 constitution had proclaimed the Croatian Littoral, including the city of Rijeka, to be part of Croatia. The highland area to its north (Gorski Kotar) was detached from the county of Zagreb and joined to this territory to form the new county of Rijeka (a new name for the old county of Severin). In 1850 a provisional county court was established in Rijeka, with authority over all the courts on this territory, hitherto subject to a variety of juridical authorities. The former district court in Rijeka became the new county court. The city thus for the first time became a proper regional capital: losing its old separate status and privileges, it acquired new responsibilities under the direction of the government in Zagreb.

Zagreb instructed the Rijeka district court to receive submissions in both Italian and Croat; but the language of the court itself, which up to then had been Italian, was now to be Croat. At the first meeting of the new court, however, its president demanded that the court should continue to work in Italian, while the local administrators insisted on the exclusive use of Croat. A group of local lawyers joined the dispute by asking that Italian should be used alongside Croat, on the grounds that few local people could speak or read Croat. They were backed by some of the leading local families, who signed a petition to the king demanding that Italian be retained as the language of Rijeka's schools and court, though the latter might be addressed also in Croat. The ministry of justice in Vienna advised the Croatian supreme court that Italian should be retained for trade, banking and maritime law, and Croat be used in civil and criminal law. It also asked for an expert opinion on the local situation, and in the meantime gave its approval for Italian to remain the language of the Rijeka county court. The expert opinion was in the end supplied by Ivan Mažuranić, a native of the area. In his submission to the government in Vienna, he sketched out the previous legal and the existing linguistic make-up of the county of Rijeka. His memorandum provides a fascinating insight into the legal complexities involved in creating a uniform juridical system from the old tangled feudal one, as well as into the implications of the state's language policy for its eventual success.[12]

Mažuranić noted that the highland area (formerly under the jurisdiction of the county of Zagreb) contained 40,000 inhabitants, all of whom were Croat, while the Littoral itself had 48,000 overwhelmingly Croat inhabitants. The latter area, however, had previously been divided between three separate jurisdictions, covering the district of Vinodol (24,000 purely Croat inhabitants), the free city of Bakar with its district (12,000 purely Croat inhabitants), and the royal free city of Rijeka with its district (around 12,600 inhabitants, 78 per cent Croat, 13 per cent Slovene and 5.5 per cent Italian). The county as a whole was thus an overwhelmingly Croat-speaking area, which justified the decision that its administration and courts should function in Croat rather than in Italian.

Although this part of the Croatian coast had never been under Venetian rule, Venice's Adriatic supremacy had ensured that its language would be used also in the ports of Rijeka, Bakar and Kraljevica. The Venetian/Italian language, however, 'being nothing but an alluvium of the Adriatic Sea', stopped at the limits of these three ports: the rest of the Littoral spoke only Croat. Knowledge of Italian along the Croatian seaboard was essentially a function of trade with Italy: in Bakar and Kraljevica it was minimal, in the city of Rijeka more widespread. Rijeka, however, was hermetically enclosed on all sides by purely Croat population; 'like all other cities of the kingdom, [it] lies on Croatian territory'.

The Vinodol district (previously a Zrinski-Frankapan possession) had hitherto been administered by the state treasury acting as feudal lord. The internal language of its administration was Latin, while Croat was used as the external language. The court also operated in Latin, not by law but by custom. It was subject in the first instance to the Rijeka *gurbernium,* and then – depending on the nature of the case – to either the ban's court in Zagreb or to the Hungarian court chancellery. In the former case evidence submitted in Italian would be translated into Latin, in the latter evidence submitted in Croat had also to be translated into Latin. In 1848, when patrimonial jurisdiction was abolished, this court's competencies were transferred to the Rijeka county court, while Croat replaced Latin throughout the kingdom.

In the case of the city and district of Bakar, the administration had previously been run by the municipal council, which was independent of the governor of Rijeka. The council appointed local judges who were directly subject first to the ban's court in Zagreb, then to the supreme court of Croatia-Hungary. The official language of this court was Latin by custom, but Italian and Croat were also used. In cases of appeal to higher courts, submissions in Italian would be translated into Latin; those in Croat, however, would be translated into Latin only if forwarded to the joint supreme court.

The city of Rijeka had around 8,000 inhabitants. For various reasons Italian had become the language of its administration and schools. In reality, however, practically every locally born citizen spoke Croat: according to church evidence, two-thirds of Rijeka's citizens made their confessions only in Croat.[13] The city had nevertheless never made educational provision for the 4,000 people who lived outside its walls, and it was only recently that it had agreed to introduce Croat into the schools. The local gymnasium was attended by students from a wide area, including the Littoral, the neighbouring islands and Istria. In 1850–1 out of fifty-five students all but one were Croat. Although the city municipality had recently agreed to introduce Croat into the gymnasium, the latter nevertheless continued teaching some subjects in Italian because of this *one* pupil. All the students at the Rijeka nautical school spoke Croat. The 'normal' secondary schools, attended only by children from Rijeka, had 253 pupils of whom 204 spoke Croat; of the remaining 49 who did not – essentially the children of state officials and military personnel – only a few were ethnic Italians. What was at stake, Mažuranić argued, was thus not the denationalisation of an Italian Rijeka, but the needs and aspirations of the overwhelmingly Croat population.

From the point of view of both historical precedent and nationality it was impossible to justify equality of the Italian and Croat languages in the public life of the county. No one wished to eject Italian totally from schools or public life, since it was the language of an important culture; but it was obvious that only use of the native language could guarantee the county population's civic rights and cultural advance. In his view the courts should conduct their business in the language of the people, which accorded with the decision of the sabor sanctioned by the king in 1850.

As for the twelve Rijeka lawyers who had complained, he went on, all but three had recently submitted proof of their knowledge of the Croat language in their reapplications for state employment. Of the remaining three, two habitually used Croat in court, while the third also appeared to know Croat. In Mažuranić's view, their insistence on the Italian language derived from their desire to retain monopoly of legal representation. As for the citizens' petition, it claimed that education and courts functioning in the Croat language would harm the city's trade; but introduction of the Croat language did not mean that Italian would no longer be taught in schools, nor that the court would refuse to accept submissions in Italian. Trade in any case was conducted in many languages. Mažuranić recommended that the official language in the county of Rijeka should be Croat in external and internal affairs, and that special provision should be made for the use of Italian in cases related to maritime, trade and banking affairs involving individuals who were not citizens of the Triune Kingdom. All relevant official decrees could be made available also in Italian.[14]

This proposal was accepted in Vienna, but it was never implemented. The city oligarchy did not wish to be ruled by Zagreb and did all it could to sabotage Croatian laws. It is true that when Jelačić became governor of Rijeka, the leading local families promptly expressed their loyalty to their 'Croatian homeland'; after Hungary's surrender they even established a Croatian Patriotic Society for the Advancement of Croatian-Slavonian Nationality in the Littoral. But the Croatian government of the period was unable to secure for the city the desired rail link to Karlovac. Vienna instead built in 1857 a rail link between Vienna and Trieste, which redirected to the latter the trade normally served by Rijeka. In 1858, when the Austrian state sold all the railways to the Society of Southern Railways along with the monopoly for building railways south of the river Danube, the idea that Rijeka with its former district should be constituted as an autonomous unit within the Austrian empire made its appearance for the first time. Rijeka's growing industry, however, which in the 1850s formed half of the Croatian total, needed fresh capital investment. This, in the event, could only come from Hungary, ensuring that Rijeka would remain loyal to Pest for the rest of the century.

A brief return to constitutional rule

Jelačić died a few weeks after Austria's proclamation of war against Sardinia-Piedmont that was aided by France. In June 1859 the Austrian armies suffered heavy defeats at Magenta and Solferino, after which Vienna was forced to sue for a peace through which it lost Lombardy, though not Venice. In March 1861 Victor Emmanuel was proclaimed King of Italy. Defeats abroad and an empty state treasury forced Vienna to return to constitutional rule, resuscitating the question of the Monarchy's internal organisation. The first step in this direction was made in May 1860, when the emperor-king convened an enlarged imperial council attended by his own advisers and by representatives of the crownlands chosen by him from among the prelates and magnates. Ambroz Vranyczány and Josip Juraj Strossmayer represented Croatia-Slavonia, while Francesco Borelli attended on Dalmatia's behalf. The enlarged council met between May and September 1860, during which time it discussed future constitutional arrangements for the Monarchy. The body soon divided into a majority made up of Slavs and Hungarians, who sought restoration of the *status quo ante*, and a minority composed mainly of German liberals, who favoured a reformed centralism.

The Hungarians demanded the unification of Croatia and Transylvania with Hungary. The Romanian Orthodox bishop Andrieu Şaguna asked for national equality within Hungary itself. Vojvodina's representative insisted on its separation from Hungary. He was tacitly supported by Strossmayer, who argued against any too strict application of the 'historic principle' in regard to Hungary. The Croatians informed the assembly that Croatia's relationship to a reorganised Austria and Hungary would be decided by its sabor, in which the Military Border and Dalmatia should be represented. Borelli defended Dalmatian autonomy, on the grounds that Dalmatia was a 'historical-political individuality' in its own right, and that its future could not be decided by reference to Croatian state right. According to Borelli, the crown of the Illyrian-Dalmatian queen Teuta had passed successively to the Roman emperors, Charlemagne, the Byzantine emperors, the Croatian and Hungarian kings, before in 1409 ending up in the possession of Venice. After the dissolution of the Venetian republic, the Dalmatian nobility and people had surrendered it to Emperor Francis I and his successors.

In October 1860 Francis Joseph issued a Diploma announcing return to constitutional rule. This would be based on cooperation between the regional parliaments and the central parliament in Vienna, in which individual crownlands would be represented. The projected division of powers between the emperor-king and the central and regional parliaments followed the concept of the March Constitution. The central government, headed by Anton Schmerling, proceeded to draft a basic law on representation in the central parliament or Reichstag, which was accepted by the emperor-king and proclaimed as Patent in February 1861. According to the February Patent,[15] the Reichstag was to be made up of two houses: the house of lords and the house of representatives. The upper house was to be composed of the aristocracy, the high ecclesiastical lords and lifelong members appointed by the crown, while the lower house would be elected by crownland parliaments. Crownland parliaments, however, were to be organised this time into four electoral colleges or curiae, representing respectively great landowners, rural districts, privileged cities and towns, and chambers of commerce. The franchise system was to be based on property qualifications that could vary in accordance to local circumstances.

The February Patent recognised Hungary's distinct status, by subdividing the Reichstag into a plenum that included Hungary and a narrower body dealing only with the Austrian lands – which now, however, included Croatia and Transylvania. Laws for Dalmatia were to await definition of its future status. To please Hungary, however, Transylvania was subsequently returned to Hungarian rule. Hungary was also promised the return of the disputed territory of Međimurje. The crownland of Vojvodina and the Banat of Temesvár was dissolved, after which its Hungarian parts were returned to Hungary and its Croatian parts to Croatia, leading to the restoration of the county of Srijem. The king also re-established the Hungarian court chancellery, though this would now no longer deal with Croatian affairs. Croatia remained under the control of the government in Vienna, exercised by way of a separate Croatian office attached to the central government.

In March 1861 the Habsburg Monarchy formally reverted to constitutional rule. The Croatian and Hungarian parliaments were recalled and instructed to come to an agreement regarding their future relationship. The return of parliamentary politics brought up the problem of representation. The Hungarian electoral law of 1848 assumed that Croatia would be represented in the Hungarian parliament. However, when Hungarian officials asked their office in Vienna whether Ban's Croatia and the Military Border should be included on the Hungarian electoral lists, Vienna advised them to omit these but to include Međimurje. The Hungarian upper house nevertheless invited the Croatian prelates and magnates to attend – but they refused to do so. Count Lazar Hellenbach from Požega declared on the magnates' behalf in the Croatian sabor: 'We have decided not to accept the invitations until the sabor decides our relationship with Hungary, since the magnates will obey the national will.'[16] Basic differences between Hungary and Croatia were thus recapitulated in advance of the convening of the two parliaments, since it was important to establish their relative spheres of authority.

The Hungarian political leader, Ferenc Deák, argued that any eventual incorporation of Croatia to Austria would be illegal, since it amounted to an attack on the territorial integrity of the lands of the Hungarian crown. Hungary denied that the rights of the Triune Kingdom amounted to statehood, on the grounds that Croatia shared the same legal and constitutional order with Hungary, established by decisions of the Hungarian parliament in which Croatia was represented. The Croatian Pragmatic Sanction was in its view superseded by the Hungarian, which Croatia itself had endorsed. Hungary also refused to accept the Croatian view that the union of Croatia and Hungary had been dissolved in 1848, and that Međimurje and Rijeka were part of Croatia. The main aim of the Hungarian government at this point, however, was to ensure participation of all the lands of the Hungarian crown in the Hungarian parliament. It was ready, therefore, to compromise on the issue of territorial autonomy for Croatia, provided that the sabor accepted the validity of the Hungarian 1848 laws. Deák's address to the Hungarian assembly expressed this conciliatory mood:

> With regard to Croatia, we do not insist that our numerical superiority should decide. Croatia has its own territory and specific position, since it has never been incorporated into Hungary but only associated with us. As our friend she has shared our rights and duties, our fortune and misfortune. If Croatia as a state wishes to participate in our legislature, if she wishes to negotiate the terms with us beforehand, if she wishes to re-align her legal status with Hungary, if she wishes to speak to us as nation to nation – we shall not reject her offers. We only demand that Croatia not be prevented from sending its deputies to our parliament and that an opportunity be given to us both to reach a constitutional agreement.[17]

This proved impossible, however, since in August 1860 the Hungarian parliament was dissolved, for refusing to accept the February Patent and elect deputies for the proposed Reichstag.

The ban's advisory conference, which met in November 1860 at the behest of the new ban, General Josip Šokčević, to draw up the electoral register for Croatia, faced a similar problem of which lands should be represented in the sabor. Its address to the king, delivered in advance of the sabor's recall, reaffirmed the basic axiom of the Croatian state right: that royal rule in Croatia rested 'exclusively on the right derived from mutual agreement' reached in 1527 and in 1712. It asked for the constitutional order of the Triune Kingdom to be restored; for incorporation of Dalmatia, the north Adriatic islands and Istria's eastern districts; for approval of the Croatian electoral law of 1848 (which embraced the Military Border, the district of Rijeka, Medimurje and the still alienated Petrovaradin regiment with its three townships); for recognition of Croat as the only official language; and for the Croatian office in Vienna to be replaced by a court chancellery with the same status as the Hungarian one. In response, the king approved Croat as the official language of the internal government, and – disregarding Hungarian protests – the creation of a separate Croatian chancellery whose head would be able to address the central government. At the suggestion of Prime Minister Schmerling, and despite the king's hesitation, the post of the chancellor was given to Ivan Mažuranić.[18] The existence of a separate judiciary for Croatia was also confirmed. The king ruled against Military Border participation in the sabor, but agreed that Dalmatia's representatives should be included in the ban's conference.

A letter drafted by Kukuljević was sent to the Dalmatians to that effect, promising Dalmatia autonomy within Croatia. Striking an emotional note, it described Dalmatia as 'the mother of our nation and the cradle of our glory', and assured 'our brothers and neighbours of Italian origin who call Dalmatia their homeland' that their rights would be preserved. The Croatians, he added, harboured the deepest respect for the language of Dante, Petrarch, Tasso and Ariosto – it was indeed the Italians' love for their language which encouraged the Croats to cherish their own.[19] Acting through the Dalmatian governor General Mamula, however, Vienna made sure that no such delegation would be sent, since Austria did not wish to see Dalmatia fall under Hungarian influence. Zagreb asked the king to use his personal prerogative to effect Croatian-Dalmatian unification, but the king left the decision to the newly established Dalmatian parliament. This body, which met before its Croatian counterpart, voted against sending representatives to Zagreb, and instead elected deputies to the central parliament in Vienna.

Rijeka, encouraged by the demands of the Hungarian counties for its 'return', also refused to attend the sabor. The king refused to accept Rijeka's takeover by Hungary, but in order to appease the Hungarians he now formally returned Međimurje to their rule.

The electoral law which the ban's conference adopted divided the country into counties, counties into districts, and these last into boroughs. As a concession to the conservatives, the counties were once again able to elect their own officials on the basis of a relatively low tax census, while the royal free cities regained their earlier self-government. Being a unicameral body, the sabor was made up of both non-elected (*virilisten*) and elected individuals. The former included the aristocracy, prelates, the county heads and other high officials. Elected deputies came from counties, royal free cities, privileged townships and districts, religious chapters and monasteries. Election in the counties was a two-step process: each district elected electors who then chose one deputy for the sabor. This electoral law was approved by Vienna. Once in session, however, the sabor invited the Military Border to elect deputies as before (four deputies per regiment and one or two deputies per military township), and sent a delegation to Vienna to reason with the king on this issue. The Croatians argued that the border had to be represented in a sabor that was to decide Croatia's constitutional relationship with Austria and Hungary. This was accepted, on condition that the border deputies return home once this part of the work had been completed. The Petrovaradin regiment was excluded, however, since it was still under the command of the military headquarters in Temesvár.

The sabor worked on the premise that all laws introduced during the period of direct rule were invalid, so had to be either revised or confirmed. It opened in an atmosphere of great enthusiasm: there was a strong feeling among the deputies that the future 'happiness of the homeland' depended on this 'national parliament', which indeed became a focus of great hopes. Everyone expected it to solve their urgent problems, and the sabor was soon flooded with demands coming from all over the country. Rijeka's refusal to attend was badly received. The bishop of Senj, Venceslav Soić, insisted that the port was Croatian by nationality and historic right. Ivan Kukuljević, now head of the county of Zagreb, noted that Rijeka as a major port was guided by economic interests in its desire to maintain a close relationship with Hungary, but hoped that it would soon realise that it could act as a port for Hungary only if Croatia itself enjoyed a friendly association with Pest. The sabor once again instructed the Rijeka magistrate to organise elections for the sabor – but a letter came back, written in Italian, refusing to do so. Dalmatia's absence was also debated. Franjo Rački, deputising for the Karlovac Catholic Church hierarchy, insisted that the Dalmatian parliament's primary duty was to elect deputies to the sabor. A challenge to the sabor's authority came also from the county of Srijem, whose two Serb representatives had been elected not in accordance with the electoral law, but by the whole county assembly. These deputies treated Srijem as part of the Serb Vojvodina that they hoped would be re-established. After some dispute the Srijem deputies were admitted 'with reservation' on the grounds that Croatia faced far more important enemies.

The border deputies, aided by the sabor's drafting commission, formulated on 5 July 1861 a special submission to the king stating their problems and aspirations. It opened with the statement that return of constitutional rule had encouraged the hope that it would apply also to the Military Border. The fact that border economy and education were poorly developed derived from the fact that laws applied to it were made without the participation of its population. The border's unification with Croatia should be granted, given that the fundamental law for the Military Border of May 1850 had acknowledged that it formed one country with Croatia-Slavonia. The question of the constitutional arrangement with regard to Hungary and Austria could not be fully settled, indeed, until the Croatian borders had been properly established. The deputies also pointed out that, while the border had been established to defend the country against the Ottomans, the recent fundamental law made it part of the imperial army, which meant that all of its population now lived under military rule. Furthermore, the law, which covered both civilian and military affairs, had left German as the only official language, creating great problems in communication between the local population and the military authorities. The Grenzers had gained the right to their land, but this gain was only nominal, given that the land remained tied to military obligations in perpetuity. The border was being treated indeed as a source of permanently available soldiers: it contributed six times as many soldiers per capita as any other Austrian land. The 1848–9 war alone had created 30,000 widows. The people of the border wanted to be treated like everyone else, that is, to enjoy the same liberties as pertained in the rest of Croatia.

The constitutional debate ended on 5 August, after which the border deputies had to leave. The sabor adopted, in their absence, Article 44/1861 announcing the border's dissolution. Its preamble stated that the Military Border had been illegally constituted, and that the sabor had repeatedly demanded the extension of constitutional rule to this part of Croatian territory. The article abolished the border 'in perpetuity', extended the Croatian constitution to it, and replaced regimental by county organisation. Three new counties – Krbava, Slunj and Petrinja – were created in the area of the former border, while the territory of the other regiments was distributed among the existing counties. Mindful of the ire this act was bound to provoke in Vienna, the article envisaged that existing border laws be retained until the necessary laws were drafted. The military penal system, however, was immediately abolished. The king refused to sanction this article as law.

Croatia and Hungary

One of the sabor's main tasks, which took up a great deal of its time, remained the clarification of Croatia's status within the Monarchy. The sabor's drafting commission opted for a union of Hungary and Croatia based solely on their having a common king. A parliamentary motion drafted by Mažuranić affirmed Croatia's state individuality and specified her real and virtual territorial extent. It stated that all previous legal ties with Hungary, apart from the king and the act of coronation, had been abrogated in 1848; and that Croatia, in addition to her separate and fundamental state and constitutional rights, considered as her own also all those rights enjoyed by Hungary prior to 1847 that did not contradict her sovereignty and independence (this was added in order to ensure Croatia's own constitutional continuity). Croatia declared herself ready nevertheless to enter into a closer constitutional relationship with Hungary, on the basis of common interests and needs, as soon as the latter recognised her borders and her independence, in which event a common legislature and government could be set up to deal with affairs that would be jointly agreed. Once the Hungarian parliament accepted these conditions, the two sides would elect committees to work out the details, which would be submitted for approval to the individual parliaments. Croatia's internal government, however, was declared non-negotiable.

Proponents in the sabor of a real union with Hungary – one based on a shared parliament, government and constitution – supported a motion submitted by the city of Zagreb. This agreed that the year 1848 had represented a legal break, and endorsed the specified territorial extent of the state (omitting, however, any reference to Međimurje); but it proposed that Croatia should begin negotiating with Hungary without preconditions. Count Julije Janković from Slavonia, speaking on the behalf of this 'unionist' current, argued that in view of its own experience of direct rule from Vienna Croatia should not remain neutral in the dispute between Hungary and the king (who had just dissolved the Hungarian parliament), but should instead join the Hungarian side. Following Vojvodina's reabsorption into Hungary, Serb deputies from Srijem too came out in support of the 'unionist' motion.

A third proposal came from Eugen Kvaternik, stressing Croatia's independence from both Austria and Hungary, based on state right and popular sovereignty. In Kvaternik's view, closer ties with Austria could be established only after the king had reunited all Croatian territory. In the event of dissolution of the German Federation, the Slovene areas too should be joined to Croatia, 'if the lands concerned so wished'. The king could rule in Croatia only as a constitutional monarch, and should be crowned separately. The Croatian prime minister would act as the link between Croatia and the central government on matters involving common interests; everything else, including state security and the army, would be autonomous. Croatia should also be ready to form a political alliance with Hungary under well-defined conditions. While many deputies approved this vision, it was rejected as unrealistic.

The majority's proposal was in the end adopted by the sabor with near unanimity as Article 42/1861. The 'unionists' walked out before the vote was taken. Forty-two of them subsequently signed a declaration protesting against their allegedly unfair treatment. They included ten magnates, the representatives of the cities of Osijek and Zagreb, and the two Serb deputies from Srijem. The sabor was left, however, with more than the necessary two-thirds quorum, and all but three deputies voted in favour. It was one of the few decisions of the 1861 sabor that the king actually confirmed.

Article 42/1861

The text of this article reads:

1. Croatia in her present territorial extent – consisting of the counties: Rijeka with the city and district of Rijeka and the rest of the Littoral, Zagreb, Varaždin, Križevci, Požega, Virovitica, and Srijem; the present Military Border consisting of eight Croatian and three Slavonian regiments: Lika, Otočac, Ogulin, Slunj, the Ban's First and Second, Križevci and Đurđevac, as well as Gradiška, Brod and Petrovaradin; and including here also the kingdom's right to Međimurje and other virtual and territorial rights – declares and confirms at its parliament held in the capital city of Zagreb that, consequent upon the events of 1848, each and every legislative, administrative and juridical tie between Croatia and Hungary

Croatian Parliament, 1861, by I. Zasche

has legally ceased to exist, with the exception that the king – who by virtue of their common laws was their common king up to 1848 – shall be crowned king of Croatia on the basis of previously and separately agreed diplomas for Croatia and Hungary and, by the free will of the nation, with the same crown and the same act of coronation as he is crowned king of Hungary, with Croatia reserving for herself in addition to her separate fundamental, state and constitutional laws also all public rights enjoyed by Hungary up to the end of 1847 other than those infringing directly or indirectly her independence and sovereignty.

2. Taking into account, however, their shared past and their previous common constitutional life, as well as their common interest in upholding and developing constitutional freedoms, Croatia – responding to the royal request no. 152 of 28 February 1891 inviting her to state her wishes and views regarding her relationship to Hungary – declares through her parliament that, guided by her interest and needs, she is ready

to enter into a closer legal association with Hungary as soon as the latter recognises in a legally valid form her independence and sovereignty as well as her real and virtual territorial extent described above.

3. The proposed legal association between Croatia and Hungary, based on the totality of their old constitutions as well as Croatia's independence and state equality, would rest on a joint legislature and government derived from it, and restricted to those affairs that shall be decided by mutual agreement.

4. The legislature and government concerned with political, educational, confessional and legal affairs as well as the judiciary at all levels are excluded from the closer association between Croatia and Hungary, hence also from negotiations regarding their mutual relationship.

5. As soon as the Hungarian parliament accepts these principles, the two sides shall create committees involving equal numbers of parliamentary deputies which shall meet at a mutually agreed place in order to draft details of the legal association which will be submitted to their respective parliaments.[20]

Croatia and Austria

The king had instructed the sabor to elect, in accordance with the February Patent, nine deputies for the central parliament and to decide the nature of Croatia's participation in it. This issue appeared on the agenda at the end of July 1861 and caused a serious split within the National Party. Archbishop Haulik, who introduced the debate, favoured endorsing both the October Diploma and the February Patent on the same grounds that the March 1849 constitution had been defended: that Austria was now ruled constitutionally; that Croatia could not pretend to be wholly independent from the Austrian nations and lands in matters such as finances, trade and defence; and that the sabor itself had in the past recognised the need for a government for the whole monarchy, which could be found only in Vienna. The Reichstag was dominated, moreover, by Slav nations and Croatian participation would strengthen further its Slav character. Participation in the work of central bodies would also aid unification with Dalmatia. This view was shared by many of the National Party deputies and leaders, who favoured closer relations with the Austrian lands provided certain conditions were met.

The nub of their position was that the sabor should recognise the validity of the October Diploma, though not of the February Patent. Their proposal, drafted by Maksim Prica,[21] stated that the Monarchy had for centuries comprised a number of kingdoms and lands, and that the time had come for their relationship to be regulated 'by way of a free mutual agreement and internal convention' in which 'common interests could be articulated without infringing the constitutional autonomies of the constituent kingdoms and lands'. Participation in the Reichstag in accordance with the February Patent, on the other hand, was to be rejected, since this body had been established without consultation with the national representatives. Ivan Mažuranić backed Prica. He believed that the constitutional order created by the October Diploma was far better for Croatia than the Monarchy's division into two halves. If dualism were once more to prevail, Croatia would find itself 'at the mercy of our autocratic neighbours across the Drava'. As he told the sabor: 'The October Diploma demands of us and Hungary nothing more than to recognise the existence of central affairs concerning all the empire's lands, and to take part in determining these together with other Austrian nations. We also know that by virtue of the October Diploma the Kingdom of Hungary has no more political rights than does the Triune Kingdom.'[22]

The seriousness of the split within the National Party was revealed by the fact that forty-six of its deputies voted in favour of Prica's motion, while sixty-nine opposed it. The majority's view was that Croatia should decide on its relationship to Austria after having talked with Hungary. At this juncture the Hungarian parliament had rejected both the Diploma and the Patent, and everyone expected its conflict with the king to escalate (the Hungarian parliament was indeed dissolved in the following month). The imminent departure of the Slav deputies from the Reichstag was also expected. What worried the National Party majority was the monarch's propensity for autocratic rule: there was no guarantee that the present constitution would not be unilaterally rescinded by the king in the future. There was also a concern that Vienna had not quite given up on the idea of joining the Monarchy to the German Federation. And finally there was the sore issue of territorial integrity. Despite their differences, both factions agreed that Croatia should not at this stage elect deputies to the Reichstag.

The sabor's address to the king adopted in late September 1861 insisted on Croatia's sovereignty and demanded that its 'thousand-year-old constitution' and territorial integrity be restored, with a promise of this being included in the coronation oath. The king was also told that 'the nation of the Triune

Kingdom' had already rejected the Hungarian laws of 1847–8, and that it wished to organise its life instead in accordance with 'state right and liberal principles'. Participation in the Reichstag, however, was precluded by the Croatian constitution. The address stressed that the crown remained the only link between Croatia and the Monarchy's other kingdoms and lands, and rejected Vienna's interpretation of the Pragmatic Sanction according to which Croatia was one of the Habsburg king's hereditary lands, stressing that Croatia was an independent state in regard to legislation and administration. The address also implied fear of a united Germany that would include the Habsburg Monarchy. Croatia's response was conveyed to Vienna by two sabor deputies. They were received by the king wearing the uniform of the commander of one of the Lika regiments. The Croatians addressed the king in Croat and the king replied in German, saying that he would soon give his answer. His ministers eventually produced a non-committal response. The king stated that his intention was not to take away from Croatia those of its rights that were 'long established and still relevant', but only to ensure changes necessary for the 'unity and strength of the Monarchy'. The sabor's refusal to send deputies to the Reichstag was qualified as 'wholly negative': it was difficult to accept that the kingdom had no interests or affairs in common with the rest of the kingdoms and lands other than the common ruler. The Triune Kingdom was represented together with them vis-à-vis the outside world, while 'the sons of the Triune Kingdom had fought many wars together with them'. In the monarch's view, 'this common life in good and bad times' had created 'real and permanent bonds' making the empire 'one and indivisible'. The sabor had also overreacted in its rejection of Croatia's identification as a 'hereditary kingdom': this term appeared in the documents of both 1527 and 1712, and the same was true for the kingdom of Hungary.

Deliberately distorting the meaning of the demand that Croatia's old constitution be returned, Francis Joseph stated that the latter's quality was neither 'in the spirit of the new era' nor 'in the interest of the kingdom itself', since it would amount to a return of feudalism, which the sabor itself had rejected in 1848. As for the demand that the Military Border be united with Croatia, while the crown recognised that the Border was part of Croatia, there were good reasons for leaving it as it was, though future administrative and other changes would seek to bring it closer to 'the mother country'.[23] Regarding Dalmatia, the king had made his views clear, but the Dalmatian sabor was against unification. However, 'as soon as the status of Croatia-Slavonia in regard to the Monarchy as a whole becomes permanently established in a manner that would respect both the interests of the Monarchy as a whole and of those of the Triune Kingdom', he was ready 'to invite once again the Dalmatian sabor to come to an agreement with that of Croatia-Slavonia in regard to establishment of closer ties', and to submit that agreement 'to our supreme decision'.[24] Just how this could be achieved was unclear, given that the letter ended by dissolving the sabor. However, the royal rescript did confirm Article 42 and, as indicated above, the creation of a Croatian chancellery (albeit of a more limited status than the Hungarian one) and separate judiciary.

The sabor in the meantime proceeded to work in haste, since the deputies expected its imminent dissolution. The importance and scope of the issues brought before it were so great, however, that it was impossible to avoid lengthy debates. Both the people and its representatives shared a hatred of 'German absolutism' and 'all-powerful bureaucracy', and there was a desire also to invest the sabor's decisions with a 'national spirit'. There was no agreement, however, as to what this might entail. The old political conflict between liberal and conservative forces which had been suppressed during the period of absolutism now erupted into the open. The liberals complained that the nobility, pursuing its own selfish interests, was using the remnants of its feudal rights to destroy the peasantry. They did what they could to undermine the power of the nobility (especially that of the 'anti-national' Slavonian aristocracy), and sought to prevent large landowners being appointed county heads. The urban 'privileged estates' also came under heavy criticism. The conservatives, on the other hand, feared that modernisation of the old constitution would destroy their class, which in their view was the historic bearer of the Croatian state right. All agreed that Croatia's self-governing institutions should be defended, but they were divided over who should be in charge of them. The sabor majority worked on the principle that one should adopt all that was good from the 'Croato-Hungarian' and 'Austro-German' laws; but the need to work fast once again prevented harmonisation of their efforts. One key problem was the Austrian tax system. The government's plea to the local authorities to collect taxes was falling on deaf ears, with the result that the army was often used instead, causing a flood of complaints against the sabor, mainly from an often hungry peasantry. The land compensation fund was constantly in arrears, so that loans had to be sought from central government. The trouble was that the sabor controlled neither the government nor the state budget, and did not even know the actual state of the Croatian state funds – previously managed by the Hungarian crown treasury and now by the Viennese ministry of finance. In the end its labours came to an abrupt end. Following the refusal of the Czechs, Magyars and Croats to accept the proposed constitution, the Monarchy reverted once again to centralist rule.

Croatia and Vojvodina

The sabor saw itself as the representative of the Croatian nation, which was the bearer of state sovereignty. This concept was now challenged, however, by the Serb concept of the nation as an essentially ethnic quality. The question of what constituted the Croatian nation became a major issue of dispute between Croat and Serb parliamentarians in 1861, provoked in fact by the fledgling Vojvodina project. In order not to alienate the Serbs altogether, the king had permitted a meeting of their representatives to discuss Serb needs, though only in relation to the kingdom of Hungary. The Serb assembly, which convened in April 1861 in Novi Sad, recognised Hungary's territorial integrity and the Hungarian state right, including the 1848 Hungarian laws contested by Croatia. Serb liberals wished to see Hungary's federalisation on an ethnic basis; and despite the fact that the Hungarian parliament of 1861 denied any such possibility, they supported its struggle against Vienna in the hope that this would ultimately pay off. Their stance was approved by the principality of Serbia. The Serb assembly, however, asked for the re-establishment within Hungary of Vojvodina in its 1848 borders, that is, including Srijem. The head of this entity or *vojvoda* would be an Orthodox Serb elected by all Serbs living in Hungary and Croatia – not by the proposed Vojvodina's population, nor indeed by the Serbs who lived on its proposed territory. Vojvodina was thus to be established as an asymmetric combination of the ethnic and territorial principles. What was new was that the establishment of this entity was now defended on the basis of 'historic right': that is, on the basis of privileges that Leopold I had granted to Serb immigrants from the Ottoman Empire, now reinterpreted as an agreement reached between the king and the Serb nation. The Serb conservatives insisted that the king should simply impose this solution on Hungary, while the Serb liberals wished to achieve it by cooperation with Hungarian liberals. The Hungarian government's nationality approach, however, excluded any solution of the Serb national question on a territorial basis.

In 1848 the sabor had been willing to give Srijem to Vojvodina, but on condition that Vojvodina would form a common state with Croatia. The Novi Sad assembly, however, had ruled out any such an alliance. The two deputies from Srijem, Jovan Živković and Mihailo Polit-Desančić, now presented that assembly's views to the Croatian parliament. Polit-Desančić pressed the deputies to formally declare that in the event of Vojvodina's revival the county of Srijem would be allowed to join it. Živković wished the sabor to declare at least that the status of the county of Srijem was an open question. The Vojvodina project was debated by the sabor in the autumn of 1861, after the dismissal of the Hungarian parliament and on the eve of the sabor's own demise. A separate committee was set up to deal with the issue. Based on its recommendations, the drafting commission came up with a concept for solution of 'the Serb question' within the Habsburg Monarchy. This involved the establishment of a self-governing Serb territory to include the southern Hungarian counties of Banat and Bačka, the Petrovaradin and German Banat regiments, and the whole of Srijem. The exact degree of Vojvodina's autonomy would be decided by the Croatian and Hungarian chancelleries without recourse to the king. The Serbs would participate in both the Hungarian and the Croatian parliaments as Vojvodina representatives. As proposed by the Novi Sad assembly, Vojvodina would be headed by a vojvoda of Orthodox faith, elected by an assembly of Serb representatives from both Croatia and Hungary. There would be a council and an assembly to run local affairs, including taxation. Vojvodina's official language would be Serb with its Cyrillic script (though other languages could also be used), and its official symbols the Serb flag and emblem.

The sabor now split between those who were ready to surrender Srijem to Vojvodina and those who felt that this was no longer a valid proposition. Jovan Živković assured the sabor that to do so would not infringe Croatia's territorial integrity, since Vojvodina would remain associated with Croatia by way of Hungary. Eugen Kvaternik, however, argued that – given that only one-fifth of the inhabitants living on the territory of the 1848 Vojvodina was Serb by nationality – a renewed Vojvodina could not be formed on the same territorial basis. The Croatians should support the Hungarian Serbs, but sentimentality in his view had no place where Croatian territory was concerned. He was supported by Kukuljević and Strossmayer. The sabor agreed to express sympathy with Serb aspirations, and proposed that the king should recall the Hungarian parliament and the Serb national assembly, which together with the Croatian parliament would draft Vojvodina's constitution.

The sabor also approved the central ministry's education reform, including the separation of children along confessional lines. Village schools were to be run by parish priests, town schools by laymen. Catholic schools had to teach the Cyrillic and Orthodox schools the Latin script. The intention to regulate schools by way of a single law caused problems, however, with regard to the competence of the Serb communal assembly associated with the Orthodox Church. The law on education that the sabor finally adopted likewise failed to gain royal assent. The same happened with the decision to transform the Zagreb Academy into a university with four departments: Catholic theology (the proposal for a similar department for Orthodox theology fell, thanks to the resistance of the Serb Orthodox hierarchy), law, medicine and philosophy. Other decisions, including codification of the land laws and civil taxation, also failed to receive royal sanction.

The re-emergence of party politics

The divisions which came to light in the course of a constitutional debate focused on Croatia's relationship to Austria and Hungary resulted in the subsequent formation of political parties. The unionist minority, involving mainly magnates and petty nobility, came together to form the National Constitutional Party, subsequently known as the Unionists. The Unionists stressed the common history, legal ties, defence needs and economic interests that Croatia shared with Hungary. The wing of the National Party that supported a conditional union with Austria formed the Independent National Party. This was composed of officers from the Border, and functionaries from the upper rungs of the civil service working in the central government in Vienna, in the Croatian judiciary and in the counties. It sought the preservation and unity of the Monarchy; recognition in principle of the existence of common affairs with the Austrian lands; and participation in the Reichstag on the basis of Article 42/1861. The mainstream National Party continued to rally the intelligentsia, the lower ranks of the civil service and the clergy. Bishop Josip Strossmayer, ably seconded by Canon Franjo Rački, now emerged as one of its leaders.[25]

A new political current also emerged in the course of the 1860s: the Party of [the Croatian state] Right, led by Ante Starčević and Eugen Kvaternik, with a programme of complete independence for Croatia. Its rise was fuelled by the reaction to absolutism, and also by the Croat-Serb polemic signalling the division of the Croatian nation into Croat and Serb components. Serb national ideologues attacked the idea of Croatian state right, as well as the Illyrian and Yugoslav ideologies, as inherently anti-Serb. They criticised the two national parties for their anti-Hungarian position and for seeking federalisation of the Monarchy. They were provoked by the Croats' refusal to accept that all *štokavian* speakers were Serbs, and by the sabor's unwillingness to acknowledge the Serbs as a 'political nation' in Croatia or to cede Srijem. The Croat side, on the other hand, remained committed to Croatia's unification and the transformation of its inhabitants into a single Croatian (Croat and Serb) nation; it was willing to make necessary concessions in regard to the name of the language and use of the Cyrillic script. The Serbs continued to grumble that affirmation of Croatia as a state and nation endangered their Serb identity, while the Croats pointed out that the Croatian Serbs were imperilled neither as citizens, nor as a faith, nor as a people.

Croatia in the meantime continued to be governed from Vienna, by way of a lieutenancy council headed by Jelačic's successor – ban and general Josip Šokčević – and the court chancellery headed by Ivan Mažuranić. During this period Zagreb acquired a link to the Vienna-Graz-Maribor-Ljubljana-Trieste railway, and also a railway connecting it with Karlovac. In 1864 a first all-Croatian trade fair was held in Zagreb. In the same year Maksim Prica and Nikola Krestić (both ethnic Serbs), working in collaboration with Mažuranić, published anonymously a pamphlet entitled *Conditionally or Unconditionally?*, the basic message of which was that, given that the sabor had voted against a real union with Hungary, Croatia should proceed to negotiate independently with the king.[26] The pamphlet condemned the dismissed parliament for its 'sheer negation' of Austria's state unity, which they argued was a precondition for the survival and advance of the non-Magyar nationalities in the lands of the Hungarian crown. Instead of building upon Croatia's existing administrative and legal autonomy, the opposition, by going against the Monarchy's vital interests, had created an 'unbearable interregnum'. The authors pointed out that Hungary itself was getting ready to give up parts of its 1848 and 1861 programmes, and called upon the future sabor to accept the existence of common bodies for the Monarchy. It also listed a number of conditions under which Croatia would be ready to negotiate with Vienna. First, an immediate restitution of Dalmatia and the north Adriatic islands, plus a guarantee that the border would be allowed to join Croatia in the near future. Secondly, as a token of royal good will, the two Varaždin regiments, the military township of Bjelovar, the district of Žumberak and the port of Senj should be immediately added to Croatia. The conditions included also a separate budget for Croatia, an increase in the number of Croatia's representatives in the Reichstag, and a guarantee that this body would not endanger Croatia's own autonomy based on Article 42/1861.

In January 1865, as the period of direct rule was coming to a close, the ban's conference was recalled with the task of producing a new electoral law. The conference was composed mainly of supporters of the Independent National Party. The new electoral law aimed to produce a smaller, more representative and pro-Austrian parliament by drastically reducing the number of *virilisten* (personal seats). The Unionists and the National Party now joined forces, both sides supporting an agreement with Hungary. Since the National Party was in contact with the Czech parties and the Unionists with Deák's Liberals, this amounted to the formation of an anti-centralist Croat-Czech-Magyar axis. In 1865, however, under the pressure of Austria's growing conflict with Prussia, Vienna decided to stabilise its domestic position by seeking a rapprochement with Hungary. In July that year Anton Schmerling's government was dismissed and pro-federalist Count Richard Belcredi appointed as the new prime minister. The February Patent was suspended and the Reichstag dissolved. Francis Joseph visited Hungary. In these circumstances the king decided not to approve Mažuranić's electoral law, and reaffirmed instead the one applied in 1861. The Military Border was once again allowed to participate, but only in the constitutional debate.

Croatian elections took place soon after this, in July and August 1865. The opposition won, taking two-thirds of the seats; but no party formed a majority in the sabor, though the National Party was the strongest. Ante Starčević, a leader of the still minute Party of Right holding violently anti-Austrian views, was elected in one of the Zagreb constituencies. The sabor included also two leaders of the Dalmatian National Party, Mihovil Pavlinović and Miha Klaić (see chapter eleven). The Dalmatian Nationals were anti-Austrian and favoured an agreement with Hungary. On the advice of the Austrian government, the king postponed the sabor's opening. On 20 September 1965 the emperor-king issued a proclamation to 'my peoples' in which he declared his intention to come to an agreement with the legal representatives of the empire's 'eastern parts'. The Croatian and Hungarian parliaments were to be offered another chance to adopt the October Diploma and the February Patent. On the eve of the convocation of the Croatian parliament Mažuranić formally retired, although he remained in his post for another year because the king delayed signing the necessary decree.[27]

NINE

The Croatian-Hungarian Compromise

In 1865 the Magyar nobility, guided by Ferencz Deák, offered Vienna a new settlement based on the Hungarian Pragmatic Sanction. Vienna responded by recognising the Hungarian constitution and the territorial integrity of the lands of the Hungarian crown. On this basis Deák's Liberal Party was able to win the subsequent elections. In his speech at the opening of the Hungarian parliament in December 1865, the king declared that the Pragmatic Sanction would form the basis of a new constitutional arrangement ensuring the unity of the Habsburg Monarchy, and within it the independence and unity of the Hungarian crown lands. In the same month the Transylvanian assembly voted to rejoin the kingdom of Hungary. As for Croatia, Francis Joseph would henceforth support its autonomy only to the extent that was acceptable to Hungary. The problem was Article 42/1861, which the king had legalised but which the Hungarians found unacceptable. He told the Hungarian parliament that the sabor had been invited to participate in its deliberations in 'the proper manner', referred to Article 42/1861 and expressed the hope that a compromise might be found. The demand that Rijeka be represented in the Hungarian parliament, however, was rejected. The Hungarian parliament declared itself ready to negotiate with the Croatian 'brotherly nation' on the basis of the – slightly modified – 1848 laws.

In his rescript to the Croatian parliament, the king stated that old constitutions should not be valued for themselves, but rather taken as a basis for progress in keeping with the spirit of the new times, which demanded that all the lands of the monarchy should have a common representation. The actual scope of common affairs could be negotiated. The sabor was invited to accept the October Diploma and the February Patent; to determine Croatia's constitutional relationship with Hungary; to elect representatives for the forthcoming coronation of Francis Joseph as king of Croatia and Hungary; and to join the Hungarian parliament in drafting the coronation document. The Military Border would be allowed to participate in the sabor's deliberations, but only in the part dealing with constitutional issues. However, the royal rescript did not mention Article 42/1861. On the eve of his retirement as Croatian chancellor, Ivan Mažuranić wrote to his brother Antun: 'So dualism, which has hitherto been shyly concealing itself, is once again raising its horned head, ready to swallow up Croatia. *Tu l'as voulu, Georges Dandin*! I am physically well, but my spirit aches when I see what is being prepared for Croatia.'[1] He left Vienna in February 1866, though not before receiving the royal endorsement for Strossmayer's Yugoslav Academy of Arts and Science. It was intended that the academy, together with the planned university, should make Zagreb a cultural centre for the South Slavs.

When the sabor met in November 1965, the two National parties united against the Unionists. The outcome was an address that rejected both the Diploma and the Patent, but admitted the existence of common affairs for the Monarchy and the need for some central institutions. Croatia's territorial integrity was emphasised, and the demand for union with Dalmatia and the Military Border repeated. Croatia was ready to negotiate with the kingdom of Hungary, provided that it was accepted it as an equal negotiating partner. Hungary, in other words, had to accept Article 42/1861 in advance of the negotiations. The address thus met some of the monarch's demands. The sabor next elected a delegation led by Strossmayer to discuss the outstanding issues with Hungary.

The delegations met soon after the start of Hungary's own negotiations with Vienna, so that the Hungarian side had no mandate to discuss the future relationship between Austria and the lands of the Hungarian crown. The Croatian delegation did not deny the existence of a state tie with Hungary, but argued that Croatia's legislative and executive autonomy was likewise a historical fact. The Hungarian 1848 idea of unity had proved too narrow and dangerous for the individuality of the Triune Kingdom, and the coronation oath should take this into account. The Hungarian laws of 1848 had not been endorsed by the sabor. The break in 1848 had thus been a product of the free will of both parliaments. Hungary should recognise Croatia's autonomy and integrity. The Croatians also insisted that the nature of the kingdom's common affairs with Hungary depended upon the outcome of the negotiations with the Austrian lands; hence common affairs with the latter too should be included in the Croatian-Hungarian talks.

The Hungarian delegation recognised that Croatia had never formed one state body with Hungary, but denied that it had ever enjoyed autonomous legislative powers. The sabor's ratification of decisions adopted by the joint parliament i.e. the Hungarian parliament sitting together with Croatia's representatives, was in its view nothing but an obligatory proclamation of them. The Hungarian parliament acting together with the king, they argued, had passed the March 1848 laws with Croatia's participation. The Hungarian delegates were ready to advise their parliament to modify the old state tie, but only if the Croatians accepted this 'fact'. In that event Hungary would be ready to contemplate a wider autonomy for Croatia. They were against separate coronation oaths for Hungary and Croatia, which in their eyes not only made no sense but were dangerous for Hungarian state unity. Nor would they accept the Croatian view that the king ruled by the will of the people, since this contradicted the Pragmatic Sanction. As for the territorial issue, they refused to accept any change resulting from the 1848 war. So far as they were concerned, Rijeka had never been part of the Croatian crown lands, while Međimurje was a Hungarian state territory. They invited Croatia to join the ongoing discussion in the Hungarian parliament on the nature of common affairs with Austria.

The Croatians insisted that the sabor had no obligation to accept laws passed by the Hungarian parliament. If it had done so in the past, that was of its own free will. The Croatian delegates in the joint parliament had always worked under the sabor's mandate. Laws in the Hungarian parliament were never made by majority vote, but only in agreement with Croatian representatives. The Hungarian parliament was indeed constitutionally prohibited from intervening in Croatia's internal affairs, which is what its parliament had done in 1848. Croatia could not accept laws that deprived it of sovereign power, or which reduced its territory to so many counties subject to the Hungarian government. The Croatian delegates, in sum, demanded a new institutional agreement in regard to a common Croato-Hungarian legislature and government. The Hungarian delegation then asked its government to change its mandate, permitting it to discuss these issues. At this point (May 1866), however, the Austro-Prussian war appeared imminent, so both sides decided to delay resumption of the negotiations in the hope that the outcome of the war would favour their particular cause.

The Austro-Hungarian Compromise

The process of transformation of the Habsburg Monarchy into Austria-Hungary accelerated under the impact of the Austro-Prussian war over the former Danish province of Holstein. In August 1866 the Monarchy was defeated at Sadová in Bohemia and forced to cede to Prussia both Holstein and hegemony within the German Federation. Although Italy (which had

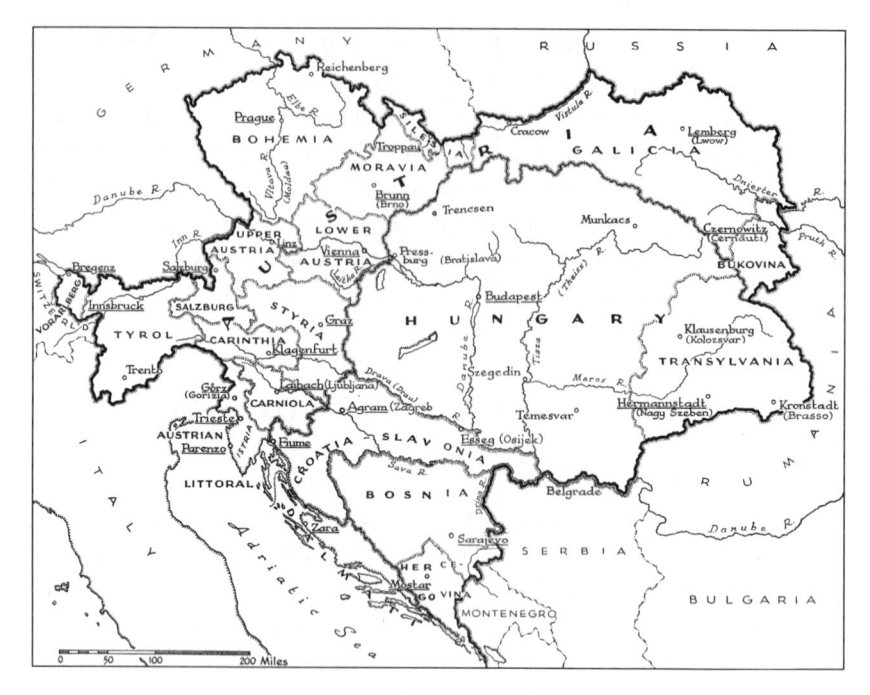

Austria-Hungary, 1867

joined the war on the Prussian side) was defeated on both land (Custozza near Verona) and sea (off the Croatian island of Vis), it nevertheless gained Austrian Venice. This outcome set the stage for a historic agreement between the Habsburgs, the Austrian German liberal bourgeoisie and the Hungarian nobility – all of whom were keen to limit the influence of the Monarchy's Slav majority – leading to the emergence of Austria-Hungary. The fundamental laws creating the Dual Monarchy, based on the Pragmatic Sanction, were passed by the Hungarian and Austrian parliaments in the spring of 1867. This Austro-Hungarian Compromise was later supplemented by two additional legal acts: the Croato-Hungarian Compromise of 1868 defining the legal position of Croatia, and the 1878 mandate of the Congress of Berlin permitting Austria-Hungary to occupy Bosnia-Herzegovina.

The Austro-Hungarian Compromise turned the river Leitha into a border between two distinct state-like entities: the 'kingdoms and lands represented in the Reichsrat' in the west, ruled by Austrian Germans, which became 'Austria' for short; and the 'lands of St Stephen's crown' in the east, ruled by Magyars, which was perceived as 'Hungary'. Ban's Croatia belonged to the latter, Dalmatia and Istria to the former – even though the existence of a single Triune Kingdom was formally accepted by both sides. The Military

Border came under the authority of the joint Austro-Hungarian ministry of defence. The legal anomaly of Croatia's position – its nominal unity, yet its division between the two entities – was thus built into the very foundations of the dualist arrangement, so that every Croatian attempt to realise state unity was viewed as subversive of the whole constitutional order.

According to the Austro-Hungarian Compromise, each of the two parts had its own territory, supreme government and citizenship. They shared the head of state, defence and foreign affairs – and the finances needed to cover the cost of these. The ministers of common affairs were responsible to two delegations elected by – and responsible only to – the Austrian and Hungarian parliaments respectively. These delegations came together every year in Vienna and Pest alternately, and communicated with each other only in writing.[2] They actually met in separate rooms, and discussed and voted separately. Common economic interests were regulated by separate inter-state agreements, reviewed every ten years. Since no superior authority existed to arbitrate differences between the two delegations, the whole system underwent periodic crises.

The precise nature of this construct remained throughout open to different interpretations. In the Austrian German view, the Austrian empire continued to exist as a supra-state, made up of two equal parts linked in a real union – given the monarch's role as the crucial constitutive factor and the existence of common bodies competent to make laws for both parts. In the Hungarian interpretation, Austria-Hungary was a union of two independent states linked only by a common ruler (that is, a purely personal union) and lacking true common bodies, since the two delegations were responsible only to the individual parliaments. What was indisputable was that in international affairs Austria-Hungary behaved as a single subject, the unity of which was symbolised by the monarch.

Austria-Hungary was based, however, not on the Pragmatic Sanction alone, but also on Hungarian insistence on the perpetuation of the Austrian constitution of 1867. The Hungarian landowning class clung to the fiction that Hungary – unlike Austria – was not a multinational state.[3] This myth could be maintained only if Vienna did not grant autonomous government to its constituent nationalities, that is, if Austria continued to be organised on the same centralised basis as Hungary. But just as there was no common understanding of the meaning of 'Austria-Hungary', so too there was no shared agreement about what either 'Austria' or 'Hungary' meant separately, especially among their component lands and nationalities.

The introduction of dualism could be likened to an earthquake, in that it resulted in a sudden and radical shift of the Monarchy's centre of gravity to the east. Hungary, or more precisely the Magyar landowners, had been the driving force behind the dualist arrangement and emerged as the dominant force within Austria-Hungary. This shift manifested itself in Ban's Croatia in the form of the political ascendancy of the Slavonian landowners. The western and eastern portions of the Monarchy would hereafter develop differently. The Austrian peoples would gain civic equality, recognition of their national individuality, and near-universal manhood suffrage. In the Hungarian crownlands, by contrast, the Magyar nationality (as represented by the nobility)[4] would reign supreme, while the suffrage remained limited to a small percentage of the population: 2 per cent in the case of Croatia, 6 per cent in that of Hungary.[5] Magyar domination encouraged national assimilation. In the 1906–10 period, for example, 91 per cent of the deputies in the lower house of the Hungarian parliament listed themselves as Magyars in the official census, but 27.5 per cent of them had been recently assimilated. Roughly the same proportions could be observed in the national make-up of the central government's officials.[6]

The Croatian-Hungarian Compromise

On its return to Zagreb, the Croatian delegation informed the sabor that negotiations with the Hungarians were leading nowhere, and advised it to deal separately with the king. The Unionists disagreed: in their view Croatia could not negotiate independently, since it did not possess a state individuality vis-à-vis the Austrian lands. It did enjoy such individuality within the lands of the Hungarian crown, however, so it should seek a compromise with Hungary on that basis. They agreed that Rijeka was part of Croatia, not Hungary, but hoped that this problem could be solved favourably if Croatia proved cooperative. The majority felt that the sabor had no duty to attend the Hungarian parliament. Starting from the premise that the Pragmatic Sanction guaranteed the unity and integrity of the Monarchy, however, the sabor agreed to recognise and participate in common bodies created on that basis. But the February Patent was rejected, on the grounds that the structures it offered did not give sufficient protection from an omnipotent royal will.

The sabor drafted an address to the king offering its own model for organisation of the common bodies. To begin with, these should result from mutual agreement among all the crownlands, negotiated by their legal representatives. The central parliament, representing all the Monarchy's lands, should be constituted as a single chamber. The executive would be responsible to it, but would act through the executives of the individual crownlands, which would be responsible solely to their national parliaments. The powers of the central parliament could not be extended without the agreement of all crownlands. This proposal pointed in the direction of an Austrian confederation. The address declared that Croatia would never participate in joint bodies unless they were created with its consent, and that the sabor would not be involved in formulating the relevant laws unless the territorial integrity of the Triune Kingdom and a government responsible to the sabor were recognised first.

The Croatians had clearly misread the implications of the war lost to Prussia.[7] Two days after this address was adopted by the sabor, the Hungarian parliament agreed to negotiate with Vienna without informing Zagreb. In March 1867 it adopted a law defining common affairs with the rest of the Monarchy, and in the following month Deák won its acceptance for Croatia's autonomy based on Article 42/1861. The king, who, backed by the army anxious to keep the Military Border, hoped for a fairer deal for Croatia, was asked not to encourage Zagreb. He was informed that Hungary was keen to achieve a legally valid union of 'the associated lands' with Hungary, and that Croatia's representatives would be included in the Hungarian state delegation. In April 1867 Rijeka with its district would pass to Hungarian control; it was to be directly represented in the Hungarian parliament.[8]

In the same month the king instructed the sabor to elect deputies to the Hungarian parliament, in order to take part in formulating the coronation oath. The sabor was also sent a copy of the position adopted by the Hungarian parliament regarding Croatia. This stated that there could be only one coronation oath, guaranteeing a common constitution for all the lands of the Hungarian crown – and in that context also the lawful rights of the Triune Kingdom. Its content would be decided by the joint parliament. Croatian representatives would be included in all bodies concerned with affairs common to the Monarchy. The sabor was asked to send a delegation to negotiate with the Hungarians, without this prejudicing the ultimate solution of the kingdom's status. As for the territorial issue, the king wrote that he wished to safeguard the totality of the 'historic rights' of Croatia within the framework of the Hungarian Pragmatic Sanction. The sabor should accept in a legal manner his agreement with the Hungarian parliament in order to remove all obstacles to a peaceful resolution of Croatian-Hungarian differences. The king refused to discuss the question of Dalmatia until after the completion of constitutional talks, and while affirming the Military Border as an integral part of Ban's Croatia refused to pronounce on its incorporation. At his express wish, Mažuranić and Strossmayer were forced to absent themselves from the sabor.[9] Tremendous pressure was exerted on the civil servants elected to the sabor to vote in favour of the royal rescript, but they all refused. The same was true of the clergy of both faiths. It was in this situation that the sabor voted to affirm Croat-Serb equality. As the deputy who introduced the motion said, it was necessary to ensure full national unity at this fateful moment.

The sabor divided along party lines in its response to the king's message. The Unionist minority accepted the Hungarian proposal, provided that Croatia's full internal autonomy and territorial extent (including Rijeka) were recognised. The majority, formed by the now reunited National Party, adopted an uncompromising position. Faced with this unpalatable choice, it decided to go down fighting. The sabor's answer to the king rejected the idea that Austria's agreement with Hungary was valid also for Croatia. Croatia stood in the same relationship to the other lands of the Monarchy as did Hungary, and should enjoy the same degree of autonomy. Stressing that Croatia's relationship to Hungary was one of personal union alone, it asked for a separate coronation oath. This would contain the following elements: dissolution of the Military Border as an exclusively military institution, and its unification with Ban's Croatia; incorporation of Dalmatia; and assurance that the Hungarian 1848 laws did not extend to the Triune Kingdom. The address rejected Croatia's participation in the Hungarian parliament, but agreed to send a delegation to negotiate with Hungary on their constitutional relationship, provided that Croatia's real territory and autonomy were recognised in line with Article 42/1861 as confirmed by the king. The sabor also declared illegal Rijeka's separate representation in the Hungarian parliament.

The deputies then proceeded to elect a delegation to negotiate with the Hungarian side. Expecting the sabor's imminent dissolution, they also voted that 'the nation of the Triune Kingdom remains bounded by the only lawfully founded electoral law of 1848 [until] a new electoral law and law on the composition of the sabor are decided by the joint will of the king and the nation'. Until such time, 'the nation will acknowledge as legal only the sabor constituted on that basis'.[10] This decision was motivated by the fear that Vienna and Pest between them might try to create a parliamentary majority for the Unionists. A week later the sabor was indeed dismissed by the king, on the grounds that the Hungarian parliament had done all it could to meet Croatian demands. On 8 June 1867 Francis Joseph was crowned with great pomp in Buda as King of Hungary and Croatia. He swore an oath as the 'hereditary and apostolic king of Hungary and the associated lands'. Leaders of the Monarchy's Slav parties, meanwhile, demonstratively attended the opening of an ethnographic exhibition in Moscow.

Ban Šokčević was now replaced by the arch-conservative and previously politically inactive Baron Levin Rauch – the first ban for a long time not to be an army general. Elections took place in November and December 1867 under strict governmental supervision. Thanks to the National Party's opposition, Chancellor Mažuranić's attempt to weed out anti-Vienna officials in Croatia had largely failed, which meant that the new regime could count on a significant number of anti-Austrian functionaries, National as well as Unionist, who saw in the reborn Hungary of the crown the best framework for Croatia. The Unionists won a huge majority, the National Party only fourteen seats. Since the Nationals commanded the support of the vast majority of the educated population, the Unionists could not have won in free elections. But the idea of union with Hungary was popular also among the masses, who had been led to believe that it would bring about a general lowering of taxes and economic prosperity. The Unionists, in fact, won not only most of Slavonia, but also the old Croatian counties of Varaždin, Zagreb and Križevci. Most of the county of Srijem, on the other hand, voted for the National Party. The National deputies moved that the sabor was illegally constituted and demanded new elections; when this was refused, all but two left the chamber. The Nationals would henceforth fight an unremitting struggle against the new ban and the Unionists, as a result of which the country entered a period of civil cold war leading to political and administrative paralysis. Many supporters of the National Party were removed from their posts and accused of being 'Panslavic agitators' in the service of the Russian tsar. The party journal *Pozor* (Observer) was banned. As Rijeka, capital of the eponymous county, slid into the hands of the pro-Hungarian party, Bakar, Kraljevica and Vinodol rose in revolt, threatening the interruption of local trade. The Unionists themselves divided between those who sought the closest union with Hungary and those who supported wider autonomy for Croatia.

The sabor formally opened on 9 January 1868. Its inaugural address recognised the legality of the king's coronation, the dualist arrangement, and the 'state association' of Croatia and Hungary. It agreed to Croatia's participation in the Hungarian delegation dealing with common affairs for the Monarchy, and hoped for an amicable agreement between the 'two free nations' based on Article 42/1861. It asked for the incorporation of Dalmatia and a gradual dissolution of the military system in the border, and declared its readiness to elect a delegation to negotiate with its Hungarian counterpart.

The delegation was this time not given any specific instructions, however, except to bear in mind the spirit of the sabor's address. Negotiations took place in Pest in April–July 1868. The Croatian delegation soon split on how much autonomy Croatia should enjoy. The Hungarians themselves were also divided on this issue.

A concept proposed by Jovan Živković won Deák's broad support. Živković sought to establish a clear separation between the common affairs deriving from the Pragmatic Sanction – such as the coronation and the royal oath – and those pertaining to the common affairs of Croatia and Hungary alone, which were subject to negotiation.[11] In regard to the former, Croatia was willing to allow the content of the common coronation oath to be decided by the joint parliament, provided that Hungary guaranteed Croatia's territorial integrity and constitution. Croatian representatives in the Hungarian state delegation would be elected by the sabor, but would not act under its mandate. As for affairs shared by Croatia and Hungary, they would be administered only in agreement with the sabor. The executive for these common affairs would form a joint Croato-Hungarian government. All other affairs, except for the postal and telegraph service, would be Croatia's internal business, for which the sabor alone would be responsible. Autonomy would apply to the Triune Kingdom as a whole. The only official language in Croatia would be Croat. The Croatian government would be responsible to the sabor. The Croatian prime minister, appointed by the king, would be included in the joint government. Croatian deputies to the joint parliament would be elected by the sabor and remain responsible to it. Croatia would have its own budget to cover its administrative needs, and would be responsible for taxation and for management of its state funds. Rijeka belonged to Croatia. The agreement between the two parliaments would not be changed unilaterally, but only by a new agreement between their delegations.

However, the Hungarian prime minister, Gyula Andrássy, supported by the Austrian prime minister, Friedrich Beust, took a different view. Andrássy was convinced that the Hungarian government's full control of state finances was the foundation stone of the 'Hungarian state idea', and that even a minimum of financial independence for Croatia would endanger it. Beust, for his part, feared that Croatia's financial independence would stimulate similar demands in the Austrian half of the Monarchy. Živković's financial proposal was consequently rejected. It was now decided that the joint parliament would be responsible for all taxation, and for the budget for running common affairs. The ministry of finance would control Croatian financial affairs through its office in Zagreb, and would also appoint and pay the latter's officials. The sabor would be informed of the revenue raised through taxation in Croatia, 63 per cent of which would go to the central treasury, from which a fixed sum would return to Croatia for its own administration while the rest would go to support common affairs with Austria. The financial agreement would be submitted to revision every ten years. As Croatia's chief executive, the ban would be appointed by the king upon the advice of the joint prime minister. The Croatian delegation made further concessions. It dropped the demands that the joint government should be responsible also to the sabor, and that the Croatian deputies in the joint parliament should be bound by the sabor's mandate. It also agreed that the status of Rijeka be decided by the king. Croatia's territorial integrity (with such significant exceptions as Rijeka and Međimurje) was confirmed, however, as well as the provision that Croat be the sole official language in Croatia and that Croatian administration be staffed only by Croatians. The two sides also agreed that the Varaždin Border should immediately be dissolved.

This provisional agreement was received with great hostility in Croatia. Its defenders argued that it was the best that could be achieved in the circumstances, and that it was better to create a state of normality than to live in a state of permanent chaos; but moderate Unionists joined the Nationals in condemning it as contrary to Croatian state interests. The Croato-Hungarian Compromise was nevertheless ratified by the sabor on 24 September 1868, with the qualification that the two delegations were unable to agree on the status of Rijeka and its district. The sabor consequently asked the king for recognition of Croatia's 'incontrovertible' right to Rijeka. The Hungarian parliament voted to adopt the agreement, however, only if Rijeka were included in Hungary. A meeting of Croatian, Hungarian and Rijeka representatives was arranged, but no agreement could be found. Francis Joseph finally decreed Rijeka a *corpus separatum* and placed it under control of the joint Croato-Hungarian – in effect Hungarian – government.

The final version of the compromise was adopted by the sabor on 18 November 1868 as Article 1/1868. It had seventy paragraphs. The indivisibility of the lands of the Hungarian crown was affirmed: Croatia and Hungary united with Transylvania formed 'one and the same state association'. The king was to be crowned with one crown, and there was to be only one coronation oath – issued in both Magyar and Croat – which would guarantee Croatia's territorial integrity and constitution. Any revision of the Austro-Hungarian Compromise would in the future have to have Croatia's agreement. Affairs common to all the Monarchy were subject to a single legislative and executive authority vested in the joint Croato-

Hungarian parliament and government. The joint ministries dealing with finances, budget, taxes, trade and defence would maintain their offices in Croatia, which would operate only in Croat. On the financial side, Croatia would pay 5.4 per cent of the Croato-Hungarian dues allocated for running the monarchy's common affairs. Of Croatia's own revenue derived from taxation, 45 per cent would be used for its internal needs, the rest for supporting the affairs run in common with Hungary. The sum involved was not linked to actual revenue, however, but fixed at 2.2 million forints for ten years; this was to change after the reincorporation of the Military Border. Hungary also guaranteed reimbursement of the old feudal dues.

Croatia was to send twenty-nine deputies to the lower house of the parliament in Budapest and two to its upper house; this number would change after the incorporation of the Border and Dalmatia. These deputies would be elected by the sabor, but would not be bound by its mandate. The joint parliament would also elect the Croatian members of the Croato-Hungarian state delegation. There would be a Croatian minister attached to the central government, who would act as link between the king and the Croatian government.

The Kingdom of Croatia-Dalmatia-Slavonia (there was initially no mention of Dalmatia, but this was later rectified)[12] was defined as a 'political nation' with its own separate territory and government. Its deputies consequently had the right to address the joint parliament in Croat. All laws passed by that parliament would be published in Croat. The common emblems of the joint ministries would consist of the emblems of both Croatia and Hungary. When common affairs were discussed – that is, when the joint parliament was in session – the building would also fly the Croatian flag. The Triune Kingdom's autonomy in 'all internal affairs, religious affairs, education and justice' (in the case of justice, maritime law was excluded) was guaranteed. The internal and external language in Croatia would be Croat (not 'Croat or Serb'). Its government would be headed by the ban, who would be responsible to the sabor. He would be appointed by the king with the consent of the joint prime minister, and would sit in the upper house of the joint parliament. He would not be a military man, nor would his authority extend to military affairs. The ban would communicate the sabor's demands and proposals to the king by way of the Croatian minister in the joint government. He had the power to introduce a state of emergency. According to Article 1/1868, while the ban and the sabor decided jointly on internal matters, the Croatian government – that is, the heads of the different departments of the Croatian administration – was responsible not to the sabor but to the ban.

Further paragraphs defined Croatia's territorial extent: the seven counties and the eleven regiments plus Dalmatia. The incorporation of Dalmatia would be sought on the basis of the rights of the Hungarian crown, but would need to have Dalmatia's consent. Help was promised for an early incorporation of the Military Border. The county of Rijeka was recognised as part of Croatia, but not the city of Rijeka and its district: this was left to further negotiations. The last paragraph stated that the agreement could not be altered by either parliament, but only in the manner in which it had been reached, namely, by way of delegations elected by the two parliaments and subject to confirmation by the king.

As in the case of the Austro-Hungarian Compromise, the Croato-Hungarian Compromise was open to different and contrary interpretations. In the Hungarian view, it was simply a fundamental law by which a unitary state transferred some of its competencies to one of its parts. The Croatian side viewed it as an agreement between two nominally sovereign states.[13] It stressed that the Croato-Hungarian Compromise was a product of negotiations between the two parliaments acting as equal partners. Croatian state right consequently remained unimpaired, since Croatia surrendered to the joint state only those affairs which it agreed to surrender, and since the arrangement could not be changed against its will. This was true also in regard to the Austro-Hungarian agreement, which could not be altered in the future without Croatia's consent. Moreover, Croatia continued to have the essential features that made it a state: territory, definition as a 'political nation', legislature and government. Croatia and Hungary formed one and the same state association only in relation to the king's other lands and the world outside. Croatian jurists pointed to the fact that there were joint Croato-Hungarian as well as separate – Croatian and Hungarian – state bodies, and that the existence of the latter qualified the existence of the former. The joint parliament, for example, existed only when Croatian deputies were present; in their absence the body became solely the parliament of Hungary.[14]

Croatia's position within the Habsburg Monarchy was indeed quite specific in that it continued to be a state, despite all the limitations imposed on its exercise of self-government. In its desire to control Croatia, indeed, Hungary would find it necessary to act contrary to the compromise, that is, to engage in non-legal methods of coercion.[15] There is no doubt, on the other hand, that the terms of the agreement limited Croatia's sovereignty in favour of Hungary. This is evident in the fact that the sabor neither nominated the Croatian prime minister nor controlled the executive; that the Croatian deputies in the joint parliament and representatives in the Croato-Hungarian delegation were not bound by the sabor's mandate; that the sabor was denied direct access to the head of state; and finally that Croatia did not have prerogatives in such affairs vital to any state as its own budgetary, foreign and defence policy. (In this last respect, however, neither 'Austria' nor 'Hungary' enjoyed full sovereignty.) There was also the curious role of the Croatian minister, who as a member of the joint government was responsible to the joint parliament but not to the Croatian sabor. The main function of his office was to act as an additional barrier to communication between the sabor and the king. Despite Croatia's formal autonomy, Hungary's control of the joint bodies secured its dominance over Croatia.[16]

The fact that Croatian deputies did not act under the sabor's mandate ensured that Hungarian wishes would prevail in the joint parliament. That parliament, moreover, had no common language – a circumstance that, given the numerical proportions, worked to Croatia's disadvantage. The Hungarian deputies spoke (or were permitted to speak) only in Hungarian,[17] a language that few Croatians knew; hence, the Croatian public could inform themselves on what was happening in the parliament at Pest only by reading German-language press reports. Since the Hungarian deputies did not understand interventions made in Croat either, the joint parliamentary sessions proved truly a dialogue of the deaf.[18]

On 8 March 1869 the king, accompanied by Andrássy, made a formal visit to Croatia, on which occasion he announced the transformation of the Zagreb Academy into a fully fledged university. Strossmayer's contribution was not mentioned. The Unionist government added this to its list of achievements, as it claimed credit also for the royal decision that year to demilitarise the Varaždin part of the border and return the area – together with Senj, Sisak and the Žumberak district – to Croatian civilian administration. The Varaždin Border area gave rise to the new county of Bjelovar, physically uniting Slavonia with the rest if Ban's Croatia for the first time since the sixteenth century.

A legal and political quagmire

The real nature of the Croato-Hungarian Compromise was revealed as soon as it started to be implemented, when it became clear that the Hungarian government reserved for itself the exclusive right to interpret its meaning and content. The first stumbling-block proved to be the relative competencies of the ban and the Croatian minister. The Croatian parliamentarians, as a result, scrutinised the text of the Compromise in order to better resist Croatia's 'absorption on the part of the Kingdom of Hungary'. A part of the Unionist bloc now joined the opposition.

The National Party believed that dualism would not last, given the resistance put up against it by Czech national leaders, who announced that the lands of the Bohemian crown were linked to other parts of the Monarchy only by the person of the king and called for a new agreement between the king and the Czech nation. A few days after the sabor's adoption of the Croato-Hungarian Compromise, Prague was placed under a state of emergency. The Czechs refused to attend the Reichsrat and resorted to organising open air or *tabor* rallies, which lasted until the autumn of 1871. The Slovenes followed their example on a programme of Slovene national unity. The start of the Franco-Prussian war in July 1870 encouraged a fear that, if Prussia were to win the war, the Monarchy might fall apart, after which the areas that used to belong to the Holy Roman Empire (which included the Slovene lands) would be joined to Germany. This strengthened pro-Yugoslav sentiments among the Slovenes – the idea that the united Slovene lands should on a federal basis join Croatia and a Serb Vojvodina.

The National Party too awaited the outcome of the Franco-Prussian War. In September 1870 France was defeated at Sedan, and in January 1871 the Prussian king, Wilhelm I, announced the birth of a united Germany. The Austrian Germans' enthusiasm for the German cause frightened the Habsburg court so much that Francis Joseph approved the unification of the lands of the Bohemian crown, on the same basis as the lands of the Hungarian crown, and agreed to crown himself King of Bohemia. This intention implied a reorganisation of the Austrian part of the Monarchy. Recognition of the Bohemian state right would strengthen the Croatian case. The National Party was also encouraged by the fact that in 1870 its Dalmatian counterpart won a majority in the Dalmatian parliament. Prompted by Rački, the Dalmatian sabor's address stated that the Unionist parliament was illegal, not least because it had been convened without Dalmatian representatives. The king was asked 'to create the necessary legal conditions which would permit Dalmatian and Croatian representatives to meet and decide on how to restore the former constitutional link between Dalmatia and Croatia-Slavonia'. The National Party was encouraged also by the fact that the Unionists proved unable to bring order to the chaotic legal and administrative situation in Ban's Croatia. In new elections conducted in May 1871 the Unionists were indeed crushed, after which they disappeared as an organised force. The National Party once again dominated the sabor.

Ivan Mažuranić was elected in the new county of Bjelovar that had replaced the dissolved Varaždin Regiment. The convening of the sabor, however, was postponed three times.

In September 1871 the National Party issued a public manifesto denouncing both the Austro-Hungarian and the Croato-Hungarian Compromises. The manifesto stated that the Croato-Hungarian Compromise was invalid, since it had been concluded 'without the participation of the greater part of our nation', and demanded that the ban be appointed without recourse to the Hungarian government. In October that year the Bohemian parliament adopted fundamental laws affirming Bohemian statehood, but it also accepted dualism. However, German representatives in the Reichsrat and the Hungarian government denounced this act as contrary to the Austro-Hungarian Compromise. Fear of Austrian German irredentism and a consequent break-up of the Habsburg Monarchy prompted Germany also to indicate its displeasure with Vienna's policy of appeasing the Czechs. In this confused situation Eugen Kvaternik, reacting to the turmoil produced in the Military Border by the arrival of dualism, attempted to organise an armed rebellion against 'German-Magyar supremacy' with the aim of establishing a transitional Croatian government prior to liberating the whole of Croatia. This ended in his own death in the Border village of Rakovica and the brief imprisonment of Starčević. Two weeks later, the pro-federalist Austrian government headed by Carl Hohenwart fell, and negotiations with the Czech parties were suspended. The emperor dismissed Beust as foreign minister and replaced him with Andrássy. Germany now became, together with the Magyar landowners, the chief guardian of Austro-Hungarian dualism.

The Croatian sabor was finally convened in January 1872, only to hear of its dissolution. The new ban, Koloman Bedaković, was asked to organise fresh elections, which in the king's view should produce 'a more constructive spirit'. The National Party was faced with the choice between remaining an impotent opposition party and accepting the Croato-Hungarian Compromise, which at least would allow it to work for its revision. The party's new cooperative mood was encouraged by the fact that a large number of Unionists, including the key city of Zagreb, switched their support to the National Party in the hope of ending the existing administrative chaos. The Nationals now submitted a memorandum to the new Hungarian prime minister, Menyhért Lónyay, in which it accepted 'an unbreakable and real union of the lands of the Hungarian crown' in return for Hungarian support for the reintegration of Dalmatia and the border, an independent

Croatian government, and revision of the financial side of the agreement. The Hungarian parliament rejected this offer.

The National Party won a handsome majority in the new elections – forty-seven seats against the Unionists' twenty-eight – but failed to command a majority, since the ban simply increased the number of *virilisten* seats to forty-seven, which gave the sabor to the Unionists. The Hungarian government knew, however, that it could not rule in Croatia without the support of the National Party. In June 1872 the Hungarian prime minister offered the possibility of revision of the terms of the Croato-Hungarian Compromise, on condition that half the Croatian seats in the joint parliament and on the Croatian part of the Croato-Hungarian delegation be given to the Unionists. A Unionist was also to be given the post of deputy speaker of the parliament. The National Party, in other words, had to fuse with the Unionists. It was an offer the National Party could not refuse. The country, as a result, acquired a more stable government run by the new model National Party – which Starčević's Party of Right quickly dubbed the Neo-Magyarones. The sabor elected Ivan Mažuranić as its speaker and Jovan Živković as his deputy. The king wrote a letter to the sabor urging reconciliation and completion of the administrative and judicial reforms, adding vague promises in regard to the building of Croatian railways.

The sabor's address once again asked for the restitution of Dalmatia and the rest of the Military Border. It also elected a new delegation to negotiate with the Hungarians. The Croatian delegation was to demand that the ban should be appointed without the involvement of the Hungarian prime minister. It was to demand, too, that the Croatian minister should not interfere in Croatia's internal affairs, but limit himself to representing Croatia in matters dealing with common Austro-Hungarian affairs. The Croatian members of the Croato-Hungarian delegation should be elected only by the Croatian members of the joint parliament, rather than by the whole parliament. Given repeated disagreements over interpretation of the Croato-Hungarian Compromise, a crown court should be established that would regulate disputes between Hungary and Croatia, similar in nature to the court established in 1867 for the lands represented in the Reichsrat. Dalmatia and Croatia-Slavonia should be allowed to negotiate their unification. The rest of the Border should also be demilitarised and returned to Croatia. The status of Rijeka should be renegotiated.

The Hungarian side rejected almost all these proposals, on the grounds that they were contrary to 'Hungarian state unity'. It disliked in particular the idea of a crown court. The duties of the Croatian minister, on the other hand, were more clearly specified: he was to forward to the ban 'without alteration or delay' communications from the king. In the event of 'ambiguities perceived from the angle of state union or common interests' which could not be removed through direct contact with the ban, the minister would be able to inform the king of his own view and that of the central government. What this meant in practice was that all decisions of the Croatian government would be scrutinised by the central ministry, and everything it did not like presented as contrary to the interests of state unity.

Given the incorporation of the Varaždin Border, on the other hand, the number of Croatian seats in the joint parliament was increased from twenty-nine to thirty-four. Croatia was also given a guarantee that the sabor would henceforth be recalled within three months of its dissolution. On the financial issue, the Croatian proposal was that the budget for Croatia's internal affairs should be separated from the joint budget. The Hungarian response was that a single financial and tax system was the foundation stone of the state association created by the Compromise. Hungary was ready, however, to permit Croatia to keep 45 per cent of its income as originally envisioned, rather than a fixed sum as before. This concession did not amount to much, since the Croatian government had no means of establishing the extent of internally generated revenue, or how much the Hungarian government spent in Croatia on behalf of joint affairs. The revision, in other words, brought little change.

When these 'revisions' were placed before the sabor, the opposition, led by Franjo Rački, refused to accept them. But the majority of the National Party argued that they should be endorsed, since without this it would be impossible to normalise the situation in Croatia. Refusal involved a continuation of administrative and judicial disarray, as witnessed in the preceding period. In the blunt words of one deputy, the position of negation led only to Rakovica – to armed rebellion. The revised Compromise was adopted on 29 September 1873 by seventy-nine votes in favour and ten against. On the same day Ivan Mažuranić was appointed ban. Jovan Živković and Nikola Krestić, both ethnic Serbs, became respectively minister of the interior and deputy ban. Serbs also held the posts of minister of justice and president of the supreme court. This was a clear sign that union with Hungary was leading also to a growing Serb influence in Croatia's domestic affairs.

Ban Mažuranić

Ivan Mažuranić was the first non-noble to hold the post of ban – and the first to shed the formal ban's apparel. He remained in this post until February 1880, by which time the modernisation of the Croatian government and civic society, begun in 1848, had been largely completed. His tactic was to avoid an open clash with the Hungarian government, and to conduct step-by-step reforms that would place Croatian autonomy on firm foundations.

Between 1872 and 1875 the Croatian parliament under his leadership passed a number of laws embracing all spheres of life, including the separation of justice and administration, a new legal system, penal and civic reforms, educational reform, and a number of other measures pertaining to the functioning of the economy and society. He introduced close supervision of the civil service to ensure its professionalism and prevent corruption. This feverish reforming activity was perceived as a threat, however, by local conservatives as well as by the Hungarian government, which saw it as a way of strengthening Croatia's independence by the back door. The ban was therefore frequently called to Pest to account for his actions. On the pretext that Croatian decisions affected the continued health of the 'Hungarian state idea', Pest insisted on approving the Croatian sabor's addresses to the king, and habitually vetted the list of Croatian deputies elected to the joint parliament through the office of the Croatian minister. Mažuranić consequently found himself between the hammer of the government in Budapest and the anvil of domestic opposition, which – faced with growing infringements of the terms of the Compromise on the part of Hungary – charged him with being too conciliatory.

One of Mažuranić's greatest achievements was to remove church influence from the schools. His educational reform was inspired by the Austrian education law of 1867, which placed schools under sole control of the state. A similar reform was undertaken also by the military authorities in the border. A single system of state schools now emerged, involving all Croatian children, which meant that all teachers became state employees. The churches retained responsibility for religious education, but even that was placed under government control. The only concession to the confessions was the rule that teachers had to be of the same faith as their pupils, or in mixed schools as the majority. The Catholic Church, including Bishop Strossmayer, was bitterly opposed to this reform. But the strongest opposition came from Serb leaders, who saw the new educational law as an attack on the Serb nation. The main problem lay in interpreting the competence of the Serb communal assembly – which administered Serb

Orthodox Church affairs, including church funds – to run schools for Serb children. The Hungarian government had confirmed Serb confessional autonomy in 1868, and it also permitted municipalities and private individuals to establish schools under the state's ultimate control. These laws were enacted before the Croato-Hungarian Compromise established Croatia's full autonomy in educational and religious affairs, following which supervision of the Serb communal bodies came under the authority of the ban. This unresolved problem of jurisdiction between the Croatian and Hungarian governments became a source of both cooperation and disagreement between the Croatian administration and the leaders of the Serb community in Croatia.

Mažuranić's law did not limit Serb confessional autonomy, and it permitted the Orthodox Church to run schools at its own expense; but these schools had to conform to a certain standard in order to be approved by the state. The growth of Serb confessional schools was limited further by his ruling that the municipalities had to provide a school in every area with more than forty children of school age, which meant that some of the funds previously used to support Serb Orthodox schools had to be diverted to state schools. The Croatian government believed that the new laws would satisfy Serb cultural and religious needs, given that all the country's schools taught the Cyrillic script and Serb literature and history. Serb leaders and the Serb Orthodox Church, however, wished to see a separate educational system for Serb children run by Serb communal bodies. They attacked Mažuranić's law as an anti-Serb measure, because their confessional schools were for them an instrument for forging the Serb nation within Croatia. Serb deputies in the sabor consequently moved that the law should not apply to Serb children. The sabor, however, did not wish to exempt education from its authority. The law was accordingly passed, with the qualification that the term 'Croat language' should be interpreted also as 'Serb language'. But Serb nationalists would never forgive Mažuranić, despite the fact that school attendance greatly improved under his government.

The Serbs found themselves with a problem in that they enjoyed a degree of autonomy in regard to their religious institutions, but in their different ways both the Croatian and the Hungarian governments were authorised to define its outer limits. The Croatian Serbs had to choose, therefore, between strengthening Croatian autonomy, in order to limit the influence of the Hungarian government in Serb communal affairs, and weakening it, in order to preserve their own freedom of action on the ground. Their actual behaviour depended on political circumstances. Both the Hungarian and the Croatian side sought to win their support, with the difference that the power of the Hungarian government was stronger than any exercised by Croatian state bodies. The fact that Serbs occupied important positions in the Croatian parliament, however – thus participating in many decisions that other Serbs saw as an attack on their nationality – prevented a complete Croat-Serb polarisation within Croatia. The policy of Magyarisation conducted in Hungary itself also aided good Croat-Serb relations.

Mažuranić's government did not interfere in elections, although at Hungarian insistence the Croatian government retained full control of the electoral process. The elections of 1875 were comfortably won by the National Party, but the tempo of reform subsequently slowed down, thanks to the hostility of the new Hungarian government headed by Kálmán Tisza. Hungarian politicians remained deeply suspicious of Croatia's autonomy, and of the modernisation of its state structure undertaken by Mažuranić. The Hungarian government consequently blocked Mažuranić's attempt to make the Croatian government responsible to the sabor, and rejected his proposal that royal decisions be countersigned by the ban rather than the Croatian minister. But fearing the advance of the 'Yugoslav idea', the continued hankering for federalisation of the Monarchy, and Austrian influence in Croatia generally, they wished to keep the peace won on the Croatian front. In the meantime they fuelled Croat-Serb quarrels over the future of the South Slavs, in line with the principle of *divide et impera*.

The fact that the Croatian deputies in the Hungarian parliament regularly voted with the government did not prevent the latter from chipping away at Croatian autonomy. At the start of Mažuranić's period in office, the Hungarian minister of transport had made Hungarian the official language on the railways and in the telegraph and postal service, in order to remove German-speaking officials; but he made no provision for employing Croat-speaking personnel. The national guard and the gendarmerie also came to wear exclusively Hungarian national insignia. Mažuranić protested that this was against the terms of the Compromise, but to no avail. There was also the problem of the Senj diocese, which included Rijeka. The Hungarian government demanded that it rather than the Croatian ban should be consulted on the appointment of the bishop of Senj. Similar problems arose also in connection with the Military Border. And in 1875 Međimurje was taken from the religious jurisdiction of the diocese of Zagreb and incorporated into the Hungarian church. The result was a growing sense of frustration in the country, and increased criticism in the sabor of the ban for his alleged appeasement of the Magyars. The sense of alienation was reinforced by the fact that the royal rescripts read out at the opening of the 1875 and 1878 parliaments failed to address the issues of Dalmatia and the Border. Croatia's autonomy was in fact increasingly treated on both the Austrian and the Hungarian sides as an unnecessary embarrassment, and there was fear that it might be abolished altogether.

The revival of the Eastern Question

The growing instability of Ottoman rule reopened the Eastern Question, producing a violent Croat-Serb polemic over the destiny of Bosnia-Herzegovina. In the summer of 1875, suppression of a widespread rebellion among the latter's Christian population led to the arrival of around 100,000 refugees in Dalmatia and Croatia-Slavonia. The Croatian press sided with the rebels, the Hungarian with the Ottoman state. The National Party's position was that if Serbia could not liberate Bosnia, it should be annexed by the Monarchy and joined to Croatia. Serb politicians insisted, however, that Bosnia was a purely Serb land, which should be joined to Serbia – along, some argued, with other 'Serb lands' such as Slavonia, Dalmatia and the Military Border.

In 1876 Serbia and Montenegro declared war against the Ottoman Empire, but were beaten back. In the same year the Austro-Hungarian foreign minister, Gyula Andrássy, seeking to prevent Serbian expansion into Bosnia, proposed to Russia a division of the Ottoman Empire's European lands: Bulgaria would go to Russia, Bosnia-Herzegovina to the Monarchy. Fearing the arrival of Serbian rule, the Bosnian Franciscans sided with Vienna. The dispute between Serbs and Croats over Bosnia's future now came to boiling point. The general excitement over the situation in that country stimulated broad support for the claim of the Party of Right that Bosnia-Herzegovina was Dalmatia's historic hinterland, hence belonged to Zvonimir's crown (though the party's leader, Ante Starčević, was against its being joined to Austria-Hungary). Zagreb university students, who now swelled the ranks of the Party of Right, in 1876 voiced support for 'the Croat people's sacred struggle' in Bosnia, and demanded that 'the Croatian king' liberate it on Croatia's behalf. They also gave full support to the Bulgarian national struggle. The growth of the Party of Right's influence among students shocked the National Party.

The Bosnian dimension of the Eastern Question was in the end resolved without either Croatia or Serbia. Russia declared war on the Ottoman Empire, and in 1877 its army reached the gates of Istanbul. Great Britain and Austria, backed by Germany, now joined efforts to keep Russia away from the Straits, and the whole venture ended with the convocation in 1878 of the Congress of Berlin, out of which three independent states emerged: Bulgaria, Montenegro and Serbia. Austria-Hungary was allowed to occupy Bosnia-Herzegovina, even though the latter remained nominally an Ottoman territory. Against the advice of Ban Mažuranić, the Croatian sabor drafted an address to the king requesting that Bosnia-Herzegovina be added to Croatia together with Dalmatia. Mažuranić would also have liked Bosnia to join Croatia as part of a general policy of uniting the South Slavs within a single framework; but he was suspicious of the true goals of imperial policy. He consequently advised the sabor not to link the Bosnian issue with that of Dalmatia. He added: 'It is being said that [Bosnia-Herzegovina] provides Dalmatia with a proper hinterland, but we don't know who will benefit from this [occupation]; whether it will serve Dalmatia or something else; we don't know the purpose of it all, or indeed that Bosnia will ever belong to the Monarchy. Given all these uncertainties, the address should not deal with such matters.'[19] The sabor nevertheless expressed the hope that 'the legal system of the newly gained provinces' would be 'gradually adjusted' in a manner that would facilitate their integration with Croatia. The king's response was that the sabor had overstepped its authority.

Serb deputies in the Hungarian parliament condemned the occupation, while Croat deputies welcomed it. In the Austrian parliament the Austrian German parties tended to condemn it, the Slav ones (with the exception of the Poles) to welcome it. In the end a majority in both parliaments approved the occupation, which Andrássy defended on the grounds that it was the only way of preventing the creation of a Yugoslav state.[20] The commission he set up to determine the administration of Bosnia-Herzegovina involved no one from Croatia. In 1879 the waiting government was placed under the authority of the Austro-Hungarian finance ministry and given a Hungarian governor. That same year Germany, Russia and Austria-Hungary created the so-called Three Emperors' Alliance. The fact that Serbia too now entered the Austro-Hungarian (in fact Hungarian) sphere of influence could only strengthen the Serbs' commitment to Croatia's continued union with Hungary.

Disappointed by the delay in returning the Military Border to Croatian administration, and finding increasingly little support at home, Mažuranić decided to withdraw. He had become a symbol of Croatia's determination to make something of its autonomy, and both Vienna and Budapest wished to see him go. He resigned in early 1880 and was replaced by the wealthy landowner Slavonian magnate Ladislav Pejačević. A poet, jurist, statesman and visionary, Ivan Mažuranić had done what he could to steer Croatia through the treacherous waters of Austria-Hungary towards the modern age. But he continued to worry about its future. As he told his son: 'We [Croats] live in the night's shadow hoping for dawn to break.'[21]

Josip Juraj Strossmayer – a troublesome priest

The conduct of the National Party in the crucial decade of the 1860s was to a large extent determined by Mažuranić's political opponent, Bishop Josip Juraj Strossmayer. The Italian statesman and twice prime minister Marco Minghetti once said that there were two of his contemporaries who 'appear to belong not to our own but to another race: Bismarck and Strossmayer'.[22] It is possible that Minghetti had met Strossmayer in the company of the English liberal thinker John Acton at the time of the First Vatican Council (1869–70), when both tried hard to prevent the council from adopting the doctrine of papal infallibility. Having challenged the will of his king, Strossmayer was ready to do battle also with the head of his church. Acton was greatly impressed by his courage: 'If the whole Council were against him and for infallibility, Strossmayer will remain firm.'[23] Acton fully shared Strossmayer's views on a whole range of issues – such as the church and the papacy, the rights of bishops and laity, the 'love of souls', and unity with Orthodox and Protestants. Felix Dupanloup, the bishop of Orleans, wrote of the Croatian bishop: 'The Council has found its man.'[24] Pope Pius IX described him as that '*caposetta Croatino*', or Croat ringleader. The delegation from Austria-Hungary included also the Slovene bishop of Trieste, Bartholomeu Legat; the Istrian Croat bishop of Poreč, Juraj Dobrila; and the Uniate bishop of Križevci, Juraj Smičiklas: they too signed the minority protest at the Council's procedures, drafted in all probability by Strossmayer.

Intellectual independence had marked Strossmayer from an early age. Having granted him a degree in theology in 1837, the head of the examining board at the University of Pest noted: 'Strossmayer is destined to become either the greatest heretic of the nineteenth century or the strongest pillar of the Catholic Church.'[25] At the Vatican Council he was indeed denounced as being not so much a heretic as a 'cursed Lucifer' – even though, unlike some members of the defeated minority, he remained loyal to Rome. He is best remembered, though, as a national leader. It is in fact difficult to separate Strossmayer's political engagement from his vision of the moral and historical mission of the Catholic Church.[26] One of the Church's duties, in his view, was to support national struggles for freedom: 'We all know that the nations of the world desire freedom and unity. Every nation forming a community by its nature, history and descent has the right to unite and seek unity in its strength, life and progress. The Church is not against this.'[27]

He was born in 1815 into a family of modest means in the then mainly German-speaking city of Osijek, which meant that he was equally at home in Croat and German. After leaving Pest he worked briefly as chaplain in the border fortress of Petrovaradin, before winning a place at the Augustineum, the elite Catholic college in Vienna. He gained a doctorate at the University of Vienna with a thesis on the East–West religious schism. In 1847–8 he served as court chaplain and as a director of the Augustineum. During his studies in Pest he had come under the influence of the Protestant Slovak pastor Jan Kollár, who advocated the idea of Slav solidarity. In Vienna he became an adherent of the Illyrian movement together with other Croat clerics who studied at the Augustineum: the future bishop of Poreč Juraj Dobrila; the future bishop of Senj Venceslav Soić; and the future historian and first president of the Yugoslav Academy Franjo Rački. Rački became Strossmayer's life-long friend and collaborator, a man whose natural caution helped to keep in check Strossmayer's own fiery temperament. During his time in Vienna Strossmayer also met the Czech national ideologues, František Palacký and František Rieger, who won him over to their Austro-Slav policy and to the conviction that constitutional government and federalisation of the Habsburg Monarchy were the only way to prevent its disintegration.

In 1850 Strossmayer was appointed bishop of Đakovo and Srijem, resurrected in this united form by Maria Theresa in 1770. Srijem was an ancient diocese, while bishops of Đakovo had for centuries been titular heads of the Bosnian Catholics. From 1851 until 1897 Strossmayer was also the apostolic vicar for Serbia. His rapport with the Orthodox population was a major recommendation for the post, as was his interest in Catholic–Orthodox relations. In his inaugural speech he characteristically linked freedom of man with national freedom and Christian ethics: 'The spirit of our time is called the spirit of freedom, the spirit of equality and brotherhood, the spirit of nationhood and patriotism.' Freedom was the most crucial quality, since 'man was created to be free', and 'Christianity protects freedom'.[28] Christianity was the force that raised humanity from slavery, while love of one's nation was natural to man.

The posts he filled imbued Strossmayer's Croat national ideology with a strongly Yugoslav spirit, and equally with a desire to unite the Catholic and Orthodox Churches under Rome. His seat in the Croatian parliament strengthened his natural inclination towards political engagement, especially during the 1860s, when he became leader of the National Party.

Josip Juraj Strossmayer

He identified absolutist rule as 'a silent [German] war against the Slavs': as long as absolutism remained a threat, he favoured Croatia's alliance with Hungary. It is on this issue that he clashed with Mažuranić. He was an ardent advocate of Croatian state right, which he saw as 'the glue binding together our nation's different parts'. As the only surviving old kingdom in the South Slav world, Croatia in his view was destined to become the centre of a Yugoslav union that would emerge once the South Slavs had been liberated from Ottoman rule. Their liberation was Croatia's – and the Monarchy's – historic and divinely inspired mission.

As bishop of Đakovo and Srijem, Strossmayer belonged to the Slavonian magnate class. Income from his wealthy see – composed of 700,000 hectares of ancient Slavonian forests, meadows and arable land, vineyards and stables – enabled him to fund all manner of national projects (though he himself lived frugally).[29] According to one account, in the last few years of his life he donated over one million forints for 'the faith', and an even greater sum for 'the nation', of which half a million was spent on the Yugoslav Academy alone. Most of the money for 'the nation' was spent in Croatia. Quite apart from funding the academy, the great art gallery he built alongside it and the University of Zagreb, he sent scholars like Rački to study Croatian and Croatia-related documents in foreign archives, especially in the newly opened ones of the Vatican. He bought shares in early banking, road and railway consortia in Ban's Croatia and Dalmatia, intended to stimulate Croatia's economic advance and political integration. He financed opposition parties and patriotic journals throughout the land; Croat-language schools and institutes where the local population was too poor to provide for them – as, for example, in Istria; and a large number of impoverished writers, artists and intellectuals. He also supported the building and maintenance of churches, monasteries and seminaries, including a seminary which he set up in Đakovo for the Bosnian Franciscans. But he also aided projects of a national character in Slovenia, Serbia, Bulgaria and Montenegro – and above all in Bosnia-Herzegovina.

Strossmayer's most expensive single undertaking, however, proved to be the cathedral of Đakovo, built in the Romanesque style on the very border between the Catholic and the Orthodox worlds. Construction began in 1866, and by the time it was completed in 1882 he had exhausted the diocesan funds – according to one estimate, he spent over 1,200,000 forints on the building, excluding the timber from his estates. It is difficult to understand Strossmayer's decision to build such a splendid cathedral in a modest place like Đakovo, with its 2,500 inhabitants, without reference to his vision of Croatia's potential role in bringing the two worlds together:

> Our country's geographical location has given it the role of binding together the West and the East. In the old days, when [Romano-Christian] civilisation and education were moving from the East to the West, our country was a main mediator between the two. The West should now return its debt to the East by transferring to it both education and Christian freedom. We [Croatians] are once again invested with a great task in this divine mission.[30]

Strossmayer was consequently ready to support Serbian intervention in Bosnia rather than see the latter left in the Ottoman Empire. While opposing any separate status for the Croatian Serbs other than in the religious sphere, he also sought to protect them from Magyarisation. Though critical of some of their leaders' claims, he remained convinced that the main danger to the Monarchy's Slavs came from Austrian German centralists, who in his view were seeking to turn them into Germans. Fighting fire with fire, so to speak, he did what he could to Croatise the Germans of Srijem by introducing

Croat into the local church, and by discouraging the use of German in local schools – whereupon his outraged German flock threatened to turn Protestant.

Strossmayer's political opponents portrayed him as a dangerous Panslavist, intent on creating a Yugoslav state outside the Monarchy. Mažuranić's successor as Croatian chancellor wrote in one of his reports: 'Bishop Strossmayer is a most dangerous Yugoslav agitator; his extreme nationalist views are detrimental to the Monarchy's interests.'[31] Strossmayer himself wrote to the German Catholic thinker Ignaz von Döllinger in the turbulent year of 1871: 'My position in my own country is a delicate one. I am close to the Church and the political affairs of my nation. The poor South Slavs are to the highest degree ill-treated by the governments of Vienna and Budapest. I am a thorn in their side and for years they have looked for some excuse to remove and silence me.'[32] Following adoption of the Croato-Hungarian Compromise he practically retired from active political life, concentrating instead on religious matters and the progress of his cathedral. After Prussia's victory at Sedan he advocated an anti-German alliance of Europe's Romance and Slav nations. He supported Italy's unification and stressed the existence of deep cultural ties between Croats and Italians. France's humiliation, however, convinced him that Russia alone could prevent German mastery in Europe. But Austria-Hungary, this 'Europe in miniature', remained in his view the fulcrum of the continental balance of power.

Seeking to bring the Orthodox world closer to Rome, Strossmayer advocated decentralisation – or, more accurately, internationalisation – of the Catholic Church, the use of Church Slavonic in Catholic liturgy, the propagation of the cult of Cyril and Methodius (the latter, after all, had been one of his predecessors), and a concordat with the Slav states. Echoing Markantun de Dominis, Catholic Church unity in his view rested on the community and authority of the bishops, rather than on that of the pope alone. A reorganised Catholic Church would, moreover, be more attractive to the Orthodox peoples. He argued at the Vatican Council that the 'Eastern schism' should be called Slav rather than Greek, since

> eighty million [Slavs] live outside the embrace of the Catholic Church. They are greatly committed to their independence and separate rights. They fear above all anything that could bring their independence and their rights into question. I live among South Slavs of whom approximately eight million are schismatics and only three million Catholics. I remain forever grateful to God's mercy that my beloved Croat nation is Catholic and, I can assure

you, remains loyal to the Holy See. But if this definition [of papal infallibility] prevails, I wonder whether this good leaven sent by God will be able to influence the Orthodox Slav masses and bring them into unity with the Church.[33]

The Croats were such a leaven as the only Catholic nation that habitually used Slav liturgy.

Strossmayer was the last Catholic bishop to publish the Vatican Council's declaration on papal infallibility, and even then he himself never endorsed it publicly. Yet this defiance did not prevent him from maintaining a cordial relationship with Pope Pius IX. His last great achievement was the encyclical *Grande Munus*, issued by Pope Leo XIII in 1880 to honour Saints Cyril and Methodius, which he helped to draft. Its appearance caused the greatest suspicion among Croatia's Orthodox clergy and Serb secular leaders, particularly since Strossmayer used the occasion to stress the essential unity of the Christian religion and to call for the two Churches to unite: the Holy Apostles' lives and work argued that 'we are one in church and religion'.[34]

During the 1870s Strossmayer worked hard to establish diplomatic relations between Moscow and the Vatican. The *Grande Munus* facilitated these negotiations. In 1888, when Russia was celebrating the 900th anniversary of its conversion to Christianity, he sent a telegram of congratulations to Kiev in which he blessed Russia and, following in the footsteps of Juraj Križanić, reminded it of its divine mission in the world. The Budapest and Vienna press roundly condemned him for this. Visiting a military exercise in Bjelovar, Francis Joseph too reprimanded him for this act 'against the Monarchy and the Church'. Strossmayer's response – 'Your Majesty, my conscience is clear' – was treated by the king and the press alike as a personal affront. He died in self-imposed exile at Đakovo in 1905, but not before being able to witness a new upsurge in the political life of his 'beloved nation'. Although this upsurge was led not by his own party but by the rival Party of Right, its leaders in Dalmatia and Istria had in the meantime adopted many of his own political postulates.

In Hungary's grip

On accepting his post, in February 1880, Mažuranić's successor in the office of ban, the wealthy Slavonian landowner Ladislav Pejačević proclaimed his adherence to the Compromise and his intention to defend it both against the Croatian opposition and Hungarian encroachments. He also promised a speedy integration of the Military Border with Ban's Croatia. Despite his Unionist background, the Hungarian government did not trust him. In Hungary itself the rights of the non-Magyar nationalities had come under sustained pressure, and there were increasing calls in the Hungarian parliament for ending Croatian autonomy. The Hungarian government knew that this could not be done: its intention was to Magyarise Croatia without the pain of abolishing its distinct status. One way of achieving this was to abolish the monopoly of the Croat language in the Croatian kingdom, using the presence of central state offices on its soil. Magyarisation of the schools and bureaucracy were in fact the most potent weapons for assimilation of the non-Magyar nationalities.[35] The Hungarian prime minister, Kálmán Tisza, now announced that the Compromise did not exclude the Hungarian language from Croatia, and proceeded to prove it. Croat officials working in central governmental offices, including the railways and the postal and telegraph service, would henceforth have to speak Magyar. In the spring of 1880 the Hungarian government appointed as head of its financial office in Croatia one Antal David, who proceeded to organise free Magyar language classes for Croatian civil servants working in the ministry of finance. He also announced that knowledge of the language would henceforth be made obligatory for those wishing to advance in the service. There was an angry reaction in the sabor, but Živković assured it that the measure would be repealed as soon as a Hungarian language department was established at Zagreb University. The majority of the National Party accepted this, but a minority of twenty-two split off to form a new Independent National Party seeking revision of the Croato-Hungarian Compromise.

The imprecisions of the Croato-Hungarian Compromise, particularly regarding the separation of Croatia's internal affairs from those which it shared with Hungary, proved most contentious in the financial sphere, given that the Croatian parliament was unable to learn the country's actual revenue or control its spending. (Financial disagreements likewise marred the relationship between the Austrian and the Hungarian parts of the monarchy.) In 1880 the Croatian delegation failed in an attempt to separate more clearly Croatia's own budget from that of the joint state. Hungary in fact found itself in grave financial difficulty at this time, which it tried to solve by taking loans and increasing domestic taxes.[36] The growing tax burden impoverished the peasantry and small landowners, and sequestration of property for non-payment of taxes became a common occurrence in Croatia. In Hungary itself tax inspectors were responsible to the local county government, so were able to prevent misuse of state power and thus prevent violent resistance; in Croatia, however, tax collection was part of 'joint affairs' over which Croatia had no influence. These 'joint bodies' thus became identified as Magyar and social revolts took the form of national resistance.

The status of Rijeka also continued to poison Croatian-Hungarian relations. In 1873 Rijeka finally acquired a rail link to Karlovac, sidelining completely its old competitor, Senj. Rijeka was becoming a major industrial, trade and financial centre – it acquired, among other things, an oil refinery and the first European torpedo factory, initiated by the British engineer Robert Whitehead – and was keen to regularise its status. This could not be achieved, however, without Croatian consent. The old Magyar dream that Rijeka could steer the Croatian Littoral in a Hungarian direction had proved vain, and the autonomist Rijeka government became worried by the rise of the Croat national movement in the Littoral and Istria, which inevitably made itself felt in the city itself. The city government consequently asked for the closure of the Croatian county office in Rijeka, as well as of the Croat-language gymnasium, which in the meantime had become a bastion of Croat nationalism. The appearance of the Party of Right journal *Sloboda* (Freedom) in the neighbouring port of Sušak suggested that there was little time to lose. Sušak, lying on the other side of the river Rječina, had replaced Rijeka as Croatia's main port on the Littoral, and was developing rapidly as a result. The Hungarian counties now pressed the Hungarian government finally to annex Rijeka, while the sabor sought to prevent a 'Magyar confiscation' of this Croatian port. The atmosphere became even more heated after the Rijeka government closed down the local county assembly. The king sided with the Hungarian government. Following the dissolution of the Military Border in 1886, the county of Rijeka was renamed the county of Rijeka-Modruš and its seat transferred from Rijeka to Ogulin, a place of modest economic and strategic importance. The enterprising mayor of Sušak, however, ensured that the Croat gymnasium, once expelled from Rijeka, would come to Sušak rather than go to Ogulin.[37]

These measures led to Rijeka being finally excluded from Croatian administrative and economic life. The city's phenomenal growth – it doubled its population between 1880 and 1900 – encouraged, however, its sense of separateness from Hungary too. Hungarian efforts to submit it to firmer control, including by replacing Italian with Magyar in its administration, were rebuffed. When in 1896 the Rijeka magistracy was denied the right (derived from its formal status as a *corpus separatum*) to confirm laws passed by the parliament in Budapest, the local leader Michele Maylender established the Autonomous Party and was in 1897 elected mayor. On assuming office he declared: 'The sole source and root of Rijeka's love for Hungary [are] to be found only and exclusively in the [Hungarian] government's respect for its autonomy. [Any] attempt to take away from Rijeka its autonomy in internal affairs and the Italian language would cut the roots of the tree of our [Hungarian] patriotism, causing it to wither. For the people of Rijeka, Hungarian patriotism is inconceivable without autonomy.'[38] Maylender was re-elected mayor three more times, until finally the Hungarian government dissolved the city council and installed its own man. At the turn of the century Italian irredentism began to capture the imagination of Rijeka's youth, leading to the foundation in 1905 of the movement *La Giovine Fiume* (Young Rijeka). By denying Rijeka to Croatia, Hungary ensured that it would become Italian.

This was still in the future. In the meantime Croatia's political prostration was feeding the advance of the Party of Right in Croatian urban centres. The party's fundamental postulates were that Croatia should seek full independence on the basis of historic and natural right; that it had to break with the 'treacherous' Habsburg dynasty; and, in sum, that the Croatians should be masters of their own fate. In 1875 the party acquired its first deputy in the sabor, Fran Folnegović from Zagreb, and in the 1878 elections four more including the party's founder Ante Starčević himself. In his maiden speech Starčević declared that all Croatian parliaments since 1865 had been illegal, since for the sabor to be legal it had to include deputies from Dalmatia and the Military Border. In 1881, despite political persecution, the party won one more seat. Four years later it would have twenty-five, as against thirteen held by the Independent National Party. Starčević's dislike of Austria led him to embrace Russia as a potential liberator of the Croatian people, thus strengthening pro-Slav sentiments among the Croatian youth. The younger generation in the party, however, broke with his view that all South Slavs other than the Bulgarians were Croats, and rejected his hostility towards the Serbs and the Yugoslav idea. They were willing to recognise the existence of a Serb people in Croatia, provided that the Serbs rallied to the cause of Croatia's unification and liberation.

Dissolution of the Military Border

There was also the perennial problem of the Military Border. The Croato-Hungarian Compromise, and the coming to power of the Unionists in 1868, caused great consternation at all levels of Military Border society. Stimulated by the National Party's anti-compromise propaganda and the Austrian military's dislike of dualism, representatives of the Croatian Border area –

composed of military officers and local notables – demanded that a new sabor be convened in which they would be represented, in order to decide the actual modality of the border's dissolution and its integration with Ban's Croatia. The National Party fuelled this resistance, hoping that it would help the party to achieve a revision of the compromise. The Hungarian government, on the other hand, struggled to ensure control of the dissolution process, as part of a general desire to assert Hungary's independence from Vienna as well as in order to prevent Croatia from escaping its domination. The continued presence of Austrian military authorities in the border remained a threat to the new Hungary. Andrássy, keen to see their departure, even offered to drop Hungary's claim to Dalmatia. The rise of a strong and well-organised movement among the border population (upon which Kvaternik had counted when he started his doomed venture) encouraged Vienna and Budapest to close ranks. There followed a purge of leading Croatian generals, some of whom were retired outright while others were sent to assume new duties outside the border.

Urban Population in the Military Border by religion in 1875[39]

Town	Catholic	Orthodox	Jewish
Petrinja	4,033	1,000	–
Kostajnica	4,000	767	–
Brod	2,126	229	84
Zemun	4,403	4,702	354
Karlovci	1,661	2,654	–
Petrovaradin	3,267	1,293	–

It was only after the stunning Prussian victory over France in 1870, however, that negotiations between Vienna and Budapest started in earnest, leading in 1871 to the dissolution of the Varaždin Border announced two years earlier. The negotiations, which also involved Croatian representatives, now became purely technical; they focused mainly on the economic aspects of the surrender of the Border area to the Hungarian half of the Monarchy, and on the legislation associated with the transition from military to civilian government. On 8 August 1873 the king formally announced the dissolution of the border regiments. The Border area was in the first instance constituted as a separate *Land,* however, with its own government located in Zagreb and headed by General Anton Mollinary.

Mažuranić had hoped for a quick unification, but was told that this would not happen. Unification faced great obstacles that would not be removed during his tenure. Chief among these was the Hungarian government's fear that addition of the border area would increase Croatian influence in the joint parliament, at a time when Hungary had become internally divided and suffered from governmental instability. According to the Croato-Hungarian Compromise, the incorporation of the Border would increase the number of Croatian seats in the lower house of the Hungarian parliament from thirty-four to fifty-five, at a time when the government had a majority of sixty-six including the thirty-four Croatian deputies. The possibility arose that the enlarged Croatian bloc would hold the balance in the joint parliament. In order to prevent this, Hungary made unification conditional upon Croatia's willingness to reduce the number of its deputies to forty. The Croatian opposition demanded that this be discussed in the presence of the border deputies, but the majority voted to accept the condition. In 1876 this prerequisite was compounded with another: that the system of railways planned for the border area would be such as to ensure a Hungarian monopoly of trade with the Balkans. General Mollinary was eventually removed because of his stubborn defence of a railway network that would run along the Sava from Zemun to Sisak, and thence by way of Ogulin to Knin in Dalmatia. Nor was Mažuranić able to prevent Hungary from redirecting Croatia's Bosnian trade to Budapest. Croatia also failed to gain control over the border's capital funds and forests, which were declared crown property.

On 15 July 1881 the Military Border was formally united with Croatia – or, more precisely, with 'the lands of the Hungarian crown'. The announcement, signed by the king and addressed to 'my Grenzer's, coincided with new elections in Croatia that were won by the National Party. Various problems associated with the transition, however, meant that final integration of the border would be completed only in 1888.[40] Most of the border area was distributed among the existing seven counties, but a new one was also created, the county of Lika-Krbava, with its capital at Gospić rather than Senj (which only deepened the latter's economic decline). The first elections in the former Border area were held in April 1883. By agreement between Zagreb and Budapest, the area was allocated proportionally fewer seats than in the rest of Croatia. The National Party won twenty-five seats, of which eighteen went to ethnic Serbs.

The Hungarian government sought to delay the appearance of the new deputies in the sabor, given the unrest in the border area associated with the transition. But then Antal David replaced the state emblems on finance

The Zrinski palace in Čakovec, 16th century.

Croatia after the Peace of Zadar (Dubrovnik not shown), 1358.

Ottoman incursions into Croatia, 1391–1490.

Croatia, 1606 (Dubrovnik not shown).

21. Croatia, 1741 (Dubrovnik not shown).

22. Trakošćan, main seat of the Drašković family after 1569.

The country house of Gornja Bistra, built by the Oršić family in 1770–75.

The castle of Sisak, ancient Siscia, onetime seat of Ljudevit of Pannonia.

Ban Khuen-Héderváry and Croatian dignitaries welcome King Francis Joseph, Zagreb, 1895

ministry buildings, previously inscribed only in Croat, with a new bilingual Croat-Magyar emblem, setting off anti-Hungarian demonstrations in Zagreb and a broad revolt in much of northwestern Croatia. The rebellion included the former (mainly Serb) Ban's Border, now integrated with the county of Zagreb. Fearing that the unrest would spread also to Bosnia, the government reacted with a violence that led to loss of life. Ban Pejačević resigned in August 1883, after which the Hungarian government imposed a state of emergency. Once the unrest had died down, the contested emblems were replaced with new ones bearing no inscription. A young Slavonian magnate named Dragutin Károly Khuen-Héderváry, a cousin of the Hungarian prime minister, Kálmán Tisza, was appointed ban. For the next twenty years he ruled like an autocrat. The Austrian Social-Democrat Otto Bauer aptly described Croatia under Héderváry's regime as the 'Hungarian Pashalik'.[41] The national initiative now passed to Dalmatia, where it would remain until the formation of Yugoslavia in 1918. On the positive side, Khuen-Héderváry's government ended a long period of administrative instability.[42]

Between 1850 and 1886, in fact, the organisational principles of administration in Ban's Croatia changed no fewer than six times. The first

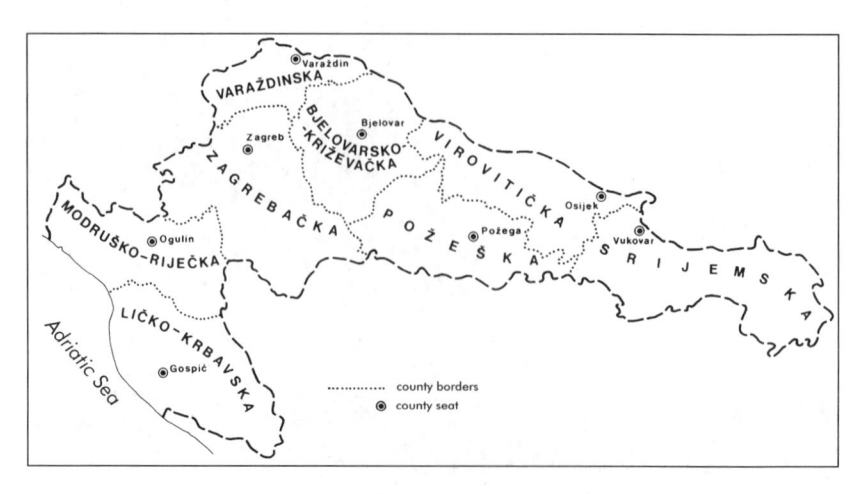

Ban's Croatia, end of nineteenth century

reform, carried out in 1850 by the Austrian ministry of the interior, created a vertical structure in which county heads were appointed by the king. The arrival of the February Patent led in 1851 to a new administrative arrangement in which the counties were run by a lieutenancy council. After the fall of absolutism in 1861, the sabor returned to the counties some of their earlier administrative and judicial powers; but, since its decisions failed to gain royal approval, they were implemented only in part. A fourth reorganisation took place after the signing of the Croato-Hungarian Compromise of 1868, when the counties again lost self-government, including the right to impose local taxes. The fifth reorganisation came in 1875 as part of the reforms instituted by Ban Mažuranić, who once again centralised the whole administration and placed it under government control; county assemblies survived, but with minimal authority. Mažuranić was unable, however, to solve the problem of financing local government in economically weak areas, while the lack of communications impeded supervision of their bodies. The reintegration of the Military Border led a sixth and final administrative reorganisation. This was finalised in 1886, when a new law on the organisation of the counties and their districts was adopted by the sabor. The counties became nominally self-governing communities, but enjoyed no executive powers. Half the county assembly was appointed by high tax payers, the other half elected. Real power was held by the central government in Zagreb – and in fact by Khuen-Héderváry. Dislike of his methods gave the Party of Right twenty-five seats in the elections of 1884.

TEN

Croatia and its Serbs

The 'Serb question' in Croatia emerged initially as an institutional problem related to the settlement of a population of Orthodox faith in lands in which the Catholic Church alone was officially recognised. During the seventeenth century the Venetian republic and the Habsburg Monarchy, guided by immediate needs and long-term political interests, tried in their different ways to accommodate the Orthodox immigrants within their administrative and ecclesiastical structures, but without arriving at a stable solution. The manner in which they approached the problem reflected their diverse historical experiences. In northern Croatia a Uniate Church was established at the start of the century for the Orthodox population of the Military Border, whose bishop resided in the monastery of Marča, built on land owned by the bishop of Zagreb. No similar institution was to be found in Venetian Dalmatia: prior to the Candian War (1645–69) the small groups of Orthodox immigrants were obliged to convert to Catholicism. The very nature of the problem changed at the end of the seventeenth century, however, when as a result of victorious wars fought against the Ottoman Empire the two states acquired substantial Orthodox populations, whose numbers were then swelled by further influx from areas remaining under Ottoman rule. In both cases the fate of the Serb Orthodox Church was ultimately decided by, respectively, the imperial court in Vienna and the Venetian senate. However, while Venetian interest in the Orthodox issue remained limited to the need to conserve territorial gains, Vienna harboured the much greater ambition of replacing Ottoman power in the Balkans. As a result, the two states arrived at different solutions to the problem of how to assimilate the Serb Orthodox Church into their legal orders. Thus, with the establishment of the Serb Orthodox Church at the end of the seventeenth century, Serbs as a people became a legally constituted subject in the lands of the Hungarian crown; but their status as a separate confessional community was to remain unresolved in Dalmatia until the very end of Venetian rule there.

An Ottoman inheritance

Both states had to take into account the particular bond between religious and secular life that informed the behaviour of the Serb Orthodox hierarchy. The Serb Church was founded by the Serbian ruler Stefan Nemanja at the start of the thirteenth century, as a condition of his realm's political independence from Constantinople, following which the clergy became an integral part of the governing structure. Its first head was indeed Stefan's brother Sava, later immortalised as St Sava.[1] As Serbian state territory expanded or contracted, so did the area under the jurisdiction of the Serb patriarch. In 1459, however, when Serbia of the Despots finally succumbed to the Ottoman armies, the Serb Church disappeared also. Its dioceses reverted to the original authority of the Orthodox archbishop of Ohrid, subject to the ecumenical patriarch of Constantinople.

Like other Christian subjects of the Ottoman state, the Serbs were allowed to keep their language and religion, provided they showed unconditional loyalty to the sultan and the new order, paid their taxes and served in the Ottoman armies. The empire's religious tolerance embraced not only individuals, moreover. But also their churches: rather than destroying these, the sultan built them into the foundations of his state. The empire consequently came to be made up of basic units or millets, each millet being a recognised religious community to whose leaders the sultan transferred some of his prerogatives. Within this system each bishop and parish priest acted also as administrator and judge among his co-religionists in matters internal to that community, arbitrating according to the customs and canons of their own church. Since the Orthodox population was officially a community of the Greek faith, all its members were treated as 'Greek', irrespective of their language or ethnicity. The Serbs, now subject to the Greek Church, also became 'Greeks'.[2] But in 1557 the autonomy of the Serb Church was restored, and Peć (Peja) in Kosovo became the seat of the Serb patriarch. All those subject to this patriarch, both Serbs and non-Serbs (Vlachs, for example), now became 'Serbs'.

The legal status of the Serb Church mirrored that of the Greek Church. Synods made up of the higher clergy and lay notables elected the patriarch and the more important bishops, and these were then confirmed by the sultan. The Serb Church regulated the civic life of its congregation and enjoyed a degree of economic independence, including the right to tax its members.³ And just as the memory of the Byzantine Empire remained alive with the Greek clergy, so the Serb Church and its patriarchs continued to identify themselves with the vanished Serbian kingdom. Echoing the titles of the Nemanjić rulers, Serb patriarchs called themselves variously 'patriarch of the Serbs, the Bulgarians and other lands'; 'patriarch of all Serb lands and the [Adriatic] Littoral'; 'archbishop of Peć and patriarch of all Serbs and Bulgarians, and of the northern and other parts'; 'archbishop of the Serb and Danubian lands'; and so forth. In the late seventeenth century the patriarch of Peć, Arsenije III, identified himself as 'archbishop of Peć and patriarch of all four points of the compass'.⁴

Mehmed II extended his protection to Bosnian Catholics, represented on this occasion by a Franciscan monk. The Catholic community became similarly part of the imperial system, and since it was a community of the Latin rite its members were called 'Latins'. But the Catholic clergy remained part of the Western world, with which the Ottoman Empire was permanently at war. The Ottoman state therefore preferred to settle Orthodox soldiers and their families, believing them to be more loyal, along the borders facing Venice and the Habsburg Monarchy, leading to the appearance of Serb Orthodox parishes and bishoprics in areas that had traditionally been wholly Catholic.⁵ The jurisdiction of the Serb Church to the north and west consequently spread as far as did the reach of the Ottoman armies. Since the Serb Church expanded into an area where the earlier political and ecclesiastical structures had been destroyed, these lands came to be treated by the Serb Orthodox clergy as Serb lands: 'Serb lands' stretched as far as the authority of the Serb bishops.

But the nominal jurisdiction of the Peć patriarch was not limited to the Ottoman Empire; it extended also beyond it, reaching into the Military Border and Venetian Dalmatia, that is, into all the territories settled by Orthodox immigrants. Bishop Simeon, the first Uniate bishop of Marča, was thus confirmed by the Peć patriarch. Orthodox monks from the Military Border, who in the seventeenth century travelled to Russia seeking financial and other assistance for their monasteries and churches, regularly stated that they came from 'Serb lands'. The perception of what constituted 'Serb lands', forged at the height of the Ottoman expansion, did not disappear with the Ottoman Empire's retreat south of the Sava and the Danube at the turn of the seventeenth century. Orthodox monks travelling to Russia in the first half of the eighteenth century habitually referred to Slavonia and Srijem as 'Serb lands'.

That this vision survived in the Habsburg Monarchy was due to the particular and in many ways unforeseen circumstances that prevailed in the last stages of the war preceding the Peace of Karlovci of 1699. When the Austrian army was routed in Kosovo a few years earlier and forced to retreat north, it was followed by thousands of Serbs and Albanians – and somewhat later also by Arsenije III, the patriarch of Peć.[6] On his arrival in Belgrade, the patriarch met the resident Orthodox clergy to formulate a request to Emperor Leopold asking for religious freedom in return for loyalty. On 21 August 1690 Leopold issued a diploma granting full autonomy to the Serb Orthodox Church. The resulting privileges were spelt out more clearly in another document, issued five years later, according to which the Orthodox population was freed from paying the usual tithe to the Catholic Church: this was to go to the Serb Church instead. Patriarchs would as before be elected at synods made up of secular and religious notables, but from now on they would be confirmed in their positions by the monarch. When issuing this diploma the emperor-king had in mind a new war against the Porte, after which the immigrants would return to their previous homes, which it was hoped would now come under Habsburg rule. But the border created in 1699 remained stable and the immigrants and their church took a permanent footing in Croatia and Hungary. The Orthodox Church had in fact gained a foothold here already in the fifteenth century, when Serbia under the despots became part of a state system linked to the Hungarian crown, following which the pope issued a special dispensation granting religious freedom to the Serbian rulers and their families, including the right to build a limited number of monasteries. The Serbs who arrived at the end of the seventeenth century brought with them the bones of their saints, including those of Lazar Hrebljenović (who had perished in 1389 at the battle of Kosovo), and added them to relics already held in Orthodox monasteries in Srijem.

This arrangement had emerged suddenly as the result of an unexpected immigration, but remained in force because the depopulated land needed colonists and the crown fresh soldiers: the war against the Ottoman Empire was not yet over. Many of the Serbs who settled in eastern Croatia and southern Hungary became soldiers in the new Military Border that emerged along the Sava and the Danube. In 1713 Karlovci in Srijem became the seat of the Serb archbishop (as he was officially called), who was invested with the wealthy manor of Dalj. Secure in its income and endowed with land in one of the most fertile regions of Europe, the Serb Church under the Karlovci patriarchs became in fact a far more important centre of Serb religious and national life than the increasingly insecure patriarchate of Peć.

Tsar Dušan crushes the Turks, 1741

In 1733 Arsenije IV, the new patriarch of Peć, followed the example of his predecessor by leaving Kosovo and settling in Karlovci instead. In 1766, when the sultan finally abolished the patriarchate of Peć and placed the Serb Orthodox bishops under the authority of the patriarch of Constantinople, the Karlovci metropolitan inherited also the title of patriarch of Peć.

The establishment of the Serb Orthodox Church ended all attempts to unite the Serb Orthodox community with Rome. Its supporters, indeed, soon ejected the bishop of Marča from his seat.[7] Relying on their church's autonomy the Orthodox Serb clergy proceeded to weld the new immigrants together with the Orthodox and Hungary population already living in Croatia into a distinct national-denominational Serb community. The war-induced transposition of the Serb Orthodox centre from Peć in Kosovo to Karlovci in Croatia altered also the church's historical perspective, in a manner illustrated by the great popularity of a work published in 1741 on the initiative of Patriarch Arsenije IV. The volume in question is a translation of *Stemmatographia* (Heraldry) written by Pavao Ritter Vitezović, which contains real and imaginary coats of arms of the 'Illyrian' (for him Croatian) lands and of several (mainly Croatian) noble families. The Serb edition reproduced all these, but added to them portraits of twenty-nine Serb Orthodox saints (mainly Serbian kings, queens and patriarchs), as well as nine Bulgarian and two Orthodox Albanian saints. The pride of place in this visual display was given to the Serbian king Stefan Dušan (1346–55), under whose rule the medieval Serbian state had acquired its greatest territorial extent. Mounted on a horse and ringed with Vitezović's 'Illyrian' state emblems, he was depicted crushing a cowering Turk – even though his rule, in fact, predates the Ottoman invasion. A portrait of Arsenije IV was placed alongside in a manner suggesting that the Serb patriarchs were legal heirs of the Serbian kings. According to the publisher's inscription, all the 'Illyrian' lands represented in the volume were in fact 'Serb lands'.[8] The belief that the area of jurisdiction of the Serb Orthodox Church formed a single and unified Serb territory, and that the Orthodox population living within it – in Croatia, Hungary, Bosnia-Herzegovina, Serbia, Kosovo and elsewhere – formed a single Serb nation, provided the foundation of the modern Serb national idea, which would be remoulded by secular national leaders recruited from the urban class arising in Croatia and Hungary in the first half of the nineteenth century.

The Orthodox question in Venetian Dalmatia

In contrast to the Croatian north, where Catholic dioceses had been re-established only recently and the whole re-conquered territory treated initially as imperial property, in Venetian Dalmatia Orthodox subjects and their clergy were faced with a stable and well-organised Catholic Church hierarchy.

During the seventeenth and early eighteenth centuries Venice waged three wars against the Ottoman Empire, all of which ended in Dalmatia's

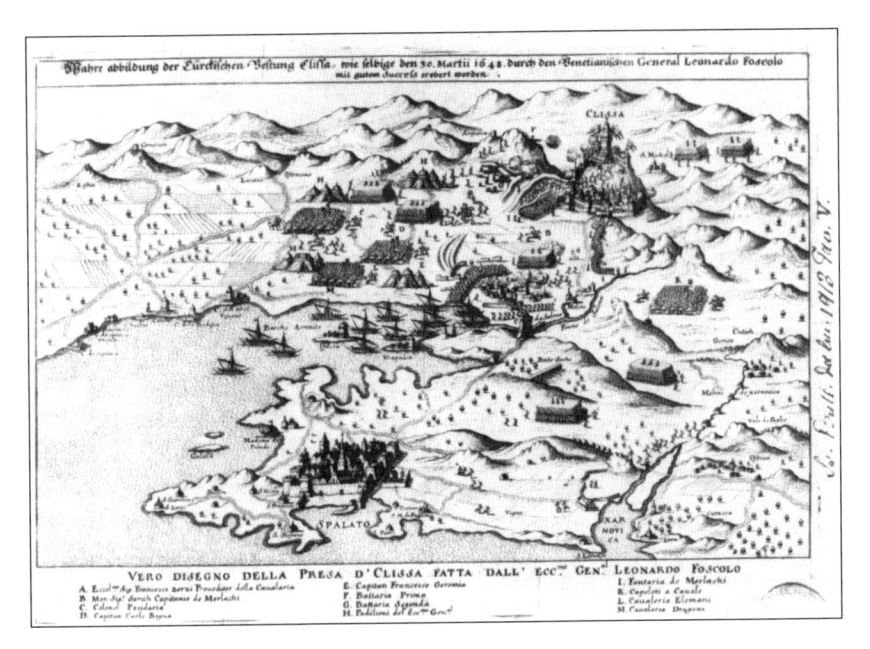

The battle of Klis, 1648

territorial enlargement and an influx of immigrants. The Candian War (1645–69) brought into the fold Klis, Omiš, and Makarska with its Littoral. Dalmatia simultaneously gained around 10,000 new inhabitants, or one-fifth of its total population. These were the so-called Morlachs (Black Vlachs), that is, Catholics and Orthodox who came from both sides of the Venetian-Ottoman border and who had actively supported the Venetian side during the conflict. With the Morean War (1684–99), Venice acquired the much larger area between the river Zrmanja and Neum (including Obrovac, Benkovac, Knin, Skradin and Metković). Dalmatia gained an additional 30,000 inhabitants, mainly Orthodox Morlachs. Finally, in the war of 1711–7, Venice obtained Imotski, and rounded up its possessions in Venetian Albania, namely the area round the Bay of Kotor. As these overwhelmingly rural areas became absorbed into Dalmatia, the Catholic bishops reclaimed their old parishes, often in the teeth of Fransciscan opposition, since the Franciscans had up to then been the official leaders of the Catholic community. The integration of the Orthodox population, however, proved a much more demanding and complicated task.

The Venetian state welcomed its new subjects as a potential source of soldiers, the Catholic Church as additions to its congregation. Both sought to convert the Orthodox among them to Catholicism. This proved easier in a diocese like Split, where the Orthodox formed a small minority among mostly Catholic settlers, than in places where the Orthodox community was numerically dominant, or had arrived alongside its clergy. The group that came to Dalmatia during the Candian War included the Orthodox bishop Bishop Stefanović and fifteen monks attached to the Orthodox monastery of Krka (then still in Ottoman territory), who had looked after Orthodox Christians in the Ottoman *sandžaks* of Lika and Klis. These clerics soon accepted the authority of Rome, it seems, with the prior approval of the Serb patriarch of Peć.[9] At the request of the Congregation for the Propagation of Faith, these Uniate clergy were given a church in the vicinity of Zadar for their use, and a promise of a monastery for the monks. To facilitate their conversion, the Congregation instructed the Dalmatian bishops to allow them to keep their Eastern rite. The Orthodox liturgical practice remained thus protected by the Roman curia, as well as by the Venetian state striving to win the loyalty of the Orthodox population in order to consolidate the new frontier against the hostile Ottoman Bosnian government.[10] But whereas under Ottoman rule the Orthodox clergy had acted freely within their religious community, they now found themselves subject to the authority of Catholic bishops.

Venetian territory contained populations of several different confessions, and the republic traditionally practised religious tolerance as much as was compatible with its Catholic nature. The arrival of so many people of Orthodox faith, however, posed a novel problem of Church jurisdiction for its government: who was to appoint a new bishop for these 'Greek Catholics' once Bishop Stefanović, who was an old man, died? There already existed a small Orthodox community in Dalmatia, consisting of ethnic Greek soldiers and their families who had arrived in the middle of the sixteenth century and settled mainly in the dioceses of Zadar and Šibenik. They were given Catholic churches for their use and placed under the supervision of Catholic bishops, but in religious matters they were linked to the Uniate bishop of the established Greek community in Venice itself. As a religious community these Venetian Greeks were formally subjected directly to the pope, but their bishops were in reality appointed by the patriarch of Constantinople, so that the Greek community came effectively under the joint jurisdiction of Rome and Constantinople. Dalmatia's Orthodox population, however, came from an area which had been under the religious authority of the Serb Orthodox patriarch of Peć. Accepting a bishop nominated by this patriarch meant establishing a church hierarchy independent of both Venice and Rome – both of which rejected this possibility. The Dalmatian bishops for their part resisted the idea that the pope himself might nominate Stefanović's successor, for this would mean introducing a hierarchy that was independent of them. In their view, the Orthodox Christians should be subject not only to the pope but also to the Catholic bishops in whose dioceses they now found themselves.

After the Morean War, however, when the Orthodox population greatly increased in size and Dalmatia came to include the Orthodox monasteries of Krka and Krupa, the Orthodox clergy felt strong enough to demand their own bishop. They were supported in this stance by the Bosnian Serb Orthodox bishop, who surreptitiously visited his congregation now living on another state's territory. In Venice, the Uniate bishop Tipaldi now stepped in with his own solution: the Morlachs of the Eastern rite would come under his authority and thereby directly under that of the pope. They would thus remain outside the jurisdictions of the Serb Orthodox patriarch as well as of the Dalmatian 'Latin' bishops. The Venetian senate found this acceptable, and one Nikodim Busović became Uniate bishop of Dalmatia, presiding over a congregation most of which lived in the districts of Zadar, Knin and Sinj. Dalmatia's Venetian governor donated to the new bishop the disused Catholic monastery of Dragović on the river Cetina with the adjacent church. This solution seemed to work well at first: the majority of the Orthodox population were happy with their new bishop and so was the state, since Bishop Busović now sought to exclude the influence of the Bosnian Orthodox prelate. But the Serb patriarch of Peć, Arsenije III, was displeased – as were most of the Dalmatian Orthodox monks, who found union with the Catholic Church unacceptable in principle. Eventually, however, the Serb patriarch recognised Busović as his bishop for Dalmatia. The relationship between Dalmatian Uniate bishops and Serb patriarchs would thereafter vary in accordance with the attitude adopted by successive Dalmatian governors: unsympathetic governors would draw the two prelates closer.

The first open protest against the new state of affairs came from the vicar of the Greek Church in Šibenik, who complained to Venice that Bishop Busović was illegally interfering in the internal affairs of the Greek community. The offensive against Busović took off properly in 1703 with the arrival of Governor Angelo Emo (1703–5), who was sympathetic to the Catholic bishops. These now complained to Rome that the 'pseudo-bishop' Busović was appropriating honours that were properly theirs: he built new churches, appropriated ruined ones, collected taxes, ordained new priests, distributed parishes and appointed their curates – all without seeking prior permission. Emo's successor proved to be an even greater supporter of the

Catholic bishops. Busović was banned from allocating parishes or appointing parish priests without permission from the Catholic bishops, whereupon he resigned and ultimately withdrew to the Krka monastery, where he died.

This failure to create a Uniate Church in Dalmatia left only two alternatives: to subject the Orthodox population and clergy to the Catholic bishops, which is what the latter had continually demanded; or to establish an Orthodox hierarchy, which was the wish of the Orthodox clergy and increasingly also of the Orthodox population. In the seventeenth century it was not clear whether an Orthodox Church could exist within a Catholic state, but once its autonomous existence was accepted in the Habsburg Monarchy the Dalmatian Orthodox clergy no longer felt the need to accede to union with Rome. This development strengthened Venice's habitual fear of the designs that its two large neighbours, the Habsburg Monarchy and the Ottoman Empire, might harbour towards its territory; so Orthodox clergy deriving from Bosnia or the Monarchy were banned from acting as parish priests in Dalmatia. This restrictive policy, however, did not solve the problem of how to regulate the religious life of the growing Orthodox population in Dalmatia. The problem became even more intractable in 1713, when Bishop Tipaldi died without leaving a legitimate successor. The senate, while keen to pacify the Orthodox element in Dalmatia, remained most unwilling to surrender any rights to the Peć patriarch, whom it saw as the representative of a foreign power. To allow a foreign patriarch confirmed by a foreign sovereign to exercise spiritual jurisdiction in Dalmatia was to invite outside interference in the internal life of a Venetian province whose borders were of recent date and might change again. This is why the senate rejected repeated requests by the Orthodox population in the newly acquired area of Herceg Novi in the Bay of Kotor to be allowed to remain under the jurisdiction of the Orthodox bishop of Herzegovina.

In 1719, however, the Peć patriarch confirmed Stefan Ljubibratić as bishop of Herceg Novi, and entrusted him with authority also over the Dalmatian Orthodox population. The energetic Dalmatian governor Alvise Mocenigo (1717–20) permitted Bishop Stefan to visit the Orthodox churches and monasteries in Dalmatia. Mocenigo's view was that the Orthodox population should have their own bishop, and that Stefan was an excellent candidate for the post. However, the news that the Orthodox had acquired their own bishop caused an uproar among the Catholic clergy, which grew in strength as Stefan began his travels through Dalmatia. The bishops warned the Vatican and the senate of the dangers inherent in establishing a 'schismatic seat' in Dalmatia. The Vatican agreed with them.

The Venetian government ordered Stefan to leave Dalmatia on the grounds that he had been invested by a foreign cleric. Unlike the Catholic bishops, the senate was not in principle against there being an Orthodox bishop in Dalmatia, provided that some politically safe mechanism could be found for his installation. Such a bishop would ideally be elected in the usual manner, that is, by the Orthodox clergy and laity, and then confirmed by the senate, which would also provide him with a suitable place of residence and a stable source of income. The senate opted, however, for a safer course by asking the Dalmatian governor to propose four candidates from whom the senate would select the most suitable person. Feeling that his side had won the battle but not the war, the Catholic archbishop of Zadar Vinko Zmajević appealed directly to the pope. The Orthodox clergy and notables, on the other hand, petitioned the senate to let them choose their own bishop. Following the pope's intervention the senate postponed its decision.

The tension between Catholic and Orthodox clergies grew as a result. Catholic bishops were prevented from visiting Orthodox churches and parishes. In 1731 a meeting of Orthodox clergy from Dalmatia and the Bay of Kotor was held in Benkovac, which ended with a demand for full autonomy of their Church. Government representatives were handed petitions asking for an Orthodox bishop, which the Dalmatian governor forwarded to Venice with a recommendation that the request be granted, since in his view an accepted religious leader would help control this 'unruly' people. The Catholic bishops petitioned the senate, too, however, and the latter again postponed its decision. In 1734 the Orthodox clergy elected their own bishop, Lav Abramović, and the senate was advised that he was a suitable candidate for the post. Dalmatia's Catholic prelates again appealed to Rome, and the senate again suspended its decision, mainly because it saw Abramović as being too close to Russia. The Orthodox community renewed its petition to the senate and was again rejected, despite the advice of the provincial government that it would serve the peace of the land for these people to have their own bishop. The rest of the century was spent in a fruitless repetition of such initiatives. Between 1748 and 1750 Dalmatia's Orthodox population again attempted to rid themselves of the Catholic bishops' control, and the Catholic bishops again sought support in Rome. The Orthodox clergy petitioned the state and wrote also to the Serb patriarch asking him to appoint a bishop of their choice. In 1751 the Bosnian Orthodox bishop invested Simeon Končarević as bishop for Dalmatia, but the Dalmatian governor banned him from assuming his duty. The new archbishop of Zadar, Mate Karaman, then visited Rome bearing a letter signed by all Dalmatian bishops outlining their opposition. Two years later Končarević was expelled from Dalmatia. In a worrying development the dissatisfied Orthodox population began to migrate to Habsburg territory, some travelling on as far as Russia.

In 1754 the Orthodox again petitioned the senate, asking that Dimitrije Novaković, the Orthodox bishop of Buda in Hungary, be appointed their bishop; but the fact that he was a bishop in another state made him unsuitable in Venetian eyes. In the absence of a Dalmatian Orthodox bishop, it was the more militant monks who came to shape the response of the Dalmatian Orthodox community: their monasteries of Krupa, Krka and Dragović emerged as bastions of Orthodox resistance against the Catholic clergy. The bishop of Šibenik reported in 1757 that of the eleven Orthodox vicars and several chaplains who served in his diocese – some of whom were, indeed, Austrian subjects – not one had presented himself for his confirmation, while he himself was denied access to their churches. Two years later the Orthodox dignitaries of Dalmatia and the Bay of Kotor again signed a petition asking for their own bishop. There was an increasing consensus in Venice that only a positive response would defuse what was fast becoming a generalised revolt of the Orthodox population; but the senate remained fearful of the Orthodox clergy's ties with Russia, which acted not only as a place of refuge but also as a supplier of liturgical books.

Catholic and Orthodox population of Dalmatia in 1761 by diocese[11]

Diocese	Catholics	Orthodox
Split	42,553	3,450
Nin	9,961	12,309
Šibenik	29,970	10,730
Skradin	4,000	2,000
Trogir	17,566	275
Makarska	21,621	568
Hvar	15,267	1
Korčula	7,000	–
Zadar	22,466	869
Krk	12,000	–
Osor	7,700	–
Total	190,104	30,202
[Kotor]	9,000	16,000

The position of the Catholic Church

The Venetian state, while not always agreeing with the Dalmatian bishops, ended on their side out of concern that an established Orthodox Church would ally itself with hostile foreign powers. But the failure to legalise the Orthodox Church in Dalmatia was to a significant extent due also to the steadfast refusal of the local Catholic prelates to accept such a possibility, leaving the senate with a feeling that the introduction of another church hierarchy would cause more divisions than it would heal. The dispute between the two churches was in essence a jurisdictional dispute. The Serb Orthodox patriarch refused to follow the example of the sultan and cede what had been part of his jurisdictional territory to another power, while the Catholic bishops understood that same territory to have always been part of the Roman Church. The struggle between the Catholic and Orthodox hierarchies was consequently fought in the name of true faith, canonical principles and historic right.

The position of the Dalmatian Catholic Church was articulated by two Zadar archbishops, Vinko Zmajević and Mate Karaman, who between them covered much of the eighteenth century (1713–71). Zmajević came from the Bay of Kotor, where he had succeeded his uncle as archbishop of Bar. Serving also as apostolic vicar for Albania, Macedonia, Bulgaria and Serbia, he was from an early age keen on union of the two churches. On becoming archbishop of Zadar his visitation of Albania and Serbia was confirmed, and in 1737 Bosnia was added to the list. Zmajević's views were accordingly treated as authoritative in the Vatican. When he died in 1745 he was replaced by his assistant Mate Karaman, a Split-born prelate who had been bishop of Osor. Their position was that clergy of the Eastern rite could not lawfully exercise jurisdiction within the borders of the Roman patriarchy.[12] The establishment of an Orthodox hierarchy in Dalmatia hence contradicted the Christian Church canons, and in particular the ruling of the Synod of Nicea that the borders of existing archbishoprics should be respected. Since the whole of Dalmatia was under two archbishops, those of Zadar and Split, it was inadmissible to split either of their jurisdictions in order to accommodate an Orthodox bishop. The mixing of bishoprics and archbishoprics, they argued, would lead to a mixing of patriarchates – ultimately at the expense of the Roman one to which Dalmatia had always belonged.

The problem, they argued, lay in the desire of the patriarch of Peć to extend his jurisdiction to Dalmatia. The Serb patriarch justified this intent by appeal to two different arguments: that he had been given jurisdiction over

Dalmatia by the patriarch of Constantinople, and that Dalmatia contained people of the Serb language and rite. But the first reason was invalid, as stated above. It was invalid also because the patriarch of Constantinople had been against the creation of a separate Serb Church, which is why the Roman patriarch refused to recognise its patriarch. The Serb patriarch of Peć, in other words, was not only wrong: he was also bogus. The patriarch's other argument – that all Serbs, wherever they lived, came automatically under his authority – was absurd, the argument went on, since this would give him an unlimited and indeterminate jurisdiction not enjoyed by other Orthodox patriarchs. It was also an ancient custom that Latin bishops could govern Christians of both rites. If one were nevertheless to allow the establishment of an Orthodox bishopric in Dalmatia, the Serb patriarch would be able to create as many Orthodox bishoprics as there were Catholic ones, and thus strengthen 'schismatic' beliefs at the expense of the Catholic Church. Dalmatia could thus be lost in the way that Bulgaria and Serbia had been lost to the Roman Church. The introduction of an Orthodox bishop, in other words, was an attack not only on the rights of the Dalmatian Catholic bishops, but also on those of the Catholic Church itself.

The Serb patriarch, finally, considered himself to be not only the religious head but also the secular leader of the members of his church. He claimed this right for himself not only in regard to the area of the old Serbian state, but also in regard to the parts of Croatia and Hungary settled by Orthodox immigrants. He now wished to do the same in regard to Dalmatia. This had dangerous implications for the Venetian state too: given that Serb bishops were also secular leaders, the introduction of an Orthodox hierarchy would lead to the formation of a state within the state – which, moreover, would ally itself with foreign powers, most particularly with Russia, which was openly dreaming of creating an Orthodox empire that would include Constantinople.[13]

The two archbishops were aware that the alienation of Dalmatia's Orthodox population derived in part from the fact that few Dalmatian bishops at this time spoke the local language. Neither of the two bishops of Šibenik, who between them covered the period 1676–1756, ever learnt Croat. The letters and directives they sent to the Orthodox clergy were written in Latin, which the recipients could not read. The archbishops, therefore, asked for the appointment of bishops who could speak the native language, and recommended that the 'Illyrian' clergy – armed with books written in the 'Illyrian' language and printed in the Glagolitic and Cyrillic scripts – be accepted as natural mediators between the Slav Orthodox parishes and Rome. This proved a vain project, however. As life normalised after decades of war and a network of Orthodox parishes emerged in Dalmatia, the Orthodox population followed its clergy in the conviction that their religious community belonged to the Serb Orthodox Church. Uninterested in the theological and historical arguments that informed the Catholic approach, the Orthodox clerics believed that their jurisdiction extended everywhere where members of their congregation lived. Dalmatia too was a 'Serb land'.

Torn between the need to placate its Orthodox subjects and apprehension regarding the possible negative consequences of having an established Orthodox Church on its territory, the Venetian government failed to come to a decision. In 1797, when the republic disappeared following its occupation by Napoleon's armies, Dalmatia was still without an Orthodox bishop. It was left to the French to create in 1808 the first Orthodox bishopric in Dalmatia, with its seat at Šibenik. In 1841 the seat was moved to Zadar, when Dalmatia came under Austrian rule where it would remain until the end of the First World War. An Orthodox bishopric for the Bay of Kotor and Dubrovnik, meanwhile, was established by the Austrian government only in 1870.

The Orthodox Church in Ban's Croatia

In 1779, as part of his rationalising drive, Joseph II united the Orthodox churches in Hungary, Transylvania and Croatia, involving Serbs, Romanians and 'Greek Orthodox' merchants of various ethnic origins coming from the Ottoman Empire. The Orthodox bishops of Bukovina and Transylvania were simultaneously subjected to the authority of the patriarch of Karlovci, although their flock was exempted from the privileges granted to the 'Illyrian', or Serb, people. Since they themselves were not invited to attend the Serb Church synods and were hence excluded from the election of the metropolitan, they refused to recognise the latter's authority. It thus emerged that a Serb metropolitan guarding jealously the Serb character of his church and congregation could not act as head of a united Orthodox Church. By the middle of the nineteenth century the Romanian bishop of Transylvania, who in the meantime had come to head the Romanian national movement, won from Vienna the right to establish a separate Romanian Church. The Dalmatian Orthodox bishop too was now excluded from the Serb Orthodox synod.[14]

In 1791 members of what was officially known as the 'Greek-disunited' Church were granted the right to own land and perform public duties. With their church fully established, the better-off burghers and merchants organised themselves into Orthodox communes. Orthodox traders of various origins – Vlachs, Macedonians, Greeks – living in Croatia were readily assimilated by the Serb Church, and many of them would acquire leading positions within the Serb national movement – on both sides of the Ottoman-Austrian border – inspired by the desire to unify all 'Serb lands'. In the early years of the twentieth century a Hungarian Serb lawyer published and distributed 2,000 copies of a map of 'Serb lands' which included, among others, Slavonia with Srijem and Dalmatia with Dubrovnik.

The early ideologues continued to grapple, however, with the problem of how to provide the nation thus conceived with clearly defined territorial and indeed ethnic borders, given that the area of authority of the Serb church had no secular equivalent.[15] The Serb patriarch might well be the 'patriarch of all four points of the compass', but what did this actually entail? In 1810, for example, Rado Vučinić – a highly educated Border officer from Karlovac (then under French occupation) – tried to persuade Napoleon to place Serbia, that is, the Serbian insurgents, under his protection; but the memorandum he submitted on this issue to the French foreign ministry contained no clear idea of who 'the Serbs' actually were. The memorandum thus talked of Serbs who formed one people with Bosnians, Montenegrins, Illyrians and Bulgarians, but it is not clear whether the Bulgarians were here conceived as ethnic Serbs, or as Slavs who had once lived under the jurisdiction of the Serb Church, or simply as a population living on the territory of Dušan's state.[16] The medieval Serb empire, the memorandum claimed, was created through common resistance of its population to 'Greek emperors', later replaced by sultans. The Serbian uprising of 1804, it implied, was but the first stage in the process of this empire's revival. By creating the Illyrian Provinces Napoleon too had contributed to this process, and it was his historic mission to ensure its completion.

The Croatian Illyrian idea was well received by the Serb officers of the Military Border, in contrast to its reception by the Hungarian Serbs and the Serbs of Srijem, who rejected it outright. The Illyrian policy – which insisted on equality of the Catholic and Orthodox Churches as well as the Latin and Cyrillic scripts, and on Croat-Serb linguistic unity – opened to the Orthodox population new avenues of social integration, symbolised by Patriarch Rajačić's assumption of a seat in the Croatian parliament. Many Croatian Catholic priests were in fact ardent Illyrians: in 1843, for example, the Orthodox bishop of Pakrac was installed with the assistance of two Catholic canons, who used the occasion to hail 'national harmony'. 'Regardless of religion (and everyone is bound to respect his own), we should love one another, since the one God who has created both the Western and the Eastern Church loves us all equally in his divine spirit. Each of us should remain faithful to his church and all of us to Christ's teaching of brotherly love, which alone can save our people divided by conflict,' wrote Ljudevit Gaj in the literary journal *Danica*. And again: 'Those of us educated in the Illyrian spirit should learn the Cyrillic script as part of our own ancient heritage, used by our forefathers of both confessions in the past. The Illyrians of the Eastern Church have conserved it under the Serb name for us too, not only for themselves.'

The Croatian mainstream failed, however, to identify Croatia's Orthodox population as Serb. Janko Drašković in his *Disertatio* published in 1832, while strongly advocating religious tolerance, saw the Orthodox population of the border as Croats. The Croatian linguist Vjekoslav Babukić wrote to his colleague Pavel Šafařík ten years later: 'Serbs live in Serbia, while those scattered in other Illyrian provinces are called Serbs only because of their church, and then only by the educated class.' In 1847 Ivan Kukuljević told Serb writers: 'The fact is that our people in Croatia, Slavonia, Dalmatia and Istria, as well as in Illyria, has never heard of the Serb name, excluding the Orthodox clergy and those who have learnt of the name from books.' A decade later still Bogoslav Šulek wrote that the population of Croatia was Croat by language – which, however, they shared with the Serbs.

As already described, the 'Serb question' was initially posed in the sabor as the 'Srijem question', namely a question of the eventual incorporation of Srijem into a Serb Vojvodina – an entity that failed, however, to materialise.[17] But it was clear by the start of the 1860s that Serb national aspirations could not be accommodated within the concept of a single, albeit pluralist, Croatian nation. The issue was faced squarely by the sabor in 1861. The debate was triggered off inadvertently by Ivan Kukuljević. Speaking about the Military Border's unification with Croatia, he stated that the time had come to unite 'all the severed limbs of our people'. If the Croatian state 'right and law' and 'the holy principle of nationality that now moves the world' meant anything, then 'one should hope that our parliament today will achieve what all of our people aspire and must aspire to: unity of our parliament and the lands of the Triune Kingdom', of which 'the most important is our Military Border. This land, historically and lawfully part of our crown and kingdom, is inhabited solely by our people', yet 'continues to suffer under the heavy burden of German absolutism and the military system at a time when all other provinces of the Austrian empire have gained constitutional freedom.'[18] Patriarch Rajačić, who was not present at the sabor, promptly wrote a letter protesting that Kukuljević had proclaimed the border population to be purely Croat. According to Rajačić, the initial population of the Military Border was initially purely Serb, and it was only later – when the Border became organised into regiments – that it came to include also a small number of Croats. It was clear that Rajačić's definition of 'Serb' included all *štokavian* speakers. Rajačić also protested against the return of Srijem to Croatia and described the planned transfer of the Varaždin regiment to Croatian jurisdiction as its enforced Croatisation. (The Varaždin Border at this time had around 156,400 inhabitants, of whom 76 per cent were Catholic.)

In his efforts to establish a clear boundary between Croats and Serbs in Croatia, he offered a picture of a wholly separate and uninterrupted history of the latter going back to the time of Tsar Dušan. Ever since that time, he argued, Serbs from 'Serbia, Bosnia, Herzegovina, Albania, Macedonia and Montenegro' had been settling in the Croatian lands, especially after the battle of Mohács, when Croats had disappeared from the Border area. By living in their own separate community, the Grenzers had managed to preserve their own Serb character. It followed from this that: 'Serbs have their own and Croats their own history; Serbs their Eastern and Croats their Western church; the Serb Grenzers their Serb and the Croats their Croat language; Serbs their Slav [Cyrillic] and Croats their Latin script. Although Serbs and Croats may be the closest of brothers, they are not one and the same nation.'[19] Rajačić overlooked the fact that half the population of the Military Border belonged to the Western church and used the Latin script. To claim 'Serb lands' such as the Military Border or Srijem for Croatia nevertheless amounted, in his view, to a claim that Serbs were Croats: the Serbs, however, would never give up their name 'for the sake of Illyrianism, Yugoslavism or Croatism'.

Kukuljević rejected Rajačić's interpretation, declaring that his term 'all our people' had included both Croats and Serbs. The Orthodox population that had settled in the Border area, he argued, was in any case originally not Serb but Vlach. He added that language did not divide Serbs from Croats, and that religion did not define a nationality. While not wishing to negate the existence of Serbs as a separate people, he denied that they constituted a 'political nation' in Croatia, that is, a people with the right to a separate territory. There was in fact only one political nation, that identified in state documents as *gens croata*. The idea that this term embraced the Orthodox population too, however, was not popular with the Serb deputies, who pointed out that the Magyars similarly identified Hungary with the Magyar 'political nation'. Franjo Rački tried to square this circle by suggesting that

Serbs and Croats were one – Yugoslav – nation, made up of two peoples which jointly formed the 'political nation' in Croatia. The Unionists at once complained to the king that the National Party was seeking to create a Yugoslav state within the Monarchy. The Orthodox bishop of Pakrac Stefan Kragujević agreed that the sabor had never denied the 'essence' of the Serb people, but felt that it would be right in the circumstances to declare that the Serbs formed a distinct people. The sabor accepted this. The proposal – 'The sabor formally declares that the Triune Kingdom recognises the Serb people living within its borders as one with – and equal to – the Croat people' – was passed by acclamation (Article 31/1861). The sabor also proclaimed the need for mutual respect and solidarity, and as proof of its good will the deputies were invited to attend Mass at the Zagreb Orthodox church, in order to commemorate Rajačić's fifty years of service.

Kukuljević accepted this conclusion, but not before mounting a veiled attack on what he understood as separatism:

> I am surprised to hear the esteemed patriarch, our Croatian countryman and native of the proud [border village of] Brinje, to hear this very gentleman – who understandably wishes to defend and protect the Serbs in regard to their holy faith – ask the assembled parliament that we as a nation deny our Croatian homeland and our gallant Croat name; that we forget our past for the sake of our brothers, however close they may be to us. We love our Serb brothers both as [Slav] brothers and as an integral part of our nation. We do not mind when the occasional Serb writer attacks us, or claims our language, lands and cultural heritage to be Serb, [since] we are convinced that the happiness and prosperity of our southern Slav people can come about only by Croat-Serb cooperation. We respect both the Western and the Eastern Church and always have done, and will defend our people's two religions with the same determination as we will their civic rights. We neither have been, nor wish to be, against the Serbs, and are indeed ready to sacrifice our own particular interest for the sake of the Yugoslav people's common good. [But] no one should demand of us to sacrifice the smallest part of our national welfare [for] the sake of some particular interest, individual or nationality, on behalf of certain aspirations of dangerous design. Let no one believe that we will support or permit the growth of the cursed seed of disunity, nor that we will sacrifice any part of our Croatian soil, including our heroic Croatian Border, for the sake of such aspirations.

In Kukuljević's view, Serbs living in Croatia should become Croatians and Croats in Serbia Serbians, because their prosperity and pursuit of happiness vitally depended on the country in which they found themselves.

The Serb issue was raised again in the course of the debate on the language, which included both a philological and a political dimension. Kukuljević described the existing situation in which Croat and German were used in the administration, schools and services, while the Catholic Church (apart from the bishopric of Senj) used in addition Latin and Italian. He proposed that the name of the official language be 'Croato-Serb', since 'it is clear that this language [belongs] to both Croats and Serbs and that these two Yugoslav peoples [form] in fact one and the same nation [whose] happiness rests on their cooperation, while their disunity leads all Yugoslavdom to a catastrophe. Since we have already acknowledged the existence of Serbs in the Triune Kingdom, it seems to me that we should also honour the Serb name by calling our language Croato-Serb.' Another deputy moved that the language be called 'Yugoslav', and that equality of the two scripts be accepted. The suggestion that the language be called Serb in areas inhabited mainly by Serbs, and Croat in areas inhabited mainly by Croats was rejected as impractical. The possibility that 'Serb' in 'Croato-Serb' might be understood to refer to *štokavian* led the sabor to reject the hyphenated form, and to vote instead that the official language in Croatia be called 'Yugoslav'. This formula was accepted also because at the time the sabor was legislating for the establishment of a Yugoslav academy of arts and sciences (for the upkeep of which Bishop Strossmayer offered a significant sum of money), a Yugoslav university, and a Yugoslav theatre. Equality of the Latin and Cyrillic scripts was also proclaimed. The Yugoslav name, however, was rejected by the Serb deputies. All this effort in regard to the status and national language of the Serbs was wasted anyway, since none of these decisions was given royal assent. Chancellor Mažuranić cut the Gordian knot in regard to the language, by ordering that the official language in Croatia be called Croat – which, he added, was the same language as Serb. (In 1888 'Croat', however, would be changed to 'Croat or Serb'.)

In 1866 the sabor again faced a debate on the 'Serb question', set off by the term 'nation' that appeared in various drafts of the sabor's formal address to the king. The majority address, drafted by Rački, referred to 'our nation' in order to avoid conflict with the Serbs over the term 'Croatian political nation'. An alternative draft produced by Nikola Stojanović, a Unionist Serb official from Virovitica, spoke of a 'Croato-Serb nation'. Svetozar Miletić, a Unionist Serb deputy from Srijem, argued that the nation could not be defined territorially, since it was a 'genetic' category. The Austrian Serbs, he went on, supported Croatia's statehood and territorial integrity, but they also felt that their own political status in Croatia should be defined more clearly. The Croat failure to recognise the Serbs as a separate 'political nation' in Croatia derived, in his view, from a desire for Croat national supremacy. Matija Mrazović of the National Party pointed out that the address avoided mentioning the Croat name, and that in Croatia Serbs enjoyed the same rights as Croats. Kukuljević suggested that 'our nation' be replaced with 'our nation called Croat and Serb'. The sabor majority, however, rejected the inclusion of the Serb 'genetic' name: the sabor's good will towards the Serbs was already manifested by the fact that the address omitted mentioning the Croat name. A Croat deputy from Karlovac remarked that the address was a political document that did not deal with 'genetic nationalities', and charged the Serb deputies with wishing to establish a Serb state on Croatian territory. The former Illyrian Dragutin Kušlan declared himself in favour of both names being used for the language, but not for the Croatian state, crown and state right. This won wide support. The sabor consequently voted in favour of Rački's 'our nation'.

Both Serb liberals and conservatives had by now fully rejected the idea of a united Croatian nation as a Croat manoeuvre. Svetozar Miletić's proposal involved an alternative political programme for the Croatian Serbs, according to which it was not enough for the sabor to recognise the Serbs as a distinct people and as equal citizens: they must also be recognised as a separate 'political nation'. This change would then be systematically applied at all levels of the administration, leading to the emergence of Serb self-governing areas that would eventually include Srijem, the Military Border and Dalmatia, that is, as Miletić wrote, 'nearly half the population' of the Triune Kingdom. Rački pointed out in his reply that Croatian Serbs did not need self-governing districts in order to safeguard their national individuality, since they already enjoyed full cultural and political rights. He rejected, moreover, the idea that all Croatia's Orthodox population was Serb, as well as any national division on a confessional basis. Miletić had charged Strossmayer, Rački went on, with using the Yugoslav idea to weaken Serb national consciousness; he had alleged that ever since 1861 Strossmayer had been trying to Croatise not only 'Serb' Slavonia and Dalmatia, but also all South Slavs, in order to create a Great Croatia. It was inappropriate to apply the term 'Great Croatian policy' to defence of the Croatian state right, or to efforts to unite the Triune Kingdom into a single state based on its 'thousand-year-old Croat character'. The Serb side referred to Leopold's privileges as sufficient grounds for being treated as a distinct 'political nation'; the Croats saw them as nothing but a promise of protection for the Eastern Church, which in any case was out of date now that all religions were legally equal. The Croat majority feared, in fact, that any recognition of the Serb name as 'diplomatic' within the Triune Kingdom would permit Serb deputies next to demand administrative demarcation and separation of Serb-majority areas – particularly dangerous since their concept of 'Serb' included a large number of Croats – which at some future date would seek incorporation with Serbia.

By the time of the Croato-Hungarian Compromise of 1868, the Croat and Serb national ideologies had been fully formed, with the Croat Yugoslav idea confronting the Serb idea of Great Serbia. External circumstances would henceforth dictate the degree of the respective parties' cooperation. The policy of the Croatian Serbs would oscillate between, on the one hand, a desire to become fully independent and, on the other, the need to cooperate with the Croat parties; between a desire to weaken Croatia and the need to defend its autonomy, since without it their own ambitions, especially in the economic field, could not be realised. Their separatist inclinations often led them into political alliances directed against Croatia's interests; but, as Kukuljević had noted, the fact that they lived in Croatia meant that they could not prosper without it. They lived everywhere intermingled with Croats, forming a bare majority only in the impoverished county of Lika-Krbava. Whether they wished it or not, they were Croatians: denial of this fact made them into a minority exposed to Croat anger. This was true especially of the urban class, which with few exceptions formed small islands in a Croat sea: in 1900 Serbs formed only 11 per cent of the town population in Ban's Croatia.

Serb policy was formed, however, not only in the Croatian and Hungarian parliaments, but also in the Serbs' own autonomous lay-clerical bodies which ran the internal affairs of this Orthodox community. Although this autonomy did not have a political form, its extent and role gave it an aspect of self-government by the Serb people that transcended the existing political borders. Decisions regarding the life of this community were made at lay-clerical assemblies elected on the basis of a wide suffrage – all literate males over the age of twenty-four could vote – that met in Karlovci. This was made up of twenty-five priests, twenty-five laymen from the Military Border and twenty-five from the civilian districts, who elected a smaller committee of eight as its executive. In the second half of the nineteenth century this structure became the focus of intense competition among Serb political parties. Following the Croato-Hungarian Compromise, however, when Croatian deputies appeared in the Hungarian parliament, it became possible to coordinate Serb policy also at that level. Croatia's integration with Hungary gave Serb politicians additional political leverage, in that they were left with a choice as to whether cooperation with Hungary against Croatia or with Croatia against Hungary would best serve their own particular interests – although, for the most part, they sought to minimise Croatian-Hungarian differences in order to maintain the unity of their own autonomous bodies. Despite Croatia's repeated efforts to defend its autonomy in religious and educational affairs, the Hungarian government retained control over the Serb autonomous bodies on its territory, thereby lessening the reliance of the Croatian Serbs on their country's own political institutions while at the same time creating an additional instrument for influencing Croatia's political life.

As Croatia gradually lost the capacity for self-government, it lost also the means with which to forge its fractious collectivity into a unified national body. During the 1860s and 1870s all hope of gaining Dalmatia in the near future was also lost, despite the clearly stated will of the Dalmatian parliament, and the same was true of the more vacuous belief that Bosnia-Herzegovina would be added to Croatia. The Croatian state, in fact, was thus waning in the west at the same time as the Serbian state was rising in the east. In the last quarter of the nineteenth century, the independent kingdom of Serbia became an alternative pole of orientation for Croatian Serbs, particularly since after the Berlin Congress of 1878 Serbia inclined towards Austria-Hungary. The fact that Serbs occupied high positions in the Croatian government acted as a brake on the Serb–Croat conflict. The latter was mainly kept in check, moreover, by the Yugoslav orientation of the dominant Croat parties, induced by their fear of German, Italian and Hungarian expansionism. Their distant goal remained a South Slav federation, but in the meantime it was necessary to ensure Serb–Croat cooperation in order to protect and strengthen Croatia's autonomy within the monarchy. This policy was rejected, however, by Starčević's Party of Right, which continued to gain in popularity after the Croato-Hungarian Compromise: it gained one deputy in 1875, five in 1878 and twenty-four in 1884. Its further progress in Ban's Croatia was checked by official hostility, but the party continued to gain in Dalmatia and Istria – where, however, its ideology would lose two of its basic premises: that no Serb nationality existed in Croatia, and that Croatia's place was outside the Monarchy (or, eventually, Yugoslavia).

Turning Orthodox Grenzers into Serbs

A new period in Croatian politics opened in 1881 with the incorporation of the Military Border, following which the proportion of the Serb population in Ban's Croatia, made up mainly of subsistence farmers, rose to 26 per cent. Up to this time Serb political activity had concentrated on Srijem and southern Hungary, but the incorporation of the Military Border argued in favour of the establishment of a new centre of political action in Zagreb itself, where – quite apart from defending the autonomy of Orthodox Serb schools – nationally minded Serbs would be in a position to influence the former Grenzers, and to combat more effectively Croatian claims to Bosnia-Herzegovina. The outcome was the formation in 1881 of the first Serb party in Croatia: the Independent Serb Party (*Samostalna Srpska Stranka*), with its own paper *Srpski glas* (Serb Voice). This organisation would in due course become the main party of the Croatian Serbs. Its starting position was that Croatian Serbs should seek affirmation of their political status in Croatia 'with the Croats, without the Croats, and if need be against the Croats'.[20]

In the election of 1883 the sabor acquired eighteen new Serb deputies from the former Military Border. A parliamentary Serb Club was formed soon afterwards – consisting of the old Serb Unionists and the new deputies – which supported the National Party. Soon after the elections, however, mass unrest broke out in Croatia, which developed into an anti-Hungarian movement and led to the declaration of a state of emergency. *Srpski glas* criticised the ensuing calls for Croat-Serb cooperation, and condemned a speech made by the Serb liberal politician Mihailo Polit Desančić in the Hungarian parliament defending Croatia's autonomy on the grounds that 'irritating the Magyars [should] not be the main aim of the Serb deputies in the Hungarian parliament'. Though formally in opposition, the Independent Serb Party became a natural ally of the Hungarian regime in Croatia.

Return to normality was followed by the appointment in December 1883 of Dragutin Khuen-Héderváry as ban. The first elections under his administration took place a year later, when the Croat opposition won thirty-seven seats (the Party of Right twenty-four, the Independent Nationals thirteen), the National Party thirty-five, the Serb Club thirty-two, and 'neutrals' three. The elections revealed a growing opposition to the compromise. Some of the ruling National Party's Croat candidates, having lost in majority-Croat districts, were elected in majority-Serb ones. *Zastava* (Flag), the voice of the Hungarian Serbs, pointed out that the National Party's relative success was due mainly to Serb votes: 'We can say that the Serb pragmatic policy [of joining the government benches] has been successful, and that without the Serbs one can no longer govern in Croatia.' The disunity within the Croat opposition ensured that the balance in the Croatian parliament would henceforth be held by the Serb Club.

The Serb Club joined the National Party's club in the sabor. The National Party thus transformed became known as Khuen's party, and the Serb Club within it as Khuen's Serbs. It was a party made up of government officials, lawyers and members of the propertied classes. In fact, because of limited suffrage and general lack of political freedoms which inhibited political action and organisation, Croatian parties could hardly be called parties in the sense in which they existed in western Europe, or indeed in the Austrian half of the Monarchy. They were simply expressions of corporate interests, reduced in the case of the opposition to publishing journals of limited circulation such as *Obzor* (Horizon), the paper of the Independent National Party. Ban Khuen-Héderváry's firm grip on the Croatian political machinery meant that the Croat opposition had no hope of playing any significant role in national politics.

The new ban's mandate was to restrain Croatian opposition to dualism (or rather to the Hungarian interpretation of it), for which he needed an obedient parliament and bureaucracy. He achieved control of the parliament by means of electoral gerrymandering, and by changing parliamentary procedure to permit the speaker to eject opposition deputies from the house for long periods at a time. He also revised Mažuranić's administrative and legal system in a manner that created an obedient justice and bureaucracy, and gained control of public debate by suspending trial by jury in cases concerning the press. Most important in the long run, perhaps, was his reliance on the Serb middle class. While he was in office, for example, the headship in four of the eight counties of Ban's Croatia were reserved for Serb members of the National Party: in Lika-Krbava (51 per cent Orthodox), Modruš-Rijeka (32 per cent Orthodox), Požega (26 per cent Orthodox) and Srijem (46 per cent Orthodox). This caused considerable Croat-Serb tensions in these areas, especially since their urban population was overwhelmingly Catholic (with Orthodox constituting 4 per cent, 1 per cent, 9 per cent and 35 per cent respectively). Hostile to the Croatian state idea, the ban also discriminated systematically against the Croat middle class, while allowing its Serb counterpart to create strong economic and especially financial institutions.[21] Serb policy, as a result, became a visible manifestation of Khuen's regime in Croatia.[22]

Since *Srpski glas*, published in Srijem, could not effectively address the newly integrated Orthodox population of Ban's Croatia, a new paper called *Srbobran* (Serb Defender) was founded in Zagreb in 1884, where less than 1,000 of the city's 28,000 inhabitants were Serbs. The paper aimed to educate the readers in an 'authentic' Serb national spirit. According to its editor, Pavle Jovanović, the paper's name summed up its policy: 'to defend and protect from all hostile attacks what has been won with our forefathers' blood, and guaranteed by imperial diplomas: the Serb name, language, church and school.'[23] Funded by Serb merchants and politicians, *Srbobran* became the main voice of the Independent Serb Party. Given that the vast majority of the Orthodox population was illiterate, the paper was directed mainly at the Serb clergy and middle class, which despite its small numbers was now playing an important role in Croatian administration and economic life. This helps explain its fiery rhetoric. The paper sold also in Serbia and Montenegro (which aided it financially), and secretly in Bosnia-Herzegovina and Dalmatia, where it was banned on account of its strident nationalism. Its most powerful tool, however, proved to be the annual calendar it published in 40,000 copies.

Jovanović advocated a strongly separatist stance for the Croatian Serbs. He was born in Zemun (36 per cent Orthodox) in the former Military Border now part of the county of Srijem, but attended the Belgrade gymnasium together with the future leaders of the Serbian Radical Party. His paper generally portrayed the position of the Serbs in the Monarchy in the darkest colours; but its favourite tactic was to present the Serbs as permanent victims of the Croats, in order to justify their separation and unification. The paper argued that 'Croat domination over the Serb nation in Croatia-Slavonia' was inaugurated by Mažuranić's educational law directed against Serb confessional schools, which educated children in the Serb spirit while at the same time protecting them from the Western civilisational invasion. Mažuranić's refusal to subsidise the Orthodox Church likewise aimed at Serb denationalisation. The University of Zagreb was equally an anti-Serb institution: a Croat trap for Serb youth. The paper's claim that Yugoslavism was a 'stew' did not prevent it, however, from attacking as chauvinism any suggestion that Strossmayer's Yugoslav Academy be renamed the Croatian Academy.

In its early days the paper criticised in particular the poor work of the Orthodox clergy, many of whom, it alleged, did not even know who St Sava – the founder of the Serb Orthodox Church – was. Some of this clergy saw themselves indeed as Orthodox Croats, preached the Croatian state idea, and used the Latin script. The Serb intelligentsia, on the other hand – 'chained by its positions and frightened by *Obzor*'s Jesuitism and Starčević's chauvinism'

Pavle Jovanović

– was leaving the Croatian Serbs 'leaderless and divided', 'lambs facing the wolf', a prey to 'Croat parties and their agitators'. Nominally in opposition, the paper carefully avoided criticising Khuen-Héderváry's regime, which it saw as the bastion of dualism, and denounced the resistance to dualism in Croatia as 'the dictatorial behaviour of a minority'. It argued that the Croato-Hungarian Compromise defended the Croatian Serbs by creating in Croatia a situation far more favourable to them than the one pertaining in Hungary, while simultaneously also preventing Croatia's unification – which, if realised, would 'create a wedge within the Serb body'. Preservation of the Compromise was hence a matter of 'the survival and advance of the Serbs and of the Serb idea'. The Independent Serb Party consequently rejected all politics based on the premise of Croatia's independence as being anti-Serb, since it involved imposition on the Croatian Serbs of a 'foreign' state idea. But the Croats' main sin, in the editor's eye, was their alleged efforts to convert the Serbs to Catholicism. Turkish transgressions indeed paled in comparison with those committed by the Croats from the moment of the Serb arrival in Croatia. Unlike the Ottomans, the Croats had for centuries imperiled the Serbs' national identity by restricting their religion, tradition, language and name.

A vital element in *Srbobran*'s construction of the Serb national identity was its interpretation of Serb history. The idea was to bolster Serb pride and prepare Serbs for the national tasks ahead. According to the paper, the Serbs were the greatest nation on earth. They had enjoyed a glorious past under the Nemanjić dynasty and a bright future awaited that would see their unification. Ever since the battle of Kosovo, Serb history had been moving in the direction of regaining the lost state. Serbia was the 'promised land', because with it the Serb people, after so much movement and resettlement, had been reborn as a nation state. It was in the harmony of church and people that the paper saw Serb strength then and now. 'Serbdom and Orthodoxy represent an identical concept for us. Loss of one entails the loss of the other.' When Tadija Smičiklas of the Independent National Party (himself of Orthodox faith), wrote in *Obzor*, that – because they had a common language – Serbs and Croats were one people, albeit with two names, two histories and three religions (including Islam), all of which should be equally honoured, the paper replied that unity between Croats and Serbs 'will not be realised until the two names, the two political histories, the two scripts and the three religions fuse into a single name, a single political history, a single script and a single religion'. It left no doubt as to which name, history, script and religion would emerge victorious. The Serb national ideology's inherent hostility towards Catholicism and Islam worked against Vuk Karadžić theory of 'one nation, three confessions' taking deeper roots in the Serb national imagination.

According to *Srbobran*, Croats were in fact originally Serbs. Their separation began with Branimir's '*coup d'etat*', which delivered Croatia to Rome. The Croats then gave up their Serb nationality together with their Serb religion. As a result two opposing camps emerged: Catholic Croatdom and Orthodox Serbdom. The Bosnian Muslims had similarly rejected their Serb religion and name, after which they too became 'the most energetic exponents of foreign ideals and enterprise directed against the Serb people and their state idea'. The view that Croats were originally Serbs was upheld also in *The History of the Serb Church*, written by the Orthodox bishop of Žiča, Nikanor Ružičić, and financed by the Serb patriarch, Georgije Branković. According to this work, it was actually Borna not Branimir who – being a blind follower of the Franks and the pope – had separated a portion of the Serb people from the Serb Church, and created a statelet which he called Croatia and a new nation which he called Croat. At that time all nations, jealous of Serb glory, were joined in a plot against the Serbs.

Srbobran endorsed the view that all *štokavian* speakers were Serbs, comparing Vuk Karadžić who had popularised this idea to St Sava, but only in order to claim certain territory or cultural achievements for the Serbs. Despite the stress on the historical and cultural divide allegedly established when the Serbs later called Croats adopted Catholicism, works produced by Catholic Croats were treated as part of Serb cultural heritage. Dubrovnik was thus a Serb city. The sixteenth-century Croat poet from Korčula, Ivan Vidal, who called Dubrovnik 'the crown of all Croatian cities', was described as 'a mere Croat champion who, like so many today still do, attempted to Croatise Dubrovnik'. The alleged Serb nature of the Dubrovnik republic, however, did not prevent the paper from listing the republic's own alleged crimes committed against the Serbs. Nor did claiming Croat achievements for the Serbs deter the paper from insisting that the Serbs had never succumbed to outside influences that would alter their nature: a Serb was 'always pure and authentic, always exclusively Serb'. Serb folk poetry was the fount of patriotic and moral values, the one-string *gusle* players national educators and missionaries. The reason why the Serbs were able to develop a strong national culture was because they 'basked in the Eastern sun'. The Croats, by contrast, had no folk culture; insofar as they had ever had any, it had been destroyed by their Western orientation. Western civilisation had sapped their national essence, making them demoralised and degenerate – and ultimately doomed. The Croats had in fact stolen the Serb language, history and culture and the Serb nation's most illustrious sons – all under the slogan of Croat-Serb brotherhood. They had invented Illyrianism and Yugoslavism with the intention of 'breaking down the vital Serb nation'. The task of *Srbobran* was to 'destroy the weed' growing from the 'murky sediment of the Illyrian mixture' (on this it agreed with the leader of the Party of Right, Ante Starčević). Croats and Poles, being wholly Catholic, were an alien presence in the Slav body. Croats were in fact 'southern Poles': Polish misdemeanours towards the Russians were matched only by Croat aggressive behaviour towards the Serbs.

It was the Orthodox faith that supplied the vital ingredient enabling the Orthodox Slavs to acquire independent states. 'Providence has placed the Serbs at the heart of the Balkans and decreed that they should dominate it politically and culturally.' The Serb people had created two Serb states, whose duty was to free the unredeemed Serb lands: their right to unite overruled the rights of other nationalities living on 'Serb' territory. Given that the other nations in the region did not agree with this vision, the paper advocated if necessary war against all of them. The paper presented the history of humanity as one of permanent conflict between the East represented by Russia, which was 'young and morally strong', and the 'putrefying' West, represented by Great Britain. The West could save itself, though, by converting to Orthodoxy. Orthodox Slavs would regenerate Europe and establish 'the principle of brotherhood and Christ's empire on earth'. Serbs and Russians had the same historic mission. After Serbia fell at Kosovo, Russia took up the banner of Orthodoxy and Slavdom. The reborn Serbia had resumed its mission, however, and now stood alongside Russia. This is why the Serbs and the Russians were the most important Slav nations: Russia's advance was also a Serb and Slav advance. The paper argued that the next major war would be one between Slavdom and Germandom. Slav solidarity (excluding the Croats and the Poles) was needed against the German *Drang*.

Srbobran's unremitting anti-Croat propaganda ultimately proved its undoing. In 1902 it published an article titled 'Serbs and Croats', penned by Nikola Stojanović, the president of the Serb cultural society in Vienna, in which the alleged natures of the Serb and Croat peoples were contrasted. The article recapitulated *Srbobran*'s main arguments but sought to give them a 'scientific' form, in that its author relied on a widely accepted theory advocated by Ludwig Gumplowitz according to which a people develops from a tribe or ethnos (*Stamm*) to a political or state people (*Volk*) and then to a culturally integrated nationality (*Nationalität*). Stojanović argued that the Serb *ethnos* had become a state people through the Serbs' resistance in Kosovo, and their subsequent common history of subjugation to a single authority. Their cultural unity, whose foundation had been laid by St Sava, found its expression in this 'magnificent resistance' which fused the 'Serb aristocratic spirit and natural democracy' into 'a wonderful and inseparable unity': 'In this sense the Serb defeat at Kosovo signified a great victory.'

The Croats, by contrast, had failed to develop a national consciousness or sense of common identity in the course of their history. Consequently, they had never become a state people. For Stojanović, the turning point came not with Borna or Branimir, but with King Tomislav. It all began with the Split synod in the early tenth century, at which the Croats rejected their Slav liturgy in favour of the Latin. The religious difference between the feudal masters and serfs, which had fuelled Serb anti-Ottoman revolts, consequently could play no such role in the Croat case, since both shared the same faith. Croat aspirations, as a result, had become represented by 'various cliques', which – though serving all interests but the Croat – had succeeded in becoming identified with the Croat people. Imitating the Hungarians, these 'cliques' had adopted the theory of political nation in order to deprive the Croatian Serbs of their right to existence. Given that the Croats lacked 'a distinct language, customary community and strong living unity', they could not be treated as a distinct nationality either. Neglecting the fact that Serb politicians were a main pillar of Khuen-Héderváry's regime in Croatia, the author insisted that 'insofar as the Croats were now offering some resistance to foreign influence, they were doing so under the influence of Serb culture'.

In fact, Stojanović argued, the more the Croats became Croat, the lesser was their power of resistance. The Croats 'typically glorify Zvonimir, who willingly became the pope's vassal; commemorate thousands of warriors who fell on the fields of central and southern Europe; and extol Ban Jelačić, who was nothing but a servant of the court in Vienna.' Oblivious to the fact that a large proportion of the Border Serbs at the time still believed that the Austrian yellow-black flag was their own national flag, and that both the imperial and Ban Jelačić's army included a large number of those whom he treated as an authentic part of the Serb nation, Stojanović insisted that 'a people which idealises the servants of foreigners cannot but imitate its ideal: to become a servant'. This subjugated Croat mass was bound to lose to the heroic Serb nation, which 'despite its democratic formation harbours an aristocratic sentiment and pride'.

The Croats were thus not a nationality, nor had they any hope of ever becoming one. 'Their drift during the nineteenth century from Gaj's Illyrianism to Strossmayer's Yugoslavism and Starčević's Croatism clearly proves this.' Their leaders, acting on behalf of foreign interests, have sought to create these various nationalities in order to assimilate the Serbs. Illyrianism was created when Austria needed a strong counterbalance to the Hungarians. When the Serbs showed not the smallest interest in it, there came along Strossmayer's Yugoslavism, which this time included also the Bulgarians. Its aim was to 'Uniate' the southern Slavs on behalf of Austria and the Vatican. And, 'when these hopes were betrayed and a single Austria was replaced by Austria-Hungary, [it] was time to apply *divide et impera*, so Starčević's Croatism was created'. Since the Croats were not and could not become a distinct nationality, they were destined to become Serbs. The process of their assimilation was unstoppable. Calls for Croat–Serb solidarity could not halt the struggle between them, because 'Serbs and Croats in their present form constitute two political parties.' Croats and Serbs were divided by 'the idea of freedom': free men became Serbs, servile ones Croats. The struggle between the Croats and the Serbs could thus end only with the annihilation of one or the other (as he put it, 'in our annihilation or yours'). 'One party must lose. That this will be the Croats is guaranteed by their small size, their geographical location, their overall situation, the fact that they are everywhere mixed with Serbs, and by the process of general evolution in which the Serb idea stands for progress.'

This message, not surprisingly, caused an outcry among the Croats. Stojanović's article stung all the more since it contained a basic truth: that in Khuen-Héderváry's Croatia Serb political and economic organisation was advancing, while the Croat ones were falling behind. In a situation in which the state institutions were in the hands of a regime inimical to Croatia, the pursuit of national unity had become practically impossible. The sabor, far from functioning as an authoritative source of national policy and a mediator between the country's various constituencies, had been turned into its opposite. The impotence of the Croat opposition ensured that politics would take to the streets. A week after the publication of Stojanović's article, there was a demonstration in Zagreb organised by university and secondary-school students which, contrary to their intentions, soon developed into an anti-Serb riot that lasted for three days. Many prominent Serbs fled the city. Two days later Zagreb and the surrounding area were placed under martial law. *Srbobran* was closed down, and its editor and printer briefly arrested. Prominent Croat and Serb leaders condemned both the riot and *Srbobran*. The 'September events', by exposing Serb vulnerability, aided the argument that Serbs could prosper in Croatia only in cooperation with the Croats.

A troubled identity

Croatia's Orthodox population was composed of four major groups: those who had come to the Military Border area during the sixteenth century; those settled by the Ottomans in their part of Croatia; the Serbs who had arrived at the turn of the seventeenth century, most of whom ended up in the Slavonian/Srijem border; and the Vlachs, embraced by the Venetian republic as it expanded into Ottoman territory. The persistence of the institution of the Military Border, combined with the establishment of the Orthodox patriarchy in Karlovci, provided the basis for the transformation of Croatia's Orthodox border population into Serbs. The fact that the authority of the Serb patriarchy embraced equally the Serbs of Hungary and Croatia worked against a proper closure of the Croatian border with Hungary in Srijem, while opening at the same time a new conduit for Hungarian interference in Croatia's internal affairs.

The isolation of the Military Border from the rest of Croatia had ended in 1848, when the Croatian parliament came to represent and speak for the Grenzers. However, Croatia had failed to gain this most important part of its territory before the arrival of dualism, which had greatly strengthened Hungary's role in the affairs of the Habsburg state, subordinated Croatia to its will and snuffed out the dream of a Serb Vojvodina – but also reinforced the ties between Hungarian and Croatian Serbs. The installation of the dualist system, followed by Serbia's emancipation from the Ottoman Empire and Croatia's integration of the Military Border in 1881, was to produce a new Serb policy in Croatia. Serbia's expansionism, on the other hand, helped to transform the Serb question in Croatia into an issue with international ramifications.

Until the Congress of Berlin, Serbia had relied on both Hungary and Croatia to aid its Eastern, that is, Bosnian, policy. Here the role of the Military Border was of crucial importance. In fact, all the interested parties – Austria, Croatia and Serbia – had counted on the Border army for their eventual entry into Bosnia. The Yugoslav orientation of Strossmayer's National Party was a reflection in part also of the hope of joint Croatian-Serbian action in Bosnia, whose liberation would provide a stepping stone towards the creation of a South Slav state. But Serbia's failure to gain Bosnia altered both Croatia's attitude to Serbia and Serbia's to Croatia. While Serbia at all times preferred to keep Croatia (hence Austria) out of Bosnia, Croatia came to count on Austria to liberate Bosnia. Following the Congress of Berlin, Croatia and Serbia were to part ways for a generation. Their mutual alienation was reflected also in an increasingly sharp divergence between the Croatian Croat and the Croato-Hungarian Serb parties. At the same time, the integration of the Military Border into Croatia soon after the Congress posed the danger that the Orthodox population of the border might be lost for Serbia, and created a need for energetic action to prevent this. The appearance of the Independent Serb Party and its paper *Srbobran* was part of that action.

The Serb national ideology acquired its final form under the dualist system, which limited the appeal of the Croatian state in the eyes of its Orthodox population. The character of Khuen's period is perhaps best illustrated by the fact that, while it was possible in Zagreb to publish virulent anti-Croat propaganda, to hail Croatia could land one in prison and to vote for the Croat opposition could lead to instant dismissal from public service. This situation permitted the Independent Serb Party to create in the Orthodox population of the former Military Border the sense of belonging to a wholly different nationality. Although the Independent Serb Party remained a minor party until the beginning of the twentieth century, the wide reach of its publications was ensured by financial support from the upper layers of Serb society – and whenever possible from the Serbian and Montenegrin governments. The Serb press taught the Croatian Orthodox population not only that they were Serbs, but also that they were Serbian Serbs. Furthermore, relying on arguments variously involving language, religion, national rights and historic rights, it sought to justify Serbia's enlargement at Croatia's expense. The Serb parties thus rejected the Croatian state idea not because it stopped them from being Serbs, but because it prevented them from being Serbians. Their struggle against the alleged non-recognition and unequal status of Serbs in Croatia was in reality a struggle over the future of 'Serb lands'.[24] By limiting its political aspirations to joining a Great Serbia, however, the Croatian Serb elite surrendered the political initiative to Belgrade.

The Serb national ideologues of the late nineteenth century did all they could to wrench Croatian orthodox population from the arms of the Croatian state and to make them feel foreigners in their own country. The immensely popular *Srbobran* calendars, for example, were filled with exclusively Serb and Serbian content, while carefully excluding all that might make the paper's readers feel part of Croatian society. In order to separate Serbs from Croats, moreover, they did not limit themselves to stressing what Serbs had in common, but sought also to make Serbs feel insecure in Croatia by presenting the Croat-Serb relationship as a permanently antagonistic one, with the Croats playing the role of aggressors and the Serbs that of victims. While such publications were successful in instilling in the Orthodox masses a strong sense of Serb unity, however, the national identity they created – or tried to create – for them was inevitably a troubled one.

These national ideologues stridently rejected such feeble attempts at assimilation as Illyrianism or Yugoslavism, let alone appeals to a common Croatian nationhood, insisting instead on a total separation of Serbs and Croats – even though this was unattainable in reality, given the ethnic distribution of both. They tried to solve this problem by arguing that Croats were in fact Serbs; yet their publications used every opportunity to cultivate a sense of organic linkage between the Serb people and the Serb Church, which automatically excluded Catholic Croats. Unlike the Croat political mainstream which viewed the Serbs as an equally valid component of the Croatian nation, Serb national ideologues insisted on their total cultural and historical opposition – while at the same time claiming the Croatian cultural heritage as exclusive Serb property. Such propaganda inevitably fanned Croat hostility, creating a sense of incipient civil war. It is true that the more extreme version of the Serb national ideology to be found in *Srbobran* and similar publications did not find support among the better-educated Croatian and Hungarian Serbs; but its premises were widely shared. Yet, notwithstanding their heady rhetoric, Serb politicians found it impossible in the end to establish a separate Serb 'political nation' in Croatia – that is, to create a clearly demarcated Serb area within which the community could govern itself independently from the rest of Croatia. Despite the stress on national unity, indeed, Serb politics in the Habsburg Monarchy in fact remained divided by the Croatian-Hungarian border, as a result of which the evolution of Croatian Serb politics would follow a different pattern from that of the Serbs in Hungary. The installation of the Khuen-Hédervary regime, and the profit initially derived from it by the rising Serb middle class, made the members of that class feel that Croatia's interests were no longer its own. They soon discovered, however, that Croatia's capacity to function as an autonomous state was a necessary condition for their own advance as well.

A sharp distinction between Croats and Serbs combined with a conviction that they were really one and the same people were elements shared by Ante Starčević, who negated the very existence of a separate Serb people in Croatia and appropriated the more heroic parts of Serb national history for the Croats. Starčević did not fall into the trap of claiming racial purity for the Croats; but he did believe that the Croats were by definition a lordly people, while the Serb name in his view denoted a slavish spirit, which is why he called the Croat proponents of Illyrism and Yugoslavism 'Slavoserbs'. As far as Starčević and his supporters at this stage were concerned, Serbs – and Slovenes too – were an Austrian invention. The charge of being an 'Austrian invention' was indeed standard political currency in the nationally contested areas of the Habsburg Monarchy.

A survey of political attitudes held by the members of the Croatian parliament shows that of the 460 deputies elected during Khuen-Hédervary's tenure, 354 were government loyalists – of whom 224 were Croats and 130 Serbs, so that there were not only 'Khuen Serbs' but also 'Khuen Croats'. The difference between the Croats and the Serbs, however, lay in the complete absence of a Serb opposition to Khuen's rule. Of 106 members of the opposition, 104 were Croats and only two Serbs. The two Serb oppositionists belonged moreover to the Independent Serb Party, which fully supported the regime's anti-Croatian policies.[25] This is why

Khuen-Héderváry was hailed by the Serb politicians as a 'Serb ban'. The usual justification offered at the time for Croatian Serb support for the government – namely, that it was a reaction to the Party of Right's anti-Serb rhetoric – could not be taken seriously, in view of *Srbobran*'s own strident denunciations of the Independent National Party, which recognised Serbs as a distinct people and sought Croat-Serb collaboration.

At the same time, it was not possible to reduce the Croat-Serb divide to confessional differences. For example, Šime Mazzura, unofficial leader at the time of Strossmayer's Independent National Party, came from a Dalmatian Orthodox family. Stjepan Miletić, director of the Zagreb National Theatre, was Orthodox too and, like Mazzura, felt Croat; he joined the Party of Right. On the other hand, Nikola Tomašić, the descendant of an old Croat noble family, converted to Orthodoxy on marriage and became active within the Zagreb Serb Orthodox community. The Croat-Serb antagonism that characterised the politics of Ban's Croatia in the last two decades of the nineteenth century derived in part from the inability of the country's elite to alter the course of Hungarian politics. Thus the old Unionist Jovan Živković, for example, deputy ban in 1873–83 and one of the strongest critics of the economic side of the Croat-Hungarian Compromise, left the National Party in 1885 and joined the Centre Party – composed of the nobility and the upper class – which formed a wing of the anti-government coalition. It was the collapse of the united opposition after its poor performance in the 1887 elections that led many Serb notables, including Živković, to concentrate on exclusively Serb affairs: in 1887 Živković became involved with the Independent Serb Party, and was to play a crucial role in all its important ventures. It was not in fact the heady nationalist rhetoric of its publications, but rather its work in bettering the life of the impoverished Serb population in the former Military Border regions that in the end gave the Independent Serb Party leadership of the Croatian Serbs. What was specific to Serb political life in Croatia and Hungary was the fact that Serb parties were able to address their national constituency through its autonomous lay-church bodies, elected on a wide suffrage and consequently far more representative than the Croatian parliament. All Croatian parties – including the Serb Independents – were essentially urban parties, with little reach into the countryside; but the Serb autonomous bodies enabled the Serb parties to maintain a closer contact with the peasant masses than was true for their Croat equivalents.

During the first twenty years of its existence the Serb Independent Party managed to gain only two deputies in the sabor;[26] but it scored an impressive success in the economic field, with the creation of a network of financial institutions centred on the Serb Bank and Serb agricultural cooperatives. The Serb Bank was established in 1895, with contributions coming from all over the Habsburg Monarchy as well as from outside it. The Serb press welcomed it as an important tool in the economic and political emancipation of the Serbs. This was a time of agricultural crisis, caused by the sale of American wheat on European markets, which was forcing peasants to leave the land and either move to the cities or emigrate: by 1914 there were over 600,000 Croatians in the USA, made up of recent arrivals and a first generation born in the country. Croatian Serb leaders tried to prevent this exodus by looking for ways to help the Serb peasants. Agricultural associations were established on the model of the German Raiffeisen cooperatives, as a form of small farmers' self-help. Peasant associations were at this time sprouting throughout Western Europe, including in the Austrian part of the Monarchy, but the Serb leaders were the first in Ban's Croatia to understand their value. The first such cooperative was established in 1897, and within a year there were enough of them to form an Association of Serb Agricultural Cooperatives in Austria-Hungary, which by 1900 had acquired sixty-seven members.[27]

The Serb Independent Party also made a great contribution to popular education by publishing technical manuals and organising lectures on good husbandry. In 1898 a monthly journal, *Privrednik* (The Economist), was established as the organ of the association, which acted as a coordinator, educator, informer and initiator of practical initiatives. Each issue carried a reminder: 'We know that the condition of the Serb people can be improved only through their own incessant and patient work. We rely on no one and are ready and determined to do our business on our own.' This multidimensional activity was made possible by a combination of regime benevolence, the practical experience of Serb shopkeepers, support from the Orthodox clergy, commitment by the Serb intelligentsia (especially teachers) and the generosity of the regime's numerically small yet influential Serb propertied class. The economic policy of the Serb Independent Party was based on what it called the 'St Sava concept' – the idea that the Serbs 'can survive only by seeking independence in all branches of public life; by relying on no one from outside; and by concentrating resolutely on their own affairs'. Unlike *Srbobran*, however, *Privrednik* avoided getting entangled in political disputes. The paper did not so much press the view that Serbs were endangered in Croatia, but preferred instead to do something more useful

The Serb Orthodox community building with the Serb Bank and the Serb Orthodox Church, Zagreb, second half of nineteenth century

for the national cause: help to create a class of independent Serb artisans and managers.

A new concept of national unity

The Croatian Serb elite, while remaining hostile to the Croatian state idea, defended their country's financial autonomy from Hungary and joined the Croat opposition in criticising the Croatian representatives' poor performance during the decennial negotiations with the Hungarians. In 1885 *Srbobran* published an analysis made by Jovan Živković disputing the view popular on the Hungarian parliamentary benches that Hungary was subsidising Croatia. The paper now concerned itself with the persistent problems created by the absence of economic investment in Croatia; the fact that the Hungarian government's transfer of tax collection to the municipalities brought the latter under its control; and the relentless Magyarisation of the postal and railway services, which led to the opening of Hungarian language schools for the children of the Hungarian railway officials. It pushed for a reduction of the Croatian contribution to joint governmental institutions, protested at discrimination against Croat and Serb candidates in appointments to joint offices, and pointed to the Magyarisation of Međimurje and Rijeka as well as to growing Magyar immigration into

Slavonia. In 1900, 12 per cent of the population of Ban's Croatia were recent immigrants, with 5.4 per cent from Hungary, 2.5 per cent from Austria.

At the outset of his rule in Croatia, Ban Khuen-Héderváry had offered the Serbs support for Serb Orthodox schools and other benefits in return for their loyalty, thereby creating the phenomenon known as 'Khuen Serbs'. But as the Serb middle class grew in size and confidence, it no longer felt dependent for political influence on the Serb autonomous bodies – which in any case were under Hungarian control. The Hungarian government recalled church synods only irregularly, omitted to implement their decisions, and imposed its will upon them. It appointed administrators within their structures who were loyal to itself, and influenced election of the patriarchs. The Serb Independent Party regularly denounced such practices, attacking the Hungarian-appointed Patriarch Anđelić, for instance, as a corrupt individual and 'friend of the devil'. The Serb Church too, however, was in a separatist mood. The structure established in the middle of the nineteenth century, giving the laity a significant influence in running church bodies, was now being challenged by a clerical hierarchy seeking to assume charge of its own affairs. Anđelić's successor, Patriarch Georgije Branković, demanded that the clerical members of the lay-clerical assembly be elected by the clergy alone, and parish priests from among candidates chosen by the church.

The increasingly open intervention by the Hungarian government in the management of the Serb autonomous bodies aided Croat-Serb rapprochement in Ban's Croatia. It was during the period of Khuen-Héderváry's rule, indeed, that Zagreb became not only the political but also the economic capital of the Croatian Serbs. Serb politics as a result developed two poles – Zagreb in the west, dominated by the Serb Independent Party, and Srijem in the east, dominated by the Radical Party – with the National Party present in both and acting as a bridge between them. Despite their differences – visible in party publications, and activated during elections to the sabor and especially to the lay-church assembly – the Serb parties cooperated closely in advancing their corporate interests, together with and against the government. 'Khuen Serbs' thus sat on the management board of the First Croatian Savings Bank, which was a bastion of Croat opposition, as well as on that of the Serb Bank held by the latter's Serb opponents.

As Zagreb became the new gravitational centre of Serb politics, the influence of the Serb Independent Party grew at the expense of the National Party. The struggle between them started in earnest after Jovanović's death in 1897, when a new generation of Serb politicians arrived to challenge the confrontational stance of the Independent Serb Party and its support for the Khuen regime. The time had come to end the Croat–Serb conflict. The new Independent Serb Party leaders came from a circle of Zagreb university students who in 1894 had begun publishing a journal called *Omladina* (Youth), open to Croat–Serb dialogue. Under the influence of more moderate members of the Party of Right, Croat and Serb students joined to form the United Croat and Serb Youth, based on respect for Serb individuality and opposition to the government. Their paper *Narodna misao* (The National Idea) embraced the view that Croats, Serbs and Slovenes were one nation, whose spirit derived from 'common sentiments, interests and beliefs'. A common language, common material and other interests, and a continuous common territory, argued that Serbs and Croats were one and the same nation. The United Youth leaders admitted that there was not as yet 'a subjective sense of unity', but believed that time would create the necessary conditions for such unity to emerge, thus negating foreign efforts to divide the 'Croat or Serb nation'. This was the old Illyrian and Yugoslav idea, albeit in a new and less tolerant form as unitary Yugoslav nationalism. But at least the Croat and Serb national ideas were no longer treated as mutually opposed. The initiative was for this reason not widely accepted, and *Srbobran* condemned an approach in which 'the Croat and Serb names are held equally dear'. Nevertheless, in 1900 Serb members of the United Youth joined the Serb Independent Party, and in 1902 they took it over, together with its paper.

Before leaving Croatia in 1903 to become Hungarian prime minister, Khuen-Hédervary chose another Slavonian magnate, Teodor Pejačević, as his successor. Nikola Tomašić became Croatian minister in Pest. The Party of Right had by now splintered into a number of mutually warring factions, divided broadly speaking between those who wished to abandon Ante Starčević's policy of total negation of the existing system and those who wished to remain in opposition. Out of this split emerged in 1895 the True Party of Right, led by Josip Frank. In this conflict over the orientation of the old party, Ante Starčević sided with Frank, a capable and active politician who was to make the True Party of Right into a serious political force.[28]

ELEVEN

Redeeming Dalmatia

The negotiating stance adopted by Vienna, following the Peace of Karlovci of 1699, towards the territories gained from the Ottoman Empire was posited on the historical right of the Habsburgs as the sovereign power in Hungary and Croatia. At the behest of the head of the imperial border commission, Luigi Marsigli, the Croatian parliament set up its own special body with the task of sifting through state and private archives for evidence that would support claims against both the Porte and Venice. It reported that in regard to Venice, the archival material showed not only that the republic had usurped places such as Sinj and Knin, but also that Dalmatia had enjoyed no legal existence separate from Croatia. Marsigli was able, therefore, to inform Leopold I that no evidence could be found that 'any place or city in Venetian Dalmatia had ever belonged to a Kingdom of Dalmatia, but only and always to the Kingdom of Croatia: Dalmatia was once, indeed, an integral part of Croatia as a whole'.[1] The Venetians, Marsigli noted in his report, were simply using Dalmatia's name to further their territorial claims, by identifying their Dalmatia with the entirety of the old Roman province.

The Venetians had initially agreed to return to Leopold all the lands in the Dalmatian hinterland that had belonged to the Croato-Hungarian crown, but after the war they simply incorporated the new acquisitions into their Dalmatia. Long after the border issue had been settled, the republic continued to guard itself against Habsburg claims by cultivating a perception of Dalmatia as an ancient Roman province and of the Dalmatian population as a distinct Dalmato-Slav nation derived from the Illyrians – who by now had become firmly identified with the Slavs. The earlier presence of the Croatian kingdom in Dalmatia survived, however, in the archives of Venetian Dalmatia itself, in the titles and deeds related to land ownership and privileges of the Catholic Church, the cities, the nobility and the villagers. When in 1620, for example, the archbishop of Split, Sforza Ponzoni, took peasants living in nearby Kaštela to the Split court over their alleged failure to render him labour and the tithe, he rested his case on a copy of King Trpimir's donation from 825. The lawyer acting for the defendants countered this claim with a copy of a document issued by King Zvonimir, according to which the land in question originally belonged to Croat freemen, hence also to their descendants, thus invalidating all other claims. The legal battle went on for decades, and was ultimately won by the farmers.[2] Such medieval documents were used also by the Dalmatian nobility to back their claims to parts of the land regained from the Ottoman Empire which the Venetian state wished to distribute among the settlers.

Following Dalmatia's final return to Austrian rule in 1817, the Croatian parliament repeated its demands for the province to be restored to its jurisdiction, whereupon Vienna adopted the earlier Venetian view of a Roman-rooted Dalmatia, in the perspective of which Francis Joseph appeared as a direct descendant of the Roman emperor Constantine and the Frankish ruler Charlemagne.[3] The Austrians proclaimed Dalmatia a separate crownland, established a centralised administration with Zadar as the capital, and redrew the ecclesiastical borders to match. The ancient bishopric of Trogir was dissolved and the archbishopric of Split reduced to the status of a bishopric, so that the whole of the Dalmatian church came under the authority of the archbishop of Zadar. The Orthodox congregation was divided into two parishes; but the attempt to push the Serb Orthodox Church into union with Rome failed, this time for good. The Dalmatian Franciscan province, established in the early eighteenth century, was left untouched and in possession of the Catholic parishes on former Ottoman territory. In 1829 primary schools in this area became attached to the monasteries. Of local origin, the Franciscans taught the children in the Croat language, and also to be Croat. They remained ardent supporters of the idea that Dalmatia should join the rest of Croatia. The Orthodox monasteries similarly became the nurseries of a Serb or, more accurately, Great Serb nationalism, since the Orthodox clergy, trained in the monasteries of the Croatian north, brought with them the conviction that all *štokavian* speakers were Serbs.

The Dalmatian cities failed, however, in their task of forging a unified Dalmatian nation, partly because they increasingly spoke Italian. Italian had been the language of the Venetian administration, but it was only during the regime of the Austrian chancellor Klemens Metternich (1821–48) that it became the exclusive language of the Dalmatian urban middle class. Keeping Dalmatia out of Croatia involved discrimination against the Croat language so that Italian became the sole language of the administration, the courts, and instruction in the secondary schools (except for the Franciscan gymnasium in Sinj) as well as in most primary schools. Laws and regulations were published only in Italian, and the local administration was filled with officials from the Austrian Italian provinces, who as a rule did not speak Croat. The teaching of Croat was considered not only useless but harmful, for it discouraged the learning of Italian. Only those who had mastered Italian could expect to be promoted. Since, in addition, practically all Dalmatian students traditionally attended the universities of Padua and Bologna, the new generation of locally recruited bureaucrats likewise found it easier to express themselves in Italian than in Croat. For good measure, the churches that still used Church Slavonic were Latinised. Niccolò Tommaseo, a native proponent of the existence of a distinct Dalmatian or Slavo-Dalmatian nation, neatly summed up Austrian policy in the phrase *Slavus nascitur, Italus fuit* – it entailed turning native Slavs into Italians.

During the early part of the nineteenth century, moreover, the earlier myth of the Slavs as the autochthonous Illyrian population was gradually dismantled, so that the Dalmatian Slavs were no longer perceived as a people whose language and culture derived from antiquity. Their numerical preponderance was not denied, but their language and culture became identified instead with the 'Vlach' world of the Dalmatian hinterland. Italo-Dalmatians now appeared as the bearers of a superior civilisation. For Tommaseo and other champions of the Italian *Risorgimento* at this time, Dalmatia was culturally an Italian province, but also one which, thanks to its Slav nature, was destined to act as a bridge between Italy and the Balkans: the eastern end of what some of them called Ausonia, an entity made up of the Italian peninsula and the Adriatic Sea. In 1848, however, the pro-Italian – and indeed pro-Venetian – options found few takers in Dalmatia. The local nobility and much of the urban middle class remained loyal to Austria, which protected their social status and gave them a sense of political importance. Immersion into Italy, they feared, would make them aliens in their own land. Nor did they wish Dalmatia to unite with Ban's Croatia.[4] The Croatian leaders of the Illyrian movement, who in the 1840s travelled through Dalmatia collecting evidence of its Croatian nature, discovered few urban supporters of union with Ban's Croatia: at this stage they could count only on the lower clergy, and the nobility of Dubrovnik mourning their lost independence. The Italian-speaking urban elite, on the other hand, could find nothing in common between Dalmatia and Ban's Croatia. When the Croatian national assembly of 1848 included in its programme

Dalmatia's incorporation into Ban's Croatia, the provincial elite declined such a prospect and raised instead their own demands for an autonomous Dalmatia with its own parliament, university and national guard, and for free municipal elections. Having opted for Austria, Dalmatia became represented in its parliament, to which it sent eleven deputies. But the revolutionary year supplied also the first generation of Croat national politicians, who would dominate the political life of the province for decades to come. Split emerged as their centre, although as late as 1860 they and their supporters would number no more than forty individuals in a town of some 13,000 inhabitants.[5]

Dalmatia versus Croatia

The suppression of the 1848 revolutions consolidated the so-called Autonomists, a current favouring Dalmatia's autonomy which included the conservative nobility and the Italian-speaking urban middle class. Those who believed in Croatia's right to annex Dalmatia on historical and national grounds became known as Annexationists, or Nationals. This division within the local elite reflected Austrian Dalmatia's composite formation. The appeal of the Slavo-Dalmatian ideology was limited largely to the urban society of the old Venetian Dalmatia, dominated by the traditional oligarchies of the city communes. The territory of the former Republic of Dubrovnik and of Boka Kotorska (the Bay of Kotor), like the peasant society of the former Ottoman lands, did not share this ideology, or only minimally so; accordingly they inclined towards the Nationals. The 'Vlach' hinterland, divided between the districts of Zadar and Split, however, contained a number of small towns struggling to maintain an urban identity which imitated the life of the larger coastal cities and so leaned towards the Autonomists.

Given the nature of their respective constituencies, the division between the Autonomists and the Nationals appeared in the first instance as a linguistic and social opposition between the Italian-speaking towns and the overwhelmingly rural Slav-speaking interior. Which of them was the 'true' Dalmatia? People like Tommaseo argued that the countryside should bow to the will of the towns. The Autonomists of pro-Italian leaning insisted that the nationality of a land was determined by the literate classes, which made Dalmatia an Italian province. In their view both the Croatian and the Slavo-Dalmatian ideologies were nothing but medieval recidivism. Antonio Bajamonti, the charismatic leader of the Split upper class, emerged as the representative of the Italian current within the Autonomist party.

Throughout their history, however, the Autonomists remained prone to fragmentation along the lines of the old city communes. Split and Zadar, in particular, fought for regional pre-eminence: in 1848 they spent much of their time disputing in the Austrian parliament which of the two cities should become Dalmatia's capital. To give itself a more central position, Zadar sought the return of the north Adriatic islands to Dalmatia; Split for that reason argued against it. Faced with the Croatian sabor's demand for the return of Dalmatia, however, the two cities united in defence of its autonomy.

The prospect of union shook Dalmatia to its foundations. According to one observer, its population divided overnight into 'Croats' and 'Italians'.[6] Rural Dalmatia was in favour, urban Dalmatia strongly against. Citizens of Zadar took to attending the theatre wearing badges inscribed with the message: 'We do not wish to be Croats'. *La Voce Dalmatica* (Dalmatia's Voice), the paper of the Autonomists published in Zadar, summed up their case in the following terms: Dalmatia did not participate in either the election of the Habsburgs in 1527 or the acceptance of the Croatian Pragmatic Sanction in 1712. It had become part of Austria not as a result of any Croatian action, but by agreement between Austria and France. Union with Ban's Croatia would not only lead to social and economic regression, it would also endanger Dalmatia's Italian component, since the 'Illyrian' language would become dominant.

The editorial board of *La Voce Dalmatica* saw itself initially as an advocate of Dalmatia's economic and cultural progress. It now divided between Autonomists and Nationals over the issue of union with Ban's Croatia, and more immediately over whether land registers – which recorded the progress of the endemic and bitter struggle between landowners and sharecroppers – should be kept only in Italian or also in Croat. The Nationals left to set up their own paper, *Il Nazionale* (hence their name), the first issue of which appeared on 1 March 1862 in Zadar. Miho Klaić, one of the National Party's founders, wrote to Ivan Kukuljević that its task was to further the cause of union, to acquaint Italian-language readers with Croatia's aspirations, and generally to present the Nationals' policy in a positive light.[7] The paper's first editor was Natko Nodilo from Split, an ardent supporter of union with Ban's Croatia. He announced that the paper's policy was to further national and political freedoms: 'We wish our homeland too to be rejuvenated through freedom's fruitful action, and that the executive should faithfully implement the liberties promised by the imperial diploma. [Then] the national identity of this province will no longer be contested, but will enter as lawful master into indisputable possession of it.'[8]

The paper argued that the nationality of Dalmatia was Slav – Dalmatia at the time had 415,458 inhabitants, of whom only 4 per cent did not speak 'Slav' – and that the Dalmatians' desire to unite with the Croatians in the north reflected their common language and history. Union with Ban's Croatia would preserve, not destroy, Dalmatia's cultural individuality; a united Croatia would guarantee, moreover, the rights of the Italian-speaking minority. The Nationals at this stage did not agree among themselves as to whether 'Slav' meant simply South Slav, or Croat, or indeed Serb – that depended on their individual understanding of Dalmatian history – but a common view was not yet required. What united them was their attachment to the native language and union with Croatia. Their Autonomist opponents evoked economic and cultural progress for their province, but overlooked the fact that popular literacy demanded education in the mother tongue. In 1861 Kosta Vojnović, a prominent National, wrote in reply to Tommaseo's appeal to the Dalmatians to reject union with Croatia that 'one cannot keep people in ignorance for long without being punished for it, for it is a crime against humanity'.[9]

The National Party in Dalmatia closely resembled the National Party in Ban's Croatia, with the difference that the Dalmatians were much more influenced by the Italian movement for national unification. The *Risorgimento* supplied a model which could be applied to Croatia, whose unity followed naturally , they believed, from the Croatian state right and the principle of nationality. Miho Klaić, who together with don Mihovil Pavlinović came to lead the party, was a typical representative of urban Dalmatia. A native of Dubrovnik, he had studied in Padua, Venice and Vienna, and was a great admirer of English and French liberal thought. Italy taught him to associate national-state unity with economic and cultural advance, technological progress (he taught physics and mathematics at the gymnasium in Zadar), and liberal democracy. In a speech to the Dalmatian parliament in 1863, he stated that the Nationals readily acknowledged their Italian education: 'Italian culture is above all a national culture. We Dalmatians, in seeking to create our national culture by removing the adverse [language] duality that divides it, will prove worthy of our noble teacher.'[10] Pavlinović, on the other hand, remained in close touch with the aspirations of the Dalmatian hinterland, which he regularly criss-crossed on horseback and on foot.[11]

The dispute between Nationals and Autonomists over the status and fate of Dalmatia was in the end resolved by the government in Vienna.

The October Diploma of 1860 had constituted a common legislature, the Reichsrat, for all the Monarchy's lands, with delegates to be elected by the crownland parliaments. Zagreb asked that Dalmatia be represented in the Croatian parliament, and promised to respect its autonomy; but Vienna made granting this demand conditional upon Croatian participation in the Reichsrat. The February Patent of 1861 temporarily exempted Dalmatia from the new arrangement and allowed for the possibility of its inclusion into Ban's Croatia – provided, however, that its parliament met to approve this step. The Dalmatian parliament was formally established on 12 February 1861. It now had to be elected.

The parliament was organised as a single-chamber body of forty-three members, of whom two – the Catholic archbishop and the Orthodox bishop – sat by virtue of their office. The right to vote was qualified by taxable wealth. The voters were divided into four electoral colleges or curiae: twenty-one seats were reserved for the landowners, the cities, and the chamber of trade and crafts, and twenty for the rural municipalities. Elections for the first three curiae were direct, and for the last curia indirect: here 500 voters elected each elector, the electors then electing the deputies. The electoral system accordingly delivered control of the parliament to the cities (where the noble landowners habitually lived), leaving the overwhelming majority of the population with only limited representation. The elections were held quickly: the electoral law was published on 8 March and the elections held between 17 and 30 March. Political agitation was prohibited. The Autonomists easily won the coastal cities, but needed police help in the villages and the small towns of the interior. The parliament, which met on 8 April 1861, was composed (in addition to the two prelates) of twelve Nationals and twenty-nine Autonomists. Dubrovnik elected two important National Party leaders, the curia of high tax-payers sending forward Miho Klaić and the city itself Niko Pucić.

The police entered Klaić in their records as 'leader of the ultra-Slav party'. In his report to Vienna, the Dalmatian governor, General Lazar Mamula, wrote that Klaić had until recently displayed a fervent sympathy for the Italian cause, but was now showing similar ardour for Dalmatia's union with Ban's Croatia, as was the Dubrovnik nobleman Niko Pucić. Pucić wrote to the king that his countrymen had elected him because they shared his conviction that union of the two parts of Croatia was 'in the spiritual and economic interest not only of your subjects, but also of the dynasty, [for] our epoch is governed by the principle of nationality'. The Serbian and Ottoman provinces were being 'set into motion by agents of states hostile to Austria,

Miho Klaić

which causes us to fear that the Illyrian nation may evolve in a direction harmful to the empire'. An Austria that relied on its Slavs, however, would 'attract these provinces once Turkey is gone'.[12] Pucić was subsequently to attack Dalmatian regionalism as a joint conspiracy of Austrian bureaucracy and Dalmatian 'pseudo-aristocrats'; the Autonomists in turn portrayed him and his electors as 'the microscopic feudal faction of Ragusa'.

The Autonomist majority voted unanimously against sending a delegation to Zagreb, and instead elected its allocated eleven deputies for the Reichsrat, which Ban's Croatia was boycotting. Only one of these came from the National Party: Stefan Ljubiša, a native of Boka Kotorska. The defeated Nationals left the same day for Zagreb, where they joined the Croatian parliamentary delegation led by Bishop Strossmayer, which was travelling to Vienna. The Autonomists sent their own parliamentary delegation to Vienna, headed by the archbishop of Zadar. At the king's request the two delegations met, but they were unable to reach an agreement. In a symbolic gesture towards national unity, Klaić and Pavlinović were coopted into the Croatian parliament. Vienna moved quickly to seal the Dalmatian outcome. On 13 June 1861 the king activated the relevant land law formalising Dalmatia's constitution as a separate Austrian crownland. The province gained a governmental structure similar to other Austrian provinces: an elected parliament with an executive committee, and a centrally appointed government (lieutenancy council or Giunta) headed by a governor, drawn as a rule from the military. Within a few years Dalmatia acquired also its own provincial court, whose business was conducted by the court of the district of Zadar.

The Croatisation of Dalmatia

Far from aiding Dalmatia's separateness as the central government might have hoped, the introduction of parliamentary democracy stimulated its Croatisation. Despite the limited suffrage, parliamentary and later also municipal elections involved previously voiceless social strata in political life, and made possible Dalmatia's own *Risorgimento*. In contrast to the Croatian north, where the cities directed the tempo of national integration, here the process moved in the opposite direction, in that the countryside became 'nationalised' before the cities. The leaders who saw this process through came from the same social layer as the Autonomists – the world of lawyers, teachers, state employees, government officials, businessmen and nobles – but they also attracted the lower clergy drawn from the rural population. The most agile pro-union faction in Dalmatia proved to be the Franciscans.

In his diaries the former French governor of Dalmatia, General Marmont, described the Dalmatian Franciscans as 'highly educated priests, who are in every way greatly superior to the rest of the clergy in the province'; their friendship, he added, was essential to any government in Dalmatia.[13] For these priests, language was the first and most visible sign of Dalmatia's Croat identity. In 1797, when Croatian Border troops first took Dalmatia, the Franciscans justified its inclusion into Croatia in terms of historical right; but later they laid the stress on national right. In 1848 they wrote to the Croatian Ban Jelačić, who at that time was also governor of Dalmatia, that as Dalmatians and Croats the people wished 'to join and be one with our brothers [in the north]'. The Dalmatian people, they insisted, 'demand and desire nothing else. It is neither just nor right to overlook and negate their large number in favour of a few thousand Italian foreigners and quasi-Dalmatians.' Union with Croatia would defeat those bent on destroying 'two of God's most wonderful gifts: language and nationality'. The Franciscans were accordingly natural allies of the National Party. They participated vigorously in the 1861 parliamentary elections, despite the fact that this made them targets of government persecution.[14]

The programme of the National Party in 1861 was a typical liberal programme with its stress on civic rights (freedom of press, assembly, organisation, equality before law), national and religious equality, economic progress – and federalisation of the Monarchy. Many of these aims were shared by the Autonomists. What differentiated the Nationals from the Autonomists was their demand for union with Ban's Croatia and for introduction of the Croat (or 'Slav') language into the schools, the courts and the administration. Their language policy brought them the loyalty of the rural interior. Rural Dalmatia provided the Nationals with a secure base that they would use to launch their campaign for control of the cities. There could indeed be no unified nation in Dalmatia so long as city walls kept the peasantry out.

Although the party at this stage united Croats and Serbs, and chose its local and parliamentary candidates by agreement and regardless of ethnicity, and although the party scored an early victory in the predominantly Serb areas, Dalmatia's 'nationalisation' inevitably meant its Croatisation. The population was 82 per cent Catholic and 18 per cent Orthodox, but the Catholics formed 93 per cent of the urban population. Serb votes were concentrated in two locations, one in the north[15] and one in the south,[16] embracing four electoral districts which together contributed seven parliamentary seats. In the elections of 1861 six of these went to the Nationals, and subsequently all seven. Most of the elected deputies were ethnic Serbs. But while the Serbs were at different times able to win additional seats in other areas or curiae, their electoral reach remained essentially unchanged at this level. This meant that the contest between Nationals and Autonomists over Dalmatia's destination would be decided by the predominantly Croat areas – and by the cities in particular, since they dominated political life. If the Nationals were to win Dalmatia, therefore, they had to win the cities; and in order to win the cities, their elites had to become accustomed to the national language. This was to be accomplished by opening 'Slav' reading rooms in all the major towns, a venture made possible by Strossmayer's patriotic largesse. The first such reading room opened in Zadar in 1863.

Major cities of Austrian Dalmatia in 1857 and 1869 by size[17]

City	1857	1869
Split	10,358	12,196
Zadar	7,560	8,292
Šibenik	6,611	6,821
Dubrovnik	4,346	6,032
Korčula	2,168	1,992
Hvar	1,904	1,930
Total	32,947	37,263

The institutional triad of reading rooms, newspapers and elections provided the necessary instruments for the pursuit of national unification. The hub of the National Party's organisation was the club of its deputies in the Dalmatian parliament, while the reading rooms acted as the party's local branches. Given the small size of the Dalmatian cities and of the electorate, the

Mihovil Pavlinović

deputies were locally known as teachers, doctors, lawyers and parish priests. At election times the parliamentary club formulated the party's programme, *Il Nazionale*, with its Croat supplement, *Narodni list*, popularised it, and the clergy would take the message to the villages. The paper reported on parliamentary proceedings, criticised the government, debated major political issues, reported on events in the Monarchy (especially in Ban's Croatia) and abroad, and generally nurtured a sense of national cohesion by stressing the bond between the towns and the countryside. Two reports, published in *Il Nazionale* and *Narodni list* in 1870, provide an insight into how this system worked. One deals with the opening of a reading room in Imotski, a small town in the Dalmatian interior. Mihovil Pavlinović, who was invited to do the formalities, was met two miles from the town by local dignitaries and the representative of the reading room at Sinj. 'It was wonderful to watch the blending of plain [peasant] caps and smart [town] hats. The carriage was drawn by horses arrayed in the Croat manner, with the Austrian flag fluttering next to the Croatian.' At ten o'clock that morning Pavlinović said the Mass in Church Slavonic in the local Franciscan church, after which he was ceremoniously conducted to the new reading room. On entering it, the correspondent continues somewhat emotionally, 'tears came to my eyes as I looked at [...] humble peasants and learned gentlemen standing squeezed against each other in order to better hear the speaker – all these people sensing their future and being aware. This nation, I felt, cannot be destroyed.' After a welcoming address by the local mayor, the guest spoke. He was heard 'in deep silence interrupted by frequent exclamations, approval, clapping, and sobs. We all followed him in embracing the banner of the Croatian [state] right.'

The second report describes elections in the Imotski district for the provincial parliament. It illustrates the importance of reading rooms on such occasions, and how disciplined the peasant constituencies could be under their own leaders. The peasants – all 843 of them who had the right to vote – arrived in Imotski led by their village heads and priests. 'Once in town, they were able to see that they all spoke the same Croat language.' The voters gathered in the reading room, then marched on to the polling station 'without a clamour or any kind of disruption, to cast their vote for electors who were bound to elect as their representative an honest and diligent man, a true native and patriot.' The forty-two elected electors, all candidates of the National Party, proceeded unanimously to elect Mihovil Pavlinović. The Autonomist minority abstained. This outcome, the journalist wrote with glee, 'should finally convince the foreigners in our country that its true sons are Croats, not Hungarians or Germans as some would have it'. When the business of voting was over, the people and their new parliamentary representative met again in the reading room. Pavlinović's speech, the journalist was able to report, 'enlightened everyone about what we once were and what we are now; and that we have the same rights and the same common purpose as our [Croatian] brothers beyond [Mount] Velebit.'[18] In the two speeches mentioned in these reports, however, Pavlinović departed from the general policy of the National Party by affirming Dalmatia as a Croat rather than a generically Slav land.

Having failed to achieve union with Ban's Croatia from above, the Nationals concentrated on realising it from below through the medium of language. Their aim was to achieve equality of the Croat and Italian languages in public life, as a prelude to the eventual total elimination of the latter. Education in the national language was indeed a priority: if Dalmatia was to have a Croat-speaking administration, its schools would have to produce a sufficient number of individuals educated in the Croat language to replace the Italian- and German-speaking bureaucrats. The Nationals broached the issue of the language during the first parliamentary session, in 1861, when Pavlinović asked that its draft laws be made available also in Croat, and that the business of parliament and government be conducted in both languages. Juraj Pulić, another National Party supporter who was rector of the gymnasium in Zadar, demanded the same for the courts and schools. The leader of the house tried to deflect these demands by referring to the cost involved, but Klaić retorted that 400,000 inhabitants deserved that this money be spent. Pavlinović's proposal was accepted, but Pulić's was forwarded to a special committee. The Nationals tried to win official support for their language policy by presenting it as a common good, as well as being in Austria's own interest. In 1863 Klaić told the parliament that a more enlightened language policy in Dalmatia would make the Habsburg

Monarchy the natural heir of the Ottoman Empire. Instead, 'by mercilessly removing the Croato-Serb language from public life, it is not only inviting Italy's expansion to this side of the Adriatic, but also erecting a Chinese wall between Dalmatia and the neighbouring land [of Bosnia-Herzegovina], where the people despite their distress can at least comfort themselves that the kadi and the mufti conduct justice in their language, while most Dalmatians do not understand either the judges or their verdicts.' Incomprehension of the judicial procedure, he went on, made ordinary people lose faith in justice and incline towards crime.[19]

In 1864 the Dalmatian parliament's drafting commission recommended unanimously that the municipalities should be able to decide which language would be taught in the primary schools in their area. In secondary schools and gymnasia – with the exception of the Sinj gymnasium, where Croat would continue to be used – Italian would remain the language of instruction; but Croat might be used for teaching certain subjects, such as history. The courts would be allowed to use Croat in civic and penal cases, and officials dealing with the public should know Croat, that is, should have passed the necessary examination; but other officials wishing to use Croat would have to obtain first permission from their superiors. On this occasion Klaić told the house that 'the use of the mother tongue is a natural and primary right of every nation and cannot, therefore, be a matter of a legal concession, let alone prohibition'. He reminded the deputies that the 1858 Austrian law on the use of national languages in schools was not being applied in Dalmatia, and asked that Croat be imposed in schools, so that future officials would know the language of the people.

The smooth passage of the new law on municipal self-government and language provision was ensured by a prior agreement between the Nationals and the Autonomists' more liberal wing, represented by the mayor of Split, Antonio Bajamonti. Once the threat of union with Ban's Croatia had receded, the Autonomists divided over local issues. Their disunity was encouraged by the fact that the Nationals proved a cooperative opposition. Convinced that the natural weight of the Slav population would sooner or later give them control of parliament, the Nationals concentrated on ensuring respect for procedure in the conduct of elections and in the work of parliament itself. Dalmatia's most important problem was its isolation from the rest of the Monarchy. Its ports were stagnating, since Austria and Hungary concentrated on developing, respectively, Trieste and Rijeka as their main trade outlets. This isolation could be broken only by a railway line to link Dalmatia with its hinterland, and here the old competition between

Split and Zadar re-emerged. Bajamonti saw his city as the heir of ancient Salona, namely as the natural centre of exchange between the Appennine and Balkan peninsulas. This could be achieved by building a railway connecting Split with Sarajevo and Belgrade – but the Austrian government rejected such a plan, for political reasons. Zadar, on the other hand, supported the Croatian parliament's proposal for a railway linking Zemun, Zagreb, Rijeka and Zadar – but Vienna, unsure at this stage whether Ban's Croatia would join Austria or remain with Hungary, would not support this project either. Various other routes were proposed at different times for a rail link between Dalmatia and northern Croatia, some going through Bosnia and others not, but the rivalry between Austria and Hungary always intervened and the link was never built.

At a deeper level the Autonomists split between supporters and opponents of Austrian centralism. Although the Nationals regularly denounced all regionalists as crypto-Italians, most of them were in fact loyal to Austria. Luigi Lapenna, head of the provincial court and a member of the Dalmatian and Austrian parliaments, who acted as an unelected leader of the loyalists, favoured centralism. He was able to count on the support of the local Austrian officials, the Church hierarchy, and the noble landowners. As an ardent Italian nationalist, Bajamonti became the leader of the opponents of centralism among the Autonomists. While for Lapenna the Dalmatian regional ideology was a useful tool against both Croatian and Italian nationalisms, for Bajamonti it was simply a tactical manoeuvre appropriate to a period that he saw as an *interregnum* at the end of which Dalmatia would join Italy. The desire to limit the central state's interference in Dalmatia's political life led to the emergence of a Liberal Alliance composed of the Nationals and Bajamonti's Autonomists. A deal was struck according to which the Nationals would abide by the will of the parliamentary majority in regard to the issue of union with Ban's Croatia, and in return Bajamonti's side would support equality of the 'Slav' and Italian languages. Bajamonti sealed the agreement with words that became the motto of the whole Autonomist movement: '*Slavi anche domani, Croati mai!*' ('Slavs gladly, Croats never!'). The Liberal Union deputies in the Reichsrat were instructed to complain of Dalmatia's parlous state; to demand separation of the civilian and military administrations joined in the person of the governor; and to vote with the moderate federalists there. The government in Vienna reacted to the emergence of the Liberal Union by dissolving the Dalmatian parliament two years ahead of its proper time. New elections took place in the summer of 1864, which the Union fought together. Seeking to weaken the Nationals, the Dalmatian governor, General Mamula, managed to persuade the Orthodox bishop Stefan Knežević – and by extension his congregation – to withdraw support from the National Party and vote for Lapenna's loyalists. The elections were handsomely won by the government in Vienna, which intervened heavily to ensure the right result. The new parliament was filled with state employees. Out of forty-three seats the Nationals gained seven and the Liberal Autonomists three.

Peasants into Citizens

However, the first municipal elections, held in 1865, undermined this parliament's legitimacy. They were organised in accordance with the law on local government that divided voters into three tax-based curiae with twenty votes each. These elections were politically more representative than those for the provincial parliament, since all voters voted directly. They were also of exceptional importance, given that the municipalities now had the right to decide the language of instruction in primary schools.

The Nationals mobilised the peasants with promises of lower taxes and redivision of land, and stressed the social divide between Slav-speaking peasants and Italian-speaking landowners. A popular cry was: 'Attack the palaces!' The Autonomists denounced the Nationals as revolutionaries who campaigned under foreign – Croatian and Russian (that is, Serbian) – flags. In the cities the main battle was fought between the liberal middle class and the conservative bureaucracy. Bajamonti easily regained Split. The Liberal Union also won Šibenik, despite the local bishop's excommunication of its leaders. In Trogir most voters abstained, leaving the city in the possession of the local patrician Fanfogna family. In Dubrovnik the Nationals won the votes not only of those who felt themselves to be Croat or Serb, but also of those who remained faithful to the memory of the Dubrovnik republic's independence. In the traditionally restless municipality of Knin, the elections took place in the presence of the army. Fearing electoral fraud, the peasants stormed the municipal hall to take from 'the Italians' what they felt was rightfully theirs, since it had been built with their taxes. The army intervened, leaving several dead and wounded. The ensuing uproar led to General Lazar Mamula being replaced with another soldier from the Military Border, General Franjo Filipović. The new governor released the rebels from the Knin prison, including the National Party's candidate, Lovro Monti, who walked from his prison cell to the town hall to assume his duties as mayor of Knin. Klaić was now convinced that the Nationals would easily win the next parliamentary elections, provided that the central government did not interfere.

A survey of electoral results shows that the Nationals had won the countryside in the very first municipal elections.[20] Dalmatia was organised into eighty municipalities, which politically could be divided into roughly two zones. The first zone comprised the hinterland and the south: its forty-four municipalities sent twenty deputies to the local parliament. The second zone consisted of the old Venetian Dalmatia: its thirty-six municipalities sent twenty-one deputies. In 1865 the Nationals won outright forty-two municipalities, all in the first zone, and shared another fifteen with Bajamonti's Autonomists. The first zone would provide the Nationals with a secure base, but it was only by winning a majority also in the second that they could be sure that Dalmatia's Croatisation would become irreversible. This second zone was not homogeneous, however. It consisted of a demographically smaller region gravitating towards Zadar and Šibenik, and the more densely populated and economically increasingly dominant region centred on Split, which included the islands of Brač, Hvar and Vis. The Zadar-Šibenik region contained twelve municipalities, which sent eleven deputies to the provincial parliament. The region of Split embraced twenty-four municipalities with ten deputies. Winning Split became a chief preoccupation of the National Party leaders.

In 1865 the Austrian prime minister Anton von Schmerling resigned and the February Patent, which he had helped to craft, was suspended. He was replaced by the federalist Richard Belcredi. Schmerling's departure removed the need for the Liberal Alliance, while the new government's federalist course made cooperation between the Nationals and the Autonomists more difficult. That year Miho Klaić and Mihovil Pavlinović were elected to the Croatian sabor. When the sabor reopened the issue of reunification, the Dalmatian Nationals responded by proposing that the Dalmatian parliament should resume negotiations with Zagreb. This was rejected: on that issue the Autonomists were united. In 1866 Bajamonti's group refused to support a proposal for equality of Croat and Italian in the secondary schools and the courts. The tottering Liberal Alliance was dealt a final blow by the Austrian-Italian war of 1866, which highlighted Dalmatia's importance for the Monarchy. On 20 July 1866 the Austrian navy, manned largely by Dalmatians, spectacularly defeated the Italian fleet at Vis. The Nationals attributed this victory not to Admiral Wilhelm von Tegethoff's martial skills but to Croat valour, decried the Autonomists yet again as crypto-Italians, and depicted the growing Italian immigration into Dalmatia as a potential fifth column. The hastily assembled territorial guard, recruited from the local population to act against a possible Italian landing, took to displaying Croat and Serb colours.

Italy's push for Dalmatia further weakened the position of the Italian-speaking Dalmatians. In an effort to prevent their marginalisation, the rising industrial class of Zadar in 1866 funded the foundation of the journal *Il Dalmata* as mouthpiece of the now formally constituted Autonomous Party, with a programme that embraced liberalism and constitutionalism. The editors wrote that they belonged to the Dalmatian party, which by definition was autonomous 'in the fullest sense', and stressed their membership of the Slav world: 'We are Slavs not only by birth, but in our hearts and feelings.' The projected party was stillborn, however. The founding meeting revealed a deep split between the liberal bourgeoisie, which wished to create a modern centralised party capable of overcoming local and class differences, and the nobility, which saw it as a corporate organisation of different social groups. Speaking two decades later, Lapenna stated that the party's chief aim had been to protect Italian language and culture, and to counter Croat propaganda portraying the Autonomists as an Italian party of irredentist orientation, hostile both to the Slavs and to the government in Vienna.

In the Croatian north, Ivan Mažuranić, who had counted on Vienna's support to achieve the union of Dalmatia with Ban's Croatia, left his post as head of the Croatian office in Vienna. The Dalmatian Nationals welcomed his departure, since at this stage they supported Croatia's alliance with Hungary; but after the Monarchy's removal from Germany, Klaić advocated a break with Hungary, and Croatian representation in the Reichsrat. Belcredi's replacement by Beust in early 1867, however, ended the period of flirtation with federalism and opened the road to dualism. In the Austrian parliament Dalmatian deputies voted in favour of the Austro-Hungarian Compromise. The Autonomists welcomed dualism because it would finally settle the issue of Dalmatia's status; the Nationals did not, for it kept Dalmatia out of Croatia. They expressed solidarity with the Croatian sabor, supported its side in the negotiation with Hungary, and expressed a desire for Dalmatia to rejoin Hungary of the crown as part of Croatia. When these negotiations broke down, they refused to participate in the elections for the Reichsrat in order to facilitate Croatia's negotiations with Vienna.

Following the conclusion of the Croato-Hungarian Compromise, the Autonomists drafted an address to the king thanking him for anchoring Dalmatia firmly to Austria. The Nationals, while criticising the terms of the Compromise, kept up their courage by an optimistic interpretation of its overall meaning. They greeted Hungary's declaration of support for Dalmatia's return to Croatia, pointed to those articles of the Compromise that treated Dalmatia formally as part of Croatia, and stressed that Vienna had never denied that Dalmatia belonged to the lands of the Hungarian crown. They stated that they were willing to accept the new arrangement, but would also seek to alter it. Their view that the 'issue of the [Croatian state] right is outside the Reichsrat's competence' was not shared, however, by the Austrian government. On 15 January 1869 the Austrian deputy prime minister, Eduard Taaffe, told the Austrian parliament that Dalmatia's union with Ban's Croatia was now a matter for it to decide. The union, in reality, was placed *ad acta* – filed away.

Winning Dalmatia

In these circumstances the National Party became Vienna's natural partner in Dalmatia. Fearing Italian irredentism, the central government removed most, though not all, remaining barriers to the advance of the Croat language. In 1866 Governor Filipović ordered that Croat be made a language of instruction in all primary schools: knowledge of Croat would henceforth be obligatory for all teachers. Croat was to be used also in the courts in cases involving Croat speakers, and knowledge of both languages would be required of state employees. In May 1868 the state introduced obligatory eight-year schooling. By the time Filipović left the province, sixty-five municipalities used Croat in the schools, while eighteen Autonomist controlled municipalities continued to resist bilingual education. Croat became the language of instruction also in the gymnasia of Dubrovnik, Kotor and Šibenik, although the gymnasia in the Autonomist cities of Zadar, Split and Korčula retained Italian.

The government directives on the use of the Croat language, however, were either disobeyed or applied only to the lower rungs of the civil service. The Autonomists verbally supported language equality in parliament, but resisted it in practice. The real problem, however, was that the existing schools were as yet unable to produce a sufficient number of Croat-speaking scholars. To ease this situation, the government permitted the import of school textbooks from Ban's Croatia. Miho Klaić, who was appointed director of schools, wrote to Franjo Rački: 'This way we can unite at a metaphysical level until the time comes when we can unite also politically. That, I fear, will not be soon, unless outside events, especially in the East, intervene. [In the meantime] I would be grateful, if you would send me the guidelines applying to your primary and secondary schools [since] I prefer to follow your example.' He promised to consult Rački in all matters so that 'we can achieve unity wherever and whenever we can'.[21] The cooperation with Zagreb scuppered Austria's feeble attempt to make 'Illyro-Dalmatian', the local Croat dialect, into Dalmatia's national language. *Il Dalmata* was forced to admit that the standard language issuing from Zagreb was winning in Dalmatia.

The battle over language now engulfed the whole of Dalmatia. Some Autonomists treated the introduction of Croat into public life as de facto union with Ban's Croatia, which they depicted as a land of 'barbarian laws, all-embracing military service and a torture'. The respected National Party supporter Vid Morpurgo was attacked in Split by Bajamonti's champions, who marched through the streets shouting 'Death to the Croats!' and tore down Croatian flags. In some cities supporters of the National Party were put on trial and dismissed from their jobs. In Sinj local Autonomists charged the Franciscans with wishing to instal Orthodoxy because they allowed visits from the Orthodox clergy. Mihovil Pavlinović toured the interior on horseback thundering against 'Italomanes' and 'bureaucrats'. *Il Dalmata*, frightened by the growing involvement of the masses in politics and the unstoppable Croatisation of the schools, repeatedly stressed its own Slav orientation. The Dalmatian identity, it wrote, was not a matter of national declaration but of civilisational standard. It was able to point to the local parliament, where Nationals with Italian surnames such as Monti, Fontana, Raimondi, Antonietti or Machiedo sat together with Autonomists bearing Slav names like Knežević, Petrović, Bujas, Buljan or Kapović.

In their reaction to dualism, some of the National leaders turned ostentatiously to Russia. In 1867 they joined other Austro-Hungarian Slavs in a visit to an ethnographic exhibition in Moscow. *Il Dalmata* denounced the Nationals as Russian spies and anarchists financed by Moscow. General Filipović, who had been sent to Dalmatia to speed up the introduction of the Croat language into public life and generally democratise the local government, was now judged to have been too successful and was withdrawn. At the same time, however, the Austrian constitution of 21 December 1867 – which underscored civic rights, independence of the judiciary, religious freedoms, national equality and protection of minorities – aided the Nationals' advance and Dalmatia's Croatisation. Although in the parliamentary elections of 1867 the reunited Autonomists won twenty-six seats and the Nationals a mere fifteen, the latter continued to gain at the municipal level.

The legal package adopted by the Reichsrat in May 1868 introduced not only schools in the national language, but also general conscription. In 1869 the government's attempt to draft men in the areas of Dubrovnik and Kotor who had previously been exempt caused a local uprising. In the ensuing battle between the army and the insurgents, several hundreds were killed on both sides. Kotor was placed under a state of emergency, and six warships with 10,000 soldiers were sent to Boka Kotorska (the Bay of Kotor). The unrest coincided with the opening of the Suez Canal. The new Dalmatian governor, General Ivan (Johann) Wagner, suggested to Vienna to extend the state of emergency throughout Dalmatia in order finally to eliminate the 'ultra-Slav party'. The Kotor area was pacified in 1870, however, after which the rebels were amnestied. Denied a place in Germany, Austria was turning towards the Balkans and the Bay of Kotor appeared an ideal southern location for the Austrian navy. Beust offered financial assistance to Montenegro, and persuaded Turkey to evacuate the last garrisons in Serbia. There were plans to build a railway line linking Vienna with Salonica. Wagner now departed to become Austrian minister of defence, and was replaced by a retired privy councillor, Joseph Baron Fluck von Leidenkorn.

In the municipal elections in the spring of 1870 the Nationals made a determined effort to gain Zadar. On election day supporters and opponents of the Autonomists fought in its streets. In the nearby town of Benkovac two voters were killed and several wounded. The Autonomists held Zadar, but the Nationals won fifty municipalities, including Dubrovnik, and shared four with the Autonomists. The feverish atmosphere carried over into the parliamentary elections of 4–9 July 1870. There was an attempt to blow up the Franciscan monastery in Sinj, but the friars nevertheless delivered both Sinj and Drniš to the Nationals. *Il Dalmata* subsequently wrote that the voters had been bribed with wine, false promises and money sent by Prague, Zagreb and Moscow; but in reality it was the central government's neutrality that made the difference. Governor Fluck's decision, prompted by Vienna, not to interfere in the elections led the Autonomists to charge him with collusion with the Nationals. He subsequently wrote that 20,000 Italian-speakers could not rule except by force over 400,000 Slavs.[22]

In the event the Nationals won twenty-nine seats and the Autonomists twelve. The pro-union party was finally in control of the Dalmatian parliament – a situation that would remain unchanged to the end of the Monarchy. The new parliament opened on 2 September 1870. The Nationals took over the running of both the assembly and the executive committee, and elected five deputies – named by the Autonomists 'Yugoslavia's Five' – to the Reichsrat. Zagreb joyfully celebrated this victory as did much of

Dalmatia. Some viewed it as the most significant and glorious national event since 1848. The euphoric Nationals declared the Autonomists 'the party of the dead'. The Autonomists, however, still retained a string of important cities, including Zadar, Split and Trogir. They also held the central Dalmatian islands of Brač, Hvar and Vis. Rural Dalmatia had contributed the lion's share of the National Party's victory: seventeen out of the twenty village seats. The cities were evenly divided, with five seats going to the Nationals and six to the Autonomists. Most of the landowners remained in the Autonomist camp, however: in the curia of high taxpayers, the Nationals won only three out of ten seats. The Dalmatian Autonomist nobility could not understand the modern phenomenon of nationalism: being Italian or Croat was to them purely a matter of personal choice. The conflict that concerned them most was the old one over land produce and labour dues. In their eyes the Nationals represented the illiterate masses and peasant republicanism. *Il Dalmata* wrote that the victory of the National Party demanded the formation of an alliance between the nobility and the middle class against 'rustic Slavs'.[23]

Italy's unification and Croatia's return to Dalmatia led to a questioning of the value of a purely regional ideology. Bajamonti argued ever more forcefully that 'it is not the culture, but the language which will in future guarantee equal rights'. This meant adoption of Italian nationality. Lapenna disagreed. In 1875, on the eve of new elections for the Reichsrat, he warned that: 'it would be a great mistake to erect in Dalmatia an Italian National Party as a counter-weight to the [Slav] National Party'. The Autonomists, now condemned to eternal opposition, renamed themselves the Constitutional Party and formed their own club in the Dalmatian parliament. Defence of the Italian language became their chief priority.

The impotence of victory

Vienna's neutrality came at a price. During the election campaign of 1869–70 Klaić, much to the annoyance of his National friends in the north, failed to mention the issue of unification. He told his intimate circle that the party's priority was to win the elections, and that the National Party should cooperate with the government in Vienna for the sake of Dalmatia's development. When the new parliament met, it was faced with the delicate problem of choosing representatives for the parliament in Vienna. The Independent National Party, which was leading the resistance to dualism in Ban's Croatia, urged them to guard Croatia's territorial integrity by refusing to participate in the Austrian parliament, and to elect instead a delegation to negotiate with the Croatian sabor. The Nationals, however, felt unable to comply. Their paper wrote that the Dalmatians could not wait for the complicated situation in Ban's Croatia to be resolved, risking their majority by attacking the Austrian constitution. Their duty was to use the means at their disposal to prepare the grounds for unification. Klaić told the parliament that sending deputies to the Austrian parliament was for Dalmatia a constitutional issue, which derived from laws older than those which had created the Reichsrat. Dalmatia's right, which rested on 'historical, juridical and natural foundations, was the right to be one state with Croatia-Slavonia. Since Croatia was not represented in the Reichsrat, Dalmatia could not be either.' But Dalmatia could not proceed towards unification under the terms of the Croato-Hungarian Compromise, which, having been reached without Dalmatia's participation, was legally invalid. The parliament should, therefore, elect deputies to the Austrian parliament, and at the same time affirm that the act in no way infringed the Croatian state right in regard to Dalmatia. Once in Vienna, the Dalmatian deputies would press the king to create the necessary conditions in the Croatian lands for their representatives to meet and decide on unification. Klaić's proposal was accepted and the delegates elected.

The Nationals vested their hopes in their control of the Dalmatian parliament, Vienna's good will, and 'world events'. They now held most of Dalmatia, but their control remained uncertain as long as the Autonomists held the two most important cities, Zadar and Split. In Zadar the parliament's deliberations were now regularly disturbed by its pro-Italian galleries, and it was not always safe for National deputies to walk through the city streets. The old pro-Autonomist bureaucracy too was hostile. Given the Autonomists' hold over the main cities and the resistance of the inherited administration to the transfer of power, the Nationals could not afford to alienate the government in Vienna. For its part Vienna accepted a National parliamentary majority, but worked to check its influence. General Gabrijel Rodić arrived as governor with the task of doing precisely that. There was to be no peace between the parliament controlled by the Nationals and the Giunta appointed by the central government. A request by National deputies in the Reichsrat for the replacement of recalcitrant officials was rejected. The landowner Antonio Fanfogna was given back his old post as mayor of Trogir, which he would keep for another fifteen years. In 1872, however, the Nationals won a by-election in the municipality of Šibenik, when the local peasants, fired by their anti-Italian propaganda, marched to the city in columns headed by the local clergy and National Party leaders.

The parliament now adopted a draft law making Croat and Italian equal in the administration and in the courts. The emblems and seals on all official documents other than those of the army, meanwhile, were to be inscribed only in Croat. The Austrian government refused to sanction this law, however, on the grounds that Dalmatia had no right to decide the state's language policy. Nevertheless, unsettled by the progressive 'nationalisation' of Dalmatia, the Autonomists felt they could no longer rely solely on reading rooms to maintain popular support in their last urban strongholds, so they turned to organising cultural and gymnastic societies, beginning with the paramilitary *Società del tiro a bersaglio* (Target-shooting Association) fashioned on the model of Giuseppe Garibaldi's volunteers. Such societies were established in Zadar and Split in 1871. The *bersaglieri* were supposed to protect 'civilisational values', but were in reality meant to guard against 'arrogant' Nationals. The Autonomists also proceeded to create labour associations, such as the *Concordia e lavoro* organised in Bajamonti's Split by don Giovanni Delich. Music bands became another favoured form of urban mobilisation.

The Nationals now set their sights on Split. In 1872 the parliamentary auditing commission (which the Autonomist press promptly nicknamed *Torquemada*) visited the city to investigate the council books, as well as Bajamonti's own company, *Associazione Dalmatica*. Unwilling to let the Nationals take Split, the Giunta declined to dissolve the city council, so Bajamonti won that round; but the war for Split continued by other means. In 1870 Vid Morpurgo, the Split notable and pro-National politician, founded the First Dalmatian People's Bank, aimed at local sharecroppers and peasants. The struggle over language also continued unabated throughout the 1870s. Klaić did not seek to exclude Italian altogether: convinced that there was no Italian nationality in Dalmatia, he believed that the language would die out naturally. In the Split gymnasium at this time, out of eighty-two Slav students only two could speak Italian. The gymnasium of Zadar had thirty Slav and eight Italian students. By the middle of the 1880s Croat became the customary language of the Dalmatian parliament and its executive, although Italian remained the language of external communication in some departments. By now practically all municipalities and schools used only Croat. The exception was the gymnasium in Zadar, which remained the only Italian-language secondary school in Dalmatia

Cooperation with Vienna promised the realisation of hitherto elusive projects such as a Dalmatian railway and drainage of the Neretva estuary, which Dalmatia could not undertake on its own, given that its income was habitually inadequate to finance the province's needs. The Nationals consequently joined the side of Hohenwart's conservative government in the central parliament. This government fell after the German and Hungarian Liberals refused to accept the agreement that Hohenwart had reached with the Czechs, in order to persuade them to end their boycott of the Reichsrat. The new government opted for another course. In 1872 it put through the Reichsrat an 'emergency elections' law permitting the emperor-king to dissolve the crownland parliaments in certain circumstances. To the disgust of the Monarchy's other Slavs, the five Dalmatian National deputies voted with the government in return for promises of investment in Dalmatia. Miho Klaić insisted that the opportunistic policy that the party had adopted in 1870, when it elected deputies for the Reichsrat, remained a political necessity. If the Nationals were to make use of their majority in the Dalmatian parliament, they had to safeguard that majority and not sacrifice it for the sake of 'political sentimentality'. The alternative, he argued, was to go into total opposition.

The new government, however, proved not to be so friendly to the Nationals. In 1873 the Austrian parliament was asked to vote for a new electoral law according to which deputies to the Reichsrat would no longer be elected by crownland parliaments, but directly. This was to be the last nail in the coffin of federalism, and the Autonomists welcomed direct elections for this reason. The Austrian Slav deputies asked the Dalmatians to join them in boycotting the measure. Although the Dalmatian National deputies were instructed by their party to vote against the law, they nevertheless voted with the government. The party leaders denounced their conduct as an attack on the party, the parliament, the nation and the Austrian Slavs, and expelled them from the party. This was good news for Governor Rodić, who had been seeking to create a new loyalist party in Dalmatia. Supported by Rodić, the ejected deputies, headed by Stefan Ljubiša, formed a National Centre Party with its own paper *Zemljak* (Countryman). Klaić declared a 'war to the end' against them, but the campaign was impeded by unforeseen events. The financial crash of that year sent the whole Monarchy into an economic decline. Projects promised by the central government were suspended. Many of the municipalities held by the National municipalities went bankrupt. The Nationals asked for a 25 per cent increase in taxes to pay for schools and hospitals, but the Autonomists refused their support. The overtaxed peasantry blamed the Nationals. The battle against Ljubiša's party was complicated also by a rising liberal-conservative conflict within the Catholic body. Suspicious of the National Party's liberalism and Slavism, parts of the

Catholic clergy started their own paper, *La Dalmazia Cattolica*. In some places the Catholic clergy opted for the conservative Autonomists rather than the liberal Nationals. For his part the Orthodox bishop denounced the Nationals as enemies of God. Putting up clerics as election candidates, on the other hand, offended the liberal voters in other areas. The Autonomists and the *Zemljak* group, moreover, sought to divide the traditional National Party 'Slav' base by initiating a dispute on Croat-Serb relations in Dalmatia, that is, by claiming that Dalmatia was a Serb land.[24]

In the winter of 1873 came the first direct elections for the Reichsrat. Klaić was a candidate in the mixed Catholic-Orthodox district of Zadar-Benkovac. Rodić tried to persuade the Autonomists to form an electoral alliance with the *Zemljak* group, but the Autonomists, directed by Lapenna, decided in the end to go it alone. This proved a sensible decision. They won five of Dalmatia's nine seats, the Nationals three (Miho Klaić, Lovro Monti and Mihovil Pavlinović), and the *Zemljak* group only one (Stefan Ljubiša). Klaić's election was subsequently declared invalid, so Pavlinović gave him his own seat. Apart from the fact that Ljubiša's party now folded up, the only good news for the Nationals was the opening of the University of Zagreb in 1874, an event attended by a large delegation from Dalmatia. Two prominent members of the Dalmatian National Party, Kosta Vojnović and Natko Nodilo, were given chairs at the new university. The Dalmatians' visit caused uproar in Vienna and Pest: the Croatians were charged with being clerical and conservative, and simultaneously with being dangerously radical in wishing to destroy dualism by creating a Yugoslav state within the Habsburg Monarchy.

Fearing the loss of majority in the parliament, Klaić sought to keep the National Party together. He drafted a programme, which the majority of its parliamentary club adopted, though Pavlinović and Vojnović did not. It included the following points: 1. the party remains strongly committed to the Croatian state right and Dalmatia's unification with Ban's Croatia; 2. the Slavs are the only nationality in Dalmatia and the club will continue to work for the latter's advance; 3. the party will do nothing that might harm other Slav nations, especially those of Austria-Hungary; 4. it will continue to uphold full political, confessional and cultural equality of Croats and Serbs in Dalmatia; 5. while remaining wholly independent of the government in Vienna, the party will support it in matters of national interest. This programme, however, did not prevent the departure of Serb politicians from the National Party.

On the other hand, the elections marked a decline of the nobility's

Arrival of Francis Joseph in Zadar, 1875

influence within the Autonomist bloc. In Zadar Niccolò Trigari, of plebeian origins, replaced Count Cosimo Begna as mayor. Trigari's victory encouraged the Italian radicals in Split to try to seize the leadership of the Autonomist Party. Bajamonti's new paper, *L'Avvenire* (The Future), argued in favour of its transformation into an Italian party – the very thing that Lapenna had tried to prevent. The steady loss of municipalities and schools during the 1870s, however, had undermined Lapenna's position. His opponents among the Autonomists insisted that there were two distinct nationalities in Dalmatia, the Slav and the Italian, which should have equal rights. By declaring themselves Italians, the Italian-speaking Dalmatians could expect support from both Austria and Italy. The majority of the Autonomists, however, could not follow in this direction. The Italianisation of the Autonomist Party actually worked in favour of the Croatisation of its Slav component, although an Autonomist residue would remain alive in Dalmatia until well into the twentieth century.

In May 1875 Francis Joseph visited Dalmatia. The speaker of parliament, Stefan Ljubiša, welcomed him in Croat/Serb, and the king replied in Italian. The Zadar *bersaglieri* greeted him in Italian, Bajamonti referred to him as 'constitutional emperor', while the Nationals hailed him as 'King of Croatia'. On the occasion of his visit to the gymnasium in Split, Humbert Borelli, son of the leading Autonomist Count Francesco Borelli, wore the Croatian tricolour on his school uniform. The teachers sang the Austrian anthem in Italian, and their students in Croat. Expecting Austrian action in Bosnia, however, the Nationals behaved as Austria's loyal subjects. They barely mentioned the issue of the union, eschewed pro-Slav rhetoric, and confined themselves to hopes of state investment in the province. The king's departure was followed by a showdown between the Nationals and the Autonomists. A delegation of Nationals returning from visiting the king on Vis was attacked in Split by Bajamonti's supporters, while Bajamonti was harassed in Šibenik by followers of the Nationals. *Il Dalmata* accused Rodić of permitting Šibenik to fall into the hands of 'illiterates': civilising the Dalmatian peasants demanded a superhuman effort of the kind the French were displaying in Algeria. The municipal elections of 1875, however, showed further gains by the Nationals: they won seventeen additional municipalities, while the Autonomists lost thirteen. Rodić's failure to create a loyalist party in Dalmatia and Austria's intervention in Bosnia Herzegovina forced Vienna to turn again to the Nationals.

Vienna's expectation that the emperor's visit would encourage an uprising in Bosnia-Herzegovina was soon realised. The Dalmatian National Party aided the insurgents with food and guns. In both parts of Croatia, support committees were established for the purpose; they invited the Slavs and their friends – and, more generally, 'friends of freedom and progress' – to help the rebellion. Most Dalmatian National deputies advocated Austria's occupation of Bosnia-Herzegovina and its addition to Croatia.[25] Expecting great changes, in February 1876 the National Party drafted an address to the king asking for a meeting between Croatian and Dalmatian representatives to discuss unification. However, before the address could be submitted to the vote, the parliament was dissolved. A few months later, in June 1876, Serbia and Montenegro declared war on Turkey, but Russia refused to aid the venture. In 1877 a secret agreement was reached between Russia and Austria-Hungary by which Russia would allow Austria to occupy Bosnia-Herzegovina in return for its neutrality in the future Russian-Turkish war.

In the 1876 elections for the Dalmatian parliament the Autonomists failed to unite around joint candidates. Bajamonti sought an alliance between Zadar and Split on a platform of Italian nationalism, but the Zadar mayor Trigari resisted the Italianisation of the party. He maintained that there was only one, albeit bilingual, nationality in Dalmatia. Divided between Trigari's and Bajamonti's supporters, the Autonomists were routed: the Nationals won thirty-one and the Autonomists ten seats. The gulf between the Italian and the Dalmatian factions within the Autonomist party grew in intensity as a result. In 1877 Trigari again won Zadar, but a large number of Autonomists abstained. The newly opened Ancona–Zadar boat line, however, now started to bring into Zadar hundreds of Italian immigrants. By 1910 the city had acquired 2,000 new ethnic Italian citizens, with another 1,000 awaiting naturalisation.

The division of the Autonomists between Dalmatians and Italians was accompanied by the split within the Nationals between Croats and Serbs. In 1870, when the National Party won a majority in the Dalmatian parliament, the province had just under 500,000 inhabitants, of whom around 78,000 were of the Orthodox faith. The 'nationalisation' of public life through use of the national language in schools, in publications and by way of reading rooms, infused this minority with the understanding that they were Serbs. This evolution was accompanied by a rise of Serb irredentism, in that the Dalmatian Serb elite identified Dalmatia as a Serb land destined to join Serbia. This idea was now frontally challenged, however, by Dalmatia's inexorable Croatisation: instead of drawing closer to Serbia, Dalmatia was increasingly behaving as a Croatian province. In contrast to the Serb national idea, where the anticipated state remained to be constructed within borders that could not easily be drawn, the Croat national ideology – in Dalmatia as elsewhere – took as its point of reference a reasonably well defined state territory: national unity meant Croatia's territorial unity. The Dalmatian Croat leaders recognised the Serbs as a distinct group, but one belonging to the same nation as the Croats. At a time when the primacy of the Italian language formed the main obstacle to national affirmation, the incongruity of the two national ideas was not readily perceived; but the arrival of parliamentary democracy supplied the tools for its manifestation.

The Croat-dominated National Party had from the start stressed national and confessional equality, and acted accordingly while in opposition and while in government. There was no endemic tension between the two confessional communities, which indeed cooperated closely during the initial, 'heroic' stage of the struggle for the national language. The force that drove the Croat–Serb conflict in Dalmatia derived, in fact, not from any local Serb grievance, but from the rivalry of the two state projects, the Croatian and the Serbian, which grew in intensity as the Serbian principality consolidated in the east. In 1844, when the Serbian prime minister Ilija Garašanin formulated a policy for Serbia's territorial expansion, its initial targets were Ottoman-held lands. But within a few years the focus widened to embrace large parts of Croatia, including Dalmatia. In order to prepare the ground for their eventual annexation, the Serbian state funded a network of spies – and propagandists of the idea of a Great Serbia – who included the speaker of the Dalmatian parliament, Stefan Ljubiša. The idea was to stimulate a Serb identity among Dalmatia's Orthodox population, and a Slav one among the Catholic. In 1865 a youth society called *Prvenac* (The First Born) was established at the Orthodox seminary in Zadar, with the task of aiding 'the spiritual unification of our dear and scattered Serb nation', that is, a recreation of Tsar Dušan's empire that would embrace 'the Serb Littoral from Budva to Zadar'. Similar societies were set up in Kotor and Risan. They were all affiliated to the United Serb Youth Organisation based in southern Hungary. These open claims to Croatian territory prompted Mihovil Pavlinović in 1869 to compose an essay entitled *Hrvatska Misao* (The Croatian Idea), which he circulated among his political friends.[26] In this essay he rejected the idea that Croats and Serbs (by which he meant the population living in, or originating from, Serbia) formed a single nation, and argued the need for the National Party to endorse an explicitly Croat national programme, based on the triple axiom of the Croatian state right: national independence, state-territorial integrity, and constitution. The territory to which this right applied included 'Turkish Croatia', specified as the part of Bosnia between the rivers Una and Vrbas. Bosnia east of that line – the territory between the rivers Vrbas and Drina – was in his view ethnically both Croat and Serb, and should belong to either Croatia or Serbia depending on which side succeeded in liberating it from Ottoman rule.

In Croatia itself, Pavlinović argued, there were no indigenous people called Serbs. The Orthodox population, whether original or settled during the Ottoman wars, was Croat, since 'they and their fathers were born in Croatia [and] spoke the Croat language'. This population had adopted the Serb name under the influence of the Serb settlers in Hungary, namely the priests and monks trained at the seminary in the Srijem town of Karlovci, as well as in admiration of Serbia's successful struggle against the Ottomans.[27] Serbia, he wrote, arose at a time when Croatia still 'slept under the Hungarian blanket'. He then posed the crucial question: 'Do we, by identifying the unity and integrity of Croatia with the unity of the Croatian nation, wish to deny the existence of Serbs in Croatia?' The answer was a decided no. In a memorable cadence of questions and answers he outlined the national policy characteristic of the Croat liberal mainstream. 'What if the Croatian citizen of the Orthodox faith prefers to call himself Serb rather than Croat? Let him do so! What if he seeks to identify that name with the religion? Let him! If he wants to call a whole people by that name? Let him do that too! And the language? That too. The script also? That as well. The Croats have no problem with any of this. Our Orthodox brothers already enjoy these rights in Croatia.'

He continued: 'As a freedom-loving people the Croats honour the freedom also of others, provided it is not used against us. The Serbs enjoy the same religious rights as we Catholics; sit with us in the same schoolrooms and courthouses; and make laws together with us. They command where we command, and serve where we serve.' However – and this for him was the crucial point – 'equal rights impose equal duties. In a state that creates no barriers to individual rights in regard to language and script, religion and rite and legal capacity, there can be none also when it comes to civic duty.' The first duty of a free citizen was loyalty to his country. 'Our Orthodox brothers who live in Croatia may not wish to call themselves Croats, but they should admit that they are Croatian by virtue of living in the Croatian land and state. All we ask of them is to uphold the integrity of the Croatian state territory. The minimum we ask of the Serbs is to understand that *the Croats are not obliged to aid the creation of a Serb state in Croatia.*' He condemned equally those who tried to make Croats into Serbs and those who pretended that Serbs did not exist as such. To deny the reality of Serbian state independence, or to seek to turn Croatia into a Serbian province, was 'foolish and counter-productive' – it was the work of 'blinded zealots'. Indeed, 'that which we seek for Croatia we do not deny to Serbia'. However, 'the only thing that the Serbs cannot demand of us is that we should create for them their Great Serbia by fragmenting Croatia'.

He situated Croatia firmly within a future Yugoslavia that would incline to the West. For this reason he condemned the Great Serbian idea: 'Serb patriots and liberals likewise are preoccupied with the recreation of Dušan's empire, oblivious to the fact that this project can only induce hatred, since all domination is intolerable even when practised by one's closest kin.' In contrast to this 'Serbian enterprise', Croatian, Slovenian and Bulgarian national aspirations do not endanger Yugoslavism, because the establishment of their national states is the necessary condition for the realisation of their unity in the future. This unity is essential for their security, 'so important to small nations situated on an [international] highway', and for their economic and cultural advance. 'The Yugoslav alliance will not only preserve the [national] identities of the Slovenes, the Croats, the Serbs and the Bulgarians, but also guarantee their independence from outside powers.' It would also meet the Western fear of the rising Russian danger. He stressed: 'Yugoslavia will be great and beautiful. It will not, however, be organised like France, Italy or Germany, but rather like federal Switzerland or the United

States of America. Yugoslavia will be organised indeed in a way that suits best a community of equal nations, a union of lasting friends.'[28]

The essence of the Croat national idea, for Pavlinović, was the transformation of the Triune Kingdom into a nation state called Croatia. Whereas many Dalmatian politicians expected Dalmatia's identity to be in some way acknowledged in the united Croatia – and even the Croatian parliament was ready in 1861 to grant Dalmatia autonomy – Pavlinović argued that the Dalmatian name should be set aside, because 'the empty name of the Dalmatian kingdom is used by foreigners to try to deny us our Croatian sea and coast', and because it 'continues to sap our people's Croat consciousness'. The Slavonian name too should be set aside, since it 'evokes Hungarian nobility and Turkish *spahis*'. National unity, in other words, demanded suppression of the kingdom's triple name in favour of the Croatian.

By identifying Serbs with Serbia and Croats with Croatia, Pavlinović was able to make also a clear distinction between the two nations. The difference between Croats and Serbs, he wrote, is not reducible to their names, as some have believed, since

> the two names denote two [distinct] histories, homelands, states, religions, cultures and scripts. Despite their common [Slav] origin and language, these realities cannot be treated as superficial: the early separation has done its work, individual evolutions have created individualities. That of the Croats is linked to the West, that of the Serbs to the East. History cannot be denied, living beings demand the right to their own individual lives. We are not concerned here with which of the two civilisations, the Western or the Eastern, will ultimately prevail, nor with how the Byzantine and Latin civilisations will influence the [future Yugoslav] association and state. What we do say is that, while all this can be harmonised and integrated within a larger [supra-national] community, it cannot be denied in the name of [some Slav or Yugoslav] singularity. [Those] who believe that national communities are essentially based on descent and language are wrong. Whence does Croatia's unity derive? From sentiment and reason; from learning and fellowship. Once a unity of these is achieved, other qualities can be added. We need to educate ourselves and to persevere, for our souls are not in chains.[29]

A critical part of this education involved setting aside the superficial 'Slav' denomination and affirming instead Dalmatia's Croat nature.[30] Speaking on the occasion of the opening of a reading room in Hvar, he declared: 'We put aside our national and political name for the sake of the Autonomists: we called ourselves Slavs rather than Croats, Nationals rather than Annexionists. What did we gain by this? The splitters who in 1861 cried that they were not yet ready for union now frontally attack it, calling it an unrealisable fairy-tale. The opponents who in 1861 denied the Croat and Slav name in favour of the Dalmatian are today painting the latter in Italian colours.' On another, similar, occasion, he said: 'We must be Croats first, and as such be close brothers of the Serbs with whom we share the same [Slav] nationality. We can best help the Slav cause, however, by being good Croats.' And he added: 'Let us give our people their self-awareness, and let us invest them with pride, so that in each of us the Croat idea, the Croat spirit, may well up with the words: I am a Croat.'[31] He argued that the political struggle in Dalmatia could not be reduced to liberal issues, for it was also a struggle for national survival. 'The urgent issue is our life, whether we are going to be a free nation and have our own national government. What kind of freedom can exist in a nation which itself is not free?' The duty of a good Catholic and Dalmatian liberal was to help the people 'become a nation, so that the people as a whole can be free to make its own laws'.[32]

Pavlinović and Klaić agreed that the 'Serb idea' stood no chance in Dalmatia, but they differed over how to respond to its increasingly vocal manifestations. The turning point came with the capture of the Dalmatian parliament by the National Party. Faced with the fact that their national idea found no appeal outside the Serb ethnic area, the Dalmatian Serb leaders decided to join forces with the Autonomists in resisting Dalmatia's union with Ban's Croatia. In the 1876 elections for the Dalmatian parliament, one of the National seats was won by Stefan Ljubiša. In his first speech before the parliament he rejected the basic tenet of the National Party's policy: union with Ban's Croatia. The Nationals' response was to invalidate his seat. Quitting the parliament, Ljubiša declared that he had never belonged to the National Party, whose very name made no sense: he himself belonged to 'the since Kosovo unlucky yet heroic Serb nation'. He also stated that he was hated because he was a Serb, but that he would nevertheless 'continue to defend the trampled rights and freedom of my people'. Klaić replied: 'One must resolutely reject the previous speaker's attempt to sow disunity within one and the same nation by presenting himself as a martyr of the Serb cause. One must fully reject the devious intention to plant hatred between the Catholics and the Orthodox.'[33]

The political gulf could not be bridged, however. Following the split within the Autonomist bloc between 'Italians' and 'Slavs', the National bloc too divided, this time into 'Croats' and 'Serbs'. In 1879 Klaić failed to be elected for the Reichsrat in the predominantly Serb district of Bukovica in northern Dalmatia, thanks to a strong campaign waged against him by the Orthodox clergy led by Bishop Knežević. The seat was instead won by an Autonomist. The 'Bukovica betrayal' and the ensuing public quarrel were followed by the Serb politicians leaving the National Party and forming their own Serb Party. Klaić experienced the rejection of the National Party's traditional position on union with Ban's Croatia as a rebellion against the party. Although he advocated a sustained offensive 'to the end' against 'the splitters' and 'neo-Serbs', he continued to hope that the split could be healed. When a Serb deputy in the Dalmatian parliament described the Nationals as enemies of the Serbs, he responded:

> As the parliamentary majority and as a political party we have never displayed any antagonism towards you. On the contrary, we tried hard to reach an agreement with you, but you rejected all our proposals and offers. We do not deny that you are Serbs [and] do not wish to call you by any other name, if that is what you want. But I will never concede that you form a separate nation in Dalmatia, with rights that are contrary to our Croat ones. You are too weak to gain what you want, but strong enough to do us injury. What have you achieved with the alliance [with the Autonomists]? Nothing at all – you have only damaged us. While you behave in this manner we shall treat you as our adversaries.[34]

He nevertheless urged the party's paper to desist from attacking the Serb leaders.

Klaić failed to grasp the full implications of the 'Bukovica betrayal'. In 1880 *Srpski list* (The Serb Journal), the voice of the new Serb Party, wrote that its programme was recognition of the Serb nationality in Dalmatia, and of the Serb language as the language of instruction and administration wherever Serbs are in a majority; rejection of Dalmatia's union with Ban's Croatia; rejection of Bosnia's union with Croatia; and support for Dalmatia's union with Bosnia. The paper reiterated the view that the Croatian coast was in fact Serb.[35] Klaić refused to believe, however, that the Croat–Serb split was permanent, and kept speaking of the 'so-called Serb movement', which he saw as a product of 'religious intolerance and mindless vanity'. He believed that if the Nationals continued to seek peace and cooperation, and avoided polemics with *Srpski list*, neo-Serbdom would disappear as the *Zemljak* group had done. In 1880, when the Croat opposition in Ban's Croatia split from the National Party to form the Independent National Party, Klaić warned its leaders of the danger that in a fragmented Croatian parliament the Serb minority would rule by holding the balance of power. In 1882, he approved Pavlinović's decision to publish *Misao hrvatska i misao srpska u Dalmaciji* (The Croat Idea and the Serb Idea in Dalmatia), which ascribed the Croat–Serb split to two incompatible state ideas, recommending that the text should show 'the absurdity and danger of raising the Serb issue in Dalmatia, and the foolishness rather than ill-intent of Serb collaboration with the Autonomists'.

The Nationals needed Serb support to destroy the Autonomists. Without that support they felt it even more necessary to draw closer to the government in Vienna, since they could not fight on all fronts. In 1879, the year in which Serb politicians left the National Party, Eduard Taaffe became Austrian prime minister, thus ending the long era of German liberal rule. In 1883 Klaić sought negotiations with Rodić's successor, General Stjepan Jovanović – who had been sent to replace the fading Italian language by German in Dalmatian offices – hoping that this would help the Nationals win a handsome majority in the provincial parliament. In May 1883 elections for the Dalmatian parliament the Nationals won twenty-five seats, the Autonomists six and the Serb Party nine. During the parliamentary debate sparked off by the closure of the Italian-language boys' school in Trogir, in which the Autonomist and the Serb deputies formed a common front, Klaić responded characteristically to a Serb deputy's claim that Dubrovnik was a Serb city.

> As for the nationality of the city and district which I have the honour to represent here, we used to call ourselves *Dubrovčani* [natives of Dubrovnik] and our language 'ours'. Others in the district, however, called it Croat. When [in 1861] constitutional rule was introduced, the Dubrovnik leaders, most of whom have since died, put forward the idea of union with Croatia. We were not concerned with the issue of nationality so much as with the union, and the language we called ours. We sought union with Ban's Croatia and politically we remained Croats, while in regard to ethnography we argued that Croats and Serbs were one people speaking the same language and having the same customs.

It may be a matter of opinion, he added, whether the city and its district were Serb or Croat, but the people of Dubrovnik would surely take note of the fact that the Serb Party was going to vote with the Autonomists against the National Party's proposal to 'remove a foreign language' from Dalmatia. He added that union with Croatia was for his party a 'political, not an ethnographic issue', and that the party would continue to call itself National until the Serb Party 'falls apart or changes into another'.[36]

Klaić continued to hope. He was encouraged by the fact that in 1886 the Serb deputies supported the Nationals over their language policy. A year later, when a Serb deputy stated in parliament that Croat was a Serb dialect and Dalmatia a Serb land, he refrained from responding at that level. In 1888 the Nationals offered a deal to the Serb politicians, according to which the two parties would act together in elections for the Reichsrat in order to keep the Autonomists out of it, and generally cooperate on all national and Dalmatian issues in both the local and central parliaments. The Serbs would be represented in parliamentary bodies in relation to their numerical weight in the province, and all differences would be peacefully resolved. This offer, however, was rejected. In the 1889 Dalmatian parliamentary elections, the Nationals won twenty-seven seats, the Serb Party eight and the Autonomists six. The National Party now renamed itself National Croat Party, but its parliamentary club reaffirmed its commitment to its programme of 1875, which advocated Croat–Serb equality as well as Croatia's right to Dalmatia. Klaić stated his party's hope that the Serb deputies would realise that they could defend their nationality only in cooperation with the Croats. In these elections, however, the Nationals lost Dubrovnik to the Serb–Autonomist alliance. According to *Srpski list*, the Serbs and the Autonomists had two aims in common: 'resistance to the Croatisation of our Dalmatia, and its incorporation into the Triune Kingdom'.[37]

Turning Spalato into Split

In the elections of 1879 for the Reichsrat, the Autonomists won only one seat. Instead of Bajamonti, the Split district sent forward Gajo Bulat, a prominent National. In the Reichsrat the Dalmatian Nationals joined the conservative Hohenwart Club, which supported the Taaffe government. The government promised them concessions in regard to the Croat language, a railway and state investment, but not union with Ban's Croatia. The Reichsrat also voted in favour of a law initiated by Bulat according to which the language commonly spoken in a given crownland would be used also in its administration and courts. In return the Nationals voted with the government for a retrograde law that reduced the period of obligatory education from eight to six years, and provided for the appointment of

The National Reading Room building in Split

teachers who were of the same religion as the majority of their students. In 1880, a letter from the emperor-king announcing the introduction of the Croat language into the two secondary schools in Split was followed by a demonstration by *bersaglieri* in Split and Zadar, during which Italy and Garibaldi were hailed. There followed a skirmish between the *bersaglieri* and the locally stationed, mainly Croat, military regiment. The Nationals took this opportunity to move against Bajamonti and his power base. The parliament's financial committee once again demanded investigation of the city council books, and in 1881 the Split municipal assembly was dissolved. The Autonomists of Zadar now rallied to Bajamonti: on his departure from Zadar a large crowd turned up to see him off, and a riot ensued. National deputies were attacked on leaving the parliament.

The Nationals' advance was aided by the fact that during the second half of the nineteenth century Dalmatia experienced a demographic boom, based on the rapid development in particular of viticulture, thanks to a temporary decline first of the Italian and then of the French wine industry caused by phylloxera, as a result of which Dalmatian wine production increased fivefold in the period between 1858 and 1898. The main beneficiary of this economic bounty was the area gravitating towards Split.[38] New elections for the Split municipality were held in July 1882, and it was the suburbs –

chaperoned by Vid Morpurgo's People's Bank – that delivered Split to the Nationals, after which victory parades were held throughout Dalmatia.[39] The capture of Split was celebrated enthusiastically also in Ban's Croatia.[40] The new city council met on 9 October 1882, the Croatian flag was ceremoniously raised over the town hall, and for the first time in the city's history the mayor's inaugural speech was delivered in Croat. One of the first acts of the new administration was to change the city's official name from the Roman Spalato into the Croat Split.[41] The capture of Split made the Nationals the true masters of Dalmatia. The fall of Bajamonti's former citadel made inevitable also the defeat of the Autonomists throughout the region. In 1886 the Autonomists lost Trogir, and in 1887 Starigrad on Hvar. Former Italians now became Croats. In 1880 the district of Split, with over 91,000 inhabitants, was the largest in Dalmatia; the city itself had 14,500 inhabitants, compared with Zadar's 10,000. Using the 'language commonly spoken' as the measure, there were 8,628 Croats, 5,280 Italians, 73 Serbs, and 178 others (mainly Jews). By 1890 the number of Split citizens who declared themselves Italian had fallen from 5,280 to 1,969. In Trogir their number dropped from 2,023 to 182; on the island of Brač from 1956 to 606; in the town of Omiš from 248 to 18. In 1900 Split had 18,547 inhabitants, of whom only 1,500 claimed to be Italian.[42] The Croat middle class, having grown in size and confidence, had in the meantime absorbed also sections of the formerly Autonomist nobility, thus completing the Croatisation of the coastal cities.

This transformation cannot be ascribed solely to the National Party's electoral success, but was due also to divisions within the Autonomist constituency. The ongoing Italianisation of the Autonomist Party was forcing a choice on its members. Some of those who spoke Italian opted to become Italian; others, especially those who did not speak Italian, became Croats or Serbs. The Fanfognas thus became Italian, the Borellis Croat.[43] As the only remaining Italian-language oasis, Zadar now acted as a magnet for the remaining 20,000 Italians – 3 per cent of Dalmatia's total population. Despite the strenuous efforts of the village clergy, enough of the peasants of the Zadar hinterland voted for its mayor Niccolò Trigari to keep him in office for twenty-five years. Dozens of Croat cultural and civic societies operated in Zadar; key Croat journals were published there; the Croatian flag flew over the provincial parliament's building; the parliament spoke mainly in Croat; and Zadar's archbishop, Juraj Rajčević, preached in Croat as well as in Italian. The beginning of industrialisation, moreover, had brought many Croats to work in the city's factories and on the railway, and to serve as local policemen, officials and administrators. Trigari took all this into account and addressed the citizens of Zadar also in Croat. Trigari was aware that the Croats had won Dalmatia for good, and for that reason he pursued a moderate course. Zadar, as a result, would remain an impregnable bastion of Dalmatian Autonomism. The Autonomist hold over Zadar was significantly aided by the presence of imperial – German and Italian – officials who felt no loyalty to Croatia, as well as by growing immigration from Italy. Another important contributing factor was the division of the National Party into its Croat and Serb components: without Serb help the Nationals were unable to win the city council in the elections of 1884. The Serb Party indeed remained the Autonomists' only local ally, which the latter greatly cherished: in 1885, for example, Luigi Lapenna established in Vienna a Society for the Support of Italian and Serb Students. The Autonomists were helped also by the fact that during 1880s the Croat vote split between the National Party and the Party of Right. All this ensured that Zadar would remain a majority Italian city up to the collapse of Austria-Hungary in 1918, despite the fact that the majority of the population of its district was Croat.

The rise of Italian irredentism

In 1884, two years after losing Split, the indomitable Bajamonti started his own paper, *La Difesa*. In its first editorial, headlined '*Alea jacta est!*', he called for Italianisation of the Autonomist Party, cooperation with Serbs and 'Slavo-Dalmatians', and defence of the cultural and language rights of the Italians, who he insisted were fighting for their very survival. He argued that in order to have schools in the Italian language, one had first to have Italians. In 1886 the first Italian Party, *La società politica Dalmata*, was set up in Split. Miho Klaić now tried to strengthen the power base of the National Party by proposing a reform of the electoral law involving the abolition of the tiny curia of trade and crafts, and more importantly a new way of assessing the category of high taxpayers. He justified this on the grounds that the tax census for this latter curia was too low (100 forints for Dalmatia and 50 for Boka Kotorska), resulting in an abnormally large number of high tax payers (700 by comparison with a little over 500 in the far richer Bohemia). This curia, he proposed, should be replaced by another that would take into account also tax on business and income. In this way the number of those who lived essentially off rent, and who in Zadar and to an extent also in Dubrovnik voted for the Autonomists, would be reduced in favour of economically active individuals, numerous especially in the Split area. He also proposed that the electoral districts be made to coincide with the judicial territorial units, which would increase the size of the Dalmatian parliament to forty-five, and that the seats be redistributed in favour of the countryside, that is, twelve seats for the cities and thirty-one for the countryside. The abolition of the two curiae and the additional seats for the rural majority would have gravely weakened the Autonomists, who by walking out of parliament had denied the majority the necessary quorum for the proposal to pass.

But Autonomism was a spent force. Left to itself, it would have died with the generation that had brought it into life. By the end of the century most of its prominent leaders – the Orthodox bishop Stefan Knežević, the former Trogir mayor Antonio Fanfogna, the Austrian loyalist Luigi Lapenna, the Zadar archbishop Pietro Maupas (popularly known as *Dalmata antico*, because he was born in Split) and the former Split mayor Antonio Bajamonti – were dead. Niccolò Trigari himself died in 1901. In the provincial parliament the party had reached a ceiling with its six deputies, all elected in Zadar. When these deputies asked for bilingual education in Trogir, they were told that there was no need for Italian to be taught in Dalmatian schools. In 1889 the Split-based *La società politica Dalmata*, popularly known as the Italian Party, became the party of Dalmatian Italians. It was the issue of the Zadar gymnasium that finally tipped the balance within the Autonomist camp in favour of its Italian component. In 1890 Klaić asked for introduction of the Croat language into the Zadar gymnasium, despite the fact that, according to the principle of 'commonly used language', twice as many of its students spoke Italian as Croat/Serb. One-third of these students came from outside, since this was now the only secondary school in the Italian language in Dalmatia. But it also meant that the Croat population of the Zadar district had to send their children to the local village of Arbanasi (originally established by Albanians fleeing Ottoman repression). The Dalmatian parliament consequently accepted Klaić's proposal, and in so doing provoked a strong and organised local resistance. This was the time when the Slovenes and the Germans were fighting over the language of the gymnasium at Celje,[44] so the Zadar action committee set up to fight the ruling received German and Italian support from all over the Monarchy. The committee complained that the Dalmatian Slavs, having adopted their 'new' Croat identity, now wished to deprive an alleged 50,000 Dalmatian Italians of their language. Its members also proclaimed 'frankly and without hesitation' their Italian identity. This Italian-speaking Dalmatian middle class had by now given up its earlier liberalism in regard to the Croats, in favour of racial stereotyping. *Il Dalmata* accused the Nationals of being preoccupied with 'hypothetical

Croatian kings and dubious historical rights', whereas the Italians had created 'a civilisation far superior to that of the Croats, a people devoid of any illustrious past or political ability'. Antonio Bajamonti, while admitting that the majority of Dalmatian population was 'Slav', argued likewise that it was eclipsed by the Italian minority's 'moral and physical individuality'.[45]

The transformation of Dalmatian Autonomism into a movement of Dalmatian Italians had in the meantime acquired crucial support from a completely new source. The establishment of the Triple Alliance of Austria-Hungary, Italy and Germany in 1882 had initiated a rapid growth of Italian national societies throughout Austria. One of these was *Pro Patria* (For the Homeland), established in 1885 and initially dedicated to the preservation of Italian language and culture in the Trentino, the Italian-inhabited part of Tyrol (this educational project is examined more closely in the following chapter). Its first Dalmatian branch was established in Zadar in 1887, and by 1890 branches had opened also in Trogir and on the islands of Hvar, Rab and Korčula. *Pro Patria* was banned in 1890 on account of its openly irredentist rhetoric, but was promptly replaced by *Lega Nazionale*, set up by Association Dante Alighieri established that same year in Rome.

The first Dalmatian branch of *Lega Nazionale* opened in Zadar in 1893, another soon after in Split, with a dozen other places including Dubrovnik following their example. Within three years the *Lega* had established Italian-language schools in Šibenik, Split and Zadar. In 1894, at the opening of a branch in Starigrad on Hvar, its local president stated that the society's purpose was to confront the German threat in Trentino and Trieste, the Slovene threat in Gorizia, and the Croat threat in Istria and Dalmatia. The number of Italian-speaking Dalmatians, nevertheless, continued to decline: there were 27,000 in 1880, and only 16,000 in 1910.

The twentieth century opened with Dalmatian cities witnessing increased fighting between radical pro-Italian and pro-Yugoslav groups. Zadar acted as a haven of Italian irredentism. Its interaction with the other coast of the Adriatic grew as a result. Its cultural and sports societies were formed as, or soon became, an integral part of the Italian network. Paramilitary sports clubs in Zadar modelled their kit on the uniforms of the Italian army. The Italian Party was not able to muster enough votes, however, to send a deputy to the Reichsrat. In 1908 young Italian radicals set up their own party, the *Partito italiano democratico* (Italian Democratic Party), a party of revolutionary nationalism that was bound to operate largely underground. Its paper, *Il Risorgimento*, portrayed the creation of any Yugoslavia as inimical to Italy's 'mission in the Adriatic', and complained that Austria had surrendered Dalmatia to the Croats. The party's leaders bore typical Slav surnames, such as Boxich, Milcovich, Delich; the paper's editor was called Bucevich. The leader of the Italian Party was equally of Slav origin – Roberto Ghilianovich. All were natives of Zadar and its hinterland. Under their influence, the Italian youth of Zadar took to marching through the streets shouting: 'Long live Italy! Down with Austria!'

TWELVE

Educating Istria

At the end of the fourteenth century Istria was divided into an area of Habsburg rule in the northeast, centred on Pazin and including the coast between Rijeka and Plomin, and one of Venetian rule in the rest. In 1815, following the end of the Napoleonic Wars, Austria gained the whole of Istria and made it part of the ephemeral Kingdom of Illyria. In 1861, however, supplemented by the islands of Krk, Cres and Lošinj, Istria was constituted as a separate crownland with its own parliament. This Istria, together with two other crownlands – Gorizia-Gradiska, and the city of Trieste with its district – formed the Austrian Littoral, administered by an imperial governor who sat in Trieste.[1] Since the department of maritime affairs was likewise located in Trieste, Rijeka and Dalmatia were in this way also included in the Austrian Littoral.

According to the Austrian census, Istria's population in 1846 consisted of some 134,500 Croats, 32,000 Slovenes and 60,000 Italians (or 74 per cent Slavs and 26 per cent Italians).[2] The Croats had been a majority in Istria ever since the Middle Ages, their ranks continuously replenished by immigration from other Venetian and Habsburg territories.[3] Slovenes were concentrated in the northwest, while Italians predominated in the small towns along the western seaboard, of which the largest were Rovinj, Piran and Koper. In the middle of the nineteenth century, however, Pula – which when the Venetian republic ceased to exist had merely 600 inhabitants – was chosen to become Austria's main naval port, after which it experienced a vertiginous growth, its population rising to over 17,000 in 1867 and to over 59,000 in 1910.[4] Lacking a historical centre of its own, Istria in the second half of the nineteenth century came under the dominance of the rapidly growing regional centres of Pula, Trieste and Rijeka, which attracted rural poor from all over Istria: in 1890 alone over 12,000 Istrian Croats moved to Trieste in search of employment.

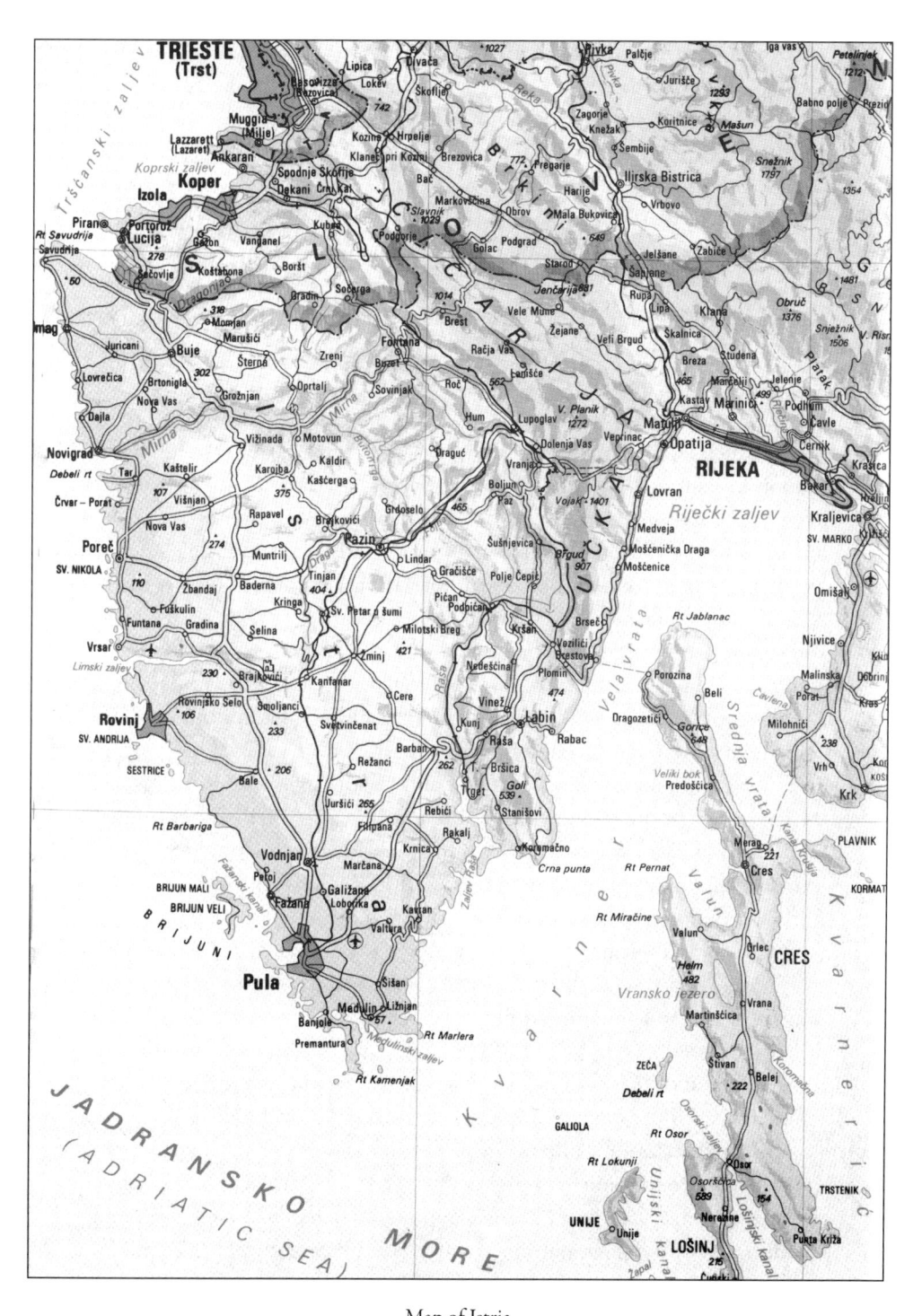

Map of Istria

Up to the nineteenth century the urban-rural division was also a national division: the towns and the large estates (excluding those held by the Catholic Church) were predominantly Italian, while most of the peasantry was Slav. The Croats lived in villages where for centuries the Mass had been said in Church Slavonic and parish records written in the Glagolitic script.[5] A few teachers and the clergy, traditionally linked with the Glagolitic centres of the Croatian Adriatic, provided the only literate layer within a society that made its living as sharecroppers working on the large estates, or as small and medium landholders. Internal social differentiation was largely inhibited by poverty and lack of education. There were only two gymnasia for the education of the local elite: one in Koper, where the language of instruction was initially German, and later Italian; the other in Pazin, which taught in German. The few Croats who passed through these schools became assimilated into the Italian middle class. Along the eastern shore, however, Croats lived also in small towns and their suburbs as traders, sailors, fishermen and artisans, and it was in this area, with its stronger ties to mainland Croatia, that the movement for national emancipation took early root. The first generation of Croat political leaders, recruited largely from the clergy, was educated outside Istria: in Rijeka, Karlovac and Zagreb as well as in Vienna or Padua. Prominent among them was Juraj Dobrila, born in the vicinity of Pazin, who in 1857 became the bishop of Poreč and Pula. He joined the Illyrian movement during his school days in Karlovac. Because he spoke Croat in public, his Italian opponents called him a 'bishop for rustics'. Mate Bastian, another clergyman and Dobrila's close collaborator, studied in Rijeka and Zagreb. Ivan Vitezić, who also belonged to Dobrila's circle of priests, was a native of Krk; he too studied in Zagreb. His nephew Dinko Vitezić was an early supporter of the Dalmatian National Party.

In Istria as in Dalmatia, political life was dominated by the Italian-speaking towns. Italian Istrian society was made up mainly of peasants, sharecroppers and town poor, but it possessed also an upper and middle layer composed of large landowners and rentiers, shopkeepers, seamen, shipowners and artisans. Italians who studied at the Koper gymnasium normally continued their education at Italian or Austrian universities, and returned to act as officials, teachers, doctors and lawyers. This educated layer gave voice to the Italian part of Istria. Istria, in their view, was Italian by language, custom, history and geography. The Italian urban elite believed at this stage in the power of the towns to assimilate their Slav hinterland: lacking their own educated class, the Istrian Slavs were bound to succumb to a superior Italian language and culture. In 1848 the Istrian representatives in the short-lived Reichstag demanded justice for all nationalities, but protested when the Austrian government, evoking the fact of Istria's Slav majority, refused their demand that Italian be made the sole official language in the province. Austria was then at war with Piedmont and relied on the Slavs to keep at bay the danger of Italian irredentism. Although Slovene and Croat formally became official languages in Istria in addition to Italian and German, it was only at the end of the nineteenth century that this law began to be implemented – and even then only in part.

The national politics of the Istrian Italians was inevitably influenced by the movement for Italian national unification. The proclamation of the Italian kingdom in 1861 reanimated their nascent irredentism, which Austria would henceforth try to temper by tolerating the Italian claim to national pre-eminence in the Austrian Littoral, where Italians were in fact a minority: 43 per cent on the eve of the First World War, according to official statistics that regularly inflated Italian numbers.[6] Austria's return to constitutional rule and the formation of an Istrian parliament in 1861 opened the door, however, to Slav participation in political life. During the 1850s the national energies of the Istrian Italians had been directed against penetration of the German language into the schools and office; but now a far more formidable Slav opposition emerged to the project of making Istria an Italian province. The struggle between Croats and Italians for mastery of Istria was to dominate the rest of the nineteenth century, and continue long after the Habsburg Monarchy had disappeared. Its forms and tempo dovetailed with the progressive democratisation of public life, which depended upon, and was stimulated by, education of the rural population. Since the political struggle at this stage was essentially a struggle within the urban middle class, the Croats entered this contest as very much the weaker side, leading to initial assimilation of those who moved to the cities by the stronger Italian one. But the subsequent rise of a Croat middle class stiffened national resistance to assimilation and made Italians into a permanent minority. However, the electoral system that Vienna introduced in 1861 – despite subsequent modifications – maintained the Italian minority's grip on the province.

The initial leaders of the Istrian Croats, recruited overwhelmingly from the Catholic clergy, were adherents of the National Party and stressed Slav cooperation. The next generation, however, which came to the fore in the last two decades of the nineteenth century, belonged to the Party of Right, which sought to join Istria to Croatia on the basis of national and historic right. Prominent among them were Matko Mandić, Matko Laginja and

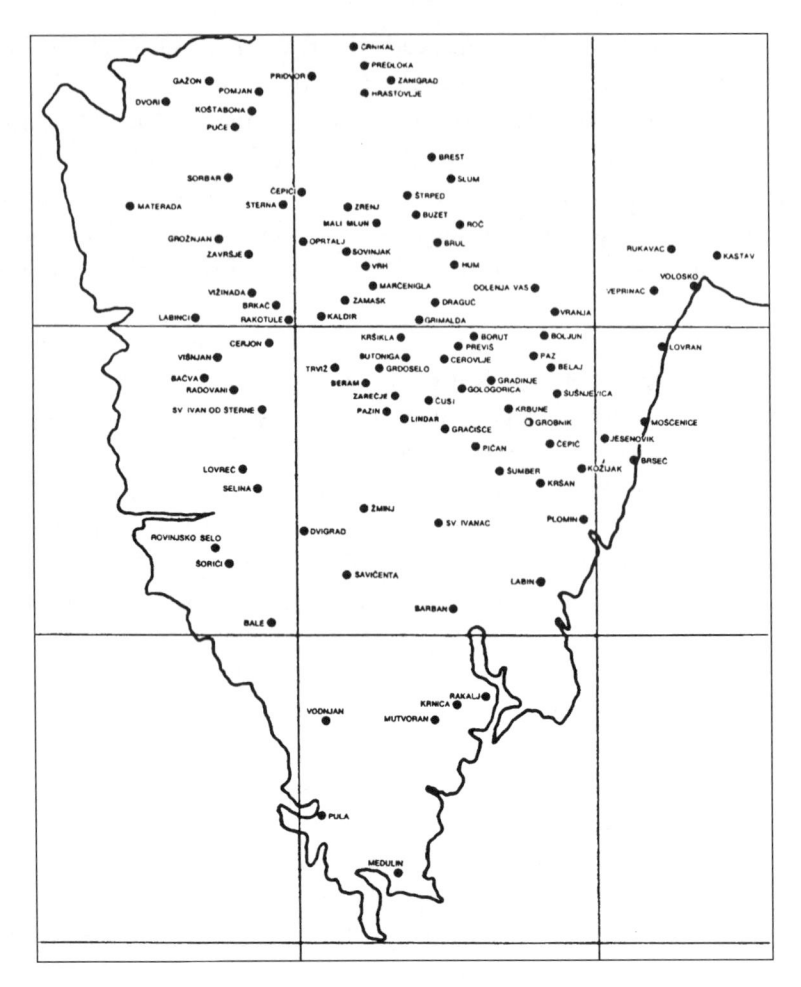

Distribution of Glagolitic inscriptions in Istria

Vjekoslav Spinčić, all born in or near Kastav, a small town east of Mt Učka which in the early decades of the nineteenth century had become a mainstay of the Istrian Croat *risorgimento*. Fearful that in the event of Austria-Hungary's break-up Istria might join Italy, they remained loyal Austrians; but inability to translate the fact of demographic majority into a correlate political power fed an Istrian Slav frustration that would finally turn against the Monarchy itself.

Parliamentary ground rules

The Istrian parliament established in Poreč in 1861 consisted of thirty members, of whom three sat by right of office: the bishop of Trieste

(Bartul Legat, a Slovene), the bishop of Poreč and Pula (Juraj Dobrila) and the bishop of Krk (Ivan Vitezić). As in Dalmatia the electoral body was divided into four electoral colleges or curiae, based on taxable wealth. Five seats were allocated to the curia of large landowners, two to the curia of trade and crafts, eight to the curia of the towns, twelve to the curia of village municipalities. In the first three curiae voting was direct, in the last indirect: 500 voters electing one elector; the electors then electing deputies. In 1861 the first curia represented 154 electors, the second 15, the third 4,200 and the fourth 14,532. Since landowners resided in the towns, the electoral system delivered control of the parliament to the towns: in effect, to Italians. This set-up ensured close cooperation between Slovenes and Croats. Only two Slavs were actually elected: Josip Samsa, a Slovene, who soon resigned on the grounds that nothing could be gained from an Italian-dominated parliament; and Franjo Feretić, a Croat canon from the island of Krk, who struggled on. Istrian Slavs were thus represented by four clerics.[7]

The parliament's main task was to elect two representatives to the Reichsrat, but the Italian deputies voted overwhelmingly against Istria's participation by inscribing *nessuno* (no one) on their electoral forms. The Slavs voted in favour. The next issue to be posed was that of the working language of the parliament and of the Istrian administration in general. Bishop Legat, backed by Bishop Vitezić, proposed that governmental bodies should be bilingual, so that they could communicate also with the Slav population. But this was declined. The parliamentary majority instead adopted Italian as the sole official language, and rejected a proposal that parliamentary records be kept in both languages. Carlo Combi, a teacher at the Koper gymnasium (who after having helped to organise the *nessuno* vote was forced to emigrate to Italy), later justified this decision in the following manner: 'Why indeed should Italian records be translated into Slav? For the reading rooms of peasants and shepherds? For villages (I know of no Slav towns in Istria) where pilgrimages are made to those who can read? And into which of the thirteen Slav dialects spoken in Istria should the translation be made?'[8] This argument overlooked the fact that most Istrian Italians at this time did not speak the standard Italian language either, because they did not attend school. As late as 1880, half the Istrian Italian population was illiterate. Pula apart, Istrian towns remained small islands in a rural sea: in 1880 Poreč and Pazin had a population of just over 3,000 each, in districts of some 40,000 inhabitants.

Following the *nesssuno* vote, the central government closed down the Istrian parliament and announced new elections. This time it invested a great effort in ensuring the return of a more compliant body, which quickly elected the two required deputies, one of whom was Bishop Dobrila. In the new parliament Dobrila asked once more for Slav-language schools and a bilingual administration, but this was again rejected. The proposal that parliamentary records should be published also in Slovene or Croat was likewise refused. Vienna refused to ratify these decisions, but they were implemented nevertheless. Speeches in Croat and Slovene would henceforth be omitted from the parliamentary records, the gaps indicated simply by the phrase *parla slavo* (speaks Slav). Slav deputies argued in vain that Italian and Slav representatives should 'show their commitment to the good of our land by cooperating and recognising that each has equal rights and duties'; and that 'justice demands that regard be shown to both equally, [not least because] the Slavs bear the same burdens and have same rights.' These words fell on deaf ears. Severely provoked, Bishop Dobrila then warned: 'The Slav nation [in Istria] may be asleep, but that does not mean it is dead. Those who sleep awake: when they do, they may do so in a manner that could be uncomfortable for the Italian element.'[9]

There was also the issue of schools. In 1863 the Italian deputy Francesco Vidulich proposed that education be conducted solely in the Italian language.[10] Dobrila countered with a proposal that schools in the Slav areas should be in Slav, with suitable provision made for Italian or German speakers. The majority voted against this. He next proposed that the gymnasium in Koper should teach also the Croat or the Slovene language, and that German be replaced by Croat as the language of instruction in the gymnasium in Pazin, given the overwhelmingly Croat nature of the district (80 per cent). Both proposals were rejected. The parliament instead forwarded to Trieste a demand that the gymnasium in Pazin be made into an Italian-language school. In the following decades Slovene and Croat deputies to the Reichsrat, backed by the Czechs, continue to argue in favour of a Croat-language gymnasium in Pazin. In the view of the Istrian parliament, however, if the Pazin gymnasium could not be Italian, it was better that it be closed down, in the interest of 'Istrian civilisation'. Each side organised their communities to petition the governments in Trieste and Vienna with their demands. When in 1898 Vienna finally decided to make it a Croat-language school, the Italian side protested that Pazin was a wholly Italian city and mobilised against the decision. In 1899, several decades after the original request was first made in the provincial parliament, a Croat gymnasium was finally opened in Pazin.[11] Having failed to prevent its opening, the provincial government proceeded to build an Italian-language gymnasium next to it –

without consulting the provincial parliament, where the project would have met Croat opposition – and this school opened in 1900.

In the 1867 elections five Slav deputies were elected to the local parliament, despite the fact that the countryside largely abstained: out of 11,544 electors, only 26 per cent actually voted (there was a similar lack of interest also in the elections for the other curiae). This time, however, Istria sent only Italians to the Reichsrat. Faced with the hostility and intransigence of the parliamentary majority, the Slav bishops ceased to attend parliamentary sessions. The parliament now decided, over the protests of the Slav deputies, to dissolve smaller municipalities by merging them into larger ones linked to the towns. Eighty-eight largely Croat and Slovene municipalities disappeared as a result. This administrative merger aided economic and linguistic penetration of the Slav villages by the Italian towns; but it also opened the towns to Slav influence.

Tilting the balance

Croat politicians understood that their most urgent task was to increase the number of Croat deputies, which meant 'awakening' the countryside. During the 1860s Slav reading rooms, which acted as local political clubs, were established: 1861 in Trieste, 1866 in Kastav and Veli Lošinj, 1869 in Pula (with Strossmayer's help) and 1870 in Koper. Their number would ultimately grow to over fifty, spread across Istria. From 1869 on the Croats, following the example of the Slovenes who had adopted it from the Czechs, also started to organise open-air rallies, where their numerical weight could be manifested – a tonic for their community's spirit and a signal to the other side. One of the most successful public rallies was organised at Kastav in 1871 by the local reading room, with thousands turning up. Messages of support came from all over Croatia. Those assembled were told that Slavs were the majority population in Istria, yet their language was nevertheless absent from the courts and offices: this was uncivilised, unjust and illegal. The provincial authorities, which insisted on Italian-language schools, were accused of seeking to destroy the Croat nation in Istria.

In 1870 the Croat national cause acquired a public voice in the shape of the journal *Naša sloga* (Our Solidarity), published in Trieste with don Mate Bastian acting as its editor. The project was initiated by Bishop Dobrila and financially aided by Bishop Strossmayer. 'We must try to stir a little our people in Istria,' wrote Dobrila from Rome, where he and Strossmayer were attending the first Vatican Council.[12] Since most Croats were illiterate, the paper was read in groups, which is why it was published

Juraj Dobrila

in a mixture of the local *čakavian* idiom and standard *štokavian* Croat. The paper reported on general events, debates in the local parliament and the proceedings of the Reichsrat. It sought, above all, to teach the villagers the importance of education and of participation in institutional politics. *Naša sloga* consequently reminded its readers that the Austrian constitution of 1867 had proclaimed the equality of all nationalities, including the right to education in their own languages. To realise this right, however, it was necessary to elect Croats to municipal bodies and to parliament. The paper was able to point to Croat successes in Dalmatia, which the Italians had also once proclaimed to be a purely Italian land. It advised its readers to address the authorities only in Croat, and to demand to be answered only in Croat, because officials were paid to serve the people.

Education was of the greatest importance, since in order to have bilingual administration it was necessary to have the requisite number of educated Croat-speaking officials and administrators. In 1872, at the start of the school year the paper appealed to parents: 'Send your child to school, give it education; send boys and girls, whether big or small; send them to school whether you live close to one or far away.' Schools were instruments of national affirmation, since they 'educate the young to become priests, lawyers, doctors, officials and employees. The nation which does not have such people of their own kin and language is in great danger, because there is no one to advocate and defend its interest, so everyone can trample upon it.' Education, in other words, was a patriotic duty. The parents should not 'regret the cost or the trouble, for one day these will, God willing, pay off. Your children will become esteemed, defenders of right and justice, light of the nation and pride of the homeland.' It was important, however, that children be sent to 'places and schools where you know they will be educated in the national spirit'. *Naša Sloga*, a paper produced by clergymen and distributed by parish priests, continued to appeal: 'Fathers and mothers, send your children to schools so that our people does not remain illiterate; send them, if you possibly can, to gymnasia so that our nation can acquire bright, educated and brave defenders. Fathers and mothers, heed this call and you will be blessed in your graves by your children and your Slav homeland!'[13]

Nation-building involved teaching a largely illiterate population election rules. In 1870 the number of elected seats in the Istrian parliament was raised to thirty, the three extra seats being added to the curia of the towns, which now held eleven seats. The Slav deputies' proposal that representation of village districts be raised from twelve to fourteen was rejected, however. The parliament again elected only Italians to the Reichsrat – the last time it was able to exercise this prerogative. The new law on direct elections for the central parliament, against which the Croat-dominated Dalmatian parliament had protested, in fact favoured the Istrian Croats, given that the Italian-dominated provincial parliament regularly elected only Italians. The new law also doubled the number of Istria's representatives in the Reichsrat to four: one each for the landowners' and city curiae, two for the villages. There was a hope that the countryside would henceforth send only Croats to Vienna: 'The village municipalities are ours: there are no Italians there.'[14] A Patriotic Electoral Committee was set up for the purpose of electoral agitation, while *Naša sloga* published special appeals for maximum participation in the coming elections: 'All of Istria is watching you!' Dinko Vitezić stood in central and eastern Istria, Bishop Dobrila in the west and north. Dobrila lost by a handful of votes, but Vitezić won. *Naša Sloga* wrote that the peasants were not to blame for this outcome, since many were not yet acquainted with the electoral rules. The elections, however, had 'strengthened the people in their national awareness' and taught them 'to know the laws and understand their importance'. Electoral work proved a thorny enterprise, however, given that the Italian-dominated administration, which organised the elections, was not above adjusting their results. Croats did nevertheless start to win some small towns in central Istria – only to encounter the problem of lack of literate people to run them. A solution was found in electing 'honest Italians' to act as mayors, but this could be only a temporary measure.

In 1878 national politics took an important step forward with the formation of a Croat-Slovene National Party. Its main opponent became the Istrian Political Society, known also as the Italian Liberal party, established in 1884 at Pazin with the aim of 'spreading Italian nationality, civilisation and culture'. Four years later the Nationals won the key town of Pazin. *Naša sloga* wrote jubilantly: 'The most powerful [Italian] opposition fortress in Istria lies in ruin, but there is a long way to go before the enemy has been crushed. We must not get drunk on this victory. Further battles lie ahead of us for other small and large fortresses, until all once again revert to us.'[15] Pazin was especially important, since it could be made into an Istrian Croat national capital. In the same year they won also the municipality of Buzet (84 per cent Croat) north of Pazin, which indicated that, having won eastern Istria, they were consolidating their position also in the central area. After the fall of Pazin and Buzet, practically all municipalities in southeastern and central Istria fell to the Nationals. During the preceding years the Nationals had won also most of the municipalities on the Adriatic islands and the coast. These gains made it possible for them in 1884 to form their own club in the provincial parliament. Their influence spread into western and southern Istria too. In 1889 they won eight of twelve village municipalities, as well as a seat (Volosko) in the curia of the towns.

Winning control of a local municipality meant winning the right to establish Croat-language schools. In 1875 the Austrian minister of education, in a reply to Dinko Vitezić, pointed out that while the government was committed to the principle of education in the mother tongue, it was not responsible for the state of education in Istria: it was the duty of the provincial parliament to decide the language of education at the request of the municipalities. *Naša sloga* redirected this message to the local Croat electorate: 'Who lawfully creates Italian-language schools for you? Your municipal representatives. Who can lawfully set up schools in your language? Your municipal representatives.' And 'whose fault is it that you are represented there not by your own people but by Italians?' The readers were instructed to elect in future only 'men who hold dear their nation and language'. They were encouraged to follow the example of Žminj in the district of Pazin, where the newly elected Croat administrators 'looked bravely into the devil's eye by declaring at their first meeting that they were masters in their own house, and would no longer tolerate their children wasting their time at school by being taught in an Italian language that they do not understand'. Žminj asked the Italian-run Pazin district educational council for a Croat-language school, but received no reply, after which it forwarded its demand to the government in Trieste.[16]

The growth of Croat-language schools was of insufficient tempo and quality, however, to prevent the spread of the Italian language beyond its ethnic borders. Many Croats and Slovenes became bilingual and, once bilingual, were classified as Italian. In the provincial parliament Croat deputies regularly complained of the absence of Istrian government support for Slav schools and students. They argued that the problem of an insufficient number of literate administrators, which in some cases led to the dissolution of local governments, could be remedied only by opening a sufficient number of Croat-language schools. By law every town or village had the right to ask for a school in its language, provided that there were at least forty children of school age. To make the law workable, however, it was necessary to have an adequate number of teachers proficient in the language. The deputies consequently complained of the lack of Croat-language teachers: in 1880, out of 250 teachers in Istria 195 were Italian, eighteen Slovene and thirty-seven Croat.[17] The provincial government, however, used the lack of Croat-language teachers to justify its policy of opening Italian-language schools in overwhelmingly Croat-speaking areas. The battle for schools was not simply over their establishment, but also over their location. The results of the 1879 elections for the central parliament showed that while purely Croat municipalities elected Croat electors, the municipalities linked to Italian-speaking towns elected Italians even where Croats were in a majority. Croats and Slovenes consequently sought the opening of their own schools in the urban centres, where their nationals were most exposed to the danger of assimilation. The Italians, on the other hand, did what they could to prevent Slav schools opening in the towns.

In the Reichsrat

Frustrated in the local parliament, Croats took their problems to the Reichsrat, where they could expect help from other Slavs. In 1874 Vitezić complained that although Slavs formed two-thirds of the Istrian population and regularly paid their taxes, Italian remained the only language of instruction in most Istrian schools. In the absence of a gymnasium in their own language, the Istrian Croats were forced to study at the Croat gymnasium in Rijeka, but its matriculation certificate was not recognised in the Austrian part of the Monarchy. Since it was contrary to the Austrian constitution for Croats to be forced to study in a foreign tongue, Vitezić invited the government to do its duty by opening at least one Croat-language gymnasium and one teacher-training college. In 1875 Croats and Slovenes gained a teacher-training college in Koper (the district was predominantly Slav), but not a secondary school.

In 1883 the government in Vienna instructed the Istrian government to introduce Croat into the courts for cases involving Croats. This was the consequence of Gajo Bulat's law originally intended for Dalmatia, which Vienna now decided to extend also to Istria. The other Istrian deputy, an

Italian elected in the landowners' curia, argued against this rule, on the grounds that, in contrast to Dalmatian Croat, Istrian Slav dialects were both too numerous and too primitive to serve justice; and that in any case it would take years to raise the necessary number of officials, notaries and attorneys in that language. Vitezić retorted that Istrian Croats spoke the same language as Dalmatian Croats. He also pointed out that in Istria the language of the majority was not used in public life, by contrast with Dalmatia where Italian, the language of a tiny minority, was an official language. The law on equality of languages, however, was not enforced in Istria. A year later Vitezić informed the Reichsrat that Italian domination of Istrian schools was being used to assimilate Croats, that the electoral law also discriminated against them, and that the Istrian governmental majority was doctoring election results. In 1890, at a meeting of Slovene and Istrian Croat deputies, Vjekoslav Spinčić advocated the union of the Croatian and Slovenian lands, and a year later during a visit to Zagreb Istria's incorporation into Croatia.

In 1897 Istrian Croat deputies tabled an emergency resolution on the situation in the Austrian Littoral, asking that the Austrian constitutional provisions be applied to Istrian Croats and Slovenes. They pointed out that 17,000 Croat children of school age did not attend schools, and that there was not a single secondary or vocational school in the Slovene or Croat language. The local administration, moreover, was refusing to accept internal correspondence written in these languages. Two years later they again protested because, despite the official position that every submission should be processed in the language in which it was submitted, this was not effected in practice. In 1901 the Dalmatian deputy, Juraj Biankini, attacked the Austrian government for its conduct towards the Istrian Croats and Slovenes: 'Two-thirds of the Istrian population suffer from governmental bias and Italian arrogance. In the Istrian parliament, representatives of the popular majority are denied the right to speak in their own language; and when they nevertheless persist, they are exposed to the most barbaric attacks.' The existing government, he concluded, 'not only refuses to honour our [Croatian] state right, but also denies us basic language rights'.[18] In 1908 the Croat Istrian deputy Matko Mandić returned again to the theme. He began by noting the absence of a Croat-language stenographer in the chamber, although the government knew in advance that it would be addressed in Croat. He next submitted to detailed scrutiny the language situation in the Austrian Littoral, where most officials did not know Slovene or Croat. The situation in the department of justice was particularly bleak: the vast majority of judges and jurors did not know the language of the majority population,

Arms of the Croatian *regnum*, 1830.

Top left: Arms of the Dalmatian *regnum*, 1701.

Top right: Arms of the Slavonian *regnum*, 1701.

Middle left: Arms of imaginary Illyria, 1701.

Middle right: Ban Jelačić's banner, 1848, Croatia's first tricolour, with the Illyrian crescent moon and star atop the spear.

Left: Banner of the Zagreb National Guard, 1848, with the Illyrian arms and the slogan 'For Constitution and National Freedom'.

Top left: Flag of the Triune Kingdom, second half of the 19th century.

Top right: Flag of the Independent State of Croatia, 1941.

Left: Arms of the Socialist Republic of Croatia, 1947.

Above: Flag of the Republic of Croatia, 1990.

The first Zagreb Christmas Fair, Ljubo Babić, 1926.

Adriatic Day, Pavao Gavranić, 1933.

Opatija, Edo Murtić, 1955.

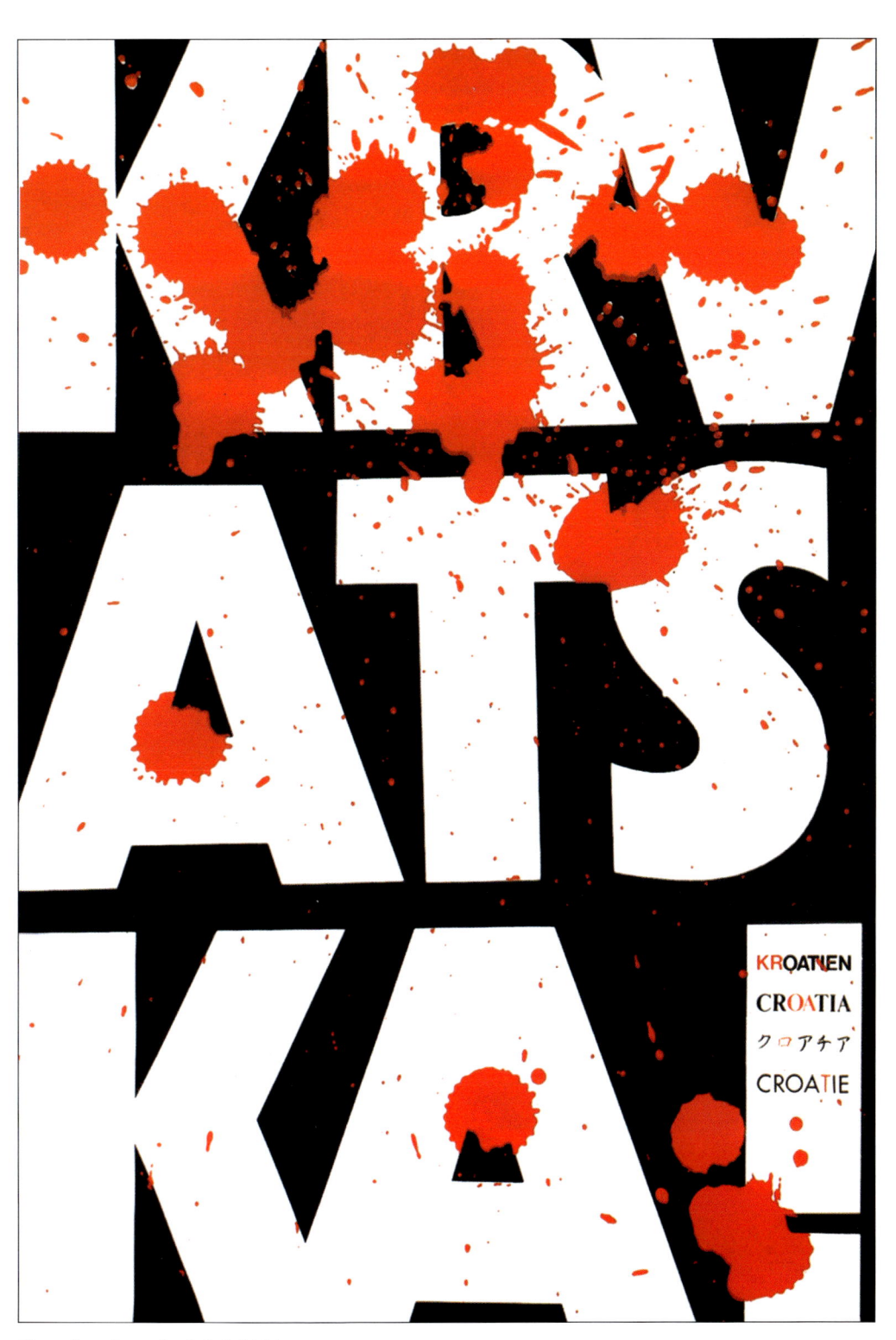

Krvatska!, Boris Ljubičić, 1991.

The 29th Split Summer Festival, Boris Bućan, 1983.

which was thereby denied elementary justice. The same situation prevailed also in the finance and tax departments, where few officials were able to deal with submissions in Croat or Slovene. The department of post and telegraph, covering an area in which 75 per cent of the population was Slav, used only Italian and German. The coast of the Austrian Littoral and Dalmatia, he continued, was inhabited overwhelmingly by Croats and Slovenes, yet in the department of maritime affairs only seventeen out of 107 officials spoke their languages. The central ministry of railways employed 180 people, of whom only twenty-seven were Slavs. To add insult to injury, the names of the stations on the Trieste-Pula-Rovinj and Trieste-Poreč routes, which passed through mainly Slav-inhabited territory, were written only in German.[19]

The language ruse

In 1880 census forms for the first time provided space for an entry meant to establish the actual national proportions in the Austrian part of the Monarchy. The form did not ask for the mother tongue, however, but for the *Umgangsprache* or 'commonly used language'. As critics pointed out at the time, a non-German living in Vienna would thus be classified as German by nationality. This highly elastic formula favoured Germans and Italians in ethnically mixed areas. Austrian Italians, while protesting against the use of the formula in the Italian areas of Tyrol, readily accepted it for Istria. Since the municipalities were given the task of collecting the census data, their manipulation especially in areas with illiterate population was widespread. Some municipalities changed their national make-up practically overnight. Data collected on this basis were consequently unreliable as an indicator of national composition; but they did nevertheless indicate growing assimilation of the Slav, mainly Croat, population. According to such data, the Italian share of the Istrian population rose from 26 per cent in 1846 to 40 per cent in 1880. Given the fact that the Slavs were overwhelmingly a rural population, their relative decline could be ascribed only to the statistical method based on 'commonly spoken language'. There followed, unsurprisingly, a string of complaints from the Croat and Slovene deputies about falsification of the nationality data. The next census, however, carried out in 1890, showed that Italianisation was slowing down, and that Croat numbers were growing faster than Italian, because of increased educational facilities in the Croat language. Census battles, however, continued to be waged every ten years.[20]

Despite the general advance of education, at the start of the twentieth century 40 per cent of the Istrian population remained illiterate, of whom the largest relative numbers were to be found in the districts of Poreč (66 per cent) and Pazin (50 per cent). The fact that the number of children attending school in the period between 1890 and 1905 grew faster in Dalmatia (from 83 per cent to 92 per cent) than in Istria (from 74 per cent to 78 per cent) was due mainly to the faster spread of Croat-language schools. As Angelo Vivante noted in his authoritative work, the surprisingly high degree of illiteracy among the Istrian population of both nationalities at the start of the twentieth century, but especially among the Croats, represented the gravest possible indictment of the Italian urban culture.[21]

War by other means

The spread of schools and administration in their own language, combined with capital accumulation realised though their savings and credit associations, led to Croat national consolidation in Istria. A new middle class emerged, which meant that Croat representation no longer had to rely on the clergy. By 1908 this layer showed a spread similar to the Italian, with lawyers, teachers, clerics, officials and landowners. This coincided with a generational change: Dobrila died in 1882, Bastian in 1885. In 1883 Matko Mandić took over as editor of *Naša sloga*. As Croats migrated to the towns, especially to Pula, the old division between a mainly rural Croat and a mainly urban Italian Istria disappeared. A growing Slav banking network weakened the earlier dependence of Slav peasants on Italian moneylenders. These changes frightened the Italian middle class. The possibility of losing their traditional dominance was experienced as an Italian existential question, and all the more so given that the Croat *risorgimento* manifested itself in its final phase as a movement for Istria's union with Croatia. Croat Istria's orientation towards Croatia was conditioned, however, not by national sentiments alone, but also by the need, in view of the persistent illiteracy in the rural municipalities, to import skilled individuals from the Croatian Littoral and Dalmatia to act as their leaders and officials.

The Italian-Croat balance had begun to shift with the introduction in 1869 of compulsory education of children between the ages of six and fourteen. Once education in the mother tongue became a right and public education bodies were obliged to ensure this for all in nationally mixed areas, the old vision of a 'natural' convergence of the peninsula's peoples into a single Italian nation had to be abandoned. The fact that the municipalities were given the right, in consultation with the provincial government, to decide the language of instruction meant that elections at all levels acquired a strong national charge. A bitter struggle ensued for each village and school, stimulating the rural population's political engagement. Italian national ideologues preferred to ascribe Istrian Slav resistance to becoming Italians not to their national sentiments, however, but to the agitation of a 'few Liburnian deputies, two or three journalists, and a host of foreign clerics who [believe] that political rights can triumph over the right of an ancient civilisation'.[22] Local Italian irredentist organisations, which grew in strength and number in the closing decades of the nineteenth century, claimed all the Austrian Littoral for Italy; they were supported in this by Italy's political and military elites, which agreed that Venice's former East Adriatic possessions should at the right moment be 'reclaimed' for Italy.

Giorgio Baseggio, an émigré from Koper living in Milan, wrote at this time:

> The uprising of the Slavs and their violent struggle against the Italian element demand a new approach. [Istrian Italians] are in no position to resist the Slav flood on their own, [while] the Austrian government is openly siding with the Slavs. [If] things continue to develop in this manner, it is my belief that within ten to fifteen years the Italian element will disappear from Istria. Compressed into their small towns along the coast, they will see their representation in the Reichsrat and even worse the local parliament's majority in Slav hands. This will mean *finis Histriae*, since for Istria to be free it must be Italian, that is, inhabited by Italians. [As] one who loves Italian Istria, I cannot bear to think of the Slavs setting up their government there; so I believe that in this situation the primary task of all patriots is to struggle against the intrepid Slav enemy: we must throw all we have against him.[23]

'All we have' included schools. Throughout the Habsburg Monarchy at this time schools were being established as national markers within contested zones. Austrian pan-Germans led the way in 1880 by creating *Der Deutscher Schulverein* (German School Association), which built schools in nationally mixed areas in order to prevent assimilation of the Germans – but also to promote the Germanisation of the non-Germans. Privately funded with money from Austria and Germany, the *Schulverein* was especially active in the Italian-speaking areas of Tyrol. Its schools, which the Italian press described as 'German sentries', became popular also among the Italians, because Italian children of poor families were supplied with clothes and other necessities. The Austrian government itself set up a similar foundation, *Der Militär-Schulverein*, which built primary and secondary schools for children of

German officers and soldiers stationed in non-German areas: well organised and equipped, these schools were meant to attract the local population as well. In 1884 the Slovenes established their own Association (*Družba*) of St Cyril and Methodius in Ljubljana, with a branch in Trieste, aimed at limiting the influence of the *Schulverein*. In 1885 a group of Trentino Italians established *Pro Patria*, quoting Article 19 of the Austrian Constitution which affirmed the Austrian nations' 'inalienable right to protect and nurture their own nationality and their own national language'. *Pro Patria* was created to protect the Italian language in Trentino, but within a year or so forty-four local branches opened throughout the Austrian part of the Monarchy, involving tens of thousands of members. In 1893 the Istrian Croats, with the aid of Franjo Rački and Josip Strossmayer, eventually established their own *Družba,* with the task of resisting the assimilation of their nationals by building Croat-language schools. Judging by the *Družba*'s audit in 1907, it received financial support from all over Croatia.[24]

In contrast to the Italians of Trentino, who sought to protect themselves against Germanisation, the Italians of the Austrian Littoral applied this model to an area where there was no threat to the Italian language, where the majority of schools taught in Italian and where Italian was the privileged medium of public communication. *Pro Patria* here was supposed to protect Gorizia and Istria 'from the inflamed Slavs who, armed by the state, are knocking at the doors of unprotected Latin cities, threatening Italian language and culture'.[25] The society's first general assembly, retrospectively described as 'the first parliament of the unredeemed lands', was consequently attended by delegates from Trieste, Gorizia and Istria. Felice Venezian, a leading irredentist from Trieste, declared on this occasion:

> People of nationality and birth different from those present here [persist] in their determination not to accept [our] civilisation and culture. We were forced to fight these adversaries on our own, courageously and stubbornly, but alone. No longer! The alarm set off from our sea shores now echoes in your mountains. Thank you for offering us the possibility of victory in the joint struggle for preservation of our language and our glorious civilisation. [. . .] Our forefathers used the *fascio dei littori* as a mark of the power of the [Roman] empire. We as its true descendants must revive this ancient symbol. Let us act as a single *fascio,* strong enough to prevent permanent loss of the immortal and glorious signs of the Roman imperial presence in our lands.

Attilio Confler from Trieste concurred: 'While you in Trentino have to

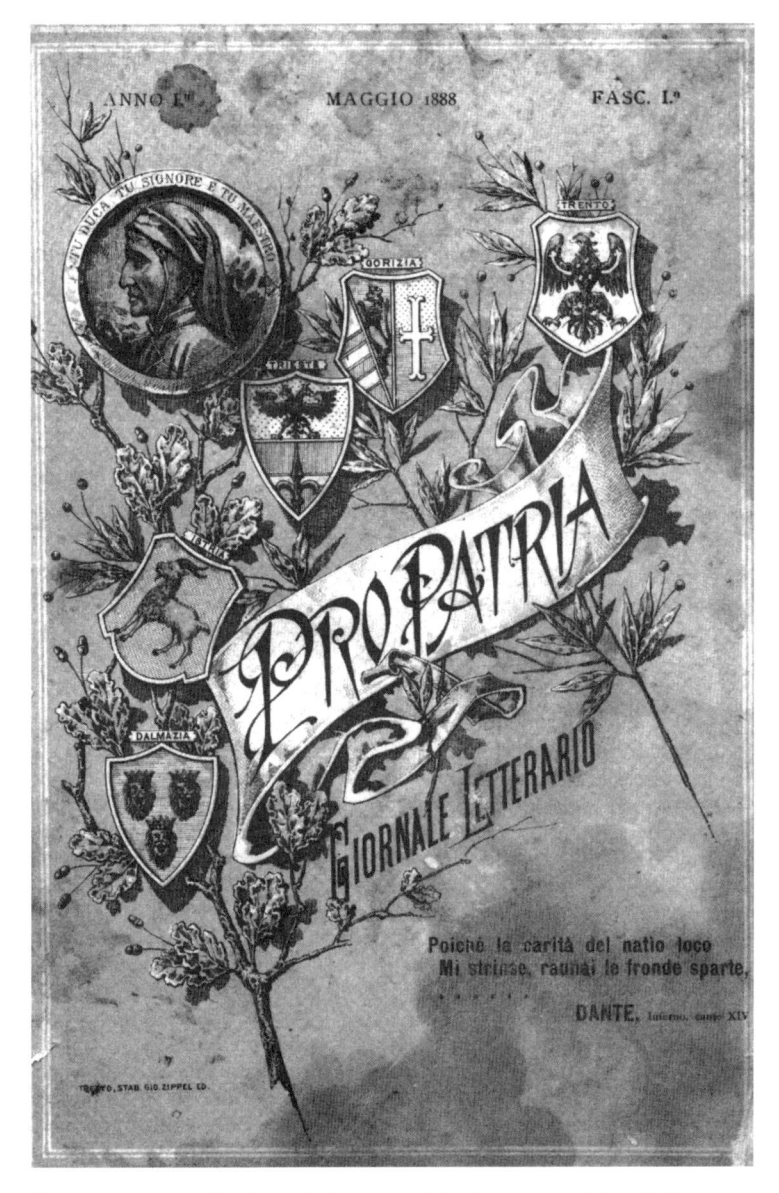

Cover page of *Pro Patria* with the arms of the 'unredeemed lands': Dalmatia, Istria, Trieste, Gorizia and Trento

defend yourselves against a nation which, though of aggressive intent, is nevertheless illustrious and educated, we have to struggle against uncultured tribes devoid of literature and tradition, and even one can say of language.'[26]

In 1890, at the founding meeting of the *Società Dante Alighieri* in Rome, the member of the Italian parliament and former minister of culture, Ruggero Bonghi was elected its president. On this occasion Bonghi declared: 'The aim is to spread our language and culture, the two sources of our life, and to join to the homeland those who remain separated from it, i.e. to free these Italians from the political bonds and states in which they live. (It) is to be expected that you will achieve this with the same ease that characterises your work in the colonies.' A large number of Italian politicians, parliamentary deputies, industrialists, trade unionists and others joined the society. *Pro Patria* in Austria and *Società Dante Alighieri* in Italy established a close cooperation.[27] In 1899 the Slovene paper *Edinost* (Unity), published in Trieste, protested against *Società Dante Alighieri*'s anti-Slav policies. Dinko Politeo, a Dalmatian journalist, wrote in 1900 in *Agramer Tagblatt* (Zagreb Daily) that: 'the society spreads political irredentism under the cover of defence of the Italian language'. *Naša Sloga* reported in the same year a speech given by the Italian senator Pasquale Villari, the society's new president, in which he stated that its task was 'to halt the German advance to Verona and Slav mastery over the Adriatic Sea', and noted Villari's claim that 'the battle for the language, as expression of the national soul, has replaced armed struggle'.[28]

During 1886 *Pro Patria* organisations spread across western Istria, to the great consternation of the Istrian Nationals. *Naša sloga* raised the alarm: 'Every Istrian Croat must bear in mind that our opponents will henceforth use money and donations received from abroad to buy your children [in order to] make new Italians and hence your enemies; that they will use money to buy your hearts, your decency and your honour. [Those] who receive it will bring damnation upon themselves, for the price will be the most shameful betrayal a human being can commit: the betrayal of his ancestors, family and progeny, his language and his decency.'[29] The Nationals, as we have seen, created in the end their own private school foundation. In 1890, however, *Pro Patria*'s irredentist sentiments became so public that the Austrian government finally banned the organisation. Its local branches were dissolved, and its schools, nurseries and libraries closed. It re-emerged almost immediately, however, under the new name *Lega Nazionale*. The trick was so obvious that the request for registration was rejected – but the German chancellor Otto von Bismarck intervened on Italy's side. *Lega Nazionale* took over the previous society's network and property, statute, activists and programme. The statute was amended, however, to allow membership to those under eighteen years of age, and to permit individuals to join a local group without necessarily living in the area – which aided the establishment of sections even in areas where there were no Italians. The

Lega financed its activities from membership fees, events, donations, etc., but money was raised also in Italy, mainly through the offices of *Dante Alighieri*, and secretly transferred to the *Lega* in Trieste. Riccardo Pitteri, one of its presidents, described *Lega Nazionale* as 'a federation of five Italian provinces in Austria: Trentino, Trieste, Istria, Friuli and Dalmatia, established for the protection of twenty centuries of Italian language and civilisation'. The *Lega* built schools in nationally mixed but also in purely Slav areas of Istria, and subsidised students attending the teacher-training college and the gymnasia in Koper and Pazin. It also funded Italian seminarists, with the aim of 'easing access to priesthood for an Italian element that would replace hostile Croat priests';[30] provided scholarships for Italian university students studying in Trieste, Florence, Graz or Vienna; and financed campaigns such as the one for establishment of an Italian university in Trieste. On the eve of the First World War the society had 45,000 members organised in 177 local branches. It was finally banned in 1915, after Italy's declaration of war against Austria-Hungary.

The functioning of the *Lega* in Istria can be illustrated by the case of the village of Labinci in the nationally mixed district of Poreč (37.5 per cent Croat according to the census of 1890), which at this time (1892) had twenty-six Italian schools but no Croat school. In Labinci, however, 'the Croats had practically drowned the Italians, to the extent that the latter were voting for Croat representatives'. In the early 1890s, therefore, the *Lega* built there a primary and a nursery school, which together enrolled 300 children. Twenty years later: 'the whole village has become once again fully Italian'.[31] Labinci, however, had been a wholly Croat village, as testified to by the use of Church Slavonic in its parish church. The *Lega* proceeded to open schools in other parts of Istria, for which the Istrian parliament donated 10,000 forints per annum, starting in 1908. The Croat deputies' request for similar support for the *Družba*, however, was rejected. Individual cities also aided the *Lega*'s activities. Pula gave it 10,000 forints to build an Italian school in the area of Buje east of Umag; Umag supported another such school further east in the area of Motovun. The appearance of well-equipped *Lega* schools fuelled national strife, especially in places where Slav villages, too poor to build their own schools, were forced to rely on an unwilling state to open a school in their language.

The territorial spread of the *Lega* schools was designed to prevent what Italian activists saw as the Slavicisation of Istria, and in particular to maintain the Italian character of the coastal towns. Attilio Tamaro, a leading Italian irredentist from Trieste, made this clear when addressing a local meeting of the *Lega*:

> Along the borders of our lands merciless German and Slav enemies stand ready for attack, deployed along a long arc stretching from the farthest valleys of the Trentino, across the Julian Alps to the ruins of Roman and Italian Split,[32] cutting across Friuli and our Istria. Along this gigantic arc millions of men are pressing against our own forces. Governed by the will to live upright and as Italians, we have established the *Lega Nazionale* to act as our shield.

He described Slav and German schools as 'alien institutions seeking our destruction', 'garrisons in which the enemy is waiting in ambush', 'enemy camps seeking to conquer', 'foreign garrisons on our own porch.'[33] In his vision, building schools was synonymous with the medieval practice of building city walls.

> If I could draw you a map of Istria, you would be able to see that the [*Lega*] schools have been built as rows of bastions, strong ramparts, veritable castles erected to defend our cities as used to be done in the past. Three cities are being protected in this way: Labin, Motovun and Poreč, [all of which] stand in the middle of, and face towards, the invading national enemy. [These] cities are the jewels which the strong arm of the Slav countryside is trying to seize by turning against them the political power of the municipalities. We have protected these cities by surrounding them with schools, by erecting perfect ramparts against this menace.

Lega schools had thus 'surrounded Labin', were 'protecting' Poreč and would 'encircle' Motovun. The Italian school in Labinci was part of the wall being built around Labin. The Italian historian Carmelo Cottone shared Tamaro's vision: 'The [*Lega*] schools formed a chain, extending all the way to the sea, of veritable military fortifications built around Italian centres exposed to the Slav danger.'[34]

Since these 'fortifications' were erected in mixed or predominantly Croat areas, the system could work only by assimilation of the local Croats. The Croat response was to erect their own ramparts. The case of the Croat village of Tar, north of Poreč, illustrates the progress of this war by other means. At the start of the twentieth century this village had an Italian primary and an Italian nursery school. The nearest Croat school, built by the *Družba* in

Kaštelir, was four miles away, so in 1901 the *Družba* opened a Croat-language school in Vabriga, just over half a mile from Tar. A year later the *Lega* opened an Italian school in Vabriga right next to that of the *Družba*, and a nursery school in the nearby village of Frati. Four Italian educational institutions thus appeared in the vicinity of three villages whose population was almost exclusively Croat. In order to understand the urgency of this school-building strategy, one must recall the earlier decision of the provincial parliament to change the administrative borders in order to bring the Croat villages under the influence of the Italian-speaking cities. This decision turned out to be counter-productive in the longer run, since the villages, having become dependent on the cities where the local administration sat, now sought to influence their governments. It was now even less possible than before to separate Croats from Italians: in the case of Labinci, not only Croats but also Italians voted for ethnic Croat officials. The answer had been sought in educating Croats to become Italians, but this was proving increasingly difficult.

Parliamentary impasse

The arrival in the early 1880s of the Party of Right hardened the stance of the Croat benches in the Istrian parliament. On 21 August 1883 Matko Laginja made history by delivering his maiden speech in Croat – or rather trying to deliver it, since he managed to say only a few words before being stopped. On leaving the parliament building in Poreč, the Croat deputies were attacked by a local mob, after which they stated that they would return only if their safety could be guaranteed. In their absence the parliamentary majority confirmed Italian as its only language of business, but the central government refused to sanction this decision.

The language struggle intensified during the 1890s. In 1896 the Croats were again prevented from speaking in their language, and the chamber again voted that the language of the parliament was Italian, so that questions, motions and proposals might be put only in the Italian language. Crowds again attacked the Slav deputies on leaving the town, and again they withdrew from parliament. The central government again refused to sanction the decision, but this time it also dismissed the parliament and moved its seat temporarily to Pula, which it wished to see made into the provincial capital. But the move made little difference, so the Slav deputies resorted to boycotting the parliament. In 1897 elections for the Reichsrat included a new, fifth curia, to be elected by all males aged twenty-four and over. Four thousand Croat peasants now marched to Poreč in order to protect their candidates. A state of emergency was proclaimed in some municipalities. Matko Laginja and Vjekoslav Spinčić were elected in the two village curiae, but the fifth curia was won by an Italian candidate. In 1898 Matko Mandić again tried to make a speech in Croat, but the speaker asked him to use Italian. The Croats again left the parliament. In 1900, under pressure from the government in Trieste, the two sides met in order to reach an agreement that would permit the parliament to function. The Slavs asked for language equality, inclusion of their representatives in parliamentary bodies and increased support for Slav schools. The Italian side refused them all. The Italian Liberals now began propagating the idea of Istrian regionalism, as an alternative to Istria joining Croatia. The Croat political movement, on the other hand, was showing signs of crisis. The 1900 census also showed that Italian numbers were again growing at Croat expense, due probably to the predominance and higher quality of Italian-language schools – most Croat-language schools in fact provided only minimal literacy.

The Istrian government had found various ways of frustrating education in the Croat language. As Cottone later admitted, 'at the time when the schools were maintained by the provincial government, those in the mainly Slav villages were established in a manner [which ensured] they could not advance'. Bilingual schools set up in nationally mixed areas actually functioned as de facto Italian schools, since few teachers knew Croat. Italian was an obligatory subject in most Croat schools, whereas only a negligible number of Italian-language schools taught Croat. Even when the government in Trieste, petitioned by the parents, ordered the opening of a Croat-language school in a particular place, the local authorities would find ways of delaying or sabotaging the instruction. In 1911, for example, the provincial government had sixty-two requests pending for new schools dating from 1906, of which nine came from Italian, eleven from Slovene and forty-two from Croat municipalities. As a poor province, Istria was unable to fund all its educational needs from its own resources; but the speed with which the Italian school in Pazin was built showed that support for Italian-language education was the priority. Another device was to use the category of 'commonly used language' to define the nationality of a place, as a prelude to building an Italian-language school. The population of Funtana in the Poreč district, for example, consisting mainly of Croats with a few Montenegrins and Albanians, was classified as Italian. In 1883, under parental pressure, the government did compromise by allowing Croat be taught in the local school; but the language of instruction remained Italian. This policy led to the spread of the Italian as the 'commonly used language' and, by definition, also of the Italian nationality. As a result the Croat population in the Poreč district officially declined by 10 per cent between 1890 and 1900.

Faced with such facts, the Croat political leaders renewed their efforts. Between 1897 and 1900 ten new reading rooms and cultural societies were established, six savings and credit associations, and three cultural cooperatives. The *Družba* built four primary schools. In 1899 a printing press was established in Pula, to which *Naša sloga* moved from Trieste. New state schools opened too, in addition to the secondary school in Pazin. Between 1901 and 1906 fifty-six new agricultural cooperatives, savings banks and trade societies were established, as well as eleven reading rooms and six 'national halls'. Three more *Družba* schools appeared. Financial aid for these projects came from Croatia. In 1906 Kastav gained a teacher-training college, after which journals for teachers and young readers sprung up in Pula. Istrian political life now also started to diversify. Slav Nationals and Italian Liberals would henceforth share the electorate with (mainly Italian) Social Christian and Social Democratic parties.

The national struggle in Istria was at all times a triangular one, with Italians and Croats joining together at times against the Austrian German-speaking government, while at other times they sought its help against each other. This was most visible in the great Austrian naval port and arsenal of Pula, which drew into its activities the local population of both nationalities. Although Italians formed less than half the city's population, they dominated the local administration and did all they could to exclude the Croat language from offices, schools, public signs – and even the graveyard.[35] As was true also of Trieste, the first generation of the Croat inflow were ready to assimilate into the urban way of life, which was Italian, in order to survive and advance. At the very basic level, in the absence of Croat-language schools one could learn to read and write only in Italian, or possibly in German. German on the other hand was not popular, since both national communities viewed Austria as Germany's outpost in the Adriatic. In 1907, when the Germans and the Italians fought over control of the city, the Croat vote split equally between the two parties. The tendency to assimilation was halted during the 1880s. One sign of this was the transfer of *Naša sloga* from Trieste to Pula, and the founding in 1888 of *Il diritto croato* (Croatian Right), a cultural journal in the Italian language. Both were printed on the large printing press owned by the patriotic Croat Krmpotić family. A year later the first *Družba* school appeared – by 1910 there were six more. During this time the number of Croat-language law firms jumped from one to five. Croats were increasingly present in the administration and courts. The National Hall built at this time became a cultural and political centre of the Pula Croats. The Istrian Croat middle class was growing in size and wealth. Dalmatia and continental Croatia contributed to this advance by sending skilled people and money, drama societies and lecturers. Time was now working in Croat favour.

In 1901 the government in Trieste tried again to mediate a compromise between Nationals and Liberals, but without success. Two years later the Italian majority once again refused to elect Slav deputies to parliamentary bodies, to which the Slavs responded with a filibuster. Their repeated attempts to speak in their own language were prevented by the Italian deputies and the Italian gallery. A possibility for compromise appeared in 1904, when the Italians sought Croat and Slovene support for an Italian university in Trieste. The Slavs, however, agreed to support only bilingual universities in nationally mixed areas. In the local parliament Croats were again prevented from speaking in Croat. Following a heated dispute on the legality of such obstruction and procedures, the minority walked out and the parliament's speaker resigned. Fearing that the new speaker might accept the use of Croat, the Italians too left the parliament, which remained closed for two years.

Failure to divide Istria

During the debate on the introduction of universal male suffrage for elections to the Reichsrat, which formally opened in 1896, the Istrian Nationals supported the reform, while the Italian party agreed on condition that its majority of representation in the central parliament was secured. Pressure from Vienna and its promise of more aid for Slav schools led to an agreement between the two sides for an equal division of the Istrian seats in the Reichsrat. Istria was consequently divided into six electoral districts, of which three were reserved for Italians, two for Croats and one for Slovenes.[36] The Italian side refused, however, to accept a bilingual parliament in return. In the 1907 Reichsrat elections Laginja, Spinčić and Mandić easily won the three Slav seats, whereas in the three Italian electoral districts no party gained a majority. Of some significance, Laginja won as many votes in the Pula district as the Italian Liberal candidate, but the Italian parties united to prevent this 'Italian' seat falling to the Croats. The easy success of the Croat deputies and Laginja's good showing in Pula were celebrated by Croat politicians as a great victory. Encouraged by the fact that these first elections based on universal male suffrage showed that the Croat and Slovene electoral districts 'were indeed Croat and Slovene', whereas 'the so-called Italian districts proved by no means wholly Italian', *Naša sloga* appeared with headlines such as: 'Istria has arisen!' and 'The people have defeated their oppressors!' Copying the rhetoric of its opponents, the paper wrote jubilantly: 'Istria is not Italian but Croat, and will remain Croat!'[37]

The introduction of universal suffrage for elections to the Reichsrat created pressure to introduce the same electoral system in elections for regional parliaments.[38] Such a measure would clearly benefit local national majorities. The Dalmatian parliament itself had voted in favour of such a reform, and in 1907 Laginja demanded in the Reichsrat that the Istrian parliament too be elected on that basis. His proposal was supported by the Istrian Social Democrats and Christian Socials; but the Italian Liberals favoured instead the introduction of a fifth curia based on universal suffrage, and as a compromise offered additional seats in the provincial parliament to the Croats and Slovenes. Vienna supported the idea of electoral reform for Istria, in the hope of thus gaining an opportunity to give the navy a greater say in the running of Pula; but it was against universal suffrage for crownland parliaments. In 1908 Istrian Croat and Italian representatives met in Vienna and, despite Spinčić's protests, accepted the Italian Liberals' offer. The new electoral law was passed by the Istrian parliament in 1908.

The law raised the number of elected deputies to forty-four. The landowners' and trades' curia kept their five and two seats respectively, but the cities increased their representation to fourteen and the villages to fifteen, while eight seats were allocated to the new curia. According to the deal reached, the Slavs would have nineteen seats: three in the city curia, twelve in the village curia and four in the new curia. The borders of existing electoral districts would be re-drawn. Decisions regarding education, agriculture and public works, and municipal demands requiring parliamentary approval or new legislation, would be made by consensus. Local parliamentary elections in 1908, however, showed that the compromise mainly served the Italian Liberals, who won twenty-four seats, while the Nationals won not nineteen, but eighteen seats.[39] Strengthened in this manner, the Italian Liberals now made implementation of the agreement conditional upon a prior compromise on a redivision of electoral districts. In 1909 the two sides agreed to postpone municipal elections for six years, or until an agreement could be reached. The parliamentary executive, which now included two Nationals, was then entrusted with the task of dividing Istria on an effectively ethnic basis, proposing a solution to the language question, and devising a more equitable sharing of the provincial budget. The Nationals wished the language issue to be settled first, while the Liberals insisted that the new administrative map be agreed first. The Italian side asked that the small isolated Italian towns in central Istria and the Croat and Slovene villages along the western coast be included in Italian electoral districts, in order to create a continuous Italian territory. This the Croats refused. *Naša sloga* wrote that they rejected a national division of Istria, since it would have left all the important towns in the west in Italian hands: the Italians wished to 'push us away from the sea on the western side of our province'.

When parliament was recalled in 1910, the Liberal deputies again insisted that National deputies should speak Italian. The chamber broke up in disorder when the executive decided to subsidise an exhibition in Koper designed to celebrate the Italian nature of Istria. The following extract from the official records for 1910 reveals all the absurdity of the Italian deputies' intransigence. The parliament's speaker is Lodovico Rizzi. Ivan Cukon, his fellow lawyer from Poreč, appears here as Zuccon.

> Hon. Spinčić: (speaks Slav).
> Speaker: Who wishes to speak next? Hon. Zuccon.
> Zuccon: (speaks Slav).
> Hon. Spinčić (interrupts, turning towards the Speaker): You are trying to provoke disorder in the House.
> Speaker: You don't have the floor, Mr Spinčić. (Interruptions and noise on the minority benches). Please continue, Mr Zuccon.
> Hon. Zuccon: (continues to speak Slav amid interruptions and comments. The Speaker intervenes several times to re-establish order. At one point Hon. Zuccon turns to the Speaker president and appears to be asking a question.)
> Speaker (interrupts): If you wish to address me that's fine, but only in a language that I can understand. It is useless to speak to me in a language I do not understand.
> Hon. Zuccon (continues in Slav among growing interruptions. At some point he stops speaking but remains standing)
> Speaker: Have you finished, Mr Zuccon? (Hon. Zuccon appears to say no.) In that case, please proceed. It is impossible to continue in this manner. Please speak or give way.
> Hon. Zuccon: (speaks several sentences in Slav) I have put a question and now await your answer.
> Speaker: I have already told you I do not understand you. (Noise) I ask you to continue to speak or to give way. (Deputies of the minority violently protest, while the Speaker repeatedly tries to make order.) Mr Zuccon, do you intend to continue or not?

> Hon. Zuccon: (speaks several sentences in Slav and then falls silent).
>
> Dr Apollonio: Don't let him proceed, by God! (Voices from the minority [Slav] benches: Bravo, Prompter!)
>
> Speaker (having rung his bell to restore order): Please continue, Mr Zuccon.
>
> Hon. Zuccon: (speaks several sentences in Slav and then stops).
>
> Speaker: Hon. Zuccon, I warn you for the last time to proceed, otherwise I shall have to stop you. (Noise and voices of protest grow in intensity. The Speaker repeatedly rings his bell.)
>
> Hon. Zuccon: (says a few words in Slav in the direction of the Speaker and then stops).
>
> Speaker: Hon. Zuccon, I must ask you to give way.[40]

It is impossible to learn from official records kept in this manner what the two Croat deputies were saying. According to *Naša Sloga*, Spinčić and Cukon were protesting against the Speaker's procedurally inadmissible decision to debate the proposal on the Koper exhibition before some fifty urgent proposals dealing with the economic situation in the province tabled a week earlier. In order to prevent the parliament from approving the subsidy for the Koper exhibition, the Croat and Slovene deputies then got up and pulled the green baize off the tables of the Speaker and the stenographer, causing papers and inkpots to scatter all over the floor. The Italian deputies then went after them, and the gallery, which was mainly Italian, joined the fray. The mêlée went on for four hours, after which the governor of the province announced that parliament was closed.

All negotiations were suspended. The parliamentary executive proceeded to make decisions without Croats, and refused to approve the budgets of Croat and Slovene municipalities. Spinčić complained in the Reichsrat about the illegality of this behaviour, and in 1911 the government invited both sides to Vienna for talks. At this meeting it was agreed that the question of Slav schools would be settled within five years, and that in the meantime the municipal budgets would be passed. The agreement was reached in time for elections to the Reichsrat, during which the Italian Liberals mobilised their constituency by conjuring up a threat of Istria's absorption into Croatia. The results were similar to those achieved in the previous elections: the Istrian east returned the Nationals, the west the Italian Liberals. The other two parties remained marginal.

The Liberals now drafted an agreement which excluded language equality, and proposed a division of municipalities that the Croats found unacceptable. In 1913 the Austrian government offered its own solution, which basically endorsed the Italian proposals. The Croats rejected it, accusing Vienna of bowing before Italy. In the local parliamentary elections of 1914 the Nationals won their nineteen seats, and 16,000 more votes than the Italian Liberals, but the parliament never met. As a result, Istria entered the First World War in a state of near-complete Italian-Slav polarisation, with each side hoping that the war would lead to the realisation of their respective national dreams. Well before the outbreak of war, however, the local Italian leaders' frustration with their inability to turn Slavs into Italians had become an 'almost psychopathic' obsession.[41]

PART THREE

Yugoslavia and Beyond

THIRTEEN

The Road to Yugoslavia

> The Germans, hitherto a 'people of state', had caused the first crisis [of the Habsburg Monarchy]; the Magyars, still a 'people of state', caused the second. Little did these privileged nations realise that a third crisis was maturing in the minds of a few Croat intellectuals, as the result of the desertion of Croatia by the dynasty and its oppression by the Magyars. Yet within ten years the South Slav question overshadowed the Austrian constitutional confusion and Magyar agitation alike; and within twenty years the South Slav challenge ended the Habsburg dynasty, German predominance, and Great Hungary.
>
> A. J. P. Taylor, *The Habsburg Monarchy 1809–1918*

At the start of the twentieth century two state ideas fought for supremacy in the South Slav lands of Austria-Hungary, one Croatian, one Serbian. Disregarding their internal contradictions and complexities of evolution, they can be summarised as follows. The Croatian idea viewed a united Croatia as the natural centre of the Habsburg Monarchy's South Slavs (identified as Slovenes, Croats and Serbs), who at some point in the future would join other South Slavs to form a Yugoslav federation. This idea appeared unfeasible already by the middle of the nineteenth century. Not only had Croatia failed to unite, but its national body had become divided into Croat and Serb components – with the latter, moreover, seeking union with Serbia. The Serbian idea was to unite all Serbs, that is, all 'Serb lands', with Serbia. This could be achieved, however, only with the dissolution of both Croatia and Austria-Hungary. This too was to prove infeasible. Croatia, albeit remaining formally divided, became politically united. Austria-Hungary was destroyed in the First World War, but it was Yugoslavia and not Great Serbia that appeared at the end of the war. This outcome was due mainly to the efforts mounted by Dalmatian Croats in the first two decades of the twentieth century. Insofar as Yugoslavia had a Piedmont, it was Dalmatia. The British historian A. J. P. Taylor rightly stressed the pivotal role played by these Croats in the dissolution of the Habsburg Monarchy, but he erred in presenting them as 'a few intellectuals'.[1] They were in fact experienced politicians, leaders of a party governing the strategically important Austrian province of Dalmatia. Their possession of Dalmatia endowed them with a political authority without which they would not have been able to initiate 'the third crisis' of the Austrian state system.

Yugoslavia was not the Dalmatians' original destination, however. It became so only after all other possibilities of realising Croatian independence had become exhausted. The persistence of dualism ended all reasonable hope that the Habsburg Monarchy could be transformed into a federal state, or that its South Slavs could unite within it as a separate unit. Dualism, an arrangement personified by Khuen-Héderváry, was a barrier also to Croatia's own unification and indeed was leading towards Croatia's political collapse. Dualism, however, was guarded by Bismarck's Germany. By the end of the nineteenth century the Dalmatians came to understand that the main threat to Croatia was in fact the German *Drang nach Osten* – Germany's domination of the Monarchy and its growing interest in the Balkans. Impelled at all times by the desire to unite their country and make it independent, the Dalmatians now sought also to protect it from the German threat. The strategy they adopted to this end led them ultimately to embrace the Yugoslav solution for Croatia.

These national strategists derived paradoxically from the Party of Right, whose ideological mentor, Ante Starčević, had resolutely rejected any Slav framework for Croatia. As it turned out, however, by winning Dalmatia for the Party of Right the strategists also took the first step on the road to Yugoslavia. They continued in fact with the old policy of state right, which they adapted creatively to the new realities. In order to understand why Yugoslavia became their preferred strategic option, and indeed why that option itself in the end proved unworkable, it is necessary to retrace the steps that led them in that direction. These involved turning Croatia against the Monarchy, and overcoming the Croat–Serb conflict within Croatia. Having achieved this, they were in a position successfully to challenge the Serbian state idea, by counterposing to it the Yugoslav concept. By erecting Yugoslavia in the path of Great Serbia, they also laid the foundations for the future emergence of the Yugoslav federation. To be sure, they were not

Winning Dalmatia for the Party of Right

The ascent of the Party of Right in Dalmatia was in the first instance due to Austria's neglect of the province.[2] As the nineteenth century drew to a close, the ruling National Party's policy of cooperation with the central government was bringing ever more meagre results. Austria's interests in the Adriatic concentrated on Trieste, which generous state aid had transformed into a major trading post, while Hungary's main interest was in Rijeka, which also underwent a spectacular growth. Both were linked by rail to the respective capitals. Dalmatia's ports, on the other hand, were stagnating. They needed railway links to Ban's Croatia and Bosnia, but for political reasons neither Austria nor Hungary wished to see these built. In their absence, earlier hopes that Bosnian trade might be attracted to the Dalmatian ports evaporated, while trade with Montenegro was discouraged for political reasons. At the end of the century Dalmatia was the least developed Austrian province. The earlier collapse of wind-driven shipping had been compensated for in the 1870s and 1880s by a sudden upsurge in viticulture and wine export; but this declined after 1891, when Austria-Hungary signed a trade agreement with Italy lowering tariffs on the import of Italian wine. By the end of the century Dalmatian wine could not sell even at cost price. To make matters worse, phylloxera appeared and devastated the wine industry.[3] The 'economic miracle' that had delivered central Dalmatia to the National Party was over. Its leaders wondered indeed whether northern Croatia would be in any position to subsidise its Dalmatian part after unification. Isolated and neglected, Dalmatia tottered on the brink of economic collapse.

The whole policy of moderation consequently came under attack, causing the National Party to split. Its failure led also to the arrival of a new political force, the Party of Right, under whose stewardship Dalmatia would take over the direction of national policy. Dalmatia's new role was made possible by the fact that the political system in the Austrian half of the Monarchy was far more liberal and democratic than that prevalent in the lands of the Hungarian crown. Dalmatia's franchise was far wider, while its municipalities enjoyed considerable autonomy. Whereas in Ban's Croatia the sabor had become a compliant tool of the Hungarian regime in Dalmatia, Vienna preferred to govern with the consent of the provincial parliament. The fact that Dalmatia elected its representatives directly to the Austrian parliament made it possible for the opposition too to be elected – by contrast with Ban's Croatia, where the obedient parliamentary majority elected an obedient

Croatian quota for the joint parliament in Pest. And whereas Dalmatian deputies could count on Slav support in the Reichsrat, Croatian deputies in the joint parliament faced a solid and, when challenged, hostile Magyar majority. Nor should one forget the fact that while the Dalmatians could speak or understand the languages spoken in the Reichsrat, there was a dialogue of the deaf in the parliament at Pest. This situation allowed the Dalmatians to pursue a more radical national policy.[4]

It was in fact a split within the National Party that gave the Party of Right its first parliamentary seats. The tension between the moderate and radical wings of the National Party came to the fore after the party had won Split in 1882. When Pavlinović, the leader of its radical wing, died in 1887, his place was taken by another priest, Juraj Biankini, the editor of the party's newpaper, *Narodne Novine*. In 1888, when the parliament debated its address to the king, Biankini asked that it should include also the demand for union with Ban's Croatia. The party leaders, Miho Klaić and Gajo Bulat, rejected this, fearing the parliament would be dismissed. Biankini, allthough the majority voted with him, withdrew his motion in the face of Klaić's threat to resign. The two leaders now made a concession to the growing radical wing by changing the party's name to National Croat Party, though they continued to hope that the Serbs would return to the fold (despite the change of name, it remained known as the National Party). In the meantime the party would use all legal means to consolidate Croat national consciousness, so that Dalmatia would be able to 'defeat Italianism and defend itself against Germanism'. In 1892 Biankini was elected to the Reichsrat. His maiden speech opened with the statement: 'It is my duty to declare that my presence here in no way prejudices the constitutional status of the kingdom of Dalmatia as part of the Croatian state.' Dalmatia was 'only temporarily represented in the Reichsrat'; it should instead be sending its representatives to the Croatian parliament, in accordance with 'natural and positive law'. He would do all he could 'for this right to be validated and implemented'.[5] His speech had a tremendous response in both Dalmatia and Ban's Croatia, particularly among young supporters of the Party of Right.

In that same year Biankini and five others left the National Party. The immediate cause of their departure was the introduction of new school textbooks published under the strict supervision of the central government in Vienna, which now replaced those imported from Zagreb. The new books were criticised for failing to educate children in the Croat national spirit. For example, children were told that their country was the Austro-Hungarian Monarchy rather than Croatia, which led Biankini to accuse the Austrian government of seeking the 'spiritual destruction of the Croat nation in Dalmatia'.[6] The students, he argued, should be told plainly who they were and to which nation they belonged. He moved that the government be invited to review the textbooks' content and ensure that the Croat name was not 'distorted', that is, coupled with the Serb as in 'Serbo-Croat'. The Autonomists took the opportunity of the ensuing debate to ask for schools for the Italian minority, only to be told that there were no Italians in Dalmatia, but only Italianised Croats. The Serb deputies, on the other hand, dismissed all talk of the Croatian state right in Dalmatia, protested against the intended removal of the Serb 'spirit, language and nationality' from the textbooks, insisted that the name of the national language was in fact Serb – and proposed that it be named 'Croat or Serb'. When this was accepted, Biankini and five others resigned from the party and formed a separate Croat Club.[7] This was a serious blow to the Nationals, since the party's paper now accused its leaders of having surreptitiously recognised the existence of a separate Serb nation in a Croatian land, and of abandoning the quest for union. The party, Biankini argued, had failed to acquire a clear national identity at a time when the Autonomists had become Italians and the Serbs were insisting on their own separate nationality.

The Nationals now faced disapproval also from the Independent National Party, its ally in Ban's Croatia which, itself critical of the Dalmatian failure to pursue the cause of unity, sided with Biankini. Klaić's answer was that denying the existence of a separate Serb nationality would only stimulate national conflict in Dalmatia, and would moreover make Croats appear uncivilised in the eyes of the outside world. As for the charge that his party had abandoned the struggle for union, Klaić felt it could do no more in that regard. As he wrote to Strossmayer, 'you must bear in mind that we are not independent and foreigners rule over us'. He added that Serb nationalism was partly to blame for the fact that the Party of Right had taken root also in Dalmatia: the maxim that all *štokavian* speakers were Serbs had caused a strong reaction in Dalmatia too. One extremism was feeding another, but 'we Croats should let the Serb extremists cool down', since if Croats were to respond with equal passion the conflict would degenerate into barbarism. The fact that the Croats were in a majority obliged them to be that much more tolerant.

A new generation of politicians had in the meantime arrived, born and brought up at the time of the National Party's rise to political dominance. Impatient with what they saw as that party's opportunism, they rallied to the Party of Right. Their leaders were Ante Trumbić and Frano Supilo.

Trumbić, a native of Split, witnessed as a child the struggle between the National Party and the Autonomists over language. He was eighteen in 1882, when the Nationals won Split. As the recipient of a Split municipal grant, Trumbić was sent to study law at the University of Zagreb, where he and other young Dalmatians succumbed to the ideas of the Party of Right. Given that the Austrian half of the Monarchy did not recognise degrees issued in the Hungarian half, Trumbić was forced to complete his studies in Vienna and Graz in order to be able to practise law in Dalmatia. In 1886, the year in which he finally returned to Split, the National Party had won the municipality of Trogir, and Trumbić became its clerk entrusted with the task of overseeing the replacement of Italian by Croat in the city's administration and schools. He ended up by setting up his own legal practice in Split. He and his co-thinkers criticised the National Party for abandoning its earlier ideals, and charged its leaders with having become Austrian 'in spirit and action'. The young rebels, however, had been formed within the liberal and tolerant National Party tradition. They rejected not only Ante Starčević's hostility towards the Serbs, but also his vision of an independent Croatia linked to the Monarchy solely by the person of the king. They embraced instead the National Party's idea of Croatia within a federalised Monarchy, as well as the possibility of its joining – at some distant point in the future – a confederation of South Slav states.

The belief that Croats and Serbs formed a single nation because they spoke the same language had by now become practically untenable, given the emergence of the Serb Party, which rejected Dalmatia's union with Croatia. The fact that in 1878 Serbia and Montenegro had become internationally recognised states, while Croatia remained subdued and divided, encouraged some Dalmatian Catholics to see Serbia as the South Slav Piedmont and adopt a Serb national identity. This phenomenon was most visible in Dubrovnik, where the Serb Party already enjoyed support among the Orthodox population that had begun to settle there after the arrival of Austrian government. Some of them had become wealthy merchants. In 1890 only 515 out of 8,000 Dubrovnik citizens were of the Orthodox faith, but they constituted a vigorous and self-contained community.[8] Aware of their small numbers, their leaders actively promoted the proliferation of Catholic Serbs by funding journals and cultural and other societies. In the 1890s, when this trend peaked, there were about eighty Catholic Serbs in Dubrovnik; they became the spearhead of the Serb Party's activity in southern Dalmatia. The Serb Party's growing presence had immediate electoral repercussions, in that the party allied itself with the Autonomists and in 1890 this alliance won in local elections. After more than two decades of National rule, Dubrovnik acquired an Autonomist mayor. This isolated Dubrovnik from its overwhelmingly Croat hinterland, which had voted for the National Party candidates.

The loss of Dubrovnik prompted the local National and Party of Right leaders to unite their efforts. In 1891 they set up a journal called *Crvena Hrvatska* (Red Croatia: 'red' here stands for 'southern') and appointed Frano Supilo its editor. Born in 1870, the year the Nationals won a majority in the Dalmatian parliament, Supilo became Austria's youngest political editor. Under his inspired leadership *Crvena Hrvatska* emerged as one of the most influential political journals in Croatia. He travelled to Split (where he met Trumbić) and to Zagreb, seeking financial support. Strossmayer and his canons bought shares in the paper. The paper's main task, Supilo informed Strossmayer, was to draw Dubrovnik back from the brink. After the Croat coalition had regained Dubrovnik in 1899, Supilo removed himself to Rijeka, to assume the editorship of *Novi list* (New Journal). It was titled thus by Supilo because 'we need a new start'. *Novi list* was to play the same role in the Adriatic north as *Crvena Hrvatska* had in the south: to 'do its duty in accordance with Croatian patriotism tempered with wisdom' – to win Rijeka from the Magyars. Rijeka was the buckle that held together Adriatic and Pannonian Croatia, the key to the door guarding Dalmatia and Istria for the Croatian state. Supilo wrote before leaving Dubrovnik: 'The Magyars need access to the sea and will seek to gain it at all costs, even at the expense of the Croatian kingdom. They must be stopped.' The idea that Rijeka was Italian, on the other hand, was 'nothing but a great, conventional lie, which can be sustained only due to its abnormal situation'.[9] Of 200 children in the city's secondary schools 197 spoke only Croat at home, yet the language of instruction was Italian. The responsibility for this state of affairs rested, in his view, with all of Croatia, down to the smallest village that voted for politicians who did not care what was happening to Rijeka. After his visit to the Croatian capital a disappointed Supilo wrote: 'Zagreb is our centre, but also our misfortune. [What it] needs is someone with courage, someone who would be able to rise above all this corruption that poisons our national life.'[10]

Like so many Dalmatian Croats, Supilo drew his inspiration from the ideas of the Italian *Risorgimento,* and from Cavour's success in bringing about Italy's unification. In fact, if Dalmatia could be described as Yugoslavia's Piedmont, then Supilo was its Cavour. Unlike Cavour, however, he had no state, army or international support, only pen and paper. But he possessed a rare talent for politics and a powerful will, a combination that would make him a national leader at the turn of the century. His supreme self-confidence was evident already in 1891, when he became the editor of *Crvena Hrvatska*.

In his introduction to the first issue, he stressed Croatian state right, which for him was 'the right of every nation to exist, defend itself, develop, and unite'. Other Slav nations should support the Croats in this endeavour, especially those closest to it, that is, the Serbs – who, however, were working against Croatia's unity. Croats and Serbs were linguistically one nation, he wrote, but all Croat efforts to reach concord with the Serbs had failed: instead of brotherly support, the Croats were offered 'un-brotherly usurpation and treachery'.[11] *Crvena Hrvatska,* he warned, would tenaciously struggle against all enemies of Croats and Croatia. He saw the difference between Serbs and Croats as political, not ethnic, and criticised the Serb policy for destroying the possibility of forging a strong nation in Croatia. The Serbs, he would later write, did not like Croatia because they wished to annex parts of it to Serbia. Serbia's quest to become the South Slav Piedmont was unrealistic, however, since the country lacked the necessary cultural and economic capacity. He also denounced dualism and the Triple Alliance of Italy, Germany and Austria-Hungary as the greatest danger to the Monarchy's Slavs.

What preoccupied him most, however, was the absence of national accord. Convinced that national salvation lay in political unity, achieving this unity became his main obsession. 'The present system does not ask of us [Croats] to engage in mutual barter', he argued, 'but to divide into two camps: those who are ready to conform and those who refuse to do so.' There was no middle way: 'we either obey or we fight back. This is why we need only one party for Ban's Croatia, Istria and Dalmatia – a single party that thinks alike, seeks the same thing, and is disciplined. Only then would we be able to realise our aims.'[12] He criticised the National parties in both north and south for being submissive to respectively Pest and Vienna, at the expense of the most important issue: national unification. Their political passivity was crippling the nation's morale. Reacting against the view that the time was inopportune, he insisted that 'the moment of union is always present, all that is needed is the will'.[13] Despite his calls for national unity, he welcomed the exit of Biankini and his co-thinkers from the National Party, hoping that this would shake it up.

Like the Nationals, Supilo sought an end to dualism and its replacement by a federal arrangement. By becoming a federal unit within the Monarchy, Croatia would make a great step towards independence. Croatia's unification, however, was only the first step towards a union of the Monarchy's South

Slav lands, including Bosnia-Herzegovina, since 'Croatia without Bosnia would always be a plaything of those who ruled in Bosnia'. At the first general conference of the Party of Right groups held in Rijeka in 1892, Supilo and Trumbić drafted a resolution seeking union of all 'Croatian lands' – Croatia with Istria, Slovenia and Bosnia-Herzegovina – on the basis of 'natural and state right'. The nation which inhabited that area was defined as 'politically Croatian'. The conference also decided that the party should seek a solution to the Croatian question within the framework of the Monarchy, but if this proved impossible go for total independence. Those coming from the Adriatic zone now pressed the two Croat opposition parties in Ban's Croatia – Starčević's Party of Right and the Independent National Party – to unite, but without success. In Dalmatia, by contrast, Supilo succeeded in a similar undertaking. In 1894 Biankini's Croat Club submitted another address to the Dalmatian parliament calling for union with Ban's Croatia, which the Nationals accepted in an amended form. But on the day the address was to be voted on, the Dalmatian governor produced an imperial order dismissing the parliament – such orders were in fact sent from Vienna in advance of every parliamentary session after 1877. The Croat Club now joined the Party of Right.

The Nationals continued to advocate the need to support the central government in Vienna on matters that were in Dalmatia's interest, and to uphold their traditional policy towards the Serbs on the grounds that Croats could not simultaneously fight on all three fronts: against the government, the Autonomists and the Serbs. While remaining a resolute opponent of Dalmatia's existence outside Croatia, Klaić never tired in his efforts to break the Autonomist-Serb alliance in Dalmatia. The Party of Right for its part continued to press for union. The following year later Biankini again asked the parliament to vote for it. Klaić was ready to support his demand, despite the fact that its adoption would lead to the parliament being closed; but he argued that Dalmatia's union with Ban's Croatia entailed a complete recasting of the Monarchy's constitution, which was unlikely: Croatia was too weak to abolish dualism on its own. There was nothing worse, indeed, than putting before the nation tasks that it could not achieve. He concluded his speech by paraphrasing the Italian national ideologue Massimo D'Azeglia: 'Let us raise Croats, and Croatia will arise of itself.' The Party of Right's proposal was rejected.

Supilo was outraged. He wrote in *Crvena Hrvatska*:

> Dr Klaić stated that, if [the address] were put on the agenda the

parliament would be closed. [Are we] to hide our programme, put off our demands, only because the government would close the parliament? [He] wants our nation to put aside its programme and principles until the government decides to be generous. But is Vienna ever going to oblige us? Will Vienna, will Austria, ever readily agree to let Dalmatia leave? If we were to follow the leader of the National Party, we would never achieve [the union]. We cannot do this – no nation behaves in this manner. We should use all our national forces and all the constitutional means available to realise our programme. Even if the parliament gets closed once, twice or thrice, the day will come when Dalmatia's voice will be heard and heeded. [If] we do not ask, we shall not be given. Jesus himself said: Ask and you will receive, knock and the door will open.

He pressed his charge:

> Mr Klaić confuses national politics with diplomacy. Governments and diplomats wait, reason and deceive each other. They can behave like that because they have power and authority at their disposal. But the policy of a nation seeking unity and independence does not possess such instruments. It must instead rely on making its intentions clear to the people, so that they can understand them, since the people are our nation's main force. Only then will its opponents take it seriously. This is why we cannot allow peace, ceasefires, delays and playing blind man's buff. The Italians did not rest until they were united.[14]

Klaić had stated, Supilo went on, that Biankini's address was 'nothing but a gesture which does not serve, but only harms the cause of union'; and that great ideas were demeaned by being constantly and light-mindedly submitted to debate. '[The] truth is that great issues are demeaned when, having been inscribed on the party's banner, they are left to slumber for thirty years or more. The nation's vital issues must instead be constantly placed before the people, whose will and consciousness alone give them force. The Party of Right engaged in no cheap demonstration: the deputies simply tried to discharge their duty [to] the people who had elected them.' The National Party had at its very birth taken the wrong position on the national issue by advocating Yugoslavism, Slavism, Serbo-Croatism and Serbism at the expense of Croatism. Now, however, a younger generation with 'sound Croat mores' had appeared, which was 'educating the nation and preparing it for a struggle that the National Party itself did not shirk at the time when it was in a minority'. That party, however, had since become a party of Austrian bureaucrats. By moving closer to the powers above, it was leaving the people behind. The National Party had aged without having brought up the next generation of Croat politicians.[15]

This last charge was manifestly true. But the National Party's strength was confirmed in the parliamentary elections of that year, when the Party of Right won only three seats. After the death of Miho Klaić (1896) and Gajo Bulat (1900), however, the former party's discipline started to fray. The Party of Right, on the other hand, grew rapidly between 1897 and 1902. In the Dalmatian parliamentary elections of 1897 it won eleven seats, the Nationals eighteen, the Serb Party and the Autonomists six each. The two Croat parties would after 1901 act in unison. The Nationals remained an important party, with the largest number of seats in the provincial parliament and nine out of eleven Dalmatian seats in the Austrian parliament, but – not wishing to risk an outright struggle with the Party of Right – it surrendered some of its seats to the latter and in 1902 agreed to enlarge the parliament's executive to accommodate it, after which this body came to be composed of two deputies from the National Party, two from the Party of Right, and one from the Serb Party. By voluntarily surrendering political leadership to the Party of Right, the Nationals ensured a peaceful generational change in the government of Dalmatia. In contrast to Ban's Croatia, where the Party of Right had fragmented and the younger generation remained marginalised, Dalmatia united under its leadership. In 1899 the party offered to recognise the Serbs as a distinct people, provided they accepted the Croatian state right and supported Dalmatia's union with Ban's Croatia – but its offer was rejected. The offer was repeated in 1902, and again rejected. The anti-Serb riot which took place that year in Zagreb, however, had greatly alarmed Supilo, who would henceforth incessantly call for Croat–Serb unity and equality. He wrote in *Novi list* that unless Croats and Serbs accepted that they were 'one and the same nation', albeit with two names, they would become each other's most dangerous enemies: the Serbs would seek to destroy Croatia in order to prevent their assimilation as Croats, while the Croats would try to destroy the Serbs in order to protect Croatia from this threat.[16]

Forging a new course for Croatia

The second step on the road to Yugoslavia was taken in 1903, when the Dalmatian Party of Right submitted its national policy to a 'fundamental revision' and adopted a 'new course' based on two axioms. One was that

Croatia's greatest enemy was the German *Drang* and the dualist system that served it. The party should consequently seek an alliance of all nations threatened by it. The other was that Croats and Serbs formed one nation not only in Croatia but wherever they lived. As Supilo told his Italian friends, the only option was 'to unite Croats with Serbs and other Balkans Slavs in a way that would transform these disunited peoples without influence or authority into a single entity outside German influence', which after the collapse of Austria-Hungary would form a common state.[17]

The revision was prompted by a popular anti-Hungarian movement that swept through the Croatian north that year – a largely anarchic mobilisation of the peasant masses triggered by the demands of the Croat and Serb opposition parties for a better economic deal for Croatia. The political energy that the movement uncovered was inspirational. It was proof in Supilo's eyes that 'our nation is true, strong and up to its task, if only its leaders and intelligentsia would do their duty'. A decade earlier he had written: 'There are only three ways in which our intolerable position can be changed: through an internal movement that would end the stasis; by way of a major crisis in the Monarchy creating the necessary conditions; or as a result of some great external change. We cannot tell which it will be. We rest our hope in all three. But we must ensure that whichever happens none finds us unprepared.'[18] He was further encouraged by indications that under its impact the Croat and Serb oppositions in Ban's Croatia had begun to cooperate. Reacting to the signs that two decades of bitter Croat–Serb conflict appeared to be ending, Supilo wrote: 'The fever has abated, the patient is on the mend. [Those] who reject their brother gain a foreign master.' The authorities responded to the popular mobilisation by heavy repression – there were people killed and wounded, and some 3,000 arrests – and the Dalmatians appealed to the king to stop it. As they expected, the king refused to intervene.

The Dalmatians now assumed responsibility for their country's fate, but in order to exercise it they had first to establish peace on the domestic front. Anti-Italian and anti-Serb articles disappeared from their press, which was made easier by the fact that the local Italian and Serb communities expressed sympathy for the movement in the north. At the end of May 1903, when it seemed that the imperial army would be used against the demonstrators, the Dalmatians decided to seek help abroad. Following a secret meeting of Croat politicians from all over Croatia, emissaries were sent abroad, including to the United States, to seek support for Croatia. These visits were a moderate success. Western Europe favoured the status quo, while Russia was increasingly concerned with the Far East. But the rivalry between Italy and Austria in the Adriatic was growing, and Italy feared that Austria would use Russia's involvement in the Far East to annex Bosnia-Herzegovina. Hostility towards Austria encouraged Italian sympathy for Croatia's plight.[19] The Croat press halted its customary attacks on Italian foreign policy and began instead to advocate a Croatian–Italian rapprochement, on the grounds that their conflict was opening the door to German ascendancy in the Adriatic and the Aegean.

In June 1903 Khuen-Hédervary finally left Croatia to become Hungarian prime minister. His task was to neutralise the Hungarian opposition, which was taking the opportunity of a new law on military recruitment to demand a separate Hungarian army. But the Hungarian opposition, however, proved stronger than its Croatian counterpart, and within months Khuen-Hédervary was replaced by Kálmán Tisza's son István, the new leader of the Hungarian Liberal Party, who shared his view that Hungary's association with Austria and Germany alone guaranteed its territorial extent and political structure. Tisza too proved unable to end the crisis, however, which entered a new stage in the autumn of 1904, when all the Hungarian opposition parties united against the government.[20] In January 1905 this opposition, organised as the Coalition, won control of the Hungarian parliament. The dualist system seemed on the verge of collapse, now being challenged not only by its victims, but also by its chief architect. This was the second crisis of the Austrian constitutional system to which the historian A. J. P. Taylor refers in his work, and the one on which Supilo himself was counting. Although the anti-Hungarian movement in Ban's Croatia had by now abated, the growing constitutional crisis inspired the hope that it might lead to a major reorganisation of the Monarchy, one that would permit Croatia's unification – provided that Croatia organised itself. The Dalmatians now got down to the business of fashioning a proper response in the north. Their task was made easier by the fact that Serbia too was in a critical state. The Austrophile Serbian king Aleksandar Obrenović and his wife were brutally murdered by army officers in the middle of 1903, after which Petar Karađorđević was installed as the new king. Faced with international censure and isolation, the new pro-Russian regime favoured Croat–Serb rapprochement.

Everything seemed to be moving in the same direction. In the autumn of 1903, seeking to placate the Croats, the Austrian governor of Dalmatia, Erasmus Handel, had offered to replace the Italian language in the province's internal affairs by Croat, but the Dalmatian parliament unanimously rejected the overture, since it was combined with introduction of the German language as the new external language of the provincial administration. This was perceived as another manifestation of German *Drang*. Knowledge of German in addition to Croat and Italian was already required for higher civil service posts in Dalmatia; if the parliament accepted Handel's proposal, adoption of German would become a general rule. Since few of the locals spoke the language, the state would import Germans or German-educated individuals who would not necessarily know Croat. The German primary school in Zadar, opened formally for children of German soldiers and officials, was expanding fast by accepting non-German children. There was a demand to open also a German-language gymnasium there. In a province in which Germans formed less than 1 per cent of the population, German-language schools were perceived as an instrument of Dalmatia's Germanisation. All three Dalmatian national communities united against Governor Handel. Trumbić now made a speech in the Dalmatian parliament in which he declared that Croats had to forge their own independent path, since the Monarchy was 'incurable'.[21] He condemned Austria for acting as the advance guard of Germany's eastward drive, which threatened all non-German nations in the Monarchy and the Balkans. He called upon the latter to unite against it, and referred to Italy and Hungary as possible Croatian allies. The traditional Croat demand that the Monarchy should federalise in order to survive was not even mentioned. Other speakers followed in his footsteps. Trumbić's party colleague Josip Smodlaka denied the existence of an eternal bond between Croatia and the Monarchy, and appealed to the Serbs for support, stressing their close link with the Croats. He approved the new readiness of the Serb parties in Ban's Croatia to advocate Croatian interests, and praised the new Serbian king as a sincere friend of Croat–Serb accord and cooperation.[22]

The announcement of the new national strategy, of a 'new course' was not complemented by any proposal about how to advance it in practice; on the other hand, no voice was raised against it in the Dalmatian parliament. Governor Handel reported to Vienna that the intention of the speakers was to separate Croatia from Austria-Hungary and turn it into an independent state. He was particularly concerned by the fact that their views enjoyed widespread support, and at his request three warships arrived at Split in December 1903, in a show of force. However, although the new course enjoyed widespread support, it was by no means universal. As Handel was able to inform Vienna, the Dalmatian Catholic Church did not approve the Croat–Serb reconciliation. Biankini, himself a liberal, could not be indifferent to the sentiments of the Dalmatian clergy, which found any policy directed against Catholic Austria essentially unacceptable. There were other problems in forging the anti-German alliance. Despite Czech efforts at mediation, Trieste Italians conditioned cooperation with Croats and Slovenes in the Reichsrat upon an admission by the latter that Istria and Trieste were unquestionably Italian – which they rejected. The new Italian prime minister, Giovanni Giolitti, for his part favoured good relations with the Dual Monarchy: the trade agreement had run out and Italy was interested in renewing it.

Governor Handel, who counted on Dalmatian political inertia to bury the new course, unwittingly brought about a revival of anti-Austrian feeling in the province by allegedly declaring that Dalmatians were habitual liars. The Croat parties announced a boycott of the parliament and municipal bodies as long as Handel remained in Dalmatia. The Serb Party and the Autonomists joined the action. In early 1905 Vienna finally replaced Handel with the first native governor, Handel's deputy, Niko Nardelli. This success led the Party of Right and the National Party to fuse, creating the Croatian Party, whose president became the old National Party leader from Dubrovnik and Supilo's erstwhile political mentor, Pero Čingrija. This party controlled parliament, most of the municipalities and practically all Dalmatian representatives in the Reichsrat. Its programme stated that the party would work for Dalmatia's incorporation into Ban's Croatia, a step leading towards the unification of all Croatian lands (without specifying which) into a separate state (without defining its status). It would promote inter-Slav solidarity and seek Slav support for Croatian national interests. Croats and Serbs were proclaimed one nation; conflicts between them should be banished. There was no mention of Italians. The party, however, would remain responsive to 'the demands of the new age', that is, it would resume its project of the electoral reform in favour of the countryside. The Serb Party remained passive, awaiting further developments

Dalmatia thus faced the dualist crisis politically united on an anti-Austrian course, whereas the opposition in Ban's Croatia had failed to achieve any meaningful consensus. The Dalmatians were now ready to give the north their undivided attention.

The imperative of Croat–Serb cooperation

After 1900 Supilo became increasingly convinced that Croatia's ability to play an autonomous role in the recomposition of the Dual Monarchy and the Balkans depended on Croat–Serb cooperation: if Croatia was to be free, it had to reach an agreement with its Serbs. Indeed, 'this whole struggle [over

Frano Supilo

the new course] started in the name of national unity of Croats and Serbs, with the clearly defined aim of rights for Croatia. Our political aim remains Croatia's liberation.'[23] The new course was based on an understanding that the Habsburg Monarchy was incapable of self-reform and would sooner or later collapse. Croatia would be set free, but it would not be able to survive on its own in the face of the *Drang* and should, therefore, seek safety within a larger South Slav state. It was indeed possible that, by joining the anti-German coalition, Croatia could play a decisive role in uniting the South Slavs. Supilo wrote to Trumbić: 'Should we Croats not be a Sardinia, which with its handful of soldiers managed to gain entry into the society of Big Powers, in order to raise on the morrow its voice for the unification of Italy? It all depends on how things work out.'[24]

If the new course was to become practical politics, however, it was necessary for the two parts of Croatia to act in unison, and this meant bringing together the Croat and Serb oppositions in the north. Ban's Croatia was represented in the joint (in effect Hungarian) parliament, and its action there could make a decisive difference. As the constitutional crisis grew in intensity so did Supilo's optimism: if Hungary was moving into permanent opposition to Austria, Croatia should be on Hungary's side, since an independent Hungary could never be such a threat to Croatia as an Austria-Hungary tied to Germany. The Hungarian opponents of dualism, on the other hand, faced the same problem as the Croatian opponents of dualism: they found no friends abroad. Like the Croatians before them, they clutched at straws, such as the possibility that the outbreak of the Russian Revolution of 1905 would soften the king's position. Francis Joseph, however, categorically refused to surrender control of the army, which he saw as the only force holding his empire together. Rather than negotiating, he appointed a caretaker government for Hungary headed by a general. The Coalition responded by proclaiming a state of 'national resistance' and appealed to Croatia for support. The opposition parties in Ban's Croatia, while attracted by Hungarian defiance, refused this, given the aggressive attitude towards Croatia displayed by Hungarian parties in the past, while the governmental National Party headed by Nikola Tomašić sided with Vienna. Given the possibility that the opposition might come to power also in Croatia, the Nationals now sought to improve their domestic position by publicly criticising Hungary's past treatment of Croatia.

Tomašić and Supilo were adversaries who attracted one another. Supilo described Tomašić as 'an exceptional political individuality', one who was not a mere leader of the National Party but its 'political brain', and 'the only real threat to our [new course] politics'. Together they represented the Janus-like twin faces of Croatian national politics, one deeply reticent, the other prone to revolutionary defiance, one defending Croatia's ties to Austria-Hungary, the other constantly seeking ways of breaking them. Polemicising with Supilo, Tomašić justified the union with Hungary on the grounds that the Magyars were the only force capable of protecting Croatia from Germanisation; but he recognised too that as soon as the German pressure was off, Hungarian power backed by dualism threatened to break Croatia's back. 'To find the right balance, to use this [Magyar] force and yet avoid conflict with it, has been the task and aim of the difficult and almost impossible struggle for survival which our nation has waged for centuries, and which is today borne by the National Party.' Supilo answered with an allusion to Goethe: Tomašić preferred to intellectualise rather then act, but all theory was grey and only the tree of life green. Tomašić believed in the 'persistence of institutions, I in their temporal limitations – and the eternal power of the idea'.[25]

Once Dalmatia sided with the Hungarian Coalition, however, the opposition in Ban's Croatia followed its lead. The Dalmatian argument was that this was a rare opportunity to demolish the system established by Khuen-Héderváry. Croatians should offer to back the Hungarian opposition in return for a promise to support Croatia's own needs. In April 1905, the month in which the imperial army chiefs of staff drew up plans for occupying Hungary, Trumbić offered Ferenc Kossuth, the leader of the Independence Party and the Coalition's largest component, a common platform. The Coalition would continue its struggle against Austria, but without for the time being calling into question the unity of the Monarchy. The Croatians would back them on the grounds that every nation has the right to liberty and independent action. The two nations would support each other and avoid all that could cause a breach between them. Their alliance would rest on the following principles: a common state framework; Dalmatia's reincorporation; strict respect for the terms of the 1868 Compromise, which would eventually be revised; Croatia's full autonomy in the joint bodies. The platform contained an implicit assumption that, if the situation were to arise in which the survival of the dynasty and the state came into question, the two sides would re-examine the agreement. Cooperation, in other words, was limited to the term of the Monarchy's existence in whatever form. The Croatian offer assumed a revision of dualism, but not its outright negation. The two states would remain together – this was a sine qua non for the Hungarian side. On the other hand, Hungary's greater autonomy from Vienna would lead to Croatia's greater autonomy from Pest – this was a sine qua non for the Croatian side. Whether the Hungarian side actually accepted this proposal is not known, but it is possible that they took it as a general orientation.

Supilo now concentrated on finding the right partner for Hungary in the envisaged anti-Austrian alliance. He was convinced that the only possible candidate was his Croatian Party, but the latter could not act without the support of political parties in Ban's Croatia. He sought to create a suitable coalition of northern opposition parties, but the fact that they were not represented in the joint parliament diminished their potential as partners for the Magyars. However, the Croatian Party – which was supposed to lead the action – proved to be in no hurry to do so, given the resistance of its deputies in the Reichsrat to accepting a common framework with Hungary, since that meant giving up the by now widely accepted 'trialist' idea of a Yugoslav unit within the Monarchy linked loosely to Hungary and Austria. The Croatian Party majority rejected as unworkable the idea that the Croatian and Dalmatian parliaments should meet together, while the proposal that the Hungarian, Croatian and Dalmatian parliaments should meet to discuss Dalmatia's incorporation was rejected by Tomašić's National Party, which refused to support any action directed against Vienna.

In the event Supilo managed in October 1905 to convene in Rijeka a meeting of fifty-five parliamentary deputies from all over Croatia, at which he asked them to approve cooperation with the Hungarian opposition. The conference adopted the so-called Rijeka Resolution, which endorsed the right of the Croatian and Hungarian nations to self-determination; Dalmatia's union with Ban's Croatia; civic freedoms; an independent judiciary; and an electoral system capable of expressing the will of the people. Two weeks later the Dalmatian Serb Party, the Serb Independent Party and the Radical Party met in Zadar, where they endorsed the Rijeka Resolution while adding to it equality of Croats and Serbs.²⁶ Their action had Belgrade's support. On his visit to Belgrade in April 1905, Supilo was able to persuade the Serbian government to discipline the divided Serb parties and press them to support the Dalmatian action. The two resolutions, secured by Dalmatia and Serbia, represent the third step on the road to Yugoslavia. They provided a basis for the formation in December 1905 in Zagreb of the Croat–Serb Coalition, uniting the Croatian Party of Right (a union of strands of the Party of Right and the Independent National Party), the Croatian Progressive Party (which derived from the Progressive Youth current), the newly formed Social Democratic Party, the Serb Independent Party, the Radical Party and several independent politicians. In its first public proclamation the coalition asked for universal suffrage, incorporation of Dalmatia, full compliance with the terms of the Croato-Hungarian Compromise, and Croat-Serb equality.

Suffrage was the most burning issue. The whole of Ban's Croatia had at this time only 51,000 voters; if the Hungarian or the Serbian electoral laws applied instead, the number would grow to respectively 140,000 and 540,000. In this situation the dependent local officials, Supilo wrote, would no longer form the bulk of the sabor deputies.

> The candle of national freedom was never extinguished in Croatia. [It] was not extinguished under the Compromise nor even during the whole time of the Khuen regime, though it has fallen very low and is in danger of being extinguished. [It] is only necessary to add a little oil to it. That oil is civic and human freedoms which we lack. The Compromise on which Croatia rests today, however small and narrow it may be, provides nevertheless a sufficient foundation on which we can rely to secure and extend our nation's rights. [We] need civil and human freedoms, and the rest will come of itself.²⁷

The Croat–Serb political alliance was potentially a serious force, since it represented the interests of domestic capital: its leaders and backers were some of the most important landowners, industrialists and bankers, including the presidents of the First Croatian Saving Bank, the Serb Bank and the Croatian Economic Chamber. They wished to see an end to Hungary's hindrance of Croatia's economic development, and in subsequent negotiations with the Hungarian government would seek the establishment of Croatia's own department of trade and industry. These leaders of industry were in turn supported by a whole host of smaller savings banks, agricultural cooperatives, and trade chambers throughout Croatia.²⁸

In February 1906, however, the king closed down the Hungarian parliament by force. He used, in fact, an even more powerful weapon to end the rebellion: a threat to extend the Austrian-style suffrage into the Hungarian part of the Monarchy. This would have spelled the end of Magyar domination of Hungary and the great privileges enjoyed by the Magyar landowning class. Informed of the king's intention, the popular masses stopped supporting the Hungarian Coalition, which soon surrendered. Francis Joseph withdrew his electoral reform programme, the Coalition its demand for a separate Hungarian army.

Now that the Hungarian rebels had made peace with the king, Croatia's help was no longer needed. It seemed that the Dalmatians' gamble had failed, since both Pest and Vienna made it clear that they preferred to work with the National Party in Ban's Croatia. Two days after the formation of the new Hungarian government, the sabor was closed down and new elections announced. Fearing that the Nationals might remain in power – due to political diffidence, inexperience, or simple ignorance of Hungarian politics on the part of the Croat–Serb Coalition – the Dalmatians, headed by Ante Trumbić, turned up in force in Zagreb and Pest. Their most immediate demand to the Hungarians was that the elections should proceed without governmental interference. Under their pressure and with the support of the anti-*Drang* wing of the Independence Party, the Hungarian prime minister, albeit acting with a heavy heart, jettisoned the National Party. In the elections of May 1906 the Croat–Serb Coalition won forty-three out of eighty-eight seats in the sabor, after which the National Party disappeared as an organised force. Dalmatia celebrated the victory of 'Mother Croatia'. The Coalition's good performance surprised both Vienna and Pest. Belgrade too was impressed. In order to be able to direct the Coalition's work in the joint parliament in Pest, Supilo had himself elected to the sabor in the mainly Serb constituency of the former border town of Glina. Under his leadership the Croat–Serb Coalition now began a struggle to implement its programme.

The new Hungarian government, however, proved no more amenable to compromise than the old Liberal one. Whatever had been promised was quickly forgotten. The Croatian parliament was soon dissolved, after which the Coalition moved into active opposition. In July 1907 it issued a proclamation in which it appealed to the nation to support its defence of 'Croatia's constitution and rights' with regard to Hungary. The Coalition deputies, however, were largely inexperienced politicians formed under the debilitating Khuen regime. Their leaders were bankers and industrialists who feared that pursuit of a confrontational policy would hurt their economic interests. Its reforming zeal soon started to crumble under Hungary's incessant pressure and Vienna's open hostility. Seeking a rapprochement with the Monarchy, Serbia too urged moderation; concerned to maintain its position within the Serb autonomous bodies controlled by the Hungarian government, the Radical Party left the battlefield.

Pressed forward by Supilo, the Croat–Serb Coalition continued to battle on for a while longer. The moment seemed propitious. That year the joint parliament was due to renew the financial side of the Austro-Hungarian Compromise, which Supilo was determined to prevent, particularly since the Hungarian government now wished to make Magyar the obligatory language on the railways even in Croatia. Supilo wrote: 'There are times in the affairs of a nation when one must throw overboard all deliberation; [when] it is a matter of life and death; when nothing exists between "yes" and "no"; when caution stands for cowardice and defeat; [when] it is better to go down fighting than to live in shame.' When in late 1907 the frustrated Croatian deputies began a filibuster in the Pest parliament the Coalition became a major problem, not least because Vienna was preparing the annexation of Bosnia-Herzegovina.[29] This was an added reason for seeking the Coalition's removal or break-up. Vienna increased the pressure on its leaders and on Supilo in particular. He was not only the Coalition's driving force but also the only one among the Croatian deputies to the joint parliament who could speak Hungarian. *Novi list* was banned and a systematic campaign in the press launched charging Supilo with sedition. The foreign editor of *The Times*, Wickham Steed, who followed these events on the spot, was told that Supilo had to be destroyed. The first step in this direction was the appointment as ban of Pavao Rauch, who in early 1908 organised new elections. The Coalition, however, this time won an absolute majority of the seats. Encouraged by the evident popular support for the policy of resistance, Supilo urged war to the end against the existing constitutional arrangement, and proposed a boycott of the joint parliament in order to paralyse its work.

The Serbian prime minister, Nikola Pašić, however, sided with Pest. Both the Serbian and the Hungarian governments pressed the Serb Independent Party to leave the Coalition. Ban Rauch for his part refused to convene the sabor. The Coalition again appealed to the nation to support its 'lawful yet unflinching struggle' for revision of the constitutional relationship with Hungary in a manner that would 'secure for Croatia its independence and freedom'. As Supilo later wrote: 'We had the Croatian delegation [in the joint parliament], we had the vast majority of the Croatian parliament, the vast majority of the youth, the people's trust and readiness to do battle, the sympathy of all Dalmatia; [we] had the numbers and position, the means and all advantages in Croatia to implement our policy.' It was necessary to use this to 'drive a nail into the so-called "normal conduct of affairs",' in order to make sure that no government in Hungary, Croatia and the Monarchy could move without first solving the Croatian question. This could have been achieved, however, 'only by constantly reminding the people of the final aim of the struggle: Croatia's liberation and its transformation into a centripetal force for the Monarchy's South Slavs.'[30] But the Croat–Serb Coalition had by now had enough of the struggle. Its main achievement was that it had survived largely intact under all this pressure. Its durability marked another step on the road to Yugoslavia.

Collapse of the Dalmatian strategy

A few months before the annexation of Bosnia-Herzegovina was formally proclaimed in October 1908, fifty-four members of the Independent Serb Party were arrested and charged with treason – that is, charged with working for Serbia. The arrests were preceded by a hysterical anti-Serb campaign waged in the Austrian and Hungarian press. As the annexation proceeded and Russia, Austria-Hungary and Serbia began to mobilise, the propaganda campaign reached its peak, targeting everything that Serbs had managed to gain and establish in Ban's Croatia. 'The Serb flag, the Cyrillic script, the emblem of the Serb patriarchy, the Serb name, the Serb schools, the Serb agricultural cooperatives, the Serb savings banks – everything, in sum, that was Serb found itself denounced as high treason [at the same time as] investigating judges were unleashed against the Serb people in Croatia with instruction to arrest as many as need be', wrote Supilo. 'The very Serb flags under which until recently Khuen's officials had been welcomed and pro-Hungarian deputies elected' were seized; 'the very Serb flasks with Serb inscriptions made by government order in the royal prisons and sold on the open market, now appeared as proof of high treason.'[31] In an ominous development, Josip Frank, leader of the True Party of Right, prompted by the Austrian government started to form 'legions' to defend Croatia from an alleged attack by Serbia. The legionaries, wearing badges with the motto 'For king and Croatia', attacked Ban Rauch's opponents. These developments broke the back of the Serb leaders' will to resist. As Supilo noted, 'unused to being at the receiving end of the system', the Serb Independent Party was worried that its community would blame the Coalition's confrontational policy for the loss of all that they had gained under the Khuen regime.

In the spring of 1909, moreover, Russia with Serbia in tow formally accepted Bosnia's annexation by Austro-Hungary. Member states of the Congress of Berlin did likewise. Although an attempt to indict the Coalition leaders, and Supilo in particular, for working with Serbia against the monarchy's interests failed spectacularly, the Coalition decided to make its peace with Vienna and Pest. This was not possible without first removing Supilo from its ranks.[32] Despite his enormous popularity among Croats and Serbs alike, Supilo was encouraged to resign from the Coalition, whose leader now became Svetozar Pribićević of the Independent Serb Party. In early January 1910 Khuen-Héderváry was appointed prime minister in Hungary and Nikola Tomašić ban in Croatia. The terms of surrender were negotiated by the new ban. The Coalition was allowed return to government and the Serbs to regain their earlier position. The Coalition would surrender six of its seats to candidates of Tomašić's choosing, and would accept him as ban; the candidates chosen by Tomašić would join its benches. Supilo wrote to his Italian friends: 'All deputies, the Croats as well as the Serbs of the Coalition (which means two-thirds of the parliament), capitulated before him. All, all of them without exception. [Khuen-Héderváry and Tomašić] have defeated and tamed them and in doing so destroyed all Croatia's resistance that had been built up during the past two-three years.' It was not simply a defeat but something much worse: 'an outright rebellion against the very idea of struggle that was shameless in its weakness'. He had to resign from the Coalition because 'our struggle was part of a sacred national contract. [We] promised the people we would fight to the end come what may. They took us at our word, elected and followed us, and made the necessary sacrifice, remaining true in their demands.' And when it seemed that only a small effort was needed to ensure a lasting victory, 'there was this sudden demoralisation, and they all capitulated'.[33]

The taming of Croat–Serb opposition to dualism dashed any hope of Croatia becoming an independent agent in regional politics. The country remained divided, while the desired anti-*Drang* coalition failed to materialise. Supilo denounced the pact reached between Tomašić and the Croat–Serb Coalition as 'surrender of an independent national policy', and held the Serb Independent Party responsible for this: 'Serb particular interests had prevailed over the idea of national unity.' He wrote that 'the struggle which began in the name of national unity of Croats and Serbs, with the clearly defined aim of Croatian rights, has suffered a fundamental defeat with this pact'. The Serb Independent Party was promptly rewarded with control over the Serb lay-clerical assembly at the expense of the Radical

Party, its traditional competitor. But the Coalition's Croat parties too had accepted that their direct attack on the system was more harmful than a policy of cooperation would be. The Croatian economy was growing at the time, especially in the banking sector, with Zagreb emerging as a major financial capital. The Coalition would remain in charge of the sabor until the end of the First World War, passively awaiting its outcome.

In the meantime it seemed that history was repeating itself. The Croat–Serb Coalition assumed the role of the former National Party, the Serb Independent Party that of the former Serb Club, Tomašić that of Khuen-Hédervary. What was new was that restoration of the status quo came as a consequence of capitulation by the very parliamentary majority that had not long before repeatedly urged the country to support its 'unflinching' battle for Croatia's independence and freedom, and to which the country had responded by delivering it control of the parliament. The surrender divested the sabor of the last vestiges of its legitimacy. As Supilo wrote, the pact was made, in fact, not with the new ban, Tomašić, but with the old ban, Khuen-Hédervary; not through the usual painful process of inter-parliamentary negotiations, but as a direct deal from which the sabor was excluded. The whole constitutional order in Croatia was placed now on probation in that Tomašić made it clear that the sabor could sit only by sufferance of the Hungarian government. The Coalition, having bowed before a *force majeure*, now internalised its status as loser. According to official records, the parliamentary majority warmly greeted Tomašić's dismissal of the parliament's right to criticise the government.

It was during this time that Supilo and Tomašić held long private conversations. In 1910 Tomašić had published his *Pacta Conventa,* defending the notion of Croatia's uninterrupted statehood. Supilo was impressed by its basic message: 'Our right is original, it belongs only to us. No one gave it to us and no one can take it from us. It can be changed and adapted to time and circumstances only by our will.' Tomašić offered Supilo the post of his deputy, arguing that the Coalition was politically incompetent. He offered a new deal on the government of Croatia, but Supilo refused: he could not work with a dualist Hungary. He wrote to his Italian friends at this time that the Serbs had become used to having privileges in exchange for supporting an anti-Croatian policy. 'I know them intimately and deny them the right to have a leading position in Croatia, because this will, as always, prove fatal. Cooperation and agreement with them yes, at all times, but not leadership and primacy in Croatia, given their behaviour.'[34]

As before, the new-old regime relied on the new-old 'Khuen Serbs', and

Serb politicians retained a decisive say in the election of over half the sabor's deputies. As before, while it was not difficult to elect government loyalists in the majority Serb districts, this proved much harder in the majority Croat areas. Voting rights were now extended to some 6 per cent of the population, but this made little difference in reality. As before, the government tried to remove from the sabor unsympathetic, mainly Croat, deputies by replacing at election times local governmental bodies with commissars, and by harassing the voters. This policy swelled the ranks of Josip Frank's True Party of Right. In the elections of 1910 the Coalition lost one-third of its seats, and a few more in 1911, when a new pro-Austrian Party of Right based on Frank's own, backed by the circle around Crown Prince Franz Ferdinand, emerged as the strongest party in the sabor.

Yet a full return to the past proved impossible. Following the annexation of Bosnia-Herzegovina the South Slav question became the most urgent problem confronting the Habsburg Monarchy. In 1910 the Austro-Hungarian governor of Bosnia-Herzegovina, General Marijan Varešanin, told the Scottish historian R. W. Seton-Watson that Croats and Serbs were one nation and that Dalmatia should be the political centre of the future Yugoslav state to be created within the Habsburg Monarchy.[35] Varešanin was in that same year the target of an assassination attempt by a Bosnian Serb student – the first such act in a series that would end with the death of the crown prince in Sarajevo in 1914. Since Bosnia-Herzegovina could not be added to either 'Austria' or 'Hungary' without destroying the balance created by the Austro-Hungarian Compromise, it remained a separate unit with limited self-government. The Serb Independent Party now favoured its unification with Croatia, provided that Serb equality was guaranteed throughout. By 1911, in fact, all the parties in Ban's Croatia, including Tomašić's revived National Party, adopted an essentially identical programme of uniting Dalmatia and Bosnia-Herzegovina with Ban's Croatia, and achieving Croatia's maximal autonomy from Hungary. In January 1912 the Party of Right called for a conference in Zagreb of all Croatian and Bosnian deputies, with the somewhat naive aim of negotiating with the king the formation of a united, independent and sovereign Great Croatian state under the Habsburgs. The Hungarian prime minister's response was to replace Tomašić with Slavko Cuvaj, who promptly dissolved the sabor.

Supilo watched as young workers and university and secondary-school students emerged as the main opposition to Cuvaj. Zagreb had become the preferred destination of students from Istria, Dalmatia and Bosnia-Herzegovina after 1904, when the earlier rule that degrees granted in

Hungary were not recognised in Austria had been abolished. The University of Zagreb became a bastion of Yugoslav nationalism. In May 1912 students organised a demonstration in Zagreb, which was followed by a strike of secondary-school students throughout Ban's Croatia. Supporting actions were mounted by students in Bosnia and Dalmatia. This led to a suspension of constitutional rule, and to the appointment of Ban Cuvaj as royal commissar. The Dalmatian Croat parties united in their condemnation of Hungarian policy. Their deputies in the Reichsrat, seconded by the Slovenes and the Czechs, demanded urgent action by the king. However, when the Austrian prime minister promised to help return constitutional rule to Ban's Croatia, since this was in the interest of the Monarchy as a whole, the Hungarian prime minister István Tisza warned against interference in Hungarian affairs by a 'foreign state'. What happened next was that the Bosnian Croat student Luka Jukić tried to assassinate Commissar Cuvaj. Jukić was caught and condemned to death by hanging, and a dozen other students (aged between fifteen and twenty-five) were imprisoned. The trial coincided with the start of the First Balkan War, fought against Turkey by an alliance of Serbia, Greece, Bulgaria and Montenegro, which ended with Turkey being divested of most of its Balkan territories. Serbia's successes greatly raised its prestige in Croatia. Dalmatian deputies, city mayors and district heads issued a proclamation stating that Serbia and Montenegro were waging a war for the liberation of a people that formed one nation with 'Dalmatians of Croat and Serb name'. Josip Smodlaka declared in the Austrian parliament that 'this is our national, truly holy war'. Mass rallies were held throughout Dalmatia, attended by local mayors and Dalmatian parliamentarians. Carrying Croat, Serb and Slovene flags, the demonstrators hailed the Balkan allies, protested against Austro-Hungarian efforts to protect Turkey, and demanded Dalmatia's union with Ban's Croatia. At the end of 1912 a meeting of 500 dignitaries – including all Croat and Serb parliamentary deputies and the heads of sixty-two Dalmatian municipalities – took place in Zadar, which welcomed the Balkan states' victory as a signal of liberation also for 'Croats and Serbs on this side of the Drina'.

Austro-Hungarian troops were in the meantime pouring into Bosnia-Herzegovina. A telling incident occurred when 700 troops were disembarked in Zadar, where they were met with great hostility until

> all at once those 700 began to sing *Hail Slavs* – they were Czechs. They changed the line 'God is with us' into 'Hus is with us'. The majority of the public, ignorant of Czech history, thought they were singing "Rus [Russia] is with us', and began to applaud

wildly. The police then assailed the public, whose defence was that they were cheering – the Austrian army. The soldiers seeing all this began to shout: 'Down with the police!' Ever since then these soldiers have been confined to barracks, and are not allowed to come to town.[36]

Throwing to the winds the old idea of unity of all South Slavs, as inscribed in the founding charter of Strossmayer's Yugoslav Academy, the Dalmatians now supported Serbia against Bulgaria in the Second Balkan War of 1913. The two Balkan wars effectively doubled the size of Serbia and increased its population by half. It acquired a large part of Kosovo and Macedonia, but at Austrian insistence was evicted from northern Albania and thus denied a seaport. Montenegro doubled its population and grew by half, incorporating the rest of Kosovo and the Albanian port of Ulcinj. The two states acquired for the first time a common border by dividing the *sandžak* of Novi Pazar between them. The Serbian prime minister, Nikola Pašić, was now able to issue a direct challenge to Zagreb, Vienna and Pest: 'The question of our liberation and unification will not be solved by the politicians of the Serbo-Croat [sic] Coalition; it will be solved by Serbia and Russia.'[37]

Supilo, too, was caught up in the great enthusiasm that swept Croatia. In his view Croatia's action in the Habsburg Monarchy and Serbia's in the Balkans were leading in the same direction, towards a common Yugoslav state. Though he refused to see Serbia as the exclusive agent of Yugoslav unification, his hope that Croatia could play at least an equal role dwindled daily. In 1913 constitutional government was restored in Ban's Croatia, after which the Croat–Serb Coalition was handed control of the sabor on condition of not rocking the Austro-Hungarian boat. Its Serb members, acting at the behest of the Serbian government, agreed to continued cooperation with Pest. Serbia was exhausted by the wars and needed a breathing space. In June 1914, however, Crown Prince Franz Ferdinand was assassinated in Sarajevo by a Bosnian Yugoslav nationalist, and within two months Europe was at war.

A week after the assassination, Croat students from Rijeka arriving in Zagreb were welcomed with the song:

> Rijeka is not Hungarian, not Hungarian,
> it is Croatian, Croatian!
> Out with them, out with them!
> We want them out![38]

Yugoslavia or nothing

Lenin noted in 1916 that 'war does not change the direction in which politics developed prior to the war; it only accelerates its development'. Had he read him, Supilo would have agreed wholeheartedly. He saw the impending war as a historic opportunity to realise the main aim of the Dalmatian strategy: the creation of a strong Yugoslav state that would block Germany's eastward drive. The coming war promised to fuse all three factors on which he had once counted: autonomous Croat, now Yugoslav, action; major changes in Austria-Hungary; and a fundamental reconstruction of the European political order. The Dalmatians' role was to ensure that this fusion would take place. Their politics was to be guided by the simple formula: 'Yugoslavia or nothing!'[39] He would have agreed also with another of Lenin's observations: that the peace following any war could be 'nothing but the accounting and registration of the actual changes in the realities of forces brought about in the course of and in consequence of the war'.[40] The Croat action was to encourage such changes in the right direction.

Immediately after the Sarajevo assassination, Supilo and Trumbić left for Italy, where they were joined by several other Dalmatians and soon also by Slovene and Bosnian Serb politicians. They saw their main task as winning over the Entente capitals to their Yugoslav programme: unification of the Monarchy's South Slav lands with Serbia and Montenegro, on the basis of the right of national self-determination. The outbreak of war had produced a new danger, however, in that it soon became clear that Italy would condition its intervention on the Allied side upon the acquisition of long stretches of the Austro-Hungarian coast inhabited overwhelmingly by Croats and Slovenes. This only strengthened Supilo in his conviction that nothing less than Yugoslavia would do. Whereas Trumbić allowed for the possibility of an independent Croato-Slovene state emerging after the war, in the event that Russia and Serbia refused to support the Yugoslav project, Supilo rejected this out of hand: it was necessary to create a large state, for otherwise 'Italy would gobble us up like macaroni'. Serbia had to be persuaded to adopt the Yugoslav programme, and all partial or temporary solutions prevented. Serbia, for its part, informed St Petersburg in September 1914 of its claims to the Slovene, Croat and Serb territories of Austria-Hungary, leaving the western half of Istria to Italy: it was an enlarged Serbia, not Yugoslavia, that was supposed to emerge at the end of the war. The prospect of Italy's entry into the war, however, placed a question mark over Serbian gains in Dalmatia. Pašić was additionally worried that the Allies might be tempted to create after the war an independent Croatia that would include Slovenia, Dalmatia and part of Bosnia. He was determined to prevent the emergence of such a Yugoslav state. Serbian politicians were also concerned that the Monarchy's South Slavs, while gravitating towards Serbia so long as the Monarchy was in existence, might opt for independence in the event of its dissolution. This fear of the Austrian South Slavs' autonomous path to national independence encouraged the Serbian government to declare in December 1914 at Niš that Serbia's war of self-defence was also a war for 'the liberation and unification of all our subject Serb, Croat and Slovene brothers'.[41] The Slovene 'brothers' had in fact been added at the last minute.[42] This was a Yugoslav programme only to the extent that it addressed the same geographical area.

Croatian exiles and Serbian politicians shared the assumption that unification would be achieved through the victory of the Entente powers, to which Russia would make a great contribution.[43] The defeat of the Central Powers would supply the necessary conditions for Yugoslav unification, since a humiliated Austria-Hungary would either break up or be forced to cede its South Slav territories. Where the two differed was on who would be the bearer of the new state idea. Starting with the premise of national self-determination, Supilo and Trumbić envisaged the new state emerging out of a national accord reached between Slovenes, Croats and Serbs, based on their full equality. While paying lip-service to the national principle, Serbian politicians by contrast were united in their view that Yugoslavia would come into being as a result of territorial compensation granted by the Allies to Serbia for participating in the war on their side. As the 'liberator', Serbia would also decide the character of the new state. In 1914, however, all this was a distant prospect. St Petersburg and Belgrade worked in the meantime for the more limited but seemingly more realistic goal of winning for Serbia the 'Serb lands' of Bosnia-Herzegovina, southern Hungary and Dalmatia, the latter providing the much-desired outlet on the Adriatic Sea. Montenegro too was to be included in this new Great Serbia.

One result of these contradictory yet convergent interests was the creation of the Yugoslav Committee in London in May 1915. The Committee, formed with Serbian support, consisted exclusively of Austro-Hungarian South Slavs, though within it Serbia could count on the loyalty of the Bosnian Serb members, who were its express delegates. Formally independent of the Serbian government, the committee would work for the creation of a post-war Yugoslav state. The conflict between the two opposing conceptions of Yugoslavia, however, would frequently paralyse its work and purpose. The struggle for mastery over Yugoslavia thus began not after the act of union in December 1918, but from the moment the Yugoslav Committee was born.

Pašić saw the Committee as nothing more than a propaganda arm of the Serbian state, directed equally against other designs on the lands claimed by Serbia and against the formation of a Yugoslavia independent of Serbia. For Supilo and Trumbić, the purpose of the Committee was to anchor Serbia to the Yugoslav project, and to become a body which in the event of Austria-Hungary's dissolution would 'appear before the public with the task of liberating all our lands as a single whole, irrespective of Serbia and Montenegro'.[44] Serbian politicians mistrusted the depth of the Austrian South Slavs' affection for Serbia, while the Croats suspected the latter of something less than full commitment to the Yugoslav programme, and feared that Belgrade might even do a separate deal with Italy in Dalmatia. The two parties, needless to say, were not of equal strength. Nikola Pašić was prime minister of an internationally recognised state fighting on the side of the Allies. Supilo and Trumbić were exiles, handicapped by lack of official status or empowerment from forces at home.

Their work was further circumscribed by the knowledge that their action had as yet little support in Zagreb. As Supilo saw things in late 1914, 'The main centre of gravity of this whole thing will be us, the *Primorci* [inhabitants of the Adriatic coast], the Dalmatians and the Istrians, while our lever will be the Bosnian-Herzegovinians. One can as yet have little if any confidence in Ban's Croatia, which will have to be dragged in, *piu confusa che persuasa* [more confused than convinced], as in 1905–6 [with the new course].'[45] In flagrant contradiction with the principle of national self-determination on which he rested his case, he was at this stage against conducting a referendum in Ban's Croatia on the issue of Yugoslavia. He agreed with Pašić that the Yugoslav Committee should work against the formation of an independent Croatian state, though for different reasons: unlike Pašić, he had first-hand experience of the Croat–Serb conflict and of its potential destructiveness. The separation of Croatia from Serbia, in his view, would lead to the emergence of Serb and Croat irredentism and ultimately to a 'fratricidal' war, not unlike the one that had pitted Serbia and Bulgaria against each other in Macedonia. This is why neither a Great Serbia nor a Great Croatia but only Yugoslavia was the desirable outcome. In the meantime, there was the question of Italy and its plans in the East Adriatic. 'Right now', he told Trumbić, 'our most urgent task is to save what, even in the event of a major Russian victory, would remain in great danger: our national Adriatic coast. Once this is secured, the rest will fall into the bag more easily.'[46]

From the moment he stepped onto foreign soil, Supilo engaged in an almost superhuman, transcontinental diplomatic activity aimed at saving the Croatian and Slovene coast from being annexed by Italy. All doors opened before this (according to British prime minister Herbert Asquith) 'elemental force'. He went first to Rome, where he visited the Serbian, French, British and Russian ambassadors; then to Bordeaux, the wartime capital of France, to talk to French officials and the Russian ambassador. He discovered that the French and the Russians knew little about Croatia or Dalmatia. He produced a whole series of memoranda which, according to Seton-Watson, amounted to the 'most competent and persuasive survey of the [Yugoslav] question that emerged during the Great War'. In October 1914 he arrived in London, to the great delight of his British friends. 'I sighed with relief', wrote Steed, 'when I saw him well and in one piece, hoping that with his and Masaryk's help we would be able to persuade the British statesmen that Austria-Hungary was the weak spot of the enemy alliance, and that Supilo's instinctive political genius would do its work.'[47] Seton-Watson wrote about how happy they were to see Supilo in London, since 'up to his arrival there was no Yugoslav in Great Britain to testify to the desire for unification'. It soon proved, indeed, that wherever he went, Supilo impressed his interlocutors with his 'understanding of the essential aspects of the European situation, his strong faith in justice and in the vital importance of the Yugoslav question for the Allies'. The main problem turned out to be the Serbian ambassador, Mata Bošković, and his strong dislike of the Yugoslav name and project. The ambassador, indeed, was greatly suspicious of anything Yugoslav. He believed that the Habsburg Monarchy's South Slavs, including those of the Orthodox faith, had been infected with a destructive, more or less Germanic, Central European culture; and he refused, for example, to attend an exhibition of Ivan Meštrović's sculptures at the Victoria and Albert Museum, because this Croat would not identify himself as a Serb.[48] The Yugoslav Committee thus found itself from the start between 'the Scylla of unintelligent Serb chauvinism (as represented by Bošković) and the Charybdis of the Italian defamation campaign'.[49]

Unlike Bošković, who was cold-shouldered, Supilo was everywhere received as someone with 'a statesman-like understanding of the Balkan problems in the broadest sense'. According to the British foreign minister, Sir Edward Grey, he would have made an excellent British foreign minister; according to Steed he had the making of a 'great European statesman'.[50] Here, then, was the Yugoslav Cavour, waging his war for unification of his imagined nation, armed with nothing but an idea. Driven by the need to save the Croatian and Slovene coast from Italy, he not only talked to everyone about it, but was also heard. The Italian ambassador, Sforza, complained of Supilo's 'quite miraculous' influence. Asquith, who had Supilo to lunch, later said: 'We were able to resist the pressure of the Serbian diplomats and arguments of bright Croatian intellectuals; but how not to waver in the face of this man's belief in his nation's existence, his contempt for the ignorance of statesmen, and the force that made one feel that the Allies' recognition of the right of a national cause was in their best interest?'[51] Seton-Watson wrote that Supilo would have achieved much more in London had he had the support of the Serbian embassy.

Serbia, however, was pursuing another cause. The fundamental difference between these two concepts of Yugoslav unification – one reducing it to annexation by Serbia, the other insisting on national accord – remained unresolved throughout the war. It was clear that the two paths to unification led also to different kinds of state: on the one hand a centralised entity riding roughshod over the national identities of Slovenes and Croats – in other words, a Great Serbia by another name – and on the other hand, a federal state respectful of different national identities. On his visit to Niš, the wartime Serbian capital, in February 1915 Supilo told Pašić and the Russian envoy Gregory Trubetskoy that the future state should be organised on the principle of a 'centralist federalism', with common institutions dealing only with foreign policy, defence, finances and transport. He told them that 'the Croats wish to have a common state with the Serbs, but also to preserve their identity in that state. The best solution would be a federation in which Serbia would be enlarged by purely Serb territories, but in which Montenegro, Croatia with Dalmatia, Slovenia, and Bosnia-Herzegovina would continue to exist as such. No other solution would work.'[52]

Up to this time Croat politicians had little knowledge of Serbia. The conversations which Supilo and Trumbić conducted in Niš in 1915 made them aware that Serbian politicians and officials viewed 'this matter of unity' in a way that 'for our Croatian, western part would be no liberation at all, but a new conquest, as a consequence of which we would find ourselves enslaved by Serb Orthodox chauvinism, and count for nothing'. The Serbian envoy to London, behaved in fact 'far worse than the most chauvinist of Magyar imperialists'. The Serbian politicians whom the Dalmatians met in Niš on the other hand, brought up within a wholly different political culture, saw the Croat quest for federalism as importation of 'the Austrian sickness', and ruled it out by appeal to national oneness: since Serbs and Croats were one and the same people, the same standards would apply to them both in the new state. In their view, this Croat 'Austrian national mentality'

Ante Trumbić

would have to be suppressed and destroyed, since the new state would not be multinational like Austria, but the state of a single nation. This is why Trumbić and Supilo decided to conduct under the auspices of the Yugoslav Committee a 'cautious yet intensive Croat action in Europe, especially in Western Europe, where criteria of justice and political motivation will find greater understanding'.[53] They knew, however, that as leading members of a body personifying Yugoslav national unity and agitating for union of the Austrian South Slav lands with Serbia and Montenegro, any public display on their part of concern for the status of Croats and Slovenes in the future state would weaken the case for Yugoslavia.

When in early 1915 Supilo asked Pašić whether Serbia was ready to give up its specific political identity for the sake of Yugoslavia, as Piedmont had done in 1859 for the sake of Italy, Pašić's answer was affirmative. Pašić's apparent readiness, however, had more to do with his sense of the unreality of the whole project than with his actually harbouring any such sentiments. For him and other Serbian politicians, Yugoslavia was a synonym for Serb national unification. Having emerged as a product of Serbia's sovereign action, it would be a state whose Serb nature would be modified only minimally and only if absolutely necessary. Throughout the war Serbia's military and diplomatic efforts were governed first of all by its own state interests. The insistence by the Yugoslav Committee that Serbia should replace its purely Serb national programme by a Yugoslav one was likewise guided by the particular national interests of the Croats and Slovenes: to save their lands from partition and to provide them with a secure existence. In a note that Supilo submitted in January 1915 to British Foreign Minister Grey, he argued that in view of the fact that the Monarchy's South Slavs formed the first barrier to Germany's expansionism, their complete liberation was a necessary condition for European peace. The trouble with this geopolitical argument was that it was not necessarily consonant with the right of national self-determination. However persuaded London, Paris and St Petersburg were of the German danger, they did not necessarily accept that this entailed the formation of Yugoslavia. Insofar as they considered this possibility, they did not much like the prospect. France and Britain viewed the creation of a large Slav state in southeastern Europe as an extension of Russian influence in the eastern Mediterranean, and they toyed for a while with the idea of an independent Catholic South Slav state centred on Croatia. Russia, on the other hand, was suspicious of Yugoslavia because it would not have the wholly Orthodox make-up of Serbia, seeing in the Croat and Slovene preference for its federal constitution an attempt by France and Britain to weaken Russian influence in the Balkans. The two Croats responded to these Russian fears by emphasising the Slav nature of the Croats and Slovenes, and pressed for Russia to defend the eastern Adriatic coast against Italian designs on the grounds that Yugoslavia would give Russia access to the Mediterranean. Serbia, on the other hand, comforted its Russian ally by exaggerating the number of Serbs living in Austria-Hungary.

The Yugoslav Committee's work was constrained above all by the fact that the Allies did not wish to see Austria-Hungary fall apart. This stance encouraged the Committee's dependence on Serbia, while maximising the latter's freedom to pursue its own separate interests. More detrimental to the Yugoslavs in the long run was the politics of annexation that welded together the anti-German alliance. The Allied plan to strip the Habsburg Monarchy of some of its territory, including the larger part of its Adriatic coast, was dictated by the need to reward existing or potential allies like Serbia and especially Italy. The case of Bulgaria, another potential ally, posed a particular problem, since its reward could come only at the expense of Serbia, which was already an allied state. In order to persuade Serbia to give up part of Macedonia to Bulgaria, Belgrade was offered compensation in Slavonia, Bosnia-Herzegovina and southern Dalmatia. Supilo strongly resisted any such idea. As he wrote to the Russian foreign minister, Sergei Sazonov: 'Serbia as such has no right to this Adriatic territory, which is Croat by composition and sentiment'; it could claim it only 'by reference to our Croat national will, our commitment to the idea of national [Yugoslav] unity.'[54] Italy, however, presented by far the greatest danger for the Croats and the Slovenes, given that it was asking for Trieste, Gorizia-Gradiska, western Carniola, Istria and Dalmatia. Italy, moreover, was vetoing the creation of Yugoslavia. The Italian ambassador told Sazonov in the spring of 1915 that such a state would be simply a Russian sentinel in the eastern Adriatic. Italy preferred to see three separate South Slav states in the

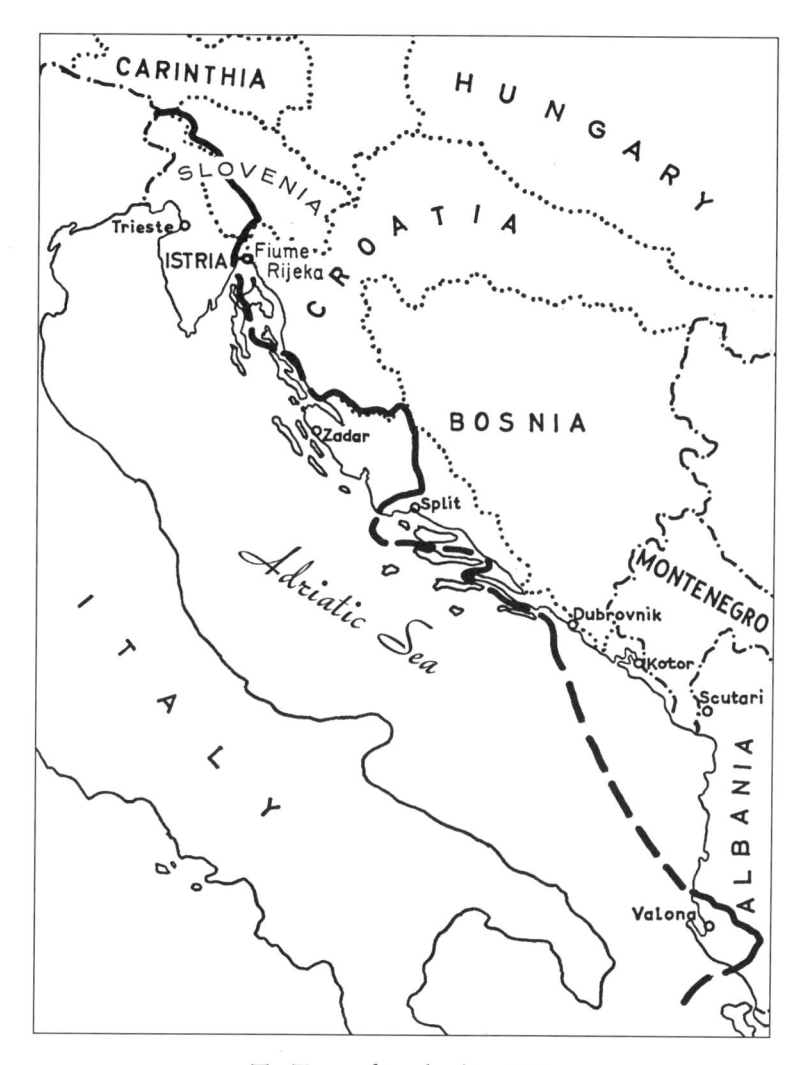

The Treaty of London line, 1915

eastern Adriatic hinterland: Serbia, Montenegro, and a truncated Croatia, with the latter possibly remaining in the Habsburg Monarchy or attached to an independent Hungary. In March 1915, France and Britain accepted Russia's demand for Istanbul and the Dardanelles in return for support of Italy's claims in the Adriatic. The treaty with Italy was accordingly signed in London on 26 April 1915.

'Some indeed believe', wrote Seton-Watson, 'that had he [Supilo] remained in London then, he could have paralysed the whole action that led to the secret treaty [with Italy] of 26 April 1915.' Grey, who was sympathetic towards the Yugoslavs, told Seton-Watson on 4 May that he was sorry that Supilo was absent at that crucial moment from London: 'it will some day be seen as a mistake. Could have used him here admirably.'⁵⁵ Supilo, however, having learned from Asquith of the nature of Italian demands, had set off to Florence to meet Trumbić and tell him about the danger that Italy might gain a large part of the eastern Adriatic coast. Convinced that Paris and London were ready to make such concessions to Italy, he decided to seek Russian help. Once in St Petersburg, Supilo was again widely received and it was here that he managed to extract from Sazonov what the Allies intended to give to Italy. He promptly alarmed Trumbić in Italy, asking him to travel immediately to London: it was important to mobilise Trumbić, since he was the leader of the parliamentary majority in Dalmatia. But Trumbić failed to get Supilo's message and went instead to Niš, with the result that the Yugoslavs got to London a week after the treaty had been signed.

Faced with this 'betrayal' by Russia, the Croat and Slovene members of the Yugoslav Committee placed their hopes in a Serbian rejection of the Treaty of London. The treaty, they argued, should be contested on the grounds not that Italy's gain was Serbia's loss, but that these territories were an inalienable part of the future Yugoslav state. Serbia, torn between its formal Yugoslav stance and its expectation of territorial reward, did nothing, however. The Croats and Slovenes, on the other hand, had nothing to gain by abstaining from struggle. A veritable battle now developed between the Allies and the Yugoslav Committee for Serbia's soul, with the former seeking to persuade Serbia to accept the treaty and the latter pressing it to repudiate it by formally raising before the Allies the issue of Yugoslav unification. In order to persuade Serbia to fall in with its plans, particularly in regard to Macedonia, the Allies at one point even dangled before Pašić the prospect of support for an eventual Serbian annexation of all South Slav territories of Austria-Hungary not promised to Italy. Asked to choose between Yugoslavia and eastern Macedonia, Pašić shocked the Committee by choosing eastern Macedonia, which he declared to be 'Serbia's best part'.⁵⁶ Serbia saw Macedonia as the fulcrum of its position in the Balkans, and as a bridge to Salonica. Pašić did protest verbally to the Allies about their failure to promise Serbia all Austria-Hungary's territories inhabited by South Slavs; but this was only a diplomatic gambit, designed largely to justify his refusal to give up any part of Macedonia.

At the same time he refused to raise the Yugoslav question formally with the Allies as the Committee pressed him to do, not only because he wished to avoid alienating the Great Powers, but also because this would have amounted to recognising the Croats and Slovenes as equal partners in the Yugoslav enterprise. The Yugoslav Committee and the Serbian government thus acted as autonomous entities throughout the war. Serbia refused to recognise the Committee formally, to seek Allied recognition of it as a representative body, to include any of its members into its own government or diplomatic personnel, or to involve them in its negotiations with the Allies. Where Serbia's own interests were directly involved, as in Dalmatia, it resisted any reference to the latter's Croat character or historic links with Croatia in the various memoranda on the Adriatic Question drafted by the Committee. Serbia also vetoed whenever possible the use of the name 'Yugoslavia' to describe the future state or the territory being claimed on the latter's behalf. Official Serbia, indeed, did not produce a single document throughout the war arguing the case for Yugoslavia. The tensions generated by this attitude did not lead to an open breach, however, since both sides were aware that they stood only to lose from it.

In the early part of the war, it seemed indeed that Serbia was following Russia in deserting the Yugoslav cause. Faced with the prospect that there might be no Yugoslavia, and that Croatia might end up being partitioned between Serbia, Italy and Austria-Hungary, Supilo now accepted the idea of a plebiscite. Such a plebiscite would make it possible, moreover, to appeal to the Italian people not to sanction 'their imperialists' misdeeds against us'.[57] He proposed to Grey that after the end of the war the Yugoslav population of the Monarchy should be allowed to decide whether they wished to join Serbia. He was convinced that they would. Grey accepted this, but in a more limited form: 'Following the end of the war Bosnia-Herzegovina, Croatia-Slavonia and southern Dalmatia will be free to decide their fate.' The plan, however, had to have Serbia's support, and Pašić vetoed it: he was unwilling to risk in any way the territories promised to Serbia. When Supilo asked the Yugoslav Committee to take a stand, frightened by the consequences of an open breach with Serbia it sided with Pašić.

Serbia in exile

Following Serbia's final defeat in November 1915 by a combined Austro-German and Bulgarian offensive, its politicians too became exiles. The Serbian government, court and army retreated across northern Albania to the Adriatic coast where they were picked up by Italian and French ships and transported to Corfu. The exodus of Serb politicians from occupied Serbia increased the possibility for meetings and debates, which served only to confirm the existence of deep differences among the future Yugoslavs.

Slovenes and Croats viewed Yugoslavia as an expression of collective will: unification made sense to them only if it included, if not all, then most of their national territories. Serbs persisted in viewing Yugoslavia as a reward for Serbia's participation in the war, and its unification as a simple extension of the Serbian state, dynasty, army and laws to the 'liberated' territory. Aware of the terror that had befallen the population of the lands gained by Serbia in the Balkan Wars – something that in the past they had chosen not to stress – the Slovenes and Croats feared 'liberation' by Serbia as much as they dreaded a Serbian defection from the Yugoslav cause.

Serbia's defeat had a pronounced effect on Yugoslav exile politics. It made Serbian politicians even more dependent on the Allies, more accommodating to their plans, and less willing to support Yugoslav unification openly. The Yugoslav Committee, on the other hand, increasingly behaved as sole representative of the Austro-Hungarian South Slavs. It pressed the Serbian government to engage in more aggressive diplomatic action on Yugoslavia's behalf, and to enter into negotiations with it over the terms of unification. This mood was reflected in the memorandum that Trumbić submitted in early 1916 to the French government, in which he elaborated anew the case for a Yugoslav state. It began by stressing that the Yugoslav idea had the support of the Austro-Hungarian South Slavs, the South Slav diaspora in both Americas, and the Serbian government. After the defeat of Serbia and Montenegro, it went on, all Yugoslav lands found themselves under foreign occupation, which meant that in liberating them the Allies would be in a position also to solve the Yugoslav 'national' question. The latter had to be viewed in the light of the future of Austria-Hungary and the Balkans. Austria-Hungary was a sick organism dominated by Germany, for whom it constituted a bridge to Istanbul and the Middle East. So it was in the Allies' interest that Austria-Hungary be dissolved. Its break-up assumed the formation of Yugoslavia. A simple restoration of Serbia would not suffice, since Serbia was too weak to resist the German *Drang* on its own. Only a Yugoslavia could do that. Serbia needed a coast, while the rest of Yugoslavia gravitated towards the Adriatic: the Adriatic coast, therefore, provided the basis of Yugoslav unity. The creation of Yugoslavia would also open the path to a peaceful resolution of inter-Balkan conflicts. Croatia's role was crucial to Yugoslav unification. The nation did not wish to stay with Hungary, nor to be partitioned between Italy and Serbia. An independent Croatia, however, lacked a *raison d'être* in the same way that Serbia did. The Slovenes, being most exposed to the pan-German drive, could survive as a people only by uniting with other Yugoslavs. Yugoslav-Italian friendship, Trumbić continued, was important for the containment of Germany. Seeking for itself a hegemonic role in the Adriatic Sea, Italy was demanding Yugoslav territories devoid of ethnic Italians. Their acquisition by Italy, however, would lead to permanent tension between the two nations. Italy did not need these lands for its own security, since the dissolution of Austria-Hungary would of itself leave Italy in a dominant position in the Adriatic. The Yugoslavs were ready to accept this, provided that Italy respected the national and territorial integrity of the future Yugoslav state.[58] Trumbić's document would provide the basis for the Allies' subsequent policy in the region.

Pašić, however, rejected this essentially Yugoslav line of reasoning. He disagreed with the view that Serbia's main interest lay in the Adriatic rather than in Macedonia and the Aegean, and rejected an approach that placed Serbia – an independent and internationally recognised state, whose occupation could be only of a temporary nature – on an equal footing with Austrian South Slav 'enslaved' territories. He also rejected Trumbić's position, stated explicitly for the first time in this memorandum, that the Yugoslav Committee represented the Austrian South Slavs and should be recognised in this capacity by the Allies. In his view only Serbia could perform that role. There was consequently no need to heed the invitation – issued originally by Supilo and now reiterated by the Committee – that the Serbian government should formally negotiate with the Committee issues of importance for the future state. In March 1916 British friends of Yugoslavia used the occasion of an official visit to Britain by Nikola Pašić and Regent Alexander to submit to the latter a memorandum warning him that Belgrade's policy of reducing Yugoslavia to a Greater Serbia would prove damaging to Serbia itself at the end of the war, since the Western Allies would see such a state as a Russian vassal and a barrier to the post-war reconstruction of Europe on a national basis. They went on to suggest that Serbia should co-opt a member of the Yugoslav Committee into its government, and appoint other members to its legations in Europe and elsewhere.[59] Their advice was ignored.

This attitude led Supilo to resign from the Yugoslav Committee in June 1916. He wrote to Sazonov that while Yugoslavia remained his ideal, if this proved unattainable: 'it would be the duty of all Croats to work for the unification with Croatia of all Yugoslav territories in which a majority of the population freely declared itself in favour of uniting with it.' This meant the creation of a second Yugoslav state centred on Croatia. Either all Slovenes, all Croats and all Serbs should be united as equals to create a single strong state, or Serb majorities should be joined to Serbia and Croat majorities to Croatia. Trumbić soldiered on, however, believing it to be the only way. The most important thing, in his view, was to keep the Committee together, since its disappearance would give Pašić a pretext for creating his Greater Serbia, in which case Italy would gain Istria and Dalmatia. Serbia would join forces with Italy, moreover, to ensure that the reduced Croatia could not survive. 'Let's swallow our pride and try to impose on Pašić our conception, which is broader and better, and which the more enlightened Serbs will sooner or later endorse.'[60]

Serbia's pursuit of hegemony in the future state led it to resist the creation of a Yugoslav army based on volunteers from the two Americas and prisoners of war. The Committee's idea was that such an army would, in the first instance, show to all concerned – and Italy in particular – that the South Slavs, far from being committed to the Habsburg Monarchy, were ready to fight on the Allied side. More importantly, these troops would serve as the army of occupation in 'our Austro-Hungarian lands', which otherwise would be occupied by the Allies, beginning with the Italians, and 'occupation by foreign troops politically inimical to our unity would allow them to act against our interests'. The Yugoslav troops, in other words, would protect Yugoslav interests in the Adriatic zone.[61] The Serbian government, however, strongly resisted the creation of any army outside its full control. It saw the Yugoslav army as a Croatian army, as an instrument of the Yugoslav Committee that, once in existence, would prevent Serbia from being the only 'liberator' and thus inhibit it from dictating Yugoslavia's internal constitution after the war. The creation of Yugoslav units would have greatly speeded up the rate of desertion of Slovene, Croat and Serb soldiers from the Austro-Hungarian army on the eastern front. Desertion in the west was not expected, since the Croatian and Slovene soldiers fighting against Italy felt they were defending their homeland. Indeed, these soldiers were largely responsible for Austria-Hungary's one great victory in the First World War, against Italy at Caporetto in October 1917. By contrast, in early 1917 after the outbreak of the Russian February Revolution it was possible to raise a major military force from the Yugoslav prisoners of war gathered at the port of Odessa. But the Serbian government's insistence that they must declare themselves Serb and fight solely under the Serbian flag led to the exodus of 12,700 Croat, Serb and Slovene volunteers from the projected Serbian Volunteer Corps. They declared that they had left because they could not tolerate the Great Serb approach to the corps command; that they remained faithful to the ideal of a federative Yugoslavia, based on national equality of Serbs, Croats and Slovenes; and that the Great Serbian idea posed a threat to Serbia's neighbours and to future peace in the Balkans.[62]

The period between Serbia's defeat (December 1915) and the entry of the United States into the war (April 1917) was the most difficult time for these future Yugoslavs. They all stood to lose in the event of a victory of the Central Powers. The Yugoslav Committee carried on with its struggle to dissuade the Allies from implementing the Treaty of London, and to convince it that the formation of Yugoslavia was in its own interest. Its credibility required Serbia's collaboration, but it now endeavoured more actively to make itself an equal and independent partner, canvassing Allied recognition for itself as chief spokesman for the Habsburg South Slavs. The Serbian government continued stubbornly to resist official recognition of the Yugoslav Committee, and sought to undermine its autonomous action and public affirmation. In contrast to the practical unity of its Polish and Czechoslovak equivalents, the Yugoslav Committee was obliged to work with an antagonistic competitor whose loyalty to Yugoslavia remained at all times contingent. The resolution of this particular Serbian-Yugoslav conflict, fought in the shadow of the larger European war, depended on events outside the participants' control. In the spring of 1917 the whole nature of the war, and hence of the future peace too, changed with the outbreak of revolution in Russia, and with the entry of the United States into the war on the Allied side. These two powers opened the door to a major reconstruction of the European state system, which would include also the creation of Yugoslavia.

A Yugoslav-Serbian compromise

The Yugoslavs' cause was greatly advanced by the outbreak of the Russian revolution and the abdication of Tsar Nicholas II, which deprived the Serbian government of its most important international support. The new Russian foreign minister, Paul Miliukov, issued a declaration, the first on the part of any Allied government, in favour of Yugoslavia. In April 1917 the Russian provisional government renounced the policy of conquest and called for a peace based on national self-determination, to which Miliukov added a demand for 'reorganisation of the Habsburg Monarchy and the liberation of her subject nationalities'. In May that year Bolsheviks declared that 'all nationalities should at once be given the opportunity to vote freely whether they wish to be independent states or parts of some other state', and called for a peace without annexations or indemnities. The Bolsheviks took power in October and removed Russia from the war by signing in December 1917 a ceasefire with the Entente's enemies. They also published the Allied secret treaties involving Russia. National self-determination now became a popular slogan in war-torn Europe, particularly since President Wilson defended the right of all nations to govern themselves. The United States, moreover, was not bound by the secret treaties. At the end of the year the British and French governments likewise decided, for reasons of political expediency, to endorse self-determination and a policy of no annexations or indemnities. These developments greatly strengthened the position of the Yugoslav Committee, which in the meantime – thanks to the support of Croat and Slovene emigrants in the two Americas – had become financially independent of the Serbian government.[63] There were changes at home too. Francis Joseph died in October 1916, after which the country acquired a new ruler in Charles I. There was a possibility that the change on the throne might lead to the Monarchy's reorganisation, thereby weakening the case for Yugoslavia. This led the Committee to proclaim itself on 18 December 1916 the only 'free representative' of the Monarchy's Yugoslavs, and to denounce any reorganisation of the Monarchy that would keep the latter within its borders. Fearing that the Allies might sign a separate peace with Austria-Hungary, the Committee urged the Serbian government to join it in raising the Yugoslav question with them formally. In March 1917 Pašić, worried that the Allies might recognise the committee or intervene to its advantage in the Serbian-Yugoslav disputes, finally agreed to organise a meeting on the island of Corfu.

At the end of May 1917, however, the Yugoslav Committee gained an important partner or possibly a competitor within Austria-Hungary itself, with the formation of a Yugoslav Club in the Austrian parliament that included all the Croat, Slovene and Serb deputies. On 31 May this club declared its intention to seek the unification of all Croat, Slovene and Serb lands of the Monarchy into a 'free, sovereign and democratic state body' under the Habsburg crown. There were now two Yugoslav actions proceeding at the same time: one led by the Yugoslav Club, the other by the Yugoslav Committee; one (formally at least) seeking the formation of a Yugoslav state without Serbia, the other a Yugoslav state that would include also Serbia and Montenegro. This outcome further softened Serbia's position on Yugoslavia.

The Corfu conference, which opened on 15 June 1917, was not properly prepared. It began informally, but soon developed into a serious discussion on how to persuade the Allies to accept the formation of Yugoslavia. Pašić insisted on Serbia's 'liberating' role. Trumbić argued that the new state should be sought on the basis of national self-determination, and his proposal was formally accepted. It was agreed also that the future state would be organised as a constitutional monarchy with a central single-chamber parliament. The Yugoslavs then proposed that it be called Yugoslavia, but the Serbians vetoed this, so it was decided that it would be called the Kingdom of Serbs, Croats and Slovenes. As for its internal organisation, Trumbić argued in effect for a federation, after which Pašić threatened to call the whole thing off: Serbia would work instead for the creation of a Great Serbia. Supilo did not take part in the conference, but he nevertheless sent a proposal according to which Yugoslavia would be a federation of five states: Serbia, Croatia, Slovenia, Bosnia-Herzegovina and Montenegro. The central parliament would deal with foreign affairs, defence, economy and communications, while the rest would be in the hands of the regional governments.[64] This document was not discussed. The trouble was that the Yugoslav Committee itself did not have a common position on the issue of the future state's constitution. Its Serb and Slovene members were in favour of a unitary system, that is, one without regional parliaments, while the majority of the Croats favoured a federal form. The division between the unitarists and the federalists reappeared during the discussion on the composition of the constitutional assembly. The federalists wished the new constitution be brought in by majority vote of the respective Croat, Slovene and Serb deputies, but after Pašić threatened again to divide the Serbs from the rest, they desisted. It was decided in the end that the constitution would be adopted by a qualified majority. It was also agreed that the Catholic, Orthodox and Muslim faiths would enjoy the same rights. These decisions formed the basis of the Corfu Declaration signed on 20 July 1917 by Pašić in the name of the Serbian government and by Trumbić in the name of the Yugoslav Committee. It proclaimed a general will to seek the unification of all Croats, Slovenes and Serbs, who formed one nation, on the basis of the national right to self-determination.

Trumbić then asked that the Serbian government demand of the governments of Britain, France and the United States to include the creation of Yugoslavia into their war aims; but Pašić refused. He was not sure that the Western Allies would agree to the Habsburg Monarchy's dissolution, in which case official Serbian support for Yugoslavia might prejudice Serb national unification. Copies of the declaration were consequently given to the foreign envoys attached to the Serbian government in exile without any explanation. The Yugoslav party, however, gained a strong ally in President Wilson, under pressure from whom Britain and France were forced to give up on Austria-Hungary. The Monarchy's capitulation on 27 October 1918 was followed by the establishment of a provisional State of Slovenes, Croats and Serbs, whose representatives proceeded to negotiate union with Serbia and Montenegro. The Kingdom of Serbs, Croats and Slovenes was proclaimed on 1 December 1918. Supilo did not live to see its birth: he died alone in a London hospital in late September 1917. The essential goals of the Croatian new course which he and Trumbić had initiated in 1903 appeared largely fulfilled. The German *Drang* had been checked; Austria-Hungary had disappeared; Croatia had joined a large South Slav state. The state he helped to create, however, carried within itself the seeds of its own destruction, since it rested on a compromise between two essentially irreconcilable state ideas. The struggle for mastery over Yugoslavia which had accompanied every step of its creation, would continue after 1918, forever questioning its very existence and purpose. Like the Habsburg Monarchy before it, Yugoslavia remained a state in permanent formation, never achieving more than temporary stability.

FOURTEEN

Between Italy and Serbia

Yugoslavia's champions, such as the Yugoslav Committee and its British supporters, Wickham Steed and R. W. Seton-Watson, invested a great deal of effort during and up to the very end of the war trying to persuade the Allies to include the creation of Yugoslavia among their war aims. To be effective, however, they needed Serbian cooperation; and Serbia, albeit claiming for itself the role of Yugoslav Piedmont, stubbornly refused to act the part. In early January 1918, Trumbić pressed Pašić to convene a conference of pro-Yugoslav forces and, armed with its mandate, to confront the Allies formally with a demand for the 'unification and liberation' of the Yugoslav people, 'on the basis of the national right to self-determination'. Pašić, however, remained adamantly opposed to any Yugoslavia that might emerge on the basis of the right to self-determination. Italy agreed with him.

In June 1918 the British and French governments proposed simultaneous recognition of the Polish, Czech and Yugoslav national committees, but the Italians vetoed any such action on behalf of the Yugoslavs, fearing that this would imperil the Treaty of London. In that same month, however, the United States announced its support for liberation of the Yugoslavs from 'German and Austrian rule'. In July 1918 the French foreign minister, Stephen Pichon, told Trumbić that France was willing to recognise the Yugoslav Committee as the representative of the Austro-Hungarian Yugoslavs. This recognition, the two diplomats agreed, would permit the establishment of Yugoslav legions in France. However, Paris could not proceed in this direction without Serbia's agreement, which Pašić refused to give on the grounds that Serbia reserved for itself the right to represent the Austro-Hungarian South Slavs. By the end of summer 1918 the French, British and American capitals recognised the London-based Czechoslovak National Committee as a de facto belligerent government, and its units as an Allied force; but not the Yugoslav Committee, or its volunteers recruited from deserters and prisoners of war, of whom 18,000 were held in Italian camps alone.

The British pro-Yugoslav lobby, acting with the support of their government, applied various forms of private and public pressure on Belgrade to alter its policy; however, Pašić and Regent Alexander stood fast. At the end of the summer the leaders of France, Great Britain and the United States indicated once again their readiness to accept the Yugoslav Committee as representative of the Austro-Hungarian Yugoslavs, but any such move was resisted by Italy and Serbia. In late August 1918, indeed, Pašić sent a note to the governments of Great Britain, France and the United States urging them not to recognise the Yugoslav Committee, and asking them to endorse instead Serbia's right to 'liberate' her 'brothers'. In early September 1918 even Rome was persuaded to acknowledge what it preferred to call 'the Yugoslav movement'; but the Serbian government could not bring itself to do even that. Any recognition, however grudging, of 'the Yugoslavs' and their autonomous right to liberation would deal a fatal blow to its conception of the new state as an outgrowth and continuation of Serbia. As Pašić told his officials: 'Serbia does not wish to be drowned in Yugoslavia; it wants Yugoslavia to submerge itself in Serbia.' Trumbić tried to reason with Pašić: since the Yugoslav question was part of the Austro-Hungarian problem, Serbia could not play the role of the Yugoslav Committee. He reminded him that by signing the Corfu agreement the Serbian government had itself recognised the Yugoslav Committee, but Pašić dismissed the Corfu Declaration as a mere exercise in public relations.

Trumbić now appealed directly to the French government to recognise the Yugoslavs as an allied nation and the Yugoslav Committee as its representative. Pichon again told him that France was willing to do so, but needed Serbia's consent. Trumbić turned next to the British foreign minister, Arthur Balfour, asking him to intercede with Pašić, which he did; Pašić remained defiant, however, insisting that the British government recognise Serbia as the only representative of 'our enslaved brothers'. This was refused: Balfour told Pašić to reach an agreement with the Yugoslav Committee. In early October 1918 the Greek prime minister, Elefthérios Venizélos, prompted by the British Foreign Office, offered a compromise that would have involved recognising the Yugoslav Committee as a temporary representative of the Habsburg South Slavs, following which a common Yugoslav-Serbian body would be established to direct war and peace policy – but this too was unacceptable to Pašić. If anything, Serbia's defiance grew as the military situation in the Balkans began to develop in

Nikola Pašić

a manner that seemed likely to permit Yugoslav unification in accordance with Pašić's plan.

The new Kingdom of Serbs, Croats and Slovenes was thus not recognised by the Allies before the start of the Paris Peace Conference on 18 January 1919, but instead was represented formally by Serbia. Non-recognition meant that its borders would be decided through negotiations between the conference's Big Four – the United States, Great Britain, France and Italy – with Italy in the role of both supplicant and judge. This outcome was due largely to the efforts of Italy and Serbia, which, united in the desire to gain parts of Austro-Hungarian territory, succeeded in blocking acceptance of the Austro-Hungarian South Slavs as an allied nation in advance of the ceasefire signed with Austria-Hungary at Padua on 3 November 1918. Their lands would hence be treated as enemy territory and potential war booty. The newly created State of Slovenes, Croats and Serbs now faced an Italian occupation of its western lands.

Trumbić tried hard to prevent Italian troops from taking part in the occupation of Yugoslav territory, and asked again that the Yugoslavs be recognised as an allied nation and his committee as their representative. He addressed a memorandum to the US State Department, laying down principles for the Allied occupation of Yugoslav territories; its main points were that the population should be treated as allies, and that nothing should be done to prejudice the territorial solutions. The memorandum stressed in particular: 'It is necessary that the interested governments of Italy and Serbia and their armies should be excluded from the temporary occupation and administration of the [contested] territories', so that the population would be able to exercise its right to self-determination.[1] The Yugoslav National Council formed in the United States besought Washington to recognise the Yugoslavs in order to prevent implementation of the Treaty of London, and asked for American troops to be sent to the contested territories. The Council also told the State Department that occupation by Serbian troops would be a great misfortune 'for both us and the Serbs', because it would sow the seeds of a civil war that would threaten European peace. They were told that the American government was willing to recognise the Yugoslav Committee, but was held back by Serbian resistance. But, like London, Washington refused to recognise Serbia as the only agent of Yugoslav unification and directed its government to reach an agreement with the Yugoslav Committee on the basis of the Corfu Declaration.

The Yugoslavs' own path to independence

Serbia's quest to be the 'liberator' of the 'enslaved brothers' and the sole subject of Yugoslav unification was in the event to remain unfulfilled, since by the time the armistice was proclaimed at Padua Austria-Hungary had fallen apart and a free State of Slovenes, Croats and Serbs had been established in Zagreb. The initiative that led to the new state's emergence did not come from Zagreb, however. On the contrary, the governing Croat–Serb Coalition resisted all moves in this direction for as long as it possibly could. This is all the more striking, given that the Hungarian and Croatian parliaments, unlike those in the Austrian half of the Monarchy, functioned throughout the war.

In the last elections before the war, held in 1913, the Croat–Serb Coalition had won 40 per cent of the votes cast, giving it forty-eight of eighty-eight seats in the sabor. It was now composed of two parties only, the Independent Croat Party, led by Ivan Lorković; and the Independent Serb Party, headed by Svetozar Pribićević. Four other parties enjoyed a considerable following: the Croat People's Peasant Party, led by Stjepan Radić (three seats); Starčević's Party of Right, led after 1916 by Ante Pavelić[2] (eleven seats); the Croatian (formerly True) Party of Right (nine seats); and the Unionist Club (twelve seats). The remaining seats went to two small parties which between them won less than 5,500 votes. The 'loyalist' bloc thus had a comfortable majority, but there was also a significant 'patriotic' opposition. On the other hand, only half the 208,411 registered voters had actually bothered to vote, indicating the sabor's irrelevance in the eyes of much of the population.[3]

With the Coalition in control, Zagreb maintained cordial relations with Budapest throughout the war. This was due largely to the influence of Belgrade, as channelled through the Independent Serb Party. In early 1914 Pašić had told Pribićević that he expected Austria-Hungary to attack Serbia within a few years, and that when this happened it was essential that Serbia should appear an innocent victim in the eyes of the world. Even after the attack, Croatian Serbs should remain passive in order to prevent repression against them. Pašić consequently advised Pribićević to be maximally accommodating in dealing with the Hungarian prime minister, István Tisza.[4] The Croat–Serb Coalition's passivity during the First World War proved a great comfort to Tisza, who whenever faced with a problem involving the Serbs felt that the Serb Independent Party would arrange everything. As a proof of his Austro-Hungarian patriotism, Pribićević even volunteered for military service in 1915, but was rejected; he spent a good part of the war living in Budapest under Tisza's protection. The sabor's political hibernation ended with the death of Francis Joseph on 21 November 1916 and the accession of Charles I, who promised to work for peace.

At his coronation as King of Hungary, Charles promised to respect the latter's constitutional liberties and territorial integrity, i.e. to uphold dualism. His oath negated the possibility of a comprehensive solution of the Yugoslav question within the Monarchy. Nevertheless, the fact that he did not swear to uphold the Austrian constitution encouraged the hope that the new emperor-king might seek a reorganisation of at least the Austrian half of the Monarchy, as a first step towards ending dualism. The return of parliamentary politics in the Austrian part of the Monarchy in the spring of 1917 prompted the Yugoslav parties to articulate their national programmes. In the last Austrian parliament before the war, the Yugoslavs held thirty-seven seats: Slovenes twenty-three, Croats twelve and Serbs two. Twenty deputies from the Slovene People's Party, three from the Dalmatian Party of Right, and three Croat deputies from Istria formed the Croat-Slovene Club. Given this distribution, the forging of the Yugoslav policy fell to the Slovene People's Party and its leaders, Anton Korošec and Janez Krek.[5]

Yugoslavia could not have been created without the active involvement of Slovene politicians. Slovenes and Croats worked closely together not only in the Reichsrat but also in the Istrian parliament, where they faced a hostile Italian majority and indifferent Austrian governors. Croat-Slovene cooperation went beyond immediate pragmatic needs, however: it was a strategic option for both nations. Ever since the stormy years of 1848–9, the idea that Slovenia should unite with Croatia revived whenever it seemed that the Habsburg Monarchy might fall apart, join Germany or undergo a reorganisation inimical to Slovene national interests.[6] That Slovenia and Croatia belonged together was at the same time a lasting tenet of the Croatian national programme, and remained embedded in the ideology of the Party of Right. At the start of their work in exile, Trumbić told Supilo that 'all Slovene and Croatian lands must be in one state, whatever its form', because 'if the Slovenes were to be separated from us, the majority of the Croats would not accept a Serbian king, and would seek their own state'. Since Italian aspirations to Slovene ethnic territory were bound to rally the Slovenes behind Vienna and hence inhibit the spread of the Yugoslav movement among them, the Yugoslav Committee felt bound to defend unconditionally the integrity of the Slovene lands. Once the war began, practically all Slovene national leaders agreed that Slovene national security would best be safeguarded in a union with Croatia. In late October 1916 the Croat-Slovene Club decided that as soon as the Austrian parliament was recalled it should ask for the Monarchy's reorganisation, in a manner that would permit the creation within it of a separate Croato-Slovene state. This was a direct attack not only on dualism, but also on perceived pan-German national interests, given that the Slovene lands linked Vienna to its main commercial port of Trieste and to its naval base at Pula, which Germany viewed as its own strategic asset.

In May 1917, during the high-level talks that preceded the opening of the Austrian parliament, the deputies of the Croat-Slovene Club informed the monarch and the Austrian prime minister, Heinrich Clam-Martinič, that they wished for a union of Slovenian and Croatian lands. Clam-Martinič assured them that the Austrian system would be reformed, but that the Yugoslav unit which they desired could be created only as part of the postwar settlement. The Yugoslav case had by now become further complicated by the fact that Serbia and Montenegro were occupied lands, so that their future too had to be taken into account by Vienna. Following further talks between Slovene and Croat politicians, it was agreed to work for Yugoslav unification outside the Monarchy, and to unite all Yugoslav deputies in the Reichsrat into a single Yugoslav Club, which would act as the counterpart of the Yugoslav Committee abroad. On 30 May 1917, the day of the opening of the Austrian parliament, the president of the Yugoslav Club, Anton Korošec, read out the following declaration:

The undersigned national deputies united as the Yugoslav Club declare that, on the basis of the national principle and the Croatian state right, they demand the union of all lands of the Monarchy inhabited by Slovenes, Croats and Serbs into an independent, sovereign and democratically established body under Habsburg rule; and that they shall work with all their strength to realise this, our united nation's demand. The signed deputies shall participate in the work of the parliament with this qualification in mind.[7]

By limiting Yugoslav unification to the Monarchy's borders, the declaration appeared to disagree with the programme of the Yugoslav Committee. But this was largely a tactical gesture, aimed at persuading those within the Slovene People's Party who resisted the idea of the Monarchy's dissolution to support the declaration. Quite apart from this, the Yugoslav Club had to bear in mind the fact that the Allies did not as yet challenge the Monarchy's existence. On the other hand, the stress on a national unity that included the Serbs left the door open to unification outside the Monarchy involving Serbia and Montenegro. The May Declaration was warmly welcomed in Zagreb by Starčević's Party of Right and by Radić's People's Peasant Party, while the Croat–Serb Coalition studiously ignored it. According to Ivan Lorković, the Serb members of the Coalition refused to consider any unity with the Slovenes.[8]

During the debate on the sabor's address to the king, which had begun in March 1917, three drafts were discussed – submitted by respectively the Croat–Serb Coalition, the Croatian Party of Right and Starčević's Party of Right. Only this last one endorsed the idea of Yugoslav unity – it was the first declaration in favour of Yugoslavia heard in the Croatian parliament. In a statement on 5 June 1917, Starčević's Party of Right insisted that national right to self-determination and free national development was the only foundation for a just peace in Europe; called for a reorganisation of the Habsburg Monarchy based on the principle of national equality; and offered its unconditional support for the unification of 'all the lands in the Monarchy inhabited by Croats, Slovenes and Serbs into a single, independent and democratically constituted state body'. It also called upon 'the whole Croatian nation' to support this aim, and invited the sabor to work for the 'great ideal of national liberty and unity'.[9]

The Yugoslav Club, urged on by Trumbić, next sought to unite all the pro-Yugoslav political parties on a platform of unity and independence. A conference to this effect was held in Zagreb in early March 1918, attended by representatives of the Yugoslav Club, Slovene political leaders, Starčević's

Party of Right, the Social-Democratic Party, two Serb dissidents from the Croat–Serb Coalition, and representatives of parties and groups from Bosnia-Herzegovina, Dalmatia, Istria and Međimurje. The Croat–Serb Coalition boycotted the event. The Zagreb conference adopted a declaration stressing that Slovenes, Croats and Serbs formed a single nation, whose unity 'should never be called into question'. This nation wished to create its own independent and democratic state on the territory where it formed a continuous and compact majority, with full cultural rights to be granted to national minorities. The Yugoslav state to be created would respect the individuality of the three Yugoslav 'branches', as well as 'the state continuity of its component parts'. The declaration singled out in particular 'the coast, ports and islands of the northern and eastern Adriatic' as an integral part of the Yugoslav state, and asked that the Yugoslav nation be invited to participate at the forthcoming peace conference.[10] The Zagreb Declaration followed that issued in Corfu in omitting all reference to the Monarchy; but differed from it by insisting on preservation of existing state/historical entities. The Zagreb meeting also decided to work for the formation of a National Council of Slovenes, Croats and Serbs that would work together with the Yugoslav Committee in London. When in April 1918 Stjepan Radić indicated his support for this programme, the Croat–Serb Coalition acquired a sizable pro-Yugoslav parliamentary opposition.

In June 1918 the pro-Yugoslav deputies moved that the sabor should demand, in the name of 'the Slovene, Croat and Serb nation', that 'the Croatian or Yugoslav question be solved on the basis of national self-determination'. The Croat–Serb Coalition refused to support the motion. The pro-Austrian Croatian Party of Right, meanwhile, insisted that Yugoslavism was nothing but a screen for Serb imperialism. But in July 1918 Ivan Lorković, leader of the Croat part of the Coalition, made a speech in which he stated that the Yugoslav idea had 'conquered our whole people like an elemental force', and called for unity of all parties agreeing with the message of the Zagreb Declaration. He ended his speech by urging the deputies to respond to the people's 'imperative call'. Pribićević, while accepting 'in principle' the idea of such an alliance, disagreed with the prospect of continued existence of separate national or historical individualities within the future state. He rejected both the proposed coalition of parties and the sabor's transformation into a Yugoslav body, arguing that it was better to maintain the present constitutional government and the sabor's control.[11] Pribićević's insistence on this occasion that the Yugoslav question was not on the agenda contrasted sharply with the US government view, publicly stated the month before, that the Yugoslavs should be freed from foreign domination. Lorković now left the Coalition, thus further strengthening Pribićević's influence within it.

Yugoslav self-organisation was nevertheless proceeding rapidly outside Ban's Croatia, fuelled by the growing paralysis of the Austrian government, the increasing war-weariness of the population, Slav revolts, and the failure of the German offensive on the western front. In that same month, July 1918, Slovene-Croat-Serb national councils were formed in Dalmatia, the Croatian Littoral and Istria. In the middle of August a Slovene National Council was formed in Ljubljana, in order to prepare the Slovene nation 'for the historic moment when it will take upon itself all rights and duties of state independence together with the Croats and Serbs'. The Yugoslav Club now declared its intention to unite all the regional national councils into a single National Council for the Yugoslav lands of the Monarchy, with the task of preparing the ground for the emergence of Yugoslavia. This body was to be organised on a territorial basis, that is, its founding conference was to be attended by representatives elected by the political regions. Its seat would be in Zagreb. It was necessary, however, to persuade the Croat–Serb Coalition to end its boycott of the Yugoslav enterprise, since otherwise the Serb areas of Bosnia-Herzegovina and Ban's Croatia might not join the proposed National Council. The Coalition refused, however, to give up its privileged position in Ban's Croatia. The whole situation changed under the impact of military developments in the southern Balkans. On 14 September 1918 French troops, backed by the Serbian army, began an offensive from Salonica and within weeks Bulgaria was forced to sue for peace. Bulgaria's collapse speeded up the political preparations, and on 5 October 1918 delegates from practically all the Monarchy's South Slav lands met in Zagreb to establish the planned National Council. The Croat–Serb Coalition was asked to send representatives, but its leaders hesitated. It finally joined the Council only after being promised a decisive role within it.

On 19 October 1918 the National Council established a presidency, with Anton Korošec as its head, and with Ante Pavelić and Svetozar Pribićević as his deputies. The presidency then issued a declaration announcing the formation of the State of the Slovenes, Croats and Serbs. It demanded the unification of all Slovene, Croat and Serb lands into a single sovereign state, and for 'our nation' to be represented at the forthcoming peace conference. It also rejected all outside claims to the Yugoslav Adriatic coast.[12] Three days later a large crowd met in central Zagreb hailing Wilson, Trumbić and Yugoslavia. The Zagreb military command informed Vienna that it was losing control of the situation throughout the land, and that Croatia was on the brink of a revolution. The administrative fabric was indeed collapsing, as civil unrest spread throughout northern Croatia under the impact of the Monarchy's military defeat and political disintegration. The new government had only just been established, while the old one had ceased to command either authority or affection. It was not clear, indeed, what the relationship was between the old and the new institutions.

At a meeting of the sabor's inner committee, Svetozar Pribićević now suggested that the sabor should proclaim an end to Croatia's union with Hungary, transfer its own powers to the National Council, and proclaim Croatia part of the State of Slovenes, Croats and Serbs. There was a strong feeling, however, that the sabor should continue to function, and that it should delegate only part of its authority to the National Council. Matko Laginja, the Croat deputy from Istria and member of the National Council, argued that the office of ban was part of the Croatian political tradition which should be respected, and that the ban should be co-opted onto the National Council. In Radić's view the ban should remain head of the Croatian government, which should be enlarged by the addition of people from the National Council. Pribićević argued that the country could not have two governments, and that the National Council should be invested with dictatorial powers. The majority agreed with him.

On 29 October, when the sabor was to reconvene, the city's streets and squares thronged with people – students carrying red banners, and soldiers the Croatian national colours on their breasts. Before entering the chamber the deputies addressed the crowd, which responded to their rousing speeches by singing the Croatian, Serbian and French national anthems. The parliamentary speaker, Bogdan Medaković of the Independent Serb Party, opened the session by telling the deputies that – since government was now in the hands of the National Council – the sabor's only remaining task was to sever all constitutional ties with Austria and Hungary, and to prepare the transition to the new order. Pribićević then proposed that the sabor should declare, on the basis of the national right to self-determination rather than the Croatian state right, that all ties between the Triune Kingdom and Austria and Hungary were severed. It should next proclaim Croatia (including Rijeka) a wholly independent state, which was joining the new State of Slovenes, Croats and Serbs to be established on all their ethnic territories between the Isonzo and Salonica (!). This was unanimously accepted. Pavelić next moved that the sabor should recognise the National Council as the supreme government in Croatia, which won the approval of the current ban, Anton Mihalovich. This too was accepted. The Croatian Party of Right then announced its own dissolution, followed by that of the Unionist Club.

On the same day, 29 October 1918, the National Council's presidency formally proclaimed the independence of the State of Slovenes, Croats and Serbs, and the creation of a national government whose task was to effect union with Serbia and Montenegro. It appointed a new government for Ban's Croatia and confirmed Mihalovich in his post. New governments were established in Slovenia and Bosnia-Herzegovina a few days later. The National Council also authorised the Yugoslav Committee to act as its representative abroad. Rather than waiting to be liberated by Serbia, the 'enslaved brothers' had established their own state six days before Austria-Hungary signed an armistice, in affirmation of the right to self-determination and in consequence of their autonomous action. Given the volatile circumstances, it was an oddly peaceful and legalistic transfer of power. The State of Slovenes, Croats and Serbs was constructed on a federal basis, in that in addition to the central National Council and its executive there existed also regional governments for Slovenia, Dalmatia, Ban's Croatia and Bosnia-Herzegovina, while the Hungarian Serbs acknowledged that the Council also represented them. However, the National Council and its executive soon lost effective power to the presidency, which – given the Coalition's grip on it – became dominated by the Independent Serb Party and its leader, Svetozar Pribićević. The new Croatian government, on the other hand, proceeded to work like the old one, without active engagement with the population and without seeking to make its own workings and decisions comprehensible to them.

The Croatian conundrum

Despite the fact that Austria-Hungary's war against Serbia was inspired by the desire to keep its South Slav dominions, the Yugoslav question was not seriously discussed by the Monarchy's leaders until the very last months of the war, because at its core lay the Croatian issue – which could not be resolved without abolishing dualism. On 3 March 1918, however, the Zagreb Declaration endorsing Yugoslavia stunned official Budapest, and forced it to consider its position. At a meeting held on the following day involving leading Hungarian politicians, the governor of Bosnia-Herzegovina, General Stjepan Sarkotić, was asked for advice. He suggested that Dalmatia be immediately given to Ban's Croatia, which should also be promised the eventual incorporation of Bosnia-Herzegovina. Two days later Sarkotić repeated this advice to Emperor Charles, who believed that the answer lay in the creation of a Yugoslav unit which would include also occupied Serbia. The Austrian government refused, however, to consider ceding Slovenia to any such a unit, because Slovenia was Austria's bridge to the Adriatic Sea. At this time, in any case, the Austro-Hungarian generals were convinced that their side was winning the war, so the Yugoslav question was once again set aside.

In May 1918, at a meeting of their own with Sarkotić, the military governors of occupied Serbia and Montenegro argued that these lands should be joined to Dalmatia and Bosnia-Herzegovina, and the resulting Yugoslav unit be constituted as a separate crownland. Sarkotić reminded them that Croats were the essential glue of any Yugoslavia. The key problem, in his view, was the Adriatic Sea: since neither the Germans nor the Magyars would permit any solution that would cut them off from the sea, it was better to create a Slovene state in Austria on the one hand and a united Croatia within Hungary on the other. Bosnia-Herzegovina could be either joined to Croatia or added as a *corpus separatum* to Hungary. Another possibility was to unite Bosnia's Croat areas to Croatia and add the resulting unit to Austria, while the Serb part of Bosnia would be joined to Hungary together with Montenegro and Serbia.

The search for a magic solution to the Croatian question within the existing dualist division of the Monarchy continued over the following months. At a meeting of the crown council in Vienna, held on the first anniversary of the May Declaration, the Hungarian prime minister, Alexander Wekerle, proposed that Dalmatia be added to Ban's Croatia – that is, to Hungary – and Bosnia-Herzegovina too as a *corpus separatum*. The Austrian prime minister, Ernst von Seidler, however, insisted that Dalmatia was part of Austria, and that the Austrian parliament would not agree to Bosnia-Herzegovina going to Hungary. General Sarkotić's view was that Dalmatia was part of the lands of the Hungarian crown and should be added to Croatia, together with Bosnia-Herzegovina. Emperor Charles proposed that the two prime ministers find a mutually acceptable solution.

At the meeting of the Austrian and Hungarian prime ministers, Sarkotić argued in favour of a complete state separation of 'the Serb and Croat elements'. A united Croatia, with Bosnia-Herzegovina loosely attached to it, would create a complex orientated towards the Monarchy rather than to Serbia. At a meeting of the joint ministry of finance held in Vienna in early September 1918, he warned that the Hungarian government was too complacent, and that the growing 'Yugoslav epidemic' demanded an urgent response. He wrote to the emperor-king that Wekerle had become a prisoner of the Croat–Serb Coalition, which should not be trusted at any time; and advised him to establish contact with 'the true Croats', namely, the Croatian Party of Right. Sarkotić ascribed the alleged 'Serbophile' orientation of the Monarchy's foreign minister, Stephen Burian (who was a Hungarian), and the premier Wekerle to the influence of István Tisza, Hungary's most powerful politician. Tisza, he wrote, should come to Bosnia to see how matters stood.

So in early September Charles asked Tisza to undertake a journey through the Monarchy's South Slav lands. On his arrival in Zagreb, Tisza was told by Dušan Popović, a close confidant of Svetozar Pribićević, that he, Tisza, ought to negotiate with Pašić a lasting solution to the Yugoslav problem. According to one account, Tisza reluctantly rejected this proposal. The royal emissary arrived in Sarajevo on 20 September 1918, feeling quite unwell as a result of the bad roads and the poor welcome he had received in Dalmatia. The Bosnian leaders presented him with a memorandum signed by all three Yugoslav 'branches'. Before reading it, Tisza complained to Sarkotić about the alleged degeneracy of the Croatian noble class, and the unpleasant atmosphere he had found in Zagreb and Dalmatia: how could this be? His mood dramatically worsened after reading the Bosnian memorandum. The memorandum criticised in blunt terms the Monarchy's treatment of Bosnia-Herzegovina, and insisted with a certain biblical flourish that 'the suffering soul of our single Serb-Croat-Slovene nation, if further broken up through violence and injustice, is ready to burn and die a martyr's death on the path to unity and freedom'.[13] Tisza declared that he had never been so insulted. On the following day he received the Bosnian delegation dressed in a military uniform decorated with many medals. He did not invite them to sit down, but addressed them standing beside a table on top of which he had placed his sabre and a whip. As he spoke he gradually lost his temper. He stated, among other things, that Britain had invented the principle of nationality – a principle which she did not apply at home in Ireland – in order to destroy Austria-Hungary. He ended his speech by pounding the table with his fist and shouting that Hungary was still strong enough to crush its enemies. The Bosnians turned their backs on him and left the room. After calming down somewhat, Tisza told Sarkotić that '[Dušan] Popović will fix it all', and that the Croatian Serbs would restrain the Bosnians. Sarkotić argued that one should think of some way of neutralising the Entente's victory, which appeared increasingly likely: it was this prospect that was feeding the Yugoslav idea. The Serbs, showing no gratitude for having been a privileged minority, were now abandoning their alleged oppressors with curses and derision. There was still a faint chance that the Croats could be won back by being offered Bosnia-Herzegovina. Tisza, however, rested his hopes upon the Croatian Serb politicians.[14]

A few days later the joint minister of finance arrived in Sarajevo, only to be informed of Bulgaria's imminent defeat. Austrian officials and generals promptly informed the monarch that the only way of saving the Slav South for the Monarchy was to confront 'the Serb element' with a united Croatian-Bosnian force. It was necessary, therefore, to unite Dalmatia and Bosnia-Herzegovina immediately with Croatia, and to add the whole lot to Hungary. This was the only way to divide Croats and Serbs. Unless Emperor Charles took this step, loyal Croats would sink forever into Yugoslav waters, at the expense of Hungary and the Monarchy as a whole. In late September 1918 General Sarkotić, having learnt of Bulgaria's intention to seek a separate peace, sent another desperate missive to Charles telling him that the Monarchy's position in the south was about to collapse, given the enthusiasm for Yugoslavia sweeping through Croatia; and that this could be prevented only by proclaiming a Great Croatia. Such solutions were by now quite unrealistic, however, even if their architects had possessed the means to enforce them; but the rulers of Austria-Hungary were living in a world quite divorced from reality. As the Allied troops marched north towards Hungary, the only thing that Hungarian prime minister Wekerle was able to promise Croatia was a modification of the 1868 Croato-Hungarian Compromise.

On 4 October 1918, the day Yugoslav politicians began assembling in Zagreb, the Austro-Hungarian government sent a note to President Wilson accepting his Fourteen Points drafted in January 1918, which since then had been radically altered to the detriment of the continued existence of Austria-Hungary. On 16 October 1918, while waiting for a reply, Emperor Charles issued a manifesto announcing Austria's federalisation, whereupon the Hungarian prime minister accused the monarch of unilaterally abrogating the Austro-Hungarian Compromise of 1867. The Hungarian parliament then gleefully declared an end to the union with Austria. Charles's proclamation was in any case quite superfluous, since by this time practically all national groups within the Monarchy – apart from the Germans and the Hungarians – were busy setting up their own national bodies. On 19 October, the day that the National Council was set up in Zagreb, the American president responded to Vienna by saying that his country had recognised Czechoslovakia, and that he welcomed the Yugoslavs' aspirations to freedom. Vienna was advised to negotiate peace with its own peoples.

Three days later the Austrian prime minister told parliament that Austria – but not Hungary – would be transformed into a federation of nation states. This final attempt to please the United States was rejected, however, by the Czechs and the Yugoslavs. On 26 October Austria-Hungary informed Germany of its intention to seek a separate peace, and on the following day it accepted all Wilson's conditions in advance. But it was all too late, since the Monarchy was falling apart. On 7 November Vienna was informed by the Allies that no further negotiations were possible, given that its former subject nations had already become independent.

Occupation

The National Council's most urgent problem was the rising chaos, and the need to establish some sort of law and order; but the army on which it could rely for this was not available. Railway traffic stopped as Hungarian workers and officials went home. In the Slavonian east, lordly mansions were torched, the passing armies resorted to pillage, and there was a good deal of settling of various local accounts. The far more popular Dalmatian government, assembled in Split, likewise found it impossible to raise a defence force: foreign soldiers went home, but so too did local recruits.[15] The Dalmatian government met in Split rather than Zadar, because Zadar was now under Italian occupation. On 27 October 1918 Trumbić had made one last, and equally unsuccessful, effort to prevail upon Pašić to allow recognition of the Austro-Hungarian Yugoslavs as an allied people; he warned him that Italy would not merely occupy the parts promised to it in 1915, but also seize the Austro-Hungarian navy and merchant shipping. Pašić, however, not only failed to reply, he even publicly disowned the National Council by pretending it did not exist.[16]

In early November, discussing the terms of the Austro-Hungarian ceasefire, the Allies had agreed not only that their troops should be allowed to move freely through enemy territory and occupy all strategic positions within it, but also that they should occupy the area that the Treaty of London had promised to Italy – and indeed further territory too if necessary to safeguard peace and order. On 3 November Anton Korošec addressed a note to the Allied governments asking for recognition of the new Yugoslav state; but Italy was strongly opposed and exerted such pressure that the British and American governments held back. On 4 November the Italian army and navy took possession of Trieste and Pula, and soon afterwards also of Gorizia-Gradiska, the rest of Istria, the islands of the north Adriatic, parts of Carinthia and Carniola, Rijeka, Zadar with a large part of its hinterland,

493

Šibenik and the coast down to Trogir, the Pelješac peninsula, and the islands of Vis, Korčula, Lastovo and Hvar. They would have entered Trogir and Split as well, but for the population's vigorous resistance.[17]

In all the occupied territories, especially in Istria, the Italian military authorities proceeded to behave as if they now belonged to Italy, dismissing local Slovene and Croat administrations, closing down Slav schools, arresting and deporting those who resisted, and harassing the Slav clergy. When the British government tried to remonstrate, the Italian ambassador, Guglielmo Imperiali, told Balfour that the Italians had won the war against Austria-Hungary practically single-handed, while the Yugoslavs had fought on the enemy side: Britain should choose which side to support. Concerned with the growing conflict in the Adriatic, the British and French governments pressed the Yugoslavs and the Serbians to achieve an early unification. On 6 November 1918 representatives of the National Council, the Yugoslav Committee, and the Serbian government, met in Geneva to discuss the terms of union. London advised the formation of a common government, and emerging from this a war cabinet – from which Pašić, however, should be excluded, since the Allies did not trust him.[18] The French president, Raymond Poincaré, added to the pressure by sending a telegram to Pašić urging him to avoid all divisions.

At the start of the conference, Korošec demanded an immediate recognition by Serbia of the National Council, given the Italian invasion in progress. Bearing in mind the admonition from Paris, Pašić finally agreed. Trumbić proposed the formation of a joint government that would be responsible for the conduct of foreign and military affairs, and which would prepare the convocation of a constitutional assembly, pending which the National Council and the Serbian government would remain responsible on their respective territories for all aspects of internal affairs not surrendered to the central government. He also proposed that ministers drawn from the National Council should swear allegiance to that body, while those elected by the Serbian parliament should do so to the Serbian crown prince. His proposal was accepted. It was also agreed to negotiate with Montenegro as to its incorporation into the new state. The Serbian government now formally recognised the National Council and Trumbić as its foreign representative, and promised to work for their recognition by the Allies. It seemed that a sound basis had finally been reached for a consensual union and, more immediately, for the formation of a sorely needed interim government. No sooner had he signed the relevant documents, however, than Pašić changed his mind. On 14 November he informed Korošec and Trumbić that his government had refused to ratify the Geneva accords. The American, British and French governments were at this time preparing to extend recognition to the National Council, but in view of this development and Italian resistance they decided to wait. When Korošec appealed to the Allies to recognise the National Council nevertheless, he was advised to seek an urgent compromise with Serbia.

Nikola Pašić and the Serbian government, backed by Svetozar Pribićević and his party, could not accept the existence of a separate authority vested in the National Council. They found it easy to abrogate the Geneva agreement, because the Serbian army had in the meantime positioned itself along the line separating the areas once offered by the Allies to Serbia from the rest of the Yugoslav territory. The French and Serbian armies had entered Belgrade on 1 November, where – informed of the collapse of the Hungarian state and the outbreak of revolution there – the French commander of the Allied eastern army, General Louis Franchet d'Esperey, decided to cross the Sava and invade Hungary. On 7 November 1918 Hungary signed a ceasefire, but the invasion continued for five more days, as a result of which by the middle of November Serbian troops had gained control of southern Hungary and eastern Slavonia. Some Serbian units moved into Bosnia-Herzegovina and Dalmatia, and arrived in Sarajevo, Dubrovnik and Split. They reached as far north as Rijeka, where they met the Italian army, and Ljubljana, which they saved from Italian occupation. Serbian troops managed also to occupy Montenegro and northern Albania.

Lieutenant-Colonel Dušan Simović of the Serbian army was appointed representative of the Allied, in effect Serbian, high command in Zagreb. On his arrival he promptly informed the National Council that Serbia would never allow another state that included Serbs to be formed on its border; and that, on the basis of the ceasefire signed with Hungary and the right of arms, Serbia claimed for itself not only the Hungarian lands of Bačka, Banat and Baranja, but also Croatian Srijem and eastern Slavonia, the whole of Bosnia-Herzegovina, and the parts of Dalmatia not promised to Italy by the Treaty of London. 'Outside this territory you can decide as you wish, whether to join Serbia or to form your own separate state.'[19] This blunt statement could not fail to make a deep impression on his hosts. According to Smodlaka, there existed a strong current among the Serbian military and politicians wishing to use this opportunity to create a Great Serbia rather than a Yugoslavia. Svetozar Pribićević, acting as the chief agent of the Serbian government in Croatia, knew this very well. Two days after the Serbian government had abrogated the Geneva accords, one of its members told Pribićević: 'We in Belgrade are becoming convinced that certain Croatian circles wish to isolate Serbia and Montenegro from the rest of our lands, in order to create in place of a unified state, which they fear would be dominated by the Serbs, an Austrian combination' – that is, a dual Yugoslav-Serbian state. It seems, the Serbian minister continued, that the Croats would accept the idea of an integral and indivisible state under the Karađorđević dynasty only by being shown quite concretely that 'unless they accept this idea quickly and sincerely, our [Serb] people will unhesitatingly join Serbia'. A unified government would soon put an end to the 'Geneva experiment, whose destructive nature was proved in the former Austria-Hungary'.[20]

Pribićević could not have agreed more. No sooner had he heard of the Geneva accords than he promptly informed Pašić that the National Council (meaning Pribićević himself) did not agree with them, and that Korošec and Trumbić had no mandate to negotiate on behalf of the Council. He indeed ensured that the National Council in Zagreb would not be informed of the Geneva agreement until it was too late. As he stated in 1925, in a speech given in Banja Luka:

> The agreement reached in Geneva was disgraceful, for it sought to create on our national territory another Austria-Hungary: one half was to be an Austrian Yugoslavia and the other Serbia. Its aim was to preclude in advance our nation's complete unification and amalgamation. [As] soon as I heard [of it], I immediately sent a telegram to Mr Pašić in Geneva stating that the National Council did not recognise the agreement, and declared on its behalf that I had not recognised it nor would ever do so. [I] took the responsibility for bringing it down, because it would have destroyed all possibility of implementing the idea of our state and national unity.[21]

The Serbian high command decided, therefore, to show the recalcitrant members of the regional governments, and in particular the Slovene and Croat parties represented in the National Council, that 'Serb lands' would be unhesitatingly joined to Serbia unless the union were accomplished promptly and irrevocably. The plan involved eliciting declarations on the part of Serb-controlled bodies in Baranja, Bačka and Banat (the three Bs), Bosnia-Herzegovina and Montenegro, that they wished to unite directly with Serbia. They were encouraged by the fact that the hard-pressed Dalmatian government, faced with Italian occupation and economic blockade, was urging Zagreb to proceed to immediate unification, threatening otherwise to do so on its own. Practically all Croats from the Adriatic area supported Dalmatia's stand.[22] The Slovene government, meanwhile, was divided between those who favoured unconditional unification and those who wished to secure for Slovenia some degree of autonomy within the future state.

The Serbian army soon managed to deliver the three Bs to Serbia. On 25 November 1918 the Serb National Council in Novi Sad, claiming to speak on their behalf, proclaimed their loyalty to Serbia. The same happened in Serbian-occupied Montenegro, despite the growing resistance of the 'separatists' – those who remained loyal to the Montenegrin king, Nikola Petrović and/or wished for Montenegro's independence from Serbia within the new state. The Serb members of the government of Bosnia-Herzegovina, however, resisted the call of pan-Serb unity, preferring instead to coordinate action with Zagreb, though the Bosnian parliament also pressed the National Council not to delay unification. On 26 November 1918 the hesitant National Council finally decided to send a delegation to Belgrade to effect union. The delegation was instructed to demand that the final organisation of the future state be decided by a two-thirds majority in the constitutional assembly, which would be convened within six months of the conclusion of peace and elected on the basis of general, direct and secret suffrage. Until that time the country would be run by a state council composed of members of the National Council, the Yugoslav Committee and an appropriate number of representatives from Serbia and Montenegro. The provisional government would be responsible to this Council, and would include representatives of the existing regions.

Josip Smodlaka's intervention in favour of an immediate union was decisive in breaking the resistance of Starčević's Party of Right. In Smodlaka's view it was better for Slovenia and Croatia to be in a large Yugoslavia, without which they would remain exposed to enemies far more dangerous than Serbia could ever be. Ignorant of the nature of the Serbian political system or Pribićević's concept of national and state unity, he believed that once the union had been achieved all other problems would be solved in a consensual manner. By this time, however, the popular masses in the Croatian north, and the soldiers of the small and increasingly unreliable 'army' of the State of Slovenes, Croats and Serbs, were increasingly turning towards republicanism. As Pribićević informed Belgrade, the vast majority of Croats and Slovenes preferred a republic to the monarchy, not least because the king was an Orthodox Serb. It was most important, therefore, that Regent Alexander should promise to rule as a constitutional monarch. The regent agreed: he knew that, notwithstanding Croatia's dire situation, it would be impossible to impose Serbian rule upon it by force.

The delegation that arrived in Belgrade was in fact far smaller than originally planned, for reasons which remain controversial. Once in Belgrade, Pavelić, Smodlaka and Pribićević met representatives of the Serbian government, and the two sides negotiated the delegation's address and the regent's response. On 1 December the leader of Starčević's Party of Right formally informed the Serbian regent that the National Council, representing 'the independent national state' of Slovenes, Croats and Serbs, had proclaimed its union with Serbia and Montenegro and wished now to realise this. The address recognised King Peter, represented by Regent Alexander, as king; called for the formation of a provisional government by agreement between the National Council and the Serbian government; and asked that the autonomous governments remain in place until the convocation of a constitutional assembly. The address also warned of the Italian threat, denounced the Treaty of London, and expressed its faith in the principle of national self-determination adopted by President Wilson and the Allies. The regent then proclaimed 'the union of Serbia with the lands of the independent State of Slovenes, Croats and Serbs as a single Kingdom of Serbs, Croats and Slovenes', and promised to rule in accordance with the widest 'constitutional, parliamentary and democratic principles based on universal suffrage'.[23] Montenegro was not mentioned, since it had already been swallowed up by Serbia. By endorsing the monarchy, the delegation disobeyed the National Council's instructions, according to which the character of the joint state would be decided by the constitutional assembly, and prejudiced the issue of its organisation by omitting the proviso that a two-thirds majority would be needed to validate the new constitution. On the other hand, Serbia had formally accepted that the union was one between two different states, a product of two different sovereign wills; and that what was created in 1918 was not an enlarged Serbia but a Yugoslavia.

A common government was soon established. As proposed by Smodlaka, backed by Korošec and Pribićević, it was agreed despite Pašić's opposition to make Trumbić foreign minister. Another proposal by Smodlaka, that Pribićević be appointed minister of the interior, was also agreed, albeit after considerable Serbian resistance. But the regent vetoed Smodlaka's further proposal that Pašić be prime minister, instead appointing Stojan Protić, the second most important leader (after Pašić) of the Serbian Radical Party. Pašić was made head of the Yugoslav delegation to the Paris

Territorial formation of Yugoslavia, 1913–9

Peace Conference. The delegation included also the Serbian envoy to Paris, Milenko Vesnić; two Dalmatian Croats, Trumbić and Smodlaka; and two Slovenes: Josip Žolger, a minister without a portfolio in the last Austrian government, and Otokar Rybarž, leader of the Slovene national association *Edinost* (Unity) in Trieste. Following the formation of the government in Belgrade, the National Council ceased to exist, as, by extension, did the Yugoslav Committee. With all powers now centralised in Belgrade, the new government proceeded to behave as a Serbian government. Trumbić was thus informed that the foreign ministry of the new state had to be 'governed by the customs of Serbia', meaning that during his stay in Paris it would be run by Prime Minister Protić. The ministry, staffed by inexperienced, prejudiced and largely incompetent Serbian personnel, would decide all important matters pertaining to the work of the Yugoslav delegation at the Paris Peace Conference.

The Adriatic Question

The Yugoslav delegation to the Paris Peace Conference represented a country that was not as yet recognised by the Allies. The proclamation of the Kingdom of Serbs, Croats and Slovenes had nevertheless greatly upset Italy, confronting it with a situation not envisaged when the Treaty of London was drawn up. The Italian foreign minister, Sidney Sonnino, with strong support from the Italian army's high command, stubbornly resisted Yugoslavia's recognition, subjected its coast to an economic blockade, sent Italian troops beyond the demarcation line established with the ceasefire at Padua, and generally sought various ways to break up Yugoslavia before it could live.[24]

The Yugoslav presence in Paris involved some twenty to twenty-five Slovenes and Croats and around ninety Serbs, drawn mainly from Serbia. The delegation consisted in fact of three different parts, Slovenian, Croatian and Serbian, acting separately from one another and often in opposite directions. The Slovenes established their own office organised just like an Austrian ministerial department. Their delegation worked closely with the National Council in Ljubljana, which had empowered the two representatives and chosen and paid their supporting staff.[25] The Serbian delegation, which kept in continuous touch with the Serbian (nominally Yugoslav) government in Belgrade, was large and idle, all the necessary work in fact being carried out by the Serbian embassy in Paris, headed by Milenko Vesnić. Having lost its Russian patron, Serbia now relied on France to defend its interests within the Allied camp. Pašić, who spoke no foreign language comprehensibly, hardly left the hotel housing the Yugoslav delegation. The Yugoslav delegation's conference room in fact led directly to his private chambers, whence he would emerge daily to preside over the delegation's meetings; since this was his only business, he took the opportunity to waste everyone else's time. On the two occasions that he met foreign heads of state (Wilson and Clemenceau), he pressed only Serbia's claims against Bulgaria, Hungary and Albania. The records of the joint meetings were regularly doctored by the delegation secretary, appointed by Pašić, who omitted statements and interventions that his chief did not like, and inserted lengthy speeches by the latter that were never actually delivered.[26]

Unlike the Slovenes, the Croats had no separate office, nor direction of any kind from a Croatian body, and were left to fend for themselves. They were helped in their work by a small staff inherited from the former Yugoslav Committee, who came from the Adriatic area. When at one point they asked the government in Belgrade to send them Ivan Lorković and another Croatian official, who were experts on the financial relationship between Croatia and Hungary, Pribićević in his capacity as minister of the interior refused to issue them with passports, allegedly because the government could not trust them. But the two Dalmatians – Trumbić and Smodlaka – established good relations with the American embassy and the experts working for President Wilson, and were additionally also able to rely on people like Seton-Watson, who attended the Peace Conference on the British side and whose opinion was greatly valued by the Americans. What concerned the Croats most was the Adriatic Question, and on this issue they managed to establish a kind of American-Croatian axis. Although the government in Belgrade changed several times during the negotiations, Trumbić remained foreign minister throughout, largely because the Serbians wished a Croat to take upon himself the odium of the expected surrender of Croatian and Slovenian territories to Italy.

The delegation was divided into two basic factions: a Slovene and Croat one, which by and large defended the principle of ethnic borders; and a Serbian one, which did not. The Serbians concentrated instead on maximising their territorial gains against Hungary, Romania, Bulgaria and Albania. Since they needed Italy's help for this, they were far more ready to accommodate the latter's demands in the Adriatic. The delegation, as a result, was unable to agree on common principles to guide its work and remained sharply divided throughout. According to Smodlaka:

> Trumbić and I, faithful to Wilson's canons, condemned borders established by force and favoured plebiscites, protection of minority rights, and agreement between democracies. Pašić, who did not take Wilson's ideas seriously, thought the opposite. [His] conduct of affairs made it clear that he trusted only in brute force [according] to which the victor takes anything he desires from the vanquished. [This] is why he did not care for plebiscites. Calling conquests 'liberation', he refused to acknowledge the right of the 'liberated' population to decide its own fate. This is why he did not shrink from trying to seize Bulgarian districts wholly devoid of Serbs, and claimed for Serbia purely Albanian lands and parts of Hungary in which the Serbs were either a tiny minority or not present at all. Practically all the Serbians shared his view. The Italians used the same approach to justify their usurpation of Gorizia, the Croat parts of Istria, and Dalmatia. Their imperialist tenets fully agreed with Pašić's own. The Italians were against plebiscites in the areas they had seized from us in the same way that Pašić rejected them for the areas claimed by Serbia.

> This inevitably led to conflict between us, though not to an open breach, since that would have made us part company, which is what we all tried to avoid. But the conflict continued to simmer, and our delegation remained throughout seemingly united but in fact divided into two opposing camps, of which one stood for Conquest and the other for National Rights.[27]

Elated by victory, the Italians sought to obtain Slovene ethnic territories in Gorizia and Gradiska, all of Istria, Dalmatia as promised to them by the Treaty of London, and now also Rijeka (here evoking the very national principle it rejected elsewhere). To agree to this, the Croats felt, would amount to national suicide, particularly since Italy's arrival on the east side of the Adriatic portended its future expansion into the Balkans. Nourished on the experience of their century-long struggle for Rijeka, rather than now give it up the Croats were ready to submit if need be to Italy's continued occupation of the territory and Dalmatia, but stubbornly resisted Italian demands for a formal surrender of sovereignty. The Serbians, while giving verbal support to the Croats and Slovenes, were inclined to listen to the French counsel that the Yugoslavs should seek a compromise with Italy in the Adriatic. The British and French were sympathetic to the Yugoslavs, but they also felt bound by the Treaty of London. In this situation the Croats turned to President Wilson. The American experts had in the meantime produced their report on the Yugoslav borders, recommending that these should be drawn in line with ethnicity (that is, language).[28] The Italian prime minister, Vittorio Orlando, was consequently informed that if the Italians insisted upon the line drawn by the Treaty of London, this would certainly mean war in the future. In early February 1919 Trumbić, acting on American advice, proposed that the delegation submit the dispute with Italy to Wilson's arbitration. Wilson accepted to act as moderator, provided that the Italians too agreed. The Yugoslavs were also informed that the United States would extend recognition to the Kingdom of Serbs, Croats and Slovenes. The Italians, however, rejected American arbitration.

Trying to break the impasse, Smodlaka next proposed that the Yugoslavs ask for a plebiscite in all territorial disputes with the Allies. This was welcomed by their American and British friends; but the Serbians, backed this time by the Slovenes, rejected it, so the plebiscite proposal was shelved. There followed long and exhausting negotiations, during which the Yugoslavs were forced to retreat step by step. In March 1919 the Americans reiterated their position on the Adriatic Question, which was that the Yugoslavs should have Istria, Rijeka and the whole of Dalmatia with its islands, but they now conceded the possibility of Rijeka becoming an international port. The Yugoslavs told them, however, that they would turn down any proposal that denied them either Dalmatia or Rijeka. On the other hand, they were no longer pressing for the inclusion of Trieste, while the Italians signalled their readiness to trade Dalmatia for Rijeka. Trumbić's response was: 'Rijeka must be ours and about this there can be absolutely no discussion.'[29]

Wilson now made an important concession to the Italians, offering them a border coinciding with the Treaty of London in the north, together with a partition of Istria along the so-called Wilson line bisecting the peninsula in a north-south direction.[30] He offered in addition the island of Lošinj, demilitarisation of the other islands, and control of the Albanian port of Valona. Rijeka could not go to Italy, because it was essential to Yugoslavia; but it could be made into a free city within a Yugoslav customs framework. His offer was rejected by Rome. The Yugoslavs now revived their idea of a plebiscite – to submit the whole Italian-Yugoslav dispute to a popular vote – but this too was rejected. Wilson then offered to make Rijeka a free city under League of Nations administration, but the Italians once again said no. The Americans made further concessions, involving eastern Istria also going to Italy and Rijeka with northern Dalmatia being placed under League trusteeship for an unspecified number of years; but the Italians refused this too, after which Wilson gave up his search for a compromise with them. He told the French and British prime ministers that the choice was between 'drawing the Southern Slavs to Western Europe and the League of Nations, or throwing them back on Russia and Bolshevism'. Offending the Slavs by satisfying the Italians would open the road 'to Russian influence and to the development of a Slav bloc hostile to Western Europe'.[31] On 23 April he issued a public statement 'Regarding the Disposition of Fiume [i.e Rijeka]', in which he explained the American position and in effect appealed to the Italian people not to support their government's demand for Rijeka. Wilson's appeal elicited a veritable nationalist storm in Italy, stoked by Mussolini's Fascists. The cry was that, if Italian demands were not met, *Italia farà da se* – that is, Italy should annex all the territories under her occupation. At a public rally, the Italian poet and adventurer Gabriele d'Annunzio called Wilson a 'Croatified Quaker'.

The British and French prime ministers, while not wishing to offend Wilson, assured the Italians that if a compromise with the Yugoslavs could not be found, they would uphold implementation of the Treaty. The American president now stood accused by Allied propaganda, and some of the press, of holding up the peace process. His expert advisors, however, now joined the battle for Rijeka:

> The Italian representatives demand Fiume and part of Dalmatia in order to emerge from the Conference with loot. [These] districts belong to Yugoslavia, not Italy. [By failing to make them] an integral part of the Yugoslav organisation [the Conference] would be charged that the principle, 'There shall be no bartering of peoples', had been publicly and cynically thrown aside. [If] Italy gets even nominal sovereignty over Fiume as the price of supporting the League, [the] League of Nations will be charged with accepting the principles of Tallyerand and Metternich. [Never] in his career did the President have presented to him such an opportunity to strike a death blow to the discredited methods of old-world diplomacy [by] a clean-cut decision against an infamous arrangement, the last vestige of the old order.[32]

The British tried to reason with the Italians, arguing that the premises which pertained in 1915 were no longer applicable, given that Austria-Hungary had ceased to exist and Russia was no longer a factor, while the United States was not a signatory to the Treaty of London. It was, moreover, unwise to include into Italy so many people against their will. The Italians, however, stuck by their demands and the Adriatic Question remained the only one which the conference could not resolve. In early June 1919 the British and French governments finally recognised the Kingdom of Serbs, Croats and Slovenes, despite Italy's objections. The Yugoslavs and Italians now accepted the idea of Rijeka becoming an independent city, after which the focus shifted to Istria. Trumbić stuck by Wilson's line, but the Italians wanted the whole of Istria and the coast up to Rijeka. The French then suggested that the city-state of Rijeka should include both Istria east of the Wilson line and the island of Krk, and that the fate of this territory be resolved through a plebiscite within fifteen years. In return Italy would be allowed to annex Zadar, Šibenik and the islands of Cres, Vis, Lošinj and Palagruža. The Americans this time agreed, amending the deal to make Zadar and Šibenik free cities under the protection of the League of Nations. State Secretary Lansing informed the Yugoslavs that they should accept this offer, since 'for the American people, Fiume cannot and must not be the sole obstacle to peace'.[33]

The Yugoslavs were placed in a difficult position. They agreed to accept free status for Rijeka, provided it included all eastern Istria and the island of Cres – making it an overwhelmingly Croat entity. They asked, however, for an earlier plebiscite; for Rijeka's twin port of Sušak and its hinterland to be allotted to Yugoslavia; and for the islands promised to Italy to be placed under the League and offered plebiscites likewise. In fact, their response denied Italy sovereignty anywhere on the eastern Adriatic coast, albeit accepting the permanent loss of western Istria. An increasingly impatient Wilson then offered Italy Lošinj, the islands off Zadar, and Lastavo and Palagruža. This was not enough, however, for the Italians. But in June 1919 the Italian Prime Minister Orlando resigned, thus removing the intransigent Sonnino from the stage.

The Treaty of Versailles was signed on 28 June 1919 after which Wilson left Paris and the French took over the representation of Yugoslav interests. In mid-August 1919 the Yugoslavs were informed that the Adriatic Question had to be settled by the end of the month. The Italians now suggested that the free state of Rijeka should be made permanently independent, and that eastern Istria with its islands, Zadar and the outer Dalmatian islands should be assigned to Italy. On 12 September, however, d'Annunzio took over Rijeka and proclaimed himself its dictator. There followed several new rounds of negotiations, during which the Italians made minor concessions, but in the end nothing came of them since the Americans refused to surrender Rijeka to Italy. By the end of December, with practically all other peace treaties having been signed, the French and British decided to truncate the Adriatic Question. They told the Italians they had to choose between the Treaty of London and Rijeka, the Yugoslavs that unless they compromised the Treaty of London would be implemented in full – an ominous threat, given that the territories it had promised to Rome were already under Italian occupation which the Yugoslavs were unable to terminate by military means. The Allies were by now aware that the Serbs were far more amenable to the deal than the Croats. In order to divide them further, in January 1920 the British offered the Yugoslavs the Albanian city of Shkodër in return for the Croatian city of Rijeka. Regent Alexander was in favour: he told Trumbić that Rijeka was not all that important, whereas Shkodër was 'vital'.[34] In June 1920 Pašić resigned from the Yugoslav peace delegation, which was then dissolved, although Trumbić remained foreign minister.

In that same month, the new Italian government, headed by Giovanni Giolitti, made a fresh offer to the Yugoslavs. Having removed the Albanian issue from the agenda by withdrawing Italian troops from Albania and recognising the country within its 1913 borders, it announced its readiness to give up Dalmatia. The French informed the Yugoslavs that they must now reach an agreement with Rome. In November 1919 Woodrow Wilson lost the presidential elections, and the Croats their only support. Trumbić finally accepted defeat. The Treaty of Rapallo, which he signed on 12 November 1920, gave Italy the whole of Istria up to and including the strategic mountain of Snežnik; all territory up to and including the nominally independent (but in fact Italian-held) Rijeka, embracing mainly the territory of the old *corpus separatum*; the city of Zadar and its immediate hinterland; and the islands of Cres, Lošinj and Lastovo. The Yugoslavs also granted special cultural privileges to their Italian minority, without winning any reciprocity for the half million Slovenes and Croats assigned to Italy. Trumbić later argued that Rapallo had been a sacrifice made 'for the sake of our [Yugoslav] national and state unity. That was the god to which this offering was made.' He now resigned his post and joined the opposition. Regent Alexander awarded him the St Sava medal, which he refused. Although in 1921 all Dalmatian Croat parties had put Trumbić on their lists for the Constituent Assembly, he had preferred to be elected as an independent candidate for the city of Split.

Making Istria Italian

The Istrian Croats waited with trepidation the outcome of the final settlement. Tomo Banko, a priest in the village of Tinjan southwest of Pazin, wrote in his diary at this time:

> The thought that the day is nearing when we shall hear the terrible judgment is quite unbearable. We shall have to live with people who do not like us and who despise us, who will pride themselves on achieving victory over us. We shall have to live in accordance with laws and customs we detest. We shall die a painful death as they tear our nationality from us bit by bit. They [the Allies] will not let us go where we belong, forcing us instead among those who are not ours. We shall have to learn to be theirs.[35]

Following the signing of the Rapallo treaty, Croat Istria flew black flags while the deputies from the lost areas declared that 'there will be no lasting peace or friendship between the Yugoslavs and the Italians [until] the rights of the former have been met by revision of the Rapallo Treaty'.[36] Don Božo Milanović, a local parish priest from the Pazin area, wrote to a fellow priest in Kastav (which was included in Yugoslavia): 'So you have become Yugoslav overnight! And we? What a bleak future! One must be a true hero not to surrender to despair. All our plans are gone, and with them joy. We shall be buried alive.'[37] His forebodings were more than justified, since these

> **P.N.F. – Comando Squadristi – Dignano**
>
> ## Attenzione!
>
> Si proibisce nel modo più assoluto che nei ritrovi pubblici e per le strade di Dignano si canti o si parli in lingua slava.
>
> Anche nei negozi di qualsiasi genere deve essere una buona volta adoperata
> **SOLO LA LINGUA ITALIANA**
>
> Noi Squadristi, con metodi persuasivi, faremo rispettare il presente ordine.
>
> **GLI SQUADRISTI**

Ban on the use of Croat by Fascists of Vodnjan, Istria, 1920

'unredeemed Italian lands' would soon be supplying Italian Fascists with an initial springboard for their conquest of Italy.[38]

The fact that the future of the former Austrian Littoral was not decided at Versailles had led to an early cooperation between Fascists and local Italian authorities directed against the Croats and Slovenes. In the early months of 1919 the Italian authorities drew up a secret list of 'Croatophiles' and 'dangerous Yugoslav propagandists' and placed the suspects under police observation. In parallel with a purge of Croat and Slovene state officials, Fascist *squadri d'azione* emerged, targeting labour organisations as well as Croat and Slovene cultural and business associations. The new authorities persecuted both by conveniently treating them as a single menace called 'Slavo-Bolsheviks', 'Croato-Communists' and so on. In 1919 the Slovene *Edinost* office was badly damaged and the Croat printing press in Pazin demolished; in 1920, in a well-coordinated action, a large number of Croat and Slovene cultural and economic institutions, schools and businesses in the former Austrian Littoral were burned down and destroyed. The pogrom continued throughout 1921 and 1922. In March 1922 a Fascist coup overthrew the Rijeka government, following which the city was occupied by Italian troops. In October 1922 Mussolini took over the government of Italy. In January 1924 the Yugoslav prime minister Nikola Pašić signed the Treaty of Rome, formally recognising Italy's annexation of Rijeka.

In the period between the end of the war (1918) and the Fascist assumption of full power in 1926, the Istrian political parties tried to adapt their organisational forms and aims to the new situation. The Italian parties joined appropriate all-Italian parties, the Croat-Slovene National Party became the Yugoslav National Party, while the mainly Slovene Yugoslav Social-Democratic Party joined the Italian Socialist Party. Several new parties appeared, including *Fascio Italiano* (after 1921 the National Fascist Party) and the Communist Party of Italy (PCd'I). The socialist and liberal parties had already withered, however, by 1926 when the Fascists introduced their dictatorship, after which state terror prevented any kind of oppositional activity. Croat and Slovene priests now become a main target of state repression. The Catholic hierarchy tried to protect them, but the government's implacable animosity towards Slav priests encouraged their replacement by Italians – who, of course, did not speak either Croat or Slovene. The *Lega Nazionale* re-emerged – in 1927 building seventy-two nursery schools in Croat areas of Istria. A year later, however, it was dissolved – to be replaced by other, more aggressive state-run institutions dedicated to strengthening the annexed population's Italian national consciousness. *Società Dante Alighieri* also became busy in the newly acquired territories. Among other things, it distributed annual prizes to non-Italian students for learning the Italian language; these were handed out on 28 October, the date of the establishment of Fascist rule.[39]

Unwilling to accept the ethnic realities in this 'eminently Italian' province, the Italian government now tried to change them through a policy of systematic denationalisation. By January 1923, as part of a school reform conducted by Benedetto Croce and Giovanni Gentile, Croat and Slovene primary and secondary schools were either closed down or turned into Italian-language schools. Children were not allowed to speak Croat or Slovene on school premises, or indeed outside them. Croat and Slovene teachers were sacked. All primers in Croat and Slovene were banned. The law initially permitted Croat and Slovene to be taught after school hours as extracurricular subjects, but only for two hours a week and then only orally – no use of books or writing materials was allowed. No Croat or Slovene teachers were provided for these classes. In the case of the few villages with resident former teachers of Croat or Slovene, it was necessary for twenty-five parents to sign a petition asking for such classes; but if they did so, they suffered severe reprisals including the burning of their homes. In the end even this purely nominal provision was withdrawn, apart from religious instruction in primary schools – which, however, was now conducted under strict supervision. As the Fascists of the Julian Region informed Mussolini in 1926, it was vital 'to cut the Slav teachers out of the schools, the Slav priests out of their parishes'.[40] The public security law and the law on protection of the state made it possible for people to be tried on the basis of mere suspicion. At the end of 1927 a special police inspectorate was established in Milan, a first step towards the creation of the notorious *Opera Vigilanza Repressione Antifascista* (OVRA), which would lead to the imprisonment and execution of thousands of Italians, Croats and Slovenes. In 1932 alone over 100 Istrians were sentenced to 1,124 years in prison, and five to death.

Between 1921 and 1927 all Slav personal and all place-names were Italianised. Andrijančić thus became Andreani; Ježić, Essi; Kranjčić, Ranci; Mogorović, Macorini; Ovčarić, Ozzori; Potočar, Pottari; Radetić, Ardetti; Vranjac, Urania; Zgrablić, Grabelli; Žužić, Sussi; and so on.[41] The actual choice was left to the individual official's imagination, which led to multiple forms of one and the same surname: Grbac in Pula became Gerba, his brother in Trieste, Gherbasi; Ivetić in Pula became Gianetti, his brother in Trieste, Vetti; Sirka in Gorizia became Sirtori, his brother in Pula, Serchi, another brother in Trieste, Sirca. With a few strokes of the pen Milan Ribarić became Emilio Pescatore. There was a mopping up operation in 1936, when the official gazette published a list of 22,000 additional new surnames for Istrian Croats, most of them in the Pula area. This was not all. Local parishes were instructed even to Italianise retrospectively Croat names in their registers, which had been kept for centuries. Croat and Slovene clergy and their congregations often boycotted these provisions, but defiance regularly invited violent reprisals from the Fascist *squadri*. Italian soon became the language of religious education as well.

A Croat Istrian writing in exile gave an audit of this policy as it applied to the Slavs. Before the war, he wrote, Croats and Slovenes of the Austrian Littoral had their Slav liturgy; 504 churches and at least that many hard-working parish priests; 581 schools and 1,350 teachers; 5 high schools; 4 teacher-training colleges and 2 trade schools; 7 printing presses; 4 dailies and 26 weeklies, reviews and occasional publications; 414 trade associations, that were the pillars of their economic strength; 19 provincial parliamentary deputies; 500 educational and sports societies; their own names and surnames; their own ancient names for local places, rivers and mountains; their ancient Glagolica monuments, books and documents; a rich literature in their languages; a large number of national halls built by their peoples' hard work; a series of municipalities in which they governed themselves.

> We had everything that a cultured and proud nation, conscious of its identity and honour, could have. All that is now gone. They have taken it all, destroyed everything, leaving us with nothing. We have not a single school; not a single church and only a tiny number of priests; not a single teacher; not a single journal; not a single book; not a single society; not a single national hall; not a single printing press; not a single bookshop; not a single deputy; not a single intellectual. They have driven them all away and imprisoned all those who remained. They have destroyed and burned down everything: our charters, our cultural monuments, even tomb inscriptions in Croat, everything in fact, including the names of our fathers and forefathers. They have taken everything from us, eradicated everything, deformed and ruined everything. [They] have systematically destroyed all that is Croat and Slovene in Istria.

This was written in 1944, after Mussolini's Italy had lost the war and the future of Istria was being considered by the victorious Allies. 'There will be [those] who will try again to argue that for state, political, strategic or economic reasons Italy needs to keep or regain control over Istria and its Gorizia hinterland. The reply of ever single Croat or Slovene [will] be one and the same: No! Never! [We] shall never again, nor at any price, accept an Italian government whether it calls itself Fascist or Democratic, Socialist or Communist, Liberal or any other. Istria's only possible destination is in Croatia, our sole place is with the rest of our Croatian brothers. [Our answer is:] Never again under Italy! Never!'[42]

Yugoslavia versus Great Serbia

The first national government of the Kingdom of Serbs, Croats and Slovenes was formed on 20 December 1919. It consisted of thirteen Serbs, four Croats, two Slovenes and one Bosniak. The government was supposed to be responsible to the new provisional parliament, but this body possessed little authority, since all effective power lay in the hands of the central government and Regent Alexander. Most Croatian parties and politicians argued that

Svetozar Pribićević, Ante Trumbić and Josip Smodlaka, circa 1920

the sabor should be recalled in order to ratify the act of union. This did not happen, however, due to adamant opposition on the part of Svetozar Pribićević. It did in fact eventually meet in November 1920 – but only to be dissolved, along with the Serbian and all other regional parliaments. As minister of the interior, Pribićević acquired practically dictatorial powers in Croatia, where he used them to establish Belgrade's full control over the administration through a combination of governmental decrees and the application of force.[43] A fanatical believer at this stage in the oneness of Croats and Serbs, he sought to create without delay a strong central state apparatus, in the absence of which he believed it would be impossible to forge the desired 'Yugoslav nation'. There were in his view only two political currents in Yugoslavia, one seeking complete state and national unity, the other – against which he declared war to the end – composed of 'separatists' or 'anti-state elements' committed to regional autonomies and national individualities. He stated in his first public speech in the new state:

> Centralism is the great principle, the great idea to which we must absolutely commit ourselves regardless of the struggle we have to pursue, if we are to serve our large nation. We wish one state, a single unified state, not a state of Serb hegemony or one in which separate provincial Slovene and Croat interests are retained, since we are against all hegemony and all separatism.[44]

The application of this 'great idea' was limited in practice, however, to the former Austro-Hungarian lands, where, quite apart from its effect on national sensibilities, Pribićević's iron-fist policy stimulated new divisions and conflicts, which compounded the disorder stemming from the collapse of the old political and economic order and from the return of hundreds of thousands of soldiers from the front.[45] What made matters worse was the fact that instead of waiting for the constitutional assembly, which alone could give it the necessary legal basis, the Belgrade government proceeded at once with an agrarian reform amounting in practice to the pillaging of the large estates by corrupt party and state officials. The former Austro-Hungarian lands in fact became the main source of income for the Serbian-dominated regime. These provinces contributed 68 per cent of the new state's population, 58 per cent of its territory, some 70 per cent of its economic assets, and a disproportionate amount of direct taxes. According to one estimate, during the period 1919–28 the average citizen of Vojvodina paid five times as much tax as the average citizen of Serbia, the average citizen of Slovenia three times, and his counterpart in the former Ban's Croatia twice as much.[46] During this time, furthermore, 79 per cent of centrally allocated investment funds were spent in Serbia, although the Habsburg area contributed over two-thirds of the state budget. The Yugoslav banking sector was dominated by four state-owned banks, all of which were in Serbian hands. Thus, for example, 196 out of 200 officials of the State Mortgage Bank were Serbs. A select number of Serbian families also held 89 per cent of the shares of the central National Bank, which brought enormous profits to their holders and to the Serbian part of Yugoslavia.[47]

The systematic and continued plunder of the former Habsburg provinces could be accomplished only within a system in which all power, military and civilian, was concentrated in Serbian hands, even though Serbians formed only 23 per cent of the total population. Up to 1937 Yugoslavia had thirty-five governments or cabinets with a total of 656 ministers, of whom 69 per cent were Serbs, 61 per cent from Serbia itself. Serbian preponderance was even greater – 83 per cent – in the four key ministries of foreign affairs, the interior, the army, and finances, with another 9 per cent of these posts being filled by Serbs from the former Habsburg area. Whereas on the eve of the First World War there were fifteen Croat generals and two admirals in the Austro-Hungarian armed forces (15 per cent of the total, far more than the national percentage), on the eve of the Second World War 161 out of 165 Yugoslav generals in active service were Serbs (Croats and Slovenes furnishing two apiece), while among 1,500 cadets studying at the military academy there were only 150 Croats and fifty Slovenes.[48] Throughout the inter-war period, in fact, power resided with the Serbian dynasty, the Serbian-dominated army and state officials, and various interest groups known as the Belgrade *čaršija*.[49] Political position was as a rule used for personal enrichment and the distribution of all sorts of favours, leading to corruption on a scale that from the outset perverted the very idea of parliamentary democracy. One consequence of the Serbian policy was that the former Habsburg territories, irrespective of their national make-up, soon united against Belgrade on a platform of Yugoslavia's federalisation.

Pribićević's main foe in Croatia became Stjepan Radić, whose party now renamed itself the Croatian Republican Peasant Party (HRSS), with a programme of establishing a state based on democratic – and in that sense republican – peasant government. Its main motto was 'We wish to be with, not under, Serbia.' Although Pribićević regularly denounced Radić's party as an enemy of the state, the Peasant Party in fact played a decisive role in preventing civil war, by directing the growing revolt of the Croat population into peaceful forms of resistance. Radić was soon arrested, however, at Pribićević's behest, and his party banned from holding public meetings. Pribićević had himself in the meantime established the Yugoslav Democratic Party, based on a programme of one nation, one state, one parliament and one government. The Democratic Party was a transnational party, in that it brought together members of the old Croat-Serb Coalition, the Serbian Independent Radical Party, the Slovene Liberal Party and a number of small parties and groups from Vojvodina, Bosnia-Herzegovina and Dalmatia. Its nominal head was the Serbian politician Ljuba Davidović, but Pribićević was its true leader and ideologue. In Croatia itself, meanwhile, Starčević's Party of Right led by Ante Pavelić, the Croat Progressive Party (Croat dissidents from the Croat-Serb Coalition) led by Ivan Lorković, and the exiled politicians from Istria, came together as the Croatian Union, with a vaguely defined aim of achieving national equality of Slovenes, Croats and Serbs within Yugoslavia.

The period leading up to the convocation of the constitutional assembly was characterised by frequent changes of government, and Radić's more or less permanent incarceration. The elections for the constitutional assembly, held in a tense atmosphere, proved to be a major turning point in Croatian politics, since for the first time in the former Ban's Croatia all adult males over the age of twenty-one gained the right to vote and be voted into office. The consequent enfranchisement of the rural population delivered the lion's share of the Croat vote in the Croatian lands to the Peasant Party, despite the fact that its leader was in prison and the party was prevented from holding public meetings. Throughout the 1920s the share of the Peasant Party grew irresistibly. What happened in northern Croatia during this decade is similar to what had happened in Dalmatia and Istria in the 1870s and 1880s, in that widening the suffrage brought the popular masses into politics, resulting in Croat political consolidation and national unification. The elections for the constituent assembly took place on 28 November 1920, a few weeks after the signing of the Treaty of Rapallo. Out of the projected 419 seats for the kingdom as a whole, the Democrats won eighty-nine, the Radicals eighty-seven, the Communists fifty-eight, while fifty-two seats went to the Peasant Party.[50] What the electoral results showed was that the country divided equally between centralists and anti-centralists, the latter including also the Slovene People's Party (twenty-seven seats) and the Bosnian Yugoslav Muslim Organisation (twenty-three seats); but the anti-centralists' position was greatly weakened by the decision of the Peasant Party to boycott the assembly, which it considered illegitimate.

The constitutional draft produced by the governmental coalition – Pašić's Radicals and the Democrats of Davidović and Pribićević – envisaged dividing the country into thirty-five regions with limited autonomy; a unicameral parliament, its quorum to be fixed at one-third of the deputies; and the right of the king to make laws (which the parliament, however, could reject). The king was also given the right to appoint and dismiss the government, and to dissolve the parliament more or less at will. The Croatian Union proposed that Yugoslavia be divided into six self-governing regions: Serbia (with Kosovo and Macedonia), Croatia (with Dalmatia, Istria and Međimurje), Bosnia-Herzegovina, Montenegro, Vojvodina and Slovenia. These entities should enjoy something close to sovereignty, in that a new constitution could be introduced, or the existing one changed, only by agreement between the centre and the regions. The plan further envisaged a bicameral parliament, one chamber of which would be made up of delegated regional representatives; and a constitutional court to adjudicate conflicts arising between the centre and the regions. The Slovene People's Party also envisaged a bicameral parliament and a division of the country into six regions, with the difference that Dalmatia was to be added to Bosnia, thereby creating three mainly Catholic regions to counterbalance three mainly Orthodox ones.

The government ensured, however, that the constitutional assembly's drafting committee would take its own constitutional proposal as the basis for discussion, and curtailed the possibility of its being amended in the assembly. The big battle over whether the constitution should be adopted by a simple majority or a qualified one as envisaged by the Corfu Agreement was won by the governmental coalition, which – faced with the likelihood of the assembly adopting a federal constitution in the event of the principle of qualified majority being adopted – simply imposed its will. The other big battle, over whether the deputies should swear loyalty to the king, thereby limiting in advance the assembly's sovereignty in favour of the monarch, was won by the government in similar fashion, that is, by fiat. In this way the ruling coalition, which together had only 176 seats, decided the new state's constitution.

The so-called Vidovdan Constitution adopted on 28 June 1921 was pushed through by the government without much debate, with the result that the Slovene and Croat parties left the assembly before the actual vote took place, on the grounds that a centralist system was being imposed on their nations. The Communists had left even earlier, in protest against the repression of their party. The government still did not have enough votes for even a simple majority; but it managed to win the support of the Yugoslav Muslim Organisation (JMO) and two smaller parties, after promising the JMO that the planned division into regions would respect the borders of Bosnia-Herzegovina. The constitution, which formalised Serbia's hegemony within Yugoslavia, was thus adopted without the representatives of the vast majority of Slovenes and Croats, who would henceforth seek its revision.[51] A first sign of this determination was the formation of a Croatian Bloc, made up of the Peasant Party, the Croatian Union, and the revived Croatian Party of Right, which had done well in Zagreb.

A few months after the adoption of the constitution, King Peter died and was succeeded by his younger son and regent, Alexander.

Svetozar Pribićević had played a major role in crafting and imposing the Vidovdan constitution. His position weakened, however, after its adoption, because he was no longer needed to pacify Croatia, which could no longer be governed, moreover, by sole recourse to police methods, given the strength of the Peasant Party. Pribićević's group, composed mainly of Croatian Serbs, retained its grip on the Croatian administration – a source of power that he feared would disappear in the event of any federalisation of Yugoslavia – but it became increasingly isolated within the Democratic Party. On the other hand, the Radical and Democrat mainstreams were based on Serbia, which despite its hegemonic position provided an insufficient base for effective government of the kingdom. Lack of domestic consensus, and the great hostility that the constitution encountered in the former Habsburg areas, led to governmental crisis that could not be solved without involvement of the Peasant Party. The problem of how to engage the Peasant Party without endangering centralism would bedevil internal politics throughout the inter-war period. Radić, for his part, was now ready to abandon his policy of abstinence. In 1922 he made an appeal to the Serbian public to support a Croat–Serb compromise, arguing that the Serbian dictatorship was 'to us Croats [a] direct call to revolution, which could lead to a terrible civil war. Do not, therefore, think of the solution to the Croat question simply as an administrative problem or a parliamentary chess move, [but rather as the need] to organise Croat–Serb relations in harmony with our centuries-old peasant Slav culture [and in a manner that] would realise the right of national self-determination, which in our case means honest and sincere recognition of the Croatian national-state individuality.'[52] The first step in that direction, he argued, would be to hold new elections, after which national deputies on both sides would sit down to negotiate a new constitutional agreement.

In the first elections after the adoption of the constitution, held in March 1923, the Radicals doubled their votes and became the leading party not only in Serbia but also in the parliament, where they acquired 108 seats largely at the expense of the Democrats. The Peasant Party doubled its vote and gained seventy seats, twenty more than in 1921, and became the second largest party in the country – a remarkable feat, given that it was not able to rely on newspapers, public rallies, or the money and sinecures distributed by the governmental parties.[53] It won, in fact, practically all Croat votes in the former Ban's Croatia, and emerged also as the strongest party in Dalmatia. The Peasant Party consequently became the gravitational centre of the Yugoslav federalist opposition: by joining forces with the Bosnian JMO and the Slovene People's Party, the Peasant Party was now in a position to guide the creation of a single federalist bloc strong enough to challenge Serbia's supremacy.[54] The Radical Party was sufficiently alarmed by the prospect of the Peasant Party ending its boycott of parliament to initiate negotiations with the federalists. These ended with the signing of a formal agreement in April 1923, by virtue of which the fragmentation of Slovenia, Croatia and Bosnia-Herzegovina into administrative districts as envisaged by the 1921 constitution would not be carried out, the administrative apparatus would be reformed, and the rule of law and constitutionality would be affirmed. The Peasant Party promised not to return to parliament immediately, in order to allow the formation of a purely Radical government – a first step, in Radić's view, towards reaching a new constitutional arrangement.

Once in place, however, the new Radical government refused to honour the agreement its plenipotentiaries had signed in Zagreb. Indeed, Pašić stated in parliament that it was essential to implement the 1921 constitution in order to undermine the political traditions inherited from Austria-Hungary and being perpetuated by the federalists. Radić now left the country and, after visiting London and Vienna, ended up in Moscow, where he declared his party's adhesion to the Soviet-dominated Peasant International. The Communist International, which met in Moscow during Radić's visit, had hitherto favoured Yugoslavia's federalisation; but it now adopted a new policy, seeking in effect the country's break-up by supporting the establishment of separate and independent republics of Slovenia, Croatia and Macedonia. However, this turn in fact owed little to Radić, who on his return to Croatia in August 1924 announced his intention to play a constructive role within the system, as well as his desire to see a Croatian republic within the Yugoslav kingdom.

During his absence the Peasant Party deputies finally arrived in Belgrade to join the parliament, whereupon Pašić resigned in the hope of provoking fresh elections. The Democratic Party now split over the Croat issue, leading Pribićević to establish his own Independent Democratic Party (SDS), which promptly allied itself with the Radicals. But the king refused to allow new elections, offering instead a mandate to the Democratic Party. The new government, based on a coalition of the Democratic Party with the Slovene People's Party and the Yugoslav Muslim Organisation, was willing to reach an agreement with the Peasant Party, and took several important steps towards placating the Croats – such as permitting the re-emergence of Croat cultural associations and tolerating the display of Croatian flags. Fearing the federalists' advance, however, the king insisted on this government's resignation – despite the fact that it enjoyed strong parliamentary backing. He gave a fresh mandate to Pašić, who promptly dissolved parliament, in order to prevent his minority government from being voted out, and announced new elections. This led the Croatian Union to give its backing to the Peasant Party, now seen as representing the Croatian nation as a whole, and to embrace republicanism.

Pašić, supported by the king, now decided to humble the Peasant Party by invoking against it the law for protection of the state. On 1 January 1925 the party was banned and its leaders imprisoned. It was nevertheless tacitly allowed to contest the elections of February 1925, albeit under tremendous political and police pressure. In the event the Pašić–Pribićević coalition won 164 and the opposition 151 seats. The Peasant Party (together with the Croatian Union) increased its vote, though winning only sixty-seven seats.

It retained its primacy in Dalmatia and made additional gains in Bosnia-Herzegovina, despite the adverse conditions under which it was operating. It did exceptionally well in the main Croatian cities, winning over 70 per cent of the vote in Zagreb and Osijek and over 60 per cent in Split and Dubrovnik.[55] These results were a clear sign that pressure from Belgrade, far from checking the party, was making it the focus of an unprecedented display of Croat national unity.

The Peasant Party now decided to enter a coalition with the Yugoslav Muslim Organisation, the Slovene People's Party and the Democrats, forming the Bloc of National Agreement and Peasant/Popular Democracy. It jettisoned its republicanism in favour of 'a monarchy and parliamentary life of the English type', and promised to play the role of a constructive opposition in parliament. In March 1925 Stjepan Radić made a historic speech denying any link with the Peasant International and recognising 'unconditionally' the monarchy, the dynasty, and the 1921 constitution – though he hoped this constitution could be changed. The Peasant Party consequently dropped the word 'republican' from its title and became simply the Croatian Peasant Party (HSS). This sudden change, which was a natural consequence of the party's decision to enter parliament, caused great confusion and consternation in Croatia. Most of the Croatian Union could not follow Radić in this direction, but remained committed to the republican idea. Radić's conversion, on the other hand, opened the door to an agreement between the two strongest parties: the HSS in Croatia and the Radical Party in Serbia. In July 1925 Radić's nephew Pavle informed the party's erstwhile coalition partners in the Bloc of National Agreement that the HSS would form a government with the Radicals, even though the agreement forming the bloc had explicitly disqualified the Radical Party as a potential partner. Since the HSS was the lynchpin of the bloc, its defection led to the latter's break-up.

The Independent Democratic Party became the victim of a similar 'betrayal'. Pribićević, who had not been informed in advance of the negotiations between Radić and Pašić, did not believe that these would lead anywhere; but once Pašić brought the government down by resigning as prime minister, he had to face reality. The Radical press now blamed Pribićević and his party for the repression against the HSS, while the HSS saw Pribićević's fall from grace as one of its most important achievements. After seven years in government Pribićević found himself in the political wilderness, his place taken by his old enemy, Radić. Without the support of the Serbian parties, the SDS could play only a minor role in Yugoslav political life. On his release from prison in July 1925, Radić sent a telegram to King Alexander praising the 'freedom-loving, constitutional and parliamentary tradition of the House of Karađorđević'. In an address to his party on the following day, he claimed that the agreement with the Radical Party showed that the latter could not rule without HSS support. Radić was right in his intuitive sense of the Radical Party's weakness, despite its control of the Serbian political machinery. Its decline would ultimately result in royal dictatorship, as the only guarantee of Serbia's domination of Yugoslavia.

On 22 July 1925 Radić arrived for the first time in Belgrade, where he was warmly welcomed. In March 1926, however, Pašić came under concentrated attack in Serbia and was forced to resign again, this time for good. He died in December of that year, leaving behind a disoriented Radical Party. The entry of the HSS into government, meanwhile, led to splits within it. Some of its members, dissatisfied with Radić's new course, created a new party – the Croat Republican Peasant Alliance – which joined the Croatian Party of Right (HSP) as a new Croatian Bloc. Others joined with the Croatian Union to form the Croatian Federalist Peasant Party (HFSS), in which Trumbić played an important role; this party too then joined the Croatian Bloc. Others again joined the circle around King Alexander. But the pull of republicanism and Croatian sovereignty exerted by the Peasant Party's social base made Radić an unreliable governmental partner, particularly since his party was given only minor ministerial posts and its legal prohibition had not been formally lifted. In February 1927 the HSS duly left its coalition with the Radicals. In September 1927 elections it nevertheless lost over 100,000 votes, even though it won sixty-one seats. The Croat electorate had punished the party for its cooperation with Belgrade. Zagreb voted for the Croatian Union, and in substantial numbers for the Communists. The Croatian Bloc, on the other hand, won only two seats: Trumbić taking one for the HFSS, Ante Pavelić (the future Ustasha leader) taking the other for the HSP. The Radicals likewise did badly in Serbia, by contrast with the Democrats, and Pribićević's SDS – benefiting from being in opposition – won twenty-two seats.[56]

A new Croat–Serb Coalition

Croatian politics took a new turn in November 1927, when Radić and Pribićević announced the formation of the Peasant-Democratic Coalition (SDK) – a revival, in effect, of the old Croat–Serb Coalition, with the difference that this time its Serb component stood in opposition to Belgrade. Pribićević even declared himself in favour of a revision of the Vidovdan

Stjepan Radić

Constitution. The SDK coalition, the two leaders argued, gave the lie to those seeking to present the conflict between Zagreb and Belgrade as a conflict between Croats and Serbs. Its creation inevitably caused a sensation, with many believing that it would not last; yet various attempts to split the HSS from the SDS all failed. Pribićević brought with him knowledge of how the Belgrade political machine worked, and under his influence the SDK mounted a vigorous offensive in the Belgrade parliament, with the aim of removing the hold of Serbian parties on the central state organs and thereby Serbia's hegemony within Yugoslavia.

The parliament now divided into two sharply opposing blocs: a centralist one dominated by the Radicals, and a federalist one led by the SDK. The conflict culminated on 20 June 1928, when the Radical deputy, Puniša Račić, shot dead two HSS deputies and wounded three more, including Stjepan Radić, who was his real target (the others were trying to protect him).[57] The SDK deputies now left Belgrade and met, according to the Coalition's statement issued on 1 August 1928, 'in the Croatian sabor in the Croatian capital of Zagreb'. It declared that the SDK had sought to win by parliamentary means 'a change of the state organisation that would secure and guarantee the equality and parity of Croatia and all [the lands of the former Austria-Hungary] with Serbia'. Given what had happened, however, it considered the parliament illegitimate in its present form. In 1918 Croatia and other 'national-political individualities represented in the National Council' had surrendered their sovereignty not to Serbia, but to 'the common state union of Serbs, Croats and Slovenes'. But the act of union of 1 December 1918 and the constitution of 28 June 1921 had been used to establish 'the hegemony of the former Kingdom of Serbia over all other lands and national parts', thereby delegitimising 'the state organisation as a whole'. The SDK would henceforth conduct a 'most determined struggle for a new state arrangement, which would ensure the full equality of all national individualities'. The declaration ended by inviting 'all political parties and groups in the [former Austro-Hungarian] lands' to join the struggle, and asked the 'Serbian peasant people' and Serbians who did not approve Belgrade's hegemonic policies, to help the realisation of 'the great principles which alone can save the state union'.[58]

Pribićević stated on this occasion that the Belgrade 'hegemonistic oligarchy' was trying to use the Croatian Serbs as gendarmes in order to 'tame the Croats and prevent their just struggle for equality'. Those who wished to create a Great Serbia through territorial amputation were hoping that it would be possible 'to mobilise the Serb part of our nation, especially in Bosnia and Vojvodina, against the Croats'. He added: 'I am well aware of the responsibility which I assume here. There is no doubt that the outcome of our struggle for [national] equality will depend to a large extent on the position assumed by the [former Habsburg] Serbs. These Serbs too should be aware of their great historical role and the attendant responsibility.' For without their support the Croats, driven to despair, would reject the common state. The Serbs outside Serbia too, moreover, were victimised by the regime. The Croat question stood in fact for the fate of all non-Serbian people and lands alike, faced not with a Great Serb, but with a Great Serbian, hegemony.[59] Yet the SDK was not united on the meaning of 'full equality of the national individualities', and the SDS found it difficult to follow the HSS in its quest for Yugoslavia's confederalisation.

It was King Alexander, in fact, who informed Pribićević of his intention to expel the Croats from the new state – a move that Pribićević likened to 'high treason'. According to his own account, the king told him that he would never agree to federation, preferring separation; to which he replied that alteration of Yugoslavia's borders would inevitably lead to foreign intervention. When Pribićević asked the king who would actually cut up the state, the king replied that this would pose no problem, and added: 'The vast majority of the Serbs would remain in their state, which would be smaller but more homogeneous. We cannot live with the Croats any longer.'[60] But any independent Croatia, however small, posed a threat to Serbia's hegemony, which is why nothing came of such plans.

Stjepan Radić died of his wounds on the night of 8 August 1928, a new martyr in the Croatian national cause, and was replaced by his deputy, Vladko Maček. The Croatian writer Miroslav Krleža, who was close to the Communist Party and highly critical of Radić's policy, wrote on this occasion that Radić 'went to the Croat peasant masses in order to *enlighten* them' and to 'teach them *Constitution*'; to 'raise their economic power in order to liberate them'; and since 'in his cosmology the peasantry and the nation were perfectly congruent', he remained convinced that peasant emancipation meant also Croat national emancipation.

> The whole thirty-year complex of the Radić phenomenon could in its various phases be viewed from the right and from the left, positively and negatively; but anyone who, on hearing the panic ringing of church bells on the night of 8 to 9 August, failed to grasp that a romantic lover of Croatia had died understands nothing of our psychological petty-bourgeois desire for Croat freedom. These days of Radić's posthumous glory have manifested in the most visible way the fact that the people returned his sincere love of them with love. He was a rare Croatian politician fated to be borne along by the elemental sympathy of the whole nation, and to be unreservedly canonised on his bier.[61]

The SDK's position now was that not the parliament but 'the nation and the king' should decide. Despite its trenchant call for 'the most determined struggle', it was held back by fear of civil war. The Radical Party's main paper was very blunt on this score: 'If they [the SDK] persist with their insane struggle, and continue to incite the ignorant masses; if they wish a war at all costs; they could lose the status of a negotiating partner and become instead the target of a war to the end, which is bound to be won by the stronger [that is, Serbian] side.'[62] On 4 January 1929 Maček and Pribićević informed the king that the crisis was not a parliamentary but a state crisis, which could be resolved only by 'the establishment of state-historical individualities with their own parliaments and governments'. The Serbian parties, however, rejected any such prospect. The king then declared that the differences between the parties were such that they could not be solved by parliamentary means: 'the moment has arrived when nothing could or should come between nation and king'.[63] On 6 January 1929 he suspended the 1921 constitution, dissolved parliament, banned all political parties, and made himself dictator. After less than a decade the Yugoslav experiment in parliamentary democracy had ended, never again to be attempted.

Maček's initial reaction to the introduction of royal dictatorship showed approval, which he would soon regret: 'The [wrongly buttoned] waistcoat has been unbuttoned. The Vidovdan Constitution, which for over seven years had oppressed the Croat nation, has been abolished.' He expressed his confidence in the maturity of the Croat people and His Majesty's wisdom,

Vladko Maček

which should 'enable us to realise the Croat national ideal: that Croats be masters in their own free Croatia'.[64] Pribićević was more cautious, but used the opportunity to declare that he remained: 'forever loyal to the Croats on the basis of the declaration of 1 August 1928. Nothing would make me waver in this loyalty, because I am deeply convinced that our state can survive and become strong only when the Croats are as happy within it as the Serbs.'[65] This was a response to those in his party who felt that the HSS had taken over the SDK, and that Serbs were being neglected in favour of Croats. The SDS continued to harbour a strong unitarist current, but for Pribićević the most important goal was to preserve Yugoslavia.[66] Ante Pavelić of the Croatian Party of Right, on the other hand, now left the country. He would in due course set up an Ustasha organisation that aimed at Croatia's violent separation from Yugoslavia.

It soon became clear, however, that the king's intention was not to solve 'the Croat Question', but to safeguard Serbia's hegemony, which was incompatible with any parliamentary democracy, even in the limited form that had prevailed in 1921–8. As a Dalmatian Croat politician wrote to Seton-Watson in October 1928:

> [The Serbians] would never consent to changes that would take hegemony from their hands. They would rather let the state fall apart than allow equality. Equality means reducing Serbia and the Serbians to their just proportion. [A] neutral, honest government would also be a death warrant to their hegemony [because Macedonia would no longer elect Serbian parties]. Montenegro too would turn against them, as would Vojvodina, most of Bosnia, Croatia and Dalmatia to the last deputy. This, of course, would transform Yugoslavia into a democratic state; it would contribute more than anything else to winning Macedonians, Germans and

Albanians for the state [and] to satisfying the Croats and the Slovenes. [But] this cannot be, because it is conditioned upon the Serbians giving up their hegemony, which in practice means giving up the exploitation of the state for the personal enrichment of a few Belgrade and Serbian families.[67]

The king now appointed a new government, headed by General Petar Živković, commander of the royal guard, which included Anton Korošec of the Slovene People's Party and some prominent Croat politicians representing Croatian financial and industrial circles. The Serbian parties would henceforth limit their demands to the restoration of political liberties, while the SDK would stress revision of the constitution. The SDK was not united, however, on political strategy: the HSS insisted on a new constitution as a precondition for joining a wider coalition against the dictatorship, while the SDS saw agreement with Serbian parties as a necessary prelude to constitutional change. In May 1929, however, Pribićević was arrested on a visit to Belgrade and interned at a small village in central Serbia: he, who in the past had sought and gained Alexander's support, became the first prominent victim of his dictatorship. At the end of July 1931, thanks mainly to pressure from Paris, he was allowed to leave Yugoslavia for Prague – never to return. In 1930 Maček was arrested and spent five months in prison. In 1931 a number of Croatian politicians were murdered by the regime, including the prominent HSP member Milan Šufflay, the HSS vice-president, Josip Predavec, and a dozen Communist activists. That year the king proclaimed a new constitution which in fact preserved royal dictatorship. The new electoral law permitted only single lists for the whole country, with the list winning a simple majority (that is, half the votes plus one) awarded two-thirds of the parliamentary seats. Only one such list was eventually passed: that of General Živković.

The SDS's response this time was that Yugoslavia must be reorganised on a federal basis. Pribićević wrote to his party colleague and close personal friend, Hinko Krizman, that state centralism and national unitarism – which he had favoured in the past – had clearly failed, and that another way must be sought. 'The most important thing for me is that a constitutional solution should be found which would enable the Croats to experience Yugoslavia as their own state, which would allow them to identify with it.'[68] He now accepted that this meant Yugoslavia's federalisation, with the central government retaining only such prerogatives as were necessary to the state's survival and development, and that this could be achieved only under a republic. 'The solution of the Yugoslav question within the framework of a

General Petar Živković, prime minister of Yugoslavia, 1929

federal republic would satisfy all its constituent elements; their satisfaction would be the foundation of its potential and force.' Only the overthrow of the monarchy could save Yugoslavia from an otherwise inevitable debacle.[69] In his view the 'best, wisest and fairest' solution would be for the Serbs to offer the Croats 'a blank sheet on which to write their demands'; anything else meant 'eternal conflicts and war that would end catastrophically for both'.[70]

Pribićević died in Prague as a guest of the Czechoslovak government on 15

September 1936. In his political testament he insisted that 'our state can exist only with Croat consent, which is what its original founders had thought. This is why I recommend [to the SDS] complete loyalty to the alliance with the HSS within the framework of the SDK, which Radić and I created on 10 November 1927 and which my friend Maček is continuing.' He wished to be buried in his birthplace in Croatia, but the Yugoslav government would not have it, so he was buried in Prague. The Communist Party of Yugoslavia contributed its own wreath; the SDS base would indeed produce the bulk of Croatian Serb Partisans in the Second World War. In 1968 Pribićević's remains were transferred to a Belgrade cemetery.

Darkening skies

In the years following Radić's death, Ante Trumbić became the Peaseant Party's advisor on foreign policy. The party to which he belonged, the Croatian Federalist Peasant Party (HFSS), was small yet influential, because it controlled Zagreb. This party had criticised the SDK declaration of 1 August 1928 as too timid: it should have promised to work for Croatia's state independence within Yugoslavia.[71] Suspicious of the king's intentions, the HSS decided to seek international support for the Croatian cause, even though the SDS was against internationalising the issue, considering it an internal Yugoslav matter. The HSS's commitment to its alliance with the SDS remained firm, however, since there was otherwise a danger that the Zagreb–Belgrade conflict would be transformed into one between Croats and Serbs.

In October 1928 Trumbić undertook a diplomatic mission for the HSS, which led him first to Vienna, where he talked to Austrian political leaders. They told him that Croatia should seek the solution of its problems within Yugoslavia, given Italy's continued territorial aspirations against it. He next proceeded to Paris, where he spent a month talking to French officials and journalists. The French foreign minister, though highly critical of Serbian politicians, advised Trumbić to rely on the king, who was the only power in the land. Trumbić's long stay in Paris prompted King Alexander likewise to pay a visit to that capital. The French government expressed to him their concern at the Yugoslav situation, and pressed him to reach an agreement with the Croats – but the king convinced them that he had the situation under control. Trumbić then proceeded to London, where he was told that Britain would not intervene. Wickham Steed and R.F. Seton-Watson, who supported the idea of Yugoslavia's federalisation, also advised patience. Trumbić wished to visit Prague too, but was asked not to: Czechoslovakia did not wish to annoy Belgrade. Contacts with Berlin proved equally fruitless.

The proclamation of the new constitution necessitated a new agreement between HSS and SDS regarding eventual SDK cooperation with the Serbian opposition. In 1932 the SDK adopted a resolution (drafted by Trumbić, who had by now joined the HSS) denouncing the dictatorship as an enhanced form of Serbian hegemony, and calling for a return to the status quo ante 1918, that is, the removal of Serbian rule from the former Habsburg lands. The resolution demanded Yugoslavia's transformation into a confederation – 'an association of interests based on the free will of its members' – and respect for the rights of national minorities.[72] The Slovene People's Party declared itself in favour of Slovenia's own statehood, while the Yugoslav Muslim Organisation reaffirmed the individuality of Bosnia-Herzegovina. The opposition in Vojvodina too asked for the latter's autonomy within Yugoslavia. In October 1934, however, King Alexander was assassinated by the Croatian Ustashe in Marseilles together with the French foreign minister, Louis Barthou. Since Crown Prince Peter was under age, royal authority came to be exercised by a three-member regency headed by Alexander's cousin Paul. On his release from prison Maček told Prince Paul that the existing parliament should be dissolved, and a neutral government established to organise elections for a new constitutional assembly; but the regent was unwilling to take upon himself this responsibility.

In 1933 the National Socialists, who favoured revision of the Versailles Treaty, had emerged as the strongest party in the German parliament, and in January 1934 Adolf Hitler became German chancellor. Hitler's assumption of power changed the whole European situation. The British were now convinced that Germany would soon annex Austria, and that this would lead Yugoslavia to move closer to Germany. In the eyes of more prescient observers, Yugoslavia's internal stability now became 'an European and a British interest'. Serbia, not Croatia, was at the root of Yugoslavia's instability: while Croatia had united solidly behind the SDK, Serbian political life was in complete disarray. The Serbian parties had by now realised that the old Vidovdan Constitution would have to be revised; but they could not agree among themselves what this entailed. According to a report produced by Seton-Watson after a visit to Yugoslavia in late 1936 (and which he forwarded to both Prince Paul and the Foreign Office), the main problem was how to transform an overcentralised state into a federation. But there was no agreement as to its make-up. The SDK proposed seven federal units: Slovenia, Croatia, Bosnia-Herzegovina, Serbia, Vojvodina, Macedonia and

Montenegro, while Belgrade would accept only the first four – and even then Bosnia-Herzegovina only reluctantly. What the Serbian parties found difficult to accept, in particular, was that the vast majority of Vojvodina's Serbs favoured its autonomy. The HSS was committed to Vojvodina's autonomy mainly, though not only, because the SDS insisted on it. Seton-Watson believed that it would be possible to reach a compromise whereby Montenegro and Macedonia would remain within Serbia as autonomous units. The main problem was that whereas Maček had a clear mandate to negotiate on behalf of Croatia, and enjoyed the confidence of the Slovenes and the Bosnians, there was no person of equivalent authority in Serbia. In October 1937, nevertheless, the SDK and the main Serbian parties did reach an agreement to create a Bloc of National Accord, whereby the Croatians would recognise the Karađorđević dynasty and the common state, while the Serbians would support a constitution acceptable to the Slovenes and the Croatians.

The Serbian parties had joined the bloc out of fear that the SDK might reach a separate agreement with Prince Paul; but they were unwilling – or too divided – to take any initiative of their own to implement the agreement reached with the SDK. Yugoslavia's inherent instability was highlighted at this time by the failure of the Yugoslav government, headed by Milan Stojadinović, to ratify the previously agreed concordat with the Vatican, thus leaving the Catholic Church alone of the recognised confessional communities without a clearly defined legal status. The decision to shelve the concordat came in response to a strident agitation against it organised by the Orthodox Church, with the support of Serbian opposition parties, which frequently took on the tone of an anti-Catholic religious war.[73] Trumbić noted at this time: 'We demand a free Croatia. We do not recognise the present situation and will not accommodate to it. Our ideal is an independent state. This is our greatest desire, the realisation of which, however, depends not on us but on outside events. If we cannot gain full independence, then we wish to be masters in our own home in regard to what is most important for our national life, and to share the rest with others.' Croatia was not eternally bound to Yugoslavia any more than it had been to the Habsburg Monarchy; everything depended on whether it would be able within Yugoslavia to gain national security and self-government.[74]

In March 1938 Germany annexed Austria, thereby acquiring a common border with Yugoslavia. Trumbić told the head of the French senate's foreign-policy committee that, due to Serbian procrastination, the Croatians were now seeking their own state 'regardless of the circumstances of its creation'.[75]

He feared a European war that would involve Yugoslavia, because the Croat population would sabotage any mobilisation ordered by a regime that they perceived as their enemy. War was indeed knocking on Yugoslavia's door. By the end of September 1939, Czechoslovakia and Poland had ceased to exist and Albania was under Italian occupation.

FIFTEEN

Reform, Reaction and Revolution

> This state has buried its own idea, and that broad Yugoslav idea of Strossmayer, Križanić and others, the great Slavic idea [is] mentioned by no one, there is not a trace of it. Nothing is left of the Slavic and Yugoslav idea.
>
> Stjepan Radić, 1927

Yugoslavia as constructed in 1921 (under the name of the Kingdom of Serbs, Croats and Slovenes) was inherently unstable and could be ruled only by non-parliamentary methods. The country changed four elected governments between 1921 and 1927, none of which fell as a result of losing the confidence of the parliament. There followed the assassination of Stjepan Radić in 1928, the installation of the royal dictatorship in 1929, and the imposition of a yet more undemocratic constitution in 1931. Eight governments came and went between November 1931 and June 1935, without recourse to new elections; in the meantime King Alexander himself was assassinated and a regency installed, headed by his cousin, Prince Paul.

In 1929 the country was renamed Yugoslavia and divided into nine departments called banovinas – all but one named after rivers – whose borders were inscribed in the Alexandrine constitution. Croatia was divided between three banovinas: the Sava, the Littoral and the Zeta. The Sava coincided with the former Croatia-Slavonia, bereft of eastern Srijem; the Littoral included most of Dalmatia and western Herzegovina; while the Zeta incorporated southern Dalmatia together with Montenegro, eastern Herzegovina and the Sandžak. Slovenia escaped fragmentation, in that it was wholly contained within the Drava banovina. Bosnia-Herzegovina, on the other hand, was divided between four units: the Vrbas (northwestern Bosnia), the Drina (eastern Bosnia and western Serbia), the Littoral and the Zeta. Each banovina was allocated a certain number of seats in the parliament. But with the old parties banned, the electoral lists of newly formed parties now had to cover the whole country. The list that won a simple majority, which could only be the one favoured by the regime, automatically gained-two thirds of all parliamentary seats. This measure was directed against nationally based parties such as the Slovene People's Party (SLS), the Yugoslav Muslim Organisation (JMO) and the Croatian Peasant Party (HSS).

Following elections in May 1935, the first in eight years, which were duly won by the regime, Milan Stojadinović of the former Radical Party became the new prime minister. His government based itself on a new party called the Yugoslav Radical Union (JRZ), uniting the Radicals with the SLS and the JMO, which had found this solution to the problem of country-wide lists. The British ambassador to Belgrade, Nevile Henderson, now informed his government that the period of 'extreme Serbianisation' was over.[1] Given Stojadinović's public commitment to pursue the late king's policy of 'state and national unity', however, it was clear that the new prime minister would concentrate on preserving the gains of 'extreme Serbianisation' implemented under the dictatorship and enshrined in the 1931 constitution.

The mainstream of the Croatian opposition believed that the system could not last, because 'it is rotten to the core; hence, we are bound to win against it provided we persevere, which is what we Croats shall do'.[2] The most important thing was to preserve national unity – which in the first instance meant the alliance between the Croatian Peasant Party (HSS) and the Independent Democratic Party (SDS) – and to maintain a common front against Belgrade. Zagreb's defiance was expressed in the Peasant–Democratic Coalition's (SDK's) declaration of 1932, which in the name of popular sovereignty denied the legitimacy of the central parliament. The dictatorship, while uniting Croatia, had on the other hand divided Serbia. A prominent Serbian politician told Seton-Watson in 1936: 'King Alexander had hoped to break the passive resistance of the Croats, and the result was to make them stronger and more united than before. He had also hoped to strengthen the Serb element in the state, and the result has been a complete disintegration of Serbian political and party life to an extent unparalleled in the history of modern Serbia.'[3]

The divisions and passivity of the Serbian parties arose mainly from their predicament in being aware of the need to give Croatia autonomy, while remaining unwilling to pay the necessary price of a corresponding diminution of Serbia's supremacy. As Trumbić noted at the time, Serbia had taken everything and stood to lose the most from any change in the status quo. By becoming the outward expression of an all-national resistance, on the other hand, the HSS had lost the character of a classical party and transformed itself into a national movement, absorbing in the process groups with political and social agendas far more radical than that favoured by its leadership. Its heterogeneity, while adding to its authority, became also a source of weakness. The unity displayed at election times would dissipate once these were over, since the HSS, excluded from government, was unable to back its political dominance in Croatia with a commensurate executive responsibility, leaving each area to find its own ways of dealing with everyday problems, including that of resistance to the over-zealous police and gendarmerie, now stiffened by Chetniks – paramilitary formations deployed against Belgrade's opponents.

The party tried to solve this problem by setting up in 1935 its own Urban and Village Guards, and forms of parallel administration that in some places became a law unto themselves. The policy of political abstinence, adopted as the only practical means of resistance, could not be maintained for long, however, since the absence of any positive resolution of 'the Croat Question' fed a national radicalism tending towards Croatia's unilateral separation from Serbia. There was some hope after Alexander's death in 1934 that it might be possible to change the constitution in a manner that would allow Croatia to regain its territorial integrity and self-government, which is why Maček decided to participate in the elections of May 1935 together with the Serbian opposition; but the Serbian parties, while agreeing in principle to constitutional revision, resisted any concrete proposal in this direction. The SDS, which acted as a bridge between the HSS and the Serbian opposition, had to admit that the latter were unable to unite on the basic issue of a constitution that would satisfy the Croats. Yet the SDS leaders, however dissatisfied they might be with Serbia's hegemony, would not countenance Croatian separation either: 'we Croats will *never* win [them] for a policy of separation, but only for a policy of state reorganisation within the existing borders'.[4]

Maček turned down Stojadinović's proposal of five seats in his government, fearing that cooperation with an unpopular regime would only compromise his party, while gaining nothing concrete in return: in wooing the HSS, Stojadinović merely wished to divide the opposition. Always present in the minds of the HSS leaders was the negative experience of Radić's positive engagement. The regime, in Trumbić's view, would not compromise unless forced, and the only force the Croatians had at their disposal was passive resistance. Forging Yugoslavia had been a strategic choice, with the aim of securing Croatia's territorial unity and winning national freedom; but this had proved impossible to achieve in view of Serbian hegemony, political persecution, and the imprisonment or murder of Croatian national leaders. The Peasant Party was seeking to change the system by peaceful means, but since even the Serbian opposition proved unable or unwilling to endorse Yugoslavia's federalisation, it seemed increasingly the case that a different Yugoslavia might in fact be impossible – in which case they should give up on it altogether.

Following the installation of the royal dictatorship, the HSS sent two representatives abroad to maintain contact with Britain and France on the one hand, and Italy and Germany on the other. This pursuit of an autonomous foreign policy aimed in the first instance to put pressure on Belgrade, but also to prepare for the eventuality of a collapse of the Versailles settlement, when Serbia – which alone had an army (albeit now called Yugoslav) – might be tempted to reconsider its commitment to Yugoslavia, and to cede, whether willingly or under military pressure, Slovenian and Croatian territories to Italy, Austria or Hungary. During the 1930s Yugoslavia's foreign and domestic policies became closely intertwined, in fact, with the attempts of Croatian and Serbian leaders to outwit each other by seeking support abroad.

Under Stojadinović's administration Belgrade drew close to Italy and Germany, largely for geopolitical and economic reasons, but also in order to avoid any compromise with the Croatians. Until Hitler's occupation of the Rhineland, France and Britain backed the Yugoslav government and court unconditionally, and refused to listen to the opposition. Encouraged by Paris and London, Stojadinović signed a pact with Mussolini's Italy in 1937 and, as evidence of Italy's support for Yugoslavia's territorial integrity, the Croat Ustasha militants harboured by Mussolini were reined in. As Italy drew closer to Germany, however, Paris changed its mind: wishing to check Yugoslavia's slide towards the German camp, it now expressed support for revision of the constitution, in the hope that this would lead to Stojadinović's removal. But by this time France had lost its earlier influence in Belgrade. Britain, on the other hand, continued with its policy of appeasing Germany, and encouraged Stojadinović and Prince Paul to do likewise.[5]

The rise of the 'Berlin–Rome axis' had met with Stojadinović's approval. Since both countries promised to respect Yugoslavia's borders, he was now convinced that this removed any need to come to terms with the Croatians. In January 1938, at a secret meeting between Hitler and Prince Paul, Germany promised to guarantee Yugoslavia's borders and protect it from Italy in return for neutrality in the event of war. Stojadinović told his interior minister, Milan Aćimović, that his pro-German policy meant that 'it is not necessary to make any concessions to the Croatians, let alone the Bulgarians'; and that 'our friendship with Germany is enough to permit us Serbs to hold in check all our opponents in the Balkans both within and outside the state boders'.[6] The British ambassador agreed with his German counterpart that autonomy for Croatia would be bad news – nothing but the Croats' outright surrender would do.

Germany's annexation of Austria in March 1938 was also welcomed by Stojadinović: the Croatian and Slovenian federalists, worried that Germany and Hungary might seek return of 'their' territories, were now bound to come to terms with Belgrade. This is what British diplomats resident in Yugoslavia advised the Croats to do.[7] The German ambassador to Belgrade, Viktor von Heeren, wrote to Berlin that it was in Germany's interest that 'Maček be forced to begin negotiations with Belgrade'; the German foreign ministry agreed – since the *Anschluss* Germany had become even more interested in having 'a strong and friendly Yugoslav nation' on its borders.[8] Maček, on the other hand, insisted that Belgrade was making a bad mistake in thinking that the German danger would force the Croats to accept the existing situation. The German threat was nothing new for the Croats, indeed it was understood better in Zagreb than in Belgrade, while the *Anschluss* had only highlighted the importance of Croatian-Serbian relations for European stability. The Croats were keen to find a solution within Yugoslavia's borders, but they would not be bullied into making unnecessary sacrifices. Croatian dissatisfaction, after all, had dangerous implications for Serbia too. The Croat leaders made it plain that in the event of war they would not defend a state that was their enemy, in which case Serbia might end up being reduced to its pre-1914 and maybe even its pre-1912 borders. Trumbić was convinced that a Yugoslavia ruled without Croatian consent was in any case bound to fall apart.[9] Maček and Trumbić continued to hope that 'the Croatian Question' could be resolved within Yugoslavia, and vested their hopes in Britain's interest in the Mediterranean, which sooner or later would prompt London to take 'the Croat Question' seriously. Ante Trumbić died on 18 November 1938, practically a pauper, before any resolution of this issue in Zagreb. He was buried in the Franciscan monastery in Split next to Thomas the Archdeacon and Marko Marulić. Forty thousand of his countrymen took part in the funeral procession. According to Josip Smodlaka, 'all his life he remained faithful to the Party of Right's programme of re-creating the old Croatian state of Trpimir and Krešimir'.[10]

The most difficult problem for the SDK leaders was how to maintain the confidence of the Croatian – Croat and Serb – population, which by 1937 was beginning to feel that the SDK's policy of passivity was leading nowhere. Stojadinović indeed encouraged radical Croat nationalists aligned with the Ustashe to challenge Maček's leadership, and permitted them to spout anti-Serb rhetoric as a way of putting pressure on the SDK alliance. The SDS urged Maček to engage more with the Belgrade opposition, and in October 1937 an agreement was reached for the two sides to seek adoption of a new constitution acceptable to a majority of Slovenes, of Croats and of Serbs – without, however, specifying its nature.[11] Following this agreement the deputy leader of the SDS, Većeslav Vilder, told the worried Czechoslovak envoy to Belgrade: 'Maček has absolute authority in the Croat population and he alone is capable of taming its radicalism. I keep saying that Maček is Yugoslavia's greatest asset. The agreement [with the Serbian opposition] was a test of his statesmanship, and it is now the turn of Prince Paul. [I] am in full solidarity with him [Maček] and we are united in our approach, with the difference that I am a Yugoslav at all costs, while he only on condition of Croatia's freedom.'[12] Maček, aware that negotiations with the divided and confused Serbian opposition was a blind alley, preferred to deal directly with Prince Paul; but their meetings led nowhere, since Paul was unwilling to sacrifice Stojadinović, with whom Maček refused to work. In August 1938 Maček visited Belgrade – the first visit by a Croatian leader since Radić's murder a decade before – and was greeted by a huge crowd. Nothing, however, came from his visit. Stojadinović publicly rejected any negotiations with 'the former HSS'. A Dalmatian correspondent wrote to Seton-Watson:

> When we remember that after Radić's death the decision was 'Never to Belgrade!', and that the decision until quite recently was still 'Never to a centralistic Belgrade!', we see that Dr Maček is making serious efforts to ease the situation for Prince Paul, and for all those elements in Serbia who honestly wish for a settlement with the Croats. Dr Maček, after all, must think about his own situation in Croatia and our [Croat] extremists. [In] order to win the Croats for a constructive policy of collaboration with Belgrade, he must have some spectacular gesture from the people in Belgrade; if his efforts fail through not finding a [corresponding] response in the governing circles in Belgrade, he will not be responsible for the unfavourable turn of events.[13]

British policy towards Yugoslavia was now beginning to change, however, and this was reflected in the attitude adopted by Prince Paul to the Croatian issue. In late September 1938 the British prime minister, Neville Chamberlain, agreed in Munich to Czechoslovakia's partition, but there was a growing unease in the country with his German policy. Through the annexation of Austria Germany had gained control of the Danube, and the Munich conference strengthened German influence in the Balkans. With Yugoslavia becoming part of the German economic zone, its neutrality was increasingly questioned and, as war approached, its future – hence, also Croatia's attitude to Yugoslavia – gained in international importance. Germany's political patronage and economic largesse, on the other hand, was making Stojadinović an increasingly independent actor, and there were signs that he might even proclaim himself a Yugoslav Duce. The prospect of losing control over his prime minister increasingly worried Prince Paul, particularly given the rumours that Stojadinović had on his own initiative negotiated a division of Albania with the Italian foreign minister. There were reports too that, in the event of war, he was ready to surrender the Croatian coast to Italy in return for recognition of the rest of Yugoslavia as a Serbian possession.[14]

Paul firmly supported the policy of neutrality, but this could be maintained only by the country becoming internally more stable, which meant overcoming the war of attrition between Belgrade and Zagreb, which demanded the removal of Stojadinović. This was not an easy decision to take, however. He was afraid that Berlin might take Stojadinović's dismissal as a provocation, but also that the Serbian political, ecclesiastic and military establishments might reject any deal with Croatia. He was after all a Serbian prince, and would be negotiating on Serbia's behalf. What tipped the balance in favour of positive action was the outcome of the December 1938 elections. Despite Stojadinović's control of the electoral process and active harassment of the Serbian opposition, the opposition list headed by Maček won 45 per cent against the governmental party's 54 per cent of the vote. It is true that this gave the government 303 seats and the opposition only sixty-seven, but the HSS got the largest number of votes in its history and the SDS did well too, prompting one of Stojadinović's candidates to complain that 'Maček's movement is growing rapidly among the Serbs; if this continues, at the next elections he would be able to win districts which had always been national [that is, loyal to Belgrade].'[15] In the Serb areas outside Serbia, Maček's list in fact had won more than twice as many votes as Stojadinović's JRZ.

The German ambassador reported that the elections had taken on a plebiscitary character in Croatia, and that Stojadinović's poor performance in Croatia and elsewhere was highly regrettable from Germany's point of view. He noted in January 1939: 'Those within and outside Yugoslavia who have a sound interest in a strong Yugoslav state must acknowledge, regardless of their sympathy for the Croats, that it is necessary to preserve Serbian hegemony within the state.'[16] His equally disappointed British colleague wrote that it might be necessary to introduce military rule, although he hoped that Stojadinović would stay: Prince Paul would surely not dismiss one who had served him so well over the past three and a half years, and who was so eminently suited to his post.[17] Stojadinović's determination not to offer anything to Croatia, however, had become a dangerous liability for Yugoslavia.

On 15 January 1939, on the eve of parliament's recall, the HSS adopted a resolution based on the principle of national self-determination and the Croatian state right. It asserted that the party would never recognise a government not responsible to the Croatian nation; alerted the Great Powers to the instability of the Yugoslav system; and hinted at the possibility that Croatians might be forced to seek their own path to independence. The SDS, meeting separately, supported the decision to boycott parliament. The declaration in fact involved a degree of bluster. The HSS had presented the elections as a historic turning point that would decide 'the fate of the state called Yugoslavia'. If the opposition failed to win, 'we Croats will seek other ways and other means to win freedom'. Although the opposition did not win, the party's electoral success encouraged great expectations in Croatia, including the possibility of recalling the sabor and forming a separate Croatian government. Anxious that in the absence of any progress on the Croatian issue the more radical elements of his party and the militants belonging to the small yet noisy Croatian Party of Right might gain in influence, and wishing to utilise the psychological impact of his party's electoral triumph, Maček now made a concession to Prince Paul: he would not insist on revision of the constitution, which Paul had stubbornly resisted throughout, as a precondition for a settlement. But Stojadinović had to go. The gambit worked. Impressed by the good showing of the opposition, Prince Paul felt it provided a convenient pretext for Stojadinović's removal.

As it turned out, this was easily accomplished. In early February 1939 Slovene, Bosnian and some Serbian ministers suddenly resigned, and the regent refused to allow Stojadinović to reconstruct his government. A new government, drawn largely from the JRZ, was formed on 6 February 1939 under Dragiša Cvetković, who stated that its particular mission was to work for consolidation of the internal situation, the most important aspect being the need to appease the Croats. The Serbian opposition parties, however, insisted that they alone represented the Serbian people, and demanded that they be given the mandate to conduct the negotiations. Maček, wishing to conciliate them, asked them to send representatives to Zagreb to establish a common basis for the coming negotiations with Cvetković – but they refused to work with the latter. Their preferred option was to return to power in the form of a government of national unity headed by Maček, and to postpone all hard questions of interest to the Croatians to some unspecified date in the future, when the international situation had improved. The HSS, on the other hand, refused to enter the government before Croatia's borders and status had been agreed.

Maček now informed the regent that an agreement could be reached on the basis of Article 116 of the existing constitution – which permitted the king to take all measures he considered necessary in the case of (unspecified) public need – and that he would accept Cvetković as a negotiator only if he spoke in Paul's name. This was accepted by Prince Paul. The negotiations between Zagreb and Belgrade began on 2 April 1939. The talks were conducted in the shadow of the approaching world war. In March 1939 German troops had occupied the rump of Czechoslovakia, following which Britain and France pledged to Poland to defend it against Germany. A few days after the start of Maček's negotiations with Cvetković, Italy invaded Albania. At a meeting in the middle of the same month, Goering and Mussolini agreed to support Yugoslavia's unity only if the latter pursued a wholly pro-Axis policy. In early February 1939, uncertain as to whether Prince Paul would engage in serious negotiations and concerned that Italy might attack Yugoslavia before any settlement could be reached, Maček had sought in Berlin protection for Croatia (in which he included Bosnia-Herzegovina). But the Italian foreign minister, Galeazzo Ciano, Mussolini's son-in-law, warned the Germans that their alliance was based on the assumption that the Adriatic Sea, hence also Croatia, belonged to the Italian sphere of influence. London, approached by HSS envoys with a request that it put pressure on Prince Paul to negotiate, had indicated that Britain would not interfere. These explorations confirmed Maček in his belief that it was necessary to settle the Croatian issue within Yugoslavia.

The Zagreb–Belgrade talks concerned two basic questions: Croatia's borders and its status within Yugoslavia. Maček, negotiating on behalf of the SDK, offered essentially two alternatives: a division of Yugoslavia into seven units: Slovenia, Croatia, Bosnia-Herzegovina, Vojvodina, Montenegro, Serbia and Macedonia; or, failing that, addition of parts of Vojvodina and

Vladko Maček and Dragiša Cvetković, Zagreb 1939

Bosnia-Herzegovina to Croatia. It was accepted early on that Croatia would include the Sava and the Littoral banovinas, as well as the Dubrovnik district; but differences remained over arrangements for the rest of the country. It was agreed in late April 1939 to proceed immediately to unification of the uncontested territory under the name of Banovina Croatia, whose final borders would be decided by a plebiscite conducted in the rest of Bosnia-Herzegovina, the Bay of Kotor, Srijem and Vojvodina. The two sides also agreed to transfer to Banovina Croatia the conduct of all affairs other than foreign policy, defence and essential central state prerogatives; to provide a constitutional guarantee of Croatia's special status; and to form a new government that would include the SDK.

Prince Paul, however, rejected the idea of a plebiscite for the Bay of Kotor and Vojvodina. Maček concurred. The regent then rejected the idea of a plebiscite in the case of Bosnia-Herzegovina too. This was due in part to protests from the JMO and the Bosnian Serb parties, but above all to opposition from the army, which disliked the idea of federalisation in general and, more specifically, the addition of any part of Bosnia-Herzegovina to Croatia. At this point the negotiations stalled. Reacting to this retreat from the agreement reached with Cvetković, the HSS met in early May and declared that the Croatian nation was being unjustly excluded from international negotiations that concerned its future too; that a just peace in central and southeastern Europe could not be reached without meeting its demands; and that the Yugoslavia created in 1918 on the premise of equality of Serbs, Croats and Slovenes had not lived up to expectations.[18]

The party now renewed its contacts with Rome. This time Foreign Minister Ciano agreed to support Croatia's independence politically and materially, provided that Croatia accepted Italian troops on its territory and, in effect, Italian overlordship. Maček then broke off negotiations and redoubled his efforts to find an agreement with the Serbian parties and the government. By the end of June 1939 he and Cvetković had managed to agree on Croatia's territorial extent, in line with the original proposals, after which the talks focused on the competencies of the Croatian Banovina's future government, which took most of the month of July. The Croatians, for example, demanded that the gendarmerie be placed under the control of the Croatian ban, which Belgrade refused. With both sides fearing an imminent outbreak of war, however, the negotiations ended with the formal announcement of an agreement on 26 August 1939, when a set of laws were passed establishing Banovina Croatia. Parliament was now dissolved and a new government formed, again headed by Cvetković, which included five HSS ministers and one from the SDS. Maček became Cvetković's deputy. The final demarcation of the borders of Banovina Croatia was left to the future, when the reorganisation of the whole state would be decided; it seemed most likely that this would take a federative form, given that the Drava banovina was identified with Slovenia.[19] For Maček and his party, Banovina Croatia was a federal state within Yugoslavia. The Ustasha emigration, meanwhile, pronounced any solution other than Croatia's complete independence as treason.

The birth of Banovina Croatia practically coincided with the outbreak of the Second World War. Three days earlier, Germany and the Soviet Union had signed a Non-Aggression Pact, following which Germany invaded Poland. On hearing the news of the Cvetković–Maček agreement, Winston Churchill, then British minister of the navy, congratulated the Yugoslav ambassador to London, adding that the agreement would permit Yugoslavia's mobilisation.[20] On the other hand, the agreement stimulated a broad debate on the eventual internal division and constitution of the Yugoslav state. The old centralist structure established in 1921 had been undermined at its weakest – Croatian – point; but there was no overall agreement on how to proceed, or who the subjects of change should be. The Serbian parties soon united against the Cvetković–Maček accords. Although they failed to reach a common stance, the majority of Serbian politicians urged the establishment before proceeding to elections of a third

Banovina Croatia, 1939–41

– Serbian – unit, which would include either the rest of Yugoslavia (without Slovenia, of course) or alternatively all 'Serb lands'. The HSS, however, made it clear that it would resist any inclusion of the rest of Bosnia-Herzegovina into such a Serbian unit. The JMO, alarmed at the loss of Bosnian territory to Croatia and the prospect of further partition of their homeland, insisted on its integrity, demanding that Bosnia-Herzegovina be recognised as a separate unit under its own government. The SDS would have liked western Bosnia (the Vrbas banovina) to have been included in Banovina Croatia, in order to augment the number of Serbs there; and it would have preferred the Yugoslav centre to retain more power than was acceptable to its HSS allies. Nonetheless, it approved the agreement and joined the Cvetković government.

The SDS had feared that the Maček–Cvetković cooperation might lead to its being sidelined in favour of Cvetković's Radicals (which is what Cvetković himself desired), but the HSS remained firmly committed to the SDK alliance: 'The SDK is the other name of the policy of [Croat–Serb] national accord. Its durability, translated into the language of Europe, means Yugoslavia's survival.'[21] The SDS leaders agreed with Maček that there was no alternative to this particular governmental coalition. New elections were promised, but – given the disagreement on whether they should come before or after an all-Yugoslav constitutional settlement had been reached, and the fundamental differences over the new constitution resolved – were never held. Since elections for the sabor were supposed to take place at the same time as those for the Yugoslav assembly, moreover, the sabor too never met. The country, as a result, would enter World War II without functioning representative institutions.

Implementation of the agreement soon ran into technical and political problems regarding the Banovinas' competencies, finances and borders. The HSS concentrated on gaining maximum independence for it within the Yugoslav framework, and remained preoccupied with the consolidation of its administration. In view of Serbian domination of the army, it sought the creation of a Home Guard as a guarantee against any unilateral alteration – or indeed abrogation – of the agreement; since this was resisted, it continued to rely on its own Urban and Peasant Guards which, in the event of a state coup in Belgrade or a war, would be able to protect Zagreb.[22] Judging by the results of the municipal elections held in Croatia in May 1940, however, the HSS was losing ground on the one hand to radical Croat nationalists and on the other to the Communists.[23]

The fall of France in June 1940, the entry of Italy into the war, and the latter's invasion of Greece in October 1940, increased the overall sense of confusion and insecurity in Yugoslavia. One after another Hungary, Romania and Slovakia joined the Tripartite Pact concluded by Germany, Italy and Japan in September 1940. Yugoslavia's rapidly deteriorating international position shook the confidence of the Serbian generals, who, unwilling to take responsibility for the poor state of an army that they had dominated from the start, sought to lay the blame on the Croats.[24] In October 1940 the German ambassador reported to Berlin:

> Rumours are circulating again of plans by the Serbian generals to stage a coup d'état and introduce military dictatorship, and if need be to replace the prince regent with the young king, which shows the presence of a deep dissatisfaction in the army and in Serbian circles with the existing Yugoslav situation.[25] The regent's policy of seeking peace with the Croats is considered to be impairing and endangering the unity of the state.[26]

As subsequent events would show, however, the agreement actually ensured that when war came the HSS would prove loyal to Yugoslavia.

The pressure on Belgrade to abandon neutrality increased after Mussolini's failure to subdue Greece, and with the consequent need by Germany to intervene in order to prevent the arrival of British troops on the Greek mainland. Germany and Britain (the latter backed by the United States) now joined battle for Yugoslavia, one pressing it to adhere to the Pact, the other to enter the war on the Greek and British side. When on 1 March 1941 Bulgaria too joined the Axis, the British redoubled their efforts to get the Yugoslavs to engage against the Italian troops in Albania, despite the fact that London would be quite unable to help when the inevitable German invasion ensued. Since, according to the Yugoslav minister of war, the country would be incapable of resisting for more than six weeks without outside help, Yugoslavia finally succumbed to Hitler's demand and, on 25 March 1941, Belgrade joined the Pact – on surprisingly favourable terms, in that nothing more was asked of it. Germany and Italy promised not only to respect Yugoslavia's independence and integrity, but also to demand no military assistance from it, not even the transit of their troops through its territory.[27] The HSS was originally against Yugoslavia signing the Pact, but in the end Maček agreed in order to avoid war on Yugoslav territory. He was greatly swayed by the Serbian military's bleak assessment of Yugoslavia's capacity to resist.[28] Leading Serbian politicians, on the other hand, agreed to the Pact on condition that Yugoslavia be ceded Salonika and its hinterland: this was included in a secret clause of the treaty.

Were it not for their tragic consequences, the events that followed the signing of the Pact could be described as farcical. On the night of 26–27 March 1941 a few Serbian air force officers staged a coup, which brought their commander, General Dušan Simović, to power. The putschists promptly deposed the regency and proclaimed the hapless Crown Prince Peter king. Berlin was informed in advance of the impending coup, but was assured by its ambassador to Belgrade that Cvetković knew about it and would be able to quash it. In the event, however, Prince Paul – fearing civil war – refused to contemplate any such action. British operatives, who had been keeping in touch with the members of the Reserve Officer Club in Belgrade, were directly involved in this venture; but they were not responsible for it.[29] The coup expressed deep dissatisfaction in Serbia with the Cvetković–Maček agreement and its implications, even though this never led to the articulation of any coherent alternative other than return to the 1921 constitution. As for the rebels, they had no idea in fact of what to do next, and were deeply divided among themselves. It never occurred to them that Germany might retaliate in the event of their success. But on 27 March, the day of the coup,

Hitler issued the order to attack Yugoslavia, which was to be quickly and mercilessly subjugated, then dismembered. The plan, known as Operation 25, involved also stoking internal tensions in Yugoslavia. At this stage Hitler and the German high command believed that the Yugoslav army would put up a strong defence, and the idea was to win over the Croats, the Bosnians and the Macedonians with promises of liberation from 'Serb dictatorship'.[30]

Having taken power, however, the putschists now faced its responsibilities – which led them promptly to adopt the very same policies against which they had mutinied. Although the political groups that joined Simović's government had all been against the Cvetković–Maček agreement, they quickly realised that this was no moment to challenge it, since their government's legitimacy depended on the support of Maček and the HSS. They assured the Croatian ban, Ivan Šubašić of the HSS, that the coup in no way changed the status of Banovina Croatia. The briefly imprisoned HSS, SDS, JMO and SLS ministers were all asked to remain in their posts, and Maček was proclaimed deputy premier (without being asked). Within days the new government passed ten laws investing Banovina Croatia with all the powers that the HSS had unsuccessfully sought in the past. Maček and Prince Paul were both in Zagreb at the time of the coup. On hearing the news Maček proposed to the prince to use the army stationed in Croatia to crush the rebellion. But all that Paul wished to do was leave with his family for Greece.[31]

In the days preceding the attack, the German foreign minister, Joachim von Ribbentrop, urged Maček and his party not to have anything to do with the new government. The HSS nevertheless decided to join it. Its leaders also decided that, in the event of war and the government having to go into exile, Maček would remain in Croatia. On 3 April 1941 Ribbentrop's envoys arrived in Zagreb and offered Maček the creation of an independent Croatia under German protection. This was refused. Nor would Maček sanction any negotiations involving partition or annexation of Slovenia. According to the German report of the conversation, he assured the Germans that Simović's government would honour the Pact, declaring:

> A sense of responsibility towards the people who for the past nine years have given me their confidence bids me do everything in my power to ensure that it has peace, since peace is mankind's greatest treasure. I am convinced that the present Serbian leaders are as sincere as I am. I am confident that despite these recent difficulties we shall be able to save the peace, and as a result bear the troubles that have arisen more easily. The rights that Croatia has gained

through cooperation [with Belgrade] have not only been secured and consolidated, they will also be enlarged.[32]

The German consul in Zagreb, Alfred Freundt, informed Berlin on the same day that Maček's efforts were divided between maintaining peace with Germany and ensuring Yugoslavia's continued survival. Maček knew, however, that war was inevitable, and feared that it would spell the end of Yugoslavia. On his arrival in Belgrade on 4 April he found his new cabinet colleagues in a state of panic; when he insisted that they had no option but to maintain adherence to the Pact, he found he was pushing at an open door. Germany and Italy, and indeed all countries with Yugoslav embassies, were accordingly informed of Belgrade's determination to remain faithful to the Pact: the new government's 'chief concern' was 'to maintain the policy of good and friendly relations with Germany and Italy' and to make 'determined steps not to be drawn into the present conflict'.[33] The British were told that Yugoslavia would not join the war on their side. But it was already too late.

In the early morning of 6 April, the German air force bombed Belgrade causing great loss of life; and within less than a fortnight the German army occupied much of the country, meeting hardly any resistance from the poorly equipped, badly led and highly demoralised Yugoslav army, which simply fell apart. On the evening of 8 April Maček told the Croatian people that the war had begun, that he would remain in the country, and that it was important to maintain discipline 'at home and in the army'. Unbeknownst to him, however, on 5 April 1941 three followers of the Croatian Party of Right, a tiny party close to the Ustasha exiles but with few followers outside the Zagreb area, together with two dissident members of the HSS had signed a declaration drafted by Edmund von Veesenmayer, one of the German officials sent to Zagreb to negotiate with Croat politicians, signalling the formation under German protection of an 'independent Croatian state' within its 'historical borders'. On 10 April 1941, as German troops were about to enter Zagreb, Slavko Kvaternik of the Croatian Party of Right announced on the radio the creation – or, as he put it, resurrection – of an independent Croatian state. He ascribed this miracle, in turn, to divine will, to the will of the German 'ally', to 'the centuries-long struggle of the Croat people', and finally to 'the great efforts' of Pavelić and his Ustashe:

> People of Croatia! By the grace of God and the will of our [German] ally, and also as a result of the strenuous centuries-long struggle of the Croatian people and the great efforts on the part

of our leader Dr Ante Pavelić and the Ustashe movement at home and abroad, today, the day before the resurrection of the Son of Our Lord, our independent state of Croatia too has risen again.[34]

Maček, faced with the collapse of his whole policy and seeking to avoid bloodshed,[35] responded by inviting the population and public officials to submit to and cooperate with the new government.[36] He then retired to his country house to wait for the western Allies to win the war. His party, after all, was represented in what would become the government-in-exile. On 14 April 1941 the Yugoslav government (in which Juraj Krnjević had replaced Maček) and the newly installed king made their way to Greece. Taken aback by the speed of the Yugoslav army's collapse, the only thing the British government could do was to offer hospitality to the Yugoslav government-in-exile. On 17 April 1941 the former Yugoslav foreign minister, Alexander Cincar-Marković, whom the putschists had dismissed for trying to keep the country out of the war, and General Radivoje Janković, forced to deputise for his absconding civilian and military superiors, signed unconditional capitulation ceding Yugoslavia – including Croatia – to Germany's absolute rule. They had hoped that Hitler would permit a solution on the lines of Vichy France, allowing a degree of self-government over part of the territory; but he had decided to destroy Yugoslavia as a state for good. Following the invasion, the country was broken up and partitioned among its neighbours. Germany added northern Slovenia to the Reich, and occupied eastern Vojvodina, Serbia and northern Kosovo. Italy took the rest of Slovenia (including Ljubljana), a large part of Dalmatia and Gorski Kotar, the Bay of Kotor and most of Montenegro. Italian-ruled Albania incorporated the bulk of Kosovo, and the Albanian-inhabited area of Montenegro. Bulgaria annexed most of Macedonia, as well as some Serbian territory and a slice of Kosovo. Hungary absorbed the rest of Vojvodina, Međimurje, and Slovene territory east of the Drava. The rest of Croatia and all of Bosnia-Herzegovina were formed into the Independent State of Croatia (NDH), the inclusion of Bosnia-Herzegovina having been agreed during German–Italian negotiations of 21–22 April 1941 in Vienna. Its territory was within days occupied by German and Italian troops, and a demarcation line drawn through its middle separating their respective zones of occupation and authority.[37]

Yugoslavia's collapse was both sudden and complete. The government had departed without having prepared the population in any way for what was about to descend upon it, leaving a power vacuum to be filled by the

Partition of Yugoslavia, 1941

advancing armies and by local forces pursuing their own separate and often conflicting plans. In the subsequent blame game, all kinds of explanation have been offered for Yugoslavia's defeat and implosion, but there is no doubt that the Serbian political class bears the lion's share of responsibility. The German *Drang*, which Supilo and Trumbić had tried to fend off by erecting in its path the Yugoslav barrier and the idea of Croat–Serb national unity, was now back with a vengeance.

Revolution of the Right: the Independent State of Croatia (NDH)

Up to the time of coup, Hitler had no intention of dividing Yugoslavia, which had long been a friendly state. Support for Yugoslavia included also support for Serb hegemony within the state. The German Nazi establishment was uniformly pro-Serbian, especially Hermann Goering, who was impressed by the warm reception he had received in Belgrade. Goering's autographed photograph indeed occupied a place of honour in the rooms of the leading plotter, Brigadier-General Bora Mirković. Hitler himself used to praise the 'brave and warlike Serbs' for their purported resistance to the Turks; his anger after the coup arose mainly from a sense of personal betrayal. And although Italy was still harbouring the Ustashe, Mussolini nevertheless sought a German–Yugoslav rapprochement, hoping to enlist Yugoslav help in his war against Greece. Nor did Germany's initial war plans include the creation of an independent Croatian state. Hitler in fact offered Croatia (by which he probably meant the Austro-Hungarian Ban's Croatia, or maybe the territory of Banovina Croatia bereft of the parts demanded by Italy) to Hungary as an autonomous entity within its borders – but Hungary was not tempted. It was only four days after the decision to attack Yugoslavia that the idea of an independent Croatia began to be considered in Berlin.[38]

Having been accustomed to dealing with Serbia, however, and acting on the assumption that Croatia was part of the Italian sphere of influence, the Germans had failed to create their own group there. Maček seemed to them the obvious choice as Croatia's leader, but Maček refused to play the role of a Croatian Pétain. As he told the German envoys, Croatia now had a stake in Yugoslavia, while any other option would lead to a Croat–Serb war. Given his refusal, the Germans were obliged in the end to rely on the HSP. According to Kvaternik himself, being unable to judge Germany's true intentions he had hastened to proclaim independence before the arrival of the German army, in order to create a fait accompli.[39] German analysts concerned with the area differentiated at this time between Pavelić's Ustashe and the Croatian Party of Right. The latter had been traditionally pro-Austrian, and was now pro-German.[40] Ante Pavelić, on the other hand, was perceived as an Italian pawn. In the end, however, they had no choice but to back him.[41]

In the Ustashe calendar, 10 April 1941 consequently marks the victory of their 'revolution'. On that day, however, Pavelić and his Ustashe were kicking their heels in Italy, where they learned the news from the local media. Mussolini, who had not been informed either of Kvaternik's involvement, was greatly put out to learn that Croatia's independence had been proclaimed in Italy's absence and under German sponsorship. He promptly claimed the NDH as Italy's own war booty, but the German army was already in possession of the Croatian capital.

It was Pavelić who named the new construction the Independent State of Croatia, which according to the radio speech he gave on 10 April would extend 'from the Mura and the Drava to the Drina, and from the Danube to the blue Adriatic'. He announced on that occasion that the German and Italian troops pouring into Croatia were accompanied by a 'bravely fighting Croat Ustashe army'; but the truth is that he and his 'storm troops', numbering no more than 200 lightly armed men dressed in Italian uniforms left over from the war in Ethiopia, made their way to Zagreb by train, chaperoned along the route by Italian officers. At their last meeting before the journey, Mussolini had told Pavelić that 'the Dalmatian cities of indubitably

Italian, i.e. Venetian, character would come under Italian sovereignty'. On their arrival in Croatia, Pavelić and his party could see that all the area from the coast up to Karlovac was already under Italian occupation. At Karlovac they were met by Kvaternik in the company of German officials, who were doubtless glad to learn from Pavelić that Croatia had been Germany's ally in the First World War, and that Croats were in any case of Gothic rather than Slav origin.

After twelve years of waiting – at times as Mussolini's guests, at others as his prisoners – the Ustashe, who had insisted throughout that their armed efforts alone would deliver national liberty, acquired the government of Croatia without firing a shot. This did not deter Pavelić from following his Italian patron's example by presenting the outcome as the Ustashe's own great victory. In his first speech on Croatian soil he thus declared:

> Thanks to the Croat people's endurance and the Ustashe's struggle and spilled blood, [we] have created a Croatian state which no one ever will be able to destroy, because we shall know how to defend our freedom. Croatia will be a land of order and of work. No one in the Croatian state will ever again be in a position to exploit its people and suck its blood. Everyone will work and answer to the Leader, who will be responsible to the Croat people alone.[42]

Rather than hurrying on to Zagreb to bring the nation the good news, Pavelić waited in Karlovac for Mussolini's envoy, Filippo Anfuso, to catch up with him. On his arrival, the Italian promptly drafted a telegram to be sent by Pavelić to Mussolini, asking him to recognise the NDH. This included the following phrases: 'The Croat people declares its deep gratitude to the glorious Italian detachments for liberating Croatia. Croatia will join the new European order under the wing and protection of Fascist Italy. In regard to the new state's borders, Italian rights in Dalmatia shall be taken into account.'[43] When shown this text, however, the welcome party revolted – the Germans in particular complaining that they, not the Italians, had done all the work. Since the Germans, moreover, controlled the telegraph lines between Karlovac and Rome, Anfuso's telegram could not be sent. Following further negotiations a new draft was produced, which this time expressed gratitude also to the German army, and was sent to Berlin for final approval. The latter agreed to Italy's acquisition of Dalmatia, but the Italian-German tug of war over the NDH would continue until Italy's capitulation in 1943. Italy's policy was to keep the NDH weak, Germany's to make it strong enough to maintain local peace. The NDH leaders likewise divided between

Slavko Kvaternik (left) and Ante Pavelić, Zagreb 1941

those who relied on Germany and those who remained bound to Italy. The schizophrenic nature of the whole set-up was an important, though not the only, factor in preventing the NDH's consolidation.

A warning from Kvaternik that Pavelić's entry into the capital might not be completely safe prevented an Ustashe march on Zagreb. Pavelić was also concerned that his 'storm troops' might fail to awe the city, so decided to enter it in the early hours of 15 April, when everyone was asleep. The only sign of the new order's advent was the replacement of the usual guard in front of the ban's palace by Pavelić's own men. Kvaternik, whom Pavelić promptly appointed field marshal, announced the Leader's arrival on the radio:

> Croat people! I am able to tell you the happy news that your victorious Leader has returned to the capital city of Zagreb, and has assumed sovereign government of the Independent State of Croatia. Our Leader sends you his greetings and offers you his heart, energy and wisdom: he will as always work for you day and night, and you will follow him so that we can always be 'Ready for the Homeland'.[44]

In the meantime Italian troops had taken possession of the entire coast from Rijeka's twin port of Sušak in the north to Kotor in the south. The local authorities, obeying instructions from Zagreb, offered no resistance; but the Italian propaganda machine typically presented the whole thing as a mighty conquest. Italian film news showed intense street fighting in Sušak, Split, Šibenik and Dubrovnik, a feat made possible by dressing up Italian soldiers in Yugoslav army uniforms and by a lavish use of blank ammunition. The cinematic projection of the 'Battle for Sušak', however, had to be withdrawn after Italian viewers noticed a mother peacefully wheeling a pram under supposed gunfire. Karlovac too was 'taken by storm'; the fact that Italian troops had in fact entered it unhindered did not prevent the new military commander of Karlovac from showing a similarly fabricated film in the local cinema.[45] A month later, on 18 May, Pavelić signed the so-called Rome Accords, ceding to Italy practically all the Dalmatian ports and islands together with a substantial part of the interior: 350,000 Croatians were surrendered at a stroke to Italian jurisdiction. The Accords practically cut Croatia off from the sea. But Pavelić viewed Bosnia-Herzegovina, not Croatia, as the core land of the NDH. In fact, as early as 27 April 1941 he had ordered that the office of the deputy prime-minister be transferred to Banja Luka, in preparation for turning the latter into the capital city. Zagreb was declared to be only a 'provisional capital city'.[46] The HSP paper, *Hrvatski narod*, thus insisted on 28 May 1941:

> The centre of the Croatian question was and remains Bosnia-Herzegovina. The solution of the Croatian question depends on the question of Bosnia-Herzegovina. It is sufficient to cast a cursory glance at the map to see that Croatia, Slavonia, Dalmatia are just the edges of historical Croatia, whose heart is Bosnia-Herzegovina. We can live like a human body without a given limb, but we cannot live without Bosnia-Herzegovina, because Bosnia-Herzegovina is our body and our heart.[47]

Pavelić and Mussolini had further agreed that the Duke of Spoleto, a cousin of the Italian king, Vittorio Emmanuel III, would be crowned king of Croatia. This event never took place, however, because the duke showed no desire to assume the honour, while Pavelić disliked the prospect of being upstaged by another sovereign. At the end of June 1941, the duke wrote a long letter to his royal cousin, in which he stated that the Ustashe were unpopular among the Croats, most of whom supported the HSS and were, therefore, republican, if not by now Communist, though something might perhaps be done with another government enjoying the support of the HSS and possibly also of the Serbs. He added for good measure that it would be impossible to make Dalmatia Italian, since only a few Italians lived there, while the Croats and their clergy were inspired by the spirit of militant Croat nationalism. All in all, he did not think that he would be much welcomed in Croatia.[48]

The Fascist government subjected its new citizens to even harsher treatment than it had meted out to the Croats and Slovenes of Istria, expelling undesirable elements, carrying out summary executions, burning villages, and opening concentration camps for civilians of all ages.[49] The high-ranking Fascist official Giuseppe Bastianini (whom the Dalmatians quickly renamed Bestianini: *bestia* = beast) was appointed governor of Dalmatia. Italian became the sole official language, and Italian teachers, judges and administrators were imported as 'pioneers of Italian civilisation'. City streets acquired Italian names (Strossmayer Promenade in Split thus become Italo Balbo Promenade, after the Fascist militia commander), Croat monuments were destroyed or removed, and there was a plan to import Italian colonists. Bastianini believed that Italy's hold on Dalmatia would be of limited duration unless the existing ethnic character of the area was destroyed, and that Croat–Serb rivalry should be fanned with that aim in mind.[50] The prefect of the Split district, Paolo Zerbino, who had taken part in the Fascist march on Rome, insisted that Italy 'did not annex, but merely regained Dalmatia, which has always been our land. At the time of the Roman empire, forward deployed Roman legions were stationed on the Dinaric Alps, whence the paths of our advance led deep into Pannonia.'[51] Dalmatians made a distinction, however, between the blackshirts – the Fascist component of the Italian army – and ordinary Italian soldiers, whom they perceived as victims like themselves and who 'sold their rice rations and ate our plants, in order to be able to send a few lire to their impoverished families'. When they captured Italian soldiers, the Croatian Partisans – the emerging Communist-led resistance – would as a rule release ordinary soldiers, who tended to be against the war and Mussolini, and kill the blackshirts.

Pavelić justified the territorial sacrifices as a political necessity,[52] but his signing of the Rome Accords was a blow from which his regime would never recover. Dalmatia became an early bastion of Partisan resistance, Split a major battlefield, where Communist bombs and assassinations directed against the invaders were answered by mass arrests of civilians. The surrender of the Adriatic coast was badly received by most Croatians, by the Catholic clergy, and even by locally born Ustashe. Stjepan Bogat, who worked in the ministry of foreign affairs, wrote in his diary on the day the Rome Accords were signed:

> The German radio reports that our leader and ministers are visiting Rome, and that an Italian prince has been proclaimed king of Croatia. Also that an agreement has been signed [by] which we have surrendered a large part of Dalmatia, nearly all of our islands, in fact our sovereignty over all of our south. Croatia is now cut off from the sea and has become a vassal state of Italy. [Everyone here] is depressed. A heavy nightmare hangs over the whole city [of Zagreb]. There is much bitterness. I could not help weeping. Have quietly taken off the [Croatian] tricolour from my coat, where I had placed it on 10 April, and will henceforth keep my own counsel.[53]

The disgust was so strong that the Italian envoy to Zagreb, Eugenio Coselschi, advised Rome that Pavelić's whole position had greatly weakened as a result, and urged greater tact in the annexed area. The ephemeral Croatian sabor, its members hand-picked by Pavelić personally, declared at one of its rare meetings that the loss of Dalmatia was unacceptable: 'Dalmatia is Croatia's cradle, we cannot ever surrender it; to forget it would mean to betray our own self, deny our own identity – we would be cursed by all generations to come.' Pavelić, on the other hand, deeply mistrusted Dalmatians: their hostility towards the Italians, to whom he owed his position, greatly irritated him. He blamed their 'Italophobia' for the growth of the Partisan movement there, and carped that Dalmatians were congenital separatists, 'ready to give up Croatia in order to save their own land'. Trumbić, indeed, had 'surrendered all of Croatia to the Serbs in order to save Dalmatia from Italy'.[54]

Being an occupied country, the Independent State of Croatia was not an independent subject at all. Nor did it ever become a state, in the sense of acquiring a government and administration capable of running the country without constant resort to terror. It had been made possible only by, and could survive only under, foreign occupation. Yet it would be wrong to reduce it wholly to its role as an instrument of foreign interests. What motivated Kvaternik and Pavelić in the first place was the conviction that Croatia's liberation from Serbian domination could be achieved only with the help of the enemies of the Versailles order. The policy of passive resistance adopted as the only possible course by the HSS leaders, and which had proved crucial for the relative stability of the inter-war Yugoslav state, had encouraged the belief in Great Britain and France that Croatia's needs and demands could be set aside. These two guardians of the Versailles order in Europe had fallen victim to the illusion that it was the Serbian army that was keeping Yugoslavia together, and that only a Serbian-dominated Yugoslavia was possible.[55] Trumbić, Radić and Maček had sought to establish a Croatian state within Yugoslavia by negotiation and through the ballot box. Kvaternik and Pavelić, by contrast, were resolutely anti-Yugoslav, preferring a unilateral – hence military – solution. Before and during World War I, the Croatian Party of Right had sought to prevent Croatia's slide in the Yugoslav (or, as they saw it, Great Serbian) direction. They wished instead to secure its autonomous existence, within its 'historical borders', in a constitutionally reformed Austria-Hungary; but this had proved impossible, and had continued to be impossible within Yugoslavia. In the 1927 elections the HSP had in fact managed to send just one deputy, Pavelić himself, to the Yugoslav parliament.

Following the introduction of royal dictatorship, Pavelić had left Yugoslavia in order to work for the cause of Croatia's independence abroad, leading him in 1932 to create his Ustasha organisation under Mussolini's protection. In his speech of 21 May 1941 he stated that the Ustasha movement had been born in direct response to King Alexander's suspension of constitutional rule: 'It was then that the Ustasha movement was born. It was obvious to me that we could not fight against those bandits with prayer books, which is why I started a movement with the intention of applying a bitter medicine to a bitter wound.'[56] The aim was to free Croatia (including Bosnia-Herzegovina) from Serbian rule by way of armed insurrection (*ustasha* means insurgent). Pavelić wrote at the time: 'Knife, revolver, machine gun and explosives – these are the bells that will herald the break of dawn, and the resurrection of an independent Croatian state.' And again: 'The Croat revolutionary or Ustasha [must] be hard and merciless, without pity or forgiveness, since his duty is to use iron, fire and blood to shorten the suffering of the Croat people, to break by force the neck of the foreign oppressor, and thereby liberate his homeland.' The Ustasha oath referred to winning and defending state independence, and to obeying Pavelić unconditionally in pursuit of this aim. Nothing came of the insurrectionist plan, since the vast majority of the Croat population continued to follow Maček and his HSS. In 1941, however, the kingdom of Yugoslavia disappeared and there suddenly appeared the possibility of an independent

Croatian state sheltering under the German New Order. Kvaternik and Pavelić seized their chance.

Various forms of collaboration with Nazi Germany in the name of national interest were common in Europe, both before and during the war. At the time of the NDH's creation major European states such as France (in its Vichy incarnation of the *État français*) and the Soviet Union were German allies. Throughout occupied Europe local governments, faced with a choice between resistance and cooperation, opted for some form of collaboration with the invaders. But the proclamation of the NDH was not simply about collaboration – it was also to be the start of an Ustasha 'revolution'. It is possible that in the early days of April 1941 people like Kvaternik did not fully grasp the likely dynamic of Ustasha rule, in combination with the occupation. He knew that the Ustashe and their supporters were few in number; as he stated after the end of the war, he had mustered the courage to proclaim the NDH only after Maček had decided not to resist, because this secured the potential cooperation of the Banovina Croatia officials and the HSS guards.[57] He took this as proof of a lawful transfer of government from the HSS to the HSP. Maček's adoption of passive resistance, however, did not amount to conferring legitimacy upon the Ustasha state. The NDH, unlike Vichy France, was neither legal nor legitimate.[58] And whereas the Italian Fascists and the German Nazis had built a substantial popular and institutional support before taking power, this was not true of the Ustashe. They were neither organisationally nor politically prepared for the power that so suddenly fell into their lap. Nor were the Ustashe able to construct post facto a popular following. As the Wehrmacht representative in Zagreb – and Slavko Kvaternik's old army colleague – General Edmund Glaise von Horstenau noted in his memoirs, the essential difference between the Nazis and the Ustashe lay in the fact that the latter never succeeded in 'ustashising' Croatian society.[59]

Civil war and the Ustasha terror

Unlike Kvaternik with his legitimist inclinations, Pavelić was a revolutionary. He did not view the NDH as Banovina Croatia's legal successor, but as a radical break with the past. His Croatia was to be a completely new state, based on 'revolutionary' Ustasha principles. All power within it would be held by the Ustashe organised on a territorial basis. The idea was that basic Ustasha cells would be established at the level of a village, or in the case of the cities a street; these would combine to form a higher unit embracing a whole municipality; the sum of these would in turn cover an entire county;

and so on. Each unit would have a leader subject to the leader of the next larger unit. This pyramidal hierarchy was to be capped by a central body, the Supreme Ustasha Office (GUS), headed by the Leader invested with absolute authority. Until Pavelić's arrival in Zagreb, however, the Ustashe never had a chance to practise their organisational talents, since they remained a group of some 500, maintained in existence only thanks to Mussolini's interest in them. The most that was achieved at the organisational level prior to their return to Croatia was the acceptance of Pavelić as Leader (enforced, when necessary, by murder of his opponents), and the constitution of GUS – of which Pavelić was in fact the only member.

Despite his long years in Italy and his great admiration for Mussolini, Pavelić never bothered to study fascism, nor did he read more than a dozen pages of Hitler's *Mein Kampf*.[60] Neither did he draw his inspiration from the Croatian political tradition associated with names such as Ante Starčević or Stjepan Radić, both of whom abhorred violent action in pursuit of political aims. Suspicious of all intellectuals, he had kept them out of his Ustasha organisation, and prided himself on being nothing but a pragmatist. It was Serbian political history that fascinated him most: he told his friends that reading the available histories of the Obrenović and Karađorđević dynasties had provided him with 'the best possible political education, far more useful than reading Machiavelli'. He admired Nikola Pašić in particular, whom he described as a 'great Serb man and statesman', indeed a 'model Balkan statesman'.[61] Unlike Pašić, however, Pavelić never led an important party, nor was he interested in any form of state-building: according to his minister for legislation, he harboured an aversion to any plan for turning the NDH into a functioning state.[62] Another 'Balkan statesman' who influenced Pavelić was Ivan Vanča Mihajlov, leader of the Internal Macedonian Revolutionary Organisation (VMRO), who like Pavelić spent many years in exile. The VMRO had indeed supplied the Ustashe with King Alexander's assassin. In May 1941 Mihajlov and his wife sought refuge in Zagreb, where they remained until September 1944. It was Mihajlov, it seems, who suggested to Pavelić the creation of a Croatian Orthodox Church[63] – in which case he only added his voice to that of the German envoy to Zagreb, Siegfried Kasche. Pavelić and Mihajlov were certainly in agreement that Serbia should be isolated by establishing a common border between Croatia and Bulgaria, the former taking the Sandžak of Novi Pazar and the latter Macedonia, on the basis of the argument that Muslims were Croats and Macedonians Bulgarians.[64]

The organisational inexperience of the Ustashe as they turned to the task of building their Ustasha state was compounded by their small numbers. It is estimated that on the eve of Pavelić's own return there were around 2,000 Ustasha members or supporters in Croatia, but despite their noisy campaigns against the Cvetković-Maček agreement, the Serbs, the Communists, the Jews and the HSS, they had failed to create an organisation or leadership. Most of them, moreover, were pro-German. Outside Zagreb they could count on the support only of rare individuals, and in parts of Slavonia on the HSS Village Guards. Maček's call to the population not to resist, combined with an initial hope among the latter that with the NDH the country would be saved from war, compensated at this early stage for Ustasha political and organisational inferiority, providing the NDH initially at least with some semblance of reality. But Maček was also their enemy: his party, though banned at home, was an important component of the Yugoslav government-in-exile. Those who, without owing allegiance to the Ustashe, nevertheless joined them in 1941 in the belief that the NDH would be a self-governing land, albeit of limited sovereignty, were soon disappointed under the impact of German and Italian occupation and the Ustasha terror.

The Ustashe were never able to overcome the essential debility that stemmed from their lack of domestic support. Their first response was to institute widespread repression. The Law on Defence of the State and Nation, introduced two days after Pavelić's arrival in Zagreb, and the system of summary courts created to back it up, made anyone and everyone liable to instant imprisonment and punishment by death. The law, the summary courts, and the concentration camps set up soon afterwards, were used also for the purpose of 'purifying' the nation by removing from it 'alien' national groups – as well as those Croats, Muslims and Serbs who disagreed with, or rebelled outright against, Ustasha rule. Since Pavelić could not count on the loyalty of the officials he had inherited, while the number of those whom he could trust was too small to create a functioning alternative, the existing administrative structure on which the NDH initially relied was soon destroyed.[65] Selected individuals were allocated to different areas according to no particular pattern, and proceeded to run them as their own fiefdoms, often warring with one another. The result was complete administrative chaos, kept under control by an ever greater exercise of violence – which bred ever more resistance. The German military soon realised that the NDH was not so much an asset as a liability.

In the absence of domestic support, Pavelić sought to achieve his revolution by investing his cohorts with untrammelled powers, that is, by making his Ustasha organisation into a state within the state – a trap into

The Zagreb synagogue, built 1867, destroyed 1941

which Mussolini never fell.[66] In his efforts to consolidate and maintain his power, he relied throughout on two institutions: the Ustasha militia, a party army formed outside the regular army (similar to the Fascist blackshirts or the Nazi SS); and the secret state security service or UNS, whose task was to oversee the work of all Ustasha and state bodies, including concentration camps organised on the Nazi model of which the largest and most notorious was that constructed at Jasenovac on the river Sava. Both institutions were from the start dominated by a small number of individuals, recruited mainly from among the émigrés, called *ras* after their Italian Fascist equivalents, or 'colonels' after their rank within the Ustasha organisation. This small and closely knit oligarchy instituted a system of comprehensive terror that did not spare even fellow Ustasha officials. One prominent *ras* was Slavko Kvaternik's son, Eugen 'Dido', a fanatical follower of Pavelić, who had joined him in emigration at the age of twenty-three and to whom he initially entrusted the direction of UNS. Eugen's proclivity for arbitrary cruelty led the Vatican envoy to the Croatian church (the Vatican never recognised the NDH) to describe him as a 'living Nero'.[67] Another *ras* was Vjekoslav 'Maks' Luburić, who ran the concentration camps. An Ustasha official subsequently wrote that the *ras* were 'Croatia's great misfortune';[68] but they were not an accidental product of the regime – they represented its essential nature, just as the Jasenovac concentration camp was 'not an exception, but the system'.[69] Eugen Kvaternik, who was dismissed in September 1942, would subsequently argue that the Ustashe had abandoned in the name of the Croatian state idea 'all moral, religious, legal and political norms and by, turning Pavelić into an idol, had reduced their "fighting revolutionary spirit" to the level of a Balkan barbarism.'[70]

Turning Serbs into Croats

According to the German ministry of foreign affairs, at the time of its creation the NDH had 6,285,000 inhabitants, of whom 52.5 per cent were Croats, 30.6 per cent Serbs, 11.1 per cent Muslims, 2.4 per cent Germans, 1.2 per cent Hungarians, 1 per cent Czechs and Slovaks, 0.6 per cent Jews, and 0.5 per cent Slovenes. In Pavelić's original conception, however, the Ustasha state was to be based on 'the consistent application of the nationality principle': only those of 'the Croat blood and descent' would enjoy political rights.[71] Once in power the Ustashe defined the Croats (a concept that included also Muslims and at times also native Serbs) as an Aryan race. Following the model supplied by Nazi legislation, two laws were introduced on 30 April 1941 which excluded Jews and Roma from the Croatian nation, with a view to their final removal from it – though an exception was made for those Jews who had in the past 'rendered service' to it. By the end of the war most of the NDH's 36,000 Jews and a similar number of Roma would be either deported or killed in local concentration camps.[72] Their extermination took place in all parts of Europe that were occupied by, or came under the direct influence of, the Nazis, and the NDH was no exception. This does not alter the fact that the destruction of the Jewish part of the Croatian nation was deemed to be a price worth paying for German support. Slavko Kvaternik thus told Bishop Janko Šimrak, who protested against the racial laws in the name of the Croatian Catholic hierarchy: 'There is little I can do, since this is a concession we must make to the Germans: their demand must be unconditionally obeyed and fully implemented.'[73] Their determination to please Hitler apart, the contribution of the Ustashe to the Holocaust seems to have been largely motivated by the desire to get hold of Jewish money and property.

By contrast, the policy they adopted towards the Serbs sprang from state-political considerations. By allying themselves with the destroyers of the Versailles order, the Ustashe had achieved their primary aim of acquiring what they called an independent Croatian state within its historical borders. The next step was to ensure permanence. Success in this direction, they believed, necessitated weakening beyond repair that element which in their view had been traditionally responsible for imprisoning Croatia within the Serbian orbit: the Serb population in the NDH. In the course of April and May 1941 the Cyrillic script was banned, Serb confessional schools were closed, and the movement of Serbs was restricted. Additional measures followed, such as the outlawing of the Serb Orthodox Church, the dismissal of ethnic Serb officials, and the sequestration of Serb property. Many Orthodox churches and monasteries were destroyed and the clergy decimated. In April 1942 Pavelić proclaimed the establishment of a Croatian Orthodox Church, with a constitution that hardly differed from that of the Serb Orthodox Church.

It is a moot point whether Pavelić intended from the start to exterminate a large part of the NDH Serbs, or whether the grafting of the Ustasha regime onto a varied and hostile population in the context of war and occupation created of itself a dynamic leading inexorably to genocide.[74] What was clear, however, was that Serbs would be allowed to live in the Ustasha state only if they ceased to be Serbs and became Croats; and that extreme measures would be taken to crush their resistance to this enforced denationalisation. And there was another consideration, too. According to Eugen Kvaternik, Pavelić's anti-Serb policy was a safety valve, which he used in order to channel the bellicosity of Croat youth, which otherwise would have revolted against his Italophile policy, his Italian protectors, and even himself. To identify a particular national group as enemies of the state was no Ustasha invention. As European borders shifted (or were expected to shift) during, or in the aftermath of, two world wars, various arguments were deployed in favour of nationally homogeneous states and against national minorities, which had either to assimilate or to leave. Yet the adoption of such a policy on the part of Pavelić's regime towards the Serbs did not automatically entail genocide.

The claim that Serbs were 'eternal' enemies of the Croats was, of course, an evergreen component of the Croatian Party of Right's propaganda. In April 1941, moreover, right-wing nationalists felt that the moment had come to take revenge for two decades of subjection to Belgrade, and were encouraged in this direction by Serb resistance in parts of the NDH to the new set-up.[75] Hundreds of Serb peasants were accordingly massacred in April and May 1941 in parts of the former Military Border. What happened next, however, was the result of a deliberate policy.

It seems that the decision to destroy a substantial part of the Serb population, and to expel or forcibly assimilate the rest, was taken at the end of May 1941, that is, after the NDH had been recognised by Italy and Germany. It also seems that it was triggered by Hitler's decision to deport from areas annexed to the Reich – to Croatia and beyond – a quarter of a million Slovenes, that is, one-third of the total number.[76] At their first meeting on 6 June 1941, Pavelić informed Hitler that the Bosnian Muslims were the 'purest' part of the Croat nation, and that Serbs too were Croats, mistakenly called Serbs only because they were members of the Serb Orthodox Church. However, Hitler told him that it made sense to settle the Catholic Slovenes in Croatia, where they would take the place of the Croatian Serbs, who should be deported to Serbia. These transfers of population were bound to be initially painful, of course, but would bring great dividends in the future. If the Croatian state wished to be cohesive, it should conduct a nationally intolerant policy for half a century, since timidity in such matters brought nothing but problems. This was a lesson that Pavelić took to heart.[77]

At the beginning of June, meetings were held in some forty towns in Croatia and Bosnia-Herzegovina, at which Ustasha leaders declared that peace demanded the removal of Serbs from the land. During June and July 1941 some 30,000 Serb men, women and children were slaughtered in the villages and towns of the former Military Border, in the Ustasha-held Dalmatian hinterland, and in western and northwestern Bosnia. The massacres were accompanied by mass deportations of Serbs to Serbia, whose numbers – swelled by those fleeing the horror – had reached around 180,000 by the end of July 1941.[78] In August 1941 Pavelić stated that the 'Serb question' was on the way to be solved 'in the best possible way', and that it had been agreed with the German authorities to send 250,000 Serbs to Serbia, while the rest would be allowed to remain. The genocide against the Serbs dovetailed with that against the Jews and Roma: by the end of the war 48,500 Serbs, 13,000 Jews, 12,000 Croats and Muslims, and 10,000 Roma, had died in the Jasenovac camp alone. It is estimated that 217,000 NDH

Serbs perished as a result of 'fascist terror', that is, at the hands of the Ustashe or the German and Italian occupying forces (including their collaborators), 93,000 of them in camps, prisons and pits.[79] Seeking to save themselves and their children, about a quarter of a million Serbs converted to Catholicism, Islam or Protestantism in 1941–2.[80]

The regime's control of the media, and the secrecy with which it shrouded the ongoing genocide,[81] meant that the population living outside its epicentres was at first unaware of what was happening, or in any case that the government was behind it. In the summer of 1941 Major Ivan Babić of Slavko Kvaternik's military staff told Hrvoje Mezulić, a member of the HSS:

> 'The Ustashe believe that it is enough to exterminate the Serb clergy, teachers, lawyers, doctors, shopkeepers, locally respected and better off peasants, etc., i.e. mainly the intellectuals and economically strong Serbs. The rest will either flee to Serbia or convert to Catholicism and accept the new situation. It would probably be enough to kill only half a million Serbs and maybe even less.' Astonished by his casual manner, Mezalić retorted: 'This is not only a horrible crime, but also sheer madness. [If] Germany loses the war, then [we] all, whether Ustashe or not, shall pay for it. If Germany wins the war, however, she will not be satisfied with destroying the Serbs, but will deport the remaining Croats and Serbs to somewhere in Russia, so these massacres make no sense, however the war ends.' Babić did not respond immediately. When prompted, he waved his hand and said: 'They do not link the solution of the Serb question with how the war will end.'[82]

That the Ustashe were using the opportunity provided by the war to 'solve the Serb question' come what may was confirmed by Eugen Kvaternik in conversation with Maček's private secretary, Branko Pešelj, at the end of July 1941. Pešelj told Kvaternik that the policy of 'cleansing Croatia of Serbs' would eventually rebound on the Croats, since Britain would probably win the war. Kvaternik answered that he too thought that Britain would win, but by that time there would be no more Serbs in Croatia and whoever won the war would have to accept the fait accompli.[83] These exchanges suggest that the Ustashe did not necessarily count on Germany winning the war, but were simply using the opportunity to achieve a certain outcome: hence the speed and ferocity with which they pursued their anti-Serb campaign.

Since a conscript army could not be used for such a purpose, the

Croatian Home Guard or *domobrani* organised by Slavko Kvaternik remained neglected throughout the war. The first call-up came in fact only after Germany's attack on the Soviet Union and in response to growing internal unrest, and even then only under Italian and German pressure. Pavelić mistrusted and despised the Home Guard, preferring to rely instead on his own militia made up of volunteers, formed in May 1941 and educated in the Ustasha spirit.[84] The HSS Guard was dissolved in that same month and its leaders arrested. A wide ideological gap divided the two wings of the NDH armed forces: the militia commanders considered the Home Guard officers, drawn mainly from the former Austro-Hungarian and Yugoslav military cadre, to be hostile to the Ustasha movement; while the Home Guard commanders despaired of Ustasha crimes, which tainted them too and lowered their troops' morale. As time went by many of the conscripts would defect to the Partisans.

The Ustashe did not plan to kill all Serbs, nor were Serbs as such excluded from their army, militia, administration or sabor.[85] Talking to Hitler in early June 1941, Pavelić, having declared that the NDH Serbs were actually Croats, noted that 'the Serb question' had appeared only 'some sixty years ago', after the demilitarisation of the Military Border.[86] Pavelić's admiration for Nikola Pašić, his appreciation of Serbian history, his belief that NDH Serbs were really Croats, all suggest that his policy towards the Serbs was not inspired by racial hatred of the kind that the Nazis felt for the Jews. The idea that moved Pavelić and his circle was not very different, in fact, from that which inspired the Italian Fascists' policy towards the Croats. The aim was not to exterminate them, but to turn them into Italians. The economic base of their separate existence was consequently destroyed, as were their cultural institutions, including their language. Those who resisted, or who might inspire resistance, were deported, imprisoned or killed. Like the Italian irredentists-turned-Fascists, the Ustashe too believed that 'the right of nationality has precedence over the right of residence, [even] if generation after generation of the intruders could prove their establishment, however undisturbed or unchallenged'.[87] They could not decide, however, whether the Serbs were indeed 'intruders', or simply lapsed Croats who should be made to 'rediscover' their original national identity and faith. This is what Pavelić set out to do. It is a paradox of his national policy that he accepted the 'Italianisation' of hundreds of thousands of ethnic Croats in order to be able to 'Croatise' hundreds of thousands of ethnic Serbs.

The NDH Serbs – and indeed much of the population of Bosnia-Herzegovina – found themselves, in fact, as largely unwilling participants in

Projected Great Serbia, 1941

a struggle for mastery of Bosnia-Herzegovina waged between Ustasha Great Croats and Chetnik Great Serbs. Bosnia-Herzegovina was the ultimate strategic prize that neither Croatian or Serbian political leaders would or could surrender to the other, nor agree on how to divide it. Serb nationalists continued to view the river Drina as 'the spine' of Serb lands, while for Croat nationalists Bosnia was 'the heart' of Croat lands. Pavelić and his inner circle, a terrorist organisation suddenly catapulted to power, saw themselves as the sword that would cut the Gordian knot binding Croatia (with Bosnia-Herzegovina) to Serbia: by forcefully assimilating the Serb population, they would remove for good the basis for any Great Serbia from the soil of what they considered to be Croatia. This historical caesura could be accomplished, however, only by a monolithic nation subject to a single will: that of Pavelić. According to him, 'our internal organisation is and will remain such that the nation, alone and sovereign, will decide its own essential and living needs without recourse to so-called democracy'.

The genocide conducted against the Serbs of Croatia and Bosnia-

Herzegovina was the Ustasha answer to the project of Great Serbia. Protected by the German armies and blinded by their easy 'victory', however, the Ustasha leaders failed to take into account that their action would cause an equally strong reaction, multiplying the number of their enemies on a daily basis. They failed to understand that Croat, Serb and Muslim communities were bound together with a myriad of ties, and that a frontal attack on any one would endanger them all; that the urban class would reject their primitive ideology of blood and soil; and that foreign occupation, which kept them in power, was widely resented.[88] The Ustasha surrender of Dalmatia, anti-Serb policy and collaboration with the Italian and German invaders would help the Communists to forge an increasingly successful armed resistance involving Croats, Serbs and Muslims. The revolution of the Right would be answered by a revolution of the Left. As early as June 1941, Glaise von Horstenau was reporting that the Ustasha militia's 'senseless outrages' had further reduced an already limited popular support for the government: instead of ensuring the peace necessary to the German war effort, the Ustasha style of government was making the NDH increasingly unstable. By the autumn of the same year Glaise doubted that the NDH could survive without German protection, not least because the Home Guard units experienced the war as fratricide.[89] At the end of 1942 Raffaele Casertano, the Italian ambassador to Zagreb, noted that the effective power of the Ustashe had been reduced to Zagreb and a few other large cities, and that the attempt to 'Ustashise' Croatia had failed, the HSS retaining control over the Croat villages.[90] Feeling that its investment in the Ustashe had proved a mistake, the Italian government now approached General Milan Nedić, the German-appointed governor of occupied Serbia, with an offer to divide the NDH between Serbia and Italy.

The Italians were prompted by the increasing conviction that they had lost Dalmatia. In the late winter of 1941/2 a local NDH administrator informed Zagreb that the Partisans were recruiting peasants from the central Dalmatian interior. In the summer of 1942 the Dalmatian governor, Bastianini, acknowledged that the Partisans were present throughout Dalmatia: the red flag planted opposite the Italian coast was for him a sign that Croatia might regain what Italy had taken. Two months later General Mario Roatta of the Italian army confided to the NDH envoy in Rome that he would be 'most glad' to withdraw his army from Dalmatia. In the autumn of 1942 Bastianini admitted that the Partisans were 'absolute masters' of the Dalmatian interior, and were threatening to isolate Zadar and Split. At the end of the year a general of the Home Guard noted the 'amazing mobility, skill and admirable persistence' of the Partisans, due to the Communists' 'steely determination, guided from a single centre': their 'propaganda is flooding the population. Their cells and action groups are found in our schools, the army and even among the Ustasha Youth.'[91] In 1943 Italian intelligence reports praised the Partisans' 'unity of thought and doctrine' and their high morale, which they ascribed to Communist leadership and ability to impose an iron discipline upon the disparate volunteers. By the end of 1943 the Croatian Partisan general staff could count on 100,000 highly motivated soldiers. In 1944 the chief of staff of the Ustasha militia, Tomislav Sertić, wrote that only two 'war religions' were to be found on the territory of the NDH: the Ustashe and the Partisans, who would fight it out to the end. The Partisans were to win this war, because, unlike the Ustashe, they had popular support.

Revolution of the Left: the Socialist Republic of Croatia

The Yugoslav Communist Party (KPJ) was created in 1919, and at once joined the Communist Third International.[92] It saw itself as a party of the working class, identified also as the proletariat, whose interests, according to the socialist tradition, transcended national borders. The party soon discovered, however, that it could not advance or indeed survive without joining the ongoing struggle over the nature and organisation of the Yugoslav state. What was specific to this party, however, was its pursuit of a comprehensive solution to what it called 'the national question'. But since its members and leaders came from different national backgrounds, the inner-party debate on the national question quickly led to a confrontation between different and opposing national traditions, as a result of which the KPJ divided along the same lines as its middle-class or bourgeois opponents. The party did extremely well in the elections of 1920 – winning, for example, 36 per cent of votes in Split, 27 per cent in Osijek and 25 per cent in Zagreb – and sent fifty-nine deputies to the constitutional assembly. However, the party was soon banned and forced to retreat into deep illegality, leading to a vertiginous decline of its membership from over 50,000 to less than 1,000. Many of its leaders emigrated to Austria, where in 1921 they set up an External Committee.

The KPJ initially upheld the idea that Croats, Serbs and Slovenes were one and the same nation, and ascribed Yugoslavia's growing internal conflict to the betrayal of this idea by the Slovene, Croatian and Serbian bourgeoisies, which in fighting for economic influence were also dividing the Yugoslav nation. The defence of national oneness consequently fell to the proletariat, and one of the party's most important tasks was to protect the latter from 'the dangerous infection of nationalism'.[93] This, in its view, could best be accomplished by disbanding the existing regional branches and trade unions based on pre-Yugoslav political divisions in favour of centrally run bodies. The party organisation thus came to mirror the centralist state structure imposed by Belgrade on Yugoslavia.

At the party's first conference held in Vienna in 1922, its leader, Sima Marković, formerly of the Serbian Social Democratic Party, explained the ongoing struggle between 'bourgeois' centralists and federalists as one between Serbian and Croatian financial circles; but such explanations were increasingly challenged, given the mass support enjoyed by the Slovene People's Party, the Croatian Peasant Party and the Yugoslav Muslim Organisation, and popular unrest in other parts of Yugoslavia. In 1922, moreover, the Communist International or Comintern decided that national movements arising from the inequities of the Versailles settlement should be supported, and set up a special commission to study the national question in Yugoslavia. That same year the Russian Communist Party, which dominated the International, adopted at Lenin's insistence and after much internal struggle the position that all nations had an inalienable right to self-determination, leading to the establishment of the Soviet federation (Union of Soviet Socialist Republics or USSR) at the end of the year – although the ruling party itself remained strongly centralised. The KPJ, faced with a similar problem of acting within a multinational state, was greatly influenced by the Russian and Soviet debates, which in turn owed a great deal to the German and Austrian Social Democratic tradition. But the most important influence came from the political battles fought within the country itself.

In 1923 KPJ dissidents offered a new view of the Yugoslav internal conflict: rather than dividing the blame equally, they ascribed it to 'the hegemony of the Serb bourgeoisie and the domination of the Serb nation over all others', and recommended that the party should agitate for the right of the Yugoslav nations to self-determination, including secession. There followed a free and wide-ranging debate in the party press (that is, in the press of its legal form, the Independent Workers' Party of Yugoslavia), the only one of such a nature to be conducted before the party's taking power in 1945. Three basic positions emerged: that the national problem as such did not exist; that it had appeared only in 1920, in consequence of the elections to the constituent assembly; and that it had been a problem from the start. According to the first view, held by a small minority concentrated in Serbia, the conflict in Yugoslavia was economic, not national in nature: the divided bourgeoisie was introducing 'artificial national problems' which the party should contest. If Serbs, Croats and Slovenes were not yet one nation, that nation was now being created. All differences between them, including their state traditions, should be abolished, because they hindered the process of national fusion. The second view, popular among the party's Serb members, was defended by Sima Marković. As the debate proceeded, he was forced to admit that Croats, Slovenes and Serbs did indeed form three different nations; but he argued that from the Marxist point of view this was of no practical consequence, since the 'the historical process' was leading to their 'natural' fusion. The only progressive national policy was one that aided this process.[94]

The third view, that the concept of national oneness was merely an expression of Serbian hegemony, was held by the vast majority of members in Croatia and Slovenia, as well as by a minority in Serbia. According to August Cesarec, a leading Croat Communist theoretician,[95] although the Serbs as a people might be oppressed by their bourgeoisie, they were nevertheless a 'ruling nation' in regard to the others. By contrast, the whole of the Croat nation, regardless of class, felt nationally enslaved. The same was true of the Macedonians, Montenegrins and Slovenes. The Slovene Communist Dragutin Gustinčić added that unless Yugoslavia accepted that it was a multinational nation, it would fall apart like Austria. He pointed out that the Austrian socialist Karl Renner had insisted that separatism was of concern only to intellectuals or bourgeois politicians, but history had proved him wrong.[96] Others pointed to the national oppression in Vojvodina directed against Germans, Hungarians and Romanians, who together formed an overwhelming majority there. The theory of national oneness was now mortally wounded. The debate next concentrated on the character of the Yugoslav state. On this issue the party divided between (mainly Serb) centralists and (mainly non-Serb) federalists. According to Cesarec, the Yugoslav state had not been created from below, 'in consequence of a linear historical evolution', but from above – by agreement reached between the Croatian and Slovene bourgeoisie, on the one hand, and the Serbian bourgeoisie and its 'militarist dynasty' on the other. It was the war that had decided the issue. The Croat national movement against Belgrade, supported by the broad masses, exhibited all the features of a 'national revolution, aiming at the creation of a nation state. A critique of this national revolution can only be a critique of the imbalance between its means and its aims.' The party should support such national movements, because they were historically progressive. Sima Marković argued, on the other hand, that 'from the point of the proletariat' federalism would have no particular justification in a democratically constituted Yugoslavia, and that 'from the working-class point of view' local autonomy was the best solution. His Slovene and Croatian critics responded that local autonomy was not enough to meet their nations' needs: the whole state had to be recast. They called for a federation made up of Bosnia-Herzegovina, Croatia, Macedonia, Montenegro, Serbia, Slovenia and Vojvodina.

Marković and his co-thinkers accepted that the 1921 constitution should be changed, since it was a major factor of Yugoslavia's instability; but as long as the Croats and Slovenes supported Yugoslav state unity, the national question remained essentially a constitutional issue. Marković argued that the organisation of the bourgeois state was for the proletariat a tactical question: everything depended on the particular political constellation. For his critics, however, the revolutionary nature of the KPJ meant that it had to provide answers to all the strategic demands of the epoch, one of which was a solution to the national question. This question could not be solved simply by altering the existing constitution: the oppressed Yugoslav nations had to be freed first, because only free nations were in a position to forge a constitution ensuring national equality for all. Marković viewed Serbia's control of the Yugoslav state, and the economic pillage of the non-Serbian lands, as compensation for its relative economic weakness; once Serbia's economic development came to match that of Slovenia and Croatia, the Serbian bourgeoisie would accept the equality of the Croats and Slovenes with the Serbs. The Istrian-born Croat Communist Ante Ciliga retorted that Serbian imperialist aims had been visible even before 1918; if Serbia had entered Yugoslavia at the same level of development as Croatia and Slovenia, its hegemony would have been even more 'violent, frightening and prolonged'.

The KPJ could not but acknowledge that the bourgeois parties had emerged as national leaders. The SLS, the HSS and the JMO were all socially heterogenous parties, whose main base was the peasantry. The KPJ's federalist wing insisted that the party should seek to win the leadership of the national movements by creating worker-peasant national fronts, and by explaining to the peasantry that their only true allies were the workers and peasants of other Yugoslav nations. Sima Marković, however, denied any revolutionary nature to the Croat, Macedonian or Slovene national movements; in his view the peasantry should be won instead by stressing its agrarian and social needs. His opponents argued that the only way the party could acquire mass support was by advocating the right of self-determination, including secession, for all the Yugoslav nations. By relying on the national movements of the oppressed nations, the KPJ would be able to create a broad front against the Belgrade regime and 'Serb hegemony'.

All those from Slovenia and Croatia who took part in the debate, as well as a small yet vocal minority from Serbia, favoured Yugoslavia's federalisation. This was rejected by Sima Marković and most Serbian Communists: national rights were one thing, the duties of the proletariat another. The most they would accept was a degree of administrative decentralisation. But the admission on their part that Yugoslavia was a multinational state meant very little without simultaneous acknowledgment that national individuality meant also state individuality: that is, that Yugoslavia should be transformed into an association of sovereign states. A logical extension of this line of thought was for the KPJ to abandon its own centralist structure in favour of an association of nationally based Communist parties, but this idea found few takers at this stage. It was agreed, though, that the party's working bodies, such as its executive committee and plenary conferences, should be constituted on a proportional basis, with each 'province' supplying a certain number of representatives. The provinces envisaged were Bosnia-Herzegovina, Croatia, Macedonia, Montenegro, Serbia, Slovenia and Vojvodina.

At its third conference held in January 1924, the party finally, and unanimously, resolved that each of the Yugoslav nations had the right of sovereign decision, including the right to secession and formation of its own state, and that Yugoslavia should be federalised on that basis. Despite interventions from Gustinčić, Ciliga and Cesarec, however, the conference did not accept that Macedonians were a separate nation. The conference resolution stated that Yugoslavia had not been united by the will of its nations, but 'under the dictatorship of the imperialist policies of the Entente and the Serbian ruling class'; and that the Serbian 'militarist clique' was 'one of the main bastions of counter-revolution in the Balkans'.[97] The conference also decided to submit this resolution to a referendum among its members. The resolution was accepted unanimously by all party branches outside Serbia. Of the eighty-four votes cast against it, eighty-one came from Serbia, with Belgrade emerging as the main centre of opposition to the KPJ's new federalist policy. This Serbian opposition argued that the national question was of interest only to the bourgeoisie; that the party's endorsement of the national movements of the non-Serb nations meant abandoning working-class struggle; that federal organisation of the state would only hinder that struggle; and that the resolution in fact 'tolerates provincial chauvinism and does not respond to the proletarian spirit'. Serbian critics of this argument, however, pointed out that Serbs were a numerical minority in Yugoslavia; that it was necessary to meet the views of the other areas, and in any case a nation that oppressed another could not itself be free. Although the Belgrade party organisation did eventually adopt the new resolution, thus allowing the KPJ central committee to declare it official policy, the opposition continued its resistance. The inner-party conflict on the national question was thus reduced to an internal Serbian dispute.[98]

The Comintern's view in the spring of 1923 was that Communist parties in states like Yugoslavia that were rent apart by national conflict should use the national dimension in their struggle against the regime. A year later the Comintern formally agreed with the KPJ majority that the concept of national oneness was 'merely a mask for Great Serb imperialism', and went a step further by declaring that the KPJ should not only recognise in principle the right to national self-determination, but actually work for the separation of Croatia, Macedonia and Slovenia from the rest of Yugoslavia. Another year on, however, it would correct this position: the right to self-determination including secession did not automatically entail the duty to separate, and the Yugoslav nations could also form a federation, if that was their will. The Comintern's policy towards Yugoslavia would henceforth fluctuate in accordance with the interests of Soviet foreign policy. Thus in 1928 the KPJ was obliged to work for an immediate breakup of the Yugoslav state, in favour of the independence of Bosnia, Croatia, Macedonia, Montenegro, Serbia, Slovenia and Vojvodina: these states were all to join a Balkan federation of worker-peasant republics. In 1934–5 the Comintern's policy shifted once again: no longer hostile to the European status quo, Moscow responded to the Nazi threat by emphasising collective security and the politics of popular fronts. The KPJ would henceforth stress Yugoslav unity. The accession of Josip Broz Tito, former secretary of the party's Zagreb branch, to the leadership in 1937 marked a new phase in the evolution of the party's national policy. The KPJ now adopted a two-pronged approach: on the one hand, a concession was made to national aspirations by creating separate Communist parties for individual national regions; on the other, these separate parties were kept under firm control by the all-Yugoslav centre. Croatian and Slovene Communist parties were formed in 1937, ones for Macedonia and Vojvodina in 1943, the rest in the 1946–8 period. Yugoslavia was to be a loose federation of Bosnia, Croatia, Macedonia, Montenegro, Serbia, Slovenia and Vojvodina – while Kosovo too would enjoy a special status. Their national parliaments would decide in a democratic manner how to organise their mutual relationship within the common Yugoslav state.

By 1930 the KPJ had practically ceased to exist as an organised body outside Zagreb, which would remain its main stronghold until the beginning of the Second World War. On the eve of the war, Croatia had more KPJ members than any other Yugoslav land, and Zagreb more than any other Yugoslav city. The KPJ's Croat nature in the 1930s is indicated by the fact that half the 1,119 Yugoslav volunteers who (according to Spanish sources) fought in the Spanish civil war were Croats. It was in Zagreb that the KPJ and its youth organisation SKOJ held their last conferences before the war, and where on 10 April 1941 – the day that Slavko Kvaternik proclaimed the NDH – it decided to organise an armed Partisan resistance against the Axis occupation of Yugoslavia. Although the leadership removed itself to Belgrade in the following month, Zagreb remained the party's organisational hub; the home of its printing press and the radio station that linked it to Moscow; the centre of communication with the Slovene Communist Party, the Serbian Provincial Committee and non-Yugoslav Communist parties; and, last but not least, the base for Soviet intelligence gathering in the region.[99] One-quarter of Zagreb's population would eventually join the Communist-led resistance, of whom around 5,000 died in combat.

In September 1941 the Croatian Communist Party (KPH) issued an appeal to the NDH Home Guards that denounced the Ustashe as 'traitors to the homeland', and adjured the 'freedom-loving Croat nation that had for centuries struggled against its oppressors' to 'expel the Fascist occupiers and the hateful government of the traitor Pavelić', so that 'Dalmatia, the Littoral and Međimurje be returned to Croatia', promising that 'from the ruins of the tyranny of the occupiers and the Frankists [that is, the Ustashe] there will rise an independent and free Croatia.'[100] Yugoslavia was mentioned only in the context of 'fraternal solidarity of all the nations of Yugoslavia', reflecting a more general policy on the part of the KPJ, which during the first two years of the war barely mentioned Yugoslavia in its public proclamations.

In Serbia, meanwhile, Tito's attempt in 1941 to form a 'popular front' with the Yugoslav army colonel Draža Mihailović and the Chetniks he led failed. Like the Ustashe, the Chetniks too would take the opportunity provided by the war to decimate or remove Croats and Muslims from what they considered to be 'Serb lands', in order to create a Great Serbia within a Yugoslav shell. In late 1941 the Yugoslav government-in-exile appointed Mihailović war minister, promoted him to the rank of brigadier-general, and named his Chetnik units the Homeland Army, not because they were fighting the Axis, but because they were fighting the Partisans – who, ejected from Serbia, were forced to retreat to eastern Bosnia, and thence in mid-1942 to northwestern Bosnia. Mihailović for his part decided to await the Allies' victory, and in the meantime revenge himself on the Croats and Muslims.[101] Much to Moscow's displeasure, the KPJ now ditched the popular front policy and opted for revolution. It appealed to the oppressed nations for their support, arguing that any return of the old regime would also be a return to national oppression: 'Versailles Yugoslavia oppressed Croats, Slovenes and Montenegrins', and 'enslaved and exposed to extermination Macedonians and Albanians'. Writing in the party's paper, *Proleter*, in 1942, Tito declared that 'the current national liberation struggle and the national question in Yugoslavia are inseparably connected'. Each one of the Yugoslav nations had the right to self-determination, including secession, but they could win it only 'gun in hand, through struggle': the national question could be solved only by the people solving it themselves. He also warned that the party would fight 'any misuse of this right by the enemies of the people'. The KPJ counterposed a federal Yugoslavia to the Ustasha NDH and the Great Serbia sought by the Chetniks; 'brotherhood and unity' of the Yugoslav nations to the genocidal policies of both; and an unswerving 'liberation struggle' to their policy of collaboration with the Axis occupiers.

The Croatian Partisan Army of National Liberation

The Partisan National Liberation Army of Yugoslavia (NOVJ), formed between the middle of 1942 and the end of the war when it was renamed the Yugoslav Army (JA), was territorially based from the start, with supranational units within it having no more than a symbolic presence. The Croatian anti-Fascist resistance was consequently a home-grown force, organised and led by the KPH, albeit acting as an integral part of the KPJ. Local circumstances, but also the skill and determination of the Croatian Communist leadership, ensured that Croatia would supply more troops to the Partisan war effort than any other Yugoslav land. Croatia took the lead in the organisation of Yugoslav Partisan forces in July 1942, a lead that it would maintain until the end of 1944, during which time a new brigade was formed every two weeks on average, beginning in Serb areas of the former Ban's Border (1942) and Dalmatia (1943). By the end of 1944 an organised Partisan army was present throughout Croatia – a unique case in the former Yugoslavia. Croatian Serbs formed a majority of the Croatian Partisan army until 1943, but its political and military leaders were largely Croat. As the war progressed, moreover, so did the Croat popular intake. At the end of

1942, eighteen out of thirty-seven Yugoslav Partisan brigades were Croatian; of these eighteen, twelve had a Serb and six a Croat majority. At the end of 1943, when the Partisan army (not counting 'people's defence' units, and a foreign nationals' brigade composed mainly of Italians) had grown to ninety-six brigades, thirty-eight were Croatian, of which twenty had a Croat majority, seventeen a Serb majority, and one a Czech majority. By early May 1944, Croatian Croats, who formed 16 per cent of the Yugoslav population, supplied 22 per cent of the Yugoslav Partisan soldiers. Half of the NOVJ elite 'proletarian' brigades came from Croatia, which also supplied, of course, the incipient Yugoslav Partisan navy.

The extent of Croatia's contribution to the Partisan war effort is shown in the following table:

NOVJ Infantry Divisions and length of war activity[102]

Federal Unit	Period				Days of activity
	End of 1942	End of 1943	End of 1944	End of 1945	
B-H	2	7	10	10	6,204
Croatia	4	11	16	15	9,892
Kosovo	0	0	0	1	98
Macedonia	0	0	5	5	1,329
Montenegro	1	1	2	2	1,345
Serbia	0	0	8	7	2,445
Slovenia	0	5	5	4	3,714
Vojvodina	0	1	3	1	1,298
Extra-territorial	2	2	2	2	1,832
% Croatia	44.4%	40.7%	31.3%	30.6%	35.1%

The fact that the Croats participated in large numbers in the resistance did not prevent the Ustashe from claiming that the Partisans were a 'Serbo-Communist' force. At the same time, the multinational character of the Partisan army was used by the Chetniks as proof of its 'anti-Serb' character. The truth is that the Croatian Partisans, irrespective of their national identity, fought throughout the war as a single People's Liberation Army of Croatia (NOVH), under the command of the Croatian general staff and the political leadership of the KPH, against the Ustashe, the Chetniks, the Germans and the Italians.[103] The Partisan movement grew so fast during 1942 that as early as January 1943 General Giuseppe Pieche, head of Italian military intelligence in Croatia, reported that it had acquired 'the proportions and character of a Croat national movement', and that the Partisans were on the point of liberating Croatia. Casertano told Mussolini a month later that 'the experiment with the creation of the Independent State of Croatia has failed'.[104] In the summer of 1942, the Croatian and Bosnian Partisans were in control of a liberated territory larger in size than Belgium. National Liberation Committees (NOOs) were established in every part of this territory to support the Partisan war effort and organise everyday life in the conditions of war. In late November 1942 it was possible to convene in Bihać, in northwestern Bosnia, the first Anti-Fascist Council of the National Liberation of Yugoslavia (AVNOJ), as the kernel of the post-war Communist government. The KPJ's plan to counterpose AVNOJ to the Yugoslav government-in-exile, however, was vetoed by Stalin, who wished to avoid a breach with the Allies. This did not prevent the KPJ from initiating a series of steps leading to the formation of a unified 'anti-Fascist' authority for Croatia. After considerable preparations, punctuated by military reverses, in June 1943, on the eve of the Allied landing in Sicily, the KPH/KPJ formally established a new government for Croatia: the Anti-Fascist Council of National Liberation of Croatia (ZAVNOH), marking the birth of the future People's (later Socialist) Republic of Croatia.[105] Mussolini was deposed in July 1943, and in the following month the Italian army announced its withdrawal from the NDH (though not from Dalmatia). Following Italy's capitulation in early September 1943, a race was joined between Partisans, Germans and Chetniks to take over the positions previously held by the Italians, and to capture their weapons. In Split and elsewhere, the national liberation committees took over the local government. The Dalmatians, in particular, disarmed 35,000 Italian soldiers, many of whom joined the Partisans: altogether 40,000 Italians joined the Yugoslav resistance, half of whom died in battle, some during the liberation of Belgrade.

Italy's surrender led Pavelić to proclaim the Rome agreements null and void; but all that happened was that the German army occupied much of Dalmatia – albeit not for long. Within months all Dalmatia was in Partisan hands. The great speed of the Partisan advance shocked the Ustashe. Bogat noted in his diary in mid-September that 'the coast is flying the Croatian flag, albeit now with a red star'.[106] The Home Guard started to fall apart. The commander of its Varaždin artillery unit dismissed his soldiers with the words: 'I absolve you of your oath. Long live Stalin! Let's join the Partisans.'[107] At its second session held in October 1943 ZAVNOH – which now included thirty-four members from the Croatian Peasant Party and the Serb Independent Party – proclaimed the incorporation to Croatia of all Istria and the entire Littoral previously held by Italy. On 29 November 1943 the second session of AVNOJ was convened at Jajce in Bosnia; a new federal Yugoslavia was formally proclaimed, within which Bosnia-Herzegovina would form a separate republic.

The Communists were now determined to challenge in a 'state-legal form' the royal government-in-exile, and to 'prevent plots by the great powers [that is, the Allies] against the national liberation struggle of the Yugoslav peoples'.[108] The government-in-exile was divested of all legitimacy, and the king banned from returning until after the war, when the people would decide the form of the state. Field Marshal von Weichs, German supreme commander for the South East, reported at this time: 'the Partisan commander Tito has created within the NDH a Soviet state enjoying a solid civilian administration. [There] exists no state authority outside Zagreb. One cannot rely any longer on the NDH forces.'[109] By the end of the year Tito's army had grown to 300,000 men and women. This large and growing armed force was to be the Yugoslav Communists' main negotiating card. At the Allied conference in Teheran, held in late November 1943, it was agreed to restore Yugoslavia to its pre-war borders (with a border correction against Italy). The relative weakness of the Partisan presence in Serbia at this point in time made the KPJ leaders fear that the Allies might use Serbia to impose their own settlement on Yugoslavia, leading to the return of the old regime. But this proved impossible.

On 1 June 1944 the Yugoslav king, acting under tremendous pressure from the British prime minister, Winston Churchill, appointed the ban of Croatia, Ivan Šubašić, prime minister of the government-in-exile, with a mandate to negotiate a settlement with the Communist government. But the Serbian politicians in exile refused to join Šubašić's government, so Šubašić became his own foreign and defence minister. The negotiations, which were held on the Croatian island of Vis in mid-June 1944, involved four Croats: the president of the new Yugoslav government, Marshal Josip Broz Tito; the ban of Croatia and prime minister of the Kingdom of Yugoslavia, Ivan Šubašić; the political commissar of the Croatian Partisan army and Tito's deputy for foreign affairs, Vladimir Bakarić; and the new Yugoslav government's representative in the Allied Control Commission for Italy, Josip Smodlaka. As a result of these talks, in August 1944 the royal government formally recognised AVNOJ and the Partisan army, and called upon all Yugoslavs to join the struggle against the Axis under Tito's leadership. Tito for his part promised Churchill, whom he met in Italy that month, not to impose Communism on Yugoslavia. The king now dismissed Draža Mihailović; but the latter refused to accept the emerging new order, and prepared to defend Serbia from the Partisans. In September 1944, however, following a meeting between Tito and Stalin in Moscow, the Soviet Red Army – aided by Yugoslav and Bulgarian troops – expelled the German army from Serbia and enabled Tito's government to take possession of Belgrade.

The Croatian Communists were now racing towards complete victory, the Ustashe towards complete defeat. In the summer of 1944 Mladen Lorković, the NDH minister of the interior, and Ante Vokić, the NDH minister of the armed forces, seeing that Germany was losing the war, had tried to persuade Pavelić to switch sides. The plan involved Pavelić's resignation and the formation of an HSS government, disarming the German army, and inviting the Western allies to land on the Croatian coast. Pavelić, however, had the two ministers arrested and executed, together with their Ustasha and HSS supporters. Along with other advocates of continued loyalty to Hitler, he counted on the possibility of a war between the Western allies and the Soviet Union, which would allow the Third Reich – and the NDH with it – to survive. In the meantime the Ustasha command prepared to defend Zagreb from the Partisans. In the event of failure to hold on, however, the Ustasha government was to follow the retreating German units to Austria, together with as much of the population as could be persuaded to leave.

At their Yalta conference in February 1945, the Allies agreed that Tito and Šubašić should form a new Yugoslav government by adding to AVNOJ some deputies of the pre-war Yugoslav parliament. The only condition put to Tito was that AVNOJ decisions would be ratified by a constitutional assembly. In March 1945 a provisional government for the new Democratic Federal Yugoslavia was established in Belgrade, and was promptly recognised by Great Britain, the United States and the Soviet Union. Hitler committed suicide on 30 April, and the German army in northern Italy surrendered on 1 May. On 5 May Pavelić suspended all his racial laws, and on the following day he and his innermost circle left for the Austrian border. The Ustasha army, accompanied by assorted Chetnik units and Slovene White Guards but also by tens of thousands of civilians, withdrew to the town of Bleiburg in Austria, where they surrendered to the Allies who turned them over to the new Yugoslav government.[110] A large number of the captives were executed on the spot; the rest were subjected to a macabre exercise in collective public punishment by being forced to undertake a long march through northern

Yugoslavia. Some were killed or succumbed on the way, others died in camps, a proportion survived. It is estimated that up to 55,000 Ustashe, Home Guards and mainly Croat and Bosnian Muslim civilians, up to 10,000 Slovene White Guards and Home Guards, and approximately 2,000 Serb and Montenegrin Chetniks, perished at Bleiburg or in its aftermath.[111] The German minority of around 100,000 practically disappeared from Croatia as a result of the war. Around 90,000 left under pressure (mainly by will of the German occupation authorities, who began the evacuation process before the end of the war), while another 2,000 perished, some in concentration camps set up for them after the war.[112] All in all Croatia lost 452,000 citizens, including 149,000 Serbs (131,000 dead) and 148,000 Croats (106,000 dead).[113]

According to the commander of his personal guard, Pavelić received the news of the British surrender of the Ustasha army to the Partisans with perfect equanimity. After a spell in Argentina, he ended up in Franco's Spain, where he died in 1959. Slavko Kvaternik was handed over to the Yugoslav authorities, and shot. His son Eugen died in Argentina in a car crash in 1962. Pavelić's chief executioner, Max Luburić, was killed by a Yugoslav agent in Spain in 1969. Vladko Maček, who left Zagreb on the same day as Pavelić, ended up in the United States, where he died in 1964. His remains were transferred to the central Zagreb cemetery in 1996.

At its third session held in Belgrade in August 1945, AVNOJ – enlarged by former parliamentary deputies 'untainted by collaboration with the enemy' – proclaimed itself the Provisional National Assembly of the Democratic Federative Republic of Yugoslavia. In January 1946 the newly elected constituent assembly proclaimed the Federative People's Republic of Yugoslavia as a 'community of equal nations who had freely expressed their will to remain united in Yugoslavia'. Croatia became a People's Republic. In 1963 Yugoslavia was renamed the Socialist Federative Republic of Yugoslavia (SFRJ), and Croatia a Socialist Republic.

Winning Istria

The case of Istria was unique in wartime Croatian history, in that it was the only Croatian land in which the KPH was not involved in organising the initial anti-Fascist resistance. Since the Comintern viewed Istria as part of Italy, the organisation of resistance consequently became the responsibility of the Italian Communist Party (PCd'I). By the mid-1920s, however, the PCd'I had been reduced to a few thousand dedicated militants working underground, and in 1926 it was banned, along with other opposition parties. At the start of the Second World War the PCd'I's links with Istria were practically severed. Given the severe repression, the party instructed its branches to go underground and desist from any direct action. Other Istrian urban anti-Fascists, isolated and lacking organisation, were equally condemned to passivity. Secret Croat and Slovene resistance groups had emerged and engaged in assassination, sabotage, diversion and so forth, but rural resistance was weakened by the draft: men from Istria were involved in all Mussolini's foreign adventures, beginning with the war against Ethiopia in 1935.

In the summer of 1941, however, a small number of Istrian members of the KPH began to return from the newly established Independent State of Croatia. They were bitterly disappointed by the fall of a Yugoslavia that they had expected one day to liberate their land. Relying on family connections, they now sought to spread the idea of the need for an armed resistance of the kind organised by the KPH in the mainland, that is, in the form of a National Liberation Movement (NOP). During 1942 they finally acquired the support of the KPH for this project. The development of an Istrian NOP crucially depended, however, on the willingness of older political generations, the former adherents of the National Party and the old Party of Right, to accept Communist leadership. The enforced passivity of the Pcd'I (now renamed PCI) further encouraged these Croat Communists to rely on the support of the Nationals. The Nationals, however, had a poor view of the local Croat Communists, who in the inter-war years had joined the PCd'I and adopted an 'internationalist' position in regard to the national question. Believing that class problems were more important than national ones, the Istrian Communists had failed to challenge the policy of stripping Croats and Slovenes of their schools, languages and names, which is why the PCd'I had never gained support in the Croat countryside. Being an urban party of pronounced secular orientation, it was also hostile to the Catholic Church and generally uninterested in the needs of the Istrian rural and mainly Croat population.

The first meeting between the veterans of an earlier phase of national struggle and the young Communists armed with the KPH's position on the 'national question' took place at the end of 1941. One National leader told later of the joy they felt at hearing the standard Communist slogan of the time: 'Death to Fascism, freedom to the people!': 'I thought that if other Yugoslav Communists were like that too, we could work and fight alongside them.' The Nationals, however, made it clear that they would support the Communists only if the NOP included national aims, and did not limit itself solely to social or class liberation. They stressed the piety of Istrian peasants and the importance of the clergy who sympathised with the people, and recommended that all talk of class struggle, Communism and revolution be avoided. Although many of them, and many Croat clerics too, now joined the NOP, few endorsed Communist ideology.

By the summer of 1942 Croat Communists had established underground National Liberation Committees (NOOs) in a number of places, including Labin, Pula and Pazin. The task of these bodies at this stage was to collect war materiel, medicine, food and so on for the Partisan army on the Croatian mainland, and to aid recruitment for its units. An early attempt to establish a Partisan detachment in Istria failed, but around 2,000 volunteers left Istria during this early period to fight against Italian troops in mainland Croatia. The arrival and spread of the KPH's organisation, however, raised the problem of territorial jurisdiction between the PCI and the KPJ. The Italian Communists believed that the KPH had no right to organise on what they saw as Italian territory. The NOP as conceived by the Croats, with its stress on national liberation, in their view harmed the class struggle in Istria. Not unreasonably, they viewed Croat Communists as nationalists harbouring territorial designs on Istria. The NOP could grow, however, only by endorsing the aim of Croat national liberation. Istrian Communists consequently divided along national lines. Croat Communists saw Istria as part of Croatia, while Italian Communists never questioned its incorporation into Italy. In mid-1942, however, Moscow had accepted that Istria should be part of the sphere of activity also of the KPH/KPJ.[114] The national leadership of the PCI dutifully accepted this decision, but its local Istrian leaders refused to accept the KPH's authority in practice. The quality of cooperation between the Italian and Croat Communists varied, in fact, from place to place. The Pula PCI branch remained passive, the Labin one joined the Croatian NOP.

During 1942 and early 1943, the NOP continued to spread in rural areas. In 1943, as the grip of the Fascist state weakened, the rural population became increasingly active, at times leading to anarchy. Local Croat Communists found themselves unable to control the situation. The much longed-for news that Italy had capitulated, on 8 September 1943, spread like wild fire throughout Istria. There followed a spontaneous all-Istrian anti-Fascist – and in the case of the Croats also national – insurrection. The Croat insurrection was an outburst of accumulated loathing of Fascism and national frustration, rather than a result of the Communists' own work. The local Communist leaders wrote in panic to the KPH's committee for the Croatian Littoral, which had responsibility also for Istria: 'The movement is escaping our control. The masses are joining us in such numbers that we are being drowned. Istria is a large area, [while] our complement of political activists is minimal. We are growing fast, and do not know how much longer we shall be able actively to lead the masses.'[115] During September Istria was flooded with soldiers returning home and trying to avoid capture by the German forces that were taking over their former ally's collapsing positions. The first Partisan detachments were formed with weapons readily surrendered by these soldiers. Rapidly formed military units proceeded to take over police stations and smaller garrisons: Buzet, Pazin, Rovinj, Poreč and Labin were soon liberated from Fascist rule. In the Croat part of Istria, all larger places were soon under Partisan control. According to one eyewitness, Pazin was 'overflowing with Croatian flags which our peasants had pulled out of their chests, where they had been hidden from Fascist raids. [There] were flags with the red star and without it, the right way up or not, but the main thing was that they were Croatian colours.'[116] In the key port of Pula, however, the Fascists surrendered to an emerging Italian civilian administration.

On 11 September 1943, the executive committee of the Slovene Liberation Front in the Slovenian Littoral declared this area's union with Slovenia, and set up its own government there. The Slovene Communists based their decision on natural and historical rights, on Wilson's 14 Points, and on the Atlantic Charter, all of which stressed the right of nations to self-determination and excluded territorial changes without the consent of the local population. Two days later the Istrian regional NOO convened an assembly in Pazin, at which Istria's union with Croatia was announced and a new Istrian government legitimised. The NOO included four Catholic clerics, one of whom was Josip Srebrenić, later to be archbishop of Rijeka. Joakim Rakovac, the NOO president and a leading Istrian Communist, opened the meeting, after which the following proclamation was read out:

> People of Istria! The spirit of Istria has remained unbroken. We refused to become obedient slaves. In these decisive moments our people have displayed a high level of national consciousness. They have proved to one and all that Istria is, and will remain, a Croatian land. [We] shall never again allow others to determine our destiny.
>
> Istrian patriots! Italian garrisons are in our hands. Italian soldiers are fleeing from our soil. For the first time in our history the people are in control. Istria is joining the motherland and declares its unity with our Croatian brothers.

Joakim Rakovac, president of the Istrian National
Council of Liberation, circa 1943

Istrians! Let us hold firmly onto our weapons. Let us stand firm in defence of liberty. We shall not surrender it to anyone. We must remain free men in our land. Let us be disciplined and obey our national authorities, our National Liberation Committees.

Long live Croatian Istria! Long live the heroic National Liberation Army! Long live ZAVNOH! Long live the Red Army! Long live the Allied armies! Death to Fascism – Freedom to the People![117]

The declarations of the Istrian Croat and Slovene NOOs were of the greatest importance, in view of the fact that the Kingdom of Yugoslavia had surrendered the territories in question to Italy in a treaty. Such proclamations were intended to influence the Allies who would decide Istria's future at the end of the war. Local Italians, however, regardless of whether they had joined the NOP or not, found it hard to accept that Istria would no longer be part of Italy, and that they would become a national minority in what they considered to be an Italian land. They consequently rejected the Pazin declaration, on the grounds that Istria had been legally annexed to Italy, and hoped that the Western Allies would help Italy keep these border territories whose populations had proclaimed secession. The PCI for its part treated the Pazin regional government as a 'forcibly imposed Croatian right'. The party had in the meantime joined forces with the Italian Socialist Party and Catholic Action to form their own Italian National Liberation Committee (CLN), which after Italy's surrender called for an armed uprising throughout the country. A number of Patriotic Action Groups (GAPs) appeared as a result, but these did not act in a unified manner, with each party preferring to create its own armed units.

The Pazin declaration was validated by ZAVNOH on 20 September 1943, on the initiative of the Croatian Communist leader, Andrija Hebrang. Ever since its formation on 1 March 1943, the ZAVNOH 'preparatory committee' had stressed the KPH's intention to join Istria to Croatia: guided by 'democratic principles and the right to self-determination', the Croatian NOP was fighting for 'the liberation of all Croatia', including those parts which 'the Italian imperialists had seized after the first [1914–18] imperialist war'. The ZAVNOH government was now able to declare that 'the people of Istria, the Croatian Littoral, Dalmatia and all the Adriatic islands, acting in unison with the Croatian national liberation army, have freed these lands from their Italian oppressors', and to formally to announce their union with Croatia:

1. All agreements, pacts and conventions forged between various Great Serb governments and Italy and leading to the surrender of the Croatian lands of Istria, Rijeka, Zadar, Lošinj, Cres, Lastovo and other Kvarner islands to Italy, are proclaimed null and void.
2. All agreements, pacts and conventions forged between the Croat national traitor Pavelić and the Italian government and leading to the surrender of parts of Gorski Kotar, the Croatian Littoral, Dalmatia and the Dalmatian islands to Italy, are proclaimed null and void.
3. All the above mentioned lands [are] hereby joined to the Croatian motherland, and through it to the new democratic and brotherly community of Yugoslav peoples for which they are fighting.
4. The Italian national minority living in these areas is guaranteed autonomy.
5. This decision is being forwarded to the Allied governments.[118]

The last decision caused confusion in Istria regarding the meaning of the term 'autonomy'. Clarification soon arrived: 'We are speaking about cultural autonomy; it must be clearly stated that there is no question of territorial autonomy.' Cultural autonomy meant Italian-language schools, press, national and cultural institutions, along with proportional representation. Both the Pazin and the ZAVNOH declarations avoided mentioning any possibility of holding a plebiscite to decide Istria's future, out of fear that this would lead to the peninsula's partition. In early October 1943 twelve Istrian representatives joined the second session of the ZAVNOH assembly. In February 1944 the border between Croatia and Slovenia in Istria was drawn up by agreement between their respective governments.

In late September 1943 the provisional National Liberation Council of Istria took further decisions. All Fascist laws against the Croat nationality were repealed; the forcibly altered surnames and names of places, streets and institutions were restored; and the opening of Croat-language schools was announced. The Council also stated: 'The Italians are to have all national rights, such as the right to their language, schools and press, and a free cultural development.' At the same time, those who had settled in Istria after 1918 were to be expelled to Italy – although in order not to penalise ones who had treated Croats well, a special commission was established to examine individual cases. In October 1943, however, the PCI issued a statement asking that the decision on the future of the Slovenian Littoral and Istria should be left until after the end of the war, when it would be submitted to a referendum. In the event, at the end of the war the PCI would join other Italian parties in signing a declaration to the effect that Slovenes and Croats in Istria and the Slovenian Littoral had no right to self-determination that included secession. The KPH, in order to deliver the promised national liberation, accordingly found it necessary to eliminate the PCI from Istria, which meant destroying its network.

The new Croatian government's decisions met, in fact, with popular resistance from local Italians. The Istrian CLNs established after Italy's collapse, largely in response to the spread of the NOOs, now began to mobilise. Their key concern was to prevent any Croatian take-over of the cities of western Istria. Meanwhile NOP leaders became convinced that the CLNs in places like Pula and Rovinj would, in the event of an Allied landing, squeeze out the existing NOOs and seize power. Both sides were aware that sooner or later differences regarding Istria's future would end in open conflict. Links forged between Istrian Italians and Slavs during the

'Long Live Croatian Istria!', 1945

struggle against the common Fascist foe were soon broken. The question of Istria's future would in the end be resolved by armed force.

The final settlement

Tito was convinced that Yugoslavia would not be able gain Istria and the Slovenian Littoral by resort to diplomacy alone, but only through military action: those with their armies on the ground at the end of the war would also decide the future of these lands. Since Italy's crumbling positions had been taken over by the German army, Istria was in fact liberated from German occupation by the Yugoslav 4th Army, in an operation that began in Lika in late March 1945 and which aimed to reach the Isonzo – the old border between Italy and Austria-Hungary – before the Western Allies, regardless of casualties. The 4th Army was made up of seven divisions from Croatia and two from Slovenia; two-thirds of its soldiers and commanders were Croats.[119] Its forward units met with New Zealand troops on the Isonzo on 1 May. By this time the whole of Istria was in Yugoslav hands, with the exception of a few pockets – the most important of which were Pula and Pazin. Both these important cities were taken within the next few days, however, together with Rovinj. The entry of Partisan units into Istrian towns was as a rule followed by systematic repression of the local Italian population, including deportations and imprisonment carried out by the Yugoslav state security service (OZNA), which had arrived from the mainland with a brief to crush all actual or potential resistance to Yugoslav rule in advance of a peace settlement. The period May–June 1945, when the new political and military order was being consolidated, was also a period of great terror.

The war for Istria was effectively won, but that was not the end: it was necessary also to win the peace. Until the entry of Italy into the war on Germany's side, the issue of revision of the Italian-Yugoslav border had not been considered by the victors of the First World War. In 1940, however, when Britain was left to fight on its own in Europe, the Yugoslav government received a hint that after the war Britain would support border revision at Italy's expense. This offer was repeated after the coup of 29 March 1941. A few days after his arrival in London, the head of the Yugoslav royal government, General Simović, told the BBC that his government had asked for 'all territories inhabited by Yugoslavs', and mentioned in this context Istria, Trieste, Gorizia, Rijeka and Zadar. This caused a strong reaction among anti-Fascist Italian politicians in exile. They were reassured by the British foreign minister, Lord Halifax, who warned the Yugoslavs not to brag in public, since there was no promise, merely sympathy for their eventual expectations.[120] It is likely that the British did not mean to go much further than that.

The issue of Istria reasserted itself, however, after Italy's capitulation and the Allied occupation of much of Italy. Britain's position at this stage was that the territory contested by Italy and Yugoslavia should be divided along ethnic lines, which, where necessary, would be established by exchanges of population. In the first instance, however, the whole area was to be occupied by the Allies, and the interested parties excluded from its government until the final settlement. This plan was thwarted, however, by the early emergence of Slovenian and Croatian governmental structures based on the NOOs. Their dense network, rooted in an armed population, excluded any possibility of a solution being simply imposed from outside.

In August 1944 Churchill sent Tito a memorandum regarding Allied plans for the area. The document envisaged the establishment of an Allied military government in the territories that at the start of the war had been under Italian control, a move that implied an automatic suspension of Italian sovereignty over them. The Allied administration was to remain in place until a decision in regard to their future had been negotiated between the interested parties. At their meeting in Naples that year, Churchill tried to convince Tito that it was not possible to decide Istria's future before the end of the war, but that Yugoslavia as a member of the anti-Hitler coalition would be in a position to demand border revisions in its favour at the peace conference. During Tito's talks with the British General Alexander, held in Belgrade in February 1945, it was agreed that the two allied armies would have the right to remain in areas they took before Germany's capitulation – hence the haste of the Yugoslav 4th Army in the last months of the war. In the event the Yugoslavs not only took Istria, but also managed to enter Trieste before the Allies, announcing on 5 May 1945 the incorporation of the city and its district to Yugoslavia as a seventh republic. Faced with the fall of Trieste to Communists, the Americans now demanded the establishment of an Allied presence throughout Italy within its 1939 borders, and rejected the British-Yugoslav agreement on the line of demarcation. President Truman's view was that Yugoslavia's occupation of Trieste would have far-reaching consequences, and that the Allies should gain full control over Trieste and Pula. The Americans also asked Stalin to remain neutral in their showdown with the Yugoslavs.

On 21 May 1945, following the application of considerable military and diplomatic pressure, the Yugoslavs accepted the so-called Morgan demarcation line dividing Istria into two zones, Zone A and Zone B. Zone A included Pula and Trieste, and was governed by the Allied Military Government in Italy. Zone B, involving the rest of Istria, was run by the Yugoslav Military Government (VUJA). In late August 1945, acting in advance of a conference of Allied foreign ministers to be held in London, the Yugoslav government asked for the incorporation to Yugoslavia of the Slovenian Littoral and the Slovene ethnic areas further to the east, Trieste, Istria, Rijeka, Zadar, and the islands of Lastavo and Palagruža. It based this demand on the principle of nationality and the right to self-determination. The Italian government also sprang into action. Its call for a conference that would grant Italy the status of an ally was set aside, however, when the Soviets asked that similar status be granted to the East European states now under their control, which had declared war on Germany before the latter's capitulation. Italian Foreign Minister, Alcide De Gasperi, then asked that the border be drawn along the line proposed by US President Woodrow Wilson at the end of the First World War, but with corrections in Italy's favour. The Yugoslav position at this stage was fairly weak, because the United States supported Italy while Stalin did not wish to weaken the position of the PCI, now a member of the Italian governing coalition.

On 19 September 1945 the Allied ministerial conference agreed to what was close to an ethnic line of division, with Trieste becoming an international port. An International Border Commission was set up to draw the new border. On its arrival in Istria in March 1946, however, the commission was handed by the Istrian NOO a memorandum approved by the Istrian assembly in Pazin. The local clergy submitted a similar memorandum, which included also a map of the relevant dioceses.[121] The border commission issued its report on 23 April 1946. At the third meeting of foreign ministers, four proposals were put forward for division of the so-called Julian Region, of which the Soviet was most favourable and the American least favourable to the Croats and Slovenes. At their fourth meeting, however, the diplomats accepted a French proposal dividing Istria into two parts: the area from Novigrad to the north was added to the Free Territory of Trieste (FTT), while the rest, including Pula, went to Yugoslavia, that is, Croatia. A provisional peace accord between Italy and Yugoslavia was signed on this basis on 10 February 1947. Ten days later the FTT area was subdivided into Zone A (Trieste to Monfalcone) and Zone B (Koper to Novigrad). The predominantly Italian Zone A contained some 63,000 Slovenes, while the predominantly Slav Zone B contained some 30,000 Italians. The British and Americans controlled Zone A and VUJA Zone B.[122]

In 1948 the Italian negotiating position greatly improved, with the Christian Democrats winning elections and Italy accepting the Marshall Plan. In 1949 Italy also joined NATO and the Council of Europe. The Yugoslav position, on the other hand, worsened due to the conflict with Stalin. However, Yugoslavia's break with the Soviet Union and the PCI's decision to side with Stalin led to a shift in Western policy. In 1951 the Allies invited Italy and Yugoslavia to negotiate a final settlement, but the two countries were unable to arrive at an agreement. In May 1952 VUJA relinquished Buje to the Croatian government and Koper to its Slovenian counterpart; the resultant border between Croatia and Slovenia was formalised on 7 October 1954. The segment of the diocese of Trieste and Koper that had ended up in Yugoslavia was now included into the diocese of Poreč and Pula.

In 1953 an Italian demand for the right to absorb Zone A led to an escalation of tensions, with the two governments massing troops along the border. The situation became even more complex after Yugoslavia in the same year signed a military pact with Turkey and Greece, both NATO members, that envisaged automatic military aid in the event of an attack on Yugoslavia. The Western Allies, wishing to resolve the Trieste crisis peacefully, pressed the two sides to compromise. On 5 October 1954 Italy and Yugoslavia accordingly signed the London Memorandum, whereby Italy gained Zone A of the FTT and Yugoslavia Zone B. National minority rights were to be

Julian Region boundary proposals, 1946

respected. The memorandum was also signed by USA, Britain and France. The Yugoslav assembly soon ratified this accord, but the Italians did not. A final settlement of the Italian-Yugoslav border issue was reached only on 10 November 1975, with the signing of the so-called Osimo Accords.

The Italian exodus

In September 1945 a convention of Italian national liberation committees (CLNs) from Trieste, Gorizia, Pula and Rijeka decided to coordinate their resistance against 'Yugoslav claims to Italian land'. In January 1946 the CLN for Istria, dominated by the Liberal and Socialist parties, issued a proclamation inviting them to form 'a united resistance front against [the] brutal and stubborn invader'. A bitter struggle for Pula followed. In Rijeka, which was now under Croatian control, the resistance was forced to operate illegally. Once it became known that Rijeka and Pula were to remain in Croatia, however, the local CLNs invited the Italian population to leave. Italian emigration from Istria was throughout stimulated by strong official and unofficial propaganda from Italy, which fanned general fear and confusion.

The Italian exodus from Istria occurred in several stages. The first wave of emigration involved local Fascists and collaborators, and started immediately after Mussolini's fall. The second began after the end of the war and lasted up to the signing of the provisional peace accord in February 1947. This wave was made up largely of middle-class elements targeted by the Yugoslav government for ideological and state reasons. The Italians of Pula left in advance of the city's surrender to Yugoslav authority in September 1947. In contrast to the Italians of Rijeka and Dalmatia, whose departure was supervised by OZNA, their exodus took place under Allied protection, which meant that they were able to take with them their movable property. The third wave occurred after the signing of the Peace Accord in 1947, since it now became necessary to choose between Italian and Yugoslav citizenship – in effect, between leaving and staying. Most people left by opting for Italian citizenship. Although these emigrants were by and large ethnic Italians, a significant number of Croats also left, motivated mainly by economic considerations, and in reaction to the new government's enforced collectivisation of farms, the nationalisation or confiscation of 'bourgeois' property, and the general economic hardship affecting Istria at the end of the war. Many others who left, however, were driven by a general fear of what the future might bring. The emigrants, or *esuli*, came from all social layers: landowners, peasants, workers, fishermen, former officials, shopkeepers, craftsmen and the free professions. Istria's loss of this urban population, especially of people involved in trades and small business, caused considerable economic problems, which became acute in 1949. The possibility of replacing these skills with new immigrants was limited at this stage, given the Communists' policy of nationalisation of small enterprises. However, it was long-standing national tensions that provided perhaps the most important cause of the Italian exodus. The behaviour of the new authorities, moreover, was designed to encourage Italians to leave. In May 1945, for example, a rally organised in the overwhelmingly Italian city of Rovinj to celebrate the arrival of Communist rule was addressed only in Croat, leading to a mass protest by the local Italian population.

Estimates of the number of *esuli* vary. The Italian *Associazione degli esuli* insists on 350,000 from Istria, Dalmatia and the Slovenian Littoral; while the Croatian Centre for Historical Research at Rovinj records the names of 201,440 people.[123] One recent estimate suggests that 119,000 native Italian Istrians left Croatia after the war.[124] The Italian emigration was but the last in a sequence of population movements that had started at the end of the First World War. In the period between 1918 (when Italy occupied Istria) and 1943 (when Fascist Italy collapsed), 53,000 Croats left, 29,000 Italians arrived and around 15,000 Croats declared themselves Italian out of fear. After the end of the Second World War, in addition to the departing native Italians, 30,000 Croats left and 23,000 Croats moved in, and (in 1948) around 20,000 frightened Italians declared themselves Croat.[125]

The Italians who remained gained the status of a national minority. The Communist government's formal position was that the Italian national question had been solved, and that the needs of the Italian population would be articulated through a newly established organisation called the Italian Union for Istria and Rijeka. The Istrian provincial government knew, however, that the proclaimed policy was not being implemented, and that the national problem in Istria had deep roots and could not be quickly solved. The rights promised to Italians, especially in the first period after the war, were in fact often disregarded in practice. In the area of Buzet, for example, Italian-language schools were opened only after repeated urging by the Italian Union. Italians were not represented in the government in accordance with their numbers, out of fear that this would hinder the inclusion of all of Istria into Croatia and Yugoslavia. The local government understood these problems, but did not know how to solve them; the Italians viewed all the problems now confronting the Istrian population as being directed against them alone.

After the war, fifty primary and twenty secondary schools were nevertheless opened for Istrian Italians, with teachers mainly coming from Italy and being sent by the PCI. Italian cultural clubs too were established. Croat became the exclusive official language, however, even though Italian remained in use in the towns. Government officials of Italian nationality now had to write in Croat, which they did not know and which they learned unwillingly and with difficulty – just as in the past Istrian Croats had had trouble in learning Italian. Over time, however, cultural interaction and increased intermarriage produced a specific Italo-Croat Istrian idiom, and with it a sense of sharing the same Istrian land. As for the Italians who left for Italy, most of them, especially the younger generation, became integrated; but an older generation has remained emotionally tied to its homeland and – awaiting a future return – has created a virtual world of its own, with elected 'mayors' and 'municipal councils' of the Istrian and Dalmatian cities it left behind.

New and old borders

Following the end of the Second World War Croatia incorporated all the coast and islands ceded to Italy in 1921 and 1941, including Istria, Rijeka and Zadar, as well as Medimurje taken by Hungary in 1941. Its frontiers with Bosnia-Herzegovina and Slovenia followed the pre-1918 outlines. The Bay of Kotor, once part of the Venetian and Austrian Dalmatias, went to Montenegro. The border with Serbia concerned mainly Srijem, to which Vojvodina too laid claim. Vojvodina's own status remained uncertain until April 1945, when it was decided – in spite of its aspirations to republican status – that it should form an autonomous province within the Republic of Serbia. In May 1945 the federal ministry for the constitution and the government of Croatia established a joint border commission to decide the Croatian-Serbian frontier. This body decided that the former Hungarian county of Baranja should be allocated to Croatia, on ethnic and economic grounds – the will of the non-Slav population being disregarded. The ethnic principle was similarly set aside in the case of northwestern Bačka, which despite its sizeable Croat population was left in Vojvodina, in order to safeguard the latter's territorial unity. Srijem, by contrast, was divided largely on ethnic grounds: Vukovar and Ilok were joined to Croatia, Šid and Zemun to Vojvodina.[126]

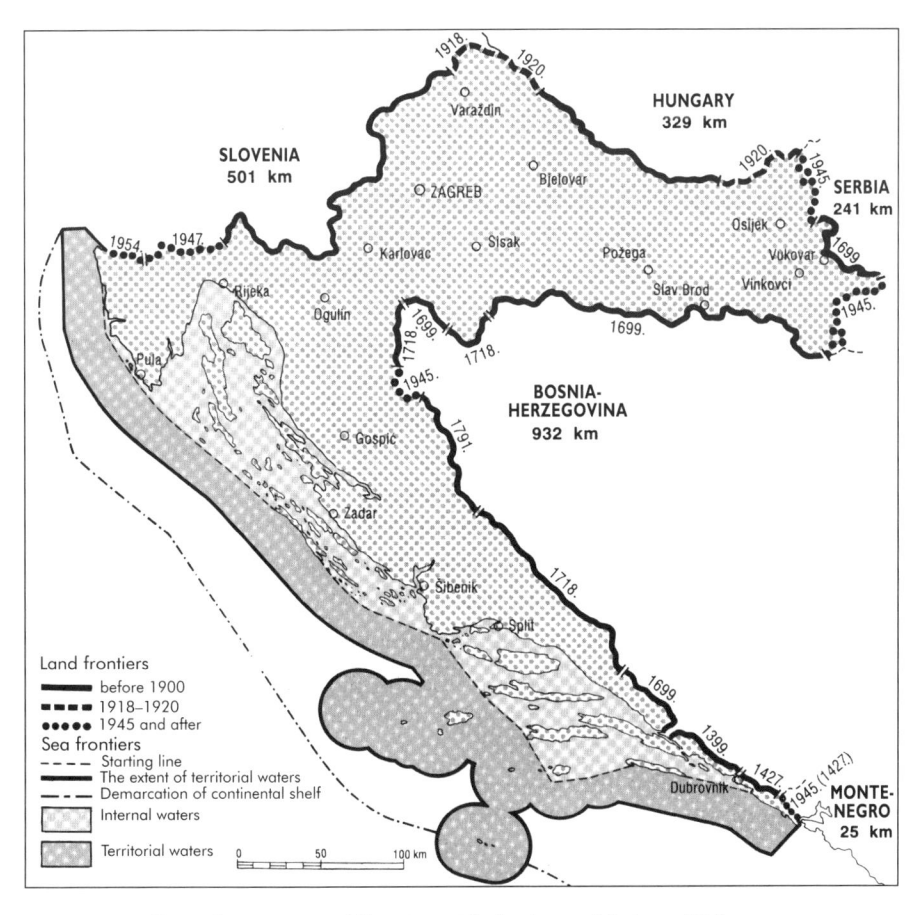

Croatia's international frontiers with the dates of their establishment
and their length in kilometres

SIXTEEN

The Promised Land

The commitment to restore Yugoslavia made the Yugoslav Communists natural partners of the Western Allies. Up to 1943, however, it was not at all certain that Yugoslavia could be reestablished. In late 1941 and early 1942, British Foreign Office staff noted that many of the exiled Yugoslav politicians had in fact given up on Yugoslavia, and were seeking alternative arrangements that would permit the emergence of separate states of Slovenia, Croatia and Serbia. The British and American governments favoured Yugoslavia, however, and in that context keeping the Croats and Serbs together. But having witnessed the speedy collapse of the Yugoslav defences in April 1941, they recognised that Yugoslavia could exist only in a form acceptable to the Croats.[1]

The Western Allies consequently endorsed the idea of Yugoslavia's federalisation, which enjoyed strong support among the exiled SLS, HSS and SDS leaders. However, this was unacceptable to the Serbian politicians who dominated the government-in-exile, and who no longer felt bound by the Cvetković–Maček agreement. By naming Draža Mihailović minister of war and his Chetnik units the Army in the Homeland, they committed themselves instead to the creation of a Great Serbia within or outside Yugoslavia. For all practical purposes, the London-based government in its various permutations became a government of Great Serbia. All efforts to persuade it to adopt a statement of aims that would encourage the Yugoslavs to cooperate at home and abroad failed, in the face of the intransigence of the Serbian parties, the king and the court – and, indeed, most of the overwhelmingly Serb military officers, diplomats and embassy employees. Their anti-Croat propaganda led the Croatian ban, Ivan Šubašić, then living in the United States, to sever all contacts with the London-based government in October 1942. In fact, given its persistent inability to unite the people it nominally represented, the Yugoslav government-in-exile never enjoyed much respect or influence, and as the Allies' interest in developments in Yugoslavia itself grew, it became ever more irrelevant. In late 1942, moreover, it acquired a competitor in the Communist-dominated Anti-Fascist Council of National Liberation of Yugoslavia (AVNOJ).

The British thus found themselves wedded to a government whose behaviour was daily diminishing the chances of Yugoslavia ever being put together again. To make matters worse, they soon learnt that Mihailović and his forces were collaborating with the enemy against the Partisans, who emerged as the only true resistance. Their long-term interest in preventing a Communist take-over clashed with the short-term need to strengthen those actually fighting the Axis. As the war flared up in North Africa in late 1942, the interest in winning the war prevailed, leading to military aid being extended also to the Partisans, with all the risks this involved for the post-war settlement. The decision to invade Italy, moreover, enhanced the importance of Croatia – in contrast to the situation in late 1918, when the Allied thrust into the Balkans from Salonica had worked to Serbia's advantage. Trumbić's view that the British could not neglect Croatia as long as they remained interested in the Adriatic proved accurate, and the first British mission to the Partisans landed in Croatia in May 1943.

The repeated efforts of the British government to make the Partisans and the Chetniks join forces failed, as was to be expected given their antagonistic political projects. A proposal to divide Yugoslavia into two operational zones, the western and the eastern under respectively Tito's and Mihailović's commands, was rejected in the Foreign Office, since this might lead to the establishment of Communist governments in Slovenia and Croatia. Mihailović now became not only a military, but also a political liability. By the end of 1943, when it became clear that the Communists would rule Yugoslavia after the war, Churchill decided to ditch Mihailović altogether and seek an accommodation with Tito and the Partisans, based on their recognition of the king and cooperation with the government-in-exile. For this strategy to work, however, it was necessary to remove the Great Serb grip on the latter, creating one that would be both more inclusive and willing to negotiate with the Partisans. But the king and the Serbian politicians remained adamantly opposed to Mihailović's dismissal, as well as to any cooperation with Tito. The British, on the other hand, could not give up the king, who remained their strongest Yugoslav card. As Communist control of western Yugoslavia became entrenched, Serbia's importance in British eyes increased. London's desire to maintain some influence in post-war Yugoslavia would henceforth take the form of defending Serb 'national interests', including the king's return. Finding a solution to this problem became more urgent with the arrival of a Soviet military mission at Partisan headquarters in February 1944. London and Washington now agreed that the ideal man for the post of prime minister of the government-in-exile was the Croatian ban, Ivan Šubašić, who shared their view of the need to work with Tito with the aim of uniting all Yugoslav resistance forces and creating a joint government. On 1 June 1944, by the will of Churchill and Roosevelt, Šubašić became Yugoslav prime minister – the first and only Croat to hold this post in royalist Yugoslavia. Yugoslavia consequently acquired two governments – AVNOJ and the royal government-in-exile – both headed by Croats.

The king and the Serbian parties, unable to contemplate having a Croat prime minister, refused to work with Šubašić. The king eventually caved in under American pressure, but the Serbian parties continued their boycott, so Šubašić's government came to be composed solely of western Yugoslavs – representatives of the SLS, HSS and SDS. Following his appointment Šubašić travelled to the Croatian island of Vis, to which the whole Partisan hierarchy – the Supreme Staff, the Central Committee of the KPJ, AVNOJ and NKOJ – had withdrawn after a major German offensive against the liberated territory in May 1944. After negotiations – from which the British ambassador was excluded, on the grounds that this was an internal Yugoslav affair – Tito and Šubašić signed an agreement that would provide the basis for the Allies' subsequent recognition of, in effect, Communist rule in Yugoslavia. Churchill and Eden were displeased with its content, feeling that Tito had overpowered their man; they agreed that Tito and Šubašić had shown an extraordinary degree of unity, as well as insufficient concern for 'the Serb point of view', which they ascribed to their common Croat nationality. The British were convinced that Serbia would strongly resist the imposition of Communist rule; in the event, though, the Chetnik forces crumbled in the autumn of 1944, under the combined pressure of the Partisans and the Red Army.[2]

Ever since the collapse of France, Britain had assumed that Yugoslavia, and the Balkans as a whole, were part of its sphere of influence. This was accepted by the United States, even though its own policy often differed from that pursued by London. But the irrepressible growth of Communist power on the ground and the unstoppable advance of the Red Army challenged this British assumption, prompting Churchill to travel to Moscow in early October 1944 in order to negotiate with Stalin a division of spheres of influence in the Balkans. After some haggling it was agreed that

Romania, Hungary and Bulgaria would be included in the Soviet sphere, Greece in the British, while Yugoslavia would be divided equally between them, with Britain having a greater say in western and the Soviet Union in eastern Yugoslavia. Churchill and Stalin agreed in fact to conduct a joint policy towards Yugoslavia, which in the first instance meant endorsing the formation of a government of coalition between the new Communist government and the royalist politicians.

The document announcing the formation of a provisional government for Yugoslavia was signed in Belgrade on 1 November 1944 by Tito and Šubašić. Yugoslavia's federalisation, and the decision of the constitutional assembly on 29 November 1945 to abolish the monarchy, ended all hope of Serbia regaining its erstwhile status. Although the KPJ was the one decisive force in securing Yugoslavia's rebirth, its success was made possible by Allied support for the country's continued existence, as well as by the loyalty which it continued to command among non-Communist Yugoslav federalists – who had created it in the first place, during the previous world war. Unlike the first Yugoslavia, however, this second reincarnation had been built from below, through an armed struggle waged jointly by its component nationalities under the direction of a party which, while pursuing its own revolutionary programme, had made the principle of national equality the foundation stone of the new state. It was this, rather than commitment to a socialist revolution, that enabled the Communist Party to win the war and emerge as the country's unchallengeable leader.

The Yugoslav federation, formed during the Second World War and accepted by the Yugoslav constitutional assembly as part of the overall war settlement, followed the outline of Supilo's old federal concept, with the difference that Macedonia became a republic in its own right, while Vojvodina and Kosovo were constituted as autonomous provinces within the Republic of Serbia. Croatia acquired its contemporary frontiers, which for the most part coincide with its historical borders. It had finally become a unified state, under the name of the People's (later Socialist) Republic of Croatia, with Zagreb as its capital. The republic's proclamation finally laid to rest the old Triune Kingdom of Croatia-Slavonia-Dalmatia: Šubašić, as it turned out, was not only the last prime minister of the Kingdom of Yugoslavia, but also the last ban of Croatia. Traditionally the link between king and parliament, his office could not survive the abolition of the monarchy. Given that the Yugoslav federation was based on the explicit recognition of its nature as a voluntary association, the new republic was a living expression of the Croatian state right. It retained its national anthem, as well as its red-white-blue tricolour forged in the revolutionary year of 1848; but its state emblem shed the old Slavonian and Dalmatian coats of arms, keeping only the red-and-white chequered shield of the old Croatian kingdom – now basking in the Adriatic Sea and carrying a red star. Don Miho Pavlinović would have strongly approved this symbolic affirmation of the primacy of the ancient kingdom.

Partisan Croatia

The new system was rooted in novel institutions. During the war the KPJ established a parallel system of government based on NOOs as the basic forms of 'government by the people'. Their task was to aid the war effort, but also to direct everyday life, including keeping law and order, on the liberated territory (though some NOOs were established also in areas under occupation). By the end of 1942 there were around 1,600 NOOs of various kinds operating in Croatia. These bodies were elected by all over the age of eighteen, though soldiers had the right to vote irrespective of their age. Yugoslav youth had made a crucial contribution to the war effort: up to the autumn of 1943, three-quarters of the Partisans were between the ages of sixteen and twenty-one. Eighty thousand members of the SKOJ (Union of Communist Youth Organisations of Yugoslavia, formed for those under the age of nineteen), died during the war, and nine-tenths of Partisan war heroes registered prior to 1951 were younger than twenty-three.[3] Women, who for the first time gained the same rights as men, fought as soldiers and political leaders and played a crucial role in the running of the NOOs, often as members of the Women's Anti-Fascist Front, within which they gained elementary political skills and literacy. The Partisan state was thus built from below under the authority of the KPH/KPJ, backed by its own military force. The KPH created also the National Liberation Front (NOF), with the aim of uniting 'all anti-Fascist, democratic and patriotic' forces.[4]

During 1942–3 the liberated territory remained largely confined to the Croatian highlands and western Bosnia, a large territory situated in the middle of the NDH where by the end of November 1943 three governments had come to be constituted: Yugoslav (AVNOJ), Croatian (ZAVNOH), and Bosnian (ZAVNOBiH). Within months of ZAVNOH's formation, Partisan Croatia was a functioning state with its own government, administration and army. This was due above all to the efforts of the central committee (CK) of the KPH headed by its secretary, Andrija Hebrang. ZAVNOH included both Croats and Serbs, and was meant to be the expression of their joint will. Although up to the autumn of 1943 the Partisan army was predominantly Serb, Croats from the start dominated the CK and the Partisan administration.

At the start of the war Serbs divided between the Chetniks and the Partisans. The area of Kordun within the former Ban's Border, where ZAVNOH was first formed, had been a SDS bastion, so most of the local peasants joined the Partisans. The Croats, on the other hand, divided between the Ustashe, the Partisans and the HSS. But the HSS leaders who remained in Croatia opted for complete passivity: they waited for Allied victory, in the meantime refusing to cooperate with either the Ustashe or the Partisans. This stance permitted the Ustashe to recruit Croat peasants into their army without meeting any challenge from a party that not so long ago had claimed to be the true national leader. In the eyes of the HSS left wing, Maček's inexplicable policy of total political abstinence amounted to collaboration. One of those who thought so was Božidar Magovac, former editor of several HSS publications. He felt that the Croats should begin an armed struggle against the Ustashe and the foreign invaders, which effectively meant joining the Partisans. He argued that the only way to safeguard the HSS position after the war was for a maximum number of its members and sympathisers to join the Partisan army, thereby diluting its Communist character.[5] Attracted by the KPJ's stress on national liberation and its approach to the national question, the left wing of the HSS soon joined the Partisans, that is, its National Liberation Front (NOF). Over fifty HSS members were present at ZAVNOH's founding conference. The KPH appointed them to the established governmental bodies, but barred all their attempts to form a separate organisation on the liberated territory. Some of the HSS agreed to surrender all claims to political autonomy, on the grounds that war demanded unity within the NOF; but others, including Magovac, tried to retain some political initiative. The KPH was caught in a dilemma. It wished to draw into the Partisan movement as many of the HSS members as possible, in order to broaden its Croat base; yet feared that unless these were firmly controlled they might pose a threat to its political monopoly. The HSS organisation that they established in 1943 within the framework of the NOF, in order to rival Maček's own, was meant to attract the leaderless Croat peasantry to the Partisans, but the KPH also wished to safeguard against any resurgence of the HSS's once powerful position in the Croatian countryside.

For much of the war Croatia was the most important country for the Yugoslav Partisans: in Tito's words, it was 'the central lever' in the Communist struggle for the mastery of Yugoslavia. If Croatia were to desert

Croatian Communist leader Andrija Hebrang on liberated territory, Croatia 1944

the Partisans, the 'Great Serb forces' and their foreign allies would be in a position to prevent Communist victory and Yugoslavia's transformation into the desired federation. The secretary of the Croatian Communist party and member of the Yugoslav Communist party's central leadership or Politbiro, Andrija Hebrang, firmly believed that his country's liberation from Serbian rule could be achieved only through the victory of Communism. Croatia's future lay in the Yugoslav association of free nation states to which the Communists were committed. He told the ZAVNOH founding conference in June 1943 that 'the Croat nation more than ever in its history now has a positive guarantee that it will win its real liberty, its true national independence'.[6] Speaking at the ZAVNOH's second session, he insisted that the body was 'the sole legitimate representative of Croatia': only ZAVNOH could speak in its name and 'make all the relevant decisions regarding Croatia's internal organisation and its relationship with other nations and states'. In May 1944 Hebrang reminded the third session of ZAVNOH, which was now called the sabor, that Yugoslavia had been originally a Croat idea; recalling Supilo, Trumbić and Radić, he insisted that Croatia could protect its state autonomy only within the Yugoslav union. The sabor was also an expression of the will of both Croats and Serbs: one of its main tasks, indeed, was to secure for the Serbs equal rights with the Croats. ZAVNOH was the tangible expression of the promise held out by the new Yugoslavia, as well as the proof that 'we ourselves decide our destiny, not the Great Powers as the fallen prophets [namely, Maček] argue'.

In May 1944 ZAVNOH consequently declared itself – 'on the basis of the sovereign will and right to self-determination of the Croat nation', and in keeping with the decisions of AVNOJ in November 1943 – that it was the only legitimate Croatian state legislature, the supreme organ of state power in Croatia, and the bearer of the sovereignty of the nation state of Croatia. A Declaration on the Basic Rights of Peoples and Citizens adopted at the same time proclaimed the equality of Croats and Serbs, and promised protection of the rights of the national minorities. Croatian citizens were proclaimed equal regardless of race and religion, women equal to men, and all civic rights were guaranteed. The declaration also affirmed the right to private property and private economic initiative, and to free education for all. It also banned all Fascist and pro-Fascist parties. A new Croatian state had been born, whose centralist form mirrored the centralist nature of the party that was shaping it. The Croatian wartime government had fourteen ministries supported by qualified experts, under whose influence the earlier period of improvisation was replaced by a stable and relatively efficient administration. As ZAVNOH consolidated, its Croat nature became more pronounced. Thus, for example, its president, Vladimir Nazor, told the representative of the Yugoslav government's press office attached to ZAVNOH, who was a Serb from Serbia:

> I have invited you to talk about something very important which I as a Croat and president of the Croatian state cannot pass over in silence. You have introduced into your bulletins the language of the Belgrade *čaršija* [market place], and are enforcing it despite the fact that you find yourself on the territory of the Croatian state. This is offensive to us Croats: we reject the language of the Belgrade *čaršija*. While you remain on our territory you are to write in Croat.[7]

The KPH jealously guarded the country's territorial integrity. Hebrang, for example, corrected a political report by Tito in late 1943, which had talked about Italy's surrender having given 'a new impulse to national uprisings in Dalmatia, Slovenia as well as in Croatia', to read 'in Dalmatia and the rest of Croatia'. At the time, in fact, the Dalmatian provincial party committee had few ties with the CK of the KPH, preferring to receive its instructions from the CK of the KPJ. This attitude was due mainly to wartime circumstances, which had led the Dalmatian Partisans to operate under the direct control of the all-Yugoslav Supreme Staff. It derived also from a resurgence of the autonomist ideology inspired by Dalmatia's particular fate under Italian occupation. Its sense of separateness was visible in the local party press, which barely mentioned Croatia, leading Hebrang to complain about Dalmatian 'regionalism' and the local Communists' undue advocacy of 'Yugoslavism'. Italy's capitulation fanned pride among the Dalmatian party leaders at their land's great contribution to the war effort and revolution. When the Yugoslav Partisan leadership removed to Vis in June 1944, the Dalmatian party committee joined them there in defiance of the Croatian party's instructions. In order to bring it to heel, the KPH reduced its status from 'provincial' to 'district', and sent Dušan Brkić – a Serb from northern Dalmatia and one of the organisers of Partisan resistance in Slavonia, who was a member of the executive council of ZAVNOH – to investigate the situation. Brkić reported that the local party felt little loyalty towards the CK KPH and ZAVNOH, and that some of its members were even seeking autonomy for Dalmatia. More generally, he said, they displayed wrong political judgements: thus, for example, they treated the Dalmatian Chetniks as essentially a political rather than a military problem, and did nothing to suppress them.

In August 1944 Ivan Krajačić, head of the Croatian security service, wrote to the CK KPJ: 'The regional committee [has] for some time now been oscillating between you and us. It refuses to recognise our authority and refers to you whenever it does not wish to obey our directives. [We] suggest that you either yourselves grapple with the Dalmatian problem or tell them that they are responsible to us.' Hebrang added: 'You either take over Dalmatia or give it to us.' A month later the Yugoslav party's Politburo replied: 'The party organisation for Dalmatia belongs to the KPH: you are responsible before the CK KPJ for its work. The regional committee is responsible to you for its work, and must coordinate with you.' The Dalmatian party secretary was then ordered to 'eliminate all damaging tendencies towards autonomism and the unsatisfactory attitude to ZAVNOH, which is the central government for Croatia'. Hebrang addressed the Dalmatians sternly: 'We consider your proposal that Dalmatia be declared [an autonomous] province to be incorrect, since there is absolutely no need for it. Those comrades who base their views on the fact that Dalmatia under Austria-Hungary had its own provincial government, so that it should again have one, are on the wrong track. Given that the aim of Austro-Hungarian policy was to destroy the unity of the Croatian nation, it cannot be used to justify Dalmatia becoming a [separate] province.'[8]

As the war drew to a close the two sovereign wills – one Croatian, the other Yugoslav – came into increasing conflict in Croatia. Tito thus condemned ZAVNOH's unilateral proclamation of the incorporation of Istria and other alienated Croatian territories, on the grounds that only AVNOJ was competent to do that; this act was in his view a sign of Croatian 'separatism'. Some of the Politbiro saw the ZAVNOH Declaration on the Rights of Peoples and Citizens as deeply indebted to bourgeois tradition and an illustration of Hebrang's endorsement of bourgeois democracy. The Slovene party leader, Edvard Kardelj, criticised also Hebrang's 'fire against the Dalmatians,' who in his view were displaying a 'more correct attitude to Yugoslavia and the CK KPJ' than Hebrang himself. Tito attacked, unjustifiably as it turned out, ZAVNOH's proposal that Croatia should have its own news agency after the war: 'You are sliding towards separatism.' Tito and Kardelj disagreed also with ZAVNOH's idea that children should be able to receive religious instruction in schools, and that the state should recognise church marriage; there was a tendency in both Croatia and Slovenia at this time to appease the Catholic clergy and to respect religious holidays.

There was also the matter of ZAVNOH's attitude towards the Croatian Serbs. In the eyes of the Croatian party leaders, ZAVNOH represented Croats and Serbs equally. The paper *Srpska riječ* (Serb Word), first published in November 1943 in the Cyrillic script and edited by a member of the SDS, was in their view sufficient to express Serb national individuality. Before the war the SDS had joined the HSS in defence of Croatia's interests in order to save the Yugoslav union, accepting that Croat national aspirations were legitimate and that the Croatian Serbs should seek to solve their own problems within Croatia. The SDS leaders in exile had protested against Great Serb tendencies within the Yugoslav government, which at times cost them cabinet seats, and had joined Šubašić's government in the late spring of 1944. Guided by the conviction that even a Red Yugoslavia was better than none, some of its members, such as Rade Pribićević, had joined the Partisans. Pribićević had become one of the three vice-presidents of ZAVNOH, alongside Andrija Hebrang of the KPH and Franjo Gaži of the HSS.

The Croatian Serbs had suffered disproportionately from the bloody onslaught by the Ustashe in 1941, which led to their armed revolt and to the establishment of a liberated territory in predominantly Serb areas. In 1943, however, as liberated territory spread and multiplied, the original area of Serb insurgency lost its earlier centrality. This, combined with the establishment and consolidation of ZAVNOH, led some local Serb leaders to complain that its structures contained more Croats than Serbs, and to wonder about the Serb fate after the end of the war. They feared, in particular, that Yugoslavia's federalisation would turn the Serbs into a subjugated minority in Croatia. Increasing desertions from the Partisan army followed, accompanied by a growing influence of the Chetniks. Pamphlets appeared attacking ZAVNOH, Croats and Communists. They described ZAVNOH as a device to save the NDH: ZAVNOH's recognition, it was said, would lead to 'obliteration of the Serb name and the completion of Pavelić's plan to exterminate all Serbs'.[9] Some local leaders favoured a return to the pre-war centralist state, others the creation of a Great Serbia. When in early 1944 German troops entered Topusko, ZAVNOH's main seat, some of the local Serb population welcomed them with flowers and gifts. A whole Partisan unit went over to the Germans. The rebellion was eventually suppressed, its leaders – true and alleged – were tried, and some were executed.

The high tide of the Croat influx into the Partisan army in the second half of 1943 thus coincided with an ebbing of Serb enthusiasm for the war. The AVNOJ executive now felt bound to intervene. In September 1943 its president, Ivan Ribar, visited Partisan Croatia and, while commending the excellence of its administration, criticised its leaders for their 'jealous affirmation of ZAVNOH' at the expense of AVNOJ, and for their lack of interest in the internal Serb struggle. In his report to Tito, Ribar recommended the creation of a Serb Club within ZAVNOH: the KPH's most urgent task, in his view, was to win the confidence of the Serbs of Lika, Banija and Kordun (Banija and Kordun being the area of the former Ban's Border). A Serb Club was consequently set up in January 1944, with Rade Pribićević as president and Dušan Brkić as secretary. Hebrang mischievously told Stanko Opačić, one of its members: 'From now on you will behave no longer as a party member, but as a member of the Serb Club, hence also as a Serb, because that is now necessary.'[10] In October 1944 Brkić and the new Croatian party secretary, Vladimir Bakarić, confirmed that Cyrillic script should be used in Serb districts, and in the following months a Serb cultural association, *Prosvjeta* (Education), was established. Purely Serb national assemblies were held in Banija and Kordun.

Yet there was no trace of any anti-Serb policy in the work of ZAVNOH or the KPH. Serbs like Dušan Brkić and Rade Žigić were made members of ZAVNOH at Hebrang's insistence. Throughout the war Hebrang's personal guard was made up of Serbs. In June 1943, again at Hebrang's insistence, the

Cyrillic as well as the Latin script was made obligatory in Croatian schools; and in Serb-majority areas children learnt the Cyrillic script first. Hebrang never missed an opportunity to stress the sacrifices that the Serbs had made for 'their Croatian homeland'. He and many Croat Communists failed to understand, however, that for many Croatian Serbs there was an essential difference between 'Croatian homeland' and 'Croatian state': one was taken for granted, the other treated with suspicion. This suspicion was fanned by people like Moše Pijade of the KPJ's Politburo, who in March 1944 proposed the creation of a Serb autonomous unit within Croatia, giving up on the idea only when it turned out that it was impossible to separate Serbs from Croats, and that such a unit would in any case not be sanctioned by Tito.[11] Such constructions were contrary, of course, to the essential concept of the Yugoslav federation, which was based not on ethnicity, but on historical territories. Hebrang obeyed the Politiburo's decisions, but was intimately against any institutions which, by separating Serbs from Croats, threatened Croatian state unity and sovereignty.

The Yugoslav Politburo now used the Serb rebellion in Kordun as a pretext to remove Hebrang from the crucial post of secretary of the CK KPH. With the Croatian Partisan army now predominantly Croat in composition, the Politburo came to view him as a political leader whose independent national base might pose a threat to its absolute authority. In March 1944 Edvard Kardelj and Vladimir Bakarić accused Hebrang of having become in effect a Croatian dictator. The Croatian party leaders were summoned to appear before the Politburo, which at the time was located in the village of Drvar in western Bosnia. Tito held a long private conversation with Hebrang, after which Hebrang informed the CK KPH that 'our work must be inspired by the spirit of new Yugoslavism so that we can better contribute to the building of the new Yugoslavia, and to the strengthening of national brotherhood and unity within it'.[12] This was not enough, however. Partisan Croatia had grown too strong, and had to be humbled. In September 1944 the Politburo members Kardelj and Milovan Đilas, Hebrang's old ideological enemy, finally persuaded Tito that he should be removed from the post of Croatian party secretary. Kardelj told Tito that although the Partisan administration of Croatia was of the highest order, things in Croatia were bound to get worse, because Hebrang's 'whole mentality and character' led inevitably to Croatia's separation from Yugoslavia. The two Politburo members charged Hebrang with nationalism and 'dislike of Yugoslavia'; with harbouring an 'extraordinary sensitivity in regard to Croatian rights', as well as 'fear that Yugoslav centralism would limit [these] rights'. Đilas accused ZAVNOH

The first Communist government of Croatia, Split 1945. In the front row: Deputy Prime Minister Franjo Gaži of the HSS, Prime Minister Vladimir Bakarić of the KPH, Deputy Prime Minister Rade Pribićević of the SDS

of preferring Croatia to Yugoslavia, and Hebrang of wishing to become, in effect, a new Maček. Kardelj proposed that Hebrang be replaced in his post by Vladimir Bakarić, which Tito accepted.

The decision to remove Hebrang from Croatia coincided, in fact, with the opening of talks between Tito and Šubašić on the island of Vis. On 13 October, the day before the Red Army entered Belgrade, Kardelj and Đilas flew from Bari in Italy to the liberated Croatian territory, where they informed the CK KPH that Hebrang was to be given a post in the new provisional Yugoslav government. Kardelj took the opportunity of this humiliation of Partisan Croatia to warn the Slovene party leadership not to fall into the same temptation as 'Hebrang and the whole of the CK KPH'. He would subsequently state that Hebrang had done nothing wrong, but that he represented a 'nationalist tendency' which had to be 'nipped in the bud'. It was better that he be brought to Belgrade, where his 'ingrained nationalist deviations' could be kept in check. From this time on any affirmation of Croatian state sovereignty would be identified with the Ustashe and their crimes.

Hebrang was appointed federal secretary for trade and industry, and soon afterwards president of the Yugoslav economic council. The consolidation of the Communist government in Croatia was accompanied by widespread terror, which did not abate for three years. Hebrang readily denounced 'the remnants of the Ustashe' who sought Croatia's separation from Yugoslavia, but also 'the remnants of the Great Serb hegemonists' who believed that Croatia had acquired too much freedom. Speaking to the Yugoslav provisional parliament in 1945, he stressed that Croatia had been the centre of opposition to Serbian hegemony in the old Versailles Yugoslavia, and was now one of the strongest bastions of the democratic and federal Yugoslavia. He continued to advocate Croatia's economic interests and defended its territorial integrity; indeed he was responsible for the vital article of the new Yugoslav constitution according to which the borders of republics and autonomous provinces could not be altered without their consent. However, Hebrang proved to be too independent also in his new post. He was arrested in early May 1948, three weeks before the breach between Yugoslavia and the Soviet Union, on the charge of having collaborated with the Ustashe. He was accused of having committed a great number of other crimes, such as delaying the insurrection in 1941, hatred of Serbs, a wrong policy towards the HSS, endorsing capitalism, conducting economic sabotage, leading Yugoslavia to an 'economic dependence on imperialist states', trying to destroy the KPJ, passing false information to the Soviet Union, being soft on the Croatian German minority – and so on. The Croatian state security service ran by Ivan Krajačić found no compromising material against him, however, so he was never formally indicted. Unable to break him, the Serbian state security service murdered him on, or after, 10 June 1949.[13] Andrija Hebrang died a victim of his own party, on behalf of which he had spent twelve years in prison in royalist Yugoslavia and another year as a prisoner of the Ustashe, at the very moment when all that he had fought for was supposedly coming to fruition.[14]

The KPH assumed the government of Croatia at the start of a Red Terror. Some of this was directed by the new authorities; some due to mindless revenge on the part of Partisan units entering 'Ustasha' towns, which the new government was unable to control. But some of it also targeted local guerrillas fighting against the new Communist government.[15] The Catholic Church also became a favoured target of the Red Terror, leading to the execution and imprisonment of hundreds of priests. Tito's attempt to turn the Catholic Church into a national church failed, thanks largely to the resistance put up by Archbishop Alojzije Stepinac, head of the Catholic Church of Croatia and Bosnia-Herzegovina. The Yugoslav Communists' aggressive attitude towards the established churches, it should be said, never reached the fervour of English Protestants, French Jacobins or Russian Bolsheviks.

The fact that Serbs formed 41 per cent of the KPH membership in the middle of 1941 meant that Serbs came to occupy important positions in the new Croatian government and administration. Dušan Brkić became deputy prime minister responsible for production, Rade Žigić minister for industry, Stanko Opačić minister for construction. Brkić and Žigić became members of the Croatian Politburo, Brkić also of the CK KPJ. Some Serb Communists took the opportunity provided by the Communist victory to avenge their people's wartime suffering by declaring everyone who had not joined the Partisan resistance to be Ustasha. Largely peasant in origin and retaining a strong suspicion of Zagreb, and of Croatian culture in general, they promptly joined the war against both, spearheaded by the then head of the federal party's Agitprop, Milovan Đilas, under the banner of struggle against bourgeois culture. A large number of Croat archeologists, writers and painters were variously denounced as 'clerico-Fascists', 'Anglophiles' and such like.[16] Hebrang's fears of separate Serb representation were confirmed by the subsequent evolution of the Serb Club, which behaved increasingly as the sole representative of Croatian Serbs. In 1945 a meeting of Croatian Serbs took place in Split at which it was decided to create an all-Serb assembly for Croatia. The first 'Serb congress' met at the end of October 1945 in Zagreb, and elected a kind of Croatian Serb presidency that included all leading Croatian Serbs. Brkić wished to celebrate the event by decorating the central Zagreb square with huge panels portraying such key moments from Serb national history as the crowning of Tsar Dušan and the Serb migration from Kosovo in the late seventeenth century, although Hebrang managed to persuade him not to proceed. The disappearance of the small Serb middle class had left the Serb Orthodox Church without its primary support, and these Communists now assumed the task of their vanquished bourgeois foe by seeking to rebuild Orthodox churches destroyed during the war and making Orthodox monasteries into Serb national and cultural centres. The founder of the Serb Orthodox Church, St Sava, reappeared as a Serb national icon. This partly organised and partly spontaneous process of restoration of the Croatian Serbs' separate cultural and political existence led also to a revival of the pre-war links with Novi Sad and Belgrade. The Croat part of Croatia resisted this in a manner that was also partly organised and partly spontaneous. Dubrovnik, for example, in 1947 banned the restoration of the Serb singing society *Sloga* (Concord), on the grounds that before the war the society had been the 'bearer of chauvinism in Dubrovnik and the crucible of religious and national hatred'. Its municipal council argued that 'the revival of this society under its old name creates in the broad popular masses the impression that it is pursuing the same cause [as] in the old Yugoslavia'. The Serb quest for institutionalised autonomy was thus quietly but firmly curtailed.

Serb Communists now found themselves in opposition to the Croat majority in the same way that Svetozar Pribićević and his SDS had in the early 1920s. This placed them in an unwinnable situation, since the Communist Party could not govern Croatia by relying on the Serb minority alone. The new government's need for administrators soon filled the KPH with mainly Croat state officials, since only party members were admitted to governmental posts of any importance. By the end of 1945 the proportion of Croat party members had jumped from 56 per cent to 65 per cent, and by the end of 1948 Croats far outnumbered Serbs.[17] Serb party leaders soon divided between those like Žigić, who followed Hebrang in defending Croatia's economic interests against the central government, and those like Brkić and Opačić, who reverted to traditional nationalism. The fear on the part of the Yugoslav leaders of a revival of national conflict in Croatia became acute in 1948, when Yugoslavia's insistence on its independence led to an open breach with the Soviet Union, after which the country found itself completely isolated internationally. Moscow decided to bring Tito down by fanning internal unrest, including national conflicts, and initiating border incidents – all this in the name of the Communist Information Bureau, or Cominform (Informbiro), established in 1947 and composed of Europe's new ruling Communist parties as well as those of Italy and France. An outright invasion appeared imminent in 1949. Stalin's attack encouraged internal criticism of Yugoslav party policy, and opened the possibility of the party breaking up along ideological lines. The Yugoslav leadership headed by Tito managed to retain full control of the KPJ, however, by resorting to widespread arrests of real, potential and imagined supporters of the Informbiro. The fear of external invasion, on the other hand, united the country and rallied the popular masses behind Tito. The USA and Great Britain, having taken the view that Tito's victory or defeat would be also their victory or defeat, now decided to extend substantial economic and military assistance to Yugoslavia. The Yugoslav leadership now severed its last psychological link with the 'socialist camp' by taking its case to the United Nations. Its delegation even condemned the invasion of South Korea by North Korea, and subsequently abstained in the crucial vote permitting the UN General Assembly to authorise the American invasion of North Korea.

Yugoslavia's new, pro-Western orientation was badly received by the three Croatian Serb leaders. Their position was further complicated by the fact that in May 1950 there was an outright rebellion in the Serb areas in central Croatia, directed in the main against the state's policy of forced collectivisation of peasant land, introduced in 1949. In September 1950 they were charged with joining the side of the Informbiro, sabotaging the economy, and generally working 'against our foreign policy, the security of our homeland, and the building of socialism'. The three were summoned to appear before a party commission composed of the Croatian Politburo headed by Bakarić, and assisted by the Serbian party leader, Aleksandar Ranković, and the Slovene party leader, Kardelj, acting in the name of the Yugoslav Politiburo. They were also accused of nationalism: according to Bakarić, their activities amounted to 'the strongest attack on [Croat-Serb] brotherhood since the end of the war'. The transcript of the hearings shows the three Serb leaders harbouring not just views typical of those – Serb or non-Serb – who for various reasons disapproved of the break with the Soviet Union, but also a growing sense of national inferiority. Brkić thus complained that 'the majority of our [Croatian] educational and cultural institutions display a negative attitude towards the Cyrillic script and Serb culture and history'.[18] The three were expelled from the party, arrested, tried, and sentenced to imprisonment in the notorious camp created for the 'Cominformists' on the island of Goli Otok. According to the official report, Rade Žigić committed suicide there on 5 February 1954. Many of the other prisoners were released in 1951, however, after the great fear had abated. The Communist Party's new sense of confidence was demonstrated in 1952 when it decided to change its name to the League of Communists of Yugoslavia (SKJ), professing a desire to give up its 'leading role' and become instead a purely ideological guide.

The Yugoslav road to socialism

The United States initially hoped to use Yugoslavia as an instrument for corrosion of the Soviet camp, following which it would return to the Western fold. This hope soon proved illusory, however, thanks to the nature of the Yugoslav system and Tito's political skill. Yugoslav leaders made it clear that in the event of a Soviet attack on the West they would come to the latter's defence, but they refused to join NATO. Unwilling and unable to join either camp, Communist Yugoslavia increasingly sought support among left-wing parties in the West and post-colonial states in Asia and Africa. Its desire to establish a position of equidistance between the two blocs was visible in its reaction to Stalin's death on 6 March 1953, when Belgrade offered the new Soviet leadership an olive branch: Yugoslavia would make peace with the

Soviet Union, provided Moscow apologised first. But Tito also made it clear that detente with the Soviet Union would not affect Yugoslavia's good relations with the West. Moscow was by now fully aware that it had made a strategic error in 1948. Stalin's death almost coincided with the signing of the Balkan Pact – involving Yugoslavia and NATO members Greece and Turkey – which, coupled with the re-armament of West Germany, threatened the Soviet Union with encirclement. Tito's highly successful official visit to London in the same month further encouraged the new Soviet leadership to seek reconciliation with Yugoslavia, offering it terms that it could not refuse. Given that NATO could not defend the Eastern Mediterranean without Yugoslavia, and emboldened by the normalisation with the East, Tito now reopened the issue of the Free Territory of Trieste. After some hesitation the Western powers finally approved what they declared would be a final settlement, according to which Istria remained in Yugoslavia while Trieste with a narrow hinterland went to Italy. Even though Yugoslavia had in reality had no hope of regaining Trieste, Tito presented this arrangement as a Yugoslav sacrifice to 'international cooperation and world peace'. His skill in promoting his country's interests impressed Western and Eastern capitals alike. During the 1950s, and indeed throughout much of the Cold War period, Yugoslavia under Tito's leadership was perceived as holding a balance of power in Europe, in the sense that its support could significantly reinforce either of the two opposing camps. This position endowed it with a real measure of freedom to pursue its own foreign policy.

In late 1954 Tito began a historic visit to South Asia, whence he returned three months later a changed man. 'Practically overnight he was transformed into a citizen of the world and a world statesman. Socialism for him now came to mean the creation of a just world, in which unity did not imply suppression of differences but their creative integration.'[19] He would subsequently engage his considerable political talents in pursuing this project, disregarding at times his own country's needs and interests. In February 1955, returning from yet another visit to Asia, he disembarked at Rijeka and proceeded to Zagreb by way of Karlovac, giving public speeches at each stop bursting with the impressions gained on his travels and with a new optimism for Yugoslavia's future. Fourteen years had passed since Pavelić had followed the same itinerary, Rijeka-Karlovac-Zagreb. The contrast between the two journeys could not have been greater; they belonged to two different worlds. Pavelić's Croatia was an occupied and fragmented land, Tito's a unified and equal republic, which now – together with the rest of Yugoslavia – was embarking upon a path leading to previously unimaginable vistas. The

Croat president of Yugoslavia told the citizens of Rijeka that his two-month stay in those countries had been 'a kind of a revelation to us, since we found there the same situation that prevails here: people making great efforts to raise themselves from backwardness. [It] is great good fortune that we have succeeded in establishing contact with them, and that we are determined to work together to do all we can to calm the growing passions in the world [because of the Cold War]. This policy, the policy of peace, is worth great sacrifice and merits our unceasing efforts.' He added on his arrival in Zagreb: '[Our journey] has produced wonderful results, we have learnt great lessons that apply to us too. [We] are becoming an industrialised land, and it is clearly of no small interest to us how and to where we can export, with whom we can realise the most profitable exchange of goods.'[20] He was referring to the fact that Yugoslavia's relationship with the West had brought it economic problems that could be solved only through diversification of its economic ties.

For Communist Yugoslavia could not join Western Europe without changing itself, or from anything but a position of inferiority. Africa and Asia, on the other hand, offered potential markets for Yugoslavia's nascent industry, and a world stage for Tito's political ambitions. The result was adoption of the 'third way' policy: 'self-managing socialism' at home, with all that this came to entail; and abroad equidistance from both blocs, based on the equality of all states. Too strong to be reduced to being a buffer state like Austria or Finland, Yugoslavia also rejected for itself the modest role of mediating between the two power blocs. Based in the first instance on bringing together the newly independent states of Asia and Africa, its new international policy came to be known as 'non-alignment'. This meant forging an active international policy guided by the idea of 'peaceful coexistence' of all nations, irrespective of their social systems, with the aim of creating an even distribution of power in the world. Thus in a December 1954 speech to the Indian parliament, Tito identified four main factors of international instability: inequality between states and nations; interference by outside powers in the internal life of others; division of the world into spheres of influence and blocs; and colonialism.

Yugoslavia's independent status was in the end accepted by both superpowers. The United States abandoned its original intention of assimilating it into the West, and concluded that a non-aligned Yugoslavia would in fact better serve its interests, particularly after Truman's policy of containment had been abandoned in favour of 'liberating' Europe from Communism and 'mass retaliation' based on nuclear weapons. Tito,

Nasser, Nehru and Tito, Brijuni 1956

convinced that Stalin's death in 1953 had marked the start of a new era in Eastern Europe, for his part tried to persuade the West that instead of seeking to overthrow Communism it should aid anti-Stalinist currents in the states of Eastern Europe, in order to make them more independent from the Soviet Union. This advice was rejected, but the United States continued to aid Yugoslavia politically, militarily and economically.

The Soviet Union too, having failed to overthrow Tito, no longer harboured a desire to include this combative state into its own bloc, which in May 1955 came to be constituted as a formal military alliance under the name of the Warsaw Pact. Following much internal struggle, a Soviet delegation headed by Communist Party leader Nikita Khrushchev finally arrived in Yugoslavia on 26 May that year – two days after the accreditation of the first Chinese ambassador to Belgrade. Khrushchev read out a letter in which he admitted that the original charges against the Yugoslav leaders had been false, for which he blamed Lavrentij Beria and other recently purged Soviet leaders. On 2 June 1955 Tito and Soviet premier Nikolai Bulganin signed the so-called Belgrade Declaration establishing correct relations between the two states. The *New York Times* described the event as a 'Soviet Canossa', arguing that Yugoslavia had won the contest. The normalisation of relations with the Soviet Union allowed Yugoslavia to begin forging a global policy in which, in addition to the West and the East, the so-called Third World would play an increasingly important role. One month after the departure of the Soviet delegation, Burma's U Nu and India's Nehru came to visit, as Tito had promised the Yugoslavs.

Tito and Kardelj were the chief architects of the policy of equidistance from West and East which secured Yugoslavia's independence and permitted it to follow its own 'road to socialism'. But this policy of non-alignment also imposed a mentality of being under permanent siege, creating the need to maintain a large army: as Tito told US Secretary of State Dean Acheson, Yugoslavia hoped for peace but in the meantime prepared for war. The policy also set ultimate limits to the development of internal democracy, in favour of continued political monopoly of the Communist Party as defender of Yugoslav sovereignty and territorial integrity. Tito typically declared in 1954 that the Yugoslav Communist Party had to retain its 'monolithic unity', because 'we have opponents and enemies on all sides. [Both] East and West are trying to destroy our Communist League, change the direction of our socialist development. The answer lies in a disciplined implementation of decisions reached.'[21] This was intended as an answer to people such as Milovan Đilas, who had suddenly turned into an oppositionist, arguing in effect that the League of Communists should stop being the ruling party. In Tito's view, with political liberalisation of the kind advocated by Đilas the Communist regime would have fallen within a year, with disastrous consequences for Yugoslavia and Europe.

Federating the federation

The struggle against Moscow weakened the party's initial concern with maintaining an internal national balance, in favour of an 'integral Yugoslavism' or unitarism. During the 1950s and early 1960s, the very expression of national individuality came to be viewed as propagation of nationalism. Federal Yugoslavia had by this time in fact become far more centralised than the Yugoslav kingdom had ever been. The Yugoslav Communists had destroyed Serbia's hegemony in order to preserve Yugoslavia, but that hegemony now revived under cover of the ruling party's organisational principle of 'democratic centralism' and policy of 'brotherhood and unity'. Once Belgrade had become the seat of an all-powerful federal party-state apparatus, it made sense for Serbian functionaries to work within it rather than in their own republican bodies, leading to an effective symbiosis between them at the level of personnel. As a result Serbia, which had played a secondary role in the formation of the new state, once again came to view itself as Yugoslavia. National conflicts returned, fuelled by a struggle over the division of state revenue. They grew ever more intense as the country entered a period of rapid industrial growth in the 1950s, when five and a half million peasants left their villages for the towns. Since the republics inevitably lobbied for their own firms and regions, disputes over the allocation of federal investment acquired an inter-republican – hence national – character.

The first post-war five-year plan had set high economic goals while banning foreign investment, so that the main burden fell on the population, for whose well-being republican party leaders inevitably felt responsible. Workers' self-management was introduced in 1953, as an ideologically safe medicine against the inefficiency of the central state's management of the economy and republican self-interest, but without any corresponding decentralisation of economic decision-making. Though a considerable proportion of federal capital was at this stage distributed to local municipalities, the federal government still decided what was to be built, where and how. Most Yugoslav financial capital remained concentrated, moreover, in a limited number of large banks, all of which were located in Belgrade, that is, in Serbia. Belgrade also became the site of several import-export firms enjoying a virtual monopoly of Yugoslav foreign trade. Having become once again the unrivalled locus of economic and political power, Belgrade resumed its old role as a nursery of Great Serb ideology, which Serbian party leader Aleksandar Ranković failed to restrain. This, combined with the fact that the Serb-dominated federal bureaucracy was becoming an arrogant and aloof power in its own right, caused enormous dissatisfaction

> OSTVARUJUĆI VELIKU MARXOVU IDEJU
> "TVORNICE RADNICIMA"
> OVDJE U "PRVOBORCU" OSNOVAN JE
> **PRVI RADNIČKI SAVJET U JUGOSLAVIJI**
> 29 PROSINCA 1949 GODINE

'Realising Marx's great idea – "Factories to the workers!"' Wall plaque at Split cement factory commemorating the establishment of the first workers' council in Yugoslavia, 1949

outside Serbia, especially in Slovenia and Croatia, which now pushed for comprehensive economic and political reform.

The main stimulus in this direction came from an understanding that the over-concentration of authority in Belgrade was leading once again to Serbian domination of Yugoslavia. The first to raise the alarm was the Slovene leader Edvard Kardelj, who wrote in 1957 that centralism – which he firmly identified with Great Serb nationalism – was resuscitating 'the old chauvinistic idea of integral Yugoslavism', namely, the negation of Yugoslavia's national diversity in favour of some 'Yugoslav nation'. This threatened fraternal relations between Yugoslavia's sovereign nations, which could endure only on the basis of their equality and close cooperation in the interest of free national development of each.[22] That Kardelj's concerns were justified was shown by the seventh party congress, held in 1958, at which proposals were voiced for abolition of the federation and for a 'gradual merging of the nationalities'. It was the onset of economic crisis in the early 1960s, however, that brought into the open the simmering conflict between pro- and anti-reform forces, between federalists and centralists, the outcome of which it was widely understood in view of Tito's advanced age – he reached seventy in 1962 – would also decide the issue of the succession. Differences over orientation at the highest levels of party and state had indeed become so fraught by this time that they threatened to tear the country apart, leading Tito to exclaim at a Yugoslav 'summit' held in the spring of 1962 and specially convened to deal with this problem: 'We must ask ourselves whether the [Yugoslav] community is capable of existence.'[23] Despite several attempts to curb the economic power of the federal state, it had grown enormously between 1957 and 1963. Political power, on the other hand, had become concentrated in the hands of Aleksander Ranković, who in 1963 became Yugoslavia's vice-president, the second most powerful man after Tito. As head of the federal party's cadre commission, he was in a position to decide (albeit in consultation with the republics) the composition equally of the federal, republican and provincial parliaments and governments. Ranković, who as federal minister of the interior had founded the state security service UDB, became a symbol not just of a police state, but also of Serbian hegemony. The Croatian secret police registered at this time a growing fear in Croatia of Tito being replaced by Ranković.

The party now divided into two broad blocs. The federalist bloc, strong in Croatia and Slovenia, sought to defeat centralism while Tito was still alive; the centralist bloc, strong in Serbia and in the federal bureaucracy, defended the status quo. The federalist bloc found its advocate in Kardelj, the centralist bloc its defender in Ranković. Bakarić agreed with Kardelj that the rising national tensions in Yugoslavia were a direct consequence of the restrictions imposed on republican sovereignty by the policy of centralism: it was necessary, he stated, to 'federate the federation'. After some hesitation, Tito sided with the reformists. At the party's eighth congress, held in 1964, he praised the third party congress held forty years earlier for its understanding that the relationship between the Yugoslav nations should be governed by the principles of national equality and voluntary association. Kardelj agreed: the party had to acknowledge that national i.e. republican economic independence was not an 'administrative category', but stood for 'the right of every nation to live and develop in accordance with the results of its labour', and that 'no power outside of it should control the fruits of its labour'. Tito responded by demanding that those who 'believe that our socialist development means that one should dispense with nations, that they should disappear' be expelled from the party.[24] This was the first party congress at which party leaders were identified by nationality. The fact that Tito was identified as a Croat rather than a Yugoslav came as a shock to some of those present.[25]

At a meeting of the federal party executive held in 1965, Tito declared himself in favour of ending the monopoly of foreign trade held by Belgrade import-export firms, to the advantage of large industrial firms; also of divesting the large banks of their capital, to the advantage of industry. Kardelj justified this change as necessary for Yugoslavia's survival. He insisted that the Yugoslav Communists were not, nor could they be, a-national: 'We [Communists] here represent our republics. [We] cannot be above our nations, or assert that advocacy of national interest is pure nationalism', because '[if] we separate ourselves from the nations we represent, what sort of political authority are we?' Nation, not class, was the basic political unit – and national sovereignty made sense only if the Yugoslav nations regulated their own economies. National equality meant republican sovereignty. After all, he said, 'we did not unite for the sake of Yugoslavia, but for the sake of socialism'. It was wrong to believe, he continued, that the relationship between the Yugoslav nations was essentially different from that which existed between other nations: 'there is nothing special in our relationship, except that fate has brought us together and [as Slavs] we are ethnically close, but [that] is true also of other nations'. Yugoslavia was held together in fact only by the socialist project. He added that restoration of a unitary state structure posed a 'mortal danger to our country's unity', and recommended that the federal system be changed in a way that would 'guarantee that no one [nation] would be in a position to rule over another'.[26]

Kardelj divided the Yugoslav republics into three blocs according to their attitudes to the concentration of economic power at the centre:

1. Serbia used federal investment funds, and administrative centralism in general, as 'an instrument of pressure on the federation'. This 'tendency' was intertwined with a 'unitarist' and 'Great Serb' ideology, which had become widely accepted in Serbia, because the Serbian leaders chose not to resist it. The relative size of the Serbian republic and the Serb population made Serbia's attitude to the federation of decisive importance, which is why it was necessary to ensure that this 'tendency' did not prevail in Serbia.
2. Bosnia, Macedonia and Montenegro favoured a degree of centralisation, out of fear that decentralisation would translate into loss of economic support. They were wrong, however, since decentralisation would create a more efficient economy and thereby greater resources for stimulating their economic development.
3. Slovenia and Croatia were irrevocably committed to decentralisation: if it were adopted, however, they would have to accept some responsibility for the development of the poorer republics.

He recommended that central allocation of the national revenue should be abolished in favour of the republics, and the role of the federation be reduced to ensuring a single market and to funnelling aid to the under-developed republics and Kosovo. What Kardelj was proposing, in fact, was that

Yugoslavia be transformed into a confederation; and this time Tito agreed with him. The growing power of the central state was not only dangerous in itself, but also threatened his own position. It was necessary to destroy the power of the federal bureaucracy on which the Great Serb revival relied. He now began in the greatest secrecy to plan Ranković's downfall. At a meeting of the federal party leadership held in June 1966 on one of Croatia's Brijuni islands, Tito attacked the UDB, comparing it to the Soviet NKVD, which as he reminded the audience was responsible for 15,000,000 deaths. A commission set up to investigate its functioning reported back that the UDB had become a closed system, outside party and state control; and that it had infiltrated, moreover, the highest state and party bodies. Ranković was accused of bearing the main responsibility for this state of affairs. He was charged with anti-state conspiracy, appeasing 'Serb chauvinism', and seeking to succeed Tito. Whether Ranković ever plotted against Tito remains to be established; but there is little doubt that he was indeed engaged in creating the right conditions for his own smooth take-over after Tito's death, in which event Yugoslavia would have drawn closer to the Soviet Union. He was expelled from the party, but was not put on trial. The fact that Ranković was Moscow's favourite candidate to succeed Tito helps to explain the latter's decision to grant him a pardon, as does his own disciplined acceptance of Tito's decision to remove him. The purge of Ranković, and that of the UDB which followed (50 per cent of the Serbian state security service was dismissed at this time), caused great consternation among the Serbian elite, who viewed them as attacks on Serbia by Croatia and Slovenia. It was left to Serbian Communists to do their best to present Ranković's overthrow as a gain for socialism and Yugoslavia. In fact, Ranković's departure did not stop the UDB from spying on the population and their leaders, but it did allow progress in the implementation of vital economic and political reforms. It also inaugurated a new policy towards the national minorities, and especially towards the long-suffering Albanian population, that would eventually lead to Kosovo and Vojvodina acquiring the status of federal members on a par with the republics.

The other closed system, the army and its counter-intelligence service KOS, was left untouched, despite Slovenian and Serbian demands to the contrary. The army was Tito's only independent basis of power, which he jealously guarded from outside interference. The Croatians supported Tito on this for largely opportunistic reasons, arguing that it would be impossible to purge both security services at the same time. Tito could not remain wholly impervious, however, to calls for reform in this sector too; but he managed to limit it to personnel changes. In order to stress republican autonomy, it was also decided in 1967 that the republican parties would henceforth hold their congresses before rather than after the congress of the federal party. Most important of all was a decision to amend the constitution in a manner that would give more powers to the republics and provinces. The second half of the 1960s was thus a period of potent innovations in the economic and political spheres, driven by the need to prepare the country for Tito's eventual departure. The trouble was that the agreed economic reforms were slow in being implemented, thanks mainly – though not solely – to the continued resistance of the federal bureaucracy and the corporate interests of Belgrade firms.

The Croatian Spring

During the 1950s political calm – or, more accurately, political passivity – reigned in Croatia. The 'class enemy' had been crushed, the Serb Partisan leaders replaced by relatively unknown and less combative individuals, and the liberal voices in the party silenced with Đilas's fall. By the end of the decade Croatia had ceased to be a largely rural society, as the percentage of peasants in its population dropped from 56 per cent in 1953 to 44 per cent in 1961.[27] Those who moved to the towns became industrial workers and officials, engineers and doctors, teachers and lawyers, while those left behind grew more prosperous once forced collectivisation had been abandoned. Thanks to Vladimir Bakarić, Croatia adopted a policy of modernising its agriculture and placing it at the service of industry, thereby stimulating agricultural productivity. During the 1960s the Croatian economy would further benefit from tourism. Yugoslavia's decision in the early 1960s to open its borders also led a large and growing number of Croats to seek work abroad, mainly in West Germany. Their remittances would become an important source of Yugoslavia's foreign currency and a bone of contention between the federal and Croatian governments over their disposition. Croatia's chief problem was its inability to finance the transition from heavy to light industry. The introduction of self-management had coincided with a transfer of federal investment funds to local industry and municipalities; but the federal bureaucracy retained the right of decision on their actual use.

The essence of Bakarić's approach was not to initiate any new policy without the approval of Tito, whom he saw as the main guarantor of Yugoslavia's federal constitution. Determined to avoid the trap of the Croatian–Serbian dualism of the pre-war era, he kept Croatia aligned with Slovenia and joined Kardelj in supporting the aspirations of other republics, and particularly the self-affirmation of Bosnia-Herzegovina. His strategy of weaning the Croatian Serbs away from reliance on Belgrade led the Croatian party to de-emphasise the Croat nature of Croatia. This 'national nihilism' fed Croat frustration. There was a growing reaction among the Croatian intellectual elite against Serbia's renewed domination of Yugoslavia, as well as against what it perceived as the federal state's deliberate neglect of Zagreb in favour of Belgrade. The fact that not a single cultural object had been built in Zagreb since the war, whereas Belgrade had gained a gallery of modern art, a theatre, a museum of medieval art and a museum of the national liberation war, caused much bitterness. Belgrade was also buying up the best sportsmen, which further raised Serbia's domestic prestige. The Croatian sense of grievance also grew, with the reappearance of the old Serbian propensity to appropriate Croatia's cultural heritage. Resentment swelled further as new accounts of Partisan resistance appeared, which glorified the contributions made by Serbia and Montenegro, while presenting Croatia as a land of collaborators. In 1963 General Velimir Terzić, a former royal officer turned Partisan, published a two-volume account of Yugoslavia's collapse in 1941, which he ascribed to a joint action on the part of Vladko Maček and his Peasant Party, Ante Pavelić and his Ustashe, the Croatian Catholic Church, and the bulk of Croat conscripts.[28] Although the SKH leaders condemned the book, it was nevertheless favourably reviewed in the influential Belgrade daily *Politika*. More ominously, perhaps, the first official history of the Yugoslav Communist Party (now the League of Communists of Yugoslavia), which covered also the wartime period, was written without Croatian involvement. This work also asserted that Maček had offered Croatia to Hitler and Mussolini. By focusing on the role of units under Tito's direct command, official historians of the war gave the impression that the Croatian Partisans, far from creating one of the most successful resistance movements in Occupied Europe, had in fact made a negligible contribution to Croatia's and Yugoslavia's liberation. That this reinvention of the past proceeded unchecked was due largely to the intense smear campaign directed against the Croatian wartime leader Hebrang, which tainted the KPH with responsibility for the NDH's crimes. Some of its members responded to such accusations by stressing their unconditional loyalty to Yugoslavia, leading to the emergence of a significant body of specifically Croat unitarists within the party.

The political apathy prevailing in Zagreb during the 1950s derived largely from the fear that any assertion of Croatia's specific interests was bound to provoke charges of 'separatism' and reviving Ustasha ideology. Bakarić's policy of national self-denial left Slovenia to fight Croatia's battles, which in turn helped to postpone the much-needed economic and political reforms in Yugoslavia. It proved impossible, however, to suppress the republic's growing sense of economic exploitation, around which all Croatians had no difficulty in uniting. Its share of federal investment was falling at the same time as its needs – thanks to industrial restructuring – were escalating. To make matters more difficult, Yugoslav industrial production began to stagnate after many years of growth. Employment fell at a time when the first post-war generation was entering the labour market. The federal state's response was to raise taxes steeply, leaving Croatian industry starved of much of its income. When the Croatian political executive met in 1960 to discuss the new five-year plan, it was presented with data showing unmistakably not only that Croatia was falling behind, but also that it would continue to do so.

This forced the SKH leaders to adopt a more active Yugoslav policy. In 1961 a new institute was set up in Zagreb on Bakarić's initiative, ostensibly to research the history of the Croatian working-class movement but in reality to defend the republic's wartime record – and thereby raise Croatia's political profile within Yugoslavia. General Franjo Tuđman, a JNA staff officer who was already fighting this particular battle, arrived from Belgrade to take charge of the institute. Another of Bakarić's moves was to recruit a team of trained economists, whose job was to survey the federal government's economic policy and its effects on Croatia. One of these was Savka Dabčević-Kučar, who eventually became what can best be described as Croatian prime minister. Then in 1962 Tito's great favourite, Miko Tripalo, returned to Croatia, after holding several important federal posts, to assume the leadership of the Zagreb party organisation – the most important in the republic – and eventually that of the SKH itself. When in 1969 Tripalo left Zagreb again in order, together with Bakarić, to represent Croatia on the newly established federal party presidency, Savka (as she became universally known) replaced him as party leader, and the mayor of Rijeka, Dragutin Haramija, became prime minister in her stead.

These three leaders, born in the Adriatic part of Croatia a few years after Yugoslavia's formation, were responsible for initiating a new movement of national self-affirmation popularly known as the Croatian Spring, which notwithstanding its brief duration created a new sense of national unity. University-educated, like Bakarić they came from well-to-do families with impeccable patriotic credentials. In 1895 Savka's father, then a law student, was arrested with Stjepan Radić for burning the Hungarian flag in central

Zagreb. He subsequently accepted Yugoslavia as Dalmatia's only refuge from Italy. Although he himself was generally anti-Communist, his three children joined the Partisans in 1943.[29] Tripalo's great-uncle was in 1870 elected a deputy to the Dalmatian parliament for the rural constituency of Sinj, together with Miho Klaić. The whole family joined the resistance in 1941.[30] Haramija, born in a merchant family from the area of Rijeka, was like so many local Croats brought up in an anti-Italian spirit, and in the belief that Rijeka and Istria belonged to Croatia. He joined the Partisan resistance in 1941.[31] Haramija brought to his new post the experience of running Rijeka, Croatia's and Yugoslavia's largest seaport. He and his team had managed to reorient Rijeka towards world markets so successfully that in the mid-1960s Rijeka's income from foreign trade was twice the Yugoslav average; the fact that three-fifths of this was taken by the federal state turned Haramija into a committed decentraliser. The fourth member of this leading team was Pero Pirker, the Croatian party's executive secretary. Born in Varaždin, he joined the Croatian Communist Party at the age of eighteen. Under their leadership Croatia became a bastion of the reform movement. This was a generation that had no experience of Stalin's 'Bolshevised' Third International: it was a product of anti-Fascist resistance rather than of the Comintern. More sensitive to the needs of good economic management and politically more liberal than their predecessors, the new Croatian leaders would use self-management as the battering ram with which to bring down the seemingly invincible citadel of the federal bureaucracy.

In the other republics too, the youngest generation of Partisan fighters assumed leading positions during the 1960s, as part of the older party leaders' deliberate policy to rejuvenate the governing structure in order to conduct reforms. Following Ranković's fall, Serbia acquired determined and talented party leaders in Marko Nikezić and Latinka Perović, who were keen to modernise their country and rid it too of the paralysing control of the federal bureaucracy. They aligned Serbia with the reformers. The desire to placate Serbia in the aftermath of Ranković's fall had led to awarding that republic such key posts as executive secretary of the SKJ's central committee (Mijalko Todorović); deputy-president of Yugoslavia (Koča Popović); president of the federal assembly (Milentije Popović). Serbia also gained 80 per cent of federal investment in the 1965–70 five-year plan, which included a railway linking Belgrade with the Montenegrin port of Bar – causing dismay among the Croatian leaders, who were hoping to see Rijeka consolidate its position as Yugoslavia's main port. The Serbian leaders now opted for a new national strategy. Rather than seeking to dominate

Latinka Perović, Savka Dabčević-Kučar and Aleksandar Ranković at Karađorđevo, 1964, photographed by Tito

Yugoslavia politically, they now wished to secure Serbia's pre-eminence by building up its economy, for which they relied on the concentration of the financial capital and foreign trade in Belgrade. Belgrade banks and foreign-trade firms, which were under Serbian management, thus held the bulk (over 70 per cent) of the Yugoslav financial capital. The concentration of foreign-trade firms in Belgrade gave Serbia 56 per cent of Yugoslav foreign trade, compared with Croatia's 18 per cent. The wealth of the Belgrade firms derived in the main from their monopoly of trade in certain areas and/or types of goods. Thus, for example, Centroprom imported oil, coffee, fats and rice; Granexport imported wheat from the United States; Yugoimport traded in arms; Jugoexport supplied the US army in Europe; Centrotekstil sold textile and footwear to the Soviet Union; Jugometal traded in industrial plant and ore; Genex engaged in general import and export. These giant firms (some of which were in fact controlled by the UDB and the JNA) were a product not of their competitiveness, but of franchises distributed by the federal state. Genex, for example, made its original fortune after having been allocated trade with the Soviet Union. The firm as a rule recruited its personnel from federal government bodies staffed by Serbians, especially from the ministries for foreign policy and foreign trade. In the struggle for such government licences, Croatian firms regularly lost out to ones from Serbia.[32] The Serbian leaders shared many Croatian views on the need for economic and political reforms; but they were unwilling to surrender the advantage afforded by Belgrade's position as the chief locus of Yugoslav capital and trade. The two republics also differed on the extent to which the economy should be liberalised: the economically more advanced Croatia demanded less state interference, while the less developed Serbia needed the state to help it industrialise. There were political differences too. Serbia sought to undermine Tito's authority, because it did not need it; Croatia relied upon it, in the knowledge that without Tito's control of the federal party machine it would be impossible to dismantle centralism.

Croatia's new leaders were ambitious and enthusiastic state builders. They sought their republic's economic integration, which demanded the creation of a consolidated transport and communication system – a most vital need for Croatia, given its peculiar shape. Italy supplied them with a model: just as the Genoa–Milan link had become the backbone of Italian industry, so too a Rijeka–Zagreb link could be the main axis of the Croatian economy. Haramija argued that the failure to achieve this now would be 'fatal both for Rijeka and for Croatia's Adriatic orientation'.[33] Investment in communications that would link Croatia on the one hand to central and northern Europe, on the other to Greece and the Aegean, became a matter of primary national importance. The emergence of mass tourism, directed mainly at the Croatian coast, made road-building even more important. Croatia, however, lacked the necessary capital. Nor did it benefit much from the central state's foreign borrowing. Yugoslavia was at this time getting cheap loans for roadbuilding from the World Bank, but Croatia got only 8 per cent of the money, which it used to build the Zagreb–Karlovac stretch of the projected motorway to Rijeka. Their plan to meet some of the cost of this undertaking by attracting foreign, mainly Italian and American, capital was vetoed by the JNA. The federal government similarly vetoed a Croatian government decision to drill for oil deposits in the north Adriatic, which it was hoped could provide a new source of revenue for investment in infrastructure and tourism. The central government also vetoed Croatia's decision to establish its own air company – in cooperation with the American firm PanAm, as part of a larger joint venture that would have involved the building of new airports and hotel chains along Croatia's Adriatic coast – on the grounds that there was already the Belgrade airline JAT. This did not prevent JAT from creating its own separate firm Air Yugoslavia; or Genex from establishing its own air company Aviogenex to complement its subsidiary Yugotours. Although 65 per cent of total Yugoslav air traffic involved Croatia (93 per cent of charter flights), the republic earned as a result only a small fraction (6 per cent) of the income derived from it.[34]

Road-building was an integral part of state-building and state-building led to a new evocation of Croatia's historical statehood. Much to Tito's displeasure, positive references to Zrinski and Frankapan re-emerged in the press, and Ban Jelačić too was rescued from near-oblivion. The projected Zagreb–Split motorway was to be called after King Zvonimir. The Croatian sabor voted also to establish a museum of sacral art in Zadar, a museum of medieval art in Split and a central national library in Zagreb. New universities were to be opened in Rijeka, Osijek and Split. These projects were very popular. The government's decision to secure the bulk of the funds needed to build the Zagreb–Split motorway by floating a public loan won enthusiastic support throughout Croatia, and especially in Dalmatia. Banners hailing the King Zvonimir Motorway would greet Savka and her team on their travels through Dalmatia. At the same time, however, the Croatian government was forced to watch on as Belgrade banks began investing in Croatian tourism, a process which soon led to political interference in the republic's internal affairs. Thus, for example, Genex offered a cheap loan to a Dubrovnik tourist firm in return for the right to buy the earned foreign currency at an artificially depressed official exchange rate, and to choose the firms that would supply the necessary building and other material. At Genex's insistence a three-member executive board was set up to run this particular enterprise, involving its own representative, a director who had to have the firm's confidence, and a representative of the firm itself. Genex's next step was to demand a say in the composition of the local government. In no time at all Genex created its own tourist firm, Yugotours, which acted as a channel for other Serbian firms wishing to share in this lucrative business.

There was now an acute feeling in Croatia that the concentration of financial capital and economic decision-making in Belgrade posed a real danger of Serbian economic domination of Croatia. At a more general level, the economics of the federal system relied on the assumption that the more developed republics such as Croatia and Slovenia would subsidise the less developed ones. The problem lay not in the idea of subsidies as such, but in these republics' inability to decide the size of their contributions or control the manner and purpose of their disposition. This state of affairs led Zagreb to insist on overall financial transparency: on the right of access to accurate economic data, such as the state of Yugoslavia's reserves, the different republics' contribution to the federal budget, the size of republican foreign debts, the level and nature of federal government spending; and so on. Croatia called for an easing of the tax burden on industry, and on the liquidation by 1971 of federal capital other than the fund for the underdeveloped republics and the province of Kosovo. Its call for financial clarity met with strong condemnation, however, on the part of the federal bureaucracy, Serbia, and the under-developed republics which for their own reasons sided with Serbia: they all chose to interpret it as an attack on Yugoslavia. In 1967 and 1968, as a result, Croatia found itself regularly in a minority on economic (though not always on political) issues. Even Slovenia, which shared many of Croatia's concerns, tended to vote against its proposals. Yugoslavia as a state system inclined towards equilibrium; taken as a whole, it discouraged any of its parts from pursuing an independent path. One consequence of the fear of radical change was that reform went nowhere, problems accumulated, and something had to give.

Convinced that they were on the side of historical progress, the Croatian leaders decided that nothing further could be gained from discussions behind closed doors and that the time had come to involve the population. Only the political engagement of the masses, they now believed, could break the passivity of the ossified federal bureaucracy. They took to touring party branches across Croatia, and spoke openly about problems and solutions. Their demand for Croatian economic equality won support from the majority of party branches, especially those in the major cities, from industrial managers, from parliamentary deputies, and from the intelligentsia. Older and less liberal party cadres too joined them in attacking the federal bureaucracy. The new leaders failed, however, to win over the army and the security service; but these branches of the state would not offer resistance, so long as Tripalo and Dabčević-Kučar enjoyed Tito's backing. The decision to seek popular support was a calculated risk. The Croatian leaders believed that the population was far ahead of the party when it came to reforms: what was needed was to find the right form for engaging it. They found this in a new version of the Popular Front, which they called 'the mass socialist movement' – a movement based on unity between the party and popular action. Popular participation in politics, however, threatened the very basis of the system, pivoted on the Communist Party's monopoly of political action – based on the belief that mass political activity, unless tightly controlled, led inevitably to anarchy and the collapse of socialism. Opposition to the new course soon emerged within the Croatian party,

Savka Dabčević-Kučar, Miko Tripalo, Pero Pirker (partly hidden) and Tito, 1968

especially within its satellite 'mass' organisations, such as the trade unions and the Socialist Alliance (former Popular Front). Nor could this sudden opening of a dialogue between the Croatian Communist Party and the nation it governed remain an internal Croatian affair.

The turning point came in May 1968, when the Croatian leaders convened a party plenum whose proceedings, contrary to usual practice, were broadcast live. The main target of criticism of the plenary discussion was the federal government, which was accused of acting as a brake on economic reform. Other targets included 'the monopoly of alienated capital held by the banks, particularly the federal ones'. The plenum demanded that the big Belgrade banks and foreign-trade firms, which were registered as autonomous 'self-managing working organisations' yet kept practically all Yugoslav capital, be closed down; and that their capital be distributed to industry once and for all. The federal government and Serbia responded by defending the position of these economic giants, on the grounds that as self-managing enterprises they were both legal and legitimate. Zagreb's challenge, however, had now gained popular backing: the struggle against Belgrade's privileged position was perceived in much of Croatia as a struggle against a Great Serb attempt to colonise it. In Serbia, on the other hand,

Croatian demands were presented as separatism and ipso facto an attack on the federation itself.

At a meeting of the Yugoslav party presidency held in June 1968, the Serbian leaders argued that Croatia's demands were actually harming their own struggle against Great Serb nationalism. The Croatians replied that the federal government, despite repeated demands, was avoiding presenting clear accounts; and that Serbia was backing it, out of a desire to secure federal financial aid needed to complete its own major projects. They now asked for a vote of confidence in the federal government. Bosnia-Herzegovina, Macedonia and Montenegro sided with Serbia and the federal government. Slovenia, which had initially supported Croatia, switched sides at the last minute after the federal government promised it additional money for its own road-building. Tito, who supported Croatia, failed to intervene; so the federal government won the confidence vote, leaving Croatia wholly isolated. Faced with such an unfavourable constellation of forces, Bakarić began to retreat, telling Tripalo that any progress was precluded in such conditions. He told his confidants that the Croatian campaign against Belgrade was beginning to look like Maček's opposition in 1937–8. But the differences between Tripalo and Bakarić, which would henceforth grow, were tactical not strategic, reflecting personal temperaments and experience.

The invasion of Czechoslovakia by Warsaw Pact armies in August 1968 temporarily ended the domestic conflict, as the Yugoslavs closed ranks. The aggression was justified in terms of the 'limited sovereignty' of socialist states in regard to the socialist bloc (that is, the USSR). The invasion created a new fear in Yugoslavia that any radical democratisation might lead to Soviet intervention. The Soviet leader, Leonid Brezhnev, informed Tito indeed that a 'counter-revolution' similar to Dubček's was taking shape in Yugoslavia too. As the Yugoslav leaders focused on the eventuality of a Soviet invasion, they discovered that the JNA's defence concept did not take this possibility into account. The disarray in the army reopened the question of its control. The Slovenes, concerned that Tito could use the army to replace any recalcitrant republican leadership, asked for Croatian support in limiting his freedom in making military appointments; but the Croatians, wishing to keep Tito on their side, refused. Slovenia and Croatia united, however, on the need to establish republican-based territorial defence forces.

Once the fear of a Soviet invasion had abated, internal conflicts re-emerged, stimulated by the opening of a debate on constitutional reform during which Yugoslavia's nature and structure came under intense scrutiny. The dispute ranged over federal powers, republican sovereignty, and national parity in the allocation of federal party, state and governmental posts, including army appointments and troop dispositions and deployment. The Croatian leaders challenged the unwritten rule that the Zagreb military district was always commanded by a Serb chosen by the JNA general staff, questioned the existing method of financing the armed forces, and supported a proposal that more conscripts be allowed to serve in their home republics. The overwhelmingly Serb character of the JNA's officer corps not only called into question the army's Yugoslav nature, but also posed serious problems for establishing a viable territorial defence, since most reserve officers were Serbs. Wartime commanders, many of whom were Croats, were being retired at this time on the grounds of age, leaving behind an ever more Serb-dominated army. The Croatian police too was overwhelmingly staffed by Serbs. It was difficult to contemplate republican sovereignty in this situation. When, in the immediate aftermath of the discussion, the Croatian leaders removed themselves briefly to a planned wartime location, Bakarić told his party colleagues that he did not wish the Lika-born General Đoko Jovanović, JNA commander of the Zagreb military district, to know where he was sleeping. Croatian Serbs constituted the core of a strong unitarist current in the army, which harboured strong suspicions against any manifestation of Croatian autonomy. The Soviet invasion of Czechoslovakia had illuminated these and related problems. As long as Tito supported the Croatian leaders, the army generals remained reasonably friendly; but they became more hostile as the Croatians continued to press for a comprehensive reform of all departments of the federal state and party.

At the ninth Yugoslav party congress, held in March 1969, it was decided to set up a party presidency made up of six representatives from each republic, three from each province, and three from the JNA. The JNA was thus treated as a separate province, not attached to any republic. The republican parties became 'autonomous' bodies within the 'single SKJ', whose authority formally derived from them. Tito remained SKJ president. This federalisation of the party created the necessary conditions for the transfer of power from the centre to the republics. Tito manoeuvred skilfully between the warring republics in order to retain personal control over the party and the army – the two institutions on which he relied for keeping Yugoslavia together. Thus, for example, in order to avoid having the Serbian politician Mijalko Todorović re-elected as his deputy – hence in a strong position to acquire control of the federal party after his death – Tito proposed the creation of an executive committee of the party presidency composed of fourteen equal members, two from each republic plus one from each province. He would head the presidency himself. Tito had a reasonable relationship with Serbia as long as he could rely on Ranković; but after Ranković's fall he gained an opponent in the Serbian leadership. He never felt at home in Belgrade, in fact, and preferred to convene important party meetings away from the federal capital. The Serbian leadership tried hard to limit his powers in regard to the party and the army, and since Tito could not be assailed publicly a trench war developed between them.

That the Serbian leaders ultimately failed was due in part to Tito's exceptional political deftness, but also to Croatian policy. Convinced that Tito alone would be able to prevail against Serbia's resistance to change, the Croatians offered him badly needed support. There was a limit, however, to how much open backing Tito could give Zagreb, in a situation characterised by Croatia being regularly outvoted four to two, or five to one, in federal bodies.[35] At the same time, Tito's growing reliance on Croatia was causing much unease in Serbia. One manifestation of this was the launching of a comprehensive and synchronised campaign against the Croatian leadership, portraying it as a threat to Yugoslavia. Nikezić and Perović refused to participate in this enterprise, but did nothing to restrain it either, possibly because their own influence was limited. At the same time, the fact that Belgrade was another state's capital made it more difficult for the others to influence its behaviour. Tito, who saw the campaign as directed against him, informed the Croatians that a plot against them was being hatched in Belgrade within the anti-reform camp. Some Serbian leaders were indeed searching for partners in Croatia, among older and increasingly marginalised party veterans such as Mika Špiljak (who in the event refused to play along), convinced Croat unitarists like Miloš Žanko, and as ever the Croatian Serbs.

At the end of 1969 Žanko – who was a member of the Croatian party's central committee and deputy president of the federal assembly – began publishing a series of strongly worded articles in a Belgrade journal, in which he talked of such things as 'the revived vampire of Croat nationalism' and criticised the Croatian leaders for their alleged tolerance towards it. This was an open invitation to the federal party to purge the Croatian party. Worried that Žanko's rhetoric could unite the opposition within Croatia itself, the Croatian leaders decided to respond to the challenge in a decisive manner, in order to discipline the Croatian party ranks and secure continued domestic support. In January 1970 the Croatian party's central committee convened its tenth session, having consulted Tito alone in advance. In a break with established practice, the session was fully televised. The meeting denounced unitarism as a cover for Great Serb hegemony, which remained the greatest threat to Yugoslavia. Bakarić identified the problem as follows:

> I wish to speak about unitarism in Croatia or, more precisely, about unitarism among the Croats. Does it exist as a concrete, real tendency in our society? I think our reply should be a firm yes, it does. It exists both inside the League of Communists and outside it. [How] are we to judge its strength? Could it form a government or at least a serious political movement? My answer is: yes! [The unitarists] could come up with a programme, find allies in Yugoslavia, and find them also outside Yugoslavia. [Their] main support would be bureaucratic centralism and Cominformism.[36]

According to Dabčević-Kučar, who as party leader gave the keynote speech,[37] unitarism was but an aspect of Great Serb nationalism, a specific form of imperialistic chauvinism. Convinced that Yugoslavia's multinational character was the main source of its weakness, the unitarists sought to suppress national identities rather than seek unity based on respect for national freedom and equality. Theirs was an 'artificial and supra-national Yugoslavia', in which the interests of the central state reigned supreme. 'This kind of Yugoslavism is a threat to Yugoslavia's cohesion.' Its bastions were the federal bureaucracy and all those who resisted reform. The Croatian people, however, were not interested in any Yugoslavia in which they would not be a free and sovereign nation. In a veiled reference to the Soviet invasion of Czechoslovakia, she added that the Croatian Communists, responsible as they were to their nation and working class, could not accept the notion of limited sovereignty. At Tito's insistence the meeting condemned not only Žanko himself, but also 'the bureaucratic and conservative forces which stood behind his activities'. This conclusion met with the unanimous support of the central committee's Croat and Serb members.

The meeting was received well in Croatia, but critically in other republics. Its verdict that unitarism was the main threat to Yugoslavia took many by surprise. The first negative reaction came from the army, which liked Žanko's austere and a-national Communism. The mainstream of the Serbian party saw the tenth session as a manifestation of Croat nationalism and an attack on Yugoslavia's integrity. The Serbian elite, in fact, habitually denounced any and every initiative designed to strengthening Croatia's sovereignty, however argued.[38] But the fact that Kardelj too was critical of the tenth session caused Bakarić to rethink not so much the policy as the tactics, in this crucial period of constitutional reform. Tito, however, sided with Croatia.

He told its leaders in May 1970: 'I have no objections and agree with your tenth session. [No one] has the right [to] deny you the right to discuss your problems in Croatia in the way you did at the tenth session. [I] will support you whenever it is needed. As you know, I am a Croat from Zagorje, from the heart of Croatia.' But he added a warning: 'Our internal problems are negligible compared with [our] international situation.'[39] Tito knew that Yugoslavia could not be kept going by relying on the idea of Yugoslavism or dictatorship. It could survive only if national, that is, republican equality was assured. Kardelj was even more clear on this. He argued that one should try out a confederation, and if that did not work one should give up on Yugoslavia. The KPJ's original thesis that Yugoslavia was an artificial creation was, in his view, far more realistic than its subsequent decision to keep the country together.[40] They both understood that the biggest enemy of the transformation of Yugoslavia into a loose federation was the ideology of Great Serbia, which endured regardless of who ran Serbia, so they sought to create strong institutional ramparts against it. In September 1970 Tito told the Zagreb party that a collective state presidency which would take over when he died was 'the only solution for our country', since it was too dangerous for any single person (other than him) to concentrate so much power in their hands.

The emerging Tito–Kardelj–Bakarić triumvirate agreed also on the pivotal role of Bosnia-Herzegovina in keeping the Yugoslav peace. Following Ranković's fall, this republic started to emancipate itself from the domination of the federal government by proclaiming the Muslims a separate national group, by reducing the repression against Herzegovina Croats initiated in 1945 and by restraining the local Great Serb forces. Seeking to protect Bosnia-Herzegovina from Serbia, Bakarić had dismissed Franjo Tuđman in 1967 from his post as head of the historical institute because of his defence of the Cvetković–Maček agreement, and of the creation of Banovina Croatia as a fair solution to the Croat national question in the Kingdom of Yugoslavia. Speaking like an old-fashioned European liberal, Bakarić argued that the Communist approach to the national question by way of federation, democratisation, and de-politicisation of the idea of nationality, was the only correct solution in such a complex area as Bosnia-Herzegovina, entailing as it did that it should no longer matter who is what, because all would enjoy the same rights. Any other path led inevitably to conflict between Croatia and Serbia over a land that could not be sensibly divided, since Bosnia was 'back to front: Serbs in the west, Croats in the east'.[41]

The tenth session of the CK SKH marked the point when the country finally rid itself of the imposed Ustasha complex. During the brief 'Spring' period Croatia started to behave like any other nation, displaying concern for its language, culture and past, its sovereignty and its economic development. Its emergence from passivity was accompanied indeed by great cultural effervescence. One aspect of the new sense of freedom was the demand that Croat be recognised as one of Yugoslavia's official languages. Although this was widely denounced at the time and some of its advocates punished, agreement was reached in the end that federal laws and acts would be published in the national languages specified by the republican constitutions. Politics was now no longer confined to party offices: practically everything discussed at the meetings of higher party bodies found its way into the public domain. The tenth session did not usher in any new policy so much as a new dialogue with the population, unknown since the end of the war. This ensured that the nation remained united behind its leaders during the decisive struggle for the constitutional reforms that would turn Yugoslavia into a de facto confederation. The push by Tito and Kardelj for this solution was a logical answer to the country's internal divisions – an attempt to ensure at least an orderly transition in the event of its disintegration. Yet they refused to contemplate the greater democracy for which social developments were pressing, partly for ideological reasons and partly out of fear of civil war. As a result, it was left to cultural institutions such as Matica Hrvatska, literary journals and the universities to organise the opposition.

The new stress on republican sovereignty inevitably reopened the Serb question in Croatia. A common argument against transformation of the republics into fully sovereign nation states was that, with the exception of Slovenia, none was nationally homogeneous. This misunderstood the issue, because sovereignty pertained to republics (and provinces too) as states, not to individual national groups living within their borders. This did not prevent Croat nationalists from arguing that, since three-quarters of the Croatian population was Croat, the Croat people were the only true bearers of republican sovereignty. In actual fact Croatia's industrialisation and urbanisation had transformed Croat–Serb relations, in that the majority of Serbs no longer lived in small and relatively homogeneous rural enclaves, but in large numbers had joined Croats in the cities. The ceding of eastern Srijem to Vojvodina, and the organised colonisation of deserted German farms in Vojvodina by Croatian Serbs after the end of the war, had reduced the Serb proportion to 14 per cent of the Croatian total, with a tendency to decline further. Out of 155 Croatian municipalities, Serbs now formed majorities in only fifteen, all of which lay in central Croatia. The Serb question, in other words, essentially concerned these fifteen municipalities, whose voice was nevertheless heard far and wide because several influential army generals had been born there.

The Croatian leadership, Croat and Serb, was of the unanimous view that Croatia was the state not just of Croats, but also of Serbs, as well as other nationalities living within it. Serb history and culture were considered to be an integral part of Croatia's heritage. As constituent people, Croatian Serbs had the right to their own language, script and cultural institutions. This position, clarified during the debate on constitutional amendments, was widely accepted. Radical Serb nationalists, including some eminent generals, favoured on the other hand the creation of a separate Serb territory, as a first step towards Croatia's break-up into several autonomous regions. But as Bakarić pointed out, this was impossible to achieve in practice unless one had in mind the fifteen municipalities – where, however, only a small minority of Croatian Serbs lived. The Croatian Serb party leaders rejected separation on the grounds that it would lead to the establishment of economically unviable Serb ghettos. They were strong opponents of Great Serbia, knowing that it entailed the break-up of Yugoslavia, in which case Croatian Serbs would be the greatest losers. There was a proposal at one point that – in order to cut the ground from under the feet of various 'defenders' of 'endangered' Croatian Serbs – it might be useful to form a Serb parliamentary caucus; but this too was rejected, because it might cause problems in other parts of Yugoslavia. Serb members of the Croatian leadership were in fact the main opponents of any such 'Serb committee for the protection of Serb rights', since that would indeed turn the Serbs into a national minority. It was decided instead that the regulation of internal national differences should be a matter for all-Yugoslav agreement.

Savka Dabčević-Kučar and Miko Tripalo nevertheless sought to reduce Serb over-representation in sensitive professions such as the police, the army and the judiciary, arguing that public services should reflect the national make-up of the population. In the Zagreb military district, for example, only three out of twenty-six regimental and brigade commanders, only nine out of fifty-three commanders of divisions and battalions, and only forty-three out of 336 commanders of platoons and batteries were Croats.[42] Croatia's foes in Belgrade quickly named this policy 'ethnic tallying', and fierce propaganda was unleashed against it in the Serbian press. Native active and retired generals living in Belgrade began to tour Serb areas of Croatia, telling the population that the Croats were out to get them, and that the Croatian government was intent on removing their 'hard-won rights'. Serbs from

Bosnia and Serbia, often fortified in their resolution by alcohol, were on suitable occasions bussed into these areas to offer their support. Their visits and fiery speeches, and the various flyers that appeared warning of a new genocide, aroused the Croats too. Conflicts began, some caused by heated responses penned by various Croat nationalists targeting Serb officials as well as 'lukewarm' Croats.

During this time, work on the new constitution proceeded apace. Tripalo became chairman of the constitutional commission established by the federal party with the task of harmonising different positions. It was finally agreed that the federation was not a supra-republican state but a union of equal republics and provinces. The economic – hence, also political – supremacy of the federal centre would be abolished. Federal organs, including the federal government, were to be formed on the basis of parity, with all higher federal officials appointed by the republics and provinces, though they had to have the confidence of other federal units. This step ensured that their primary loyalty would henceforth lie with the republics and provinces. The army, however, escaped these provisions; it was agreed merely to strive for greater parity within the officer corps. The main principle guiding the new constitution was that citizens realised all their fundamental rights in the republics and provinces in which they lived, while at the federal level they realised only those rights specified explicitly by the constitution as having been agreed by all republics and provinces. In its final draft, the Yugoslav constitution thus defined Croatia as 'the national state of the Croat people, the state of the Serb people in Croatia, and the state of the national minorities who live in it'. Its citizens exercised their sovereign rights within Croatia, and within Yugoslavia only to the extent agreed by all Yugoslav republics and provinces as being in their common interest.[43] All federal elected bodies were formed on the basis of parity, with the exception of the lower chamber of the federal assembly, whose powers were relatively negligible. A federal presidency was also established, composed of three representatives from each of the six republics and two from each province, chosen by them albeit formally confirmed by the federal assembly. In March 1971 the amendments were adopted by the party presidency, and the basic principles also by the federal assembly – although the final constitutional text was to be ratified and pass into law only in 1974.

The strongest resistance to the proposed changes came from Serbia, whose elite did not like among other things the loss of powers on the part of the central bodies, the new status of Vojvodina and Kosovo, the collective nature of the Yugoslav state leadership, or the decentralisation of financial capital. The Belgrade press protested that Serbia was being presented with a fait accompli. But finally Serbia too accepted the changes, thanks to the efforts of Marko Nikezić and Latinka Perović on the one hand, and to Kardelj's hard work and patience on the other. Perović subsequently explained the Serbian leaders' position as follows:

> Given the ingrained view within the Serbian population that Yugoslavia was primarily the state of the Serb nation, and given that the forces of centralism had always looked to Serbia for support, we believed that it was necessary continuously to offer proofs to the other nations of the existence in Serbia of another conception of Yugoslavia. This was not a question of our generosity, but of our own democratic need. It was necessary [to open processes] that would persuade the Serbian population that centralism was contrary also to Serb national interests, and that equal responsibility of all nations for common affairs was a condition for the existence of both socialist democracy and Yugoslavia's unity. This is why the central committee of the Serbian League of Communists agreed on 26 December 1968 to support the constitutional changes.[44]

Nikezić, faithful to his role as Serbia's representative, stated in 1971 that Serbia would accept the amendments, although it did not agree with all of them. The amendments, especially those concerning Kosovo and Vojvodina, had in a sense been imposed on Serbia; this should not happen in future, he argued, since the power of Great Serb reaction should never be underestimated. His criticism was in fact directed at Tito. The idea of altering the constitution had come from Tito and Kardelj, but it was Tito who had made sure that it would be adopted by all in this form. Kardelj's argument was that the federation's great powers were causing inter-republican conflicts, which were paralysing the work of the federal government. Nations as a rule found it easier to accept discipline imposed by their own state than by the federal centre. The belief that the Yugoslav nations were not proper nations, and that only the federation should be sovereign, was in his view a 'very dangerous illusion'. These nations had not only different but also conflicting interests, and the only way to overcome the inevitable strains was through negotiation and search for compromise. Kardelj was right to argue that the earlier practice of the federal state and party leaders deciding everything could not last long. But such a decentralised state also needed an arbiter, so Tito as

Yugoslav president was confirmed in his role as the supreme authority. His power in fact grew as that of the federal state and party declined.

Yugoslavia's leading politicians knew that Yugoslavia was falling apart. Frightened by the prospect of renewed fratricidal war and mutual extermination, they engaged in constructing a complex set of defence works against such an eventuality. They were defending not only Yugoslavia, but the Communist system itself, the two being inextricably linked. The new constitution consequently affirmed the leading role of the Communist Party for the first time, while the JNA was given a seat on the party presidency. It was a gesture towards an old order that had outrun its time. Within each republic, the economic reform had undermined the earlier dominance of political functionaries in favour of so-called 'techno-managers' – the people running industrial and agricultural concerns, trade, banks, insurance companies and communications – whose power derived from the market, dressed up as self-management. The republics and provinces also stimulated concentration of industrial and financial enterprise within their borders, which then competed for influence within the wider Yugoslav area. This stimulated their internal enclosure and national cohesion. The arrival of educated younger politicians who saw themselves primarily as modernisers and democratisers had signalled, moreover, the start of a generational struggle for power within the existing political structure, which in turn awakened political interest in society as a whole. Responding to these challenges, the Communist Party legitimised the republics' growing quest for independence, but sought also to restrain it, since it contained the seeds of its own negation. There was a limit too on how far decentralisation and democratisation could proceed in a Europe frozen by the Cold War.

The beginning of the end

The new constitutional provisions were welcomed in Croatia as the necessary minimum. But they shocked the Serbian political and cultural establishment. The passing away of a system that had ensured Serbia's domination reanimated calls for the republic to abandon Yugoslavia. According to one characteristic argument: 'Yugoslavia has become a mere geographical concept, now that several independent and indeed mutually incompatible states have been established on its soil – or, more exactly, on its ruins – under the pretext of promoting national equality.' The federal arrangement, the argument continued, had already placed the Serb nation 'in a position of inferiority in regard to other Yugoslav nations'. The new constitution would only aggravate this, because it was 'directed against the

Serb nation's most vital living interests [and] leads inevitably to its total disintegration'. There was no time to lose: Serbia should expand its borders so as to include the whole Serb nation: 'The present Serbian borders are evidently neither national nor historical borders of the Serb nation. [Today] it is more necessary than ever that the Serb nation should rid itself of past illusions [in regard to Yugoslavia]. If the Serb nation is to survive all these challenges, [it] must turn to itself and begin the struggle for recovery of its much imperilled national identity.'[45] The transformation of the republics, and in effect the provinces too, into self-governing states was presented as a knife thrust into the heart of the Serb nation. Such sentiments would eventually lead Serbia into war against the rest of Yugoslavia. The backlash was not an expression of Serbia's perceived weakness, however, but rather of its regained self-confidence. One leading Serbian politician, Draža Marković, who himself resisted the confederal aspects of the new constitution and sought to change them – especially those pertaining to the new position of the provinces – wrote at the time:

> The conviction that Serbia did not need Yugoslavia ... evolved in parallel with Serbia's growing strength and development, and became widespread in response to implementation of the policy of national equality. Its roots are to be found in resistance to this policy of national equality. While unitarism remains a permanent danger in the case of the Serbs, Serb nationalist separatism is no less vital or dangerous. The idea of Great Serbia, understood as territorial expansion coupled with assimilation of other nations, [and] the Yugoslav unitarist idea in fact represent two sides of the same coin. This is the ideology of the Chetniks and the Serb Cultural Club, a political platform in whose name the Chetniks did their killing and for whose sake the idea of fratricidal war and mutual extermination was sown.[46]

The Serb Cultural Club was a great Serb organization set up in response to the establishment of Banovina Croatia. One of its prominent members was Draža Mihailović's adviser, Stevan Moljević, whose work *Homogena Srbija*, published in mid-1941, argued for the creation of an ethnically homogenous Great Serbia that would include most of Yugoslavia.[47]

The acrimony with which the battle over the new constitution was fought is well illustrated by the 'spy affair'. In the autumn of 1970 Croatian leaders were informed that the branch of the UDB attached to the federal ministry of foreign affairs was distributing 'reliable information', both at home and abroad, according to which they and the Ustasha wing of the Croat emigration were working together to create an independent Croatia under Soviet protection. The Croatians promptly demanded an official investigation. The inner-party commission set up to discover who was behind it all confirmed the existence of 'enemy propaganda aimed at discrediting the Croatian leadership', and recommended further investigation. This, however, never took place. The federal minister of the interior blamed Great Serb circles in Belgrade, but the Serbian leaders, concerned with internal divisions within their own party, sought to divert attention from their republic. Although it was agreed at the highest level that the affair should not be made public, the worried Croatian leaders did precisely that. In April 1971 the Croatian party central committee issued a public statement revealing the plot against the Croatian leaders, for which they blamed 'the unitarist, centralist and bureaucratic forces in the country' acting through 'certain federal state organs'. This caused quite a stir, with the Croatian public up in arms and the federal prime minister and foreign minister threatening to resign. The Croatians were charged with breaking party discipline and destabilising the country. Yugoslavia's leaders now divided between those who supported the Croatians (Kosovo, Macedonia), those who stood back (Serbia, Slovenia), and those who were against them (Bosnia-Herzegovina, Montenegro). The Croatian leaders told an appalled Tito that Yugoslavia would fall apart after his death unless the federation was radically transformed and the political system subjected to democratic control.

The attempt to discredit the Croatian leaders by charging them with Ustasha connections was part of a wider effort to derail the proposed political reform. It was intended as both a provocation and a warning. It proved difficult, in the event, to penetrate the security and intelligence services and locate the actual instigators. Zagreb's continuing insistence that this be done if anything served the plotters' purpose. Kardelj told the Croatians that they and their Serbian counterparts were destabilising Yugoslavia by tolerating nationalist campaigns within their republics, and that unless they desisted it would be necessary to remove them both. Tito also felt that the Croatians should let go of the issue for the sake of Yugoslav national interests. Bakarić was ready to sacrifice the current Croatian team in order to secure the passing of the constitutional changes; but Tito hesitated, worried that replacing them would strengthen the anti-reform bloc in Serbia.

A meeting of the federal party presidency called to discuss the situation took place in late April 1971 at Tito's Croatian residence on Vanga island in the Brijuni archipelago. Prior to the start of the conference, a visibly upset

Tito told Tripalo (who was to chair the meeting) that it was 'illusory to think that he would behave like Dubček' – that is, like the Czechoslovak leader who, by not suppressing the Prague Spring himself, provided a pretext for foreign troops to occupy his country. He, Tito, was ready to establish order by using the army, and would find in each republic people who would support him in this action.[48] He held a separate meeting also with Savka, Tripalo and Pirker. The Croatians spoke frankly and at length, hoping to keep him on their side. When Tito said: 'You must be doing something wrong, when everyone was against you', they kept pressing him: how could it be that Croatia, whose Partisans had fought for its freedom, after so many years felt unhappy with Yugoslavia? Was he himself not a Croat? The underdeveloped republics were against Croatia because they wanted more than Croatia could give them; uncontrolled spending on the part of the federal bodies was bound to end in economic catastrophe; Croatia's economic needs were being thwarted, and so on. Tito's concluding words were: 'You are probably right, but you lack statecraft.'[49]

Tito's address to the federal party presidency painted a bleak picture of the situation in the country. His message was that unless the Yugoslavs themselves imposed order, someone else would do it for them. The most important thing was to ensure the passage of the new constitution. In the debate that followed, the Croatians were surprised by the strength of the Slovene reaction, as well as by Bakarić's failure to defend them. The increasingly heated debate was suddenly interrupted by a call from Brezhnev. Tito retired to take the call. While waiting for his return they were able to read a confidential report indicating that the Soviet leaders expected a purge of recalcitrant leaders. The Soviet press at the time was full of news about unprecedented nationalist passions tearing Yugoslavia apart, and of warnings that Moscow would not remain indifferent to Yugoslavia's fate.[50] On his return Tito told the meeting that Brezhnev had offered help, which he had declined as unnecessary. The only way to remove the suspicion that the situation in Yugoslavia was running out of control was for each republic and province to arrest a handful of troublemakers. The Croatians, he told Savka, should 'supply' a dozen. Bakarić maliciously told a shocked Savka that she was Ranković's true successor in Croatia. But, as she informed Tito, she refused to arrest anyone unless they could be lawfully convicted. The same was true of the Serbian leaders: they too refused to supply their quota.

Reacting against Soviet interference, the meeting ended with a compromise resolution. Tito welcomed it, calling for unity. Unity in the first instance meant an agreement between Croatia and Serbia; but for various reasons their leaders failed to establish their own separate channel of communication. The Serbians preferred discussions to take place within the federal bodies, where they could enlist the support of other republics. They probably felt too that the Croatian leaders were playing a losing game, and would soon be replaced.[51] The Croatians, while more inclined to bilateral talks, remained suspicious of the Serbians' true intentions. Tito now tried to persuade Tripalo to desert the Croatian leading team, thus ending Croatia's confrontational policy, by promising him positions 'of which he could only dream' – but Tripalo was not tempted. That Tripalo should have declined an important federal post on this occasion reflected a new reality: as the power of the centre waned, it proved increasingly difficult to attract important republican politicians to top federal posts. Both Savka and Latinka Perović refused Tito's offer of the federal premiership, which they interpreted as an effort to weaken respectively Croatia and Serbia. Slovenia and Macedonia likewise declined the honour of filling this post with one of their key leaders.

The summer of 1971 was characterised by a growing gulf between Tito and Serbia. At a formal gathering held in Belgrade to commemorate the thirtieth anniversary of the Partisan uprising in Serbia, Tito had been denied the customary standing applause. He now felt that he was being marginalised in Croatia too. The great popularity of the combative young leaders was much on display there, culminating with a gathering of tens of thousands at the main square in Zagreb in May of that year. They felt unable and unwilling to follow the policy of gradual advance through the structures favoured by Tito and Kardelj. Bakarić by now felt that the Croatian 'national euphoria' and conflict with other republics were dangerous, given the international circumstances and the hostility on the part of the JNA. For Tripalo and Savka, however, only the involvement of the whole nation could secure the necessary reforms without which it would be difficult to justify Croatia's continued membership of the Yugoslav federation. The SKH, after all, embraced only a small minority of the population. The differences between them and Bakarić involved not so much aims as means; but the means they chose were inevitably dividing the Croatian political body, including on a national basis, since democratisation was allowing all kinds of radical positions to be aired for the first time. Convinced that their purge was inevitable, Bakarić placed himself at the head of the internal party opposition. A pragmatist by temperament, he believed that one should never fight losing battles and should always have a ready alternative in one's pocket. But how is one to know, Tripalo argued against him, which battles are lost in advance, if one never chooses to fight any? Like Frano Supilo confronting Miho Klaić, he too believed that the doors of heaven open only to those who knock.

In June 1971 Tito asked the Croatian leaders once again to arrest a few 'enemies of socialism', and they again refused. In July he asked them to resign, for otherwise he would call in the army: better to have the JNA than the Red Army. He argued that – intentionally or simply out of incompetence – they were encouraging all kinds of counter-revolutionaries, and furthermore frightening the local Serbs. The Croatians denied that their republic had become ungovernable, or that the public display of differences was a sign of their tolerance of counter-revolution. Their self-confidence moved Tito to change tactics and to appeal to them as fellow Croats. At a formal dinner held on Slovene territory, he told Dabčević-Kučar: 'You think that I have no national feelings, that I do not feel myself a Croat, that having left as an impoverished youth my adherence to proletarian internationalism has removed all my sense of national belonging. To be sure I am an internationalist, since we Communists must be internationalists, but I am also a Croat!' He continued: 'You could, if you wished, put an end to it [that is, popular engagement], but you choose not to heed my words.' He added: 'I would rather be with you than without you, since you alone can influence the people. But you refuse to heed me.'[52]

He had counted on Croatia as his secure base, but no longer. Croatia, as he told Tripalo, had turned out to be the weak link in his plans for Yugoslavia. He was afraid that supporters of total independence might win popular support in Croatia, leading to Yugoslavia's collapse, civil war and foreign intervention. Riding the wave of popular support, however, the Croatian leaders failed to understand what they felt was an old man's pessimism. In September 1971 Tito's mood changed once more, after having received a warm welcome everywhere, especially in Zagreb, during a tour of Croatia. At a formal dinner held in Zagreb, which was attended also by Kardelj, he praised Croatia and its leaders for this, adding that the stories about the alleged flourishing of Croat nationalism were clearly wrong.[53] He ended by expressing his full support for Croatia's economic demands. The unexpected rapprochement between Tito and the Croatian leadership triggered off a new – and by far the most ferocious yet – campaign against the latter in the Belgrade press, which Nikezić and Perović found hard to restrain. The Croatian leaders were accused in turn of being chauvinists and even Fascists, anti-Yugoslav and anti-party elements, sponsors of a pro-Western and pro-capitalist orientation – and so on. Pamphlets were circulated targeting individual Croatian politicians (both Croat and Serb). Demands to reassess the character and role of the Chetniks, Serbia's existing borders and the status of the autonomous provinces re-emerged.

Neither the pro-reform nor the anti-reform forces were homogenous constructs. The reformers within the Communist Party were divided essentially between older revolutionary leaders like Tito, Kardelj and Bakarić, who endorsed change in order to maintain the existing order, and a younger generation of leaders who sought the latter's radical reconstruction by means of a political democratisation of society as a whole – something which, if consistently applied, would entail the disappearance of both the SKJ and Yugoslavia. Faced with the problem of the Communist Party's rapidly declining influence, Kardelj and Bakarić sought a solution in the concept of 'associated labour', that is, in a radical application of self-management to all levels of the society. This became distilled into so-called 'workers' amendments' to the new constitution, whose chief aim was to neutralise the new powers ceded to the republican states. According to Bakarić, the main idea behind these amendments was to prevent the state from imposing itself on society; indeed, 'to eliminate the state [and] replace it with the self-organisation of society'. Their other main aim was to set clear limits on the functioning of the market, in order to prevent greater social differentiation. In his debates with the younger Croatian leaders, Bakarić counterposed state-building to 'the emancipation of man', and criticised them for believing that the state was the foundation of nation-building.

Savka and Tripalo, while agreeing with Bakarić on the desirability of withering away of the state, nevertheless insisted that the state was a necessary instrument in creating the right conditions for the process of human emancipation to continue. The economic and political reforms, they argued, would help the Croatian state to become a more efficient instrument of the constitution and functioning of the self-managing community. If the Croatian state was to play this role, however, it had to be fully sovereign; it had to become the primary focus of loyalty of its citizens of whatever ethnic origin, as well as the ultimate authority for its officials. This was the raison d'être of the struggle against Yugoslav unitarism. The realisation of Croatian statehood, they kept reminding their opponents, was the one great achievement of the war of national liberation: this, after all, was what the Yugoslav federation was all about. In Tripalo's words: 'Croatia does not demand any privileges for itself, nor does it wish to grant any to others. What it demands is full equality, consensual decision-making, and that Yugoslav policy be made democratically, by agreement reached through democratic discussion. Croatia will never allow itself to be deprived of the right to its own views on all that constitutes federalism, since the federation does not belong to anyone in particular but is our common property.'[54] The Croatian leaders' efforts to overturn an entrenched system of political and economic privilege that was holding back their country's advance had placed them at the forefront of the struggle for reform; notwithstanding their conviction that what was good for Croatia was good also for the rest of Yugoslavia, however, they failed to forge a winning trans-Yugoslav coalition. Moreover, the fact that resistance to reform proved much stronger than expected added a national charge to the Croatian pro-reform movement.

Croatia's isolation was threatening to jeopardise the constitutional reform, however, while Tito's support for its leaders was undermining his position as the Yugoslav arbiter. The state security service now set up a special group to collect information that could be used against the Croatian leaders, and to circulate alarming disinformation about their intentions.[55] Kardelj managed to persuade Tito that they had to act soon, for otherwise they would lose control of the country. In late October 1971 he warned that the SKJ was becoming increasingly marginalised, and that the political situation was moving towards a point when it would be unable to resist 'the torrent of anarchy that will sweep us all away'. New political forces were coming forward to assume the leadership of society, he argued, and the SKJ would become a victim of this tide unless it achieved unity in action. Nationalism coming from all sides represented the main threat, though not in equal measure: the most dangerous was Great Serb nationalism, manifested in 'imperialistic, hegemonistic, unitarist and centralist tendencies'.[56]

Having unsuccessfully appealed to the Croatians to 'end so-called liberalism, for you are destroying Yugoslavia', Kardelj met them again in the middle of November in Zagreb. He told them that the lack of unity within the SKJ was causing a crisis that could lead to its collapse, and to Yugoslavia being reduced to the status of a Soviet satellite. He supported their struggle against centralism, but told them they were wrong to think that such problems could be solved by spontaneous mass movements. Nationalism in Croatia was 'child's play' in comparison with Great Serb nationalism, which was very strong among the Serbian intelligentsia and present to a significant degree also in the army and the state security, and which the Serbian leadership was resisting only feebly. Unintentionally or not, for reasons good or bad, the Croatians were exciting a Great Serb reaction that might end in a neo-Stalinist coup backed by the Soviet Union. It was fear of this outcome that explained the unprecedented growth of anti-Croat sentiment in Slovenia. The Slovenes were not happy with their position in Yugoslavia either, Kardelj added, but they saw no better alternative to Yugoslavia in its present form. The only solution, he argued, lay in uniting the SKJ around the reforms, which once in place would prevent Croatia from being repeatedly outvoted or having its interests systematically neglected. Kardelj also warned that Slovenia would not accept any eventual Croatian domination of Yugoslavia either. He and the other Slovene leaders had to take into account the possibility that Croatia's new assertiveness might lead to a fresh Croatian–Serbian agreement, with a consequent division of Yugoslavia into two respective spheres of interests, once again diminishing Slovenia's role and influence. What Slovenia, and by extension Yugoslavia, needed was balance, a relationship of forces that would prevent Croatia and Serbia alike from dominating the federation. This meant that if the Croatian leadership refused to obey Tito and had to be removed, the Serbian leadership too would have to be deposed.

The Croatians refused to be panicked. The main problem, in their view, derived not from the existence of extremists in Croatia or Serbia, but from resistance to change within the SKJ. To give up vital Croatian interests at this stage, especially those in the economic sphere, would only create new dissatisfaction with Yugoslavia in Croatia. Amid growing rumours of the Croatian leadership's imminent downfall, Tripalo made a defiant speech at the Dalmatian port of Vis in late November 1971: 'Our opponents think that our policy can be changed by replacing the leadership. For that to happen, however, it would be necessary to replace thousands of officials in Croatia, and to change the mood and thinking of the vast majority of Communist Party members, of the working class, and of the nation. It would be necessary to do the impossible – to change the whole nation together with its working class – but that is impossible.'[57]

By the end of the autumn of 1971 Tito was ready to move against the Croatian leaders. He would later tell Savka that he had been given no choice, that the army was putting great pressure on him to yield them up, and that it was either him or them. The Soviet Union and the United States were appraised of his intentions in advance. An otherwise inoffensive student strike at Zagreb University, which began on 22 November in defence of Croatia's economic interests, supplied a good excuse.[58] At the end of the month Tito instructed the army to be ready to intervene in Zagreb, only to be told that the units were already in position. On 1 December 1971, the anniversary of Yugoslavia's formation, he convened a meeting of the federal party presidency at Karađorđevo in Vojvodina. Only some of those invited were told of the meeting's purpose. The Croatians were still determined to resist any call to use repression, but their negotiating position was greatly weakened by the fact that they arrived split into two opposing factions, one led by Savka, backed by the majority of the central committee, the other led by Bakarić who enjoyed majority support on the central committee's executive body. Tito met with the Croatians before the conference, and held them in conversation for twenty hours, with short breaks for meals. The exchange was calm and polite; he would later say that the Croatian leaders had almost succeeded in 'tricking him' again.[59] He did not enjoy the prospect of removing such a popular leadership. He was ready to use the army to crush any eventual resistance, but was worried about the effect this would have on his, and Yugoslavia's, international prestige. At the meeting of the federal presidency, most of those who intervened attacked the Croatians; but Nikezić and Perović did not, mindful that they themselves were likely to be the next target, instead insisting that the Croatians be left to decide how to proceed, because only this would produce a valid and lasting solution. That was the view also of the Macedonian leader, Krste Crvenkovski, one of those who had not been informed beforehand of the meeting's agenda, since like a majority of Macedonian leaders he backed Croatia on most political issues. On 8 December Tito asked for the resignations of Savka and Pirker, on the grounds that they had lost the confidence of the federal party leadership – ignoring the fact that they enjoyed the confidence of their own party. Tripalo told Tito that he too would resign.

The three resignations, written in a manner designed to discourage any mass action on their behalf, were submitted to the Croatian party's central committee, which met four days later. They were joined by other resignations. The mass purge that followed was accompanied by a hysterical campaign against 'nationalists', 'separatists' and 'counter-revolutionaries'. According to one estimate, the purge led the party to lose half its membership, and the state 60–70 per cent of officials, judges, heads of industry, media directors and journalists, retired and active generals.[60] Some 2,300 people were convicted of criminal acts against the people and the state. Many of those who were now hounded for their 'counter-revolutionary activity' had fought in the Spanish Civil War and/or had been honoured for their contribution to the Partisan resistance. Most Croats experienced this as an attack on their state and their national liberty. Many blamed Serbs for it, finding proof of this in the writing of the Belgrade press, and in the behaviour of many Croatian Serb Communists who, fearful of Yugoslavia's break-up, took upon themselves to lead the struggle against 'Croat nationalism and separatism'.

Although some rural Serbs too joined the anti-Croat campaign – under the influence of unscrupulous propaganda portraying the Croatian Communist leaders as followers of the Ustashe, intent on the mass extermination and/or deportation of the Croatian Serbs – most of the Serb population refused to become involved.

The deposed Croatian leaders were expelled from the Party in May 1972. Their names were deleted from publications, their images from official photographs and television reports, the years of their rule expunged from the Party's official history. The revanchism did not spare their families.[61] The suppression of the Croatian Spring permitted Tito to move also against the Serbian leadership, who were likewise backed by their party's central committee. In October 1972 Nikezić and Perović resigned, after which Serbia too was subjected to an extensive purge. Smaller purges were conducted also in Slovenia and Macedonia. To prevent a unitarist or Great Serb backlash, however, the process of constitutional change was speeded up, and the new constitution finally adopted on 2 February 1974.

The federal assembly was henceforth to be composed of two chambers, the Council of Republics and Provinces and the Federal Council. The former body was made up of twelve deputies from each of the six republics and eight from each of the two provinces, elected by – and responsible only to – their individual parliaments. The Federal Council brought together thirty delegates from each republic and twenty from each province, elected by local municipal assemblies. The individual republican and provincial parliaments, meanwhile, were each now composed of three chambers, representing respectively 'associated labour', the municipalities and 'sociopolitical' bodies. Much of the capital held in Belgrade banks was dispersed to other republics and provinces, in the name of the rights of 'associated labour'. The republics and provinces acquired their own presidencies, as indicators of their autonomy and sovereignty, which brought them also their own constitutional courts, departments for foreign affairs, national banks, and territorial armed forces. The federal presidency was reduced to nine members: one from each republic and province plus Tito as Yugoslavia's lifelong president. Although the federal state retained some prerogatives, these were limited by the right of the republics and provinces to veto any of its measures which they considered inimical to their interests.

With the federal party weakened beyond repair, its executive committee too was reorganised and became in effect Tito's office for party affairs. The federal bodies functioned partly on the basis of inter-republican agreement, but mainly by obeying Tito. These changes left President Tito himself as the only federal institution, together with the army, upon which his power rested. Tito had kept the army away from all civilian control, with the result that military influence would henceforth seep into purely civilian bodies. The army intelligence service KOS now alone covered the whole country. In reality, however, Tito's ability to influence events was rapidly declining, due to his advanced age but also to the absence of any instrument (other than the army) which he could use to enforce his will. His authority was put to the test in 1975, when the new Serbian presidency asked for revision of the new constitution on the grounds that the provinces' new status prevented Serbia (meaning the Republic of Serbia, which formally still included the provinces) from constituting itself as a nation state. The provinces, as was to be expected, resisted any diminution of their powers. The dispute went on till 1977 when a so-called Blue Book appeared, marked 'top secret' and containing Serbia's proposals. Unable to agree, the opposing parties asked for Tito's arbitration – whereupon Tito sided with the provinces. Serbia accepted his decision, but left the impression of its intention to change the constitutional order once Tito was gone.

Following the resignations of Savka and Tripalo, Bakarić ruled unchallenged in Croatia until his death in 1983. Despite his role in putting an end to the Croatian Spring, he continued to defend the tenth session of the SKH central committee which had given birth to it. Within weeks of the resignations, he told the party paper *Komunist* that there was no return to the status quo ante: 'At its tenth session the CK SKH made a clean break with the unitarism present in our ranks, which at this stage of our socialist development assisted Great Serb aspirations present at the centre. This remains a lasting achievement of that meeting.'[62] Two years later he warned against a highly dangerous unitarist faction emerging within the Croatian party, whose victory would be bound to lead to civil war. Although Bakarić had no chance of replacing Tito, Kardelj did – and with Tito's attention fixed on foreign affairs he increasingly 'deputised' for him at home. But Kardelj died in early 1978, leaving Tito with the problem of finding his successor as party leader. This was more complicated than the issue of the federal state leadership, since the principle of 'democratic centralism' denied full autonomy to republican and provincial parties; it was also more portentous, given that practically all state functionaries were party members. The problem was solved by the introduction in 1978 of a rotating post of president of the federal party presidency. In that same year, asked to predict Yugoslavia's future, Tito stated: 'Yugoslavia no longer exists.' He added that the Communist Party too was gone.[63] He died two years later, on 4 May

Tito on bier, May 1980

1980, hoping in vain that the 1974 constitution would facilitate the peaceful break-up of Yugoslavia.

Beyond Yugoslavia

Tito's death removed the only authority that the constituent states had agreed to obey. The Serbian leadership now felt free to re-launch its offensive against the 1974 constitution. Initially limited to abolishing the autonomy of the two provinces, the campaign became ever more comprehensive in its aims, eventually turning into an open bid for the mastery of Yugoslavia. One of its earliest victims was Liberal Serbia. Why this Great Serb 'tendency' against which Kardelj had warned actually prevailed remains to be established. According to Latinka Perović, right-wing nationalists defeated in the Second World War, Stalinist dogmatists repressed in 1948, members of the state security service purged in 1966, and a radical Left seeking a return to 'Communist ideals', formed a potential 'revanchist bloc' that in 1987 crystallised into a strategic alliance.[64] Its ascendancy was confirmed when Slobodan Milošević became leader of the Serbian Communist Party, after which the party was purged of all opposition to Serbia's new course, in what was a third re-structuring of its political elite in just over two decades.

But whatever explanation is adopted for Serbia's behaviour in the late 1980s, the fact remains that only a near-independent state – a government in full control of the media, administration, economy, police and defence – could have organised a frontal attack on the existing federal order.

With the adoption of its new constitution in 1990, Serbia ceased to be part of Yugoslavia. Belgrade became solely the capital of Serbia: Yugoslav lawmakers and federal functionaries were now able to work in Belgrade only with Serbia's tolerance. Some were subjected to physical violence. Serbia had by this time swallowed up Vojvodina and Kosovo, and gained control also of Montenegro.[65] Aggressive moves against other federal states, however, demanded a more robust involvement on the part of the JNA.[66] The decision by the Slovene and Croatian leaders in 1989 to introduce multi-party democracy had been stimulated by the general process of change in Eastern Europe and the Soviet Union; but the timing had owed much to fear of Serbia's hostile stance. The functional coalition that Tito and his supporters had sought to create against such an outcome by means of constitutional reform was essentially defensive in nature, but was nevertheless strong enough to prevent Milošević from seizing control of the League of Communists of Yugoslavia in early 1990. The party now fell apart, signalling the demise of both Communism and Yugoslavia. Despite the increasingly divergent fates of Yugoslavia's component states, their unity survived long enough to prevent the introduction of a state of emergency in March 1991, a measure sought by Serbia and the JNA that would have nipped in the bud any transition to parliamentary democracy. Bosnia-Herzegovina's refusal to back their demand proved decisive. The pressure for the overthrow of Communism within Serbia itself, which manifested itself at this time, sealed a compact between Milošević's regime and the JNA, thus opening the road to war. The anti-Albanian and anti-Slovene hysteria that engulfed Belgrade in the late 1980s, and which in the first instance was directed against the idea of political pluralism, was a first step along that road.

Analyses that seek to grapple with the momentous changes that occurred in the Yugoslav area after Tito's death – the rise of Great Serbia and the break-up of the federal state; the fall of Communism and the dismantling of the system based on 'social ownership'; the end of the post-war peace and the advent of a war accompanied by genocide – by recourse to terms like 'nationalism', 'secessionism' or 'ethnic hatred' (rather than the categories normally used to describe times of systemic political crisis affecting a state association such as as legitimacy, constitution, party politics, aggression or defence) run the risk of mystifying history. The nationalism exhibited by the Yugoslav states was no different from that which governs the conduct of all states as they resist dilution of their sovereignty, seek to control their economies, and generally pursue their national interests, sometimes in harmony and at other times in conflict with one another. Yugoslavia broke up under the pressure not of some generic 'ethnic nationalism', but of divergent and conflicting political projects. This is perhaps best illustrated by the different responses of Slovenia and Serbia to the possibilities opening up with the fall of the Berlin Wall in late 1989. Slovenia united behind the slogan 'Forward to Europe!'; Serbia behind the idea of an ethnically homogenous Great Serbia.

Nor did ethnicity play a significant role in the political confrontations leading to Yugoslavia's collapse. Bosnia-Herzegovina's last representative on the federal presidency was Bogić Bogićević, a Serb who was to remain throughout one of Milošević's and Great Serbia's most steadfast opponents. And it was the Serb head of the League of Communists of Croatia, Stanko Stojčević, who cast the decisive vote in favour of introducing a multiparty system at the meeting of the Croatian Party presidency in December 1989. The speech he made on that occasion, part of which is reproduced below, illuminates the Croatian leaders' sense of historic responsibility, which led them to surrender power to the people as citizens.

> The problem of the relationship between the individual [citizen] and the state is never finally resolved. It involves on the one hand the citizens' identification with the political system in which they live, and on the other the legitimacy of the state which rules over them. In modern communities [that is, nation states], both are secured through a democratic procedure and above all in free elections. The League of Communists of Croatia takes the issue of the government's legitimacy extremely seriously. This is why the central committee of the SKH has initiated changes to the law on civic associations and the electoral law. Our aim is to create in advance the necessary legal conditions for free and democratic elections to take place in the spring of next year, in which all political subjects may participate on an equal basis, in order to ensure free expression of the political will of our citizens and working people.[67]

The SKH central committee went on to adopt a resolution which, alluding to the Second World War and the Croatian Spring, included the following:

> Yugoslavia finds itself today at a crossroads. Croatia's policy towards Yugoslavia must be based on the expressed will of its citizens. The SKH has won its position in a struggle with the nation and for the nation. Today too it does not wish to exercise its responsibilities or lead the country unless the working people and citizens – Croats, Serbs and others who live in Croatia – confirm it as the force capable of securing a stable, peaceful and prosperous life for them all. We won their trust in battle half a century ago, when our country was also at a crossroads. At several critical moments in the postwar period our legitimacy to institute changes has rested on our people's indisputable support. Without their support we neither can nor wish to take responsibility for the changes that lie ahead.

The central committee concluded by declaring the SKH's readiness to fight to win that support, and expressed confidence in its 'capacity to ensure Croatia's stability, territorial integrity and sovereignty, as well as the realisation of its potential within Yugoslavia'.[68] The SKH thus opted for a democratic transition, in defiance of threats coming from Serbia and the JNA. It argued that a peaceful transformation of the existing order was both possible and desirable. Serbia, on the other hand, entered the war with the opposite aim: to turn the clock back to 1966 and beyond. As Latinka Perović notes:

> The fact that the Serbs lived with other nations, which have vital interests too, should have steered them towards cooperation, compromise and tolerance. The Serbian elite, however, did not raise itself to the level of its historic responsibility, in that it failed to grasp the fact that it was in the Serb national interest to surrender all imperial ambitions. Once events in Eastern Europe had made the dominant Communist ideology untenable, Serbian rulers started to fan the flames of nationalism. Their initial programme for the Serbianisation of Yugoslavia provoked resistance, however, and encouraged other Yugoslav nations to seek independence. Serbia's response to this was war. The main war aims were clearly defined: redrawing of internal borders, exchange of populations, and re-composition of the Balkan political space.[69]

Serbia's new leaders justified the war against other Yugoslavs on the grounds of the right of all Serbs to live in the same state; but the vagueness of this ethnic formula suggested the intention to seek a maximal territorial

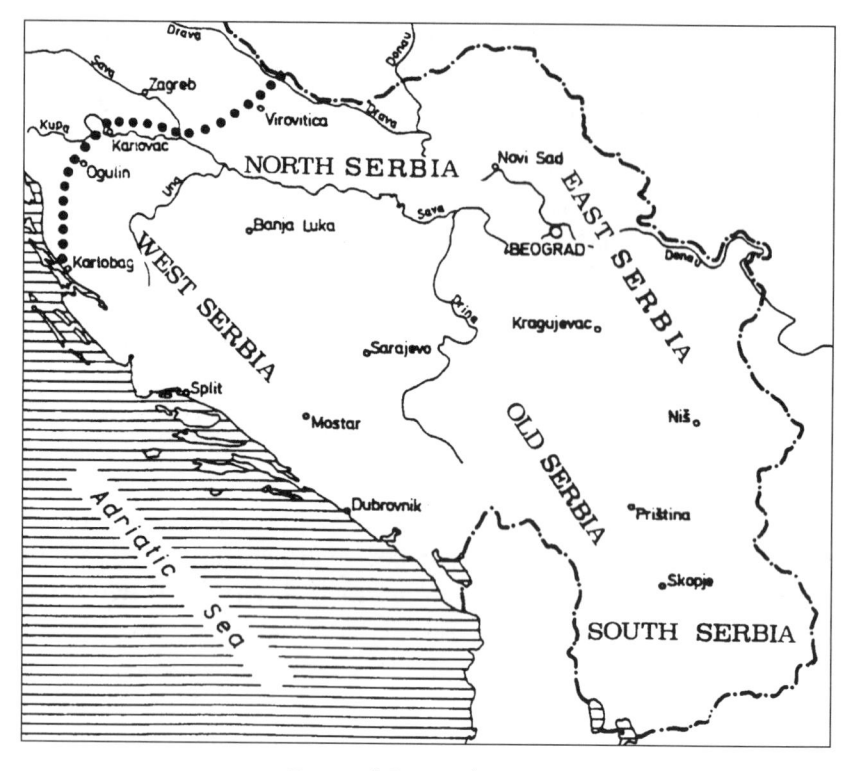

Projected Great Serbia, 1991

expansion. The formula 'all Serbs in the same state' consequently came to be filled with various and contradictory descriptions of what constituted 'Serb lands': lands that in the fourteenth century had belonged, or were alleged to have belonged, to the Serbian kingdom; lands inhabited by peoples who were 'originally Serbs' (the Macedonians and *štokavian*-speaking South Slavs); lands that would have become Serb but for their enemies' villainous behaviour. Had the fortunes of war favoured it, Serbia would have annexed – in addition to Vojvodina, Kosovo and Montenegro – the whole of Macedonia, Bosnia-Herzegovina and two-thirds of Croatia in a grand replay of the Ottoman invasions of the fifteenth and sixteenth centuries. Since Serbia also wished to end up as a more or less ethnically homogeneous state, its aggression from the start involved the forcible removal of non-Serb populations from the occupied areas. This policy was first put into practice in 1991, when Serbia managed to seize a sizable portion of Croatian territory, from which all non-Serbs were summarily expelled. On the eve of the war this territory was inhabited by just under half a million people, of whom some 204,000 were Croats and 288,000 Serbs: by 1993 all but a few non-Serbs had been expelled, while many thousands had been killed. The number of Serbs whom the area encompassed, meanwhile, amounted to less than half the total number (581,663) of Serbs living in Croatia at the time.[70]

Western democracies appeared ready to sanction the annexation, and the idea of 'ethnic' reconstruction in this part of Europe. In early 1992 this 'ethnically cleansed' part of Croatia became a United Nations Protected Area (UNPA). Removed from Croatian jurisdiction, the area was in effect handed to Serbia, which organised and maintained its army and administration. Protected by UN troops, the occupied territory was consolidated under the grandiloquent name of the Serb Krajina Republic (RSK), which survived until the summer of 1995 when it was destroyed by the Croatian army. The fact that this 'republic' hugged the Croatian frontier with Bosnia-Herzegovina suggests that Western politicians at that point in time were ready to accept the incorporation also of all or most of Bosnia-Herzegovina into a Great Serbia, with all the horrors that this would clearly entail in light of the Croatian precedent. By tacitly endorsing the forcible redrawing of state borders and the policy of 'ethnic cleansing', Western democracies stimulated the replacement of the earlier territorial concept of nationhood by one based on ethnic homogeneity and racial supremacy. They endorsed such a change less willingly than Hitler did in 1941, more out of negligence than intention. But the effects were not very dissimilar.

As a kind of additional safeguard, meanwhile, Milošević proposed to the new Croatian president, Franjo Tuđman, that Serbia should share Bosnia-Herzegovina with Croatia.[71] In the war that followed Serbia established an 'ethnically pure' Serb republic on its territory, and Croatia an 'ethnically pure' Croat Community (later republic) of Herzeg-Bosna. In 1995, the Dayton Accords brokered by the United States led to the absorption of this Herzeg-Bosna into the Federation of Bosnia-Herzegovina, while the Serb entity survived in a reduced form within Bosnia-Herzegovina. By the end of 2006, with all the former Yugoslav republics having become internationally recognised states and with Kosovo too set on the road to independence, Great Serbia had been reduced to a union of Serbia and Vojvodina.

A new republic

The acquisition of independence inevitably entailed a new understanding of the national constituency. This was as true for a relatively homogeneous state in national terms like Slovenia as it was for a nationally heterogeneous one like Bosnia-Herzegovina. Slovenia's new constitution, for example, affirmed the country as the state of the Slovene nation, recognised the existing rights

Birth of the Second Republic, Zagreb 1990

of Italian and Hungarian minorities, and offered Slovene citizenship to resident citizens of other former Yugoslav states. Croatia's new constitution defined it as the national state of the Croat people, and of other national groups whose members were Croatian citizens – Serbs, Bosniaks, Slovenes, Czechs, Slovaks, Italians, Hungarians, Jews and others. The adoption of a Western-type parliamentary system imposed also new ways of perceiving the Croatian nation, by the very fact of introducing a new system of political representation. The former parliament had been made up of three chambers, representing respectively 'associated labour', the municipalities, and socio-political associations (the Communist Party and its various offshoots). The new Croatian constitution replaced these bodies with two chambers, both territorially based: the House of Representatives and the House of Counties (abolished in 2001), elected on the basis of direct, secret and equal adult suffrage. The earlier different socio-political identities were thus fused into one, the economic sphere separated from the political, while political power became concentrated in parliament, which chose to share it with a directly elected president. The former 'ethnicisation' of politics by way of a 'national key' – a policy of national quotas, practised in order to ensure that the administration would reflect the ethnic make-up of the population – was replaced by ethnically based parties. Various social and regional interests that had earlier found expression within the confines of a single party now emerged into the open. The whole structure of the Croatian state in fact underwent a sudden and in many ways disturbing de-construction, as the earlier well-regulated and sophisticated Communist administration began to be replaced by a confused and chaotic new order.

One main difference between the old and new definitions of Croatia was that the Serbs were now defined as a national minority. This was a novelty that they found hard to accept. According to the 1981 census Serbs formed 11.6 per cent of the Croatian population, supplying in the mid-1980s 21.4 per cent of political leaders at the municipal level, 13.8 per cent at the level of regional associations, and 24.8 per cent at the republican level. Serbs were over-represented in the political sphere, under-represented among technical intelligentsia and craftsmen, while their ethnic weight was reflected appropriately among peasants and industrial workers.[72] These data show that Croatian Serbs, far from being under threat, were actually well integrated into Croatian society. Indeed, the very absence of discrimination was deemed by Great Serbs, including the Serb Orthodox Church, to pose the greatest threat to their national identity. During the nineteenth century, successive Croatian parliaments introduced a series of laws making Croatian Serbs – as individuals and as a collectivity – equal in every respect to Croatian Croats. At the time of Yugoslavia's formation in 1918, Croatia was governed by a coalition of Croat and Serb parties. Between the two world wars, the two dominant Croat and Serb parties – the HSS and the SDS – were joined in a coalition. During the period of the NDH, Croatian Serbs were indeed subjected to mass murder and deportation – but the NDH was brought down through joint Croat and Serb efforts. As indicated above, on the eve of the 1991–5 war Croatian society had succeeded in integrating its previously rural Serb population into a functioning national community. It was the Croatian leadership's fear of inflaming Croat–Serb relations that was responsible for the notorious 'Croatian silence' in the second half of the 1980s, when Croatia left Slovenia and Kosovo to bear, in their different ways, the main burden of resistance to Serbian provocations. No anti-Milošević – let alone anti-Serb – demonstrations took place in Croatia at that time, despite the fact that Serbia was organising nationalist rallies in Serb-populated areas of Croatia, with the aim of intimidating the Croatian leadership and dividing the Serb community. Serbia's virulent nationalism greatly strengthened pro-independence sentiment among the Croats; but the growing urge to part with Serbia did not embrace the idea of expelling the Serb population, nor for that matter of uniting all Croats within a Great Croatia.

The main political division in Croatia at the end of the 1980s was not ethnic, but political: between those who felt that the necessary reforms could be realised within the Yugoslav framework (orthodox Communists, and supporters of the Croat politician and Yugoslav prime minister, Ante Marković) and those who disagreed. The emergence of separate Croat and Serb parties in 1990 did not signal any imminent breakdown of Croat–Serb peace, given that Croatia had traditionally produced integrated as well as separate national parties. The issue of whether Croatia would or would not remain in Yugoslavia was decided not by ethnic Croats, but by a majority of Croatia's adult citizens. The first parliamentary elections held in 1990 reflected the national mood quite accurately. A relative minority – 42 per cent – of the Croatian electorate voted for the pro-independence Croat Democratic Union (HDZ). A coalition of liberal Croat national parties won 15 per cent. Significant numbers of both Croats and Serbs voted for the Party of Democratic Reform (SDP, former Communists, now Social Democrats), which emerged as the second largest party with 35 per cent of the popular vote. A small minority of Serbs voted for the Belgrade-sponsored Serb Democratic Party (SDS), which won less than 2 per cent.[73] These electoral results show that Croatian Serbs did not vote for separation from Croatia. But Serbian pressure on the one hand, and the 'winner-take-all' attitude of the HDZ on the other, combined to encourage a Croat–Serb divide. Soon after the elections, the SDS left parliament to concentrate on creation of the RSK, after which a number of Serb SDP deputies decided to join it. When, however, in September 1991, immediately prior to Serbian invasion, a commission arrived from Belgrade to investigate the situation in the Serb areas under JNA control, it found that the SDS leader Jovan Rašković saw the Croatian Serbs' future exclusively in Croatia; that the leader of the small Serb National Party, Milan Đukić, was also behaving 'treacherously'; and that 20 per cent of males at most expressed their readiness to fight against their country.[74]

Nevertheless, the acquisition of independence coupled with the transition to a Western-style parliamentary system was bound to reinforce the state's Croat identity. Whereas in Yugoslavia Croatian Serbs had belonged to a nation twice as numerous as the Croat one, they were greatly outnumbered in independent Croatia. In a consensual dissolution of the Yugoslav federation, Serb fears of becoming a minority – fanned by memories of the NDH and even more by Belgrade propaganda – might have largely been alleviated, but the transition would still not have been painless. The disappearance of Yugoslavia was inevitably experienced by the Croatian Serbs as a loss, to an extent that was not true for the Croats. But

The ever-present past: Croatian banknotes in 1994, with images of (clockwise) Ivan Mažuranić, Marko Marulić, Josip Jelačić, Stjepan Radić, Ivan Gundulić, and Ante Starčević

this difference was neither absolute nor permanent. The majority of Croats neither held radical nationalist views nor felt that Serb national rights should be removed. The majority of Serbs would certainly have preferred to remain in a state that also included Serbia – but that did not mean they would have gone to war for it. A significant number in fact voted with the majority in favour of independence, around 10,000 of them subsequently fighting, often as volunteers, in the Croatian army.[75] This does not detract from the fact that the decision to choose independence was a Croat decision, and that in the view of the Croat majority Serb national rights could not extend to a right of

Dubrovnik burns, December 1991

veto on such an important issue as state independence. Extrapolating from the previous constitution in the light of the new reality, the new Croatian constitution made this explicit by defining Croatia as primarily a state of the Croats.

The outgoing Communist administration, meanwhile, had produced an electoral law ensuring that whichever party won a relative majority would dominate the parliament. The intention was to create a strong government, capable of holding the country together at a dangerous time in its history. Since Croat voters showed a relatively strong preference for the HDZ, as the only party advocating outright independence, it thus won control of the national parliament and its leader, Franjo Tuđman, became Croatian president with substantial powers, which he proceeded to amplify by various subterfuges. Previously banned Ustasha insignia reappeared, as did a number of Ustasha supporters. The tendency to treat Serbs as a real or potential fifth column became widespread under the HDZ administration. In view of these changes, Serb fears were real and justified. But so too were Croat fears, since both the JNA and Serbia refused to recognise the new Croatian government. The HDZ, at all events, was not so much a party as an amalgam of different ideologies and interests. Despite its dominant parliamentary position, it produced a weak not a strong government. During the initial fourteen months of HDZ rule, for example, Croatia had two prime ministers, two ministers of defence, three foreign ministers, two ministers of the interior, two ministers of information, two 'welfare' ministers. Its weakness indeed became the main problem for Croats and Serbs alike. The government's debility was reinforced by the refusal of Belgrade and the JNA to treat it as legitimate, and by various measures they took to sabotage its functioning, including organising armed rebellion on its territory. The result was the emergence of a dual power, which by the middle of 1991 had taken on a territorial form: the Croatian government functioned on a restricted territory, while the rest was controlled by the JNA pretending to act on Yugoslavia's behalf.

The war, with all its novel and shocking violence, the loss of territory and the initial international refusal to recognise Croatia's independence, led to a closing of Croat ranks. Croatia's difficult situation served to excuse the deficiencies of a government under which the country was sliding into chaos and lawlessness. During 1991 the unoccupied part of Croatia became fragmented into discrete areas of more or less improvised authority with varying degrees of legitimacy. This was most visible in the domain of defence, with each area being forced to fend for itself. Persuaded that the JNA would not attack Croatia, Tuđman initially had refused to create an army or a defence plan, as a result of which the country came close to defeat in 1991. Matters improved only in the late summer of that year, when the HDZ government was replaced by a national coalition and the Croatian army (HV) was formed. Within months the HV came close to expelling

Serbian forces from Croatia, but Tuđman was once again persuaded not to seek a military victory. Had the HV been permitted to win the war in 1991 or soon after, conditions would have been created for national reconciliation. In the event, the Croatian president's decision – taken without knowledge of the national parliament – to allow the establishment of UNPA in the part of Croatia controlled by the JNA prolonged the war for another four years, and consolidated both HDZ rule and the Croat–Serb divide symbolised by the RSK. Croatian government policy towards the Serb population in the area under its control made it more difficult for Serbs in the occupied area who might wish to break from Belgrade to do so. In the event, most of the population of RSK left Croatia in August 1995. The decision that they should do so was taken by the defence council of the RSK on 4 August 1995.[76] The exodus was planned and organised by Belgrade, albeit with Tuđman's approval. Serbia's use of the Croatian Serb population as an instrument of war proved disastrous for this old Croatian community: according to the Croatian census of 2001, the number of Serbs in Croatia has been halved as a result.

More generally, the outbreak of war had created conditions for the concentration of unrestrained power in the hands of a president who saw himself as embodying the national will. Tuđman's strategic alliance with Milošević, and his effort to create an enlarged and ethnically homogenous Croat state, resulted in the dispossession of all Croatians both as citizens and as a sovereign people. The extent of this political dispossession is indicated by the fact that Tuđman was able to invite in foreign troops, wage war against Bosnia-Herzegovina, and barter with Croatian state territory, without consultation with or approval by the national parliament. Replacement of a predominantly state-territorial by an ethnic concept of nationhood during the Tuđman period was thus accompanied by subversion of the institutions through which citizens were able to influence the articulation of state politics and control the exercise of state power. This became possible only after his death in 1999, when a democratic Croatian polity finally began to function.

For Croatia, 22 May 1992, the day when it became a member of the United Nations, marked a symbolic end of the journey on which it had embarked a century and a half before, in 1848. Its oldest citizens were born in Austria-Hungary. Their fathers fought in the First World War, which ended with the dissolution of Austria-Hungary; they themselves in the Second World War, which ended with the creation of a federal Yugoslavia; their Yugoslav-born children and grandchildren in the war of 1991–5, which ended in the

Looking to the future. Head of a young woman, Šibenik cathedral, fifteenth century

dissolution of Yugoslavia and the establishment of an independent Croatian republic. To their great-grandchildren growing up in this independent state, Yugoslavia appears just as nebulous as Austria-Hungary did to their parents and grandparents. This suddenly unfamiliar past is now being re-explored and rethought. The country, in the meantime, waits to join the European Union – a new Croatia in a new Europe committed to peace. It is a good moment to close this book.

Acronyms

AVNOJ	Antifašističko Vijeće Narodnog Oslobodenja Jugoslavije – Anti-Fascist Council of National Liberation of Yugoslavia
BBC	British Broadcasting Corporation
CK	Centralni Komitet – Central Committee
CLN	Comitato di Liberazione Nazionale – National Liberation Committee
DAI	De administrando imperio – On the Administration of the Empire
FTT	Free Territory of Trieste
GAP	Gruppi d'Azione Patriottica – Patriotic Action Groups
GUS	Glavni Ustaški Stan – Supreme Ustasha Office
HDZ	Hrvatska Demokratska Zajednica – Croatian Democratic Union
HFSS	Hrvatska Federalistička Seljačka Stranka – Croatian Federalist Peasant Party
HRSS	Hrvatska Republikanska Seljačka Stranka – Croatian Republican Peasant Party
HSP	Hrvatska Stranka Prava – Croatian Party of Right
HSS	Hrvatska Seljačka Stranka – Croatian Peasant Party
HV	Hrvatska Vojska – Croatian Army
JA	Jugoslavenska Armija – Yugoslav Army
JAT	Jugoslavenski Aerotransport – Yugoslav Airlines
JMO	Jugoslavenska Muslimanska Stranka – Yugoslav Muslim Party
JNA	Jugoslavenska Narodna Armija – Yugoslav People's Army

JRZ	Jugoslavenska Radikalna Zajednica – Yugoslav Radical Union
KOS	Kontraobavještajna Služba – Counterintelligence Service
KPH	Komunistička Partija Hrvatske – Communist Party of Croatia
KPJ	Komunistička Partija Jugoslavije – Communist Party of Yugoslavia
NATO	North Atlantic Treaty Organisation
NDH	Nezavisna Država Hrvatska – Independent State of Croatia
NKOJ	Nacionalni Komitet Oslobođenja Jugoslavije – National Committee of Liberation of Yugoslavia
NKVD	Narodnyi Komissariat Vnutrennikh Del – People's Commissariat of Internal Affairs
NOF	Narodno-oslobodilačka fronta – National Liberation Front
NOO	Narodno-oslobodilački Odbor – National Liberation Committee
NOP	Narodno-oslobodilački Pokret – National Liberation Movement
NOVH	Narodno-oslobodilačka Vojska Hrvatske – National Liberation Army of Croatia
NOVJ	Narodno-oslobodilačka Vojska Jugoslavije – National Liberation Army of Yugoslavia
OVRA	Opera Vigilanza Repressione Antifascismo – Department for Surveillance and Repression of Antifascism
OZNA	Odjeljenje za Zaštitu Naroda – Department of Public Safety
PCd'I	Partito Comunista d'Italia – Communist Party of Italy
PCI	Partito Comunista Italiano – Italian Communist Party
RSK	Republika Srpska Krajina – Serb Krajina Republic
SDK	Seljačko-Demokratska Koalicija – Peasant-Democratic Coalition
SDP	Stranka Demokratskih Promjena – Party of Democratic Reform

SDS	Samostalna Demokratska Stranka – Independent Democratic Party
SDS	Srpska Demokratska Stranka – Serb Democratic Party
SFRJ	Socijalistička Federativna Republika Jugoslavija – Socialist Federal Republic of Yugoslavia
SKJ	Savez Komunista Jugoslavije – League of Communists of Yugoslavia
SKOJ	Savez Komunističke Omladine Jugoslavije – League of Communist Youth of Yugoslavia
SLS	Slovenska Ljudska Stranka – Slovene/Slovenian People's Party
SSS	Samostalna Srpska Stranka – Independent Serb Party
UDB	Uprava Državne Bezbjednosti – Directorate of State Security
UN	United Nations
UNPA	United Nations Protected Area
UNS	Ured za Nacionalnu Sigurnost – National Security Bureau
VMR	Vnatrešna Makedonska Revolucionerna Organizaciya – Internal Macedonian Revolutionary Organisation
VUJA	Vojna Uprava Jugoslavenske Armije – Yugoslav Military Government
ZAVNOBiH	Zemljsko Antifašističko Vijeće Narodnog Oslobođenja Bosne i Hercegovine – Country-wide Anti-Fascist Council of National Liberation of Bosnia-Herzegovina
ZAVNOH	Zemaljsko Antifašističko Vijeće Narodnog Oslobođenja Hrvatske – Country-wide Anti-Fascist Council of National Liberation of Croatia

Notes

Chapter One
1. John J. Wilkes, *Dalmatia*, Routledge & Kegan Paul, London 1969, pp. 78–80.
2. Ejnar Dyggve, *Povijest salonitanskog kršćanstva*, Književni krug, Split 1996, p. 27; Ivo Babić, *Prostor između Trogira i Splita*, Muzej grada Trogira, Trogir 1984, pp. 45–71.
3. Radoslav Katičić, *Litterarum studia*, Matica hrvatska, Zagreb 1998, pp. 75–6.
4. Most of his and his co-ruler Maximian's statues were subsequently destroyed by order of Emperor Constantine. Of the thousands of inscriptions of his name which once dotted the region, only one has been found in Salona and not a single one in his palace in Split. Joško Belamarić, 'Egyptian mementos in Diocletian's palace', *Most/ The Bridge*, 1–4, Zagreb 1999, pp. 209–16.
5. Katičić, *Litterarum studia*, pp. 75–83; Mirjana Matijević Sokol, *Toma Arhiđakon i njegovo djelo*, Institut za hrvatsku povijest, Zagreb 2002, pp. 65–6.
6. George Ostrogorsky, *History of the Byzantine State*, Blackwell, Oxford 1980, p. 35. The timing of the emergence of Byzantium as a distinct empire is a matter of dispute. Here the year 800 is taken as the turning point, as in Judith Herrin, *The Formation of Christendom*, Fontana Press, London 1989.
7. 'In technical terms they were not *laeti*, subjects of the empire, but *foederati*, a foreign state bound by treaty to Rome.': A. H. M. Jones, *The Decline of the West*, Longman, London and New York 1966, p. 68. See also Herwig Wolfram, *History of the Goths*, University of California Press, Berkeley 1990, p. 133.
8. Ostrogorsky, *History of the Byzantine State*, p. 52; *The Cambridge Medieval History*, Cambridge 1957, pp. 34–5. I am grateful to Dr László Péter for drawing my attention to this aspect, as well as for allowing me to consult his *Verfassungsentwicklung in Ungarn* in manuscript form.
9. Herwig Wolfram, *The Roman Empire and Its Germanic Peoples*, University of California Press, Berkeley 1997, pp. 116–19.
10. Radoslav Katičić, *Uz početke hrvatskih početaka*, Književni krug, Split 1993, p. 26.
11. Pierre Cabanès, 'L'Adriatique, de l'unité impériale à l'affrontement Est-Ouest', in Pierre Cabanès, ed., *Histoire de l'Adriatique*, Seuil, Paris 2001.
12. Constantine Porphyrogenitus, *De administrando imperio*, Dumbarton Oaks, Washington 1967. This confidential guide to Byzantine diplomacy was first published in Leyden in 1611.
13. Toma Arhiđakon, *Historia salonitana*, Književni krug, Split 2003, pp. 32–3.
14. Mate Suić, 'Pristupna razmatranja uz problem etnogeneze Hrvata', in Neven Budak, ed., *Etnogeneza Hrvata*, Matica hrvatska, Zagreb 1995, pp. 13–27; John Wilkes, *The Illyrians*, Blackwell, Oxford 1995, pp. 270–1.
15. They are summarised and elaborated in Ivan Jurić, *Genetičko podrijetlo Hrvata*, Zagreb 2003.
16. Antun Dabinović, *Hrvatska državna i pravna povijest*, Matica hrvatska, Zagreb

1990, pp. 49–56; Neven Budak, *Prva stoljeća Hrvatske*, Hrvatska sveučilišna naklada, Zagreb 1994, pp. 80–2.
17. The tradition of fitting unfamiliar peoples into Romano-Christian categories continued well into the twentieth century. See, for example, the Zulu *origo gentis* in Patrick H. Geary, *The Myth of Nations: The Medieval Origins of Europe*, Princeton University Press, Princeton 2002.
18. Herwig Wolfram, 'Razmatranja o origo gentis', in Budak, *Etnogeneza*, pp. 50–1.
19. Evgen Paščenko, *Etnogeneza i mitologija Hrvata u kontekstu Ukrajine*, Meditor, Zagreb 1999, p. 63.
20. Florin Curta, *The Making of the Slavs*, Cambridge University Press, Cambridge 2001.
21. Edward James, *The Franks*, Blackwell, Oxford 1994, pp. 6–7.
22. Petar Skok, *Etimologija hrvatskog ili srpskog jezika*, JAZU, Zagreb 1972, p. 216.
23. Katičić, *Uz početke*, pp. 47–8; Skok, *Etimologija*, pp. 690–2.
24. Paščenko, *Etnogeneza*, pp. 74–86.
25. Walther Pohl, 'Osnove hrvatske geneze: Avari i Slaveni', in Budak, ed., *Etnogeneza*, p. 218. On the other hand, the only mention of the Croats in connection with the Avars is found in *DAI* – where, however, they appear as Avar enemies. See Petar Štih in the same volume.
26. Budak, *Prva stoljeća*, pp. 68–9.
27. Lujo Margetić, *Dolazak Hrvata*, Književni krug, Split 2001, p. 95.
28. Petar Šimunović, *Istočnojadranska toponimija*, Književni krug, Split 1986, pp. 45–6.
29. Dabinović, *Hrvatska državna i pravna povijest*, pp. 49–56.
30. Petar Šimunović, 'Onomastička svjedočanstva nakon doseobe', in Ivan Supičić, ed., *Hrvatska i Evropa*, vol. 1: *Rano doba hrvatske kulture*, Školska knjiga, Zagreb 1997, pp. 401–14. For a survey of the debate on when the Croats were converted to Christianity, see Katičić, *Litterarum studia*, pp. 211–27, and Budak, *Prva stoljeća*, pp. 79–84.
31. Mladen Ančić, *Hrvatska u karolinško doba*, Muzej hrvatskih arheoloških spomenika, Split 2001, p. 10.
32. Peter Štih and Vasko Simoniti, *Slovenska zgodovina do razsvetljenstva*, Korotan, Ljubljana, 1966, pp. 29–43.
33. Roger Collins, *Charlemagne*, University of Toronto Press, Toronto 1998, p. 95.
34. Ančić, *Hrvatska u karolinško doba*, pp. 26–7.
35. Quoted in Katičic, *Uz početke*, p. 180. Dates of the reign of individual Croatian kings are based on Stjepan Antoljak, *A Survey of Croatian History*, Orbis/Laus, Split 1996. They are not always firmly established.
36. Gottschalk (c. 803–867/9), having fled the monastery of Fulda, went to Italy and Croatia. His doctrine of double predestination led to his life-long imprisonment on his return to Germany. Marcia L. Colish, *Medieval Foundations of the Western Intellectual Tradition*, Yale University Press, New Haven 1999, pp. 72–3. His visit to Croatia is described in Katičić, *Litterarum studia*.
37. Ivan Beuc, *Povijest institucija državne vlasti Kraljevine Hrvatske, Slavonije i Dalmacije*, Pravni fakultet, Zagreb 1985, ch. 1; Franjo Smiljanić, 'Prilog proučavanju županijskog sustava Sklavinije Hrvatske', in Budak, *Etnogeneza*, pp. 178–90.
38. Their names are inscribed in the Gospel of Cividale, a sixth-century Latin evangelistary kept originally in one of the Aquileia monasteries.
39. The proportion of Roman names in the Zadar upper class fell from 23 per cent in the tenth to 13 per cent in the thirteenth century. Ivo Goldstein, *Hrvatski rani srednji vijek*, Zavod za hrvatsku povijest, Zagreb 1995, p. 331.
40. Joan Dusa, *The Medieval Dalmatian Episcopal Cities,* Peter Lang, New York 1991;

Lujo Margetić, *Srednjovjekovno hrvatsko pravo*, Pravni fakultet Zagreb and Pravni fakultet Rijeka, Zagreb etc. 1983.

41. The investiture of Pope Hadrian II had coincided with the downfall of Rome's determined enemy Photius, patriarch of Constantinople, which led to reconciliation with Byzantium. Constantinople in fact took little interest in the brothers' mission to Moravia. Alexander M. Schenker, *The Dawn of Slavic Studies: An Introduction to Slavic Philology*, Yale University Press, New Haven 1995, p. 39.
42. The name of the script, derived from the Slav for 'word', appears indeed to be a Dalmatian invention. Schenker, *The Dawn of Slavic Studies*, p. 177.
43. Lujo Margetić, *Iz ranije hrvatske povjesti*, Književni krug, Split 1997, pp. 207–29.
44. Dimitri Obolensky, *The Byzantine Commonwealth: Eastern Europe 500–1453*, Orion, London 1971, pp. 137–8.
45. Matijević Sokol, *Toma Arhiđakon*, pp. 102–6.
46. Eduard Hercigonja, *Tropismena i trojezična kultura hrvatskog srednjovjekovlja*, Školska knjiga, Zagreb 1994.
47. Donald M. Nicol, *Byzantium and Venice: A Study in Diplomatic and Cultural Relations*, Cambridge University Press, Cambridge 1988, pp. 43–4.
48. Tomislav Rukar, *Hrvatsko srednjovjekovlje: Prostor, ljudi, ideje*, Školska knjiga, Zagreb 1997, p. 47.
49. Igor Fisković, *Reljef kralja Petra Krešimira IV.*, Muzej hrvatskih arheoloških spomenika, Split 2002.
50. R. W. Southern, *Western Society and the Church in the Middle Ages*, Penguin, London 1990, p. 102.
51. Fisković, *Reljef*, pp. 181–2. The dedication was removed in the eighteenth century during one of the recurrent battles between the Split municipal government and the archbishop of Split.
52. Ivo Goldstein, ed., *Zvonimir, kralj hrvatski*, HAZU, Zagreb 1997, pp. 52–3.
53. The retreat of St Benedict's order in the twelfth century led to an irreversible decay of Krešimir's church. The marble relief and other artefacts were transferred to Split in the same century, during which time the font was constructed and the cathedral's bell-tower was begun. The relief was placed in its present position in 1935 as part of a revival of interest in Croatian national heritage. Fisković, *Reljef*.
54. Valentin Putanec, 'Tri priloga za proučavanje prvog postanka zagrebačke biskupije', in Antun Škvorčević, ed., *Zagrebačka biskupija i Zagreb 1094–1994*, Nadbiskupija zagrebačka, etc., Zagreb 1995, pp. 124–5; Mladen Ančić, 'Desetljeće od godine 1091. do 1102. u zrcalu vrela', *Povijesni prilozi* 17, pp. 223–32, Zagreb 1998.
55. Lujo Margetić, 'Kritička rašclamba vrela najstarije povijesti zagrebačke biskupije', in Škvorčević, ed., *Zagrebačka biskupija*.
56. John V. A. Fine, Jr., *The Early Medieval Balkans*, The University of Michigan Press, Ann Arbor 1981, p. 278.
57. Jean Bérenger, *A History of the Habsburg Empire 1273–1700*, Longman, London and New York 1994, p. 12.
58. The bishop of Zagora, who may have acted as a mediator between the Croatian nobility and the Hungarian king, accompanied Coloman during his first visit to Zadar. Lujo Margetić, *Zagreb i Slavonija*, HAZU, Zagreb/Rijeka 2000, pp. 33–45.
59. Ančić, 'Desetljeće', pp. 223–32; Beuc, *Povijest institucija*, pp. 73–85. This latter source contains a summary of conflicting views on the origin and nature of the document. See also Stjepan Antoljak, *Pacta ili Concordia od 1102.*, Sveučilište u Zagrebu, Zagreb 1980.
60. Al-Idrisi visted Senj, Knin, Biograd, Šibenik, Trogir, Split, Ston and Dubrovnik. His

map marks twenty-five places in Croatia. A copy of the map is kept in the Bodleian Library, Oxford.
61. Lujo Margetić, 'Zagrebačka biskupija prema Arpadovićima i Anžuvincima', in Škvorčević, ed., *Zagrebačka biskupija*, pp. 163–8.

Chapter Two
1. These two, and a third one produced in the second half of the thirteenth century by one Martin da Canal, are reproduced in Petar Skok, *Tri starofrancuske hronike o Zadru u godini 1202*, JAZU, Zagreb 1951. The story is retold in Marcus Tanner, *Croatia, A Nation Forged in War*, Yale University Press, New Haven 1997, pp. 19–20.
2. Emerik had his son Stephen also crowned separately as king in each of the kingdoms. Ferdo Šišić, *Pregled povijesti hrvatskog naroda*, Matica hrvatska, Zagreb 1962, pp. 174, 179.
3. David Abulafia, *The Western Mediterranean Kingdoms 1200–1500: The Struggle for Dominion*, Longman, London 1997, pp. 162–6.
4. Raukar, *Hrvatsko srednjovjekovlje*, p. 81.
5. Zdenka Janeković Roemer, *Višegradski ugovor, temelj dubrovačke republike*, Golden Marketing, Zagreb 2003, pp. 52–60.
6. Ibid., pp. 11–21.
7. These statutes are examined in Antun Cvitanić, *Iz dalmatinske pravne povijesti*, Književni krug, Split 2002.
8. '[Charles's] assumption that he could rule both Hungary and southern Italy at a time of extreme disorder in Italy, schism in the papacy, and uncertainty in the central European monarchies, indicates a lack of practical political vision.' Abulafia, *Western Mediterranean Kingdoms*, p. 169.
9. Tomislav Raukar, *Zadar u XV stoljeću*, Institut za hrvatsku povijest, Zagreb 1977, pp. 30–4.
10. Mladen Ančić, *Putanja klatna: Ugarsko–hrvatsko kraljevstvo i Bosna u XIV stoljeću*, HAZU, Zagreb and Mostar 1997, p. 94.
11. Nikola Jakšić, *Hrvatski srednjovjekovni krajobrazi*, Muzej hrvatskih arheoloških spomenika, Split 2000.
12. Danilo near Šibenik was the site of an ancient culture linked to that of Vučedol in eastern Croatia which flourished around 3,000 BC. The chequerboard forms part of a pattern found in a priestly grave in Vučedol.
13. Nada Klaić, *Povijest Hrvata u srednjem vijeku*, Globus, Zagreb 1990, p. 310.
14. Nikola Jakšić, *Zemunik: Srednjovjekovni zadarski kaštel i turska kasaba*, Muzej hrvatskih arheoloških spomenika, Split 1997.
15. Mirko Tomasović, *Marko Marulić-Marul*, Erasmus, Zagreb/Split 1999, p. 173.
16. Variants of 'Hrvat' (Croat) as a personal name became a frequent choice of the local nobles at this time. Mladen Ančić, *Jajce*, Muzej hrvatskih arheoloških spomenika, Split 1997, pp. 34–43. See also Ančić, *Putanja klatna*.
17. Vladimir Košćak, 'Jadranska orijentacija feudalne Hrvatske', *Forum*, Zagreb April–May 1969.
18. Mačva, the territory between the rivers Sava, Drina and Kolubara, was established as a separate *banatus* in 1269 to protect Hungary and Slavonia from Serb incursions.
19. Lujo Margetić, 'Državnopravni položaj Hrvatske u doba Krbavske bitke', in Dragutin Pavličević ed., *Krbavska bitka i njene poslijedice*, Hrvatska matica iseljenika, Zagreb 1997, pp. 28–35.
20. Stanko Andrić, *The Miracles of St John Capistran*, CEU Press, Budapest 1999.
21. Francis Dvornik, *The Slavs in European History and Civilisation*, Rutger University Press, New Brunswick 1962, p. 205.

22. The village of Zapolje, the original seat of the family, lies east of Nova Gradiška, established in 1750 as the successor of Gradiška, an ancient crossing on the river Sava.
23. Unless otherwise stated, quotations in what follows are from Lujo Margetić, 'Cetinski sabori u 1527', *Senjski zbornik*, 17, pp. 35–46, Senj 1990.
24. The Hungarian jurist at this point referred to the Byzantine emperor Manuel I's investiture of the Hungarian king Bela III in 1164 as ruler in Croatia–Dalmatia. Legitimacy of rule was typically referred back to the Roman Empire. Dabinović, *Hrvatska državna i pravna povijest*, p. 352.

Chapter Three

1. Halil Inalcık, *An Economic and Social History of the Ottoman Empire*, Cambridge University Press, Cambridge 1994, vol. 1, p. 14.
2. Milan Kruhek, *Krajiške utvrde hrvatskog kraljevstva tijekom 16. stoljeća*, Institut za savremenu povijest, Zagreb 1995, p. 54.
3. Ibid. p. 55.
4. Ive Mažuran, *Hrvati i Osmansko carstvo*, Golden Marketing, Zagreb 1998, pp. 50–1.
5. Kruhek, *Krajiške utvrde*, p. 52.
6. Vedran Gligo, ed., *Govori protiv Turaka*, Logos, Split 1983, p. 344.
7. Kruhek, *Krajiške utvrde*, p. 52.
8. Most of its defenders and population moved to Senj to become uskoks: see Catherine Wendy Bracewell, *The Uskoks of Senj: Piracy, Banditry, and Holy War in Sixteenth Century Adriatic*, Cornell University Press, Ithaca NY 1992.
9. The Erdödy family, of Hungarian descent, held estates in both Hungary and Croatia, producing a Hungarian and a Croatian branch.
10. Nenad Moačanin, 'Upravna podjela hrvatskih zemalja u sklopu Osmanskog carstva' in Ivo Goldstein, ed., *Hrvatske županije kroz stoljeća*, Školska knjiga, Zagreb 1996.
11. Michael R. Hickock, *Ottoman Military Administration in the 18th century*, Brill, Leiden etc., New York and Köln 1997, ch. 2.
12. Bracewell, *The Uskoks*, pp. 33–7.
13. Nenad Moačanin, *Turska Hrvatska*, Matica hrvatska, Zagreb 1999, p. 38.
14. Nenad Moačanin, *Slavonija i Srijem u razdoblju osmanske vladavine*, Hrvatski institut za povijest, Slavonski Brod 2001.
15. Mažuran, *Hrvati i Osmansko carstvo*, p. 219.
16. Franjo Šanjek, *Kršćanstvo na hrvatskom prostoru*, Kršćanska sadašnjost, Zagreb 1996, p. 317.
17. Moačanin, *Slavonija i Srijem*, p. 43.
18. This section relies on the following sources in particular: Karl Kaser, *Slobodan seljak i vojnik*, vol. 1: *Rana krajiška društva (1545–1745)* and vol. 2: *Povojačeno društvo (1754–1881)*, Naprijed, Zagreb 1997; Kruhek, *Krajiške utvrde*; Dragutin Pavličević, ed., *Vojna krajina*, Liber, Zagreb 1984; Gunther E. Rothenberg, *The Austrian Military Border in Croatia 1522–1747*, University of Illinois Press, Urbana–Champaign 1960.
19. For an introduction to Vlach origin and history, as well as the debates that surround these, see Zef Mirdita, *Vlasi u historiografiji*, Hrvatski institut za povijest, Zagreb 2004. See also Gordana Žigman, 'Vlaška kolonizacija na području hrvatskih zemalja', *Lucius*, 1, vol. 1, Zagreb 2002; Noel Malcolm, *A Short History of Bosnia*, Macmillan, London 1997, pp. 70–92.
20. Raukar, *Hrvatsko srednjovjekovlje*, pp. 138–9.
21. Nenad Moačanin, 'Vlasi u požeškom sandžaku 1545–1558', in Pavličević, ed., *Vojna Krajina*, p. 197.

Chapter Four

1. Josip Adamček, 'Ekonomsko-društveni razvoj u Hrvatskoj i Slavoniji u 16. i 17. stoljeću', in Mirjana Gross, ed., *Društveni razvoj u Hrvatskoj od 16. do početka 20. stoljeća*, Liber, Zagreb 1981, p. 29.
2. Josip Bösendorfer, *Agrarni odnosi u Slavoniji*, JAZU, Zagreb 1950, pp. 52–3; Josip Adamček, *Bune i otpori: Seljačke bune u Hrvatskoj u XVII. stoljeću*, Globus, Zagreb 1987.
3. Adamček, 'Ekonomsko-društveni razvoj', p. 31.
4. Ivan Beuc, *Povijest institucija državne vlasti u Hrvatskoj (1527–1945)*, Arhiv Hrvatske, Zagreb 1969.
5. Nenad Moačanin, *Turska Hrvatska*, Matica hrvatska, Zagreb 1999, p. 32.
6. Nataša Štefanec, *Heretik Njegova Veličanstva: Povijest o Jurju Zrinskome IV. i njegovu rodu*, Zagreb 2001, pp. 131–6.
7. Vladislav Minčetić, *Trublja slovinska*, in Mihovil Kombol and Slobodan Prosperov Novak, *Hrvatska književnost do preporodnog doba*, Školska knjiga, Zagreb 1995, p. 277.
8. Štefanec, *Heretik*, p. 159.
9. For this 'Habsburg' aristocracy see R. J. Evans, *The Making of the Habsburg Monarchy 1550–1700*, Oxford Univresity Press, Oxford 1979.
10. Beuc, *Povijest institucija*, p. 4.
11. Štefanec, *Heretik*, p. 234.
12. For a recent glowing tribute to this Nicholas Zrinski, see Lázslo Kontler, *A History of Hungary*, Palgrave Macmillan, New York 2002, p. 174.
13. Košćak, 'Jadranska orijentacija'.
14. A letter that Nicholas wrote (in Latin) to a high official of county of Zagreb at this time expressed the family's intimate identification with their Croat roots: 'Since I am not untrue to my bloodline, I know myself to be a Croat – and clearly a Zrinski.'
15. Kontler, *A History of Hungary*, p. 176.
16. Zrinski cannon were taken to Kanizsa. The burning of the Süleyman bridge and the battle for Kanizsa are described in some detail in Rhoades Murphy, *Ottoman Warfare in 1500–1700*, Routledge, London 1999, pp. 122–9.
17. Quoted in Anđelko Mijatović, *Zrinsko-frankopanska urota*, Alfa, Zagreb 1992, pp. 64–5.
18. Luc Orešković, *Louis XIV. i Hrvati: Neostvareni savez*, Dom i svijet, Zagreb 2000. Others favoured a Rákóczi as a 'national' king. Kontler, *History of Hungary*, pp. 173–5.
19. For a list of estranged property see Mijatović, *Zrinsko-frankopanska urota*, pp. 102–3. According to the author, King Leopold acquired Petar Zrinski's jewellery, clothing, weapons, horse and hunting outfits, carpets – and even his bedcover.
20. John P. Spielman, *Leopold I of Austria*, Thames and Hudson, London 1977, p. 65.
21. Lučić was able to supply Petar Zrinski with copies of documents charting the transformation of the Bribirski Šubić family into the Zrinski. Miroslav Kurelac, *Ivan Lučić Lucius*, Matica hrvatska, Zagreb 1994, pp. 119–22.
22. Mažuran, *Hrvati i Osmansko carstvo*, pp. 243–7.
23. For an account of this campaign see Hickock, *Ottoman Military Administration*.
24. Kaser, *Slobodan seljak*, vol. 1, p. 173. There was also a group of 'Old Vlachs', who most likely came from the area of Stari Vlach southeast of Belgrade. Among them was a family called Pavelić, one of whose descendants would play a prominent role in Croatian politics in the middle of the twentieth century. See also Mirela Slukan, *Kartografski izvori za povijest Triplex Confiniuma*, Hrvatski državni arhiv, Zagreb 1999.

25. Gunther E. Rothenberg, *The Military Border in Croatia 1740–1881: A Study of an Imperial Institution*, The University of Chicago Press, Chicago 1966, p. 56.
26. Kaser, *Slobodan seljak*, vol. 2, p. 51.
27. All quotations here are from Drago Roksandić, *Vojna Hrvatska – La Croatie Militaire: Krajiško društvo u Francuskom carstvu, 1809–1813*, Školska knjiga, Zagreb 1988, vol. 2, pp. 169–223.

Chapter Five
1. The tablet is named after the nearby place of Baška.
2. He was born in all probability in the Roman municipality of Tarsatica, established at the mouth of the river Rječina, now part of the Croatian port of Rijeka. Tarsatica was an important staging post between Dalmatia and Aquileia.
3. Radoslav Katičić, *Na kroatističkim raskrižjima*, Sveučilište u Zagrebu, Zagreb 1999, p. 173.
4. Herzigonja, *Tropismena i trojezična kultura*, p. 74 He ended his life as a canon in Tours, leaving all his property to the city cathedral with the request that an annual Mass be said for him on the day after St Jerome's Day in the calendar.
5. Ivo Banac, 'Main trends in the Croat language question', in Riccardo Picchio and Harvey Goldblatt, eds, *Aspects of the Slavic language Question*, vol. 1, New Haven 1984.
6. Eduard Peričić, *Sclavorum regnum Grgura Barskoga*, Kršćanska sadašjnost, Zagreb 1991, pp. 256–7.
7. Mihovil Kombol and Slobodan Prosperov Novak, *Hrvatska knjiženvost do preporodnog doba*, Školska knjiga, Zagreb 1995, pp. 41–2.
8. Hercigonja, *Tropismena i trojezična kultura*, pp. 116–7.
9. Vladimir Vratović, *Hrvatski latinizam i rimska književnost*, Matica hrvatska, Zagreb 1989.
10. For his life and work see Žarko Dadić, *Herman Dalmatin – Hermann of Dalmatia*, Školska knjiga, Zagreb 1996.
11. At the time when Canaletto was painting *Riva degli Schiavoni* (Riva of the Slavs), the catalogue of the eighteenth-century Venetian printer family Occhi, which had specialised in publishing books in the Croat language, called it *Riva od Harvatou* (Riva of the Croats). Lavorka Čoralić, *U gradu svetoga Marka*, HAZU, Zagreb 2001, pp. 116–7.
12. Josip Leonard Tandarić, *Hrvatsko-glagoljska liturgijska književnost*, Kršćanska sadašnjost, Zagreb 1993, pp. 116–7.
13. Henry read Marulić even after his conflict with Rome, as is shown by a 1529 copy of *Evangelistarium*, kept in the British Library, in which the marginal notes were written by the king himself. The widespread translation and diffusion of Marulić's works in the sixteenth and seventeenth centuries, fuelled by the Catholic-Protestant schism, are presented in Charles Béné, 'Marulić and Europe', *Most/The Bridge*, Zagreb 2000.
14. One of his followers wrote in Goa in 1549 that 'Father and Master Francis reads and studies only from this book of his.' Leo Košuta, 'Fortunes and misfortunes of one of Marko Marulić's books', ibid., p. 141.
15. Ibid.; see also the essay by Franjo Šanjek in the same work.
16. Mirko Tomasović, *Marko Marulić Marul*, Erasmus, Split 1999, p. 188. The year before, in 1500, Marulić translated into Croat *De imitatione Christi*, ascribed to Thomas à Kempis.
17. Ibid., p. 235.
18. A polemical text against Italian authors claiming that St Jerome was Italian, however,

was written in Latin. Marulić protested: 'Why should some Italians suddenly seek to deny us the right to celebrate the fact that St Jerome was born in our land?' Marulić himself wrote a biography of St Jerome in 1507. Ibid., p. 89.

19. Published in Pesaro in Italy in 1601, it was allegedly used by Shakespeare when composing *The Tempest*. For Orbini's Dubrovnik see Zdenko Zlatar, *Our Kingdom Come*, East European Monographs, Boulder CO 1992. See also Robin Harris, *Dubrovnik, a History*, Saqi, London 2003.

20. Deborah Howard, *Venice and the East: The Impact of the Islamic World on Venetian Architecture 1100–1500*, Yale University Press, New Haven 2000, p. 17. *Della Mercatura et del Mercante perfetto* ('On Trade and the Perfect Merchant'), written in 1458, was published in 1573 in Venice by Francis Petrić (Francisus Patricius or Petris), his countryman from Cres.

21. Zlatko Vince, *Putovima hrvatskog književnog jezika*, Matica hrvatska, Zagreb 1990, p. 28.

22. Hanibal Lucić (1485–1553), quoted in Ivo Banac, 'Main trends', p. 203.

23. Branko Fučić, *Terra incognita*, Kršćanska sadašnjost, Zagreb 1998, pp. 64–6.

24. Francoise Waquet, *Latin or the Empire of a Sign*, Verso, London 2001, p. 49.

25. Mijo Mirković, *Matija Vlačić-Ilirik*, Hrvatska naklada, Pula and Rijeka 1980.

26. Diarmaid MacCulloch, *Reformation*, Allen Lane, Penguin, London 2003, pp. 349–50. Mijo Mirković, Flacius's inspired Croatian biographer, himself born not far from Labin, ascribes his ideological tenacity to the mentality of Istria's small city communes forged in hard work on land and sea.

27. Patrick Collinson, *The Reformation*, Weidenfeld and Nicolson, London 2003, p. 133.

28. Quoted in Mirković, *Matija Vlačić-Ilirik*, pp. 196–7.

29. According to the family tradition, the family descended from the Frankapan. The first mention of its presence dates to 1166, when one Dominic joined a delegation sent by Rab to Venice. De Dominis were ennobled by Emperor and King Sigismund at the end of the fourteenth century. Markantun's father Jerome was a prominent poet and jurist.

30. Noel Malcolm, *De Dominis (1560–1624): Venetian, Anglican, Ecumenist and Relapsed Heretic*, Strickland and Scott Academic Publications, London 1984.

31. MacCulloch, *Reformation*, pp. 411–2.

32. *Hrvatski biografski leksikon*, Leksikografski zavod 'Miroslav Krleža', Zagreb 1993, vol. 3, p. 497.

33. Adam Nicolson, *Power and Glory: Jacobean England and the Making of the King James Bible*, Harper Collins, London 2003, p. 227.

34. It appeared under the name of Antun Senjanin. The argument that Senjanin was actually Vlačić is presented in Mirković, *Matija Vlačić-Ilirik*, pp. 214–30.

35. Stanko Jambrek, *Hrvatski protestantski pokret u XVI. i XVII. stoljeću*, Matica hrvatska, Zaprešić 1999, pp. 151–3.

36. Ibid., pp. 327–8.

37. Despite the widespread endorsement of Protestantism by the Hungarian noble class, the Hungarian Bible appeared only in 1590, three decades after the Croat and a whole century after the Czech.

38. Franjo Glavinić, the guardian of the Franciscan monastery at the Frankapan city of Trsat (now part of Rijeka), writing in 1628. Quoted in Vince, *Putovima*, p. 36.

39. Dudić was a man of great talent and wide interests. He ended up as a highly tolerant Protestant. MacCulloch, *Reformation*, p. 263. The Dudić family, originally from Sinj, moved to northern Croatia to escape from the Ottomans. Its social ascent began in the service of the Croatian ban John Corvinus and his wife Beatrice Frankapan. He attended the Council of Trent in 1562–3 as bishop of Knin.

40. After leaving Zagreb he became bishop of Györ and royal chancellor, and in 1584 governor of Hungary. He died in 1585 on his way to Rome, having declined to become a cardinal.
41. According to a report from 1627 supplied by the archbishop of Zadar, there were 113 parishes with Slav liturgy in Venetian Dalmatia. Miroslav Granić et al., eds, *Život i djelo Bartola Kašića*, Općina Pag and Hrvatsko filološko društvo Zadar, Zadar 1994, p. 52.
42. Quoted in Elizabeth von Erdmann-Pandžić, 'Warum wurde die Bibelübersetzung von Bartol Kašić nich gedruckt?', in ibid., p. 197.
43. Kašić's *Biblia Sacra – Versio Illyrica Selecta* was published for the first time in 1999–2000 by F. Schöningh at Paderborn, as *Kroatische Bibel des Bartol Kašić*. Its language is a more archaic yet easily understandable version of contemporary Croat.
44. A member of the commission entrusted with the preparation of the new translation wrote: 'The Ritual we are preparing is nothing but the fourth edition of Kašić's Ritual, corrected in line with the development of the Croat language.' Granić, ed., *Život i djelo Bartola Kašića*, p. 100.
45. The nature of the relationship between the two is still being debated, the prevalent view being that both the Slovene and the Croat forms derive from an older common Slav speech. Vince, *Putovima*, pp. 29–32. The story of the Trubar-Skalić dispute is told in Katičić, *Na kroatističkim raskrižjima*, pp. 115–29. Skalić is the author of *Encyclopaediae, seu Orbis disciplinarum*, published in Basel in 1559, in which the word 'encyclopaedia' is for the first time used in the modern sense.
46. Dalibor Brozović, *Neka bitna pitanja hrvatskog jezičnog standarda*, Školska knjiga, Zagreb 2006.
47. The author was stimulated by a similar work – *The Treasure of the History of the Illyrian or Croatian People and Language* – published by Filip Grabovac, another Dalmatian Franciscan, in Venice in 1747. Since in this work Grabovac called Dalmatia a Croatian province and advocated Croat patriotism, he was promptly imprisoned by the Venetian state. He died two years later, confined to a Franciscan monastery.
48. Katičić, *Na kroatističkim raskrižjima*, p. 89.
49. Ivan Golub, *Ivan Paštrić*, Kršćanska sadašnjost, Zagreb 1986.
50. Katičić, *Na kroatističkim raskrižjima*, pp. 184–5.
51. For the life and thought of Juraj Križanić, see Ivan Golub, 'The Slavic Idea of Juraj Križanić', *Harvard Ukrainian Studies*, no. 3–4, Cambridge MA, 1986; Ivan Golub, *Križanić*, Kršćanska sadašnjost, Zagreb 1987; Radovan Pavić, ed., *Život i djelo Jurja Križanića*, Kršćanska sadašnjost, Zagreb 1974.
52. Golub, *The Slavic Idea*, p. 467.
53. Golub, *Križanić*, p. 39. Križanić's *History of Siberia*, dedicated to the Polish king Jan Sobieski, became an influential work on the subject. Pavić, ed., *Život i djelo*, p. 100.
54. Vjekoslav Klaić, *Život i djelo Pavla Rittera Vitezovića (1652–1713)*, Matica hrvatska, Zagreb 1914; Zrinka Blažević, *Vitezovićeva Hrvatska između stvarnosti i utopije*, Barbat, Zagreb 2002.
55. Blažević, ibid., p. 116.
56. Ivo Banac, 'Uskrsnula Hrvatska Pavla Rittera Vitezovića', *Kolo* 2, Zagreb 1996, p. 18.
57. Vince, *Putovima*, p. 325.
58. Ibid., pp. 325–78.

Chapter Six
1. Trpimir Macan, *Povijest hrvatskog naroda*, Matica hrvatska and Školska knjiga, Zagreb 1992, p. 259.

2. C. A. Macartney, ed., *The Habsburg and Hohenzollern Dynasties in the Seventeenth and the Eighteenth Centuries*, Walker & Co., New York 1970, pp. 82–5; 88–91.
3. Jaroslav Šidak, *Hrvatski narodni preporod – Ilirski pokret*, Školska knjiga, Zagreb 1998, p. 15.
4. Robert A. Kann, *The Multinational Empire*, Columbia University Press, New York 1950, vol. 1, p. 207.
5. This 'Croatia' stands for the territory governed by the sabor at the height of the Ottoman expansion. It is placed between inverted commas in order to avoid confusion with Croatia as a whole.
6. For the relevant documents referred to here and below see *Fontes*, 1, Zagreb 1995.
7. Stanko Andrić, 'Klaićev udio u raspravama hrvatske i mađarske historiografije', *Zbornik radova sa znanstvenog skupa o životu i djelu Vjekoslava Klaića*, Hrvatski institut za povijest, Slavonski Brod and Zagreb 2000.
8. As argued in C. A. Macartney, *The Habsburg Empire 1790–1918*, Weidenfeld & Nicolson, London 1968, p. 228.
9. Šidak, *Hrvatski narodni preporod*, p. 16.
10. Ibid.
11. Miroslav Šicel, ed., *Riznica ilirska*, Zagreb and Ljubljana 1985, p. 139.
12. Josip Horvat, *Politička povijest Hrvatske*, vol. 1, August Cesarec, Zagreb 1990, p. 33.
13. Šicel, ed., *Riznica*, p. 139.
14. Ibid., p. 164.
15. Ibid., p. 140.
16. Rudolf Bićanić, *Doba manufakture u Hrvatskoj i Slavoniji (1750–1860)*, JAZU, Zagreb 1951, pp. 328–9.
17. Macartney, *The Habsburg Empire*, p. 228.
18. The rise of the Hungarian Liberal Party, its social base and organisation, and its transformation from a pressure group into a party of government are explored in Andrew C. Janos, *The Politics of Backwardness in Hungary 1825–1945*, Princeton University Press, Princeton 1982. For the national proportions see pp. 68–9.
19. Bićanić, *Doba manufakture*, p. 332.
20. Memorandum submitted to the Commercial Commission of the Hungarian parlaiment in 1843, quoted in Janos, *The Politics of Backwardness*, p. 67.
21. Bićanić, *Doba manufakture*, p. 389.
22. Jaroslav Šidak, *Studije iz hrvatske povijesti XIX. stoljeća*, Školska knjiga, Zagreb 1973, p. 5.
23. Ibid.
24. From a poem written in Latin by Tito Brezovački, quoted in Vince, *Putovima*, p. 268.
25. Horvat, *Politička povijest*, vol. 1, p. 28.
26. Unless otherwise stated the figures quoted below are from Jakov Gelo, *Demografske promjene u Hrvatskoj od 1780 do 1981*, Globus, Zagreb 1987. The part of medieval Croatia which has remained in Bosnia-Herzegovina is not included in this account.
27. The table relates to the territory of contemporary Croatia, which differs somewhat from that of Croatia in the middle of the nineteenth century. Baranja, Međimurje and the Croatian Littoral with its islands and the port of Rijeka are included here in 'Civilian Croatia'. 'Dalmatia' includes the territory of the Dubrovnik republic but not the Bay of Kotor (now in Montenegro). 'Military Croatia' excludes the Petrovaradin regimental area (now in Vojvodina). The population figures are based on the census of 1850–1. Source: Gelo, *Demografske promjene*.
28. Vince, *Putovima*, p. 209.
29. Grga Novak, *Povijest Splita*, vol. 3, p. 117, Matica hrvatska, Split 1965.

30. Petar Korunić, *Jugoslavenska ideologija u hrvatskoj i slovenskoj politici: Hrvatsko-slovenski politički odnosi 1848–1870*, Globus, Zagreb 1986, pp. 95–6.

Chapter Seven

1. Šicel, ed., *Riznica*, pp. 121–7. The text has been slightly shortened. Not all Illyrians were patriotically engaged all the time, however. Thus an otherwise ardent Illyrian, the Slovene poet Stanko Vraz, wrote 'In Reply to Those Who Wish Me to Sing Patriotic Songs': 'I chose [to sing of King] Krešimir, but my lute would not. I started to intone Ljudevit and the mighty Zrinski, but my lute's strings would sing only of Violet's beauty.'
2. The teacher was Ferencz Császár, who in 1832 became a member of the Hungarian Academy of Science. In a letter to his friend Ferencz Toldy-Schedel, Császár described his work in the Rijeka gymnasium in the following terms: 'I am propagating here as a true apostle my country's language, not only by my written grammars and other less important works, but also by way of the living word – so successfully, indeed, that my likely successor will be one of my pupils, [a] real Croato-Italian boy, who is spending this year at a school in Győr improving his spoken language.' Milorad Živanović, *Ivan Mažuranić*, Matica srpska and Globus, Novi Sad and Zagreb 1988, pp. 27–30.
3. Ivan Mažuranić, *Izabrani politički spisi*, Golden Marketing and Narodne novine, Zagreb 1999, pp. 179–80.
4. Šidak, *Hrvatski narodni preporod*, pp. 145–6.
5. Bogoslav Šulek, *Što namjeravaju Iliri?*, in Šicel, ed., *Riznica*, pp. 189–190.
6. Šidak, *Studije iz hrvatske povijesti*, p. 136.
7. Dragutin Rakovac, 'Mali katekizam za velike ljude', in Šicel, ed., *Riznica*, pp. 135–44.
8. Bogoslav Šulek, 'Što namjeravaju Iliri?', ibid., pp. 208–9.
9. He wrote to his dismayed father about his reasons for leaving the army: 'Should I, if war breaks out, join in the killing and harassing of [the French and Italian] nations that are so much more civilised than our empire, nations which we treat as our teachers, which have done so much to elevate the human spirit, and which have done no harm to my own nation and country?' Horvat, *Politička povijest*, vol. 1, p. 78.
10. Jaroslav Šidak, *Studije iz hrvatske povijesti*, p. 225.
11. Ibid., pp. 135–44.
12. Ivan Mažuranić, Hrvati Mađarom, in Šicel, ed., *Riznica*, pp. 229–41.
13. Mažuranić had 2,000 copies of this 'letter' printed at his own expense for distribution in Hungary and Austria, hoping to gain allies for the Croatian cause.
14. Jaroslav Šidak, *Studije iz hrvatske povijesti za revolucije 1848–49*, Školska knjiga, Zagreb 1979, pp. 44–52; Tomislav Markus, *Hrvatski politički pokret 1848–1849 godine*, Dom i svijet, Zagreb 2000, p. 61.
15. According to the 1857 census, the Ogulin regiment contained around 39,000 Catholic and round 34,000 Orthodox inhabitants. The Military Border taken as a whole had just under 450,000 Catholics and just over 587,000 Orthodox. Mirko Valentić, *Vojna krajina i pitanje njezina sjedinjenja sa Hrvatskom 1849–1881*, Liber, Zagreb 1981, p. 45. Apart from Drašković, all other proposed candidates were army officers from the border.
16. Markus, *Hrvatski politički pokret*, pp. 75–9.
17. Vladimir Košćak, 'Mađaronska emigracija 1848', *Zbornik*, Zagreb 1950, nos 1–4, pp. 39–124.
18. Ivo Perić, *Hrvatski državni sabor*, vol. 1, p. 142, Hrvatski institut za povijest, etc., Zagreb 2000, p. 142.
19. Ibid, p. 142.
20. Grga Novak, *Povijest Splita*, vol. 3, pp. 112–29.

21. Perić, *Hrvatski državni sabor*, vol. 1, p. 171.
22. External language is that used in communication with other bodies of the monarchy.
23. Mažuranić, *Izabrani politički spisi*, pp. 193–6.
24. The Czech politician, František Palacký, presented this position in a letter to the German *Vorparlament* assembled in Frankfurt, in which he rejected Bohemia's participation in its deliberations aimed at establishing a constitution for a united Germany.
25. For an English translation of the text see William H. Stiles, *Austria in 1848–9*, Arno & The New York Times, New York 1971, pp. 381–4.
26. Karl Marx and Friedrich Engels in their paper *Neue Rheinische Zeitung* famously called for an 'implacable struggle, a war to the death, against the [Austrian] Slavs', and associated their physical obliteration with the march of historical progress. Hans Kohn, *Panslavism: Its History and Ideology*, Vintage Books, New York 1960, p. 100.
27. Stiles, *Austria*, pp. 397–8.
28. Markus, *Hrvatski politički pokret*, pp. 183–92.
29. Živančević, *Ivan Mažuranić*, p. 91.
30. Ibid., p. 87
31. Ibid., pp. 79–80.
32. Šidak, *Studije iz hrvatske povijesti*, p. 249.
33. Markus, *Hrvatski politički pokret*, pp. 303–7.
34. Tomislav Markus, ed., *Korespondencija Bana Jelačića i Banskog vijeća 1848–1850*, Hrvatski institut za povijest, Zagreb 1998, pp. 267–8.
35. Ibid., pp. 269–70.
36. This debate is presented at some length in Markus, *Hrvatski politički pokret*.
37. Juraj Batlja et al., *Zagrebački biskupi i nadbiskupi*, Školska knjiga, Zagreb 1995, p. 466.
38. Jaroslav Šidak, *Studije iz hrvatske povijesti*, p. 149.
39. Ibid., pp. 269–70.

Chapter Eight
1. Croats also formed the majority in the overwhelmingly Catholic province of Istria.
2. Mirjana Gross and Agneza Szabo, *Prema hrvatskome građanskom društvu: Društveni razvoj u civilnoj Hrvatskoj i Slavoniji šezdesetih i sedamdesetih godina 19 stoljeća*, Globus, p. 34.
3. The county of Osijek was the former county of Srijem without its three eastern districts, which were included in the unit made up of Vojvodina and the Banat of Temesvár.
4. Valentić, *Vojna krajina i pitanje njezina sjedinjenja*, p. 46. This table excludes the Petrovaradin regiment and its townships, which at this time did not belong to the Croatian-Slavonian Military Border.
5. Mirjana Gross, *Počeci moderne Hrvatske: Neoabsolutizam u civilnoj Hrvatskoj i Slavoniji 1850–1860*, Globus, Zagreb, p. 47. This table excludes the cities.
6. Gross, ed., *Društveni razvoj* p. 234.
7. Valentić, *Vojna krajina i pitanje njezina sjedinjenja*, pp. 45–6. This table excludes the townships.
8. See Ivo Banac, *Hrvatsko jezično pitanje*, Mladost, Zagreb 1991.
9. Bogoslav Šulek, 'Srbi i Hrvati', in Vince, *Putovima*, p. 292.
10. Ibid., p. 301.
11. The tendency in the central administration was to classify documents as 'Croato-Illyrian' or 'Serbo-Illyrian' depending on whether they were written in the Latin or Cyrillic scripts. Gross, *Počeci moderne Hrvatske*, p. 371.

12. Ivan Mažuranić, *Sabrana djela*, vol. 3, Liber and Matica hrvatska, Zagreb 1979.
13. The evidence would have come from the bishop of Senj, Venceslav Soić, whose diocese included all the Croatian Littoral. Soić had studied at the Augustineum in Vienna together with the cardinal and archbishop of Kalocsa Ludwig Haynald, the bishop of Đakovo Josip J. Strossmayer, the bishop of Pula and Trieste Juraj Dobrila, and Strossmayer's close collaborator Canon Franjo Rački. Dobrila came from Istria, Rački and Soić from the Croatian Littoral. All these churchmen were to play important roles in the lives of their nations.
14. A number of well-known Croat personalities from this period had studied at the Rijeka gymnasium, including Antun Mihanović, who wrote the text of the Croatian national anthem; Franjo Rački, first president of the Yugoslav Academy of Arts and Science; Antun and Ivan Mažuranić; Eugen Kvaternik, who helped to establish the Croatian Party of Right; Josip Pančić, founder of the Serbian Academy of Arts and Science; and Erazmo Barčić, a local patrician and the city's leading Croat nationalist. It is reported that two portraits hung on the wall over Barčić's bed: one of the Russian emperor Alexander III, the other of Giuseppe Garibaldi. Irvin Lukezić, *Fijumanske priče*, Izdavački centar Rijeka, Rijeka 1991, p. 55.
15. The term 'Patent' refers to a royal decree issued without recourse to the existing parliaments.
16. Perić, *Hrvatski državni sabor*, vol. 1, p. 266.
17. Horvat, *Politička povijest*, vol. 1, p. 165.
18. Francis Joseph deeply mistrusted Mažuranić, whom he considered to be a separatist harbouring dangerous democratic ideas. The initial candidate was the privy councillor Baron Metel Ožegović, but the Hungarians would not have him, while the Slavonian magnate Petar Pejačević was unacceptable to Vienna. Schmerling stood up for Mažuranić, describing him as a first-class legal brain.
19. Horvat, *Politička povijest*, vol. 1, p. 161.
20. Mažuranić, *Izabrani politički spisi*, pp. 242–3. The final paragraph of the article dealing with diplomatic courtesies is omitted here.
21. Deputy for the Otočac regiment from Lika, Prica was Ban Jelačić's secretary in 1848–9. An ethnic Serb and ardent Illyrian, he took part in the Slav Congress in Prague convened at that time and helped edit the journal *Slavenski jug*.
22. Mažuranić, *Izabrani politički spisi*, pp. 101–6. It is possible that Schmerling had given him to understand that Croatia's endorsement of the Diploma and the Patent would facilitate the integration of Croatian territories; but Mažuranić's stance derived from his own deep conviction that Croatia's interests would best be served in a united Hasburg Monarchy, and that Croatia could not modernise its administration without the help of the central state bureaucracy.
23. Vienna attempted to pacify the demand for abolition of the border, hinting that the border army would be used in the near future to seize Bosnia, after which Bosnia would be joined to Croatia. Valentić, *Vojna krajina i pitanje njezina sjedinjenja*, p. 105.
24. For this exchange between the sabor and the king see Mažuranić, *Izabrani politički spisi*, pp. 264–75.
25. William Brooks Tomljanovich, *Biskup Josip Juraj Strossmayer: Nacionalizam i moderni katolicizam u Hrvatskoj*, HAZU and Dom i svijet, Zagreb 2001, pp. 119–21.
26. The pamphlet was conceived at a conference held by Mažuranić with the county heads. Nikola Krestić was a young lawyer from Zagreb. Jaroslav Šidak, *Studije iz hrvatskoj povijesti*, p. 297.
27. Francis Joseph typically showed little gratitude to one of his most able officials by granting him a minimal state pension. Mažuranić, increasingly depressed about

Croatia's prospects, had tried to resign back in 1861 when Hungary was given Međimurje, but rescinded his decision in the face of strong protests from the Illyrian old guard. His letter of resignation castigated the monarch for playing around with state borders which Mažuranić saw as the main source of conflict between Hungary and Croatia. Živančević, *Ivan Mažuranić*, pp. 106–8.

Chapter Nine

1. Ibid., p. 114. The reference is to Molière's eponymous play in which Dandin, having married a woman far wealthier than himself and finding himself bossed about as a result, blames himself for his predicament: 'Vous l'avez voulu, Georges Dandin.'
2. A. Kann, *The Multinational Empire*, Columbia University Press, New York 1950, vol. I, p. 22. See also Louis Eisenmann, *Le Compromis Austro-Hongrois de 1867*, Academic International, Paris 1971.
3. On the eve of the First World War 'Hungary' had about 21 million inhabitants, of which 48.1 per cent were Magyar (54.5 per cent without Croatia). Paul Lendvai, *The Hungarians*, Princeton University Press, Princeton 2003, p. 286.
4. Up to the end of Austria-Hungary roughly 80 per cent of the deputies in the Hungarian parliament were permanently drawn from the landowning classes. Kontler, *A History of Hungary*, p. 281.
5. Jaroslav Šidak et al., *Povijest hrvatskog naroda 1860–1914*, Školska knjiga, Zagreb 1968, p. 124. On the eve of the First World War this percentage went up to around 7 per cent in both cases.
6. Janos, *The Politics of Backwardness*, p. 112.
7. They were not alone in this. There was a widespread belief that the defeat would lead to the federalisation of the Monarchy. A meeting of Austria's Slav politicians in Vienna in the summer of 1866 accepted a Czech proposal that the Monarchy be transformed into a federation of five states, of which one would be South Slav (Yugoslav).
8. The Hungarian prime minister, Gyula Andrássy, told the king that he himself should decide the status of Rijeka, but 'on no account leave its population a choice, since this could become a dangerous precedent leading to many wrong interpretations'. Vasilje Krestić, *Hrvatsko-ugarska nagodba 1868*, SANU, Belgrade 1967, p. 247.
9. The king, after informing Strossmayer of the Hungarian proposal for Croatia and his own response, stated: 'It is my will and command that you publicly endorse the Hungarian programme. If you will not, you cannot attend the sabor. I wish to make it clear to you that if you resist I am ready forcibly to constrain you.' Strossmayer refused and left the country. Josip J. Strossmayer and Franjo Rački, *Politički spisi*, Znanje, Zagreb 1971, pp. 53–4.
10. Martin Polić, *Parlamentarna povijest Kraljevina Hrvatske, Slavonije i Dalmacije*, Komisiona naklada F. Suppan, Zagreb 1899, vol. I, p. 274.
11. Deák apparently told Živković that common history and interests made it necessary for the two countries to unite, but that the terms of union should include only what was absolutely necessary for the maintenance of unity. Deák also allegedly told Živković: 'I know that some in Croatia, like for example Bishop Strossmayer, dream of a South Slav empire. It is a dream that Zagreb likes to dream, but in my view it is unrealistic. If it ever came to fruition, however, Belgrade not Zagreb will be its centre.' Horvat, *Politička povijest*, vol. I, p. 191.
12. The fact that the agreed autonomy also included Dalmatia prompted a question in the Reichsrat as to how a land represented in that body could be listed as a land of the Hungarian crown. The Austrian prime minister stated that this merely reflected

informal support on the part of Hungary for Croatia's demands, and had no bearing on actual reality.
13. Eisemann, *Le Compromis Austro-Hongrois*, pp. 541–4. See also Josip Pliverić, *Spomenica o državnopravnih pitanjih hrvatsko-ugarskih*, Komisiona naklada L. Hartmann, Zagreb 1907.
14. Ferdo Čulinović, *Državnopravna historija jugoslavenskih zemalja 19 i 20 soljeća*, Školska knjiga, Zagreb 1956, vol. 1, p. 130.
15. Krestić, *Hrvatsko-ugarska nagodba*, pp. 324–30.
16. Ivan Beuc, *Povijest institucija*, Zagreb 1985, p. 280.
17. As late as 1910, of the 413 deputies in the Hungarian parliament only eight represented the nationalities, whereas according to the population figures there should have been 198. Lendvai, *The Hungarians*, p. 292.
18. 'Is it not monstrous', wrote Rački in 1883, 'that in debates on important state questions Croatians and Hunagrians cannot understand each other, yet both vote?' The Hungarian argument, Rački added, that the problem would be easily solved by Croats learning Hungarian was naive, since the Hungarian language had never had nor would it ever command the status enjoyed by German in the Monarchy. As soon as Magyar replaced Latin in Hungary, the old state link between the latter and Croatia became unviable. *Politički spisi*, pp. 438–9.
19. Mažuranić, *Izabrani politički spisi*, p. 151.
20. Looking into the future, however, one might say that – contrary to Andrássy's intimation – the occupation of Bosnia-Herzegovina laid the foundation stone of the future state of Yugoslavia.
21. Živančević, *Ivan Mažuranić*, p. 119.
22. R. W. Seton-Watson, *The Southern Slav Question and the Habsburg Monarchy*, Constable and Co., New York, 1969, p. 118.
23. Roland Hill, *Lord Acton*, Yale University Press, New Haven 2000, p. 218.
24. Ivo Padovan, ed., *Hrvatski domoljub Josip Juraj Strossmayer*, Ogledi, Zagreb 1995, p. 122.
25. Tomljanovich, *Strossmayer*, p. 36.
26. Thus he wrote to the British prime minister, William Gladstone, in 1879 that the Church should be 'capable of entering into the most delicate matters touching upon the universal conscience of mankind and leading them to a happy solution corresponding to the real needs of the society'. Hill, *Lord Acton*, p. 219.
27. Tomljanovich, *Strossmayer*, p. 339.
28. Padovan, ed., *Hrvatski domoljub*, pp. 24–5.
29. In 1864 alone, for example, the vineyards produced 400,000 litres of wine. Timber was another great source of income, bringing 400,000 forints in one single transaction in 1876. The pure-bred horses from his stables made attractive gifts to friends, politicians and members of foreign royal families. Tomljanovich, *Strossmayer*, pp. 122–3.
30. Padovan, ed., *Hrvatski domoljub*, p. 48.
31. Tomljanovich, *Strossmayer*, p. 182.
32. Hill, *Lord Acton*, p. 455.
33. Tomljanovich, *Strossmayer*, p. 364. Criticising the grip of the Italian clergy on the Vatican, Strossmayer went so far as to state: 'So far as my people and its future are concerned, it seems to me that one day it will free itself from the burden of Rome's despotism.' Ibid., p. 368.
34. Padovan, ed., *Hrvatski domoljub*, pp. 34–5.
35. By the end of the dualist period over 78 per cent of the lower schools and over 90 per cent of the gymnasia in Hungary taught mainly in Magyar. Oscar Jászi, *The

    Dissolution of the Habsburg Monarchy, Chicago University Press, Chicago 1971, p. 329. Between 1869 and 1910 the proportion of Germans in Hungary fell by 22 per cent and of Slovaks by 21 per cent. According to one Magyar nationalist, schools and public administration were parts of one big machine into which 'one feeds a Slovak child on one side, and on the other out comes a Hungarian gentleman.' Janos, *The Politics of Backwardness*, p. 111.
36. Its economic predicament would grow thanks to the arrival of cheap American wheat on the world market, as a result of which grain prices fell by 36 per cent in the 1880s and again by 48 per cent in the 1890s. Ibid., pp. 120–1.
37. The Hungarian law on education permitted the opening of private schools; this law was not applied to Rijeka in order to prevent the establishment of Croat-language schools. Milivoj Čop, *Riječko školstvo 1848–1918*, Izdavački centar Rijeka, Rijeka 1988, pp. 116–9.
38. Igor Žić, *Kratka povijest Rijeke*, Adamić, Rijeka 2001, p. 100.
39. Mirko Valentić, *Vojna Krajina i pitanje njezina sjedinjenja*, p. 317.
40. Šidak et al., *Povijest hrvatskog naroda*, p. 80.
41. Lendvai, *The Hungarians*, p. 298.
42. For a positive view of Ban Khuen-Héderváry's government see Iso Kršnjavi, *Zapisci: Iza kulisa hrvatske politike*, Mladost, Zagreb 1986.

Chapter Ten
1. John V. A. Fine, Jr, *The Late Medieval Balkans*, University of Michigan Press, Ann Arbor 1994, pp. 116–17.
2. Radoslav Katičić in László Hadrovics, *Srpski narod i njegova crkva pod turskom vlašću*, Globus, Zagreb 2000.
3. For these 'church nations', see Božidar Jezernik, *Wild Europe*, Saqi, London 2004, pp. 179–81.
4. Hadrovics, *Srpski narod*, pp. 44–5, 88–92.
5. The Orthodox monasteries of Krka, Krupa and Dragović in Dalmatia appear for the first time in Turkish documents of the sixteenth century. Drago Roksandić, *Srbi u Hrvatskoj*, Vjesnik, Zagreb 1991, pp. 36–46.
6. For the circumstances of this migration, see Noel Malcolm, *Kosovo: A Short History*, Macmillan, London 1998, pp. 139–62.
7. For the English translation of Leopold's Privilege issued to 'the Rascians of the Greek rite of the Eastern Church', see Macartney, ed., *The Habsburg and Hohenzollern Dynasties*, pp. 79–82. The former Marča diocese would re-emerge in 1777 as the Uniate diocese of Križevci, which in 1852 would be joined to the archbishopric of Zagreb.
8. Ivo Banac, *Grbovi – biljezi identiteta*, Grafički zavod Hrvatske, Zagreb 1991, pp. 17–20.
9. Mile Bogović, *Katolička crkva i pravoslavlje u Dalmaciji za mletačke vladavine*, Kršćanska sadašnjost, Zagreb 1993, provides a systematic account of the Orthodox Church under Venetian rule.
10. Gligor Stojanović, *Dalmatinske krajine u XVIII vijeku*, Prosvjeta, Zagreb 1987, pp. 7–10.
11. Bogović, *Katolička crkva*, p. 21 (table corrected).
12. Ibid., pp. 111–26.
13. Karaman pointed out that the Montenegrin archbishop called himself 'ruler of Montenegro', ibid., p. 122.
14. Gross, *Počeci moderne Hrvatske*, p. 356.

15. Nicholas Miller, *Between Nation and State: Serbian Politics in Croatia before the First World War*, University of Pittsburgh Press, Pittsburgh 1997, p. 19.
16. Roksandić, *Vojna Hrvatska*, vol. 2, pp. 130–2.
17. Mato Artuković, 'Pitanje Srijema u Hrvatskom *sabor*u 1861', in Mile Budak et al., *Zbornik Mirjane Gross*, Filozofski fakultet Zagreb, Zagreb 1999, pp. 161–72.
18. *Dnevnik sabora trojedne kraljevine Dalmacije, HPrvatske i Slavonije godine 1861*, Zagreb 1862, p. 66. Unless otherwise stated, all quotations concerning the work of this sabor are from this source.
19. Perić, *Hrvatski državni sabor*, vol. 1, p. 315.
20. Quoted in Mato Artuković, *Ideologija srpsko-hrvatskih sporova: Srbobran 1884–1902*, Naprijed, Zagreb 1991, p. 21.
21. Natalija Rumenjak, 'Čelni ljudi u novčanim zavodima Banske Hrvatske 1990 godine – osvrt na srpsku elitu 1881–1900 godine', *Povijesni prilozi*, no. 18, Zagreb 1999, pp. 161–239.
22. Miller, *Between Nation and State*, p. 37.
23. All quotations from *Srbobran* are in Artuković, *Ideologija*.
24. According to the *Ethnographic Map of the Serb Lands* published in 1892 by the Serbian ministry of education, 'Serb lands' included all of Croatia, southern Hungary, Serbia, Kosovo, Bosnia-Herzegovina, Montenegro, Macedonia and western Bulgaria. Such maps inspired Stojanović's essay.
25. Frano Supilo, *Politika u Hrvatskoj*, Kultura, Zagreb 1953, pp. 113–4.
26. One of these was Pavle Jovanović, the editor of *Srbobran*, who won his seat in 1892 with the help of Khuen-Hédérváry's National Party. Two years later he refused to attend a meeting of parliamentarians in Budapest because the invitation identified him as a member of the Croatian parliament. In his view only Croat chauvinists called the sabor 'Croatian parliament.' Artuković, *Ideologija*, p. 191.
27. The advance of the Serb community in the economic field is examined in Mato Artuković, *Srbi u Hrvatskoj (Khuenovo doba)*, Hrvatski institut za povijest, Slavonski Brod 2001.
28. Mirjana Gross, *Izvorno pravaštvo*, Golden Marketing, Zagreb 2000, pp. 805–28.

Chapter Eleven
1. Zrinka Blažević, *Vitezovićeva Hrvatska*, pp. 249–50.
2. Vjeko Omašić, *Kaštela od prapovijesti do početka XX stoljeća*, Muzej grada etc., Kaštela 2001, vol. 1, pp. 247–60.
3. Josip Vrandečić, *Dalmatinski autonomistički pokret u XIX stoljeću*, Dom i svijet, Zagreb 2002, p. 58. See also Ivan Pederin, *Jadranska Hrvatska u austrijskim i njemačkim putopisima*, Matica hrvatska, Zagreb 1991.
4. Novak, *Povijest Splita*, vol. 3, p. 144.
5. Duško Kečkemet et al., eds, *Hrvatski narodni preporod u Splitu 1882*, Logos, Split 1984, p. 9.
6. Vrandečić, *Dalmatinski autonomistički pokret*, p. 88. This work is exceptional in its ability to recreate the cultural and political ambience of Dalmatia in the nineteenth century.
7. Trpimir Macan, *Miho Klaić*, Matica hrvatska, Zagreb 1980, p. 72.
8. Natko Nodilo, *Izabrani spisi*, Književni krug, Split 1982, p. 46.
9. Kečkemet et al., *Hrvatski narodni preporod*, p. 65.
10. Macan, *Miho Klaić*, p. 122.
11. Nikša Stančić, ed., *Mihovil Pavlinović u politici i književnosti*, Globus, Zagreb 1990.
12. Mihovil Pavlinović, *Misao hrvatska i misao srpska u Dalmaciji*, Laus, Split 1994, pp. 11–12. Pucić envisaged the introduction of the Croato-Hungarian constitution and

county system into Dalmatia, and a single parliament for the united Croatia headed by the ban's council that would include a minister for Dalmatia.
13. Maršal Marmont, *Memoari*, Logos, Split, 1984, p. 104.
14. The Autonomist paper *La Voce Dalmatica* wrote that they were 'not clergymen and Austrians, but Croats and Russians [i.e. friends of the Orthodox clergy]' engaged in spreading 'religious fanaticism and peasant communism'. Vrandečić, *Dalmatinski autonomistički pokret*, p. 102.
15. They were present in the two rural districts of Benkovac (58.8 per cent) and Knin (51.4 per cent). The small towns of Benkovac and Knin were predominantly Croat, however (75.4 per cent and 65.6 per cent). Ivo Baučić et al., eds, *Političko-geografska i demografska pitanja Hrvatske*, Savez geografskih društava Hrvatske, Zagreb 1991, p. 208.
16. Here they were represented in two curiae: that of the landowners, and that of the villages of Kotor, Herceg Novi, Risan and Budva. This area is now part of Montenegro.
17. Božena Vranješ-Šoljan, 'Demografsko-socijalne prilike u Dalmaciji i Banskoj Hrvatskoj u drugoj polovici 19. stoljeća', in Nikša Stančić, ed., *Mihovil Pavlinović u politici i književnosti*, Globus, Zagreb 1990, p. 412. In 1910 the six Dalmatian cities taken together had 69,000 inhabitants while Zagreb alone had 74,703.
18. Josip Grbavac, 'Izbori u Imotskoj krajini i Mihovil Pavlinović', in Stančić, ed., *Mihovil Pavlinović*, pp. 169–71.
19. Macan, *Miho Klaić*, pp. 116–17.
20. Nikša Stančić, 'Pobjeda Narodne stranke na općinskim izborima u Splitu 1882 god. i problem periodizacije narodnog preporoda u Dalmaciji', in Kečkemet et al., eds, *Hrvatski narodni preporod*, pp. 21–45.
21. Macan, *Miho Klaić*, p. 135.
22. Vrandečić, *Dalmatinski autonomistički pokret*, p. 159.
23. Ibid., p. 161.
24. Macan, *Miho Klaić*, p. 228.
25. This was not true of Klaić. He did not believe that Austria would unite Bosnia-Herzegovina with Croatia, in which case it was better in his view to support Bosnia's autonomous development within the Ottoman Empire. Indeed, if the Austrian action resulted in the 'liberation of these provinces and their unification with Croatia, then we will approve it, but even then we will not welcome it. But if it turns out that, as I expect, it is nothing but an Austrian deed and enterprise, then we will protest.' He later changed his mind. Macan, *Miho Klaić*, pp. 224–5.
26. First published in *Historijski zbornik*, 15–16, pp. 306–21, Zagreb 1972–3. The quotations below are from the Split 1994 edition, pp. 87–112.
27. As a young seminarist active within a secret patriotic society that he helped to establish in Split in 1846–7, Pavlinović planned to escape to the 'free land' of Serbia and once there help it to unite Serb or Yugoslav lands: at this stage he did not differentiate between the two. Stančić, ed., *Mihovil Pavlinović*, pp. 16–7. A number of well-known Italian and Croat writers and political leaders of this period had studied at the Split seminary, including Ugo Foscolo, Nikola Tommaseo, Luka Botić, Natko Nodilo, Ante Kuzmanić and Antonio Bajamonti.
28. *Misao hrvatska*, p. 108.
29. Ibid.
30. Pavlinović, like Strossmayer, was in fact a strong supporter of the Slav liturgy, which he invariably used. Once, during a session of the Austrian parilament of which he was a member, while guest of the Croatian noble Metel Ožegović at the latter's estate in Hitzing near Vienna he was asked to replace the absent local vicar. He proceeded

to conduct Mass in Church Slavonic before the astonished German peasants. He was also a great stickler when it came to use of the Croat language. His party colleagues, who knew Italian better than Croat, felt obliged to write to him in Croat in order to avoid his admonitions.

31. Stančić, ed., *Mihovil Pavlinović*, p. 22.
32. Ibid.
33. Macan, *Miho Klaić*, pp. 270–2.
34. Ibid., p. 374.
35. *Srpski list* was in fact inspired by the same ideas as *Srbobran* in Ban's Croatia. Sofija Božić, *Politička misao Srba u Dalmaciji*, Institut za noviju isstoriju Srbije, Belgrade 2001.
36. Macan, *Miho Klaić*, pp. 300–1.
37. Božić, *Politička misao Srba*, p. 102.
38. Josip Defilippis, *Dalmatinsko selo u promjenama*, Avium, Split 1997, pp. 54–5.
39. Novak, *Povijest Splita*, vol. 3, pp. 353–63.
40. For the euphoria generated by the news see ibid., pp. 353–63.
41. The central government, however, called it Spljet, in conformity with the official *ijekavski* standard. But the city council stuck to Split, and in 1921 Spljet was finally dropped from official use in favour of Split.
42. Tereza Ganza-Aras, 'Prilog upoznavanja društva splitskog kraja u doba pohrvaćenja splitske općine', in Kečkemet et al., eds, *Hrvatski narodni preporod*, pp. 175–80.
43. According to the archeologist Ivan Bulić, one of the first to be taught in Croat at the Split gymnasium, the first sentence in the Latin primer used in the school was: 'Croatiam amo' (I love Croatia). It was habitual to decline this sentence aloud, with the whole class joining in. Duško Kečkemet, *Hrvatski narodni preporod u Splitu: Zbivanja i likovi*, Glas Dalmacije, Split 1999, p. 74.
44. For the German-Slovene battle over the school in Celje, which became emblematic of the Slav-German conflict in the Austrian half of the Monarchy, see A. J. P. Taylor, *The Habsburg Monarchy 1809–1918*, Hamish Hamilton, London 1948, p. 171.
45. Vrandečić, *Dalmatinski autonomistički pokret*, p. 235.

Chapter Twelve

1. The Italians called this construction *Venezia Giulia*, the Croats and Slovenes *Julijska Krajina*. After Austria's loss of Lombardy in 1856 and Venice in 1866, the Italians became the smallest nationality of the Habsburg Monarchy.
2. Ante Cukrov, *Između obrazovanja i denacionalizacije*, C.A.S.H., Pula 2001, p. 18.
3. Miroslav Bertoša, *Istria: Doba Venecije (XVI–XVII stoljeće)*, Zavičajna naklada 'Žakan Juri', Pula 1995. See also Ivan Jurković, 'Hrvatski identitet plemstva austrijskog dijela Istre krajem XV. stoljeća', in Marino Manin et al., eds, *Identitet Istre: Ishodišta i perspektive*, Institut društvenih znanosti, Zagreb 2006, pp. 49–59.
4. In 1910 the naval personnel formed just under 17,000 of Pula's total population. Mate Balota, *Puna je Pula*, Čakavski sabor etc., Pula-Rijeka 1981, p. 56.
5. Branko Fučić, *Terra Incognita*, Kršćanska sadašnjost, Zagreb 1998.
6. In the crownland of Gorizia-Gradiska, Slovenes outnumbered Italians by two to one. Only in Trieste did the Italians form an absolute majority, followed by substantial Slovene and German minorities. Kann, *The Multinational Empire*, vol. 2, p. 423; Angelo Vivante, *Irredentismo Adriatico*, Edizioni Italo Svevo, Trieste 1984, pp. 183–5.
7. On the preponderance of Croat and Slovene clergy in the Istrian church see Antonio Miculin, 'Il diritto di nazionalità in Istria e nel litorale austriaco della seconda metà del XIC agli inizi del XX secolo', in Manin et al., eds, *Identitet Istre*, pp. 114–9.

8. Quoted in Cukrov, *Izmedu obrazovanja i denacionalizacije*, p. 43. In the early 1860s Combi published two books: *Etnografia dell'Istria* and *La frontiera orientale d'Italia e la sua importanza,* in which he presented arguments for Istria's Italian nature and why it should be joined to Italy. Vivante, *Irredentismo*, p. 7.
9. Fran Barbalić, *Prvi istarski sabori (1861–1877)*, JAZU, Zagreb 1954, pp. 325–6.
10. The Vidulich/Vidulić family from the island of Lošinj had both Croat and Italian branches. For Francesco Vidulich's political career see Petar Strčić, 'Iredentizam dr Francesca Vidulicha (1819–1889)', *Radovi*, Zagreb 1991, vol. 24, pp. 109–18.
11. In 1905, thanks to the help of the bishops of Zagreb and Đakovo, the municipality of Kastav, the Croat-held saving bank in Volosko, and the Dalmatians, enough money was collected for building a residence hall for its students, who came from all over Istria, but the necessary permission was granted only in 1914. Ernest Radetić, *Istarski zapisi*, Grafički zaavod Hrvatske, Zagreb 1969, pp. 233–8.
12. Josip Bratulić, *Istarske književne teme*, Istarska naklada, Pula 1987, p. 145.
13. Josip Percan, *Obzori istarskog narodnjaštva*, Čakavski sabor etc., Pula and Rijeka 1986, vol. 2, p. 161.
14. *Obzori*, vol. 1, p. 80.
15. Ibid., p. 109.
16. Ibid., vol. 2, p. 169.
17. Ibid., p. 204.
18. Ibid., pp. 124–8.
19. Ibid., pp. 137–46.
20. In 1890, according to Italian figures the Croat share went down to 37.5 per cent while Croatian analysts insisted on 45.2 per cent. Cukrov, *Izmedu obrazovanja i denacionalizacije*, pp. 26–31.
21. Vivante, *Irredentismo*, p. 162.
22. Giuseppe Caprin in 1895, quoted in Cukrov, *Izmedu obrazovanja i denacionalizacije*, p. 82.
23. Ibid., pp. 121–2.
24. *Naša Sloga* of 4 July 1907, quoted in *Obzori istarskog naradonjaštva*, vol. 2, p. 257.
25. Paolo Boselli, quoted in Cukrov, *Izmedu obrazovanja i denacionalizacije*, p. 119.
26. Ibid., pp. 122–3.
27. Ibid., p. 131.
28. Cukrov, ibid, pp. 133–5.
29. Ibid.
30. Ibid., p. 292
31. Carmelo Cottone, *Storia della scuola in Istria da Augusto à Mussolini*, Capdoistria (Koper) 1938, p. 118. Cottone, who came from Sardinia, served under the Italian Fascist government as head of a *Dante Alighieri* primary school in Pula and as school inspector for the Pula area; he was a member of various Fascist groups. Francesco Facin, the local *Lega* president, who taught in the Labinci school, was decorated after the Italian occupation of Istria in 1918 for promoting Italian language and culture. The Poreč authorities, who recommended him for this award, stressed that: 'when he came to Labinci, the village spoke only Slav; but thanks to his hard work and commitment a correct and mainly Italian language is spoken there today.' Cukrov, *Izmedu obrazovanja i denacionalizacije*, pp. 163–5.
32. According to Tamaro, 'Marco Maroli', i.e. Marko Marulić, was in fact an 'Italian humanist'. The fact that 'Maroli' wrote *Judith* and 'some insignificant religious poetry' in Slav did not make him Slav any more than Goldoni was French because he published some works in French. *Italiens et Slaves dans L'Adriatique*, Éditions Georges Crès & Cie, Zurich 1917, pp. 199–200.

33. *Per la Lega Nazionale,* Trieste 1911, pp. 5–6; quoted in Cukrov, *Između obrazovanja i denacionalizacije,* pp. 182–4.
34. Ibid., p. 185.
35. In 1901, for example, the administration refused to permit the initials P. U. M. ('Rest in Peace') to be carved on the gravestone of a *Naša Sloga* typesetter. Mate Balota (Mijo Mirković), *Puna je Pula,* Čakavski sabor etc., Rijeka 1981, p. 91.
36. This electoral gambit, which at the time must have appeared as a temporary arrangement, would later be interpreted as an indicator of Istria's ethnic distribution. Bogdan Novak, *Trieste 1941-1945: The Ethnic, Political and Ideological Struggle,* University of Chicago Press, Chicago 1970, p. 5.
37. Percan, *Obzori,* vol. 1, pp. 139–40.
38. Why this never happened is explored in William Alexander Jenks, *The Austrian Electoral Reform of 1907,* Octagon Books, New York 1974.
39. Šidak et al., *Povijest hrvatskog naroda,* p. 256.
40. Reproduced in Cukrov, *Između obrazovanja i denacionalizacije,* p. 47.
41. Dennison I. Rusinow, *Italy's Austrian Heritage 1919–1946,* Clarendon Press, Oxford 1969, p. 29.

Chapter Thirteen

1. Taylor, *The Habsburg Monarchy,* p. 194.
2. An Austrian official, visiting Dalmatia for the first time in 1892, noted: '[We] govern Dalmatia without any real affection. I do not believe that anyone could visit Dalmatia and not ask himself: What might not be made of this region?' Joseph Baernreither, *Fragments of a Political Diary,* Macmillan & Co., London 1930, p. 11.
3. Defilippis, *Dalmatinsko selo,* pp. 49–62.
4. Rene Lovrenčić, *Geneza politike 'Novog kursa',* Institut za hrvatsku povijest, Zagreb 1972.
5. Marjan Diklić, *Pravaštvo u Dalmaciji do kraja Prvog svjetskog rata,* Matica hrvatska, Zadar 1998, p. 218.
6. Ibid., p. 223.
7. In their view, the logic of the dual name for the language led to the Croatian state right becoming 'Croat or Serb', and to Croatia's transformation into 'Croatia or Serbia'. Given Serb hostility towards Dalmatia's union with Croatia, they said they were left with no other option but to resign.
8. Ivo Perić, *Mladi Supilo,* Školska knjiga, Zagreb 1966, p. 51; Ivo Banac, *Raspad Jugoslavije,* Durieux, Zagreb 2001, pp. 67–113.
9. Josip Horvat, *Supilo,* Tipografija, Zagreb 1938, p. 57.
10. Ibid., p. 72.
11. Frano Supilo, *Politički Spisi,* Znanje, Zagreb 1970, pp. 99–100.
12. Ibid., p. 150.
13. Perić, *Mladi Supilo,* p. 87.
14. *Crvena Hrvatska,* no. 4, Dubrovnik 1885; quoted in Perić, *Mladi Supilo,* pp. 89–90.
15. Ibid.
16. Frano Supilo, *Politika u Hrvatskoj,* Kultura, Zagreb 1953, pp. 124–5.
17. Supilo, *Politički spisi,* p. 28.
18. Ivo Petrinović, *Politička misao Frana Supila,* Književni krug, Split 1988, p. 33.
19. At this time the Austro-Hungarian army began to prepare defensive positions along the Austrian-Italian border. David G. Herrmann, *The Arming of Europe and the Making of the First World War,* Princeton University Press, Princeton, 1996, p. 34.
20. Joerg K. Hoensch, *A History of Modern Hungary 1867–1994,* Longman, London and New York, pp. 62–3.

21. Ante Trumbić, *Izabrani spisi*, Književni krug, Split 1986, p. 53.
22. Tereza Ganza-Aras, *Politika 'Novog kursa' dalmatinskih pravaša oko Supila i Trumbića*, Matica hrvatska, Split 1992, p. 209.
23. Petrinović, *Politička misao*, p. 117.
24. Ibid., p. 72.
25. Horvat, *Supilo*, pp. 113–7.
26. The texts of the two resolutions are reproduced in Supilo, *Politika u Hrvatskoj*, pp. 317–9. See also Ranka Gašić, *Novi Kurs Srba u Hrvatskoj: Srbobran 1903-1913*, Zagreb 2001.
27. Supilo, *Politički spisi*, pp. 297–301.
28. Mirjana Gross, *Vladavina hrvatsko-srpske koalicije 1906–7*, Institut društvenih nauka, Belgrade 1960, pp. 23–43.
29. In the case of the sabor being dissolved before the parliament in Pest, the previously elected Croatian delegates remained in the latter until confirmed or replaced by the new sabor.
30. Supilo, *Politika u Hrvatskoj*, pp. 197–8.
31. Ibid., p. 208.
32. This was the famous 'Friedjung trial', which revealed the deep involvement of the Austro-Hungarian government in fabricating the evidence offered by the Austrian historian Heinrich Friedjung against Supilo and the others. Supilo's friend Tomáš Masaryk, who subsequently became the first president of Czechoslovakia, acted as part of the defence team. For the trial see Seton-Watson, *The Southern Slav Question*, chapter 10. Following the end of the trial Wickham Steed invited Supilo to become the Balkan correspondent for *The Times*, but Supilo refused: he had to stay in Croatia.
33. Horvat, *Supilo*, p. 311.
34. Ibid., p. 320.
35. Ljubo Boban et al., eds, *R. W. Seton-Watson and the Yugoslavs: Correspondence 1906–1941*, vol. I, British Academy and Institute for Croatian History, London and Zagreb 1976, p. 19.
36. Boban et al., *Seton-Watson and the Yugoslavs*, p. 122.
37. Quoted in Janko Pleterski, *Nacije, Jugoslavija, revolucija*, Izdavački centar Komunist, Belgrade 1985, p. 115.
38. Josip Horvat, *Živjeti u Hrvatskoj- zapisi iz nepovrata: 1900–1941*, Liber, Zagreb 1984, p. 46.
39. Dragovan Šepić, *Supilo diplomat*, Naprijed, Zagreb 1961, p. 11.
40. Arno J. Mayer, *Political Origins of the New Diplomacy 1917–1918*, Vintage Book, New York, 1959, pp. 6, 8.
41. Ferdo Šišić, ed., *Dokumenti o postanku Kraljevine Srba, Hrvata i Slovenaca*, Matica hrvatska, Zagreb 1920, p. 10.
42. Dragoslav Janković, *Srbija i jugoslovensko pitanje 1914–1915*, Institut za savremenu istoriju, Belgrade 1973, pp. 471–2.
43. Trumbić's letter to Supilo of 9 September 1914 in Dragovan Šepić, 'Iz korespondencije Frane Supila', *Arhivski vjesnik I*, Zagreb 1958, p. 263.
44. Letter from Trumbić to Supilo of 9 November 1914, in Šepić, *Supilo diplomat*, p. 48.
45. Ibid., pp. 49–50.
46. Letter from Supilo to Trumbić of 15 November 1914, ibid., p. 50.
47. Quoted in Horvat, *Supilo*, p. 358.
48. Boban et al., eds, *Seton-Watson and the Yugoslavs*, p. 24.
49. R. W. Seton-Watson, quoted in Ivo Petrinović, *Ante Trumbić*, Književni krug, Split 1991, p. 93.

50. Horvat, *Supilo*, p. 360.
51. Ibid.
52. Šepić, *Supilo diplomat*, p. 87.
53. Ibid., p. 51.
54. Letter from Supilo to Sazonov of 2 July 1916, ibid., p. 197.
55. Boban et al., eds, *Seton-Watson and the Yugoslavs*, Zagreb 1976, p. 24.
56. Pašić to Sazonov in May 1915, quoted in Šepić, *Supilo diplomat*, pp. 129, 141; Janković, *Srbija i jugoslovensko pitanje*, pp. 478–9.
57. Supilo to Pašić, quoted in Šepić, *Supilo diplomat*, p. 145.
58. Šišić, ed., *Dokumenti*, pp. 50–8.
59. Boban et al. eds, *Seton-Watson and the Yugoslavs*, pp. 265–6.
60. Šepić, *Supilo diplomat*, p. 191.
61. Dragovan Šepić, *Italija, saveznici i jugoslavensko pitanje 1914–1918*, Školska knjiga, Zagreb 1970, pp. 193–4.
62. Ibid.
63. Ivan Čizmić, *Jugoslavenski iseljenički pokret i stvaranje jugoslavenske države*, Institut za hrvatsku povijest, Zagreb 1974.
64. Horvat, *Supilo*, pp. 387–8.

Chapter Fourteen

1. Šepić, *Italija, Saveznici i jugoslavensko pitanje*, p. 273.
2. This Ante Pavelić should not be confused with his namesake, the head of the Independent State of Croatia created in 1941.
3. Bogdan Krizman, *Hrvatska u prvom svjetskom ratu*, Globus, Zagreb 1989, p. 383.
4. Ibid., pp. 45–7.
5. Janko Pleterski, *Prvo opredeljenje Slovenaca za Jugoslaviju*, Nolit, Belgrade 1976, p. 163; Momčilo Zečević, *Slovenska ljudska stranka i jugoslovensko ujedinjenje 1917–1921*, Institut za savremenu istoriju, Belgrade 1973, pp. 67–8.
6. Pleterski, *Nacije, Jugoslavija, revolucija*, pp. 70–1; Petar Korunić, *Jugoslavenska ideologija*, p. 383.
7. Pleterski, *Prvo opredeljenje*, p. 164.
8. Ibid., p. 135.
9. Horvat, *Politička povijest*, vol. 2, pp. 25–6.
10. Krizman, *Hrvatska u Prvom svjetskom ratu*, p. 156.
11. Ibid., p. 205.
12. Bogdan Krizman, *Raspad Austro-Ugarske i stvaranje jugoslavenske države*, Školska knjiga, Zagreb 1977, p. 60.
13. Krizman, *Hrvatska u Prvom svjetskom ratu*, p. 257.
14. Jasna Adler, *L'Union Forcée : La Croatie et la création de l'état yougoslave (1918)*, Georg Éditeur, Chêne-Bourg 1997, p. 209.
15. The government in Split tried to prevent the local soldiers from leaving their posts by locking them up, but during the night they jumped through the barrack windows and returned to their villages. Marko Kostrenčić, ed., *Zapisi Dra Josipa Smodlake*, JAZU, Zagreb 1972, p. 63.
16. Interview with Reuters on 28 October 1918, quoted in Ivo Lederer, *Yugoslavia at the Paris Peace Conference: A Study in Frontier-making*, Yale University Press, New Haven 1963, pp. 41–2.
17. A mixed Allied force had in the meantime arrived in Split headed by an American admiral and a French vice-admiral. According to Smodlaka: 'The danger that Italy, which had already occupied half of Dalmatia, could also seize Split from Yugoslavia did not bother the Frenchman at all. When we told him that for Yugoslavia the loss

of Split [was equivalent to France losing] Marseilles, he jumped up and said that Marseilles had been French for centuries, whereas we had only recently gained Split.' Kostrenčić, ed., *Zapisi*, p. 73.
18. Šepić, *Italija, Saveznici i jugoslavensko pitanje*, p. 389.
19. Krizman, *Hrvatska u Prvom svjetskom ratu*, p. 337.
20. Ibid., p. 205.
21. Svetozar Pribićević, *Izabrani politički spisi*, Golden Marketing, Zagreb 2000, pp. 190–1.
22. Neda Engelsfeld, *Prvi parlament Kraljevstva Srba, Hrvata i Slovenaca*, Globus, Zagreb 1989, p. 25.
23. Krizman, *Hrvatska u Prvom svjetskom ratu*, pp. 358–9.
24. Lederer, *Yugoslavia at the Paris Peace Conference*, pp. 71–5.
25. Kostrenčić, *Zapisi*, pp. 120–1.
26. Ibid.
27. Ibid., pp. 93–4. Smodlaka, who had so ardently sought Croatia's union with Serbia, now felt greatly disappointed in 'Pašić and democratic Serbia as I had imagined them, since I discovered that the Serbian politicians, both in government and in the opposition, far from being democrats as they claimed were in fact imperialists.' Ibid.
28. They also recommended the creation of a federated Yugoslavia made up of the Austro-Hungarian territories, Serbia and Montenegro. Lederer, *Yugoslavia at the Paris Peace Conference*, pp. 136–7.
29. Ibid., p. 193.
30. A. E. Moodie, *The Italo-Yugoslav Boundary*, George Philip & Co., London 1945, p. 170.
31. Arno J. Mayer, *Politics and Diplomacy of Peacemaking: Containment and Counter-Revolution at Versailles 1918–1919*, Weidenfeld & Nicolson, London 1968, pp. 693–4.
32. Ibid., p. 696.
33. Lederer, *Yugoslavia at the Paris Peace Conference*, p. 215.
34. Ibid., p. 278; Kostrenčić, *Zapisi*, pp. 109–10.
35. Darko Dukovski, *Rat i mir istarski: Model povijesne prelomnice 1943–1945*, C.A.S.H., Pula 2001, p. 58.
36. Petrinović, *Ante Trumbić*, p. 215; Božo Milanović, *Moje uspomene (1900–1976)*, Istarsko društvo Sv. Ćirila i Metoda etc., Pazin 1976, p. 38.
37. Milanović, *Moje uspomene*, p. 38.
38. For the close link between Italian irredentism and fascism see Rusinow, *Italy's Austrian Heritage*.
39. One recipient thus wrote: 'My parents have put in a request for the correction of our name from Soldatich to Soldati. [The] money received has given me additional strength to engage in an even deeper study of our beautiful Italian language so that I can proudly call myself Italian.' Cukrov, *Između obrazovanja i denacionalizacije*, p. 208. For the enforced Italianisation of Croat personal and place names see also Hrvoje Mezulić and Roman Jelić, *O talijanskoj upravi u Istri i Dalmaciji od 1918. do 1943.*, Dom i svijet, Zagreb 2005.
40. Rusinow, *Italy's Austrian Heritage*, p. 200.
41. Ernest Radetić, *Istra pod Italijom 1918–1943*, Matica hrvatska, Zagreb 1944, pp. 158–9.
42. Ibid., pp. 272–5.
43. Bosiljka Janjatović, *Politički teror u Hrvatskoj 1918–1935*, Hrvatski institut za povijest, Zagreb 2002.
44. Hrvoje Matković, *Svetozar Pribićević*, Hrvatska sveučilišna naklada, Zagreb 1995, p. 75.

45. Ivo Banac, *The National Question in Yugoslavia: Origins, History, Politics*, Cornell University Press, Ithaca NY 1984, pp. 248–54.
46. Rudolf Bićanić, *Ekonomska podloga Hrvatskog pitanja i drugi radovi*, Pravni fakultet u Zagrebu, Zagreb 1995, p. 51.
47. Ibid.
48. Jozo Tomasevich, *Peasants, Politics, and Economic Change in Yugoslavia*, Stanford University Press, Stanford 1955, pp. 241–2; Joseph Rothschild, *East Central Europe between the Two World Wars*, University of Washington Press, Seattle 1974, p. 279.
49. A first-hand account of the scramble for wealth and influence in the rapidly growing city of Belgrade is provided in Louis Adamič, *The Native's Return*, Parper & Brothers, London 1934.
50. Branislav Gligorijević, *Parlament i političke stranke u Jugoslaviji 1919–1929*, Institut za savremeny istoriju, Belgrade 1979, p. 110.
51. Ferdo Čulinović, *Jugoslavija izmedu dva svjetska rata*, JAZU, Zagreb 1961, vol. 1, pp. 321–52.
52. Horvat, *Politička povijest*, vol. 2, p. 243.
53. Mark Biondich, *Stjepan Radić, The Croat Peasant Party and the Politics of Mass Mobilization, 1904–1928*, University of Toronto Press, Toronto 2000, p. 188.
54. This prospect led to speculations in Serbia on the possibility of 'amputation': i.e. of a division of Yugoslavia along the line Virovitica–Šibenik, following which the northern portion would be ejected from Yugoslavia and the rest organised as a Great Serbia. Vatroslav Slavko Cihlar, *Hrvatsko pitanje i amputacija - The Croatian Question and Amputation*, Zagreb 1928.
55. Gligorijević, *Parlament i političke stranke*, p. 195.
56. Ibid., p. 242.
57. Račić was arrested and executed by the Communists following their entry into Belgrade in 1945. Zvonimir Kulundžić, *Atentat na Stjepana Radića*, Stvarnost, Zagreb 1969, p. 576.
58. Horvat, *Politička povijest*, vol. 2, p. 351–2.
59. Matković, *Svetozar Pribićević*, pp. 208–10; Ljubo Boban, *Svetozar Pribićević u opoziciji (1928–1936)*, Institut za hrvatsku povijest, Zagreb 1973, pp. 36–9.
60. Svetozar Pribićević, *Diktatura kralja Aleksandra*, Globus, Zagreb 1990, pp. 67–9.
61. Miroslav Krleža, *Deset krvavih godina*, Zora, Zagreb 1957, p. 257.
62. Horvat, *Politička povijest*, vol. 2, p. 358.
63. Čulinović, *Jugoslavija izmedu dva svjetska rata*, vol. 2, pp. 7–9.
64. Ljubo Boban, *Maček i politika Hrvatske seljačke stranke 1928–1941*, Liber, Zagreb 1974, p. 44.
65. Boban, *Svetozar Pribićević u opoziciji*, p. 49.
66. He wrote to Seton-Watson in 1932: 'I must work with them [HSS] and maintain the closest links with them, since our cooperation is one of the strongest guarantees of Yugoslavia's survival.' Boban et al., eds, *Seton-Watson and the Yugoslavs*, vol. 2, p. 235.
67. Ibid., p. 180.
68. Matković, *Svetozar Pribićević*, p. 245.
69. Pribićević, *Diktatura kralja Aleksandra*, pp. 230–1.
70. 'Letter to the Serbs', in Matković, *Svetozar Pribićević*, pp. 303–8.
71. Petrinović, *Ante Trumbić*, pp. 289–90.
72. Ibid., pp. 352–3.
73. Ivan Mužić, *Katolička crkva u Kraljevini Jugoslaviji: Politički i pravni aspekti konkordata izmedu Svete Stolice i Kraljevine Jugoslavije*, Crkva u svijetu, Split 1978.
74. Petrinović, *Ante Trumbić*, pp. 397–8.
75. Ibid., pp. 379–80.

Chapter Fifteen

1. Todor Stojkov, *Vlada Milana Stojadinovića 1935–1937*, Institut za savremenu istoriju, Belgrade 1935, p. 37. It was widely believed in Yugoslavia that Stojadinović was Britain's choice. Ambassador Henderson was convinced that British interests in Yugoslavia were best served by having a strong government in Belgrade.
2. Petrinović, *Ante Trumbić*, p. 370.
3. Quoted in R. W. Seton-Watson's memorandum to the Foreign Office of 10.11.1936, Boban et al., eds, *Seton-Watson and the Yugoslavs*, vol. 2, p. 321.
4. Trumbić in Ljubo Boban, *Maček i politika*, vol. 1, p. 139.
5. The new British minister in Belgrade, Sir Ronald Campbell, agreed with Stojadinović that the Croat Question could only be solved over time; noted with approval that Stojadinović enjoyed Prince Paul's confidence; and expressed the hope that this would continue. Report to Anthony Eden in November 1936, quoted in Boban, *Maček i politika*, vol. 1, p. 212.
6. Ibid., p. 386.
7. Petrinović, *Ante Trumbić*, pp. 402–5.
8. Boban, *Maček i politika*, vol. 1, p. 424.
9. In March 1938 Trumbić told the British consul in Zagreb, T. C. Rapp, that any active Yugoslav policy on part of the Peasant Party would result in civil war, but also that in the event of war the Serbian-dominated Yugoslav army would not defend the western lands, that is, Slovenia and Croatia. Petrinović, *Ante Trumbić*, pp. 401–5.
10. Smodlaka, who joined him in opposition to Belgrade, survived long enough to join the Communist government after the Second World War. He witnessed not only the 're-creation' of the Croatian state, but also Italy's expulsion from Croatian lands. Smodlaka died in 1956 and was buried in Klis, his family's place of origin.
11. The text of the agreement is in Boban, *Sporazum Cvetković-Maček*, Institut za društvene nauke nauke, Belgrade 1965, pp. 291–2.
12. Boban, *Maček i politika*, vol. 1, p. 312.
13. Boban et al. eds, *Seton-Watson and the Yugoslavs*, vol. 2, pp. 344–6.
14. Vladko Maček, *In the Struggle for Freedom*, Spellers & Sons, New York 1957, pp. 187–8; Ivan Meštrović, *Uspomene na političke ljude i događaje*, Matica hrvatska, Zagreb 1969, pp. 255–6; Ljubomir Antić in *Izvještaj komisije za ispitivanje odgovornosti*, quoted in Boban, *Maček i politika*, vol. 2, p. 477.
15. Boban, *Maček i politika*, vol. 1, p. 385, fn. 57.
16. Ibid., p. 444.
17. Report to Halifax of 19 December 1938, quoted in ibid., p. 370.
18. Ljubo Boban, *Sporazum*, pp. 167–8.
19. Dragiša Cvetković, 'Srpsko-hrvatski sporazum 1939', in *Srpsko-hrvatsko pitanje i putevi sporazuma*, Paris 1952. I wish to thank here Bajtullah Destani for drawing my attention to this publication. In an interview given in 1956, Maček stated: 'I remain convinced that the 1939 agreement could have inaugurated not a federalisation but a confederalisation of Yugoslavia and the rest of the Balkans, including Bulgaria and Albania.' Boban, *Maček i politika*, vol. 2, p. 303.
20. Boban, *Sporazum*, p. 191.
21. Ibid., p. 347.
22. Fikreta Jelić Butić, *Hrvatska seljačka stranka*, Globus, Zagreb 1983, p. 36.
23. Ibid. p. 326.
24. J. B. Hoptner, *Yugoslavia in Crisis 1934–1941*, Columbia University Press, New York 1962, p. 161.
25. The earlier occasion had been during the struggle over the concordat with the Vatican

in 1937, when sections of the Serb Orthodox Church, the army and some politicians had plotted to bring down the Stojadinović government.
26. Boban, *Sporazum*, p. 357
27. Hoptner, *Yugoslavia in Crisis*, p. 220.
28. Boban, *Sporazum*, pp. 357–8.
29. Hoptner, *Yugoslavia in Crisis*, pp. 254–64.
30. *Zbornik dokumenata NOR-a,* II/2, p. 473, quoted in Fikreta Jelić-Butić, *Ustaše i NDH*, Globus, Zagreb 1978.
31. They were to spend the next two years in Kenya as, in effect, British prisoners of war. Neil Balfour and Sally Mackay, *Paul of Yugoslavia*, Hamish Hamilton, London 1980 provides a rare insight into the relationship between the Anglophile prince and the British government.
32. Boban, *Sporazum*, pp. 369–70.
33. Hoptner, *Yugoslavia in Crisis*, p. 284.
34. Jelić-Butić, *Ustaše i NDH*, p. 70.
35. According to a German report of 5 April 1941, 'Maček has all the appearance of a broken old man. He spoke with difficulty, expressing his thoughts more with gestures than in words. The basic point of his exposition was: "I cannot find the way out." He is clinging to a vague hope, knowing full well that it is impossible to avoid war. He has done what he could to prevent it, since in his view it leads to the state's break-up.' Boban, *Sporazum*, p. 371.
36. Boban, *Maček i politika,* vol. 2, pp. 410–2.
37. Jozo Tomasevich, *War and Revolution in Yugoslavia, 1941–1945*, Stanford University Press, Stanford 2001, pp. 61–3.
38. Jelić-Butić, *Ustaše i NDH*, p. 64.
39. Slavko Kvaternik in Nada Kisić-Kolanović, ed., *Vojskovođa i politika: Sjećanja Slavka Kvaternika*, Golden Marketing, Zagreb 1997, p. 143; Tomislav Jonjić, *Hrvatska vanjska politika 1939–1942,* Libar, Zagreb 2000, pp. 255–60.
40. Kvaternik was married to Olga, daughter of Josip Frank, founder of the Croatian Party of Right, formerly the True Party of Right.
41. Bogdan Krizman, *Ante Pavelić i ustaše*, Globus, Zagreb 1986, pp. 356–63; p. 380.
42. Krizman, *Pavelić i ustaše,* p. 405.
43. Ibid. p. 409.
44. Ibid., p. 412.
45. Nada Kisić-Kolanović, *NDH i Italija: Političke veze i diplomatski odnosi*, Naklada Ljevak, Zagreb 2001, p. 50.
46. Marko A. Hoare, *The Chetnik-Partisan Conflict and the Origins of Bosnian Statehood*, Yale University doctoral thesis, UMI Dissertation Services, Ann Arbor 2000, pp. 183–4. Pavelić was born in Herzegovina; his parents came originally from Lika.
47. Jonjić, *Hrvatska vanjska politika,* p. 484.
48. Bogdan Krizman, *Pavelić između Hitlera i Mussolinija*, Globus, Zagreb 1980, pp. 105–6.
49. One such camp was Kampor on the island of Rab, where Slovene civilians were also interned. Ivan Kovačić, *Kampor 1942–1943*, Rijeka 1998; Davide Rodogno, *Il nuovo ordine mediterraneo: Le politiche di occupazione dell'Italia Fascista in Europa (1940–1943)*, Bollati Boringhieri, Torino 2003, pp. 419–22.
50. Radogno, *Il nuovo ordine*, pp. 332–3.
51. Kisić-Kolanović, *NDH i Italija*, p. 130.
52. See his speech of 21 May 1941, in which he insisted that 'a nation which refuses to give up anything cannot exist'. Pavelić also stated on that occasion that Italy was bound to

respect Croat language, culture and property. Jonjić, *Hrvatska vanjska politika*, pp. 482–3; Krizman, *Pavelić između Hitlera i Mussolinija*, p. 76.
53. Kisić-Kolanovic, *NDH i Italija*, pp. 107–8.
54. Ibid., pp. 135–9.
55. François Grumel-Jacquignon, *La Yugoslavie dans la stratégie française de l'Entredeux-Guerres (1918–1935): Aux origines du myth serbe en France*, Peter Lang, Bern 1999.
56. Krizman, *Pavelić i Ustaše*, pp. 39–40.
57. Kisić-Kolanović, ed., *Vojskovoda*, pp. 29–30.
58. For the argument that the NDH was both legal and legitimate because of Kvaternik's allegedly autonomous action and Maček's acquiesence, see Kazimir Katalinić, 'The declaration of Croatian independence in the light of internal documents', *Journal of Croatian Studies*, no. 28–9, New York 1987–8. For the French 'national revolution' and collaboration, see in particular Julian Jackson, *France: The Dark Years 1940–1944*, Oxford University Press, Oxford 2001.
59. General Glaise von Horstenau, a staff officer in the Austro-Hungarian army and minister in the two Austrian governments preceding the Anschluss, was sent to Zagreb because he knew the Croatian military well. He committed suicide after the end of the war while a prisoner of the International Military Court established at Nuremberg. His memoirs were published posthumously in P. Broucek, *Ein General im Zwielicht: die Erinnerungen Edmund Glaises von Horstenau*, Wien-Köln-Graz, 1988.
60. Kisić-Kolanović, *NDH: Italija*, pp. 74–5.
61. For the negotiations between the HSP leaders and Nikola Pašić in 1922–5, during which Pavelić offered to give up many of his party's tenets in return for the government of Croatia, see Hrvoje Matković, *Studije iz novije hrvatske povijesti*, Institut za hrvatsku povijest, Zagreb 2004, pp. 180–98.
62. Kisić-Kolanović, *NDH: Italija*, p 62.
63. For the relationship between Pavelić and Mihajlov, see Kisić-Kolanović, *Zagreb-Sofija: Prijateljstvo po mjeri ratnog vremena*, Dom i svijet, Zagreb 2003.
64. Ustasha units in fact invaded the Sandžak in early May 1941, but had to abandon it under Italian pressure. Hoare, *The Chetnik-Partisan Conflict*, p. 182.
65. Jelić Butić, *Hrvatska seljačka stranka*, pp. 51 ff.
66. Denis Mack Smith, *Mussolini*, Weidenfeld and Nicoloson, London 1987.
67. Kisić-Kolanović, ed., *Vojskovoda*, p. 71. When General von Horstenau told Slavko Kvaternik that his son was 'the most hated man' in Croatia, the latter responded by saying that Eugen was not his but Pavelić's son, and accused Pavelić of 'turning honest youths into sadists'.
68. Ivo Rojnica, *Susreti i doživljaji*, DoNeHa, Zagreb 1995, vol. I, p. 256.
69. Ilija Jakovljević, *Konclogor na Savi*, Konzor, Zagreb 1999, p. 270. Jakovljević, a well-known lawyer, author and journalist, spent 1941–2 in the concentration camp of Nova Gradiška on the Sava, which 'specialised' in murdering Serb women and children.
70. Eugen Dido Kvaternik, *Sjećanja i zapažanja*, Starčević, Zagreb 1995, p. 241.
71. Jelić-Butić, *Ustaše i NDH*, p. 23.
72. The fate of the Jewish community in Zagreb is described in Ivo Goldstein, *Holokaust u Zagrebu*, Novi Liber, Zagreb 2001.
73. Kisić-Kolanović, ed., *Vojskovoda*, pp. 46–7.
74. Marko A. Hoare, 'The Ustasha Genocide', *The South Slav Journal*, vol. 25, London 2004.

Chapter Fifteen

75. Fikreta Jelić-Butić, *Četnici u Hrvatskoj 1941–1945*, Globus, Zagreb 1982; Jozo Tomasevich, *The Chetniks*, Stanford University Press, Stanford 1975.
76. For the German policy in occupied Slovenia, see Tomasevich, *War and Revolution: Occupation and Collaboration*, Stanford University Press, Stanford 2001, pp. 85–7.
77. Krizman, *Pavelić između Hitlera i Mussolinija*, p. 49.
78. Jelić-Butić., *Ustaše i NDH*, pp. 166–70.
79. Vladimir Žerjavić, *Population losses in Yugoslavia 1941–1945*, Dom i svijet, Zagreb 1997, pp. 91–2. See also Bogoljub Kočović, *Žrtve Drugog svetskog rata u Yugoslaviji*, Naše delo, London 1985.
80. Jelić-Butić, *Ustaše i NDH*, pp. 174–5.
81. This secrecy was maintained even in camps like Stara Gradiška; see Jakovljević, *Konclogor na Savi*.
82. Krizman, *Pavelić između Hitlera i Mussolinija*, pp. 76–7.
83. Kvaternik, *Sjećanja*, p. 249.
84. Nikica Barić, *Ustroj kopnene vojske domobranstva Nezavisne Države Hrvatske 1941–1945*, Hrvatski institut za povijest, Zagreb 2003, pp. 29–30.
85. For a critique of the view that the Ustasha attitude to the Serbs was akin to that of the Nazis towards the Jews, and that the Ustasha genocide was essentially similar to the Holocaust, see Hoare, 'The Ustasha genocide', pp. 34–6. For the drafting of Serbs into the NDH Home Guard, see Barić, *Ustroj kopnene vojske*, pp. 181 ff.
86. Krizman, *Pavelić između Hitlera i Mussolinija*, p. 49.
87. Rusinow, *Italy's Austrian Heritage*, p. 56.
88. Marko Attila Hoare, *Genocide and Resistance in Hitler's Bosnia: the Partisans and the Chetniks 1941–1943*, Oxford University Press, Oxford 2007, pp. 26–7.
89. Krizman, *Pavelić i NDH*, p. 507.
90. Kisić-Kolanović, *NDH i Italija*, p. 330.
91. Ibid., pp. 327–9.
92. It renamed itself Communist Party of Yugoslavia at its second congress, held in Vukovar in 1920: much of the city was destroyed in 1991 by the nominally Yugoslav People's Army.
93. Quoted in Latinka Perović, *Od centralizma do federalizma*, Globus, Zagreb 1984, p. 239.
94. Marković's views are set out in *Tragizam malih naroda*, Filip Višnjić, Belgrade 1985. Marković died in one of Stalin's concentration camps in or after 1937.
95. Cesarec and most other Croatian Communist leaders were shot by the Ustashe soon after their arrival in power. Ivan Jelić, *Tragedija u Kerestincu*, Zagreb 1986. Cesarec's articles on the national question are in August Cesarec, *Rasprave, članci, polemike*, Zora, Zagreb 1970. See also Zorica Stipetić, *Argumenti za revoluciju – August Cesarec*, Centar za društvenu djelatnost, Zagreb 1982.
96. Perović, *Od centralizma do federalizma*, pp. 272–5. Unless otherwise stated the citations below are taken from this work and the works quoted above.
97. The text of the resolution is in Marković, *Tragizam*, pp. 167–71.
98. According to a party branch from Slovenia: 'We in Slovenia are not well acquainted with the conflict within the party, since in the first place we are ignorant of the situation there [in Serbia], and secondly because the party organ is printed in Cyrillic, which we cannot read. [It] seems to us inappropriate to transfer the party conflict to Slovenia.' Perović, *Od centralizma do federalizma*, p. 344.
99. Ivan Jelić, *Komunistička partija Hrvatske 1937–1941*, Institut za historiju radničkog pokreta, Zagreb 1982.
100. *Zbornik dokumenata i podataka o narodnooslobodilačkom ratu jugoslovenskih naroda*, Belgrade, pt 4, vol. 1, doc, 208, pp. 457–8.

101. Vladimir Velebit, *Tajne i zamke II. Svjetskog rata*, Prometej, Zagreb 2002, p. 160. The Velebit family originated from the Croatian Military Border. The work provides an invaluable insight into Mihailović's military 'strategy'.
102. Branko Dubravica, *Vojska anti-fašističke Hrvatske 1941–1945*, Biblioteka Albatros, Velika Gorica, p. 39. 'Extra-territorial' refers to the 1st and 2nd proletarian divisions recruited from all over Yugoslavia and attached to the central main staff.
103. Marko Attila Hoare, 'Whose is the Partisan movement? Serbs, Croats and the legacy of shared resistance', *The Journal of Slavic Military Studies*, vol. 15, no. 4, December 2002.
104. Kisić-Kolanović, *NDH i Italija*, pp. 337–8.
105. Hodimir Sirotković, *ZAVNOH*, Dom i svijet, Zagreb 2002, contains both the chronology and the relevant documents.
106. Kisić-Kolanović, *NDH i Italija*, p. 387.
107. Ibid., p. 392.
108. Branko Petranović, *AVNOJ - Revolucionarna smena vlasti*, Nolit, Belgrade 1976, pp. 207–8.
109. Quoted in Dušan Bilandžić, *Hrvatska moderna povijest*, Golden Marketing, Zagreb 1999, p. 151.
110. The Ustasha leaders' retreat from Croatia is described in Bogdan Krizman, *Pavelić u bjekstvu*, Globus, Zagreb 1986.
111. Žerjavić, *Population Losses*, p. 38.
112. Vladimir Geiger, *Nestanak Folksdojčera*, Hrvatski institut za povijest, Zagreb 1997.
113. The respective Croat and Serb demographic losses are 178,000 and 159,000. Žerjavić, *Population Losses*, p. 151.
114. Novak, *Trieste*, p. 67.
115. Dukovski, *Rat i mir istarski*, p. 66.
116. Berto Črnja, quoted in John Peter Kraljić, 'Ethnic relations and sovereignty in Istria, 1945–1947', manuscript.
117. Dukovski, *Rat i mir istarski*, pp. 69–70. The declaration does not mention Yugoslavia.
118. Sirotković, *ZAVNOH*, p. 234.
119. Dubravica, *Vojska antifašističke Hrvatske*, p. 58.
120. Bogdan Krizman, ed., *Jugoslavenske vlade u izbjeglištvu, 1941–1943*, Globus, Zagreb 1981, vol. 1, p. 16.
121. Milanović, *Moje uspomene*; Stipan Troglić, 'Katolička crkva i diplomatsko-politička borba za priključenje Istre Hrvatskoj (1945–47)', in Marino Manin et al., eds, *Identitet Istre*, pp. 347–96.
122. Novak, *Trieste*, p. 261.
123. Dukovski, *Rat i mir istarski*, pp. 230–1.
124. Vladimir Žerjavić, 'Koliko je osoba iselilo iz područja pripojenih Hrvatskoj i Sloveniji nakon kapitulacije Italije i završetka Drugog svjetskog rata', *Časopis za suvremenu povijest*, Zagreb 1997, vol. 29, no. 1, p. 153.
125. Dukovski, *Rat i mir istarski*, p. 229.
126. M. Štambuk-Škalić, 'Hrvatska istočna granica u dokumentima 1941–1945', *Fontes*, vol. 1. Zagreb 1995, pp. 153–329.

Chapter Sixteen
1. Dragovan Šepić, *Vlada Ivana Šubašića*, Globus, Zagreb 1983.
2. Branko Petranović and Sava Dautović, *Jugoslavenska revolucija i SSSR (1941–1945)*, Narodna knjiga, Belgrade 1988, pp. 268–9.

3. Dušan Bilandžić, *Historija Socijalističke Federativne Republike Jugoslavije: Glavni procesi*, Školska knjiga, Zagreb 1979, p. 88.
4. Katarina Spehnjak, *Javnost i propaganda: Narodna fronta u politici i kulturi Hrvatske 1945–1952*, Hrvatski institut za povijest, Zagreb 2002.
5. Zdenko Radelić, *Božidar Magovac: S Radićem između Mačeka i Hebranga*, Hrvatski institut za povijest, Zagreb 1999.
6. Nada Kisić-Kolanović, *Hebrang: Iluzije i otrežnjenja, 1899–1949*, Institut za suvremenu povijest, Zagreb 1996, p. 83.
7. Ibid., p. 83.
8. Ibid., pp. 113–4.
9. Čedomir Višnjić, *Kordunaški proces: Fragmenti iz historije nestajanja*, Prosvjeta, Zagreb 1997, pp. 151–5.
10. Kisić-Kolanović, *Hebrang*, p. 125.
11. Ivo Banac, *With Stalin against Tito*, Cornell University Press, Ithaca NY 1988, p. 106.
12. Kisić-Kolanović, *Hebrang*, p. 128.
13. The official date of his death, entered in November 1957, is 11 June 1949. Zvonko Ivanković-Vonta, *Hebrang*, Scientia Yugoslavica, Zagreb 1988. Mrs Hebrang learnt of her husband's death only in 1952.
14. Olga Kohn Hebrang, who lost her first husband, her infant son, and over fifty members of her family in the Holocaust, was also charged with collaborating with the Ustashe, and sentenced to twelve years in prison. She was released nine years later, when her surname was officially changed to Markovac: she was able to resume her married name only in 1983.
15. Zdenko Radelić, *Križari: Gerila u Hrvatskoj 1945–1950*, Hrvatski Institut za povijest, Zagreb 2002.
16. Čedomir Višnjić, *Partizansko ljetovanje: Hrvatska i Srbi 1945–1950*, Prosvjeta, Zagreb 2003.
17. Ibid., pp. 114–5.
18. Višnjić, *Partizansko ljetovanje*, pp. 327–41.
19. Darko Bekić, *Jugoslavija u Hladnom ratu*, Globus, Zagreb 1988, p. 674.
20. Ibid., pp. 674–5.
21. Ibid., p. 588.
22. Edvard Kardelj, *Razvoj slovenačkog nacionalnog pitanja*, Komunist, Belgrade 1973.
23. Bilandžić, *Hrvatska moderna povijest*, p. 417.
24. Ibid., pp. 471–2.
25. Dobrica Ćosić in Slavoje Đukić, *Lovljenje vetra: Politička ispovest Dobrice Ćosića*, Samizdat B92, Belgrade 2005, p. 79.
26. Bilandžić, *Hrvatska moderna povijest*, pp. 485–6.
27. Ibid., p. 436.
28. Velimir Terzić, *Jugoslavija u aprilskom ratu 1941*, Grafički zavod, Titograd 1963.
29. Savka Dabčević-Kučar, *'71: Hrvatski snovi i stvarnost*, Interpublic, Zagreb 1997, vol. I, pp. 34–8.
30. Miko Tripalo, *Hrvatsko Proljeće*, Globus, Zagreb 1989, pp. 12–3.
31. Milovan Baletić, ed., *Ljudi iz 1971 – Prekinuta šutnja*, Vjesnik, Zagreb 1990, pp. 319–20.
32. Ibid., pp. 61, 326; Tripalo, *Hrvatsko Proljeće*, p. 171; Dabčević-Kučar, *Hrvatski snovi i stvarnost*, vol. I, pp. 250–1. Baletić, ed., *Ljudi iz 1971*, p. 326.
33. Ibid.
34. Croatia's economic problems at this time are presented in some detail in the works by Baletić, Tripalo, and Dabčević-Kučar cited above.

35. The Croatian leaders' sense of isolation was highlighted by Tripalo in early January 1969: 'We Croats are under strong pressure from all the five republics. I have recently read a book about Radić's assassination, and it seems to me that the current situation is the same as then, with the difference that they are as yet not shooting.' Bilandžić, *Hrvatska moderna povijest*, p. 528.
36. Vladimir Bakarić, *Društvene klase, nacije i socijalizam*, Školska knjiga, Zagreb 1976, pp. 232–3.
37. Dabčević-Kučar, *Hrvatski snovi*, vol. 1, pp. 140–5.
38. A common position was that 'we do not care if 100,000 Slovenes demonstrate against Yugoslavia. But we rise as one if a most insignificant anti-Yugoslav article appears in Croatia.' Bilandžić, *Hrvatska moderna povijest*, p. 572.
39. Dabčević-Kučar, *Hrvatski snovi*, pp. 172–3.
40. Bilandžić, *Hrvatska moderna povijest*, p. 577.
41. Darko Hudelist, *Tuđman: Biografija*, Profil International, Zagreb 2004, p. 346.
42. Dabčević-Kučar, *Hrvatski snovi*, vol. 1, p. 429.
43. 'Ustav Socijalističke Federativne Republike Jugoslavije', *Službeni list SFRJ*, Belgrade 1974, p. 283.
44. Latinka Perović, *Zatvaranje kruga: Ishod rascepa 1971–1972*, Svjetlost, Sarajevo 1991.
45. Bilandžić, *Hrvatska moderna povijest*, p. 581.
46. Draža Marković, *Život i politika*, Belgrade 1987, vol. 1, p. 182.
47. Stevan Moljević, 'Homogena Srbija', in *Zbornik dokumenata i podataka o narodnooslobodilačkom ratu naroda Jugoslavije*, vol. 14, bk. 1: *Dokumenti četničkog pokreta Draže Mihajlovića*, Belgrade 1981, pp. 1–10, see map on p. 564.
48. Tripalo, *Hrvatsko Proljeće*, p. 149.
49. Dabčević-Kučar, *Hrvatski snovi*, vol. 1, p. 552.
50. Ibid., p. 560.
51. This was the view also of the chief Soviet intelligence officer in Belgrade, who, protective of the Yugoslav UDB, forecast an early demise of Tripalo and Savka. According to Tripalo, it is possible that Tito, in order to forestall further Soviet interference, was prepared to sacrifice the young party liberals in order to protect Kardelj and Bakarić. Tripalo, *Hrvatsko Proljeće*, p. 152.
52. This was in direct response to comments made (and evidently overheard) during a conversation between Savka and Pirker in her home on the previous day. Dabčević-Kučar, *Hrvatski snovi*, vol. 2, p. 667.
53. Ibid., p. 682.
54. Bilandžić, *Hrvatska moderna povijest*, p. 611.
55. The powerful Croatian war veterans' association was thus informed that 2,000 postman's uniforms had been made for the use of assassins directed to liquidate opponents of the Croatian leadership. Tripalo, *Hrvatsko Proljeće*, p. 196.
56. Bilandžić, *Hrvatska moderna povijest*, p. 647. Tito was away at the time visiting Iran (which was celebrating 2,500 years of empire), India and Egypt.
57. Tripalo, *Hrvatsko Proljeće*, p. 192.
58. Student demands to the constitutional commission, as formulated on 12 May 1971, included: that Tito should be elected president of Yugoslavia for life; that foreign currency should belong to those who had earned it; that JNA training should be conducted in the language of the republic in which units were stationed; that three-quarters of conscripts should do military service in their own republic; that the name of the Yugoslav state should be changed from Federal Republic of Yugoslavia to Union of Yugoslav Self-governing Republics; and that the capital should be New Belgrade. Bilandžić, *Hrvatska moderna povijest*, p. 585. See also *Preporod hrvatskih sveučilištaraca*, Izdanje *Kritika*, Zagreb 1971.

59. Tito complained on this occasion that 'for you Croats the state comes first. I wish you would tell me what kind of state you want, [the] classic state of King Tomislav [or] a socialist community [of] Croatian citizens.' Bilandžić, *Hrvatska moderna povijest*, p. 651.
60. Dabčević-Kučar, *Hrvatski snovi*, vol. 2, p. 996.
61. The deeply traumatised Pero Pirker died in July 1972. Savka's and Tripalo's spouses both lost their jobs. Tripalo's dying father was refused admission to a Split hospital. Though herself a Serb, Tripalo's wife was denounced as a Croat nationalist and expelled from the party for refusing to condemn her husband.
62. Bilandžić, *Hrvatska moderna povijest*, p. 682.
63. Ibid., p. 693.
64. Latinka Perović, *Ljudi, događaji i knjige*, Helsinški odbor za ljudska prava u Srbiji, Belgrade 2001, p. 100 (text translated in *Bosnia Report*, no. 21/22, London January-May 2001).
65. In 1992 this small Great Serbia was to adopt the name Federal Republic of Yugoslavia.
66. The term 'JNA' used here applies to the generals who ran the Yugoslav army in the late 1980s. Their quest for control of Yugoslavia is described by General Martin Špegelj in Branka Magaš and Ivo Žanić, eds, *The War in Croatia and Bosnia-Herzegovina 1991-1995*, Frank Cass, London 2001: General Špegelj was Croatia's first minister of defence. See also Veljko Kadijević, *Moje viđenje raspada – vojska bez države*, Politika, Belgrade 1993: the Croatian-born General Kadijević was Yugoslavia's last minister of defence.
67. Darko Hudelist, *Banket u Hrvatskoj*, Globus International, Zagreb 1991, p. 218. The meeting took place on 10 December, International Human Rights Day, which explains the reference to the rights of the individual as citizen.
68. Ibid., p. 222.
69. Perović, *Ljudi, događaji i knjige*, p. 100.
70. Serbia's territorial claims against Croatia are sketched out in Branka Magaš, *The Break-Up of Yugoslavia*, Verso, London 1993, pp. 310–3.
71. The offer was a purely tactical move designed to prevent a Croatian-Bosnian alliance. Rusmir Mahmutćehajić in Magaš and Žanić, *The War in Croatia and Bosnia-Herzegovina*, p. 142.
72. Slaven Letica, *Obećana zemlja*, Globus, Zagreb 1992, pp. 71–2.
73. Mirjana Kasapović, *Izborni i stranački sustav republike Hrvatske*, Alinea, Zagreb 1993, p. 47.
74. Milislav Sekulić, *Knin je pao u Beogradu*, Nidda Verlag, Bad Vilbel, 2001, p. 32. General Sekulić was one of the commanders of the RSK's army. His book provides a detailed account of the collapse of this entity in 1995.
75. Anton Tus in Magaš and Žanić, eds, *The War in Croatia and Bosnia-Herzegovina*, p. 49.
76. The text of the announcement is in Sekulić, *Knin je pao u Beogradu*, p. 179.

Select Bibliography

Abulafia, David, *The Western Mediterranean Kingdoms 1200–1500: The Struggle for Dominion,* Longman, London and New York, 1997.
Adamček, Josip, *Agrarni odnosi u Hrvatskoj od sredine XV. od kraja XVI. stoljeća,* JAZU, Zagreb 1980.
____ *Bune i otpori: Seljačke bune u Hrvatskoj u XVII. stoljeću,* Globus, Zagreb 1987.
Adamič, Louis, *The Native's Return,* Parper & Brothers, London 1934.
Adler, Jasna, *L'Union forcée: La Croatie et la création de l'état yougoslave (1918),* Georg Editeur, Chêne-Bourg 1997.
Alberti, Mario et al., *Italy's Great War and her National Aspirations,* Alfieri & Lacroix, Milan 1917.
Alexander, Stella, *Church and State in Yugoslavia since 1945,* Cambridge University Press, Cambridge 1979.
Ančić, Mladen, 'Desetljeće od godine 1091 do 1102 u zrcalu vrela', *Povijesni prilozi* 17, pp. 233–59, Zagreb 1998.
____ *Jajce,* Muzej hrvatskih arheoloških spomenika, Split 1999.
____ *Hrvatska u karolinško doba,* Muzej hrvatskih arheoloških spomenika, Split 2001.
____ *Na rubu Zapada: Tri stoljeća srednjevjekovne Bosne,* Dom i Svijet, Zagreb 2001.
____ *Putanja klatna: Ugarsko-hrvatsko kraljevstvo i Bosna u XIV. stoljeću,* HAZU, Zadar-Mostar 2007.
Anderson, Benedict, *Imagined Communities: Reflections on the Origins and Spread of Nationalism,* Verso, London 1983.
Anderson, Perry, *Lineages of the Absolutist State,* Verso, London 1974.
Andrić, Stanko, *The Miracles of St John Capistran,* CEU Press, Budapest 1999.
____ 'Klaićev udio u rasprama hrvatske i mađarske historiografije', in Milanović, Dragan and Andrić, Stanko, *Vjekoslav Klaić: Život i djelo,* Hrvatski institut za povijest, Slavonski Brod and Zagreb 2000.
____ *Potonuli svijet: Rasprave o slavonskom i srijemskom srednjevjekovlju,* Hrvatski institut za povijest, Slavonski Brod 2001.
____ 'Upravna zasebnost i društvene osobine srednjovjekovne Slavonije', in Kruhek, Milan, ed., *Hrvatsko-mađarski odnosi 1102–1918,* Hrvatski institut za povijest, Zagreb 2004.

Select Bibliography

____ 'Područje Požeške županije u srednjem vijeku', in Budak, Neven, ed., *Raukov zbornik: Zbornik u čast Tomislava Raukara*, F. F. Press, Zagreb 2005.
Antić, Ljubomir, *Naše iseljeništvo u Južnoj Americi i stvaranje jugoslavenske države 1918*, Školska knjiga, Zagreb 1987.
____ ed., *Hrvatska politika u dvadesetom stoljeću*, Matica hrvatska, Zagreb 2006.
Antoljak, Stjepan, *Pacta ili Concordia od 1102.*, Sveučilište u Zagrebu, Zagreb 1980.
____ *Hrvati u prošlosti*, Književni krug, Split 1992.
____ *A Survey of Croatian History*, Orbis/Laus, Split 1996.
____ et al., eds, *Kninski zbornik*, Matica hrvatska, Zagreb 1993.
Arhiđakon, Toma, *Historia salonitana*, Književni krug, Split 2003.
Artuković, Mato, *Ideologija srpsko-hrvatskih sporova: Srbobran 1884–1902*, Naprijed, Zagreb 1991.
____ 'Pitanje Srijema u Hrvatskom saboru 1861.', in Budak, Neven, ed., *Zbornik Mirjane Gross*, F. F. Press, Zagreb 1999.
____ 'Srbi u Hrvatskoj: Statistički pokazatelji (1883–1903)', *Časopis za suvremenu povijest*, 32, Zagreb 2000.
____ *Srbi u Hrvatskoj (Khuenovo doba)*, Hrvatski institut za povijest, Slavonski Brod 2001.
Avramovski, Živko, *Britanci o Kraljevini Jugoslaviji 1931–1938*, 2 vols, Arhiv Jugoslavije and Globus, Zagreb 1986.
Babić, Ivan et al., eds, *Život i djelo Jurja Križanića*, Liber, Zagreb 1974.
Babić, Ivo, *Prostor između Trogira i Splita*, Muzej grada Trogira, Trogir 1984.
Baernreither, Joseph M., *Fragments of a Political Diary*, Macmillan & Co., London 1930.
Bakarić, Vladimir, *Društvene klase, nacije, socijalizam*, Školska knjiga, Zagreb 1976.
Baletić, Milovan, ed., *Ljudi iz 1971.: Prekinuta šutnja*, Vjesnik, Zagreb 1990.
Balfour, Neil and Mackay, Sally, *Paul of Yugoslavia*, Hamish Hamilton, London 1980.
Balota, Mate, *Puna je Pula*, Čakavski sabor etc., Pula-Rijeka 1981.
Banac, Ivo, *The National Question in Yugoslavia: Origins, History, Politics*, Cornell University Press, Ithaca NY 1984.
____ 'Main trends in the Croat language question', in Riccardo Picchio and Harvey Goldblatt, eds, *Aspects of the Slavic Language Question*, vol. 1, New Haven 1984.
____ *With Stalin against Tito: Cominformist Splits in Yugoslav Communism*, Cornell University Press, Ithaca NY 1988.
____ *Grbovi-Biljezi identiteta*, Grafički zavod Hrvatske, Zagreb 1991.
____ *Hrvatsko jezično pitanje*, Mladost, Zagreb 1991.
____ *Dubrovački eseji*, Matica hrvatska Dubrovnik 1992.
____ 'Uskrsnula Hrvatska Pavla Rittera Vitezovića', *Kolo*, no. 2, pp. 5–18, Zagreb 1996.
____ *Raspad Jugoslavije*, Durieux, Zagreb 2001.
Barac, Antun, *Književnost Istre i Hrvatskog primorja*, Matica hrvatska, Zagreb 1968.
Barbalić, Fran, *Prvi istarski sabori (1861.–1877.)*, JAZU, Zagreb 1954.
Barbero, Alessandro, *Charlemagne: Father of a Continent*, University of California Press, Berkeley 2004.

Barić, Nikica, *Ustroj vojske domobranstva Nezavisne Države Hrvatske 1941–1945*, Hrvatski institut za povijest, Zagreb 2003.
____ *Srpska pobuna u Hrvatskoj 1990–1995*, Golden Marketing, Zagreb 2005.
Barker Elizabeth, *British Policy in South Eastern Europe in the Second World War*, Macmillan, London 1976.
Bartlett Robert, *The Making of Europe: Conquest, Colonization and Cultural Change 950–1350*, Penguin, London 1994.
Batelja Juraj et al., *Zagrebački biskupi i nadbiskupi*, Školska knjiga, Zagreb 1995.
Baučić Ivo et al., ed., *Političko-geografska i demografska pitanja Hrvatske*, Savez geografskih društava Hrvatske, Zagreb 1991.
Bekić Darko, *Jugoslavija u Hladnom ratu*, Globus, Zagreb 1988.
Belamarić, Joško, 'Egyptian mementoes in Dicoletian's Palace', *Most/The Bridge*, 1–4, pp. 209–16, Zagreb 1999.
Bellamy, Alex J., *The Formation of Croatian National Identity: A Centuries-Old Dream?*, Manchester University Press, Manchester 2003.
Benković, Vlaho, ed., *Zbornik radova o Vinku Foretiću*, Matica hrvatska, Dubrovnik-Korčula.
Berend, Ivan T. and Ránki, György, *Evropska periferija i industrijalizacija 178 –1914*, Naprijed, Zagreb 1996.
Bérenger, Jean, *A History of the Habsburg Empire 1270–1700*, Longman, London and New York 1994.
____ *A History of the Habsburg Empire 1700–1918*, Longman, London and New York 1997.
Bertelli, Carlo et al., eds, *Bizantini, Croati, Carolingi: Alba e tramonto de regni e imperi*, Skira Editore, Milano 2001.
Bertoša, Miroslav, 'Pogledi Carla Combija na povijest Istre i etnički sastav njezina pučanstva', *Časopis za suvremenu povijest*, no. 3, pp. 25–38, Zagreb 1974.
____ *Istra: Doba Venecije (XVI–XVIII stoljeće)*, Zavičajna naklada 'Žakan Juri', Pula 1995.
Beuc, Ivan, *Povijest institucija državne vlasti u Hrvatskoj (1527–1945)*, Arhiv Hrvatske, Zagreb 1969.
____ *Povijest instutucija državne vlasti Kraljevine Hrvatske, Slavonije i Dalmacije*, Pravni fakultet Zagreb, Zagreb 1985.
Bibó, István et al., *Regije evropske povijesti*, Naprijed, Zagreb 1995.
Bićanić, Rudolf, *Doba manufakture u Hrvatskoj i Slavoniji 1750–1860*, JAZU, Zagreb 1951.
____ *Economic Policy in Socialist Yugoslavia*, CUP, Cambridge 1973.
____ *Ekonomska podloga Hrvatskog pitanja i drugi radovi*, Pravni fakultet Zagreb, Zagreb 1995.
Bilandžić, Đušan, *Historija Socijalističke Federativne Republike Jugoslavije: Glavni procesi*, Školska knjiga, Zagreb 1979.
____ *Hrvatska moderna povijest*, Golden marketing, Zagreb 1999.
____ *Povijest izbliza: Memoarski zapisi 1945–2005*, Prometej, Zagreb 2006.
Biondich, Mark, *Stjepan Radić, the Croat Peasant Party and the Politics of Mass Mobilization 1904–1928*, University of Toronto Press, Toronto 2000.

Select Bibliography

Black, Jeremy, *Maps and History: Constructing Images of the Past*, Yale University Press, New Haven, 1997.
Blažević, Zrinka, *Vitezovićeva Hrvatska između stvarnosti i utopije*, Barbat, Zagreb 2002.
Bloch, Marc, *Feudal Society*, 2 vols, The University of Chicago Press, Chicago 1961.
Boban, Ljubo, *Sporazum Cvetković-Maček*, Institut za društvene nauke, Belgrade 1965.
____ *Svetozar Pribićević u opoziciji (1928–1936)*, Institut za hrvatsku povijest, Zagreb 1973.
____ *Maček i politika Hrvatske seljačke stranke 1928–1941*, 2 vols, Liber, Zagreb 1974.
____ et al., eds, *R.W. Seton-Watson and the Yugoslavs: Correspondence 1906–1918/ 1918–1942*, British Academy and Institut za hrvatsku povijest, Zagreb and London 1976.
____ *Hrvatska u arhivima izbjegličke vlade 1941–1943*, Globus, Zagreb 1985.
____ *Kontroverze iz povijesti Jugoslavije*, 3 vols, Školska knjiga, Zagreb 1987/1989/1990.
Bogdanov, Vaso et al., eds, *Jugoslavenski odbor u Londonu*, JAZU, Zagreb 1966.
Bogović, Mile, *Katolička crkva i pravoslavlje u Dalmaciji za mletačke vladavine*, Kršćanska sadašnjost, Zagreb 1993.
____ ed., *Krbavska biskupija u srednjem vijeku*, Kršćanska sadašnjost, Rijeka–Zagreb 1993.
Borak, Neven *Ekonomski vidiki delovanja in razpada Jugoslavije*, Znanstveno in publicistično središte, Ljubljana 2002.
Bösendorfer, Josip, *Agrarni odnosi u Slavoniji*, JAZU, Zagreb 1950.
Bošković, Ivan J., *ORJUNA: Ideologija i književnost*, Hrvatska sveučilišna naklada, Zagreb 2006.
Bozanić, Antun, *Biskup Mahnić: Pastir i javni djelatnik u Hrvata*, Kršćanska sadašnjost, Zagreb and Krk 1991.
Božić, Sofija, *Politička misao Srba u Dalmaciji: Srpski list/glas 1880–1904*, Institut za noviju istoriju Srbije, Belgrade 2001.
Bracewell, Catharine Wendy, *The Uskoks of Senj: Piracy, Banditry, and Holy War in the Sixteenth Century Adriatic*, Cornell University Press, Ithaca NY, 1992.
Brandt, Miroslav et al., *Izvori velikosrpske agresije*, August Cesarec/Školska knjiga, Zagreb 1991.
Bratulić, Josip, *Istarske književne teme*, Istarska naklada etc, Pula 1987.
Braudel, Fernand, *The Mediterranean and the Mediterranean World in the Age of Philip II*, 2 vols, Collins, London 1972.
Brozović, Dalibor, *Standardni jezik*, Školske novine, Zagreb 1970.
____ *Neka bitna pitanja hratskog jezičnog standarda*, Školska knjiga, Zagreb 2006.
Brubaker, Roger, *Citizenship and Nationhood in France and Germany*, Harvard University Press, Cambridge MA 1992.
Buczynski, Alexander, *Gradovi Vojne krajine*, 2 vols, Hrvatski institut za povijest, Zagreb 1997.
Budak, Neven, *Gradovi varaždinske županije u srednjem vijeku*, Nakladna kuća 'Dr

Feletar', Zagreb–Koprivnica 1994.
____ *Prva stoljeća Hrvatske*, Hrvatska sveučilišna naklada, Zagreb 1994.
____ *Karlo Veliki, Karolinzi i Hrvati*, Muzej hrvatskih arheoloških spomenika, Split 2001.
____ et al., *Zbornik Mirjane Gross*, Filozofski fakultet Zagreb, Zagreb 1999.
____ et al., *Habsburzi i Hrvati*, Srednja Europa, Zagreb 2003.
____ and Raukar, Tomislav, *Hrvatska povijest srednjeg vijeka*, Školska knjiga, Zagreb 2006.
____ ed., *Etnogeneza Hrvata*, Nakladni zavod Matice hrvatske etc., Zagreb 1995.
Burg, Steven L., *Conflict and Cohesion in Socialist Yugoslavia*, Princeton University Press, Princeton 1983.
Burić, Tonči, *Brbir: srednjevjekovno sijelo Šubića*, Muzej hrvatskih arheoloških spomenika, Split 1997.
Bush, Michael L., *Noble Privilege. (The European Nobility*, vol. 1), Manchester University Press, Manchester, 1983.
Butorac, Franjo et al., ed., *Povijest Rijeke*, Skupština općine Rijeka etc, Rijeka 1988.
Cabanès, Pierre, *Histoire de l'Adriatique*, Éditions du Seuil, Paris 2001.
Carter, April, *Democratic Reform in Yugoslavia*, Princeton University Press, Princeton 1982.
Cesarec, August, *Rasprave, članci, polemike*, Zora, Zagreb 1970.
Chirot, Daniel ed., *The Origins of Backwardness in Eastern Europe*, University of California Press, Berkeley 1989.
Ciliga, Ante, *Crise d'État dans la Yugoslavie de Tito*, Danoël, Paris 1972.
____ *Svjedok najvećih laži dvadesetog stoljeća*, Dora, Zagreb 2001.
Ciliga, Vera, *Slom politike Narodne stranke (1865–1880)*, Matica hrvatska, Zagreb 1970.
Clissold, Stephen, ed., *Yugoslavia and the Soviet Union 1939–1973*, Oxford University Press, Oxford 1975.
Colish, Marcia L., *The Medieval Foundations of the Western Intellectual Tradition 400–1400*, Yale University Press, New Haven 1998.
Collins, Roger, *Charlemagne*, University of Toronto Press, Toronto 1998.
Collinson, Patrick, *The Reformation*, Weidenfeld & Nicolson, London 2003.
Cottone, Carmelo, *Storia della scuola in Istria da Augusto a Mussolini*, Focardi, Capodistria (Koper) 1938.
Crkvenčić, Ivan and Klemenčić, Mladen, eds, 'Geographical and demographical issues of Croatia',
Geographical papers, no. 8, Zagreb 1991.
____ et al., eds, *Croatia: A New European State*, University of Zagreb, Zagreb 1993/4.
Cukrov, Ante, *Između obrazovanja i denacionalizacije*, C.A.S.H., Pula 2001.
Curta, Florin, *The Making of the Slavs*, Cambridge University Press, Cambridge 2002.
Cvitanić, Antun, *Iz dalmatinske pravne povijesti*, Književni krug, Split 2002.
Čermelj, Lavo, *La minorité slave en Italie: Les Slovènes et Croates de la Marche Julienne*, Union Yougoslave des Associations pour la Société des Nations,

Ljubljana 1938.
Čizmić, Ivan, *Jugoslavenski iseljenički pokret u SAD i stvaranje jugoslavenske države*, Institut za hrvatsku povijest, Zagreb 1974.
Čolaković, Rodoljub et al., *Pregled istorije Saveza komunista Jugoslavije*, Institut za izučavanje radničkog pokreta, Belgrade 1963.
Čop, Milivoj, *Riječko školstvo (1848–1918)*, Izdavački centar Rijeka, Rijeka 1988.
Čoralić, Lovorka, *Put, putnici, putovanja*, AGM, Zagreb 1997.
____ *U gradu Svetoga Marka*, HAZU, Zagreb 2001.
____ *Hrvatski doprinosi mletačkoj kulturi*, Dom i svijet, Zagreb 2003.
Črnja, Zvane, *Kulturna historija Hrvatske*, Epoha, Zagreb 1964.
Čubrilović, Vasa et al., ed., *Naučni skup u povodu 50-godišnjice raspada Austro-Ugarske Monarhije i stvaranja jugoslavenske države*, JAZU, Zagreb 1969.
Čulinović, Ferdo, *Slom stare Jugoslavije*, Školska knjiga, Zagreb 1958.
____*Jugoslavija između dva rata*, 2 vols, JAZU, Zagreb 1961.
Čušić, Dmitar, *Tragom predaka: Srbi u Vojnoj krajini*, Belgrade 1987.
Ćosić, Stjepan, *Dubrovnik nakon pada Republike 1808–1848*, HAZU, Dubrovnik 1992.
Dabčević Kučar, Savka, *'71 – Hrvatski snovi i stvarnost*, 2 vols, Interpublic, Zagreb 1997.
Dabinović, Antun, *Hrvatska državna i pravna povijest*, Matica Hrvatska, Zagreb 1990.
Dadić, Žarko, *Povijest egzaktnih znanosti u Hrvata*, 2 vols, Liber, Zagreb 1991.
____ *Herman Dalmatin – Hermann of Dalmatia*, Školska knjiga, Zagreb 1996.
Deakin, F. W., *The Brutal Friendship: Mussolini, Hitler and the Fall of Italian Fascism*, Weidenfeld & Nicolson, London 1962.
Defilipis, Josip, *Dalmatinsko selo u promjenama*, Avium, Split 1997.
Dekanić, Igor, *Demokratizacija Hrvatske*, Prometej, Zagreb 2004.
Despalatović Murray, Elinor, *Ljudevit Gaj and the Illyrian Movement*, East European Quarterly, Boulder CO, 1975.
Diklić, Marjan, *Pravaštvo u Dalmaciji do kraja Prvog svjetskog rata*, Matica hrvatska, Zadar 1998.
Dobronić, Lelja, *Templari i Isusovci u Hrvatskoj*, Kršćanska sadašnjost, Zagreb 2002.
Dragosavac, Dušan, *Zbivanja i svjedočenja*, Globus, Zagreb 1987.
Dretar, Dražen et al., *Varaždinski dani rata*, NIŠP Varaždin, Varaždin 1991.
Dubravica, Branko, *Vojska antifašističke Hrvatske (1941–1945)*, Bibiloteka Albatros, Velika Gorica 1986.
Dukovski, Darko, *Rat i mir istarski: Model povijesne prijelomnice 1943–1955*, C.A.S.H, Pula 2000.
Dusa, Joan, *The Medieval Dalmatian Episcopal Cities*, Peter Lang, New York etc., 1991.
Dvornik, Francis, *The Slavs in European History and Civilisation*, Rutger University Press, New Brunswick NJ 1962.
Dyggve, Ejnar, *Povijest salonitanskog kršćanstva*, Književni krug, Split 1996.
Đukić, Slavoje, *Lovljenje vetra: Politička ispovest Dobrice Ćosića*, Samizdat B92,

Belgrade 2001.
Džaja, Srećko, *Politička podloga jugoslavenstva*, Svjetlo riječi, Sarajevo 2004.
Eisenmann, Louis, *Le compromis Austro-Hongrois de 1867*, Academic International, Paris 1904.
Engelsfeld, Neda, *Prvi parlament Kraljevstva Srba, Hrvata i Slovenaca*, Globus, Zagreb 1989.
____ *Povijest hrvatske države i prava*, Pravni fakultet, Zagreb 1999.
Erjavec, Tonči, *Španovica*, Novi Liber, Zagreb 1992.
Eterovich, Francis and Spalatin, Christopher, *Croatia*, 2 vols, University of Toronto Press, Toronto 1964/1970.
Evans, R. J. W., *The Making of the Habsburg Monarchy 1550-1700*, OUP, Oxford 1979.
Favretto, Tito and Greco, Ettore, *Il confine riscoperto*, Franco Angeli, Rome 1997.
Feldman, Andrea, ed., *Žene u Hrvatskoj*, Ženska infoteka, Zagreb 2004.
Feletar, Dragutin, *Podravina*, Muzej grada Korpivnice, Koprivnica 1988.
Fine, John V.A., Jr. *The Early Medieval Balkans*, The University of Michigan Press, Ann Arbor 1981.
____ *The Late Medieval Balkans*, The University of Michigan Press, Ann Arbor 1994.
Fisković, Igor, *Reljef kralja Petra Krešimira IV.*, Muzej hrvatskih arheoloških spomenika, Split 2002.
Fletcher, Richard, *The Conversion of Europe,* Harper Collins, London 1997.
Fortis, Alberto, *Travels into Dalmatia*, Arno Press/The New York Times, New York 1971.
Franolić, Branko, *A Survey of Croatian Bibliographies 1960-2003*, Croatian Information Centre, Zagreb 1985.
Frejdenberg, Maren, *Židovi na Balkanu na istoku srednjeg vijeka*, Dora, Zagreb 2000.
Fučić, Branko, *Terra Incognita*, Kršćanska sadašnjost, Zagreb 1998.
____ *Fraške*, Kršćanska sadašnjost, Zagreb 2000.
Fućak, Jerko, *Šest stoljeća hrvatskog lekcionara u sklopu jedanest stoljeća hrvatskog glagoljaštva*, Kršćanska sadašnjost, Zagreb 1975.
Ganshof, F.L., *Feudalism*, University of Toronto Press, Toronto 1996.
Ganza-Aras, Tereza, *Politika 'Novog kursa' dalmatinskih pravaša oko Supila i Trumbića*, Matica hrvatska, Split 1992.
Garde, Paul, *Vie et mort de la Yugoslavie*, Fayard, Paris 2000.
Gašić, Ranka, *Novi kurs Srba u Hrvatskoj: Srbobran 1903-1914*, Prosvjeta, Zagreb 2001.
Gazi, Stephen, *A History of Croatia*, Philosophical Library, New York 1973.
Geary, Patrick, J., *The Myth of Nations*, Princeton University Press, Princeton 2002.
Geiger, Vladimir, *Nestanak Folksdojčera*, Hrvatski institut za povijest, Zagreb 1997.
____ *Nijemci u Đakovu i Đakovštini*, Hrvatski institu za povijest, Zagreb 2001.
Gelo, Jakov, *Demografske promjene u Hrvatskoj od 1780. do 1981. god.*, Globus, Zagreb 1987.
____ et al., eds, *Narodnosni i vjerski sastav stanovništva Hrvatske 1880-1991*, 5 vols,

Select Bibliography

Državni zavod za statistiku Republike Hrvatske, Zagreb 1998.
Georgijević, Krešimir, *Hrvatska književnost od XVI do XVIII stoljeća u sjevernoj Hrvatskoj i Bosni*, Matica hrvatska, Zagreb 1969.
Gizdić, Drago, *Dalmacija 1941–1945.*, Agencija za fotodokumentaciju, Zagreb 1966.
Gligo, Vedran, ed., *Govori protiv Turaka*, Logos, Split 1983.
Gligorijević, Branislav, *Parlament i političke stranke u Jugoslaviji 1919–1929*, Institut za savremenu istoriju, Belgrade 1979.
Goffart, Walter, *Barbarians and Romans*, Princeton University Press, Princeton 1980.
Goldstein, Ivo, *Bizant na Jadranu*, Zavod za hrvatsku povijest, Zagreb 1992.
___ *Hrvatski srednji vijek*, Zavod za hrvatsku povijest, Zagreb 1995.
___ *Holocaust u Zagrebu*, Novi Liber, Zagreb 2001.
___ *Židovi u Zagrebu 1918–1941*, Novi Liber, Zagreb 2004.
___ et al., eds, *Hrvatske županije kroz stoljeća*, Školska knjiga, Zagreb 1996.
___ ed., *Zvonimir, kralj hrvatski*, HAZU, Zagreb 1997.
Golec, Ivica, *Povijest grada Petrinje: 1240–1592–1992*, Matica hrvatska/Školska knjiga, Zagreb 1993.
Golub, Ivan, 'The Slavic idea of Juraj Križanić', *Harvard Ukrainian Studies*, no. 3/4, Cambridge MA 1986.
___ *Križanić*, Kršćanska sadašnjost, Zagreb 1987.
___ *Ivan Paštrić*, Kršćanska sadašnjost, Zagreb 1988.
Grakalić, Marijan, *Hrvatski grb*, Matica hrvatska, Zagreb 1990.
Granić, Mate, *Vanjski poslovi: Iza kulisa politike*, Algoritam, Zagreb 2005.
Granić, Miroslav et al., eds, *Život i djelo Bartola Kašića*, Općina Pag etc., Zadar 1994.
Grdešić, Ivan et al., *Hrvatska u izborima '90*, Naprijed, Zagreb 1991.
Greguric, Franjo, *Vlada demokratskog jedinstva Hrvatske 1991–1992*, Naklada Zadro, Zagreb 1998.
Grgin, Borislav, *Počeci rasapa: Kralj Matijaš i srednjevjekovna Hrvatska*, Ibis grafika, Zagreb 2002.
Grijak, Zoran, 'Problem odvajanja riječke župe od Senjsko-modruške biskupije (1891–1913.)', *Časopis za suvremenu povijest*, no. 3, Zagreb 1996.
Grlica, George, *Odessa in 1917 from a Croatian Perspective*, New York 2000.
Grmek, Mirko et al., *Le nettoyage ethnique*, Fayard, Paris 1993.
Gross, Mirjana, *Vladavina Hrvatsko-srpske koalicije 1906–1907*, Institut društvenih nauka, Belgrade 1960.
___ 'Nacionalne ideje studentske omladine u Hrvatskoj uoči Prvog svjetskog rata', *Historijski zbornik*, no. 21–2, Zagreb 1968–9.
___ *Počeci moderne Hrvatske: Neoabsolutizam u civilnoj Hrvatskoj i Slavoniji 1850–1860*, Globus, Zagreb 1985.
___ *Izvorno pravaštvo*, Golden Marketing, Zagreb 2000.
___ and Szabo, Agneza, *Prema hrvatskome građanskom društvu: Društveni razvoj u civilnoj Hrvatskoj i Slavoniji šezdesetih i sedamdesetih godina*, Globus, Zagreb 1992.
___ ed., *Društveni razvoj u Hrvatskoj*, Liber, Zagreb 1981.

Grumel-Jacquignon, François, *La Yougoslavie dans la stratégie française de l'Entre-deux-Guerres (1918–1935): Aux origins du myth serbe en France*, Peter Lang, Bern 1999.
Guldescu, Stanko, *History of Medieval Croatia*, Mouton, The Hague 1964.
Gulin, Ante, *Hrvatski srednjevjekovni kaptoli*, Golden Marketing, Zagreb 2001.
Hadrovics, László, *Srpski narod i njegova crkva pod turskom vlašću*, Globus, Zagreb 2000.
Harris, Robin, *Dubrovnik: A History*, Saqi Books, London 2003.
Haselsteiner Horst, *Ogledi o modernizaciji u Srednjoj Evropi*, Naprijed, Zagreb 1997.
Hastings, Adrian, *The Construction of Nationhood: Ethnicity, religion and Nationalism*, CUP, Cambridge 1997.
Hercigonja, Eduard, *Nad iskonom hrvatske knjige*, Liber, Zagreb 1983.
____ *Tropismena i trojezična kultura hrvatskog srednjovjekovlja*, Zagreb 1994.
____ ed., *Hrvatska i Evropa*, vol. 2: *Srednji vijek i Renesansa*, AGM, Zagreb 2000.
Herrin, Judith, *The Formation of Christendom*, Fontana Press, London 1989.
Herrman, David, *The Arming of Europe and the Making of the First World War*, Princeton University Press, Princeton 1996.
Hickock, Michael R., *Ottoman Military Administration in the 18th Century*, Brill, Leiden etc., 1997.
Hill, Roland, *Lord Acton*, Yale University Press, New Haven, 2000.
Hinsely, F. H., *Sovereignty*, CUP, Cambridge 1986.
Hoare, Marko Attila, *The Chetnik-Partisan Conflict and the Origins of Bosnian Statehood*, Yale University doctoral thesis, New Haven, 2000.
____ 'Whose is the Partisan Movement? Serbs, Croats and the Legacy of a Shared Resistance', *The Journal of Slavic Military Studies*, vol. 15, no. 4, London 2002.
____ 'The Ustasha Genocide', *South Slav Journal*, vol. 25, nos 1–2, London 2004.
____ *How Bosnia Armed*, Saqi Books and The Bosnian Institute, London 2005.
____ *Genocide and Resistance in Hitler's Bosnia: The Partisans and the Chetniks 1941–1945,* Oxford University Press, Oxford 2006.
____ *The History of Bosnia*, Saqi Books, London 2007.
Hoensch, Jörg K., *A History of Modern Hungary 1867–1994*, Longman, London and New York 1996.
Hočevar, Toussaint, *The Structure of the Slovenian Economy 1848–1963*, Studia Slovenica, New York 1965.
Hoffman, George W. and Neal, Fred W., *Yugoslavia and the New Communism*, The Twentieth Century Fund, New York 1962.
Holjevac, Željko, *Brinjsko-lički ustanak 1746*, Meridijani, Samobor 2004.
Hoptner, J. B., *Yugoslavia in Crisis 1934–1941*, Columbia University Press, New York 1962.
Horvat, Josip, *Supilo*, Tipografija, Zagreb 1938.
____ *Ljudevit Gaj*, Liber, Zagreb 1975.
____ *Živjeti u Hrvatskoj: Zapisi iz nepovrata 1900–1941*, Liber, Zagreb 1984.
____ *Preživjeti u Zagrebu: Dnevnik 1943–1945*, Liber, 1989.
____ *Politička povijest Hrvatske,* 2 vols, August Cesarec, Zagreb 1990.

Select Bibliography

___ *Povijest novinstva Hrvatske 1771–1939*, Stvarnost, Zagreb 2003.
Horvat, Rudolf, *Lika i Krbava*, Matica hrvatska, Zagreb 1941.
Hoško, Franjo Emanuel, *Franjevci u kontinentalnoj Hrvatskoj kroz stoljeća*, Kršćanska sadašnjost, Zagreb 2000.
Howard, Deborah, *Venice and the East: The Impact of the Islamic World on Venetian Architecture 1100–1500*, Yale University Press, New Haven 2000.
Hrvatski biografski leksikon, vols. A-Kal, Leksikografski zavod 'Miroslav Krleža', Zagreb 1983–2005.
Hrvatsko Proljeće: Presuda Partije, Dom i svijet, Zagreb 2003.
Hudelist, Darko, *Banket u Hrvatskoj*, Globus International, Zagreb 2001.
___ *Tuđman: Biografija*, Profil International, Zagreb 2004.
İnalcık, Halil, *An Economic and Social History of the Ottoman Empire 1300–1600*, CUP, Cambridge 1994.
___ *The Ottoman Empire: The Classical Age 1300–1600*, Phoenix, London 1994.
Irvine, Jill A., *The Croat Question: Partisan Politics in the Formation of the Yugoslav Socialist State*, Westview Press, Boulder CO, 1993.
Išek, Tomislav, *Djelatnost Hrvatske seljačke stranke u Bosni i Hercegovini do zavođenja diktature*, Svjetlost, Sarajevo 1981.
___ *Hrvatska seljačka stranka u Bosni i Hercegovini 1929–1941*, Institut za istoriju, Sarajevo 1991.
Ivanković-Vonta, Zvonko, *Hebrang*, Scientia Yugoslavica, Zagreb 1988.
Jackson, Julian, *France, The Darkest Years: 1940–1944*, Oxford University Press, Oxford 2001.
Jakovljević, Ilija, *Konclogor na Savi*, Konzor, Zagreb 1999.
Jakšić, Nikola, *Zemunik: Srednjevjekovni zadarski kaštel i turska kasaba*, Muzej hrvatskih arheoloških spomenika, Split 1997.
___ *Hrvatski srednjevjekovni krajobrazi*, Muzej hrvatskih arheoloških spomenika, Split 2000.
Jambrek, Stanko, *Hrvatski protestantski pokret u XVI. i XVII. stoljeću*, Matica hrvatska, Zaprešić 1999.
James, Edward, *The Franks*, Blackwell, Oxford 1994.
Janeković Römer, Zdenka, *Višegradski ugovor, temelj dubrovačke republike*, Golden Marketing, Zagreb 2003.
Janićijević, Miloslav, *Stvaralačka inteligencija međuratne Jugoslavije*, Institut društvenih nauka, Belgrade 1984.
Janjatović, Bosiljka, *Politički teror u Hrvatskoj 1918–1935*, Hrvatski institut za povijest, Zagreb 2002.
Janković, Dragoslav, *Društveni i politički odnosi u Kraljevstvu Srba, Hrvata i Slovenaca*, Institut društvenih nauka, Belgrade 1969.
___ *Srbija i jugoslovensko pitanje 1914–1915*, Institut za suvremenu istoriju, Belgrade 1973.
___ and Krizman, Bogdan, *Građa o stvaranju jugoslovenske države*, Belgrade 1964.
Janos, C. Andrew, *The Politics of Backwardness in Hungary 1825–1945*, Princeton University Press, Princeton 1982.
Jareb, Jere, *Pola stoljeća hrvatske politike 1895–1945*, Institut za suvremenu povijest,

Zagreb 1995.
Jászi, Oscar, *The Dissolution of the Habsburg Monarchy*, Chicago University Press, Chicago 1971.
Javorović, Božidar, *Velikosrpska najezda i obrana Hrvatske*, Bibiloteka Defimi, Zagreb 1955.
Jelačić, Aleksije, *Seljački pokret u Hrvatskoj i Slavoniji godine 1848–9*, Tipografija, Zagreb 1925.
Jelavich, Charles, *South Slav Nationalisms*, Ohio State University Press, Columbus 1990.
Jelić, Ivan, *Komunistička Partija Hrvatske 1937–1941*, Institut za historiju radničkog pokreta, Zagreb 1972.
____ *Jugoslavenska socijalistička revolucija (1941–1945)*, Školska knjiga, Zagreb 1979
____ *Tragedija u Kerestincu*, Globus, Zagreb 1986.
Jelić-Butić, Fikreta, *Ustaše i NDH*, Globus, Zagreb 1978.
____ *Hrvatska seljačka stranka*, Globus, Zagreb 1983.
____ *Četnici u Hrvatskoj 1941–1945*, Globus, Zagreb 1986.
Jenks, William Alexander, *The Austrian Electoral Reform of 1907*, Octagon Books, New York 1974.
Jezernik, Božidar, *Wild Europe*, Saqi Books, London 2004.
Johnson, Ross A., *The Transformation of Communist Ideology*, Harvard University Press, Cambridge, MA 1972.
Johnston, William M., *The Austrian Mind*, University of California Press, Berkeley 1972.
Jones, A. H. M, *The Decline of the Ancient World*, Longman, London, 1966.
Jonjić, Tomislav, *Hrvatska vanjska politika 1939–1942*, Libar, Zagreb 2000.
Jovanović, Aleksandar, *Rat Srba i Hrvata*, Belgrade 1994.
Jović, Borisav, *Posljednji dani SFRJ*, Politika, Belgrade 1995.
Jugoslavia, Geographical Handbook Series, Naval Intelligence Division, 3 vols, London 1944.
Jurić, Ivan, *Genetičko podrijetlo Hrvata*, Zagreb 2003.
Kadijević, Vjeko, *Moje viđenje raspada*, Politika, Belgrade 1993.
Kaličanin, Zoran, ed., *Republika Srpska Krajina*, Belgrade 2006.
Kampuš, Ivan and Karaman, Igor, *Tisućljetni Zagreb*, Školska knjiga, Zagreb 1994.
Kann, Robert, *The Multinational Empire*, Columbia University Press, 2 vols, New York 1950.
____ *A History of the Habsburg Empire 1526–1918*, University of California Press, Berkeley 1980.
____ and Zdeněk, David V., *The peoples of the Eastern Habsburg Lands*, University of Washington Press, Seattle 1984.
Karaman, Igor, *Privreda i društvo Hrvatske u 19. stoljeću*, Školska knjiga, Zagreb 1972.
____ *Industrijalizacija građanske Hrvatske (1800–1941)*, Naprijed, Zagreb 1991.
____ *Požega u srcu Slavonije*, Naklada Slap, Jasterbarsko 1997.
____ *Hrvatska na pragu modernizacije 1750–1918*, Naklada Ljevak, Zagreb 2000.
Karatay, Osman, *In Search of a Lost Tribe: The Origins and Making of the Croatian*

Nation, Karam, Çorum 2003.
Kardelj, Edvard, *Razvoj slovenačkog nacionalnog pitanja*, Komunist, Belgrade 1973.
Kasapović, Mirjana, *Izborni i stranački sustav Republike Hrvatske*, Alinea, Zagreb 1993.
____ ed., *Hrvatska politika 1990–2000*, Fakultet političkih znanost Zagreb, Zagreb 2001.
Kaser, Karl, *Slobodan seljak i vojnik*, vol. 1: *Rana krajiška društva (1545–1745)*, vol. 2: *Povojačeno društvo (1754–1881)*, Naprijed, Zagreb 1997.
Katalinić, Kazimir, 'The declaration of Croatian independence in the light of internal documents', *Journal of Croatian Studies*, nos 28–29, New York 1987–8.
Katičić, Natko, *More i vlast obalne države*, Jadranski institut, JAZU, Zagreb 1953.
Katičić, Radoslav, *Novi jezikoslovni ogledi*, Školska knjiga, Zagreb 1986.
____ *Uz početke hrvatskih početaka*, Književni krug, Split 1993.
____ *Litterarum Studia*, Matica hrvatska, Zagreb 1998.
____ *Na krotističkim raskrižjima*, Sveučilište u Zagrebu, Zagreb 1999.
Katušić, Ivan, *Vječno progonstvo Nikole Tommasea*, Liber, Zagreb 1975.
Kečkemet, Duško, *Hrvatski narodni preporod u Splitu: Zbivanja i likovi*, Glas Dalmacije, Split 1999.
____ et al., eds, *Hrvatski narodni preporod u Splitu 1882*, Logos, Split 1984.
Kesar, Jovan et al., *Geneza maspoka u Hrvatskoj*, Književne novine, Belgrade 1990.
Kisić Kolanović, Nada, 'Drama vojskovođe Slavka Kvaternika', *Časopis za suvremenu povijest*, no. 3, pp. 379–397, Zagreb 1996.
____ *Hebrang: Iluzije i otrežnjenja 1899–1949*, Institut za suvremenu povijest, Zagreb 1996.
____ *NDH i Italija:Političke veze i diplomatski odnosi*, Naklada Ljevak, Zagreb 2001.
____ *Zagreb-Sofija: Prijateljstvo po mjeri ratnog vremena 1941–1945*, Dom i svijet, Zagreb 2003.
____ ed., *Vojskovođa i politika: Sjećanja Slavka Kvaternika*, Golden Marketing, Zagreb 1997.
Klaić, Nada, *Povijest Hrvata u srednjem vijeku*, Globus, Zagreb 1990.
Klaić, Vjekoslav, *Život i djela Pavla Rittera Vitezovića (1652–1713)*, Matica hrvatska, Zagreb 1914.
Knezović, Pavao et al., ed., *Zbornik o Pavlu Posiloviću*, Šibenik-Zagreb 2001.
Kočović, Bogoljub, *Žrtve Drugog svetskog rata u Jugoslaviji*, Naše delo, London 1985.
Kohn, Hans, *Panslavism: its History and Ideology*, Vintage Books, New York 1960.
Kolanović, Josip, *Šibenik u kasnom srednjem vijeku*, Školska knjiga, Zagreb 1995.
____ et al., 'Državno-pravni položaj Slavonije i Srijema u dokumentima 1699–1848', *Fontes 1*, Zagreb 1995.
Kolarz, Walter, *Myths and Realities in Eastern Europe*, Lindsay Drummond, London 1946.
Kolumbić, Nikica et al., *Zbornik radova o Šimunu Kožičiću Benji*, Novi Liber, Zagreb 1991.

Kombol, Mihovil, *Povijest hrvatske književnosti do narodnog preporoda*, Matica hrvatska, Zagreb 1961.

____ and Slobodan Prosperov Novak, *Hrvatska Književnost do narodnog preporoda*, Školska knjiga, Zagreb 1995.

Kontler, László, *A History of Hungary*, Palgrave Macmillan, Basingstoke 2002.

Koprivica, Veseljko, *Sve je bilo meta*, Monitor, Podgorica 1996.

Korade, Mijo et al., *Jesuits and Croatian Culture, Most/The Bridge*, Zagreb 1992.

Korunić, Petar, *Jugoslavenska ideja u hrvatskoj i slovenskoj politici*, Globus, Zagreb 1986.

Kostrenčić, Marko, ed., *Zapisi Dra Josipa Smodlake*, Zagreb 1972.

Košćak, Vladimir, 'Madžaronska emigracije 1848', *Historijski zbornik*, no. 104, Zagreb 1950.

____ 'Jadranska orijentacija feudalne Hrvatske', *Forum*, Zagreb April–May 1969.

Koštunica, Vojislav and Čavoški, Kosta, *Stranački pluralizam ili monizam 1944–1949*, Veselin Masleša, Sarajevo 1983.

Košutić, Ivan, *Hrvatsko domobranstvo u Drugom svjetskom ratu*, Matica hrvatska, 2 vols, Zagreb 1992, 1994.

Kovač, Mirko, *Francuska i hrvatsko pitanje 1914–1929*, Dom i svijet, Zagreb 2005.

Kovačević, Ivan, *Ekonomski položaj radničke klase u Hrvatskoj i Slavoniji 1867–1914*, Institut za savremenu istoriju, Belgrade 1972.

Kovačić, Ivan, *Kampor 1942–1943*, Adamić, Rijeka 1998.

Kraljević, Rudolf, *Vinogradarski slom i demografski rasap južne Hrvatske u osvit 20. stoljeća*, Književni krug, Split 1994.

Kraljić, John Peter, 'Ethnic relations and sovereignty in Istria, 1945–1947', manuscript.

Krašić, Stjepan, *Dominikanci: Povijest reda u hrvatskim krajevima*, Hrvatska dominikanska zajednica, Zagreb 1997.

Krestić, Vasilije, *Hrvatsko-ugarska nagodba 1868.*, SANU, Belgrade 1969.

____ *Srpsko-hrvatski odnosi i jugoslavenska ideja*, Partizanska knjiga, Belgrade 1983.

____ *Istorija Srba u Hrvatskoj i Slavoniji*, Zavod za udžbenike, Belgrade 1991.

Kriste, Petar, *Iznevjereni grad: Dubrovnik 1991*, Golden Marketing, Zagreb 2000.

Krišto, Jure, *Katolička crkva i Nezavisna Država Hrvatska 1941–1945*, Hrvatski institut za povijest, 2 vols, Zagreb 1998.

Krizman, Bogdan, 'Građa o talijanskoj okupaciji Rijeke, Istre i Hrvatskog primorja 1918 godine', *Jadranski zbornik*, Rijeka-Pula 1956.

____ *Raspad Austro-Ugarske i stvaranje jugoslavenske države*, Školska knjiga, Zagreb 1977.

____ *Pavelić između Hitlera i Mussolinija*, Globus, Zagreb 1980.

____ *Ustaše i Treći Reich*, Globus, Zagreb 1983.

____ *Pavelić i ustaše*, Globus, Zagreb 1986.

____ *Pavelić u bjekstvu*, Globus, Zagreb 1986.

____ *Hrvatska u Prvom svjetskom ratu*, Zagreb 1989.

____ ed., *Jugoslavenske vlade u izbjeglištvu 1941–1943*, vol 1, Zagreb 1981.

Krleža, Miroslav, *Deset krvavih godina*, Zora, Zagreb 1957.

Kršnjavi, Iso, *Zapisci: Iza kulisa hrvatske politike*, Mladost, 2 vols, Zagreb 1986.

Select Bibliography

Krstić, Kruno, *Doseljenje Arbanasa u Zadar*, Mjesna zajednica Arbanasi, Zadar 1988.
Krtalić, Ivan, *Hrvatske književne afere*, August Cesarec, Zagreb 1987.
Kruhek, Milan, *Krajiške utvrde hrvatskog kraljevstva 16. stoljeća*, Institut za suvremenu povijest, Zagreb 1995.
Kučerová, Kvetoslava, *Hrvati u Srednjoj Evropi*, Matica hrvatska and Matica slovenská, Zagreb 1998.
Kulundžić, Zvonimir, *Atentat na Stjepana Radića*, Stvarnost, Zagreb 1967.
____ *Politika i korupcija u kraljevskoj Jugoslaviji*, Stvarnost, Zagreb 1968.
Kurelac, Miroslav, *Ivan Lučić Lucius*, Matica hrvatska, Zagreb 1994.
Kužić, Krešimir, *Povijest dalmatinske Zagore*, Književni krug, Split 1997.
Kvaternik, Dido Eugen, *Sjećanja i zapažanja*, Starčević, Zagreb 1995.
Lajić, Ivan, *Stanovništvo dalmatinskih otoka*, Consilium and Institut za migracije i narodnosti, Zagreb 1992.
Laušić, Ante, *Postanak i razvitak poljičke kneževine*, Književni krug, Split 1991.
Lazić, Mladen, *Reprodukcija društvenih grupa u Hrvatskoj*, Institut za društvena istraživanja, Zagreb 1986.
Le Goff, Jacques, *The Birth of Europe*, Blackwell, Oxford 2005.
Lederer, Ivo J., *Yugoslavia at the Paris Peace Conference: A Study in Frontier-making*, Yale University Press, New Haven, 1963.
Lendvai, Paul, *The Hungarians*, Princeton University Press, Princeton 2003.
Lengel-Krizman, Narcisa, ed., *Dva stoljeća povijesti i kulture Židova u Zagrebu i Hrvatskoj*, Židovska općina, Zagreb 1998.
Letica Slaven, *Obećana zemlja*, Globus, Zagreb 1992.
Libal, Michael, *Limits of Persuasion: Germany and the Yugoslav Crisis, 1991–1991*, Texas A&M University Press, 1997.
Lingelbach, William E., *Austria-Hungary*, Arno Press, New York 1971.
Lipošćak, Višnja and Sučić, Stjepan, *Ogulin*, Matica hrvatska, Zagreb 2002.
Lisac, Josip, *Hrvatski jezik i njegovi proučavatelji*, Književni krug, Split 1994.
Ljerka, Racko, 'Spaljivanje mađarske zastave 1895. u Zagrebu', *Radovi*, vol. 23, pp. 233–245, Zagreb 1990.
Lopašić, Radoslav, *Dva hrvatska junaka - Marko Mesić i Luka Ibrišimović*, Matica hrvatska, Zagreb 1888.
Lovrenčić, Rene, *Geneza politike 'Novog kursa'*, Institut za hrvatsku povijest, Zagreb 1972.
Lučin, Bratislav, ed., 'Dossier Marko Marulić', *Most/The Bridge*, 1–4, Zagreb 1999.
Lukežić, Irvin, *Fijumanske priče*, Izdavački centar Rijeka, Rijeka 1991.
Lukic, Renéo, *Les relations soviéto-yougoslaves de 1935 à 1945*, Peter Lang, Bern 1996.
____ *L'Agonie Yougoslave (1986–2003)*, Les Presses d'Université Laval, Québec 2003.
Lydall, Harold, *Yugoslav Socialism: Theory and Practice*, Clarendon Press, Oxford 1984.
____ *Yugoslavia in Crisis*, Clarendon Press, Oxford 1989.
Macan, Trpimir, *Miho Klaić*, Matica hrvatska, Zagreb 1980.
____ *Povijesni prijepori*, Matica hrvatska, Dubrovnik 1992.
____ *Povijest hrvatskog naroda*, Matica hrvatska and Školska knjiga, Zagreb 1992.

Macartney, C. A., *The Habsburg Empire 1790–1918*, Weidenfeld & Nicolson, London 1968.
____ ed., *The Habsburg and Hohenzollern Dynasties in the Seventeenth and Eighteenth Centuries*, Walker & Co., New York 1970.
MacCalloch, Diarmaid, *Reformation: Europe's House Divided 1490–1700*, Penguin/Allen Lane, London 2003.
Mack Smith, Denis, *Mussolini*, Weidenfeld & Nicolson, London 1987.
Maček, Vlatko, *In the Struggle for Freedom*, Spellers & Sons, New York 1957.
____ *Memoari*, Dom i svijet, Zagreb 2003.
Magaš, Branka, *The Destruction of Yugoslavia: Tracking the Break-up 1980–92*, Verso, London 1993.
____ and Žanić, Ivo, eds, *The War in Croatia and Bosnia-Herzegovina 1991–1995*, Frank Cass, London 2001.
Malcolm, Noel, *De Dominis (1560–1624)*, Strickland and Scott Academic Publications, London 1984.
____ *Bosnia: A Short History*, Macmillan, London 1994.
____ *Kosovo: A Short History*, Macmillan, London 1998.
Mamula, Branko, *Slučaj Jugoslavija*, CID, Podgorica 2000.
Mandić, Ante, *Fragmenti za historiju ujedinjenja*, JAZU, Zagreb 1956.
Manin, Marino, ed., *Talijanska uprava na hrvatskom prostoru i egzodus Hrvata (1918–1943)*, Hrvatski institut za povijest, Zagreb 2001.
Manin, Marino et al., eds, *Identitet Istre: Ishodišta i perspektive*, Institut društvenih znanosti, Zagreb 2006.
Margetić, Lujo, *Iz vinodolske prošlosti*, HAZU, Rijeka 1980.
____ *Srednjovjekovno hrvatsko pravo*, Pravni fakultet Zagreb and Pravni fakultet Rijeka, Zagreb 1983.
____ 'Cetinski sabori u 1527', *Senjski zbornik*, 17, Senj 1990.
____ *Iz ranije hrvatske povijesti*, Književni krug, Split 1997.
____ *Zagreb i Slavonija*, HAZU, Rijeka 2000.
____ *Dolazak Hrvata*, Književni krug, Split 2001.
Marković, Dragoslav Draža, *Život i politika 1967–1978*, Rad, 2 vols, Belgrade 1987.
Marković, Mirko, *Descriptio Croatiae*, Naprijed, Zagreb 1993.
____ *Slavonija*, Golden Marketing, Zagreb 2002.
____ *Hrvatski otoci na Jadranu*, Jesenski i Turk, Zagreb 2004.
Marković, Sima, *Tragizam malih naroda*, Filip Višnjić, Belgrade 1985.
Markus, Tomislav, *Hrvatski politički pokret 1848–1849 godine*, Dom i svijet, Zagreb 2000.
____ ed., *Korespondencija Bana Jelačića i Banskog vijeća 1848–1850*, Hrvatski institut za povijest, Zagreb 1998.
Marmont, Maršal, *Memoari*, Logos, Split 1984.
Maticka, Marijan, *Agrarna reforma i kolonizacija u Hrvatskoj 1945–1948*, Školska knjiga, Zagreb 1990.
Matić, Milan and Janjić, Dušan, eds, *Savez komunista Jugoslavije i politika nacionalne ravnopravnosti*, Belgrade 1982.
Matijević Sokol, Mirjana, *Toma Arhiđakon i njegovo djelo*, Institut za hrvatsku

povijest, Zagreb 2002.
Matijević, Zlatko, *Slom politike katoličkog jugoslavenstva 1919-1929*, Institut za hrvatsku povijest, Zagreb 1988.
Matković, Hrvoje, *Svetozar Pribićević i Samostalna demokratska stranka do šestojanuarske diktature*, Institut za hrvatsku povijest, Zagreb 1972.
____ *Povijest Nezavisne Države Hrvatske*, Naklada Pavičić, Zagreb 1994.
____ *Svetozar Pribićević*, Hrvatska sveučilišna naklada, Zagreb 1995.
____ *Povijest Jugoslavije: Hrvatski pogled*, Naklada Pavićić, Zagreb 1998.
____ *Studije iz novije hrvatske povijesti*, Golden Marketing, Zagreb 2004.
Matković, Stjepan, *Čista stranka prava 1895-1903*, Hrvatski institut za povijest, Zagreb 2001.
Mayer, Arno J., *Policy and Diplomacy of Peacemaking: Containment and Counter-Revolution at Versailles 1918-1919*, Weidenfeld & Nicolson, London 1968.
____ *Political Origins of the New Diplomacy 1917-1918*, Vintage Books, New York 1970.
____ *The Persistence of the Old Regime: Europe to the Great War*, Pantheon Books, New York 1981.
Mažuran, Ive, *Srednjevjekovni i turski Osijek*, HAZU, Osijek, 1994.
____ *Hrvati i Osmansko carstvo*, Golden Marketing, Zagreb 1998.
____ ed., *Od turskog do suvremenog Osijeka*, HAZU etc., Osijek 1996.
Mažuranić, Ivan, *Sabrana djela*, Liber and Matica Hrvatska, Zagreb 1979.
____ *Izabrani politički spisi*, Golden Marketing and Narodne novine, Zagreb 1999.
Meier, Victor, *Yugoslavia: A History of Its Demise*, Routledge, London 1999.
Mercier, Jacques, *Vingt Siècles D'Histoire du Vatican*, Éditions Lavauzelle, Paris 1976.
Meštrović, Ivan, *Uspomene na političke ljude i događaje*, Buenos Aires 1961.
Mikolić, Mario, 'Istra 1943', *Časopis za suvremenu povijest*, no. 3, Zagreb 1973.
____ *Istra 1941-1947: Godine velikih preokreta*, Barbat, Zagreb 2003.
Milanović, Božo, *Moje uspomene (1900-1976)*, Istarsko društvo Sv.Ćirila i Metoda etc., Pazin 1976.
Miller, Nicholas, *Between Nation and State; Serbian Politics in Croatia before the First World War*, University of Pittsburgh Press, Pittsburgh 1997.
Milosavljević Olivera, *U tradiciji nacionalizma*, Helsinški odbor za ljudska prava u Srbiji, Belgrade 2002.
Minić, Miloš, *Četnici i njihova uloga u vreme narodnoslobodilačkog rata 1941-1945*, Belgrade 1982.
Mirdita, Zef, *Vlasi u historiografiji*, Hrvatski institut za povijest, Zagreb 2004.
Mirković, Mijo, *Matija Vlačić-Ilirik*, Hrvatska naklada, Pula-Rijeka 1980.
Mirošević, Franko, *Počelo je 1918: Južna Dalmacija 1918-1929*, Školska knjiga, Zagreb 1992.
Moačanin, Nenad, *Turska Hrvatska*, Matica hrvatska, Zagreb 1999.
____ *Slavonija i Srijem u razdoblju osmanske vladavine*, Hrvatski institut za povijest, Slavonski Brod 2001.
Moguš, Milan, *Povijest hrvatskog književnog jezika*, Globus, Zagreb 1995.
Molinari, Fulvio, *Istria contesa*, Mursia, Milano 1996.

Moodie, A. E., *The Italo-Yugoslav Boundary*, George Philip & Son, London 1945.
Muggeridge, Malcolm, ed., *Ciano's Diary 1939–1943*, Heinemann, London 1947.
Munić, Darinko, *Kastav u srednjem vijeku*, Izdavački centar Rijeka, Rijeka 1998.
Murphey, Rhoads, *Ottoman Warfare 1500–1700*, Routledge, London 1999.
Mužić, Ivan, *Katolička crkva u Kraljevini Jugoslaviji*, Crkva u svijetu, Split 1978.
____ *Podrijetlo Hrvata*, Marjan Tisak, Zagreb 1989.
Nejašmić, Ivica, *Depopulacija u Hrvatskoj*, Globus, Zagreb 1991.
Nenadović, Aleksandar, *Razgovori s Kočom*, Globus, Zagreb 1989.
Nicolson, Adam, *The Power and the Glory: Jacobean England and the Making of the King James Bible*, Harper Collins, London 2003.
Nikitović, Časlav et al., *Srpsko-hrvatsko pitanje i putevi sporazuma*, Paris 1952.
Nobilo, Mario, *Hrvatski feniks*, Globus, Zagreb 2000.
Nodilo, Natko, *Izabrani spisi*, Književni krug, Split 1982.
Nouzille, Jean, *Histoire de frontières: l'Autriche et l'Empire ottoman*, Berg International, Paris 1999.
Novak, Bogdan, *Trieste 1941–1954: The Ethnic, Political and Ideological Struggle*, The University of Chicago Press, Chicago 1970.
Novak, Grga, *Povijest Splita*, Matica hrvatska, 3 vols, Zagreb 1957, 1961, 1965.
____ *Hvar kroz stoljeća*, Savjet za kulturu Hvar, Zagreb 1960.
____ *Prošlost Dalmacije*, Golden Marketing, Zagreb 2001.
____ ed., *Šišićev zbornik*, Zagreb 1929.
Obad, Stijepo et al., *Južne granice Dalmacije od XV. stoljeća do danas*, Državni arhiv, Zadar 1999.
Obolensky, Dimitri, *The Byzantine Commonwealth: Eastern Europe 500–1453*, Orion, London 1971.
Okey, Robin, *The Habsburg Monarchy*, St Martin's Press, New York 2001.
Omašić, Vjeko, *Kaštela od prapovijesti do početka XX. stoljeća*, 2 vols, Muzej grada etc., Kaštela 2001.
Orešković, Luc, *Louis XIV i Hrvati: Neostvareni savez*, Dom i svijet, Zagreb 2000.
Ostrogorsky, George, *History of the Byzantine State*, Blackwell, Oxford 1980.
Oštrić, Vlado, 'Opaske o opsegu izbornih prava u Hrvatskoj i Slavoniji do Prvog svjetskog rata', *Časopis za suvremenu povijest*, nos 2–3, Zagreb 1971.
Padovan, Ivo ed., *Hrvatski domoljub Josip Juraj Strossmayer*, Ogledi, Dom i Svijet etc., Zagreb 1995.
Pasquale, Iuso, *Il fascismo e gli ustascia 1929–1941*, Gangemi, Roma 1998.
Paščenko, Evgen, *Etnogeneza i mitologija Hrvata u kontekstu Ukrajine*, Meditor, Zagreb 1999.
Pavličević, Dragutin, *Narodni pokret 1883 u Hrvatskoj*, Liber, Zagreb 1980.
____ 'Sjevernoistočne hrvatske granice', *Kolo*, no. 5–6, pp. 89–158, Zagreb 1991.
____ *Povijest Hrvatske*, Naklada Pavičić, Zagreb 1994.
____ ed., *Vojna Krajina*, Liber, Zagreb 1984.
____ ed., *Povijest Hrvatske*, Zagreb 1997.
Pavlinović, Mihovil, *Hrvatski razgovori*, Naklada Pavičić, Zagreb 1994.
____ *Misao hrvatska i misao srpska u Dalmaciji 1848–1882*, Laus, Split 1994.
Pavlović, Dragiša, *Olako obećana brzina*, Globus, Zagreb 1988.

Select Bibliography

Payne, Stanley G., *A History of Fascism 1914–1945*, University of Wisconsin Press, Madison 1995.
Pederin, Ivan, *Mletačka uprava, privreda i politika u Dalmaciji (1400–1797)*, Matica hrvatska, Dubrovnik 1990.
____ *Jadranska Hrvatska u austrijskim i njemačkim putopisima*, Matica hrvatska, Zagreb 1991.
Pejaković Mladen and Gattin Nenad, *Starohrvatska sakralna arhitektura*, Kršćanska sadašnjost/Matica hrvatska, Zagreb 1988.
Percan Josip, *Obzori istarskog narodnjaštva*, Čakavski sabor etc., Pula–Rijeka 1986.
Perica, Vjekoslav, 'Dva spomenika jedne ere. Političke konotacije izgradnje pravoslavne crkve i katoličke konkatedrale u Splitu, 1971–1991', *Časopis za suvremenu povijest*, Zagreb 1991.
Perić, Ivo, *Mladi Supilo*, Školska knjiga, Zagreb 1996.
____ *Hrvatski Državni sabor 1848–1918*, 2 vols, Golden Marketing, Zagreb 2000.
____ *Hrvatska državotvorna misao u XIX. i XX. stoljeću*, Dom i svijet, Zagreb 2002.
Peričić, Eduard, *Sclavorum regnum Grgura Barskoga*, Kršćanska sadašnjost, Zagreb 1991.
Peričić, Šime, *Razvitak gospodarstva Zadra i okolice u prošlosti*, HAZU, Zadar 1999.
Perović, Latinka, *Od centralizma do federalizma*, Globus, Zagreb 1984.
____ *Ljudi, dogadaji i Knige*, Helsinški odbor za ljudska prava u Srbiji, Belgrade 2000.
____ *Zatvaranje kruga: Ishod rascepa 1971–1972*, Svjetlost, Sarajevo 1991.
____ ed., *Marko Nikezić-Srpska krha vertikala*, Helsinški odbor za ljudska prava u Srbiji, Belgrade 2003.
Peršen, Mirko, *Ustaški logori*, Globus, Zagreb 1990.
Peršić, Ivan, *Kroničarski spisi*, Državni arhiv, Zagreb 2002.
Petranović, Branko, *Politička i ekonomska osnova narodne vlasti u Jugoslaviji za vreme obnove*, Institut za savremenu istoriju, Belgrade 1969.
____ *AVNOJ i revolucionarna smena vlasti*, Nolit, Belgrade 1976.
____ and Dautović Sava, *Jugoslovenska revolucija i SSSR*, Belgrade 1988.
____ ed., *Jugoslovenske vlade u izbeglištvu 1943–1945.*, Globus, Zagreb 1981.
Petrinović, Ivo, *Ante Trumbić*, Književni krug, Split 1991.
____ *Politička misao Frana Supila*, Književni krug, Split 1998.
Petrović, Ljubomir, *Jugoslovenska država i društvo u periodici 1920–1941*, Institut za savremenu istoriju, Belgrade 2000.
Pleterski, Janko, *Prvo opredelenje Slovenaca za Jugoslaviju*, Nolit, Belgrade 1976.
____ *Nacije, Jugoslavija, Revolucija*, Izdavački centar Komunist, Belgrade 1985.
Plevnik, Danko, *Hrvatski obrat*, Durieux, Zagreb 1993.
Pliverić, Josip, *Spomenica o državnopravnih pitanjih hrvatsko-ugarskih*, Komisiona naklada L. Hartmann, Zagreb 1907.
Polić, Bobić, Mirjana, *Medu križom i polumjesecom: Dubrovačke dojave španjolskome dvoru o Turcima u XVI. stoljeću*, Naklada Ljevak, Zagreb 2000.
Polić, Martin, *Parlamentarna povijest kraljevina Hrvatske, Slavonije i Dalmacije*, 2 vols, Komisiona naklada F. Suppan, Zagreb 1900.

Popović, Miodrag, *Vidovdan i časni krst*, Bibiloteka XX. veka, Belgrade 1998.
Popović-Obradović, Olga, *Parlamentarizam u Srbiji 1903–1914*, Službeni list, Belgrade 1998.
Porphyrogenitus, Constatine, *De Administrando Imperio*, Dumbarton Oaks, Washington 1967.
Posavac, Zlatko, *Filozofski rukopisi 18. stoljeća u franjevačkim samostanima Slavonije*, Hrvatska sveučilišna zaklada, Zagreb 1993.
Potrebica, Filip, *Požeška županija za revolucije 1848–1849*, Centar za povijesne znanosti, Zagreb 1984.
Požar, Petar, *Hrvatska pravoslavna crkva u prošlosti i budućnosti*, Stvarnost, Zagreb 1955.
Predojević, Vaso, *Dnevničke zabilješke o razbijanju Partije, Armije i Države*, Dan Graf, Belgrade 1997.
Preporod hrvatskih sveučilištaraca, Kritika, vol. 8, Zagreb 1971.
Preveden, Francis R., *A History of the Croatian People*, Philosophical Library, 2 vols, New York 1955, 1962.
Pribićević, Svetozar, *Diktatura kralja Aleksandra*, Globus, Zagreb 1990.
____ *Izabrani politički spisi*, Golden Marketing, Zagreb 2000.
Prunk, Janko, *Slovenski narodni vzpon: Narodna politika 1768–1992*, Državna založba Slovenije, Ljubljana 1992.
Radelić, Zdenko, *Hrvatska seljačka stranka 1941–1950*, Hrvatski institut za povijest, Zagreb 1996.
____ *Božidar Magovac: S Radićem između Mačeka i Hebranga 1908–1955*, Hrvatski institut za povijest, Zagreb 1999.
____ *Križari: Gerila u Hrvatskoj 1945–1950*, Hrvatski institut za povijest, Zagreb 2002.
____ *Hrvatska u Jugoslaviji 1945–1991*, Školska knjiga, Zagreb 2006.
____ et al., *Stvaranje hrvatske države i Domovinski rat*, Školska knjiga, Zagreb 2006.
Radetić, Ernest, *Istra pod Italijom*, Matica hrvatska, Zagreb 1944.
____ *Istarski zapisi*, JAZU, Zagreb 1969.
Radogono, Davide, *Il nuovo ordine mediterraneo: Le politiche di occupazione dell'Italia fascista in Europea (1940–1943)*, Bollati Boringhieri, Torino 2003.
Rakovac, Milan, 'Riva i druži', Globus, Zagreb 1983.
Ramet, Pedro, *Nationalism and Federalism in Yugoslavia, 1963–1983*, Indiana University Press, Bloomington 1984.
Raukar, Tomislav, *Hrvatsko srednjevjekovlje: Prostor, ljudi, ideje*, Školska knjiga, Zagreb 1997.
____ *Zadar u XV. stoljeću*, Institut za hrvatsku povijest, Zagreb 1977.
Regan, Krešimir, ed., *Hrvatski povijesni atlas*, Leksikografski zavod, Zagreb 2003.
Rendić-Miočević, Ivo, *U potrazi za hrvatskom kolijevkom*, Književni krug, Split 2000.
____ *Hrvatski identitet*, Adamić, Rijeka 2006.
Rice Eugene F., Jr, *Saint Jerome in the Renaissance*, The Johns Hopkins University Press, Baltimore 1985.

____ and Grafton Anthony, *The Foundations of Early Modern Europe, 1460–1559*, W. W. Norton & Co., New York 1994.
Roberts, Walter E., *Tito, Mihailović and the Allies, 1941–1945*, Duke UP, Durham NC, 1987.
Rojnica, Ivo, *Susreti i doživljaji*, DoNeHa, 2 vols, Zagreb 1995.
Roksandić, Drago, *Vojna Hrvatska/La Croatie Militaire: Krajiško društvo u Francuskom Carstvu (1809–1813)*, Školska knjiga, 2 vols, Zagreb 1988.
____ *Srbi u Hrvatskoj*, Vjesnik, Zagreb 1991.
____ *Srpska i hrvatska povijest i 'Nova historija'*, Stvarnost, Zagreb 1991.
Rossos Andrew, *Russia and the Balkans: Inter-Balkan Rivalries and Russian Foreign Policy, 1908–1914*, University of Toronto Press, Toronto 1981.
Rothenberg, Gunther E., *The Austrian Military Border in Croatia, 1522–1747*, University of Illinois Press, Urbana-Champaign 1960.
____ *The Military Border in Croatia, 1740–1881*, The University of Chicago Press, Chicago 1966.
Rothschild, Joseph, *East-central Europe between the Two World Wars*, University of Washington Press, Seattle 1983.
Rubinstein, Alvin Z., *Yugoslavia and the Nonaligned World*, Princeton University Press, Princeton 1970.
Rudolf, Davorin, *Rat koji nismo htjeli*, Globus, Zagreb 1999.
Rumenaj, Natalija, 'Čelni ljudi u novčanim zavodima Banske Hrvatske 1900. godine: osvrt na srpsku elitu 1882.–1900.', *Povijesni prilozi*, 18, Zagreb 1999.
Rusinov, Dennison, *Italy's Austrian Heritage 1919–1946*, Clarendon Press, Oxford 1969.
____ *The Yugoslav Experiment 1948–1974*, University of California Press, London 1977.
Salopek, Hrvoje, *Stari rodovi ogulinsko-modruške udoline*, Matica hrvatska, Zagreb 2000.
Sanader, Mirjana, *Antički gradovi u Hrvatskoj*, Školska knjiga, Zagreb 2001.
Schenker Alexander M., *The Dawn of Slavic Studies: An Introduction to Slavic Philology*, Yale University Press, New Haven 1995.
Schlesinger, Rudolf, *Federalism in Central and Eastern Europe*, Kegan Paul, London 1945.
Sedlar, Jean W., *East central Europe in the Middle Ages, 1000–1500*, University of Washington Press, Seattle 1994.
Sekulić, Ante, ed., *Slavonija, Srijem, Baranja, Bačka: Zbornik*, Matica hrvatska, Zagreb 1993.
Sekulić, Milisav, *Knin je pao u Beogradu*, Nidda Verlag, Bad Vibel 2001.
Seton-Watson, Hugh, *Eastern Europe 1918–1941*, CUP, Cambridge 1945.
____ and Seton-Watson, Christopher, *The Making of a New Europe: R. W. Seaton-Watson and the last years of Austria-Hungary*, Methuen, London 1981.
Seton-Watson, R. W., *Absolutism in Croatia*, London 1912.
____ *The Balkans, Italy and the Adriatic*, Nisbet & Co., London 1915.
____ *The Southern Slav Question and the Habsburg Monarchy*, Constable & Co., New York 1969.

Shaw, Stanford, *History of the Ottoman Empire and Modern Turkey*, vol. 1, Cambridge University Press, Cambridge 1976.
Shoup, Paul, *Communism and the Yugoslav National Question*, Columbia University Press, New York 1968.
Sirotković, Hodimir, 'Stvaranje federalne Hrvatske u narodnooslobodilačkoj borbi', *Časopis za suvremenu povijest*, nos 2–3, Zagreb 1971.
____ *ZAVNOH, Dom i svijet*, Zagreb 2002.
Sklevicky, Lydia, 'Organizirana djelatnost žena Hrvatske', *Povijesni prilozi*, no. 3, Zagreb 1984.
Skok, Petar, *Slavenstvo i romanstvo na jadranskim otocima*, JAZU, Zagreb 1950.
____ *Tri starofrancuske hronike o Zadru u godini 1202.*, JAZU, Zagreb 1951.
____ *Etimologija hrvatskog ili srpskog jezika*, 4 vols, JAZU, Zagreb 1972.
Skrulj, Stjepan and Lučić, Josip, *Hrvatska povijest u dvadeset pet karata*, AGM, Zagreb 1996.
Slukan, Mirela, *Kartografijski izvori za povijest Triplex Confiniuma*, Hrvatski državni arhiv, Zagreb 1999.
Southern, R. W., *Western Society and the Church in the Middle Ages*, Penguin, London 1990.
Spehnjak, Katarina, *Javnost i propaganda Narodnog fronta u politici i kulturi Hrvatske 1945–1952*, Hrvatski institut za povijest, Zagreb 2002.
Spielman, John P., *Leopold of Austria*, Thames and Hudson, London 1977.
Spinčić, Vjekoslav, *Crtice iz književne kulture Istre*, Kršćanska sadašnjost, Zagreb 1926.
Stančić, Nikša, ed., *Mihovil Pavlinović u politici i književnosti*, Globus, Zagreb 1990.
____ *Hrvatska nacija i nacionalizam u 19. i 20. stoljeću*, Barbat, Zagreb 2002.
Stanković, Đorđe Đ, *Nikola Pašić, Saveznici i stvaranje Jugoslavije*, Nolit, Belgrade 1984.
____ *Nikola Pašić i jugoslovensko pitanje*, Nolit, Belgrade 1985.
Stanojević, Gligor, *Srbija u vreme Bečkog rata 1683–1699*, Belgrade 1976.
____ *Dalmatinske krajine u XVIII. vijeku*, Prosvjeta, Zagreb 1987.
Stavrianos, L. S., *The Balkans since 1453*, Holt Rinehart, New York 1958.
Steinberg, Jonathan, *The Roman Catholic Church and Genocide in Croatia 1941–1945*, Clarendon Press, Oxford 1992.
Stiles, H. William, *Austria in 1848–49*, Arno & The New York Times, New York 1971.
Stipetić, Vladimir, ed., *Konavle u prošlosti, sadašnjosti i budućnosti*, HAZU, Dubrovnik 1998.
Stipetić, Zorica, *Argumenti za revoluciju-August Cesarec*, Centar za društvenu djelatnost, Zagreb 1982.
Stojadinović, Ljubodrag, *Film koji je zapalio Jugoslaviju*, Studio Design, Belgrade 1995.
Stojkov, Todor, *Vlada Milana Stojadinovića 1935–1937*, Institut za savremenu istoriju, Belgrade 1985.
Stokes, Gale, *Politics as development*, Duke University Press, Durham NC and London 1990.

Select Bibliography

Strčić, Petar, 'Iredentizam dr. Francesca Vidulicha (1819–1889)', *Radovi* HAZU, vol. 4, pp. 109–118, Zagreb 1991.
Strecha, Mario, *Katoličko hrvatstvo: Počeci političkog katolicizma u banskoj Hrvatskoj (1897–1904)*, Barbat, Zagreb 1997.
Strossmayer, Josip J. and Rački, Franjo, *Politički spisi*, Znanje, Zagreb 1971.
Stulli Bernard, *Iz prošlosti Dalmacije*, Književni krug, Split 1992.
Sugar, Peter F., *Southeastern Europe under Ottoman Rule, 1354–1804*, University of Washington Press, Seattle, 1977.
____ et al., eds, *A History of Hungary*, Indiana University Press, Bloomington 1990.
Suić, Mate, *Antički grad na Istočnom Jadranu*, Golden Marketing, Zagreb 2000.
Supičić Ivan, ed., *Hrvatska i Evropa*, vol.1: *Rano doba hrvatske kulture*, Školska knjiga, Zagreb 1997.
Supilo, Frano, *Politika u Hrvatskoj*, Kultura, Zagreb 1953.
____ *Politički spisi*, Znanje, Zagreb 1970.
Suppan Arnold, *Oblikovanje nacije u građanskoj Hrvatskoj 1835–1918*, Naprijed, Zagreb 1999.
Šanjek, Franjo, *Crkva i kršćanstvo u Hrvata: Srednji vijek*, Kršćanska sadašnjost, Zagreb 1993.
____ *Kršćanstvo na hrvatskom prostoru*, Kršćanska sadašnjost, Zagreb 1996.
____ ed., *Povijest Hrvata*, vol.1: *Srednji vijek*, Školska knjiga, Zagreb 2003.
Šarac, Nedim, *Uspostavljanje šestojanuarske diktature*, Svjetlost, Sarajevo 1975.
Šarinić, Hrvoje, *Svi moji tajni pregovori s Slobodanom Miloševićem*, Globus International, Zagreb 1999.
Šarinić, Josip, *Nagodbena Hrvatska*, Matica hrvatska, Zagreb 1972.
Šentija, Josip, *Razgovori s Mikom Tripalom o Hrvatskom proljeću*, Profil International, Zagreb 2005.
Šepić Dragovan, *Supilo diplomat*, Zagreb 1961.
____ *Italija, Saveznici i jugoslavensko pitanje 1914–1918*, Školska knjiga, Zagreb 1970.
____ 'Talijanski iredentizam na Jadranu', *Časopis za suvremenu povijest*, 1, Zagreb 1975.
____ *Vlada Ivana Šubašića*, Globus, Zagreb 1983.
Šetić, Nevio, *O povezanosti Istre s ostalim hrvatskim krajevima: Naša Sloga 1870–1915*, Dom i svijet Zagreb 2005.
Šicel, Miroslav, ed., *Riznica ilirska*, Cankarjeva založba and Matica hrvatska, Zagreb and Ljubljana 1985.
Šidak, Jaroslav, *Studije iz hrvatske povijesti XIX stoljeća*, Školska knjiga, Zagreb 1973.
____ *Studije iz hrvatske povijesti za revolucije 1848–49.*, Školska knjiga, Zagreb 1979.
____ *Kroz pet stoljeća hrvatske povijesti*, Školska knjiga, Zagreb 1981.
____ *Hrvatski narodni preporod: Ilirski pokret*, Školska knjiga, Zagreb 1988.
____ et al., *Povijest hrvatskog naroda g. 1860–1914.*, Školska knjiga, Zagreb 1968.
Šimončić-Bobetko Zdenka, *Agrarna reforma i kolonizacija u Hrvatskoj 1918–1941*, AGM, 2 vols, Zagreb 1997.
Šimunić, Petar, *Načertanije: tajni spis srpske nacionalne i vanjske politike*, Globus,

Zagreb 1992.
Šimunović, Petar, *Hrvatska prezimena*, Golden Marketing, Zagreb 1995.
Šišić, Ferdo, *Vojvoda Hrvoje Vukčić Hrvatinić i njegovo doba*, Zagreb 1902.
____ *Dokumenti o postanku Kraljevine Srba, Hrvata i Slovenaca 1914–1919*, Matica hrvatska, Zagreb 1920.
____ *Jadransko pitanje*, Matica hrvatska, Zagreb 1920.
____ *Pregled povijesti hrvatskog naroda*, Matica hrvatska, Zagreb 1962.
Škrbec, Stanislav, *Riječka zvijezda Gutenbergove galaksije: Tiskarstvo Rijeke i hrvatske glagoljske tiskare*, Tiskara Rijeka, Rijeka 1995.
Škvorčević, Antun, ed., *Zagrebačka biskupija i Zagreb 1094–1994*, Nadbiskupija zagrebačka etc., Zagreb 1995.
Šlabek, Stjepan, *Banovina Hrvatska*, Matica hrvatska, Kutina 1997.
Šošić, Hrvoje, *Za čiste račune*, Matica hrvatska, Zagreb 1970.
Špegelj, Martin, *Sjećanja vojnika*, Znanje, Zagreb 2004.
Štambuk-Škalić, M., 'Hrvatska istočna granica u dokumentima 1945–1947', *Fontes* I, Zagreb 1995, pp. 153–329.
Štefanec, Nataša, *Heretik njegova veličanstva: Povijest o Jurju IV. Zrinskom i njegovu rodu*, Barbat, Zagreb 2001.
Štih, Peter and Simoniti, Vasko, *Slovenska zgodovina do razsvetiteljstva*, Korotan, Ljubljana 1996.
Strčić, Petar, 'Iredentizam dr Francesca Vidulicha (1819–1889)', *Radovi*, vol. 24, Zagreb 1991.
Šufflay, Milan, *Srbi i Arbanasi: Njihova simbioza u srednjem vijeku*, Belgrade 1925.
Šuvar, Mira, *Vladimir Velebit*, Razlog, Zagreb 2001.
Tamaro, Attilio, *Italien et Slaves*, Éditions George Crés & Cie., Paris 1908.
Tandarić Josip Leonard, *Hrvatskoglagoljska liturgijska književnost*, Kršanska sadašnjost, Zagreb 1993.
Tapié Victor-L., *The Rise and Fall of the Habsburg Monarchy*, Pall Mall, London 1969.
Taylor, A. J. P., *The Habsburg Monarchy 1809–1918*, Hamish Hamilton, London 1948.
____ *The Struggle for Mastery in Europe 1848–1918*, Oxford University Press, Oxford 1980.
Terzić, Velimir, *Jugoslavija u Aprilskom ratu 1941*, Vojnoistorijski institut, Belgrade 1969.
Todorović, Dragoljub, *Knjiga o Ćosiću*, Treći milenijum, Belgrade 2005.
Tomasevich, Jozo, *Peasants, Politics and Economic Change in Yugoslavia*, Stanford University Press, Stanford 1955.
____ *The Chetniks*, Stanford University Press, Stanford, 1975.
____ *War and Revolution in Yugoslavia, 1941–1945*, Stanford University Press, Stanford 2001.
Tomasović, Mirko, *Marko Marulić-Marul*, Erasmus, Split 1999.
____ and Novaković, Darko, *Latinsko pjesništvo hrvatskog humanizma*, Školska knjiga, Zagreb 1994.
Tomljanovich, William Brooks, *Josip Juraj Strossmayer: Nacionalizam i moderni*

Select Bibliography

katolicizam u Hrvatskoj, HAZU and Dom i svijet, Zagreb 2001.
Trdina, Janez, *Bahovi husari i ilirci*, Grafički zavod, Zagreb 1980.
Tripalo, Miko, *S poprišta,* Centar za aktualni politički studij, Zagreb 1971.
____ *Hrvatsko proljeće*, Globus, Zagreb 1990.
Trogrlić, Stipan, 'Katolička crkva u Istri u nacionalno-političkim i ideološkim previranjima 1900–1014', *Časopis za suvremenu povijest*, no. 3, pp. 283–301, Zagreb 1996,
Trotsky, Leon, *The Balkan Wars of 1912–1913*, Anchor Foundation, New York 1980.
Trumbić, Ante, *Suton Austro-Ugarske i Riječka rezolucija*, Obzor, Zagreb 1936.
____ *Izabrani spisi*, Književni krug, Split 1986.
Turčinović, Josip, *Antun Vramec*, Kršćanska sadašnjost, Zagreb 1995.
Ustavotvorni sabor Narodne Republike Hrvatske: Stenografski zapisnici, Zagreb 1949.
Ustav Republike Hrvatske, CIP, Zagreb 1991.
'Ustav Socijalističke Federativne Republike Jugoslavije', *Službeni list SFRJ*, Belgrade 1974.
'Ustav Socijalističke Republike Hrvatske', *Narodne novine*, Zagreb 1974.
Utješenović Ostrožinski, Ognjeslav*, Kućne zadruge, Vojna Krajina*, Školska knjiga, Zagreb 1988.
Valentić, Mirko, *Vojna Krajina i pitanje njezina sjedinjenja sa Hrvatskom 1849–1881*, Liber, Zagreb 1981.
____ and Lovorka Čoralić, eds, *Povijest Hrvata*, vol.2: *Od kraja 15. stoljeća do kraja Prvoga svjetskog rata*, Školska knjiga, Zagreb 2005.
Valiani, Leo, *The End of Austria-Hungary*, Secker and Warburg, London 1996.
Večerina, Duško*, Talijanski iredentizam*, Zagreb 2001.
Velebit, Vladimir, *Tajne i zamke II. Svjetskog rata*, Zagreb 2002.
Vidaković, Krinka, *Kultura španskih Jevreja na jugoslovenskom tlu*, Sarajevo 1990.
Vince, Zlatko*, Putovima hrvatskog književnog jezika*, Matica hrvatska, Zagreb 1990.
Višnjić, Čedomir, *Kordunaški proces: fragment iz historije nestajanja*, Prosvjeta, Zagreb 1997.
____ *Partizansko ljetovanje: Hrvatska i Srbi 1945–1950*, Prosvjeta, Zagreb 2003.
Vivante, Angelo, *Irredentismo adriatico*, Edizioni Italo Svevo, Trieste 1984.
Vlajčić, Gordana, *Jugoslavenska revolucija i nacionalno pitanje 1919–1927*, Globus, Zagreb 1984.
Vojinović, Aleksandar, *NDH u Beogradu*, Naklada Pavičić, Zagreb 1995.
Vrandečić, Josip*, Dalmatinski autonomistički pokret u XIX stoljeću*, Dom i svijet, Zagreb 2002.
Vranješ-Šoljan, Božena, *Stanovništvo Banske Hrvatske na prijelazu stoljeća*, Školska knjiga, Zagreb 1991.
Vratović, Vladimir, *Hrvatski latinizam i rimska književnost*, Matica hrvatska, Zagreb 1989.
____ *Hrvati i latinska Evropa*, Matica hrvatska, Zagreb 1996.
Vrbanić, George Franz, *The Failure to Save the First Yugoslavia*, Ziral, Chicago 1991.
Vrhovac, Maksimilijan, *Dnevnik*, vol.1: *1801–1809*, Kršćanska sadašnjost etc, Zagreb 1987.
Waquet, Françoise, *Latin or the Empire of a Sign*, Verso, London 2001.

Wertheimer-Baletić, Alica, *Stanovništvo Vukovara i vukovarskog kraja*, Globus, Zagreb 1993.
Wilkes, John J., *Dalmatia*, Routledge & Kegan Paul, London 1969.
____ *The Illyrians*, Blackwell, Oxford 1995.
Wolfram, Herwig, *History of the Goths*, University of California Press, Berkeley 1990.
____ *The Roman Empire and its Germanic Peoples*, University of California Press, Berkeley 1990.
Woloch, Isser, *The New Regime: Transformations of the French Civic Order, 1789 –1820*, W. Norton & Co., New York 1994.
Wright, Jonathan, *The Jesuits*, Harper Collins, London 2004.
Zbornik dokumenata i podataka o narodnooslobodilačkom ratu naroda Jugoslavije, Belgrade 1981.
Zečević, Momčilo, *Slovenska ljudska stranka i jugoslovensko ujedinjenje 1917–1921*, Institut za savremenu istoriju, Belgrade 1973.
____ *Na istorijskoj prekretnici: Slovenci u politici jugoslovenske države 1918–1929*, Prosveta, Belgrade 1985.
Zelić-Bučan Benedikta, *Članci i rasprave iz starije hrvatske povijesti*, Hrvatsko društvo Sv. Jeronima, Zagreb 1994.
Zeman, Z. A. B., *The Break-up of the Habsburg Empire 1914–1918*, Oxford University Press, Oxford 1961.
Zimmermann, Warren, *Origin of a Catastrophe*, Times Books, New York 1996.
Zlatar, Zdenko, *Between the Double Eagle and the Crescent: The Republic of Dubrovnik and the Origins of the Eastern Question*, East European Monographs, Boulder CO, 1992.
____ *Our Kingdom Come: The Counter-Revolution, the Republic of Dubrvnik, and the Liberation of the South Slavs*, East European Monographs, East European Monographs, Boulder CO, 1992.
Znidarčić, Lav, *Alojzije Stepinac*, Matica hrvatska, Zagreb 1998.
Zsoldos, Attila, 'Hrvatska i Slavonija u kraljevstvu Arpadovića', *Povijesni prilozi*, 17, Zagreb 1998.
Zorić, Mate, *Književna prožimanja hrvatsko-talijanska*, Književni krug, Split 1992.
Žanić, Ivo, *Mitologija Inflacije: Govor kriznog doba*, Globus, Zagreb 1987.
____ *Smrt crvenog fiće: Članci i ogledi 1989–1993*, Studio grafičkih ideja, Zagreb 1993.
____ *Flag on the Mountain: A Political Anthropology of War in Croatia and Bosnia-Herzegovina*, Saqi Books, London 2007.
____ 'South Slav Traditional Culture as a Means of Political Legitimation', in Resić, Samir and Törnquist-Plewa, eds, *The Balkans in Focus: Cultural Boundaries in Europe*, Nordic Academic Press, Lund 2002.
____ 'The Symbolic Identity of Croatia in the triangle Crossroads-Bulwark-Bridge' in Pål Kolstø, ed., *Myths and Boundaries in South-Eastern Europe*, Hurst & Co., London 2005.
Žerjavić, Vladimir, *Opsesije i megalomanije oko Jasenovca i Bleiburga*, Zagreb 1992.
____ *Population losses in Yugoslavia 1941–1945*, Zagreb 1997.

Select Bibliography

____ 'Koliko je osoba iselilo iz podrucj pripojenih Hrvatskoj i Sloveniji nakon kapitulacije Italije i Drugog svjetskog rata', *Časopis za suvremenu povijest*, 1, Zagreb 1997.
Žic, Igor, *Kratka povijest grada Rijeke*, Adamić, Rijeka 2001.
Žigman, Gordana, 'Vlaške kolonizacije na području hrvatskih zemalja, *Lucius* 1, vol.1, Zagreb 2002.
Živančević, Milorad, *Ivan Mažuranić*, Globus and Matica srpska, Zagreb and Novi Sad 1988.
Žubrinić, Darko, *Hrvatska glagoljica*, Hrvatsko književno društvo Sv. Jeronima, Zagreb 1996.
Županov, Josip, *Zaboravljeni rat: Sociologija jednog sjećanja*, Irida, Zagreb 1998.

Sources

The maps of 'Croatia after the Peace of Zadar, 1358', 'Ottoman incursions into Croatia, 1391-1490', 'Croatia, 1606' and 'Croatia, 1741' are reproduced from Ive Mažuran, *Hrvati i Osmansko carstvo*, and printed here by kind permission of the publisher, Golden Marketing, Zagreb. The map of 'Europe under Charlemagne, 9th century' is reproduced from Alessandro Barbero, *Charlemagne: Father of a Continent*, by permission of the University of California Press.

Index

Subheadings are arranged in ascending page order. Italicised references indicate illustrations. Austria, Croatia, Dalmatia, Hungary, Serbia, Slavonia, Split, Vienna, Yugoslavia and Zagreb are not indexed.

Aachen, Peace of 34, 38
Abramović, Bishop Lav 333
Acheson, Dean 614
Aćimović, Milan 534
Acquaviva, Claudio 170
Acton, John 310
Agramer Tagblatt 422
Ahmed II, Sultan 136
Ahmed-pasha Köprülü, Grand Vizier 129
Al-Idrisi 53, *128–9*
Albania 26, 58, 6, 86, 135, 335, 340, 461, 471, 495, 500–501, 505, 529, 536, 538, 543, 546; Venetian Albania 205, 329
Albrecht Habsburg, Duke 59
Albert Habsburg, King 73–4, 87
Aldefred, Bishop of Salona 38
Aleksandar Obrenović, King 447
Alexander, General Harold 587
Alexander II, Pope 45
Alexander VI, Pope 88
Alexander (Aleksandar) Karađorđević, King 473, 480, 498, 505–6, 510, 515, 521–2, 524, 526–7, 531
Alexius I Comnenus, Emperor 49, 51
Álmos Árpád 48–9
Anđelić, Patriarch German 361
Andrássy, Gyula 296, 302, 308–9, 319
Andreossy, General Antoine-François 149
Andrew II Árpád, King 58, 71, 137
Andrew III Árpád, King 59
Anfuso, Filippo 549
Anjou dynasty 51, 58–61, 63–4, 71, 73, 81, 85–6, 88
Anti-fascist Council of National Liberation of Yugoslavia (AVNOJ) 575–8, 595–6, 598, 601, 603–4
Anti-fascist Council of National Liberation of Croatia (ZAVNOH) 575, 582–4, 598–605
Aquileia 37–8, 40–41, 151
Árpád family 47, 52, 54, 56, 59, 65–6, 72, 137
Arsenije III, Patriarch of Peć 325–6, 331
Arsenije IV, Patriarch of Peć 327–8
Asquith, Herbert 465–6, 470
Augsburg, Peace of 125, 163, 170
Autonomists 366–72, 375–90, 394, 401, 439–40, 443, 445, 449
Avars 20, 23–4, 26, 28–9, 31–2, 39, 52

Babenberg, Friedrich of 71
Babić, Ivan 562
Babonić family 53, 96
Babonić, Bishop Stephen (Stjepan) of Zagreb 53, 154
Babukić, Vjekoslav 203, 339
Baden, Ludwig of 134–5
Bag: *see* Karlobag
Bajamonti, Antonio 366, 375–8, 381, 383, 385, 388–9, 397–402
Bakar 77, 119–20, 123, 125, 127, 130, 189, 206, 210, 266–7, 295
Bakarić, Vladimir 576, 604–6, 610, 617, 620–22, 629–30, 632–3, 635, 640–42, 644, 647, 649
Balbo, Italo 552
Balfour, Arthur 480, 494
Balkans 137, 149, 181, 248, 20, 323, 351, 365, 376, 382, 436, 446, 448–9, 460–61,

465, 468, 470, 472, 474, 480, 487, 502, 534, 536, 556, 559, 570–71, 595–6, 611, 653; Balkan Wars 460–61, 472
Banija 604
Banja Luka 92, 137, 496, 551
Banko, Tomo 506
Baranja 72, 121, 211, 495–6, 592
Barthou, Louis 527
Baseggio, Giorgio 419
Basil I, Emperor 40–41
Basil II, Emperor 43
Bastian, don Mate 406, 411, 418
Bastianini, Guiseppe 552, 565
Batthyány, Balthazar 125
Batthyány family 122
Batthyány, Ban Francis (Franjo) 96
Batthyány, Lajos 227, 238, 241
Bauer, Otto 321
Bavaria 24, 31, 39, 60, 133, 190
Bayezid I, Sultan 63, 89
Beatrice Aragon of Naples 77
Bedaković, Ban Koloman 302
Begna, Cosimo 388
Bela III Árpád, King 57–8
Bela IV Árpád, King 53, 58–9, 66, 71
Belcredi, Richard 286, 378
Belgrade, 19, 72, 74–5, 79, 86–7, 89–90, 134–7, 251, 260, 326, 348, 356, 376, 453–4, 463–4, 468, 473, 480, 483, 495–501, 511–13, 517–21, 524, 526–8, 531–6, 538, 540, 543, 545, 547, 561, 567–8, 570–72, 575, 577–8, 587, 597, 601, 606, 608, 610, 614–17, 620–26, 628–9, 631, 635, 637, 640, 642–3, 647–8, 651, 658, 661–2; Peace of Belgrade 137
Benedictine Order 38, 45–6, 49, 153
Benkovac 329, 333, 382, 387
Beria, Lavrentij 614
Berlin 227, 527, 533–4, 536, 538, 542–3, 545, 548–9, 652; Congress 290, 309, 345, 355, 457
Beust, Friedrich von 296, 302, 379, 382
Biankini, Juraj 416, 438–9, 442–4, 448
Bihać 72–3, 88, 90, 96, 103, 133, 575
Biograd 36, 44–8, 51, 56–7
Bismarck, Otto von 310, 422, 436
Blahoslav, Jan 163
Bleiburg 577–8
Bogat, Stjepan 552–3, 575

Bogićević, Bogić 652
Bohemia 24–5, 73, 75–9, 83, 87, 92, 173, 188, 190, 194, 289, 301–2, 400
Boka Kotorska: *see* Kotor
Bologna 62, 154, 178, 365
Bonghi, Ruggero 422
Borelli, Francesco 269, 388
Borelli, Humbert 388, 399
Borna, Duke of Dalmatia 33, 34, 350, 352
Bosnia 19, 33, 60–61, 63–4, 66–71, 73, 75–7, 86–7, 89–90, 92, 94–6, 98–9, 106, 113, 120, 129, 132–7, 140, 145, 167, 171, 174, 176–7, 203–5, 208, 222, 247, 251, 261, 290, 308–9, 311, 313, 320–21, 325, 328, 330–33, 335, 338, 340, 345–6, 348, 350, 355, 375–6, 389, 391, 395, 437, 443, 447, 455–7, 459–64, 466, 468, 471, 477, 486–7, 489–92, 495–7, 510, 513–16, 518, 521, 523, 527–8, 530, 537–9, 541, 544, 546–7, 551, 554, 561, 563–4, 569–71, 573, 575–6, 578, 592, 598, 605, 607, 618, 621, 629, 633, 636, 640, 651–2, 654–6, 665
Bošković, Mata 465
Brač 56, 61, 63–4, 378, 383, 399
Branimir, King 38, 40–41, 68, 350, 352
Branković, George 86
Branković, Patriarch Georgije 350, 361
Brenz, Johann 167
Brezhnev, Leonid 629, 641
Bribir 29, 59, 65–6, 68–9, *224–5*
Bribirski family 65–71, 154; *see* Šubić
Bribirski, George (Juraj) 66
Bribirski, Gregory (Grgur) I 65–6
Bribirski, Miroslav 65
Bribirski, Mladin 66
Bribirski, Ban Mladin II 66–8, 70
Bribirski, Mladin III 69
Bribirski, Ban Paul (Pavao) 59, 66, *67*, 68
Bribirski, Stephen (Stjepan) 65–6
Bribirski-Zrinski, George (Juraj) III 69
Brkić, Dušan 602, 604, 608–10
Bucevich, Antonio 403
Buda: *see* Budapest
Budapest: (Buda) 63, 74, 90, 92–4, 98–100, 113, 118, 122, 129, 134, 294, 334; (Pest) 203, 208–9, 224, 227–8, 230, 341, 252, 269, 273, 291, 294, 296, 300, 305, 310–11, 362, 387, 438, 442, 452, 454–5, 457, 461; (Budapest) 254, 298, 305, 309, 314–15, 317, 319–20, 483, 489

Bukovica 395
Bulat, Gajo 397, 415, 438, 445
Bulganin, Nikolai 614
Bulgaria 28–9, 32, 40–42, 47, 75, 308–9,
  313, 318, 325, 328, 335–6, 338, 353, 392,
  460–61, 464, 468, 471, 487, 492,
  500–501, 534, 543, 546, 556, 577, 597
Burian, Stephen 491
Busović, Bishop Nikodim 331–2
Buzet 414, 581, 591
Byzantium 24–5, 27, 29–31, 33–4, 36–7,
  39–45, 47, 49–51, 55–8, 61, 63, 65, 70,
  175, 269, 325, 393

Čakovec 93, 102, 119, 123, 126, 130, 168,
  320–21
Caporetto, Battle of 474
Caraffa, General Antonio 138
Carinthia 9, 104, 112, 147, 173, 177, 205, 237,
  493
Carniola 21, 33, 71, 80, 87, 93, 96, 101, 104,
  107, 112, 130, 147, 173, 177, 205, 237, 247,
  468, 493
Casertano, Raffaele 565, 575
Cavour, Count Camillo di 441, 465
Celjski, Ban Herman 73, 75, 86
Celjski, Ban Ulrich 75
Cesarec, August 568, 570
Cetin (Cetingrad) 72, 79–80, *80*, 83, 137
Cetina, River 29, 33, 48, 71–2, 106, 167, 331
Chamberlain, Neville 536
Charlemagne 24, 31–4, 36, 39, 151–2, 269,
  364
Charles of Anjou, King of Naples 58
Charles Habsburg, Archduke 94, 104
Charles II of Durazzo, King 63
Charles I Habsburg, King and Emperor
  476, 483, 490–92
Charles II Anjou, King of Naples 58–60, 68
Charles III (VI) Habsburg, King and
  Emperor 187–8
Charles III, Emperor 40
Charles IV, Emperor 153
Charles Martel of Anjou 59
Charles Robert of Anjou, crowned Charles
  I 59, 66, 68
Charles V, Emperor 93, 162
Chetniks 532, 572–5, 577–8, 595, 599, 602,
  604, 639, 644
Christopher of Württemberg 166

Churchill, Winston 540, 576–7, 586, 595–7
Ciano, Galeazzo 538, 540
Ciliga, Ante 569–70
Cincar-Marković, Aleksandar 546
Čingrija, Pero 449
Cipicco, Jerolim 159
Clam-Martinič, Heinrich 484
Clari, Robert de 57
Clemenceau, Georges 500
Clovis, King of the Franks 27
Coloman Árpád, Herzeg 53
Coloman Árpád, King 51–2, 56, 61, 68–9,
  198
Combi, Carlo 409
Communist Party of Croatia (KPH, SKH)
  572–5, 577–80, 583–4, 598–609, 621–3,
  627–8, 631–3, 640, 642, 646–9, 652–3,
  656–8, 660–61
Communist Party of Italy (PCd'I, PCI)
  508, 578–80, 583–4, 587–8, 609
Communist Party of Serbia (KPS, SKS)
  619, 637, 650, 653
Communist Party of Yugoslavia (KPJ, SKJ),
  566–73, 575–6, 594–600, 602–3, 605,
  607, 610, 612, 614–15, 617, 621, 623, 630,
  633, 638, 643–6, 649, 651
Confler, Attilio 420
Congress of Berlin 290, 309, 345, 355, 457
Congress of Vienna 150, 212
Constantine, Emperor 20, 22, 364
Constantine: *see* St Cyril
Constantine VII, Emperor 24, 42
Constantinople 22, 31, 36, 40–41, 44, 47,
  57–8, 87, 148, 324, 327, 330, 336
Corfu 471, 476–7, 480–82, 486, 515
Corvinus, Ban John (Ivaniš) 77–8, 89
Coselschi, Eugenio 553
Cottone, Carmelo 424, 426
Council of Trent 125, 161–2, 165, 170
Cres 25, 61, 160, 162, 404, 504, 506, 583
Croat Club 439, 443
Croat-Serb Coalition 453–8, 461, 482–3,
  485–7, 491, 513, 519–20
Croat-Slovene Club 483–4
Croat-Slovene National Party 413–14, 508
Croatian Bloc 515, 518, 519
Croatian Party 449, 452
Croatian Party of Right 453, 485–6, 489,
  491, 515, 519, 523, 537, 545, 548, 554, 560
Croatian Peasant Party 518–21, 523–4,

526–8, 531–3, 535–45, 551–5, 557, 562–3, 565, 567, 569, 576–7, 594, 596, 599, 603, 606–7, 657
Croatian Republican Peasant Party 513–18
Croce, Benedetto 508
Crvena Hrvatska 441–4
Crvenkovski, Krste 647
Cukon (Zuccon), Ivan 430–31
Custozza, Battle of 240
Cuvaj, Ban Slavko 459–60
Cvetković, Dragiša 537–41, *539*, 543–4, 557, 594, 633
Czechoslovakia, Czech Republic 26, 492, 526, 529, 536, 538, 629–30, 632

Dabčević-Kučar, Savka 622, 624, *624*, 626–8, *628*, 632, 635, 641–2, 644, 646–7, 649
Đakovo 73, 92, 96, 134, 203, 234, 251, 311–13, 315
Dalmatin, Herman 154–5, *155*
Dalmazia Cattolica 387
Dandolo, Doge Henrik 57
Danica 203, 220, 339
D'Annunzio, Gabriele 503, 505
Danube, River 21–2, 26–7, 31, 72, 74, 87, 90, 96, 123, 135, 141, 145, 149, 167, 177, 197, 207–8, 268, 325–6, 536, 548
David, Antal 316, 320
Davidović, Ljuba 513–14
Dayton Accords 655
D'Azeglia, Massimo 443
De Dominis, Archbishop Markantun of Split 164–6, *166*, 168, 170, 314
De Gasperi, Alcide 587
Deák, Ferenc 271, 287, 293
Delich, Don Giovanni 385
Della Bella, Ardellio 174
Delmatae 25
Derkos, Ivan 212
D'Esperey, General Louis Franchet 495
Đilas, Milovan 605–6, 608, 614, 620
Diocletian, Emperor 19–20, *128–9*, 152
Dobrila, Bishop Juraj of Poreč-Pula, Trieste-Koper 310–11, 406, 409–13, *412*, 418
Dollhopf, Gustaf 213–14, 241
Döllinger, Ignaz von 314
Domald of Sidraga 58, 65–6
Dominican Order 53
Donji Kraji 70

Drašković family 140, 170
Drašković, Bishop and Ban George (Juraj) 125, 169–70
Drašković, Ivan 187
Drašković, Ban Ivan (John) II 126
Drašković, Janko 202–4, *202*, 208, 210, 231, 339
Drava, River 21, 25, 33, 37–9, 42, 48–9, 51, 54, 72, 90, 92–4, 96–8, 109, 111, 123, 129, 133, 151, 175, 190, 197–8, 207, 240, 254, 279, 546, 548; Banovina 530, 540
Drina, River 87, 135, 391, 460, 530, 548, 564
Dubček, Alexander 629, 641
Dubrovnik 25, 30, 36–7, 43, 50, 53, 56, 60–61, 63–4, 113, 120–21, 126, *128–9*, 136, 147, 160, 168, 171, 173–5, 182–4, 197, 205, 211–12, 233, 260, 265, 337–8, 351, 365–6, 368–9, 372, 377, 380, 382, 396–7, 400, 402, 440–41, 449, 495, 518, 539, 551, 608, 626, 660, *660*
Dudić, Andrew (Andrija) 170
Duh, Bishop of Gradec (Zagreb) 49
Đukić, Milan 658
Dupanloup, Bishop Felix of Orléans 310
Dušan, Tsar (King Stefan) *327*, 328, 340

Eden, Anthony 596
Edinost 422, 499, 507
Elisabeth Habsburg, Queen 74
Elisabeth Luxemburg, Queen 63
Emerik Árpád, King 58
Emo, Angelo 331
Erdödy family 140
Erdödy, Ban Nikola 135
Erdödy, Ban Peter (Petar) (16th C.) 93, 96, 123, 135, 168
Erdödy, Ban Peter (Petar) (18th C.) 200
Erdödy, Bishop Simeon of Zagreb 81, 96
Eric of Friuli 33–4, 37
Esterházy, Bishop Emeric of Zagreb 187
Eugene of Savoy, Field Marshal 136

Fanfogna, Antonio 377, 384, 399, 401
Fascists 503, 507–10, 549, 552, 555, 558, 561, 563, 572–3, 580–81, 584–6, 590–91, 601, 643
February Patent 255, 270, 272, 278–9, 286–7, 292, 322, 369, 378
Ferdinand Habsburg, Archduke 108
Ferdinand I Habsburg, King and Emperor

79–83, 89–90, 92–4, 97, 100–103, 167, 169–70, 187, 233–4, 238, 242
Ferdinand II Habsburg, King and Emperor 108–11, 119, 127–8
Ferdinand V Habsburg, King and Emperor 225, 227–8, 230–34, 236–40, 242
Feretić, Franjo 409
Filipović, General Franjo 377, 380, 381
Fluck von Leidenkorn, Joseph 382
Folnegović, Fran 318
Fowler, John 159
France 45, 57–8, 79, 92, 129–30, 147–50, 152, 156, 159, 175, 183–4, 190, 194, 197, 202, 204–5, 207, 220, 222, 301, 314, 319, 337, 367–8, 371, 389, 392, 398, 465, 468–9, 471–2, 476–7, 479–81, 487–8, 494–5, 500, 502–5, 526–8, 533, 538, 542, 546, 554–5, 588, 590, 596, 607, 609
Francis I Habsburg, King and Emperor 201, 205
Francis II Rákóczi 141
Francis Joseph Habsburg, King and Emperor 242, 269, 280–81, 286–7, 294–5, 297, 300–301, 315, 321, *321*, 364, 388–9, *388*, 450, 454, 476, 483
Franciscan Order 53, 99, 174, 183, 308, 313, 329, 364, 371, 382
Frank, Josip 362, 456, 459
Frankapan, Bartul 71
Frankapan, Bernardin 77, 89–90, 119
Frankapan, Ban Christopher (Krsto) 79, 81
Frankapan, Christopher (Krsto) Vuk *91*, 127–8, *128*
Frankapan, Dujam 71
Frankapan family 71–3, 76–9, 86–8, 90, 92, 103, 112–13, 119, 122–3, 127, 130, 132, 154, 161, 166, 169, 173, 180, 185, 206–7, 219, *224–5*, 267, 626
Frankapan, Francis Christopher (Fran Krsto) 130–31
Frankapan, Ban John (Ivan) 76
Frankapan, Julia 132
Frankapan, Ban Nicholas (Nikola) 72, 86, 167
Frankapan, Ban Stephen (Stjepan) 76–7
Franks 24, 26–7, 29, 31–41, 151, 350, 364
Franz Ferdinand Habsburg, Crown Prince 459, 461
Fraternity of St George and St Triphonis 155
Frederick II, Emperor 58–9

Frederick III, Emperor 74–5
Freundt, Alfred 545
Friuli 33–4, 36–7, 89, 423–4

Gaj, Ljudevit 182, 203–4, 208, 210, 224, 252, 339
Garašanin, Ilija 390
Gaži, Franjo 603
Gentile, Giovanni 508
George of Slavonia 152
Germany 26, 64, 92, 109, 122–3, 159, 162, 164, 166, 168, 237, 249, 280, 301–2, 308–9, 379, 382, 392, 402, 419, 436, 442, 447, 450, 472–3, 484, 493, 527–8, 533–4, 536, 538, 540, 542–3, 545–6, 550, 555, 561–2, 577, 587, 611, 620
Géza I Árpád, King 47
Ghilianovich, Roberto 403
Giolitti, Giovanni 449, 505
Glaise von Horstenau, Field Marshal Edmund 555, 565
Goering, Marshal Hermann 538, 547
Gorizia 205, 237, 402, 404, 420–21, 468, 493, 501–2, 509–10, 586, 590
Goths 22–5, 153, 549
Gottschalk of Orbais 34, 36
Grado 37, 56
Grbac-Garbitius, Matthias (Illyricus) 162
Greece 26, 86, 460, 542–4, 546–7, 588, 597, 611, 625
Gregory (Grgur), Archbishop of Bar 153
Gregory (Grgur), Bishop of Nin 42
Gregory I, Pope 31
Gregory VII, Pope 45, 47–8, 52
Gregory IX, Pope 53
Gregory XV, Pope 165, 168
Grey, Edward 465, 467, 469–70, 471
Gučetić, Nikola 156
Gumplowitz, Ludwig 352
Gundulić, Ivan 260
Gustinčić, Dragutin 568, 570

Hadrian II, Pope 39
Halifax, Lord 586
Handel, Erasmus 447–9
Haramija, Dragutin 622–3, 625
Haulik, Bishop Juraj of Zagreb 230, 234, 249, 251, 278
Havichsburg, Count of 50

Hebrang, Andrija 583, 598, 600, *600*, 603–9, 621
Heeren, Viktor von 534
Hektorović, Petar 156
Hellenbach, Lazar 271
Henderson, Nevile 531
Henry IV, Emperor 47
Henry V, Emperor 50, 206
Henry VIII, King of England 156, *157*
Heraclius, Emperor 24, 29
Herzeg-Bosna 655
Herzegovina 58, 87, 136, 259, 261, 332, 530, 633
Hitler, Adolf 527, 533, 544, 546–7, 556, 561, 577
Hodidjed 86–7
Hohenwart, Carl 302, 386
Honorius II, Counter-Pope 47
Horvath, István 199
Howard, Philip, Earl of Arundel 159
Hrabowski, General Johann 232–4, 238
Hrebljenović (Hrebeljanović), Lazar 326
Hrvatin 70
Hrvatinić, Hrvoje Vukčić 70–71
Hrvatinić, Vukac 70
Hrvatski narod 551
Hrvatske novine 203
Hunyady, John 75, 87
Hus, Jan 153
Hvar 56, 61, 63–4, 334, 372, 378, 383, 394, 399, 402, 494

Iapodes 25
Il Dalmata 379, 381–3, 389, 401–2
Il diritto croato 427
Il Nazionale 367, 373
Il Risorgimento 402
Ilirske Narodne Novine 203
Illyria (ancient): see Illyricum
Illyrian College 175–6
Illyrianism, Illyrian Movement 155, 157, 170–71, 174, 176–84, 202–8, 210–14, 217–27, 229, 231, 233, 235, 237, 239, 241, 243, 245, 247, 249, 251–3, 259–60, 263–5, 269, 284, 311, 328, 336–40, 343, 351, 353, 356, 362–3, 365, 367, 370, 406, *416–17*
Illyrian Provinces (Napoleonic) 147–50, *148*, 184, 204–5, 207, 222, 338–9

Illyricum 19–21, *21*, 25–6, 32, 37, 39, 50, 132, 175–7, 180
Imotski 136, 329, 373–4
Imperiali, Guglielmo 494
Independent Democratic Party 517, 524, 526, 532, 536, 541
Independent National Party 284–5, 316, 358, 396
Independent Serb Party 346–7, 349, 355–9, 361, 452–3, 455–8, 482–3
Independent State of Croatia 546–50, 553–4
Informbiro (Cominform) 609–10
Innocent III, Pope 58
Innocent IV, Pope 152
Ishaković, Isa-beg 87
Istria 29, 31, 33, 37, 405–32, *405*, *408*, 502–10, 578–92, *585*
Italy 22–3, 29, 31, 34, 40, 44, 47, 3, 76, 121–3, 125, 159–60, 167, 227–8, 238, 266–9, 289, 365, 368, 376, 388, 392, 398, 400, 402–3, 408–9, 419, 422–3, 432, 437, 442, 447–50, 462, 464–5, 467–74, 479–83, 493–5, 500–508, 510, 533, 536, 538, 542–3, 545–53, 556, 561, 565, 575–8, 580, 582–8, 590–92, 595, 606, 609, 611, 623, 625

Jagiełło, Albert John 78
Jajce 75, 86–7, 89, 92
James I (VI), King of England (Scotland) 165
Janković, Julije 275
Janković, General Radivoje 546
Jarnević, Dragojla 217–18
Jasenovac 103, 135; concentration camp 558–9, 561
Jelačić, Ban Josip 203, 231–5, 237–42, *242*, 249–51, 253, 264–5, 268–9, 353, 371
Jelačić, Stephen (Stjepan) 140
Jesuits 157, 164, 170, 180, 183
Joanna, Queen of Naples 60, 63
John Habsburg, Archduke 207, 238
John of Ravenna 52
John V Palaeologus, Emperor 63
John VIII, Pope 39–41
John X, Pope 42, 175
Joseph I Habsburg, King and Emperor 187
Joseph II Habsburg, King and Emperor 137, 183, 189–91, *191*, 206, 211, 337
Jovanović, General Đoko 630

Index

Jovanović, General Stjepan 396
Jovanović, Pavle 348–9, *349*, 361
Jovanović, Bishop Evgenije of Karlovci 264
Jukić, Luka 460
Justinian, Emperor 23

Kačić Miošić, Andrija 175
Kara Mustafa, Grand Vizier 132–3
Karadžić, Vuk 259, 261–2, *261*, 265, 350, 351
Karađorđević, Regent Paul (Pavle) 527–8, 533, 535–7, 539, 544
Karaman, Archbishop Mate of Zadar 333–5
Kardelj, Edvard 603, 605–6, 610, 614, 616–19, 632–3, 637, 640, 644–5, 649
Karlobag (Bag): 90, 94, 139, 143, 145, 206
Karlovac (Karlstadt) 94, 102–5, 112, 123, 127, 130, 140, 142–7, 149, 169, 205–8, 217, 219, 233, 263, 268, 274, 285, 317, 338, 343, 406, 549, 551, 611, 625
Karlovci 143, 235, 238, 258, 319, 326–8, 337, 344, 354, 391; Peace of Karlovci 136, 140, 180, 195, 326, 363
Karlović family 88, 90
Kasche, Siegfried 556
Kašić, Bartol 100, 170–72, *172*, 175
Kažotić, Bishop Augustin of Zagreb 154
Keglević family 140
Khuen-Héderváry, Ban Dragutin (Károly) 321–2, *321*, 346–7, 357–8, 361–2, 436, 447, 457
Klaić, Miho 286, 367–9, *370*, 374–5, 378–84, 386–7, 394–7, 400–401, 438–9, 443, 445
Klis 19, 34, 38, 66, 69, 90, 92, 94, 98, *128–9*, 133, 164, 329–30, *329*
Knežević, Bishop Stefan of Dalmatia 377, 395, 401
Knin 38, 48, 50, 65–6, 69, 72, 79, 89, 96, 133, 152, 169, 320, 329, 363, 377
Kollár, Jan 311
Kommunist 649
Končarević, Bishop Simeon 333, 334
Kopitar, Jernej 258
Korčula 61, 63–4, 334, 351, 372, 380, 402, 494
Kordun 599, 604–5
Korošec, Anton 483–5, 487, 493–5, 498, 524
Kosovo 87, 99, 135, 324, 326–8, 350, 352, 394, 461, 514, 546, 571, 574, 597, 608, 618–19, 627, 636–7, 640, 651, 654–5, 657; Battle of 326, 350, 352
Kossuth, Ferenc 451
Kossuth, Lajos 209–10, 227, 238, 241–2
Kotor 20, 25, 30, 43, 63, 136, 154, 167, 175, 205, 258, 329, 332–5, 337, 366, 370, 380, 382, 391, 400, 539, 546, 551, 592
Kotruljević (Cotrugli), Benedict 160
Kragujević, Bishop Stefan of Pakrac 341
Krajačić, Ivan 602, 607
Kraljevica 125, 266, 295
Krbava 29, 88–90, 92, 94–6, 98, 106, 134–6, 139–40, 152, 154, 168, 275, 320, 344, 347; Battle of 88
Krčelić, Balthazar 182
Krek, Janez 483
Krešimir III, King 44
Krestić, Nikola 241, 285, 304
Kristijanović, Ignac 183
Križanić, Juraj, 177–9, 181, 315
Krizman, Hinko 524
Krk 25, 43, 56, 61, 66, 71–2, 76–7, 90, 152, 11, 219, 334, 404
Krleža, Miroslav 521–2
Krmpotić family 427
Krnjević, Juraj 546
Khrushchev, Nikita 614
Kukuljević, Ivan 199, 203, 208, 210–11, 221, 224–5, *224*, 239, 241, 243–4, 246–7, 252, 265, 283, 339–42
Kupa, River 33, 50, 54, 94–5, 103, 119, 136, 140, 145, 149, 167, 207–8
Kurelac, Fran 239
Kušlan, Dragutin 253, 343
Kuvrat, King of the Bulgars 28
Kuzmanić, Ante 184
Kvaternik, Eugen 276, 283–4, 302
Kvaternik, Eugen 'Dido' 559, 562, 578
Kvaternik, Slavko 545, 548, 550, *550*, 555, 559, 562, 578

La Società politica Dalmata 400–401
La Voce Dalmatica 367
Labin 162, 424, 580–81
Labinci 423–5
Ladislav, Duke of Dalmatia 34
Ladislav I Árpád, King 48–50
Ladislav IV Árpád, King 58–9
Ladislav of Durazzo 64, 71
Ladislav V Habsburg, King 74–5

Laginja, Matko 407, 425–6, 428–9, 488
Langendorf, Adam Petri de 159, 175
Lansing, Robert 504
Lapenna, Luigi 376, 379, 383, 387–8, 400–401
L'Avvenire 388
Lawrence, Archbishop of Split 45, 47–8
Lega Nazionale 402, 422–4, 508
Legat, Bishop Bartholomeu of Trieste 310, 409
Lenin, Vladimir Ilyich 462, 567
Lenković, George (Juraj) 123
Leo III, Emperor 31
Leo VI, Pope 41
Leo XIII, Pope 315
Leopold I Habsburg, King and Emperor 128, 130, 132, 134–5, 137, 179, 326
Leopold II Habsburg, King and Emperor 192
Liburnia 29, 31, 33, 419
Lika 29, 72, 88, 90, 92, 94, 96, 98, 106, 133–6, 139–40, 146, 154, 168, 184, 258–9, 276, 280, 320, 330, 344, 347, 585, 604, 630
Lio, Gaspar de 160–61
Lippay, Archbishop George of Esztergom 130
Lisinski, Vatroslav 204
List, Friedrich 209
Ljubibratić, Bishop Stefan of Herzeg Novi 332
Ljubiša, Stefan 370, 386–8, 390, 394
Ljudevit of Pannonia 33
London 165, 463, 465–6, 468–70, 475, 478–9, 482, 486, 493–5, 498, 500, 502–5, 517, 526, 533–4, 538, 540, 543, 586–8, 594, 596, 611; London, Treaty of 469–70, *469*, 475, 479, 482, 493, 495, 498, 500, 502–5
Lónyay, Menyhért 302
Lorković, Ivan 482, 485–6, 500, 513
Lorković, Mladen 577
Lošinj 404, 411, 503–6, 583
Lothar, King of Italy 34
Louis I of Anjou, King 51, 60–61, 63, 69–71, 85
Louis II Jagiełło, King 79, 89
Louis XIV, King of France 127, 130
Luburić, Vjekoslav 'Maks' 559, 578
Lučić, Hanibal 156

Lučić, Ivan 70, 132, 177–8, 180
Lupetina, Balthazar (Baldo) 162
Luther, Martin 159, 162, 166

Macedonia 20, 26, 86, 135, 335, 340, 461, 464, 468, 470, 473, 514, 517, 523, 527–8, 538, 546, 556, 569–71, 574, 597, 618, 629, 640, 642, 648, 654
Maček, Vladko 521–4, *523*, 527, 532, 534, 537–8, *539*, 540–1, 544–5, 548, 578
Machiavelli, Niccolò 157
Magovac, Božidar 599
Magyars 42, 197, 209, 220–25, 229, 234, 241, 243–5, 286–7, 292, 302, 317, 321, 340, 360, 435, 438, 451, 454, 466
Magyarones 221–2, 225, 232, 252
Mainard, Abbot 44–5
Makarska 96, 329, 334
Mamula, General Lazar 246, 272, 369, 377
Mandić, Matko 407, 416, 418, 426, 428
Manuel I Comnenus, Emperor 51
March Constitution 242–5, 248–9, 255
Maria Theresa Habsburg-Lorraine, King 139, 189, 206
Mariočić, Colonel Josip 264
Marković, Ante 658
Marković, Sima 567–9
Marmont, General Auguste 148–9, 183, 371
Marsigli, Luigi Ferdinando 180, 363
Marulić, Marko 70, 156–9, *157*, *158*, 167, *224*–5
Mary of Anjou, Queen of Naples 59
Mary of Anjou, King 63
Masaryk, Jan 465
Matafar, Bishop Nicholas of Zadar 175
Matthias Corvinus, King 75–7, 87, 103, 115, 161, 170, 198
Maupas, Archbishop Pietro of Zadar 401
Maximilian Habsburg, King and Emperor 78–9, 83, 88, 94, 119, 173
Maylender, Michele 317–18
Mažuranić, Antun 203, 220, 264, 288
Mažuranić, Ban Ivan 203, 219–20, 228–30, *228*, 233, 239, 242, 244, 246, 266–8, 272, 275, 285–6, 288, 294, 304–7, 309, 322, 379
Mazzura, Šime 358
Medaković, Bogdan 488
Medina, Pedro de 156
Medo, Antun 156

Index

Medimurje 93, 96, 119–20, 122–4, 127, 130, 201, 211, 227, 238, 240, 247, 270–73, 275–6, 289, 297, 307, 360, 486, 514, 546, 572, 592
Mehmed II, Sultan 75, 87, 99, 325
Mehmed-pasha Sokolović, Grand Vizier 93
Melachthon, Philip 162, 163, 167
Metković 329
Metternich, Klemens von 364
Meštrović, Ivan 465
Mezulić, Hrvoje 562
Mihailović, General Draža 572–3, 577, 594–5
Mihalov, Ivan Vanča 556
Mihalovich, Ban Anton 489
Mihanović, Ivan 203
Milanović, don Božo 506
Miletić, Stjepan 358
Miletić, Svetozar 342–3
Military Border (*Vojna Krajina*) 85, 94, 97, 100–113, 117, 119, 122–3, 125–6, 130, 132–3, 135–47, *141*, 149, 173, 178, 180, 182–3, 185, 189, 191–2, 196, 198, 200, 202–3, 206–7, 211–12, 222, 227–8, 230, 232–4, 236–7, 241, 244, 246–51, 257–8, 261–4, 269–70, 272–4, 280, 284, 286, 288, 291, 293–4, 297–300, 302–4, 307–9, 315, 317–23, 325–6, 338–41, 343–4, 346, 348, 353–5, 358, 371, 377, 561, 563, 573, 588, 599, 604
Miliukov, Paul 475
Milošević, Slobodan 650–51, 655, 662
Minghetti, Marco 310
Mirković, General Bora 547
Mocenigo, Alvise 332
Modruš 71-2m 76, 87, 90, 96, 119, 123, 175, 317, 347
Mohács, battle of 79, 90, 340
Moljević, Stevan 639
Mollinary, General Anton 319–20
Monteccucoli, Field Marshal Raimondo 129
Montenegro 26, 64, 308–9, 313, 340, 348, 382, 389, 437, 440, 460–64, 466–7, 469, 472, 476–7, 484–5, 489–90, 494–8, 514, 523, 528, 530, 538, 546, 569–71, 574, 592, 618, 621, 629, 640, 651, 654
Monti, Lavro 377, 387
More, Thomas 156
Morlachs (Black Vlachs) 329, 331

Morosini, Albert 59
Morpurgo, Vid 381, 385, 399
Mostar 87
Mrazović, Matija 343
Muncimir, King 38
Mura, River 93, 104, 119, 548
Murat II, Sultan 74, 75, 87
Mussolini, Benito 503, 508–10, 533, 538, 543, 547–8, 551, 556, 575
Mustafa II, Sultan 136

Nádasy, Francis 130–31
Napoleon Bonaparte 147–9, 338
Nardelli, Niko 449
Narodna misao 362
Narodne Novine 438
Narodni list 373
Naša sloga 411–14, 422, 427, 429, 431
National Liberation Army (NOVJ) 573–4, 576, 582–3
National Party 221–2, 224–6, 252–3, 278–9, 284, 286, 295, 301–3, 371–3, *398*, 454; in Dalmatia 286, 366–8
Nazor, Vladimir 601
Nedić, General Milan 565
Nehru, Jawaharlal 614
Nepos, Emperor Julius 19
Neretva, River 33, 44, 61, 71, 87–8, 136, 385
Nicholas, Bishop of Senj and Modruš 175
Nicholas II, Pope 44–5
Nicholas II, Tsar 475
Nicholas IV, Pope 59
Nicopolis, Battle of 63, 86
Nikezić, Marko 623, 631, 637, 643, 647–8
Nikola Petrović, King of Montenegro 496
Nin 38, 40, 42–3, 48, 61, 64–6, 69, 152, 334
Nodilo, Natko 367, 387
Normans 44, 47, 51
Novaković, Bishop Dimitrije of Buda 334
Novi list 440, 445, 455
Novi Sad 282
Novi Zrin 101–2, *102*, 129–30
Nugent, Field Marshal Laval 207–8

Obzor 347–8, 350
Odoacer (Odovacar), King of Italy 22
Ogulin 112, 142–3, 231, 236, 258, 276, 317, 320
Omladina 362
Opačić, Stanko 60, 604, 609

Orbini, Mavro 160, 175, 177
Orlando, Vittorio 502, 505
Orseolo, Doge Peter II 44
Orthodox Church (Greek) 99, 178, 337–8; *see* Serb Orthodox Church
Osiander, Andreas 136
Osijek 90, 94, 98, 128–9, *129*, 132–5, 138–9, 207, 232, 257–8, 263, 276, 311, 518, 566, 626
Osor 43, 4, 56, 61, 64, 152, 334–5
Ostrogoths 22–3
Otočac 103, 142–3, 233, 258, 276
Otto III, King of Bavaria 60
Opera Vigilanza Repressione Antifascista (OVRA) 509
Ottoman Empire 12, 22, 63, 70–72, 74–9, 85–149, *89*, 155, 157, 159, 164, 167–9, 171, 174, 178–9, 181–2, 186, 191–2, 195, 197, 219, 237, 248–9, 251, 274, 282, 308–9, 312–13, *320–21*, 323–6, 328–30, 332, 337–8, 349, 352, 354–5, 363–4, 366, 369, 375, 390–91, 401, 654
Ozalj 72, 119, 123–4, 127, 130, 169, 173, 178, *224–5*

Pacta Conventa 51–2, 65, 69, 81, 198–9, 458
Padua 64, 125, 154, 164, 170, 365, 368, 406, 481–2, 500
Pag 61, 90, 170
Pakrac 94, 98, 135, 338, 341
Palacký, František 242, 311
Palatin, Vicko 156
Pannonia 19, 20–2, 24; Savia 21–3; Secunda 21, 33
Pannonius, Janus 76
Paris 53, 130, 148, 150, 152, 154–5, 227, 468, 470, 479, 481, 494, 498–500, 505, 524, 526, 533; Paris Peace Conference 499–505
Partisans 526, 552–3, 563, 565–6, 572–8, 580–81, 585, 595–6, 598–600, 602–8, 620–21, 623, 641–2, 647
Partito italiano democratico 402
Party of Right 284, 286, 303, 308, 315, 317–18, 322, 345, 351, 358, 362, 400, 407, 425, 436–41, 443–5, 449, 453, 459, 482–6, 489
Pašić, Nikola 455, 461–4, 466–7, 470–71, 473–4, 476–7, 479–81, *481*, 483, 491, 493, 498, 500–501, 505, 508, 514, 517–19, 556, 563
Paštrić, Ivan 177
Paštrić, Jeronim 177
Paul V, Pope 164–5
Pavelić, Ante (Party of Right) 482, 487–8, 498, 513
Pavelić, Ante (Croatian Party of Right, Ustasha) 519, 523, 545–6, 548–57, *550*, 559–61, 563–4, 572, 575, 577–8, 583, 604, 611, 621
Pavlinović, Mihovil 286, 368, 370, 373–4, *373*, 378, 381, 387, 391–4, 396, 438, 598
Pazin 211, 404, 406, 409–10, 413–14, 418, 423, 426–7, 506–7, 580–85, 588
Peasant-Democratic Coalition (SDK) 519–22, 527–8, 531, 535, 541
Peasant Party: *see* Croatian Republican Peasant Party, Croatian Peasant Party
Pejačević, Ban Ladislav 309, 315, 321
Pejačević, Ban Teodor 362
Perović, Latinka 623, *624*, 631, 637, 643, 647–8, 653
Pešelj, Branko 562
Pest: *see* Budapest
Peter (Petar), Archbishop of Split 38
Peter the Great, Tsar 179, 181
Peter (Petar) I Karađorđević, King 447, 496, 498, 515
Peter (Petar) II Karađorđević 527, 543, 576, 595
Peter (Petar) Krešimir IV, King 44–7
Peter (Petar) Trpimirović 38
Petrinja 73, 140, 275, 319
Piccolomini, Enea Silvio (later Pope Pius II) 175
Pichon, Stephen 479–80
Pieche, General Guiseppe 575
Pijade, Moše 605
Pippin, King 31
Pirker, Pero 623, *628*, 641, 647
Pitteri, Riccardo 423
Pius II, Pope 75
Pius IX, Pope 310, 315
Podiebrad, King George of Bohemia 75
Poincaré, Raymond 494
Poland 24–6, 63, 79, 133, 229, 529, 538, 540
Polit-Desančić, Mihailo 282, 346
Politeo, Dinko 422
Politika 521

Ponzoni, Archbishop Sforza of Split 363
Popović, Dušan 491
Popović, Koča 623
Popović, Milentije 623
Poreč 30, 310–11, 406, 408–9, 417–18, 423–7, 430, 581, 588
Požarevac, Peace of 136–7
Požega 72, 92–4, 96, 98–9, 106, 134–5, 138–9, 195, 206, 232, 257–8, 263, 271, 276, 347
Pozor 295
Praevalis 20
Pragmatic Sanction 188, 192, 237, 240, 243, 271, 280, 287, 289–93, 296, 367
Predavec, Josip 524
Pribićević, Rade 603–4
Pribićević, Svetozar 457, 482, 486–9, 495–8, 501, 511–13, *511*, 515, 521, 524–6
Pribojević, Vinko 176, 181
Prica, Maksim 279, 285
Pro Patria 402, 420–22
Procopius 27
Proleter 573
Propaganda Fide 168, 171, 178
Prosvjeta 604
Protestants 99, 125–6, 158, 161–4, 166–70, 173, 178, 185, 195, 310–11, 314, 562, 607
Protić, Stojan 498
Prvenac 391
Pucić, Niko 369–70
Pula 404, 406, 409, 411, 417–18, 423, 425, 427–9, 484, 493, 509, 580–81, 584–5, 587–8, 590
Pulić, Juraj 374

Rab 25, 43, 56, 61, 64, 90, 152, 164, 402, 406, 409, 504
Račić, Puniša 520
Rački, Franjo 265, 274, 301, 304, 311, 313, 340–43, 380–1
Radetzky, Field Marshal Johann 207, 238, 242, *242*
Radić, Pavle 518
Radić, Stjepan 482, 486, 488, 513, 516–17, 520–21, *520*
Rajačić, Patriarch Josif 234–6, *235*, 240, 250, 252, 338–40
Rajčević, Archbishop Juraj of Zadar 399
Rákóczi, Francis 130–31
Rákóczi, Francis II 141

Rakovac, Dragutin 204, 222–3
Rakovac, Joakim 581–2, *582*
Ranković, Aleksandar 610, 615, 617, 619, *624*, 631
Rapallo, Treaty of 506, 514
Rašković, Jovan 658
Rattkay, Canon Juraj 177, 180
Rauch, Ban Levin 295
Rauch, Ban Pavao 455
Renner, Karl 568
Ribar, Ivan 604
Ribbentrop, Joachim von 544
Rieger, František 311
Rijeka 31, 72, 77, 119, 123, 127, 188–9, 193, 205–8, *207*, 210, 219, 227, 233, 238, 240, 243–4, 247, 257–8, 263, 265–9, 271–3, 276, 287, 289, 292–7, 299, 303, 307, 317–18, 347, 360, 375–6, 404, 406, 415, 437, 441, 443, 452, 461, 488, 493, 495, 502–6, 508, 551, 581, 583, 586–7, 590–92, 611–12, 622–3, 625–6
Rizzi, Lodovico 430
Roatta, General Mario 565
Robert of Anjou, King of Naples 60
Robert of Ketton 154
Rodić, General Gabrijel 384, 386–7, 389
Romanus IV Diogenes, Emperor 44
Rome 20, 24, 31, 36, 39–43, 47–8, 50, 53, 72, 130, 132, 151, 162, 165–6, 168, 171, 175–9, 310–11, 314, 328, 330–33, 337, 350, 364, 402, 411, 421, 465, 480, 503, 505, 508, 533, 540, 549, 551–3, 565, 575; Rome Accords 551–3, 575; Rome Treaty 508
Roosevelt, Franklin 596
Rudolph I Habsburg, Emperor 59
Rudolph II Habsburg, King and Emperor 94, 104, 122, 126, 185
Russia 137, 149, 171, 178–9, 188, 190, 237, 308–9, 314–15, 318, 325, 333–4, 336, 352, 381, 389, 446, 456–7, 460–63, 468, 470–71, 474–5, 503–4, 562
Russian Communist Party 567
Ružičić, Bishop Nikanor of Žiča 350
Rybarž, Otokar 499

Sacra Romana Rota 177
Šafařík, Pavel 258, 339
Sagrojević, Nikola 156
Şaguna, Bishop Andrei of Transylvania 269
St Barbara 30

St Cyril (Constantine) 39, 151–3, 315, 420
St Domnius 20, 42, 46, 52
St Euphemia 46
St Francis of Assisi 157
St Francis Xavier 157
St Isidorus 30
St Jerome 152, *176, 224–5*
St John Capistran 75
St Laurentius 30
St Martha 30
St Methodius 39, 151–2, 314–15, 420
St Peter 30, 45, 52
St Sava 324, 348, 351–2, 359, 506, 608
Salona 19–20, *20*, 22–4, 38, 40, 42–3, 46, 52, 152–3, 376
Salzburg 37, 39
Samsa, Josip 409
Sarkotić, General Stjepan 489–92
Sarpi, Paolo 165
Sava, River 19, 21, 33, 72, 89, 92, 97–9, 103, 109, 111, 134–6, 138–9, 141, 145, 147–9, 197, 205, 207–8, 320, 325–6, 495, 530, 558; Banovina 539
Savonarola, Girolamo 157
Sazonov, Sergei 468, 470, 473
Schmerling, Anton von 270, 272, 286, 378
Schulverein 419–20
Schwarzenberg, Prince Felix 243
Seidler, Ernst von 490
Selim I, Sultan 89
Senj 76–7, 90, 103, 205
Serb Agricultural Cooperatives 359
Serb Bank 261, 359, 453
Serb Club 346–7
Serb Cultural Club 639
Serb Independent Party: *see* Independent Serb Party
Serb Krajina Republic 655, 658, 662
Serb Orthodox Church 235, 284, 305–6, 323, 326–8, 332–3, 335, 337, 341, 348, 360, 364, 560–61, 608, 657
Serb Party (in Dalmatia) 395–7, 400, 440, 445, 449, 452, 456
Sertić, Tomislav 566
Seton-Watson, R.W. 459, 465–6, 469–70, 479, 501, 523, 526–7, 535
Sforza, Carlo 466
Šibenik 36, 44, 56–7, 60–61, 63–6, 68–9, 87, *128–9*, 133, 152, 180, 330–31, 334, 336–7, 372, 377–8, 380, 384, 389, 402, 494, 504, 551, *663*
Sigismund of Luxemburg, King and Emperor 63–4, 71–3, 86–7
Simeon, King of Bulgaria 42
Simeon, Bishop of Marča 325
Simović, General Dušan 495, 543–4, 586
Šimrak, Bishop Janko of Križevci 559
Sinj 89, 134, 331, 363, 365, 373, 375, 381–2, 623
Sisak 21–3, 43, 49–50, *95*, 102–3, 105, 135, 145, 149, 207, 300, 320, *320–21*; Battle of 95–6
Sixtus V, Pope 176
Šižgorić, Juraj 156
Skalić, Paul (Pavao) 174
Skradin 43, 56, 60–61, 65, 69, 72, 89, 169, 329, 334
Škrlec, Adam 200
Slankamen, Battle of 132, 135
Slavac 50
Slavenski Jug 213, 241, 253
Slavonia 21, 29, 48, 54, 72–81, 138–9, 186, 193, 195–9
Sloboda 317
Slovakia 26, 252, 542
Slovene People's Party 483–4
Slovene White Guards 577–8
Slovenia 26, 33, 73, 167, 203, 227, 244, 252, 301, 313, 392, 416, 443, 462, 466, 477, 484, 489–90, 497, 500–501, 512, 514, 516–17, 527, 530, 533–4, 538, 540–41, 544, 546, 568–71, 574, 581, 584–8, 591–2, 594–5, 601, 603, 616–20, 622, 626–7, 629, 634, 640, 642, 645–6, 648, 652, 655, 657
Slunj 72, 142, 258, 275–6
Smičiklas, Bishop Juraj of Križevci 30, 310
Smodlaka, Josip 448, 460, 495, 497–8, 500–501, *511*, 534, 576
Snačić (Svačić), Petar 50–51
Sobieski, King Jan of Poland 133, 179
Società Dante Alighieri 402, 421–3, 508
Società del tiro a bersaglio, 385, 388, 398
Soić, Bishop Venceslav of Senj 273, 311
Šokčević, Ban and General Josip 272, 285, 295
Solin (formerly Salona) 43, 46–8
Sonnino, Sidney 500, 505
Špiljak, Mika 631

Spinčić, Vjekoslav 408, 416, 426, 428–31
Spoleto, Aimone Duke of 551–2
Srbobran 348, 350–2, 354, 356, 358, 360
Srebrenić, Archbishop Josip of Rijeka 581
Srijem 21, 72–3, 93, 96, 98–9, 134–6, 139, 143–5, 182, 195, 323, 236, 247, 251, 270, 274, 276, 282–4, 295, 311–13, 325–6, 338–40, 342–3, 346–8, 354, 361, 391, 495, 530, 539, 592, 634
Srpska riječ 603
Srpski glas 346–7
Srpski list 395, 397
Stalin, Joseph 575, 577, 587, 597, 609–10
Starčević, Ante 259–60, *260*, 265, 284, 286, 302, 308, 318, 351, 357, 362, 436, 440
Starčević, Šime 184
Steed, Wickham 455, 465, 479, 526
Stefan Nemanja, King of Rascia (Raška) 324
Stefanović, Bishop Epifanije 330
Stephen II Árpád, King 47–8, 50, 56
Stephen V Árpád, King 58–9
Stephen (Stjepan) I Držislav, King 43, 53
Stephen Habsburg, Archduke 241
Stephen (Stjepan) Kotromanić, King of Bosnia 86
Stephen II, Pope 31
Stephen V, Pope 41
Stephen (Stjepan) Tomašević, King of Bosnia 87
Stepinac, Archbishop Alojzije 607
Stojadinović, Milan 528, 531–2, 534–7
Stojanović, Nikola 342, 352–4
Stojčević, Stanko 652
Strossmayer, Bishop Josip Juraj 203, 240, 249, 251, 269, 283–4, 288, 294, 305, 310–15, *312*, 372, 411
Sts Cyril and Methodius Association 420
Stulli, Joakim 183
Styria 71, 73, 87, 92–4, 101, 104, 107–10, 123, 125, 127, 130, 139, 166–7, 173, 177, 237
Šubašić, Ban Ivan 544, 576–7, 594, 596–7
Šubić family, counts of Bribir (Bribirski) 65–70, 119
Šufflay, Milan 524
Šulek, Bogoslav 203, 221, 241, 243–4, 260, 339
Süleyman II, Sultan 79, 89–90, 92–4
Supilo, Frano 439, 441–5, 449–58, *450*, 462, 464, 466, 473, 477–8

Sušak 317, 505, 551
Svištovo, Peace of 137
Szatmár, Peace of 141
Széchenyi, István 209

Taaffe, Eduard 380, 396
Talovac, Ivan 74
Tamaro, Attilio 423–4
Tattenbach, Hans 130–31
Taylor, A. J. P. 436, 447
Tegethoff, Admiral Wilhelm von 378
Terzić, General Velimir 621
Theodoric, King of the Ostrogoths 22
Theodosius, Bishop of Nin 41
Theodosius I, Emperor 22
Thököly, Imre 131
Thomas, Archdeacon of Split 24–5, 49, 51–2, 62, 66, 153, 157
Thurns, Johann 123
Tipaldi, Bishop Melezio of Venice 331–2
Tisza, István 447, 460, 483, 491–2
Tisza, Kálmán 307, 316, 321
Tito, Josip Broz 269, 571–3, 576–7, 586–7, 596–7, 603, 605, 611–14, *613*, 616–17, 619, *628*, 630–33, 637, 640–41, 643, 649–50, *650*
Todorović, Mijalko 530, 623
Tomašić, Ban Nikola 358, 362, 451, 457–8
Tomislav, King 42, 352
Tommaseo, Niccolò 365–6, 368
Topal-pasha, Hussein 135
Trentino 402, 420, 423–4
Treviso, Battle of 60
Trieste 205–6, 268, 285, 310, 375, 402, 404, 408, 410–11, 414, 417, 420–24, 426–8, 437, 449, 468, 484, 493, 499, 503, 509, 586–90, *589*, 611
Trigari, Niccolò 388–9, 399–401
Tripalo, Miko 622–3, 627, *628*, 629, 635–6, 641–2, 644–5, 647
Tripartite Code 82–3
Tripartite Pact 542–5
Trogir 25, 36–7, 47, 56–7, 60–61, 63–4, 66, 68–70, 132, 152, 154, 175, 180, 334, 364, 377, 383–4, 396, 399, 401–2, 440, 494
Trpimir, King 34–6, 38, 40, 364
Trpimirović dynasty 52
Trubar, Primož 173–4
Trubetskoy, Gregory 466
True Party of Right 362, 456, 459

Truman, Harry S. 587
Trumbić, Ante 439–40, 448, 451, 454, 462, 464, 467, *467*, 472–4, 477, 480, 493, 499, 501, 506, *511*, 526, 528–9, 534
Tuberon, Louis (Ludovik) Crijević 175
Tuđman, Franjo 622, 633, 655, 661–2
Turopolje 222, 224–5
Tvrtko Kotromanić, Ban of Bosnia 71
Tvrtko II Kotromanić, King of Bosnia 86

U Nu 614
Ukraine 26, 171
Una, River 72, 86, 93–4, 96, 98, 103, 133, 135–7, 140, 167, 179, 391
UDBA 617, 619, 639
Ugrin, Archbishop of Split 154
Ungnad, John 166–7, 173
Unionists (National Constitutional Party) 284, 286, 292, 294–5, 301, 303
United Nations Protected Area (UNPA) 655, 662
United States of America 475–6, 479, 481, 493, 587, 610, 612–13, 655
Urban II, Pope 48, 50
Urban IV, Pope 58
Urban VI, Pope 63
Urban VIII, Pope 165, 178
Ustashe 519, 523, 527, 533, 535, 540, 545–52, 554–66, 572–5, 577–8, 599, 603, 606–8, 621, 634, 640, 648, 661
Utišenić, Cardinal George (Juraj) 169–70

Varaždin 72–3, 81, 93, 100–101, 105, 130, 140–44, 146, 196, 206–7, 217, 233, 240, 251, 257, 263, 276, 285, 295, 297, 300, 302, 304, 319, 340, 575, 623
Varešanin, General Marijan 459
Varna, Battle of 87
Vasvár, Peace of 129, 132, 137
Veesenmayer, Edmund von 545
Venezian, Felice 420–1
Venice 34, 43–4, 46–7, 50, 53, 55–61, 63–6, 68–72, 76–7, 79–81, 85, 87–90, 94, 96, 112–13, 120, 125–7, 130, 132–6, 139, 154–6, 158, 160–62, 164–5, 171, 175, 179–80, 186, 197, 211, 213, 224–5, 266, 269, 290, 323–5, 328–31, 333–7, 354, 363–4, 368, 404
Venizélos, Elefthérios 480
Versailles, Treaty of 505

Vesnić, Milenko 499–500
Victor Emmanuel II, King of Italy 269
Victor Emmanuel III, King of Italy 551
Vidal, Ivan 351
Vidulich, Francesco 410
Vilder, Večeslav 535
Villari, Pasquale 422
Villehardouin, Geoffrey de 57, 175
Vinodol 71–2, 77, 119, 123–4, 127, 136, 189, 206–7, 266–7, 295
Virovitica 72–3, 93, 98, 133–4, *133*, 138–9, 195, 232, 238, 240, 252, 276, 342
Vis 56, 290, 378, 383, 389, 394, 504, 576, 596, 602, 606, 646; Battle of Vis 378
Visigoths 22
Vitez, John (Ivan) of Sredna 76
Vitezović, Pavao Ritter 175, 180–83, *181*, 185, 328
Vitezić, Dinko 406, 413–14
Vitezić, Bishop Ivan of Krk 406, 408, 415–16
Vlachs 100, 106–9, 140, 354, 365; Vlach Code 109–12
Vlačić, Matija (Matthias Flacius Illyricus) 162–4, *163*, 166
Vladislav I Jagiełło, King 74–5, 87
Vladislav II Jagiełło, King 77–9, 82, 88–9
Vojnomir of Pannonia 33
Vojnović, Kosta 368, 387
Vojvodina 234–9, 244, 251, 265, 269–70, 274, 276, 282–3, 301, 339, 355, 512–14, 521, 523, 527–8, 538–9, 546, 568–71, 574, 592, 597, 619, 634, 636–7, 646, 651, 654–5
Vokić, Ante 577
Vrančić, Faust 160–61, *161*, 177
Vranyczány, Ambroz 208, 269
Vrbas, River 21, 33, 70, 136, 179, 391, 530; Banovina 541
Vrboska *224–5*
Vučinić, Rado 338
Vukotinović, Ljudevit 204, 252
Vukovar 72–3, 92, 134, 139, 207–8, 592

Wagner, General Ivan 382
Weichs, Field Marshal Maximillian von 576
Wekerle, Alexander 490, 492
Werböczy, Istvan 82
Wesselényi, Ferenc 128, 130
White Croatia 24, 26

Whitehead, Robert 317
Wilhelm I, King and Emperor (Kaiser) 301
Wilson, Thomas Woodrow 475–7, 487, 492, 498, 501–503, 505
Windischgrätz, Prince Alfred 207, 241–3, *242*

Yugoslav Academy for Arts and Science 288, 312, 342, 348, 461
Yugoslav Club 476, 484–5, 487
Yugoslav Committee 463–4, 467, 470, 475–6
Yugoslav Communist Party, Yugoslav League of Communists: *see* Communist Party of Yugoslavia
Yugoslav Muslim Organisation (JMO) 515–16, 527, 539, 541
Yugoslav People's Army (JNA) 629, 630, 649, 651, 661

Zadar 24–5, 34, 36–8, 40, 42–3, 46–7, 50, 53, 56–8, *57*, 60–68, *62*, 70, 87, 94, *128–9*, 133, 152–3, 175, 180, 184, 233, 330–31, 333–5, 337, 364, 366–8, 370, 372, 374, 376, 378–80, 382–5, 387–91, *388*, 398–403, 448, 452, 460, 493, 504–6, 565, 583, 586–7, 592, 626; Peace of Zadar 61, *320–21*
Zagreb Academy 201, 203, 220, 226, 263, 284, 300
Zagreb Declaration 485–6, 489
Zakmardi, Ivan 177
Žanko, Miloš 631–2

Zapolya, John 79–80, 83, 90, 92, 100
Zapolya, Stephen 78
Zastava 346
Zdeslav, King 41
Zemljak 386–7
Zenta, Battle of 136
Zerbino, Paolo 552
Zeta Banovina 530
Žigić, Rade 604, 608–10
Živković, General Petar 524–5, *525*
Živković, Jovan 282–3, 296, 304, 316, 358, 360
Zlatarić, Dominko 126
Zmajević, Archbishop Vinko of Zadar 333, 335
Žolger, Josip 499
Zora dalamatinska 184
Zoranić, Petar 156
Zrinski family 71–2, 77, 79, 88, 92–4, 103, 112–13, 119–27, *124*, 130–32, 154, 166, 168–9, 173, 178, 180, 185, 189, 206–7, 267, *320–21*, 626
Zrinski, Adam 130, 132
Zrinski, Catherine (Katarina) 119, 131
Zrinski, George (Juraj), 122–3, 126
Zrinski, Helen (Jelena) 131–2
Zrinski, John (Ivan) 132
Zrinski, Ban Nicholas (Nikola) of Sziget 93–4, 96, 101, 105, 119, 121–3
Zrinski, Ban Nicholas (Nikola) 126–30
Zrinski, Ban Peter (Petar) 127, 130–31, *131*, 141, 173, 180
Zsitva, Peace of 95
Zvonimir, King Demetrius 47–8, 52, 152–3, 364